£35.00

British Military Flintlock Rifles 1740–1840

With a remarkable wealth of data about the Riflemen and Regiments who carried these weapons

by De Witt Bailey, Ph.D.

ANDREW MOWBRAY PUBLISHERS P.O. BOX 460 LINCOLN, RHODE ISLAND USA

LIBRARY OF CONGRESS
CONTROL NUMBER: 2002108590
   De Witt Bailey
   British Military Flintlock Rifles: 1740–1840
   Lincoln, R.I.: ANDREW MOWBRAY INCORPORATED – PUBLISHERS
   264 pp.

ISBN: 1-931464-03-0

© 2002 De Witt Bailey

All rights reserved. No part of this book may be reproduced in any form
or by any means without permission in writing from the author and publisher.

To order more copies of this book, or to receive a free catalog
of other fine arms collecting publications, call 1-800-999-4697 or 401-726-8011.
Email us at orders@manatarmsbooks.com or visit our web page at www.manatarmsbooks.com

Printed in the United States of America.

This book was designed and set in type by Stuart C. Mowbray.
The typeface chosen for the text was New Baskerville, a modern
interpretation of classic Georgian letterforms created in the 18th century
by English printer and typographer John Baskerville.

First Edition

1 2 3 4 5 6 7 8 9 10

This work is Dedicated to my oldest friend, the late

GUY BUXTON ARNOW

who taught me muzzle-loading
and so very much else

TABLE OF CONTENTS

Acknowledgements 6
Introduction 7

CHAPTER 1
The Beginnings: 1740–1772 11
    The Seven Years War 1755–1764 12

CHAPTER 2
The American War, First Phase 21
    The Hanoverian-made Pattern 1776 Rifle 22
    The Birmingham-made Pattern 1776 Rifle 25
    Issues 31
    Ammunition 34

CHAPTER 3
The Ferguson Rifle from Manufacture to the Battle of Monmouth Court House 35
    Ammunition 55

CHAPTER 4
German Riflemen and their Rifles in the American War 59
    Hesse-Cassel 59
    Hesse-Hanau 61
    Ansbach-Bayreuth 62
    Brunswick-Wolfenbüttel 63
    Anhalt-Zerbst 63
    Summary 63
    Rifles 64
    Ammunition 68

CHAPTER 5
Loyalist Riflemen 1775–1783 69

CHAPTER 6
Indian Rifles in British Service to 1783 75

CHAPTER 7
Rifle Development in the Interwar Years, 1783–1793 87
    The Pattern 1785 Crespi-Egg Breech-loading Light Dragoon Carbines 87
    The Pattern 1793 Royal Horse Artillery Pistol-carbine 90

CHAPTER 8
The British Rifle and Rifle-armed Units during the French Revolutionary Wars, 1793–1802 93
    The Prussian Rifle Muskets 94
    Captured Foreign Rifles 94
    "Not a has-been, just a never-was" 102

CHAPTER 9
The Baker Infantry Rifle, 1800–1814 105
    Early Baker Production 107
    Pattern 1800 Rifle 107
    Pattern 1801 Rifle for West India Regiments 114
    Pattern 1805 Infantry Rifle 114
    Pattern 1810 Musket-bore Infantry Rifle 116
    Dublin-made Baker Rifles? 117
    Possible Modifications 118
    Pattern 1807 Rifled Wall Piece 118

CHAPTER 10
Cavalry Rifles, 1790s–1828 121
    British Cavalry Rifles 1793–1802 121
    Pattern 1801 Life Guards Rifle 121
    Pattern 1803 Cavalry Rifle 122
    Pattern 1812 Life Guards Rifled Carbine 124
    Pattern 1813 Cavalry Rifle 125
    Pattern 1813/27 Cavalry Rifle 127

CHAPTER 11
Postwar Baker Rifles 129
    Pattern 1800/15 Baker Rifle altered for socket-bayonet 129
    Pattern 1820 Baker Rifle 131
    The Royal Manufactory Enfield — Background 131
    Pattern 1823 Baker Rifle 131
    Pattern 1823 Shah of Persia

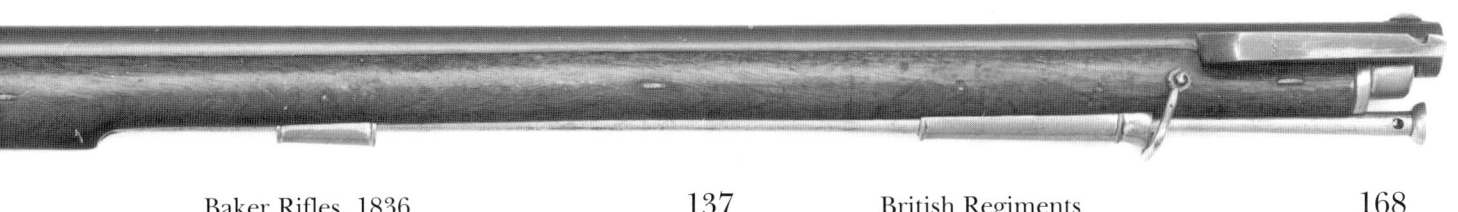

Baker Rifles, 1836	137
The Victorian Baker Rifle	138

CHAPTER 12
Baker Rifle Bayonets, 1800–1838 — 141

Pattern 1800 (First Pattern)	141
Pattern 1801 (Second Pattern)	141
Pattern 1806 Saw-back	142
Pattern 1815 Socket Bayonet	142
Pattern 1816 Saw-back Rifleman's Sword	143
Modified Duke of Richmond's musket bayonets for Pattern 1800/15 and Pattern 1820 Baker Rifles	144
Pattern 1823 Hand Bayonet	144
Pattern 1825 Hand Bayonet	144

CHAPTER 13
Accoutrements and Ammunition for the Baker Rifle — 145

Rifle Tools and Maintenance	145
Accoutrements	146
Powder Horns	147
Powder Flasks	148
Powder Chargers	149
Ball Bags	149
Mallets	149
Cartridge Pouches	150
Lock Caps (Covers)	150
Bayonet Scabbards	151
Tools and Accoutrements for the Shah of Persia's Baker Rifles, 1836	151
Bullet Moulds	151
Baker Rifle Ammunition	151

CHAPTER 14
Rifle Corps in the British Army, 1798–1841 — 155

The 60th Regiment of Foot	155
The Rifle Corps (1800), 95th Foot (1802), Rifle Brigade (1816)	158
The 7th, 9th, 10th, 14th, 15th, 18th and 23d Light Dragoons	163
The King's German Legion	164
The Ceylon Rifle Regiment	165
The Royal Canadian Rifle Regiment	166
The Portuguese Caçadores	166
Other Foreign-based Rifle Companies post-1800	167
Ad-hoc Rifle Companies in British Regiments	168
The British Militia	169
Bulk, non-specific, rifle issues	169

CHAPTER 15
British Army Rifle Marksmanship with the Flintlock Rifle — 171

CHAPTER 16
Rifles for Indians in British Service, 1783–1840 — 177

The Board of Ordnance 1813 Contract Indian Rifles	179
The Tatham Rifles of Captain Norton, 1816	180
The Last of the Government-gift Flintlock Trade Rifles	187

CHAPTER 17
A Miscellany of Unexplained British Military Rifles — 189

— Appendices —

1. Technical Specifications of British service rifles	198
2. British Rifle Gunmakers	212
3. The composition of Ferguson's force at King's Mountain	214
4. First Muster Roll of the Queen's Rangers Rifle Company, 1780	217
5. Muster Roll of the New York Volunteer Rifle Company, 1780–1781	218
6. British Pattern 1776 and Ferguson Rifle performance judged by test-firing modern replicas	219
7. Contract between Lieut. Col. DuPont and A.H. Thornbeck for rifles for the Prince of Orange's Corps, 1800	222
8. Alphabetical list of Ordnance Contractors for Baker Rifles and Carbines, 1800–1838	223
9. Baker Rifle Production 1800–1839	235
10. Extract from the Regulations for the Exercise of Riflemen and Light Infantry	237
11. Cloathing Regulations for Riflemen, 1800–09	240
12. Inspection Returns for Rifle-carrying Regiments, 1817–1852	241
13. Volunteer Rifles and Volunteer Corps described as "Rifle Men" or "Sharp Shooters"	249

Endnotes Listed by Chapter — 253
Bibliography of Printed Works — 260
Index — 262

ACKNOWLEDGEMENTS

A very large number of people have contributed to the making of this book, both individuals and the curators and staffs of many libraries and museums. Outstanding amongst those who have encouraged me to create this particular work are Herman Benninghoff II and the late Clifford Lewis III, to both of whom I owe an immense debt of hospitality, never-ending questions, and unflagging encouragement to organize and put down on paper the information on British rifles which has been accumulating in my files these many years. I guess Cliff's "Yes, but did the British actually use Ferguson's rifle at Brandywine?" and Herman's "What is this rifle?" are really the chief reasons for the appearance of this work. The late Kit Ravenshear, master gun smith, whose enthusiasm and thirst for background knowledge of the pieces he so skillfully recreated was another spur in moving me towards actual creation of text, and his excellent reproduction of the Pattern 1776 Rifle has enabled me to carry out careful test firing of this rifle to determine what its performance may have been. I am also extremely grateful to my long-time friend and fellow-sufferer from primary source research, David F. Harding, who has shared the task of studying the work force and methods of the 18th-century English gun trade with me while working on a magnificent history of East India Company small arms, for his insights and discussions which have helped immensely to clarify our joint paths through the morass of records and what they contain, and in particular for information on Asiatic-theatre British military use of the rifle.

Going back over the years, it was the late Anthony D. "Chuck" Darling who first suggested in a 1972 *Canadian Journal of Arms Collecting* (vol. 10, No.2) article that a certain rifle might indeed be the ones described in Howard Blackmore's *British Military Firearms, 1650–1850*, but it was not possible to confirm this until additional examples, bearing the markings which could only relate to rifles of the American War period, were located. For this we have to thank Maurice A. Taylor, Robert D. Cheel Jr., David A. Stewart, Richard J. Whittaker and James M. Gaynor for locating examples and communicating pictures and details to me.

The staffs of many institutions have contributed to the location and supply of vital, often unique information. Foremost amongst these must be Galen R. Wilson, Robert S. Cox and their assistant Melissa Johnston of the William L. Clements Library at the University of Michigan, Ann Arbor, without whose interest, dedication and hours of work on my behalf, this work and others to follow, could not have appeared. To Mary Robertson, John H. Rhodehamel and Mary Wright of the Henry E. Huntington Library a similar debt of gratitude for their research and sympathetic co-operation. In the United States the staffs of the Libraries at Colonial Williamsburg, the Historical Societies of New-York and Pennsylvania, the Library of Congress and National Archives, and in Britain the British Library, Public Record Office, National Army Museum, Royal Artillery Institution Library, National Library of Scotland, and Edinburgh University Library have all made possible the examination of primary source materials vital to this study. For several invaluable ammunition references, as well as enormously valuable and enjoyable discussions, I am greatly indebted to the late Capt. Adrian B. Caruana.

In studying the weapons themselves, I am greatly indebted to H.M. The Queen for gracious permission to examine and to publish pictures of the two pairs of Huhnstock pistol-carbines and the Peter Traille longrifle from the Royal Collection. To numerous private collectors including B.G.S. Coles, D. Cooper, T.A. Edwards, Dr. Ross Macinnes, Gary E. Mikelson, Dr. George Shumway, David G. Timpany, the late D.B. Tubbs, and others who remain anonymous by choice, as well as to the collections at the West Point Museum, Colonial Williamsburg, the Milwaukee Public Museum, the Royal Armouries, the National Army Museum, Sotheby's, Christie's and Phillips my sincerest gratitude for their valuable contributions in allowing me to examine weapons and in supplying photographs on request. I am particularly indebted to Joni Heyne, and James L. Kochan, then-Curator of the Morristown National Historical Park for the opportunity to examine the then-unique military Ferguson rifle in their collections, and for photographs of this example. For identifying the long-known Ferguson rifle in the Nunnemacher Collection as being an Ordnance piece, we are all indebted to Jesse Melot, and to Curator John B. Lundstrom of the Milwaukee Public Museum for making available information and photographs of the second-known military Ferguson rifle. To Charles Salerno our gratitude for sharing with us the only known physical Ferguson artifact recovered from American soil, the only physical proof of its having been there. For making available the results of their test-firing of an excellently and authentically engineered reproduction of the Pattern 1776 Ferguson breech-loading rifle, I am greatly indebted to Ernest E. Cowan and Richard H. Keller. For access to two key German rifles my grateful thanks go to Dr. phil. Arnold Wirtgen and the Blücher Museum in Kaub, Germany, and to my old friend and fellow rifleman Piero Vergnano.

My wife Sarah has contributed to this work not only through proof-reading, but by asking awkward questions, and by getting me through various computer-related crises, and by her constant understanding, support and encouragement of my research and writing. Where she is concerned, gratitude is always an inadequate word.

De Witt Bailey

Introduction

...before the close of the war, every battalion in America had organized a rifle company for itself.

E.E. Curtis
The British Army in the American Revolution.

The above was written in 1926, itself taken from a secondary though widely respected source, Sir John Fortesque, the official historian of the British Army. The statement, and its import seems, however, since 1930 (when it was quoted by Lieut. Col. F.E. Whitton in his history of the American Revolution), to have been comprehensively forgotten.

The role of the rifle in combat prior to its general adoption by all line infantry regiments in the mid-19th century is perhaps one of the most under-researched, misunderstood and misrepresented developments in the entire field of military history. Most of the technical analysis has been heavily clouded by hindsight, and distorted by far too much politics and patriotism entering into examinations of its prevalence and effectiveness in any given war or campaign. There appear to be military historians still producing works who are unaware that the rifle was not generally adopted for infantry until the third quarter of the 19th century, who refer to any small arm in the hands of infantry as a "rifle" regardless of date. Most seem to be unaware that the military use of the rifle can be traced at least as far back as the personal bodyguard of King Christian IV of Denmark (dated rifles between 1611 and 1622) and Duke William of Hesse in 1630. French cavalry flankers had rifles from the 1670s, the French in Canada had a few rifles from the mid-1690s, the Norwegians armed their ski-troops with them from 1712, Prussia established its first rifle-corps in 1740 (permanently from 1744), and the Piedmontese army issued rifles in 1743. In the first year for which we have firm evidence for the presence of rifles in British military hands, an English translation of the French military writer Le Blond's *A Treatise on Artillery* was published. Illustrating a fairly typical attitude and knowledge about rifles in military circles, and revealing some very interesting details in their loading, Le Blond wrote:

The Carabine is a sort of musketoon, the barrel of which is riffled spirally from the breech to the mouth, so that when the ball which is forced into it is again driven out by the strength of the powder, it is lengthen'd about the breadth of a finger, and mark'd with riffle of the bore.

The barrel of the carabine is three foot long, and the piece is four foot long, including the stock; it has an iron rammer, and the bullet is first driven into the mouth of the piece with a short iron pin, called a driver, striking it on the end with a small hammer ready for that purpose.

The carabine has a much greater range than the fusil, or musket, because the riffle of the barrel impedes the ball, which by that means makes the greater distance at the first inflammation of the powder, and giving time for the whole charge to take fire before it goes out of the bore, it is at length thrown out with a greater force than from the common musket.[1]

Le Blond's description contains two "classic" rifle features of the early period: a naked, unpatched, ball driven in with mallet and short-starter, and suggests that rifles in French service at the time (modifications of the Model 1733 Cavalry carbine) were not loaded with paper cartridges. Amazingly, Captain George Smith in his *An Universal Military Dictionary* published in London in 1779, was apparently unable to improve on Le Blond's description, and simply includes it as his own. By the time the Baker rifle was introduced at regimental level in the British army in 1800, more than 1400 rifles had been in official issue during two major wars. Unfortunately, military historians in general (with several brilliant exceptions in the post-1960 era) seem to have been woefully unaware of the weapons carried by the subjects of their research, and that bearing and using such weapons was the chief *raison d'etre* for foot soldiers.

Thanks to the voluminous efforts of United States historians writing nationalistic, patriotic encomiums of their troops' valiant performance during the War for American Independence, (chiefly in the 19th century), the British army in general, and the role of the rifle in particular have been very considerably distorted or ignored. These writers often conveyed the idea that the victory of the American forces was due largely to the widespread use of the rifle with its superior marksmanship against the outmoded dullard troops and tactics of the tyrant-king. Fortunately most of this misinformation has died out in books written since the end of World War II, but its effects are still with us, and the fact remains that from any sample bookshelf of volumes dealing with the American War only a handful would even begin to present the true situation.

The object of the present work is to begin a redressing of the balance by presenting a combination of original research and gleanings from printed sources which reveal the reality of the introduction and use of the rifle

— 7 —

by British forces (including their allies) in the years prior to the permanent establishment of rifle-armed companies in the 1790s, to the end of the flintlock era in the early 1840s. Because of the large amount of primary source material which appears here for the first time in many cases, and for the first time in context in many others, and due to space limitations, narrative has been kept to a minimum in order to present the maximum of fact and a minimum of unnecessary interpretation.

Since they are an integral part of the story of the use of rifles in British service, American Loyalist and German rifles and riflemen are discussed, with particular emphasis upon the composition of these units in order to clarify the use of the rifle and its widespread presence throughout the British regular and militia forces. To complete the coverage, rifles carried by the American Indians allied with the British, and by the white officers who led them, are also discussed.

Why was so little written about the British use of rifles during the American War? The answer seems to be twofold. Firstly, when compared to contemporary American commentary on their riflemen (which, from military sources was almost entirely derogatory), the absence of British comments is less marked: it is the mass of American writing after the event which makes the British dearth seem so great. Secondly, the attitude of British military commentators seems to have been one of informed acceptance of the rifle as an integral, and not separate, part of their tactical equipment. Knowledge of rifles amongst the officer corps must have been fairly widespread, given the amount of park deer shooting which took place on country estates throughout England and Ireland, and deer stalking and poaching in the Highlands of Scotland from at least the 1740s, and of officer exposure to rifles in Continental use during the wars of 1740–48 and 1756–63. In British service rifles appear to have been at first confined to the engineers, but during the American War for Independence widely dispersed amongst the rank and file of the light infantry of the regular regiments; only amongst the Loyalist Provincial corps were rifles sometimes concentrated in identifiable rifle companies, (e.g. Emmerich's Chasseurs and the Queen's Rangers) and were therefore (as with so much else to do with the Loyalists) not singled-out for comment. Sniping, or 'marking-down' officers and gun-crews was accepted as necessary, but was not an activity to brag about. It is intriguing to note that while the influences which brought the use of the rifle to the attention of British military authorities by 1740 were of European origin, yet the operational use of the rifle by British forces before 1800 appears to have been almost entirely confined to the Western Hemisphere, and very largely to North America untill the 1790s when rifle companies were active in the West Indies. Thereafter the use of the rifle by British and British-allied forces was widespread both in rifle-armed companies and in regular line and light infantry regiments with rifles forming a percentage of their armament.

Research for this work developed as part of a larger study of British military small arms of the 18th century carried on for more than thirty years, involving libraries, archives, public and private arms collections in Great Britain, the United States and Canada. Since it is offered as a "state of the art," but initial study, it is hoped and expected that further materials may come to light as the result of readers' increased awareness and curiosity and further research. This additional material will, it is hoped, appear in future enlarged editions of this work and will be included as well in the larger comprehensive works in progress by this writer, including the forthcoming *The British Army and their Small Arms in North America 1737–1783; Dublin Castle and the Irish Board of Ordnance in the Eighteenth Century;* and ultimately *British Military Small Arms 1689–1840*.

NOTE ON THE TEXT

Much of the material in this work consists of quotations from 18th-century documents, written long before the movement to standardize spelling originated. There is nothing more irritating or distracting than the frequent insertion of [sic] to denote incorrect spelling, and since this type of error is almost always obvious in the context of the materials quoted in this work, no use has been made of this distracting device. In fact, no alterations to the original spelling or punctuation have been made save in very rare instances where, for the sake of essential clarity, a comma or full-stop may be inserted. In all cases where something has been added by the writer in an original quote, brackets [ ] are used, while for editorial comments in the narrative text the usual parentheses ( ) are used.

CURRENCY AND PRICES

Prices are normally shown in British Pounds Sterling, using the symbols £ for pounds, d. for pence and / for dividing shillings from pence. The pound unit was reckoned in five divisions: pounds, shillings, pence, halves and quarters of pence. Hence the sum of five pounds 15 shillings two and a half pence will be shown as £5.15.2 1/2. Prices of less than a pound, say sixteen shillings and five pence, are shown as 16/5; sixteen shillings only is shown as 16/-.
£ 1 = 20 shillings
1 shilling = 12 pence
1 penny = 4 farthings
The guinea was a gold coin, as well as a method of expressing cost, and was equal to £1.1.0. or 21/-. Fifteen guineas (expressed as 15 gns.) was equal to £15.15.0.

The guinea as a coin was replaced by the sovereign of £1 value in 1816.

The major currency in daily use in North America was the Spanish (actually South American in origin) real or peso, which was minted in silver coins of 8, 4, 2, 1 and 1/2 real. The 8 real piece (the famous "piece of 8") was usually called the "dollar" in Britain and America, and officially established by the British Government at 4/8. In other words, the dollar passed current for four shillings and eight pence for payments such as British Army salaries, contracts &c. This figure of 4/8 did not apply to the different colonies, only to British Governmental transactions. Very occasionally it varied by a penny or two, but 4/8 was the equivalent for most of our period.

The term "buck" as an equivalent for the dollar originates from the equivalent value of one buckskin being 4/8, which was the official equivalent of the Spanish milled dollar.

Sr.   3d June 1746.

In return to your Letter to the Board of the 30th Ult: I have received their Commands to acquaint You

That they approve your buying One hundred Rounds of Ball for the Rifled Carbines, and desire you will order Mr. Parry to pay for them and for Fifty Small Bags to keep them in, the Charge of which they will allow in your Disbursmt.

They likewise approve your leaving the Two Sick Bombardiers under the Care of the Respective Officers at Portsmouth.

They think it reasonable Mr. MacCulloch Lieutenant Fireworker should have Pay as Adjutant since he does the Duty, and they consent Two Women may be admitted on the Neptune, as the other Six Transports have each of them that Number I am Sr.

      Your most Obedient
      humble Servant
      Charles Bush

Thomas Armstrong Esqr. Commander in Chief of the Train going on the present Expedition &c. at Portsmouth

Board of Ordnance letter to Thomas Armstrong, 3 June 1746, containing first reference to the presence of rifles in British military hands. *Public Record Office, W.O.55/1813.*

CHAPTER 1

The Beginnings, 1740–1772

A Board of Ordnance proportion of 14 March 1740 for stores required for the Caribbean expedition commanded by Lord Cathcart includes "Rifled Carbines - 30". Next to this entry in the margin, in red ink, is written: "Wall pieces sent in lieu of," which information is confirmed in the subsequent account of stores added to the original proportion. This first reference to rifles in the Ordnance records, while negative, poses several intriguing questions: what did the person applying for these arms expect to receive? What was the background for such a specialized request? The substitution of 100 wall pieces suggests that the intended use of the rifles was from a static position rather than by light troops, and also that long-distance shooting was in contemplation.[1] This awareness of the military utility of the rifle within British military circles in the very same year that Frederick of Prussia established his first military rifle corps, and well before the rifle apparently achieved more than local renown in British North America, suggests either a British or possibly a European origin of this awareness.

The first recorded acquisition of rifled arms for the use of the British army occurred in 1746 as part of the preparations for the expedition to relieve Louisbourg under the command of General St. Clair. No evidence survives in the Board of Ordnance or War Office records to indicate that the rifles were specially manufactured, and it is most likely that this small group of 60 rifled carbines was purchased in the open market, probably from German sources. There is no evidence pointing to the particular inspiration for adding rifles to the British armament, but at this date it must have been European rather than American. The French had used rifled carbines for selected cavalry troops since early in the reign of Louis XIV, and indeed an inventory of the public stores in Quebec of 1743 lists five *"carabines rayees,"* or rifled carbines. These were possibly Model 1733 cavalry carbines, but for what purpose they might have been intended by the Canadian authorities is not known.

The earliest mention of the British rifles occurs in a list dated 7 May 1746 of the stores for the train of artillery to be shipped on board seven transports bound for the relief of the newly captured French fortress of Louisbourg. They appear again on the Ordnance's own proportion of stores for the St. Clair expedition, dated 10 May 1746: "Rifled Carbines 50".[2] On 3 June 1746 the Ordnance wrote to Thomas Armstrong, commander of the train of artillery for the expedition, already at Portsmouth preparing to embark:

In return to your Letter to the Board of the 30th Ulto: I have received their Commands to acquaint you
That they approve your buying One hundred Rounds of Ball for the Rifled Carbines, and desire you will order Mr Parr to pay for them and for Fifty Small Bags to keep them in, the Charge of which they will allow in your Disbursements.[3]

So little did the Board of Ordnance have to do with this first acquisition of rifles, that they did not even supply ammunition or the means of carrying it, but merely approved its purchase by the officer responsible for artillery supplies, and allowed for its payment from public funds. The records have not revealed any payment of the bill to the individual who purchased the rifles, presumably on instructions from either the Board of Ordnance (no instructions recorded), or General St. Clair or some other lesser officer.

The St. Clair expeditionary force was too long delayed in England. Its destination and its commander were changed: under General Lestock the force landed at the French port of L'Orient on the Brest peninsula, headquarters of the *Compagnie des Indes*, early in October 1745. It was a futile raid, and the force was re-embarked with a loss of about 100 men. There is no indication about the possible use of the fifty rifled carbines.

Sometime between 13 December 1746 (when only 10 rifles are recorded in the Stores) and 31 December 1747 (when the war had effectively ended) the rifles were taken into store at the Tower of London, and they appear regularly, variously described in the annual inventory of small arms in the Tower as "Rifled Bullet Guns, Bullet Guns with Rifled Barrels, Rifled Bullet Guns of Sorts, serviceable, 60"[4] until the outfitting of the North American expedition commanded by General Edward Braddock. The "of Sorts" in the above inventory suggests that there may have been more than one design of rifle in store. One rifle was withdrawn from store sometime during 1753, as the inventory of 31 Dec.

— 11 —

Entry in the Deputy Paymaster General's accounts giving description of the first bulk order of rifles obtained for British Army use in North America, 2 March 1757.
Public Record Office, PMG14/1.

1753 shows only 59 remaining,[5] one perhaps for retention as a pattern piece.

In July 1747, Admiral Boscowen, in his list of requirements for a train of artillery for an expedition to India, included "Rifled Carbines, 50" but the Ordnance list of items actually to be included (called a "Proportion") drawn up on 14 October of that year did not include these items.[6] But the idea of rifles as useful military arms had caught on in the British service, and would remain in evidence in varying degrees through the rest of Britain's 18th-century wars until the official adoption of rifles of a fixed pattern at Board of Ordnance level in 1800.

THE SEVEN YEARS WAR

On 2 November 1754, the Duke of Cumberland's secretary, Colonel Napier, informed the Board of Ordnance that the Quarter Master of the American Expedition then fitting out under the command of General Braddock, Sir John St. Clair, had requested that a dozen rifled barrel carbines be included in the expedition's stores. The Ordnance responded by supplying "12 Rifled Barrel Guns with their proper Moulds, 4 Barrels of Powder, 1/2 cwt of Lead" from those still in store of the 1746 purchase.[7] The ammunition mentioned amounted to four hundred pounds of powder and fifty-six pounds of lead; no references to an improved quality of powder have been noted. The withdrawal of the rifles from Store was confirmed by the inventory of Tower small arms, dated 31 December 1754, which shows 47 rifles remaining in Store.[8]

The rifles issued for the Braddock expedition were intended to be used by the engineers accompanying the force, and since these selected troops formed part of the spearhead of the marching column, they were very near the front of the force when the French and Indian party literally ran into them on 9 July 1755.[9] Given the propensity for booty evinced by both the French and the Indians, it is highly likely that this dozen of rifles, the first to be used in combat by British forces, vanished into Indian and/or French hands, and were probably used up in the course of the long war which followed. There is one eyewitness report of the battle on 9 July which suggests that the French/Indian force were already using rifles. The unidentified British officer wrote that the British vanguard's fire was returned "...not in a regular manner, but like Poping shots, with little explosion, only a kind of Whiszing noise; (which is a proof the Enemys Arms were riffle Barrels) this kind of fire was attended with Considerable execution,..."[10] The same effect would have been achieved (and was noted by other contemporary writers) by the small powder charge used by the Indians in their trade guns, often with ill-fitting balls. The most interesting point here is that the officer was sufficiently familiar with rifles and the characteristic sound of rifle-fire to note this difference.

The fate of the balance of the 1746 rifles, 47 still in store as of 1 January 1756, is unknown since no inventories taken during the war years have survived. They may have joined the other rifles which were shortly to appear in service in America, or they may have accompanied British troops to Germany in 1758, to be used by selected marksmen, or handed over to German allies whose *chasseur* (*jäger*) troops may have used them. Or they may simply have remained in store in the Tower and been disposed of by public auction sale in 1764. None have been identified at the time of writing.

On 2 March 1757, the Deputy Paymaster General of H.M. Forces in North America paid Colonel Jacques (James) Prevost £900 for 300 rifled carbines "for the use of His Majestys Troops." Prevost had been commissioned colonel commandant of the newly created 62nd (Royal American) Regiment on 4 January 1756, and in fulfilling part of the conditions for his commission he had spent most of 1756 recruiting for the regiment in the German States. Since there is no suggestion in the records that the rifles were made by or for the Board of Ordnance, it can safely be assumed that they were made in Germany, and were brought to North America by Prevost on his arrival at New York City on 20 January 1757. The Commander-in-Chief, North America, and Colonel Commandant of the regiment for whom Prevost had acquired the rifles, was not altogether pleased when Prevost arrived with the rifles and demanded payment. Lord Loudoun noted in one of his notebooks on

The Beginnings, 1740–1754

The Commander-in-Chief's warrant to Comptroller of the New York Ordnance Office to receive into Store the rifles purchased from Colonel James Prevost, 3 March 1757.
Henry E. Huntington Library, LO 2961.

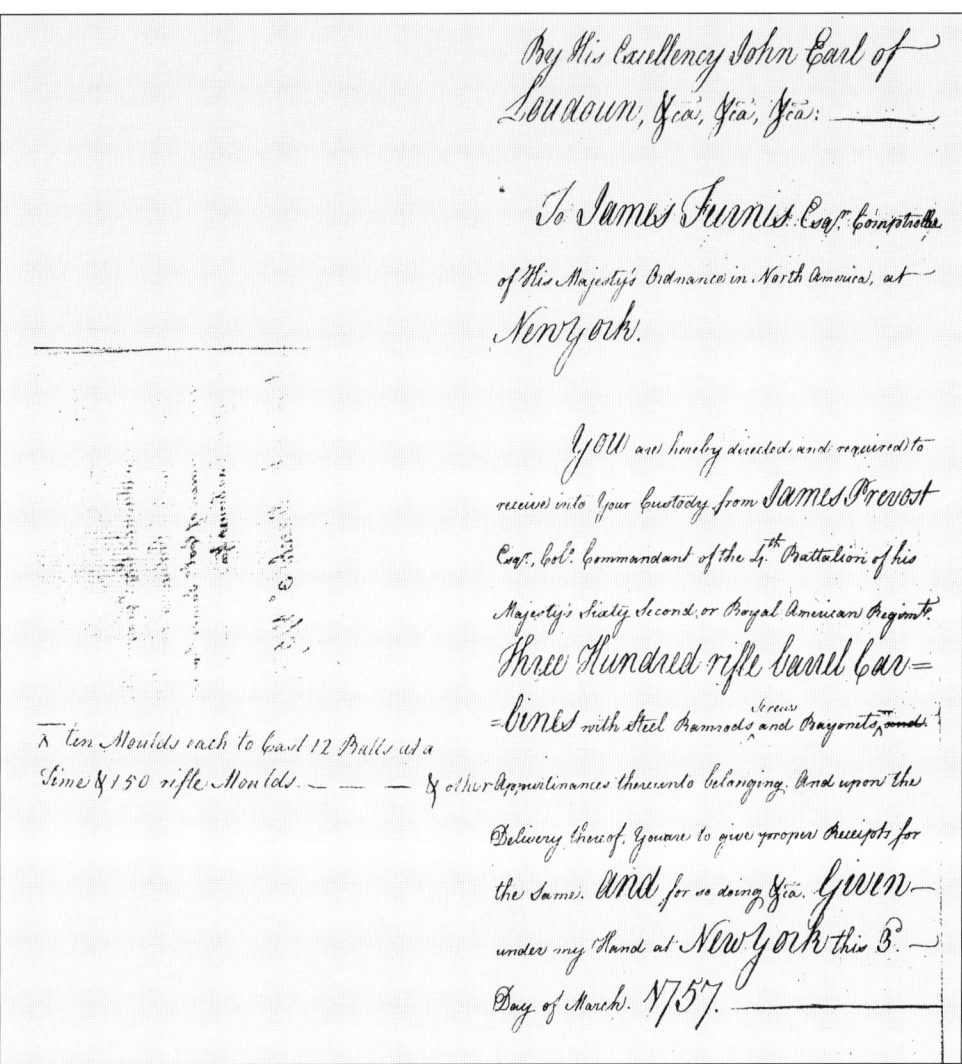

24 Feb. 1757 under headings of a visit from Prevost:

Riffeld Pices is to show me a Pattern has been offered £3- on which Price he is about 18d [ ] in each [11]

and a few days later on 3 March, he noted:

Col Prevost. Gave him a Warrant for £900 for 300 Riffeld Carabines which he had provided on the first plan of the German Regt [the 62d, Royal Americans] with Bayonets Iron Ramers Screws and moulds for making Balls.

These he proposed at London to deliver over here said he could dispose of them H R H [the Duke of Cumberland] if he could then I should allow him to Despose of them

He has since brought them here and askes £3 for them and on examining them by a rank man they are reported to me to be worth £7 Currency and I have left the price to M G Web to settle who thinks I may pay the £3 for them which is about £: :18 for the rest and of ...original price and I hope to have them as I find they will be of some use in the Service here. Mr. Furnis. Signed an order to him to Receve the above Riffeld Carabines in the Kings Stores. [12]

These confused and partly illegible jottings indicate that while rifles may have played a part in the original plans for the Royal American Regiment, by the time Prevost arrived with them in New York changes had been made, and the price of the arms varied from what had been previously suggested. However, Loudoun accepted them and they were delivered into the Ordnance Stores at New York, to Mr. Commissary James Furnis, from whence their distribution can be partly traced from various Stores inventories.

Their first appearance is in a Return of Arms at New York 19 Apr. 1757, which shows 296 Carbines and 296 Bayonets received from Col. Prevost still in Store.[13] Four have already disappeared, presumably in issue. On 14 May 1757 the first official issue is ordered: to James Hockett, stores for an expedition include:

Carbines with Riffle barrels, steel Rammers screws and bayonets - 100. Riffle Moulds for Do. - 100[14]

Hockett was the Ordnance assistant Storekeeper at Albany at the time. By 6 September 1757, all 100 of these arms had been turned into Ordnance Stores at Fort Edward, New York, though only 50 of the moulds accompanied them.[15] On 7 January 1758 in the Ordnance Stores in New York City, 190 rifled carbines and 190 bayonets for them were available.[16] When Major General James Abercromby took over the command-in-chief from Lord Loudoun, the meticulous record keeping which had characterized Loudoun's every move ceased, and tracing the rifles becomes even more haphazard.

For the campaign of 1758, we have Abercromby's warrant of 4 May 1758 to Furnis to issue to Colonel Henry Bouquet 16 rifled carbines for the Forbes expedition against Fort DuQuesne and the Board of Ordnance Indenture signed by Bouquet which clearly describes the rifles. On 25 May General John Stanwix wrote to Bouquet:

Mr Ourry indented for the 16 Rifled Barrel Fuzees as deliver'd to the first Battalion [R.A.R.] of wch ten are sent round

(above) The Commander-in-Chief's Warrant for the issue of 16 rifled carbines, 4 May 1758. *Henry E. Huntington Library, AB109.* **(below)** The standard printed Board of Ordnance Indenture used when issuing arms from Store. Records the issue of sixteen rifles to Colonel Henry Bouquet at New York, 6 May 1758. *British Library, Add. Mss. 21,640.*

to Philadelphia with some Stores, the Box is directed to you. The other six is with our six Comps & we must be responsible for them.[17]

On 15 May 1758, Abercromby ordered Furnis to issue stores for an expedition from Albany, the genesis of the Fort Ticonderoga campaign. These included 176 Carbines with Rifle Barrels and Bayonets &c.[18]

The following month an anonymous officer on the Fort Ticonderoga expedition wrote at Fort Edward:

...and that there might be a less Expense of Provisions orders were given on the 12th [June] to reduce the Allowance of every person in the Army to one Ration, and 10 Rifled Barrelled Guns were delivered out to each Regiment to be put into the hands of their best Marksmen.[19]

This was confirmed in General Order for 12 June 1758:

Fort Edward Camp. Each Regt to receive ten riffled pieces from the store, & to return the like number of firelocks for them.[20]

The regiments encamped at Fort Edward at this date included the 27th, 42d, 44th, 46th, 55th, 60th, Gage's Light Arm'd Foot (80th), and Bradstreet's armed batteaumen, suggesting a total issue of at least 70 rifles. Later that month it was ordered that

The men of each regiment, who have rifled barrel pieces, to fire three rounds each at six tomorrow morning in the front of the 42d.[21]

The troops having moved on to a camp at Lake George, on 1 July 1758 orders announced:

Capt Shepherd's Company of Rangers to discharge their pieces between 3 and 5 this afternoon. The Regts may try their riffles at the same time.[22]

On this same 1 July a new deployment was ordered which appears to have included the above-mentioned riflemen or others selected for similar reasons:

The Landing of the Regulars Settled and a Company of the best Marksmen picked from Each Regiment and the...Company of Marksmen and Light Infantry to be divided into four Platoons, two in the Front of each Flank, and two in the Front of the Right and Left hand interval, marching in two files and forming a Rank intire–...[23]

Abercromby's orders for the attack on Fort Carillon (Ticonderoga) specified that from the regiments with an establishment of 1,000 men, a company of 100 marksmen was to be chosen; from those established at 700 men, a company of 80 men; the 1/60th a company of 60 men. There were to be two subaltern officers for each company and the 46th was to contribute a captain and one subaltern. Gage's Light Arm'd Foot were to be divided: two captains, five subalterns and 120 men to the Inniskilling Brigade, a like number of the Brigade of the 44th, and a further captain and four subalterns to the Brigade of the 42d. The orders, dated 3 July, agree with the orders quoted on 1 July, but specify that the light infantry and companies of marksmen were to form two in the rear of each flank and two in the rear of the right and left-hand intervals. It also notes that "the whole Army is to have their Hats cut as Colonel Bradstreet's is, that they may know one another from the Enemy."[24] It may be reasonably accepted that British regulars carried rifles during this disastrous engagement, possibly to the number of the entire 176 issued and available to the forces.

With the army back in winter quarters, the regiments around Albany were subjected to the usual paperwork, including one of the last indications of rifles in this area on 12 February 1759:

The Returns of Arms wanting & of Riffled pieces according to Genll Amherst's Order of 23d Janry., to be given in to the Brigade Major as soon as they can be made out.[25]

The westernmost reference to a rifle in the northern sector is also the last: on 4 Sept. 1759, an advertisement in daily orders stated:

...a waist belt & Rifle Byonet Dropt or misLaid who ever brings it to the Serjeant major of the 60th Regiment shall be handsomely Rewarded.[26]

No rifles appear to have accompanied the expedition against Louisbourg in 1758, despite this operation seeing the organization of the first British light infantry companies. On 24 May 1758, James Wolfe wrote to Lord George Sackville (then Lieutenant General of the Ordnance) from Halifax:

As here are no spare arms, nor no rifled barrel guns, the firelocks of these regiments will be so injured in the course of the siege that I doubt if they will be in any condition of service after it is over.[27]

The Forbes campaign across Pennsylvania to Fort DuQuesne certainly did include riflemen, both regulars carrying the 1756 rifles and provincials carrying their own rifles. Writing from Carlisle, PA on 3 June 1758, Col. Henry Bouquet advised that

until arms should arrive from England, I think it advisable to persuade every Man that has a Good Gun, or Rifle to bring it with him, and it shall be Appraised, that in case it shou'd be lost, or destroyed on real Service, the owner may be paid the just Value of his Arms.[28]

Paying for arms lost or destroyed on actual service was standard Board of Ordnance procedure, which applied to regular regiments as well as private individuals. In writing to Gen. Forbes a few days later, Bouquet noted that:

A large part of the provincials [Pennsylvanians and Virginians, with some Marylanders] are armed with grooved rifles and have their molds. Lead in bars will suit them better than bullets – likewise the Indians – but they also need fine powder FF.[29]

A useful insight not only on the prevalence of rifles with their own moulds, but the need for FF-grade powder for them. Bouquet said that cartridge boxes were inconvenient for all of the provincial troops and that they were too slow in making paper cartridges. He recommended the encouragement of powder horns and bullet pouches, reserving cartridge boxes "to use in case of a sudden or night attack." Problems in obtaining the required numbers of bullet pouches in leather caused Col. George Washington of the Virginia Regiment to have them made of Raven duck.[30] Washington noted on 3 July that he had managed to find 330 powder horns and 339 leather shot pouches to replace the linen ones of which they had a full supply.[31] Forbes informed Bouquet on 19 June that he was sending from Philadelphia 28 dozen powder horns and a further 20 dozen by the end of the week.[32] Philadephia's horn workers must have had a busy time (or were they imported from England, and being bought-up in the retailers' shops?) These accoutrements were used with both muskets and rifles, and the evidence is that the majority of the provincials carried muskets during this and the subsequent campaigns.

The final reference to rifles during 1758 occurs in November:

Bouquet's Camp. A return to be given in of the best Marksmen in each Corps also the Number of Rifles in each Corps.[33]

In March 1759, an officer of the 60th described a session of firing at marks by that regiment, some "Hylanders" and some of the Pennsylvania troops, with a significant footnote on the latter: "All the Penss that fire have not Riffles, nor do those that have make the best Shots."[34]

The rifle shown on the following page may have seen service during the Cherokee War of 1760, being the property of the commanding officer of this expedition, Archibald Montgomery, 11th Earl of Eglinton and colonel of the 1st Highland (63d/77th) Regiment. Its design is a combination of German and English features, the bore accepts the .693-in. musket ball, current at the time, with a patch suited to the depth of the rifling, and the presence of sling swivels — most unusual for English rifles — suggests a military function. Its details are given in Appendix 1.

❧ ❧ ❧ ❧ ❧ ❧ ❧ ❧

In the continental European phase of the Seven Years' War, Britain relied on her German allies and auxiliary troops for her rifle-armed light forces until 1761. Of these, Prussia and Hanover fought as allies, while Hesse-Cassel and Brunswick participated as "foreign troops in British pay." Bückeburg participated as an auxiliary of Hanover, not Britain.

Prussia had her own *feldjägercorps*, but no references have been found to any of its companies serving with the British and allied forces commanded by Prince Ferdinand of Brunswick. Between 1757 and 1762, Hanover supplied the largest force of riflemen to the allied forces, beginning with two companies of mounted and four companies of foot *jägers*, at first commanded by Major General Graf von der Schulenburg, and later by the famous Heinrich Wilhelm von Freytag who had raised the first company of Hanoverian *jägers* in 1757. By April 1759, this force had increased to three companies of mounted and six companies of foot *jägers*. Colonel von Wintzingerode also commanded a unit of mounted and foot *jägers*, as well as some Brunswick *jägers* during the campaign of 1762. Hesse-Cassel supplied two companies of foot *jägers* for the campaign of 1758, and two further companies were added by April 1759. A further two squadrons of mounted *chasseurs* and another two companies of foot *jägers*, each of 100 men, were added by 1760. Brunswick raised a "corps" of *jägers* for the 1759 campaign and a second one in 1760. A battalion of Buckeburg *jägers* is mentioned during the campaign of 1760, but as indicated these were paid as auxiliaries of Hanover, although serving alongside British troops. What percentage of these various units were entirely rifle armed, and which carried a mixed armament of light smoothbore bayonetted carbines as well as rifles, is yet to be determined. All of them fought extremely well and provided a sound basis for the British to build upon in setting up their own rifle-armed forces.[35] At this time, none of the rifles carried by these units has been positively identified.

Fraser's Chasseurs

After three years of campaigning in company with the German *jägers* mentioned above, the British command in Germany apparently felt it was time to set up their own unit during the campaign of 1761. Fraser's

The Beginnings, 1740–1754

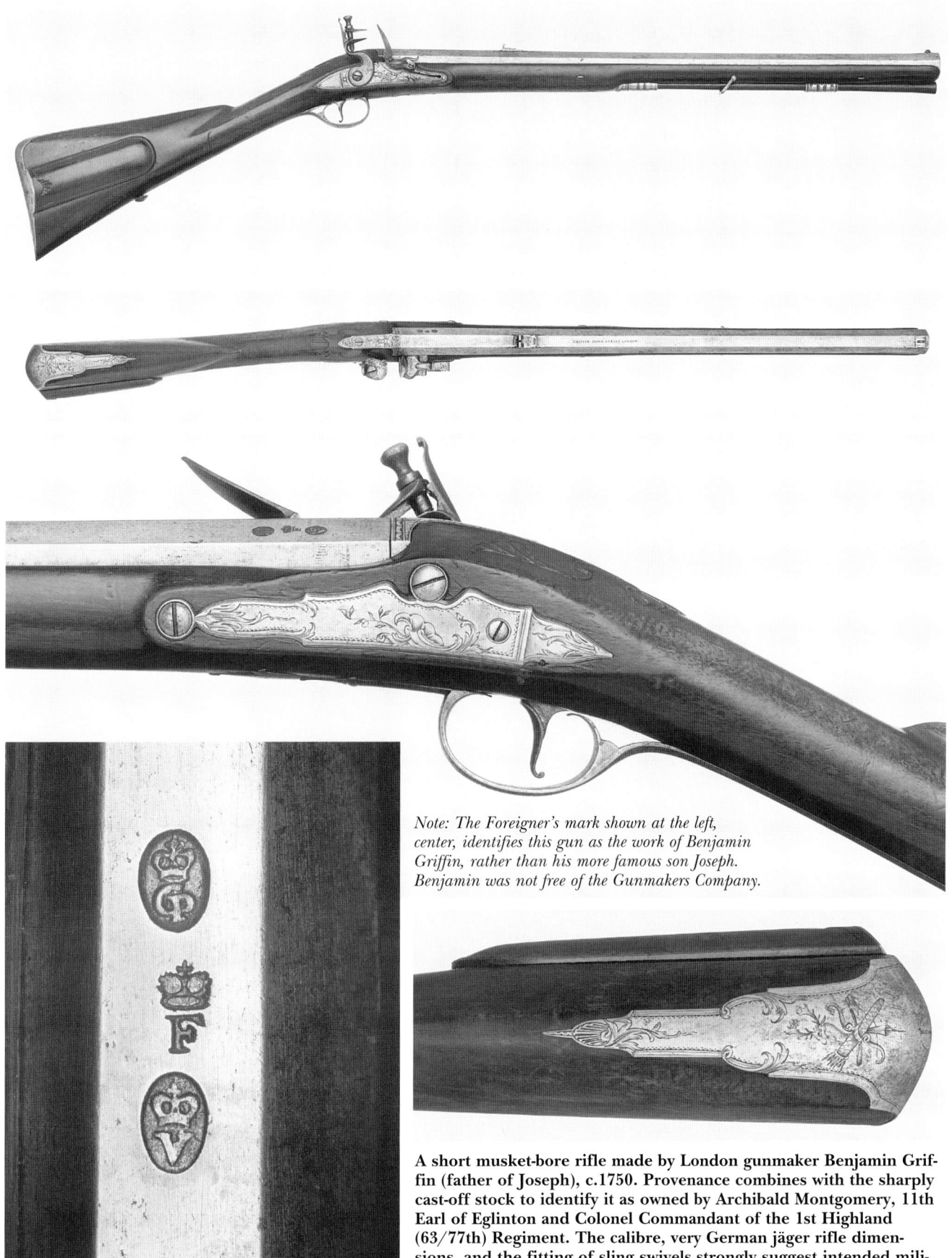

Note: *The Foreigner's mark shown at the left, center, identifies this gun as the work of Benjamin Griffin, rather than his more famous son Joseph. Benjamin was not free of the Gunmakers Company.*

A short musket-bore rifle made by London gunmaker Benjamin Griffin (father of Joseph), c.1750. Provenance combines with the sharply cast-off stock to identify it as owned by Archibald Montgomery, 11th Earl of Eglinton and Colonel Commandant of the 1st Highland (63/77th) Regiment. The calibre, very German jäger rifle dimensions, and the fitting of sling swivels strongly suggest intended military use. *Private collection.*

— 17 —

Chasseurs, commanded by Major Fraser, first appears with Prince Ferdinand's army in October 1761, and next, acting in Column "A" with other British troops commanded by Lord Granby at the Battle of Wilhelmsthal on 24 June 1762, when they suffered 1 killed and 12 wounded.[36] The unit's commander was almost certainly Major Simon Fraser of the 24th Foot, who was subsequently killed, reputedly by an American rifle bullet, at Bemis Heights in 1777. The unit is described in a General Order of 23 May 1762, as composed of selected men from twelve British line regiments then serving in Germany. There was one subaltern, one serjeant, one corporal, one drummer and thirty privates from each of the regiments, giving a total force of a dozen subalterns, serjeants, corporals and drummers and 360 privates. Three fifers were added to each battalion. They were to bring their own arms as well as tents and camp equipage, two bread wagons and an infirmary wagon per brigade. It was specified that:

...none to be sent on this Service that are not perfectly in health, good marchers and Every way fit for the Elertest part of the Service.[37]

Commanding officers were to pay particular attention to accustom their men to patrols and ambushes. On 9 June the organization of the new unit is described. Each battalion was divided into three companies by brigades, with each company being sub-divided into four divisions. The battalions were to form line two deep. As to uniforms, the hat lace was to be removed and the men were to wear green cockades. Grenadier regiments were to furnish their Chasseurs with hats in place of grenadier-caps.[38]

After the Battle of Nauheim on 30 August 1762, 98 of Fraser's men were reported missing. On the other hand, Fraser was praised by Colonel von Riedesel (commanding Hessian *jägers*) for the handling of his troops during the repulse of a French attack near Wenzen on 9 November 1761.[39]

Although there is no clear statement that this new unit carried rifles, it is significant that they were brigaded with a four-battalion unit referred to as "Cavendish's *jägers*" or "*jäger* brigade" commanded by Major-General Lord Frederick Cavendish, which included Hanoverian, Hessian and Brunswick *jägers*, both mounted and foot, during August and September 1762.[40] The unit probably purchased German rifles at regimental level, or they may have been at least partially armed with the residue of the 1746-purchase rifles in Store in the Tower at the beginning of the war. In either case, no records are known to survive supporting these suggestions. Some part may also have been equipped with Pattern 1760 Light Infantry Carbines.

British reaction to the outbreak of Pontiac's Rebellion in 1763 included the organization of a force to penetrate into the heart of Indian country and destroy the villages and crops which supported the attacking warriors. Henry Bouquet was to command this force, and as part of the recruiting for it he issued an order for the local recruiting of Rangers for the expedition:

By Henry Bouquet Esqr Colonel of Foot and Commanding His Majesty's Troops in the Southern District. To Captain Lemuel Barret. You are hereby authorized to engage thirty Woodmen, or Hunters, to march with the Troops under my Command, to Fort Pitt, and be employed as Rangers... The said Rangers are to furnish themselves each with a good Rifle, & ammunition to serve them to Ligonier, where they are to join me, on the 1st August next at furthest...
Fort Bedford, 25 July 1763.[41]

Once again American-made rifles were brought temporarily into British service. No references have yet been found to the use of the 1756 rifled carbines after the 1758 campaign, but there is no reason to doubt that they continued in use until the close of hostilities.

There is no indication that any of the 1756-purchased rifles were ever sent into Store in the Tower. Problems must have been encountered in the use of the bayonets with these rifles, or possibly it was realized from their field use that their role did not require them, for when the Ordnance came to order its own muzzle-loading rifles in 1776, the bayonet was omitted from the specification.

Having almost certainly been purchased in Germany, these 1756 rifles probably resemble closely the typical German military *jäger* rifle of the time, with a swamped octagonal barrel of something under thirty inches in length and of a calibre which did not take either British Government musket (.693") or carbine (.615") ball, since moulds had to be issued with the rifles; full stock with a wooden-covered buttbox and heavy brass furniture, including some form of grip-rail triggerguard, with sling swivels through fore-end and guard bow. There is no indication that they were ever subjected to the King's Proof, but since Prevost took ship for New York on 21 October 1756 from Cork in Ireland, it is possible that some form of official examination may have been carried out on the rifles en route, and they may bear some form of inspector's view or Storekeeper's marking applied to them by Ordnance officials at New York, Albany or Philadelphia, but this is pure speculation since we do not know the route of the rifles from point of purchase to New York. Whether they may carry markings to the Royal American Regiment is another unanswered question, but regimental

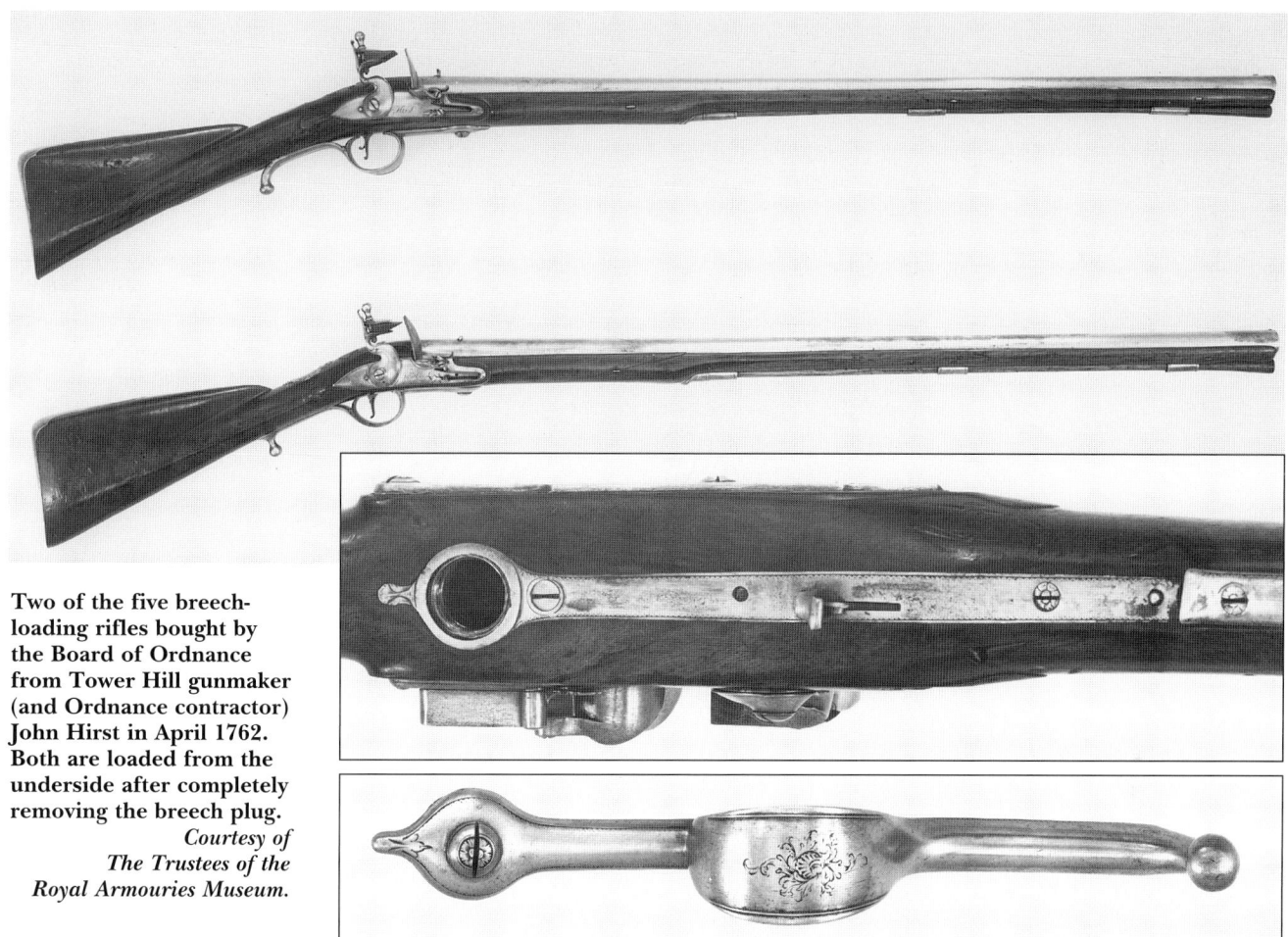

Two of the five breech-loading rifles bought by the Board of Ordnance from Tower Hill gunmaker (and Ordnance contractor) John Hirst in April 1762. Both are loaded from the underside after completely removing the breech plug.
Courtesy of The Trustees of the Royal Armouries Museum.

markings are always a very questionable feature upon which to base any certain identification.

Having written to the Portsmouth Ordnance officers on 13 February 1762 about rifles, on 14 February 1762, the Surveyor General of the Board of Ordnance ordered that 10 rifled barrel pieces, 60 flints, 10 bullet moulds and 84 pounds of lead be packed up and sent to Portsmouth "and added to the proportion for the Expedition under the Command of the Earl of Albemarle," i.e. for the Siege of Havana. They were intended for the use of engineers, as with Braddock's force.[42] To date no accounts of the use of these rifles during the siege have been located. It is assumed that the rifles were part of the 1746 purchase which had remained in store at the Tower, an assumption supported by the speed with which "1 Chest Rifled Barrel Guns arrived, at 3 p.m." at Portsmouth on 20 Feburary.[43]

During 1762, the Ordnance made its first experiments with breech-loading rifles. Five rifles on two different systems were provided by the Tower Hill gunmaker and Ordnance contractor John Hirst. They are described as:

Two Rifeld Bullet Guns, pluged at the Handles, &
Steel Mounted   15. 15. ..
Two Do plug'd at the upper Side of the Britch &
Steel Mounted   14. 14. ..
One Do plug'd at ye Handles & Mounted wth Brass
  5. 5. ..[44]

All were of the so-called screwplug system, two with a short plug screwed into the top of the barrel with the rear sight formed like a wing-nut for removing the plug, and three with the plug fixed to the front of the trigger-guard, *(see photos)* on which the guard is unscrewed to load on the underside of the piece. Experiments with these pieces were apparently satisfactory, for in December 1763, an order for twenty additional "Bullet Guns with best Rifel'd Barrels compleat at £6. each" was given to Hirst. From the price, these are assumed to have been breech-loading, but of the system used we know only that they were "agreeable to the Pattern this day produced to the Board."[45] Clearly the Board were well aware of the concept of the breech-loading rifle, its possible utility and its military limitations by the time Cap-

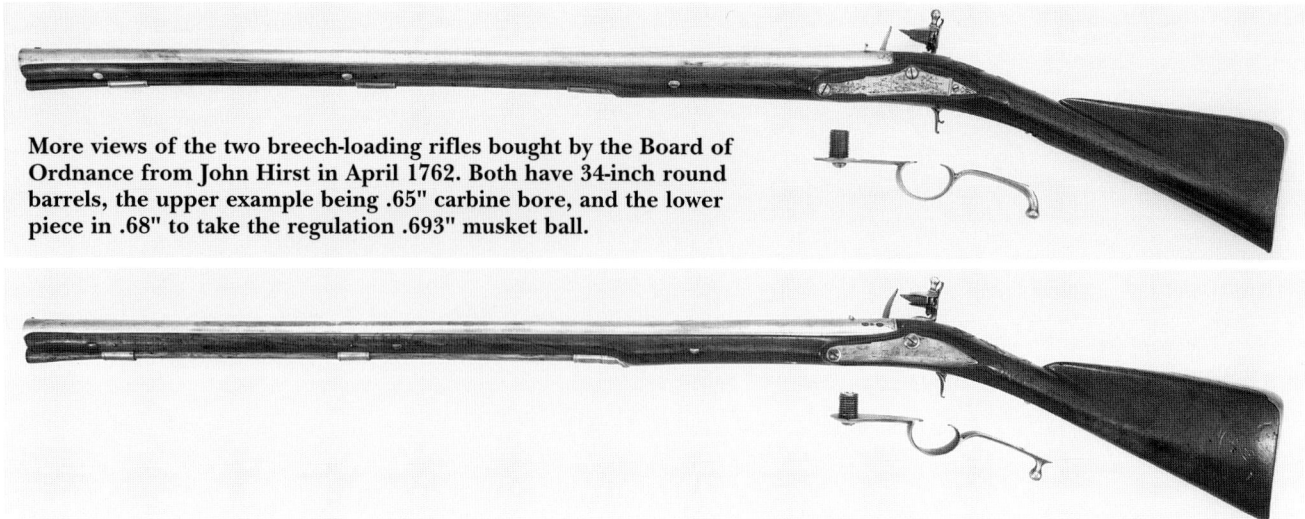

More views of the two breech-loading rifles bought by the Board of Ordnance from John Hirst in April 1762. Both have 34-inch round barrels, the upper example being .65" carbine bore, and the lower piece in .68" to take the regulation .693" musket ball.

tain Patrick Ferguson appeared on the scene thirteen years later.

These twenty-five breech-loading rifles were almost certainly connected with an unfulfilled scheme for the establishment of a specially trained corps of Military Artificers and Pioneers, the serjeants, corporals, cadets, artificers and pioneers of which were to be armed with

a musket of no more than 30-inches in the barrel, which is to be rifled and loaded at the guard [my emphasis] which will avoid the troublesome, dangerous and noisy motion of drawing and returning their rammers before an enemy, besides the advantage of loading on their backs and firing on their bellies without being exposed.

In addition they were to be subjected to intensive

Practice of firing dextrously at a mark standing, kneeling,and almost lyeing on the ground. To be taught to load quick on their backs and at one time. To fire together by signals in the day and by particular whistles in the night, as their services may require it often.[46]

This project was put forward in great detail by one of the Engineer officers who had served in America during the Seven Years' War, probably Patrick McKellar. The idea for such a corps came to naught at this time, probably because of peacetime economy measures.

On 20 Jan. 1764 the Ordnance Clerk of the Stores proposed to the Board that "35 Rifled Bullet Guns of different patterns" be included in the next public auction sale of unserviceable stores from the Tower.[47] The Board approved the order, and it seems that with this sale the last of the 1746 purchase of rifles disappeared into private hands.

Between their first appearance in 1746, and the sale of 1764, the British army had acquired a total of 360 muzzle-loading rifles, through two foreign purchases, with an additional 25 breech-loading rifles being supplied by John Hirst for experimental purposes. While the breech-loaders were retained by the Board for experimental purposes, the initial purchase of 60 rifles were probably issued to the Louisbourg/L'Orient force, certainly to Braddock's expedition and probably to Albemarle's Havana force, and the remnant were disposed of directly from the Tower. The fate of the 300 rifles purchased by Colonel Prevost in 1756, and used throughout the French & Indian War, remains unknown, although it seems likely that they remained either in the possession of the Royal Americans or in various Ordnance Stores in North America. Apart from the breech-loaders shown here, none of these rifles have been identified at the time of writing.

In the early 1770s, the rifle barrel makes a brief appearance, in connection with a new carbine for the two regiments of Light Dragoons commanded by Generals John Burgoyne and George Augustus Eliott, originator (if not designer) of the Eliott Carbine and Pistol. On 2 August 1772, the Adjutant General of the Army, Edward Harvey, wrote to General Henry Seymour Conway, Lieutenant General of the Ordnance, saying:

I am also desired by them to mention, that they much wish for a Rifled Barrell Carbine to be made, as a Pattern, as they apprehend it may be well worth considering, if Rifled Barrels for the Light Dragoons, will not be essentially usefull for His Majesty's Service.[48]

There is no recorded response to this in the Ordnance records and no evidence that anything of this type was ever made by them. However, several years ago a rifled carbine said to resemble an Eliott carbine (but apparently of musket-bore) was reported in a private collection. If details of this piece became available, then detailed examination might possibly suggest it to be connected with the desires of the two cavalry generals.

CHAPTER 2
The American War, First Phase

Did the threat of the rifle loom large in the thoughts of the British when the American War broke out in 1775? The answer is elusive, since only American newspapers and correspondents seem to have originated comment in print about the effectiveness of the rifle, as obvious propaganda; these comments were then occasionally quoted by anti-Government journals in England. A typical example from the firm of W. & T. Bradford of Philadelphia was printed in the *London Chronicle* of 17–19 August 1775:

This province has raised 1000 rifle-men, the worst of whom will put a ball into a man's head at a distance of 150 or 200 yards, therefore advise your officers who shall hereafter come out to America, to settle their affairs in England before their departure.[1]

This type of article does appear to have created a certain degree of concern, largely outside military circles. For those in the field, apprehension proved of short duration. Some days later Lieut. Evelyn of the 4th Foot recorded in Boston that

The rebels have got some reinforcements of riflemen from Virginia and Pennsylvania, mostly Irishmen. They have made some little attempts upon our out-parties, without success; and we have taken one or two of them prisoner.[2]

The *Leeds Mercury* informed its readers on 5 September that "A correspondent observes that the riflemen amongst the Americans are held in the same degree of terror, as the broadswords were in the year 1745," a particularly apt comparison given the rapid demise of the broadsword as an infantry weapon, and the suggestion that it was the Americans themselves who feared the riflemen as much for their appearance and behaviour as for their accurate shooting. General Thomas Gage at Boston confirmed the frequent desertion of rebel riflemen in a letter to the Secretary of State for America, Lord Dartmouth, on 20 Sept. 1775:

There are many Irish in the Rebels Army, particularly amongst the Rifle-Men, brought here from the Frontiers of Virginia and Pennsylvania, who take every opportunity to desert to us, notwithstanding the Danger & difficulty of doing it.[3]

Two months later, on 4 November 1775, Benjamin Thompson, (later Count Rumford), an acute observer, noted that

Of all useless sets of men that ever encumbered an army, surely the boasted riflemen are certainly the most so. When they came to the [American] camp they had every liberty and indulgence allow'd them that they could possibly wish for. They had more pay than any other soldier; did no duty; were under no restraint from the commands of their officers, but went when and where they pleased, without being subject to be stopped or examined by anyone, and did almost intirely as they pleased in every respect whatsoever. But they have not answered the end for which they were designed in any one article whatever. For instead of being the best marksmen in the world, and picking off every regular that was to be seen, there is scarcely a regiment in camp but can produce men that can beat them at shooting, and the army is now universally convinced that the continual fire which they kept up by the week and month together has had no other effect than to waste their ammunition, and convince the King's troops that they were not really so formidable adversaries as they would wish to be thought.

Mr. Washington is very sensible of this, and has not only strictly forbid their passing the advanced sentries to fire at the King's troops, without particular orders for that purpose, but has lately obliged them to do duty as other troops. And to be sure there never was a more mutinous and undisciplined set of villains that bred disturbance in any camp.

The whole number of these men in the camp may be somewhere about 650;...[4]

The Battle of Long Island seems finally to have dispelled any lingering concern felt in the British army about the rebel riflemen. There was a force of some 1,500 riflemen in action, and they were very badly defeated by British light infantry and Hessian troops. The Captain of the 33rd Foot's Light Infantry company, William Dansey, wrote after this battle:

I was lucky in my Escape for I had my right hand Man wounded and left hand Man kill'd and Six wounded in my Company in about three moments [,] having fallen in with about 400 Rifle men unawares. They are not so dreadful as I expected or they must have destroyed me and my whole Company before we were supported by anybody else. Afterwards they were all either kill'd or taken,...[5]

And the same writer, from Newport, Rhode Island, 11 January 1777:

Its astonishing to think how the Leaders of this Rebellion have made the poor ignorant People believe that because they are brought up to Gunning, as they call it, [Lieut. F. McKenzie notes 19 April 1775, "These fellows were generally good marksmen, and many of them used long guns made for Duck Shooting."[6]*] they must beat everything, but now they are convinced that being a good Marksman is only a trifling requisite for a Soldier, indeed I myself saw them beat as Marksmen at Frogneck [Throg's Neck] (12 October 1776). I was engaged having mine own and another Company under my Command (with 150 or 200 Riflemen), for upwards of seven hours at their favourite Distance of about 200 yards. They were better covered than we were, having a House a Mill and a Well. We had only Trees. They got the first fire at us before I saw them. I bid my men cover themselves with the Trees and Rocks and turn out Volunteers among the Soldiers to go to the nearest Trees and keep up the fire with the Hessian Riflemen who came to us but did not stay above an hour. I continued the popping fire at them and they at us and we had the Satisfaction of knocking several of them down and had not a man hurt. This kind of popping continued two or three days between the Light Infantry and the Riflemen across a Water Hill. We kill'd an Officer of them besides several Men and had not one of ours wounded and they at last fairly gave up firing finding themselves beat in their own way, which showed that a good soldier with a good Firelock was beyond a Rifleman and all his skill, but such a Bugbear were they at first our good Friends thought we were all to be kill'd with Rifles.*[7]

Two months later he wrote this concerning his own marksmanship:

You know I never was a famous shot but I made a very good one at the Skirmish we had on the 23rd of last month of which I wrote Mr. Gwilliam an Account. A Fellow jumped up from behind a bush near me ran behind a Tree and presented a Rifle at me. I up with my Fiwzee and knock'd him as a Cockshooter wou'd a Cock.[8]

This is the only account in which the writer has found fusil or fuzee spelt in the above ingenious manner.

THE PATTERN 1776 INFANTRY RIFLES

By the end of 1775, whatever the reality of the situation in America, there was a clear interest in getting rifles into the hands of the British troops to be sent to quell the disturbances. Apparently, some Scotch officers had aired their views to the American Secretary, and some enquiries had been made through Colonel William Faucitt, then in northern Germany to negotiate treaties with various princes for the hire of troops, including riflemen, to act with the British troops in America. Months before any Government-made rifles appeared on the scene, the Guards had apparently decided to introduce war games that included riflemen, although from the following it is not clear whether they actually had rifles:

Yesterday Morning some of the parties of the Guards, who had been learning the exercise of bush fighting, had a sham attack on Kensington Gravel Pits, which their Officers called Bunkers Hill; some of the soldiers were called riflemen and had a target fixed to exercise their dexterity at, but alas! there was not one hole in it. However, they made the thistles fly that surrounded it and peppered the gravel pit with a vengeance.[9]

THE HANOVERIAN-MADE PATTERN 1776 INFANTRY RIFLE

On 26 December an Ordnance labourer was sent with "two Riffle Guns to Capt. Tovey at Woolwich" and was paid £6.10.0. expenses, suggesting that he may have assisted Tovey in carrying out trials of the weapons.[10] From a letter quoted below, it is clear that these pattern rifles had come through Faucitt from Germany, indicating that the idea had probably originated as far back as the autumn of 1775. By the end of the month, the Master General of the Ordnance, Lord Townshend, was writing to the Secretary of State for America asking him to get the King's permission to order some light artillery pieces and 1,000 rifles for the troops in America, and giving at least some of the reasons for the requests:

...and also for 1000 rifled Barrel pieces (which I apprehend from a letter from Colo Faucit) may be purchased the cheapest and best in Germany, and also of some experiments I have made of them at Woolwich.

The Highlanders who have many marksmen & Deer Killers amongst them are particularly desirous of having 5 of those pieces per Company, I am persuaded they would be of great use in America, Colo Harcourt desires also the same proportion, and I would submit whether every Battalion Engaged in this Service should be provided with this much boasted weapon of that Country.[11]

George, 1st Marquess Townshend, had served with the British army in America, being one of the "three Brigadiers" with Wolfe at Quebec in 1759, and was a man of very decided opinions; he was Master General of the Ordnance from 1772 to 1782 and was responsible for a number of innovations in small arms and artillery. It is clear that he had experimented with rifles prior to the arrival of the new patterns from Hanover. Lieutenant-Colonel William Harcourt at this time commanded the 16th (Burgoyne's, Queen's) Light Dragoons. Having experimented with the Hanoverian pat-

The American War: First Phase

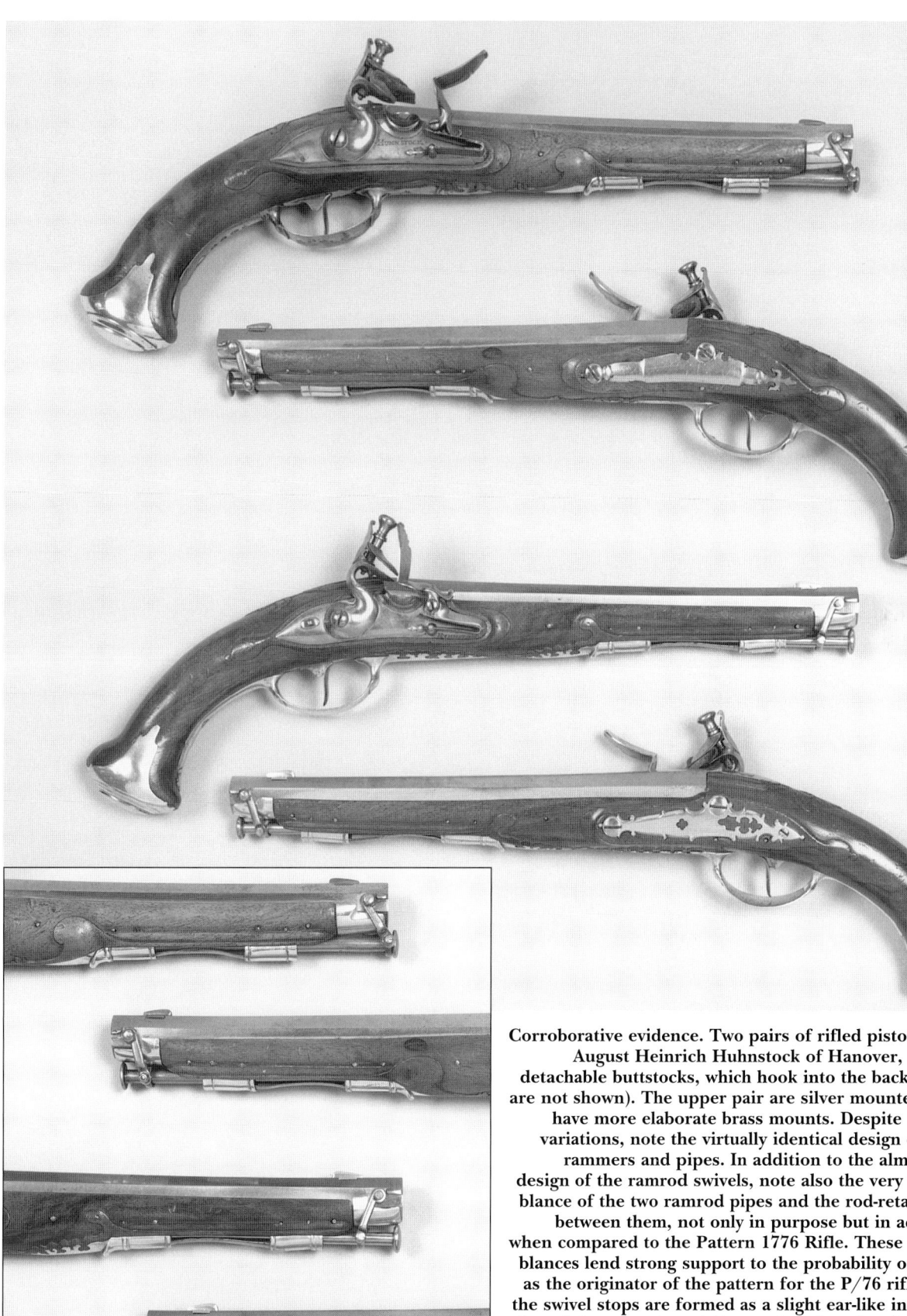

Corroborative evidence. Two pairs of rifled pistol-carbines by August Heinrich Huhnstock of Hanover, c.1776. (The detachable buttstocks, which hook into the back of the grips are not shown). The upper pair are silver mounted, the lower have more elaborate brass mounts. Despite these styling variations, note the virtually identical design of the swivel rammers and pipes. In addition to the almost identical design of the ramrod swivels, note also the very close resemblance of the two ramrod pipes and the rod-retaining spring between them, not only in purpose but in actual design, when compared to the Pattern 1776 Rifle. These close resemblances lend strong support to the probability of Huhnstock as the originator of the pattern for the P/76 rifle. Note that the swivel stops are formed as a slight ear-like integral extension of the upper barrel flats, rather than the simpler, cheaper and more readily replaceable screws of the service rifle.
Royal Collection, Windsor Castle, reproduced by gracious permission of Her Majesty The Queen.

British Military Flintlock Rifles

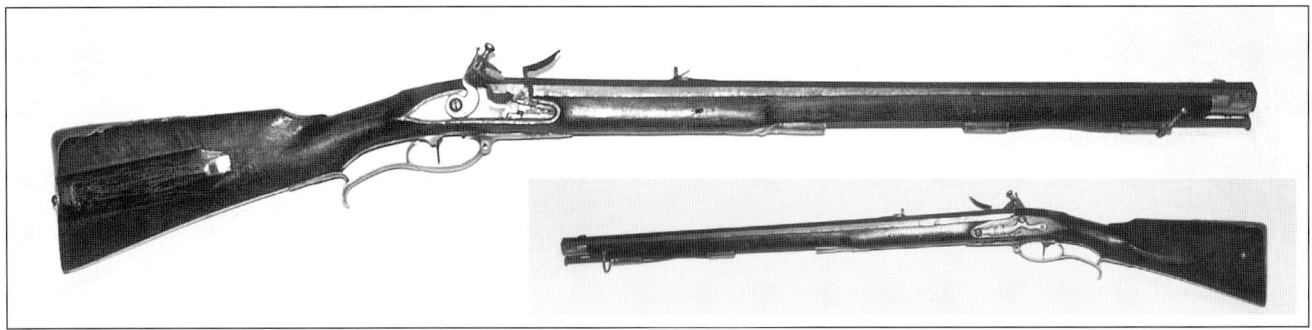

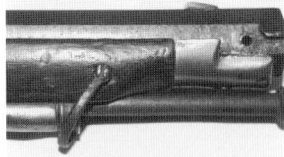

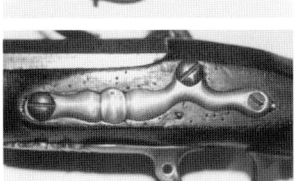

Pattern 1776 Rifle made in Hanover by August Heinrich Huhnstock early in 1776. Many Germanic military rifles of the last quarter of the 18th century have brass furniture of this general pattern, but the salient feature of this rifle, the design of the swivel rammer and its fittings and retaining spring clearly identify it as one of the 1776 Huhnstock production. These rifles served as the pattern from which the Birmingham-made rifles were adapted to a more typical British Ordnance appearance in the lock and butt areas of the rifle.
Private collection.
Photographs courtesy
E.E. Cowan.

tern-rifles, and obtained the King's approval, the Master General was now able to confirm an order to Col. Faucitt in Hanover:

The two Riffles which you were so good as to send me arrived safe last week [the week of 26 Dec. 1775], as I saw no Proof Marks on the barrel of the new Pattern pieces I thought it prudent to order them to be proved at the Tower. The old Barrel stood but the new one burst into pieces and upon Examination the metal appeared to be very badly tempered, the workmanship seemed extremely well Executed & had the Barrel stood, there could be no doubt of its answering perfectly well, as indeed the other has done upon tryal. As I wish to have some of them in store to answer any sudden demand, and our People here are not Sufficiently acquainted with that Sort of work to depend solely on them for a large number I must take the liberty of troubling you further to order 200 to be immediately put in hand, of the same Construction with that which you sent, or such others as you think can be best recommended for their service & portableness- at the same time it will be essentially necessary before they are received to have satisfactory tryals made with them upon the Spot, in order to ascertain their Strength as well as their Execution. I have been informed that the Germans often use Cast Iron for their Riffles, which I imagine they are obliged to do when they are confined to a low price; but as the advantages which their Pieces are supposed to have over Musquets will be lost if the exactness of their Construction & the goodness of the materials are not particularly attended to, I could wish that the price may be Settled so as that neither of these points may be neglected. Genl Williamson who I have requested to try some Riffles at Woolwich has expressed a desire to know what proportion of ingredients the Germans use in their Gunpowder. If you could inform yourself of this Circumstance and send over when an opportunity offers a Sample of the Powder in common use where you are, and of the materials of which it is composed you will much oblige me. I shall make no further apology for being so troublesome as I am sure your Zeal for His Majestys Service renders it unnecessary.

You will be so good as to direct that these pieces may be furnished immediately as they probably will be called for very soon they may be sent by 50 at a time as they are finished.[12]

It is clear that the Master General and Secretary of State had already ironed out the details by the middle of January 1776, when Lord George Germain (the new Secretary of State for America) committed progress to paper:

It is also His Majesty's further Pleasure that Your Lordship do give the necessary Directions that 12 Light Feild Peices such as are described in your Lordship's letter to me of the 31st December be prepared and sent to Major General Howe, & also 1000 Rifle barrelled Muskets to be distributed among the different Corps as proposed by Your Lordship. ...[13]

In view of the correspondence that mentions patterns sent from Germany at the earliest stages, it is clear that the pattern adopted originated with the Hanoverian gunmaker August Heinrich Huhnstock, who supplied the two hundred rifles ordered by Faucitt in Hanover. Apart from comparing the Hanoverian and English rifles themselves, support for this attribution is given by two pairs of pistol-carbines by Huhnstock in the Royal Collection at Windsor (L395, L457,464), incorporating an identical

— 24 —

form of swivel rammer to that on the rifle, which is the first swivel rammer in British service, and amongst the earliest of swivel rammers.

The rifle shown earlier in this section and described in detail in Appendix I is without reasonable doubt one of the 200 rifles supplied by August Heinrich Huhnstock of Hanover in the Spring of 1776, on a contract of January 1776, prior to the delivery of the balance of 800 ordered from the four Birmingham contractors. Basically this rifle is a straightforward "typical" German military rifle of the period, except for the modifications made in fitting a swivel ramrod. The example illustrated is numbered 184 on the barrel tang. The rifling of the Hanoverian contract apparently retained the rapid pitch typical of German rifles of the period — one turn in the length of the barrel — rather than the one turn in 56 inches adopted for the Birmingham version of this pattern described below.

THE BIRMINGHAM-MADE PATTERN 1776 INFANTRY RIFLE

Before the end of January, orders for rifles had been placed in Birmingham[14] and by the end of the month the Board was able to give specific instructions to its local examining officials:

Ordered that the Viewer at Birmingham give directions to such of the Barrel and Lockmakers as can give most despatch & be Relied upon to provide 600 Rifled Barrel Guns according to a Pattern sent to Mr. Grice who had ingaged for 200 Exclusive of the above 600 and that he Report the Price &c in what time they can be made.[15]

Although William Grice of Birmingham was a leading contractor to the Board for locks, barrels and ramrods, this is the first time since a single contract of 1742 with his father, that he was asked to supply complete weapons. It suggests strongly that Grice was already familiar with rifle manufacture.

A few days after official correspondence makes it clear that the manufacture of the Government rifles was just beginning, the popular press came out with another "red herring":

The guards are every day practising the use of the rifle gun in Hyde Park. The barrels of these new fangled instruments of death are on so particular a construction that a pistol carries 300 yards; and some of the men are already so dextrous, that they can hit the centre of a small target at that distance.[16]

What rifles had the Guards acquired for this practice? Left-overs from the Prevost purchase of 1756 are unlikely in view of the auctions just after that war; perhaps the rifled pistol-carbines by Huhnstock, bought by officers and lent to their men (strange the mention of a "pistol" in the above). This is another of the many unanswered questions relating to early British rifle use.

A month later, William Grice requested payment of £3.5.0. for his pattern rifle, and having been inspected by the Ordnance Furbisher and Clerk to the Surveyor General, they pronounced it worth two shillings less, or three guineas, which payment to Grice the Board authorized on 8 March.[17] For many years it was thought that the rifle shown on the following page was the pattern by Grice referred to; it may in fact have been an initial pattern, but is certainly earlier in design and far more Germanic than the design ultimately manufactured in 1776.

The Master General appears to have originated the idea that the Commander-in-Chief, as the man on the spot, should have the final decision as to who received rifles, and on 12 March 1776, he was able to write to General Howe at Boston that the King agreed with him:

...and a Quantity of Rifles of the best sort which are making in Germany and at Birmingham, applications have been made for the one and the other by many officers according to their fancy, but His Majesty has thought it best that they should be sent to you to dispose of as you shall judge best for the Service. Burgoynes and the Highlanders were promised some before I received these orders.[18]

This letter clearly states that, whatever rifles Howe may subsequently choose to issue on local demands, those earlier requested by the Highland regiments (the 42d and two battalions of the then-raising 71st) at five per company, as well as those to the 16th Light Dragoons, were to be issued.

Meanwhile manufacture of the rifles at Hanover had been agreed and was in progress by mid-February, as Faucitt informed Townshend on the 28th:

Colo Faucitt having in his Letter to the Master General dated at Hanover 28th ultimo represented that agreeable to his Lordship's desire he has agreed for the Riffle Barrel Guns to be made & therefore requested that a proper person may be sent over to inspect the workmen and attend the Proof of the said Riffle Barrels.

Ordered a Letter to acquaint the Master General that the Board are of opinion it will be less expensive to send the Rifled Barrel Guns to England and prove them afterwards. A Letter to Colo Fawcett to acquaint him therewith.[19]

This clearly indicates that the German-made rifles will bear the King's Proof marks on the barrels, and the Storekeeper's mark on the butt as well. Production having commenced, Faucitt was able to delve into more technical and financial details:

British Military Flintlock Rifles

Military pattern rifle by William Grice, 1776. This is probably the pattern rifle submitted by Grice to the Board of Ordnance, which was rejected in favour of the design of the Hanoverian gunmaker Huhnstock. In proportions it is English in design, but the details are German. .54 calibre, 36¾" swamped octagon barrel 1⅛" across flats at breech, 8 groove square rifling half the width of the lands, making ½ turn in the barrel, or 1 turn in 73½".
Courtesy of The Trustees of the Royal Armouries Museum.

Ordered that Colo Faucitt be acquainted that he may draw upon the Board from time to time for money to pay for the Rifle Barrel Guns & that they are to be sent to the Tower without proving for the Resons set forth already & that he will take proper receipts & transmit them to this Office.[20]

Colo Faucitt having in return to Mr. Boddington's Letter of 26 ultimo represented in his Letter of the 4 instant that the Riffle Barrel Guns for which he contracted for at Hanover shall be Compleated & sent over as soon as possible but that it will be necessary to send to America a finer sort of Powder than what is furnished for the musquetry for the particular use of the Hessian & Brunswick Chasseurs who are all armed with Riffle Barrel Guns who had informed him would be useless unless they are supplied with a Powder Superior in Quality and Fineness to the ordinary kind used by the Infantry.[21]

Faucitt had written to the Board on 17 April about obtaining a higher quality and finer grain of powder for the new rifles. Thomas Hartwell, the Ordnance Proofmaster, was instructed to advise and to give a proportion of 200 rounds for 1,000 men, as was done for English muskets.[22]

On 24 April, the Board wrote to John York, the Viewer at Birmingham, to report progress on the rifles and when they would be finished. Bridges, Eade and Wilton, operators of the Ewell powder mills on the Hogsmill River in Surrey, notified the Board that they could furnish fifty barrels (5,000 pounds) of S.D.S. (superfine double-strength) powder in ten days, at a cost of £7.10.0. per barrel, provided they were paid ready money. A warrant was issued on the same day, confirming that the question of rifle powder was promptly dealt with:

Messrs Bridges, Eade & Wilton. Superfine powder S D S Barrels with 100 lbs each, 50 @ £7.10.0. per barrel. Powder Barrels for do., whole 28, half 44, quarter 200.[23]

followed by a letter of 10 May informing Faucitt that the powder had been ordered, and that the rifles are needed as soon as possible.[24]

Production was moving but the Viewer at Birmingham informed the Office on 3 May that no rifles would be ready before July, a date confirmed by Grice himself in a letter to the Board on 6 May.[25] The Board must have been cheered by a second letter from Viewer York of 17 May saying that all the rifles, not just Grice's, would be completed before July; "upwards of 100 ready in a few Days." The Board told him in reply that they "must be sent to the Tower as fast as finished."[26]

An unfortunately undated diary entry from about this time gives us some interesting details on the rifles:

The Gun manufactory is pretty; the forging, scraping and boreing, pleas'd me much. The Rifle Guns are handsome pretty pieces, 800 are nearly finish'd on government account at three pounds three shillings each. A Gentleman, with one of them at a distance of 150 yards shot a Ball 6 times out of 8 within the circumference of the crown of my hat; at 400 yards he shot within half a yard of the mark.[27]

Given that the average crown of a hat of the period was about six inches in diameter, this is first-class shooting, and we do not know how proficient the "Gentleman" was. This remains the only contemporary reference to the accuracy of the Pattern 1776 rifles.

Although as yet no rifles had been completed, on 16 May a projection was made of Ordnance materials required for General Howe's army in America. Under the heading of "For the use of the Troops" we find:

Rifle Barrel Guns	1000
Glazed Powder, Whole Barrels	90
Carbine Ball	18 tons, 10 cwt
Flints	10,000
Formers	200[28]

The inclusion of formers for making up paper cartridges is the only clue we have as to how the rifles were intended to be loaded. Since they were using carbine ball and formers, it is reasonable to think they may also have used a carbine charge of 3 drams of powder (82½

— 26 —

grains), or thereabouts, considering it was a much stronger powder than that issued with carbines. The above proportions represent 763,636 charges of 3 drams for 828,800 carbine ball, with 10 flints per rifle and one cartridge former for every five rifles – the projected number of rifles to be issued to each infantry company. An exact proportion of ball to powder would give a powder charge of 76 grains, just over 2¾ drams, which might represent the true charge put down the barrel after deducting for priming which was done first in the loading process.

There is no indication of any hangers or other sidearms in lieu of a bayonet being either intended, manufactured or purchased for the use of the riflemen, but as it was intended the rifles should be part of a company's armament, it could be assumed that the intention was for the remainder of the bayonet-equipped company to back them up in the conventional manner of light infantry. It may also be that despite this intention which was carried into practice, hangers or short-swords may have been purchased at regimental level, a standard practice.

By early June the arrival of the first half of the Hanoverian rifles was imminent:

Read a Letter from Colo Faucitt at Stade dated 28th Ulto reporting that 100 of the Riffle Barrel Guns bespoke at Hanover pursuant to the Master Genls Orders are finished & sent to Bremen to be forwarded to the Tower by the first Ship that sails from thence [.] that he had examined the said Barrels & find them exceeding good ones all which had been proved with Double Loading & that the other 100 Rifle Barrels would be ready in about a month when they should be forwarded to the Tower & hoped his proceedings would meet with the Boards approbation.

Ordered that a Letter be wrote to the Lords Commissrs of the Treasury to Acquaint their Lordships that 100 Rifle Barrel Guns made at Hanover for His Majesty's Service in America are daily expected from thence. The Board therefore desire their Lordships will be pleased to obtain His Majesty's Licence for the Importation thereof.[29]

Problems with Customs were to plague the Board throughout the war not only in receiving foreign-made arms, but in moving arms and powder around the coasts and to Ireland for troop transports.

It would appear that this first batch arrived during the following three weeks, for on 21 June the Board ordered:

...that 50 Riffle Barrel Guns be sent to Genl How and 50 to Genl Burgoine with proper ammunition & that they be sent to Portsmouth by Land carriage as soon as they arrive from Germany.[30]

On 27 June, the Ordnance officers at Portsmouth harbour notified the Board that they had received "by Clark's Waggon," two cases [50 to a case seems doubtful, probably the standard 25] of guns and eight quarter-barrels of glazed powder, three hundredweight of carbine ball and 540 carbine flints for onward transmission to Generals Howe and Burgoyne. Two days later they informed the Board that they had shipped on board the Ordnance Transport *Lovely Mary* one chest of arms, four quarter-barrels of glazed powder, 1½ hundred-weight of carbine ball and 270 carbine flints, consigned to General Howe. The arms and powder for General Burgoyne remained with them because the Canada Fleet had sailed prior to the arrival of the waggon from London. The Board replied that they should be shipped by the first opportunity.[31] A month later Burgoyne's rifles still remained unshipped, and the Ordnance wrote to the Board of Admiralty in hopes of speeding up the movement. On 1 September, the Admiralty replied that they had ordered the arms and powder sent to Quebec on the Navy Transport *Mellish*, which was finally done on 4 September.[32]

Gunpowder for the rifles continued to arrive: ten barrels (1,000 lbs.) were received in the Tower from Bridges, Eade & Wilton by 10 July.[33]

On 24 June the Master General ordered that no more muzzle-loading rifles than had already been ordered be manufactured, so that production of Ferguson's rifle could be commenced as soon as possible.

On 30 June, Master Armourer John Wilkinson at Woolwich was billed for "38 Pr of Moulds for Rifle Barrel Guns 1/- ea, £1.18.0."[34] This is curious in that moulds normally originated from the maker of the rifle, or were at least produced to his immediate orders. Obviously the Board preferred to produce its own to ensure uniformity with existing carbine-bore ammunition.

In Hanover, production required stimulation by additional payments:

Colo Faucitt having in his Letter dated Hanover 12th July 1776 represented that he had that day drawn on the Board 2 Bills of Exchange the one for £200 & the other for £182.6.0. payable one month after date to Messrs Michl David & Son or Order on acct of Rifle Barrel Guns and that the last 100 of this Contracted for are on the way from thence to Bremen in Order to be Shipped for England.

Ordered that the Bills be accepted.[35]

On 24 August 1776, the Bill books record the first payment at three guineas (£3.3.0.) each, for a first batch of 97 of the muzzle-loading rifles, to William Grice & Son.[36] This was followed on 30 September by other initial payments to the remaining three Birmingham contractors for their initial batches:

British Military Flintlock Rifles

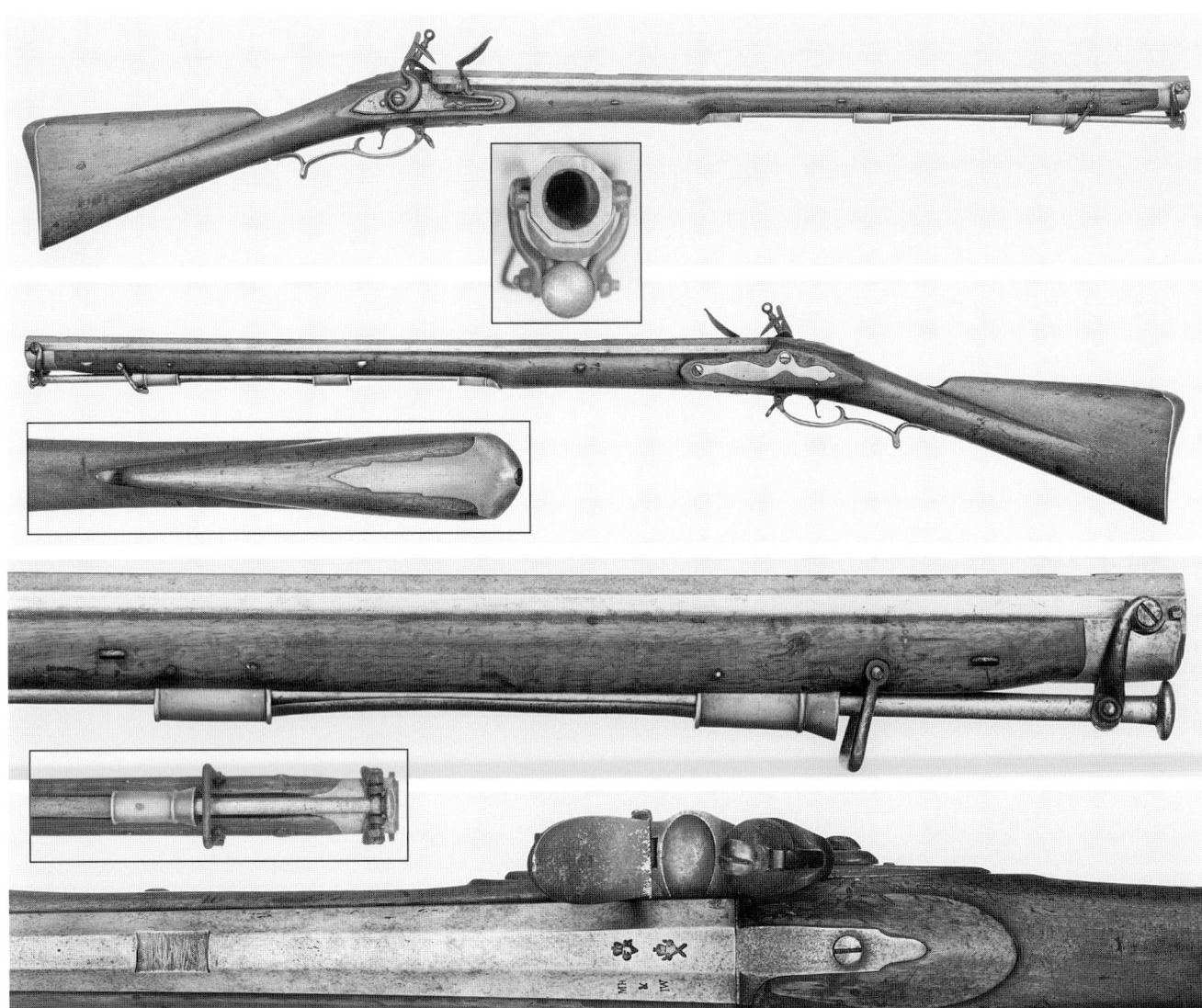

Pattern 1776 rifle, the regulation military rifle used by the British Army in North America from late 1776. 800 were made in Birmingham during the summer of 1776, and another 200 in Hanover of the same general design. The muzzles of all examples examined have been deliberately relieved while retaining the rifling. The proofmarks are the standard King's Proof, and the maker's mark on the left identifies Matthias Barker & John Whately who supplied 200 rifles.
Courtesy of R.J. Whittaker; other views from private collection, D.A. Stewart and Messrs Phillips.

Benjamin WILLETTS
    Rifled Bullet Guns 108 @ £3.3.0.
Matthias BARKER
    Rifled Bullet Guns 122 @ £3.3.0.
Samuel GALTON & Son
    Rifled Bullet Guns 102 @ £3.3.0.[37]

The 800 rifles produced by the four Birmingham contractors bear a strong resemblance to the Hanoverian pattern, being almost identical ahead of the lock, but clearly "Anglicised" from the lock to the butt. The design of English civilian rifles of the period is often virtually indistinguishable from that of fowling pieces, but where military experience is concerned the trend was strongly towards the German origins of the rifle. As one would expect, their dimensions are extremely close (see Appendix 1).

On 11 October orders for the further shipment of rifles to North America were recorded: "Ordered that the Riffle Barrel Guns with ammn to be sent to Halifax to be forwarded to Genl Howe."[38] This was in addition to the 50 Hanoverian-made P/76s shipped earlier. A week later the Master Carpenter to the Board had prepared 40 chests for carbines (at the standard 25 per chest, a total of 1,000 arms), which may well have been for the rifles:

— 28 —

The American War: First Phase

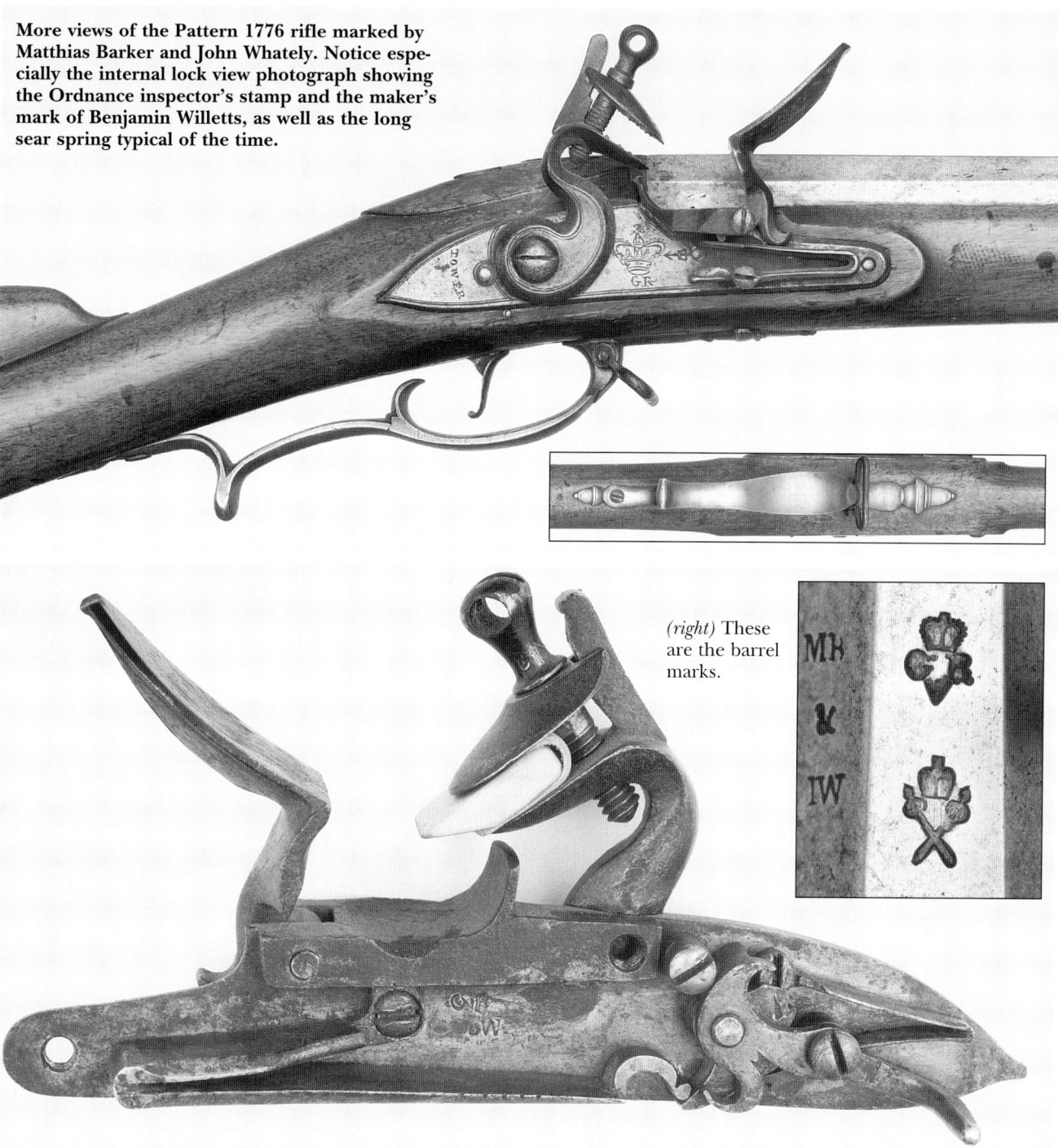

More views of the Pattern 1776 rifle marked by Matthias Barker and John Whately. Notice especially the internal lock view photograph showing the Ordnance inspector's stamp and the maker's mark of Benjamin Willetts, as well as the long sear spring typical of the time.

(right) These are the barrel marks.

To James Morris, Master Carpenter, by Warrant of Justification of 7 Feb. 1777, allowed 19 Oct. 1776: 40 Carbine Chests @ 10/- each.[39]

A Warrant of Justification was official permission for work to be done after it had actually been completed. At the end of October a bill for the loading of transports, including the *Lord Townshend* Ordnance transport, suggests the timing of the shipment and the vehicle:[40] bill for loading transports for America, 27 days.

Also for loading the *Lord Townshend*, a bill on 30 September.

Gunpowder was not overlooked, and the timing of the order is directly related to the general movement of the rifles to America. On 18 October, Bridges Eade & Wilton were ordered to supply 72 barrels of 100 lbs. each of "Superfine powder" at £7.10.0. per 100 lbs., as well as 144 full bound half-barrels to contain the powder at 2/6 each. Of this amount, 43 whole barrels (4,300 lbs, or 364,848 carbine charges) were shipped in

— 29 —

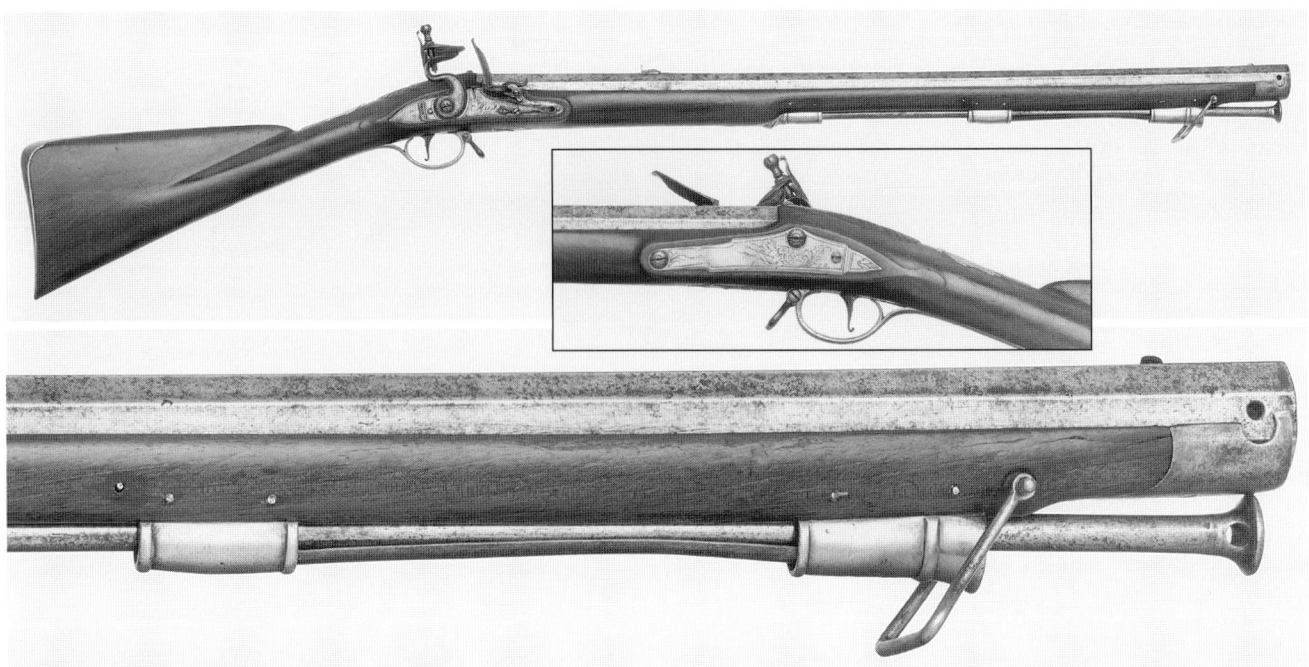

Hirst officer's rifle. A very close up-market copy of the Pattern 1776 Rifle, most probably made for an officer in one of the regiments to whom the P/76s were first issued. The proofmarks are the "private Tower proof" marks introduced in 1751, often confused with private Birmingham marks. *Courtesy of The Trustees of the Royal Armouries Museum.*

the *Lord Townshend*.[41]

In Hanover, settling-up for the 200 rifles made there earlier in the year was still going on, and although the final account was entered on 18 October 1776, it was not paid to Faucitt until 1784!

To Lt Genl Wm Faucett, the sum of Three hundred eighty four pounds 1/10 for the following disbursements on acct of Rifle Barrel Guns purchased in Hanover by Order of Lord Townsend & delivered at the Tower p. Certificate indorsed – 1776 July 12. Pd Aug: Heinrich Huhnstock for 200 Rifle

Barrel Guns at 11 Rx is	Rx 2200 - Groats 36
Proving & packing the same in 4 chests	16 23
Ludolph Johann Kumme for Freight of do to Bremen	11 30
Daniel Tietie for Charges on Shipping the same for London	9 24
Hanover post Master 1 Box from Narden	2 12
	Rx 2240 17

at an Exchange of Rx 5 5/6 p # Sterlg is £384.1.10¾.[42]

On 1 December 1776, the final batches of muzzle-loading rifles, long since delivered, were billed:

Matthias BARKER
  Rifled Bullet Guns 78 @ £3.3.0.
Samuel GALTON & Son
  Rifled Bullet Guns 98 @ £3.3.0.
William GRICE
  Rifled Bullet Guns 103 @ £3.3.0.

Benjamin WILLETTS
  Rifled Bullet Guns 92 @ £3.3.0.[43]

Despite having launched themselves into the purchasing and domestic manufacture of military rifles, the Board of Ordnance retained a degree of scepticism over their utility, and late in January 1777, set up an experiment to determine the value of rifling. They ordered

A Plain Barrel to be made of the same Dimensions of a good American Rifle, to be tried against it, and to be mounted in the same manner.[44]

Most unfortunately, no subsequent references to the results of this trial have been found. The smooth-rifle made by John Christian Oerter and dated 1775, captured by the British, carried by Royal Artillery Captain Peter Traille, and now in the Royal Collection (L276), (shown later in this book), would suggest that the idea was still considered at this time to possess some utility. What were known as "Ball guns" or "Bullet guns" (as distinct from "rifled bullet guns") had been in use in England since the 17th century.

A PATTERN 1776 OFFICER'S RIFLE?

A rifle closely connected to this period is a short sporting rifle by John Hirst, the Tower Hill gunmaker who had supplied all of the English-made rifles acquired by the Ordnance prior to 1776. Apart from closely

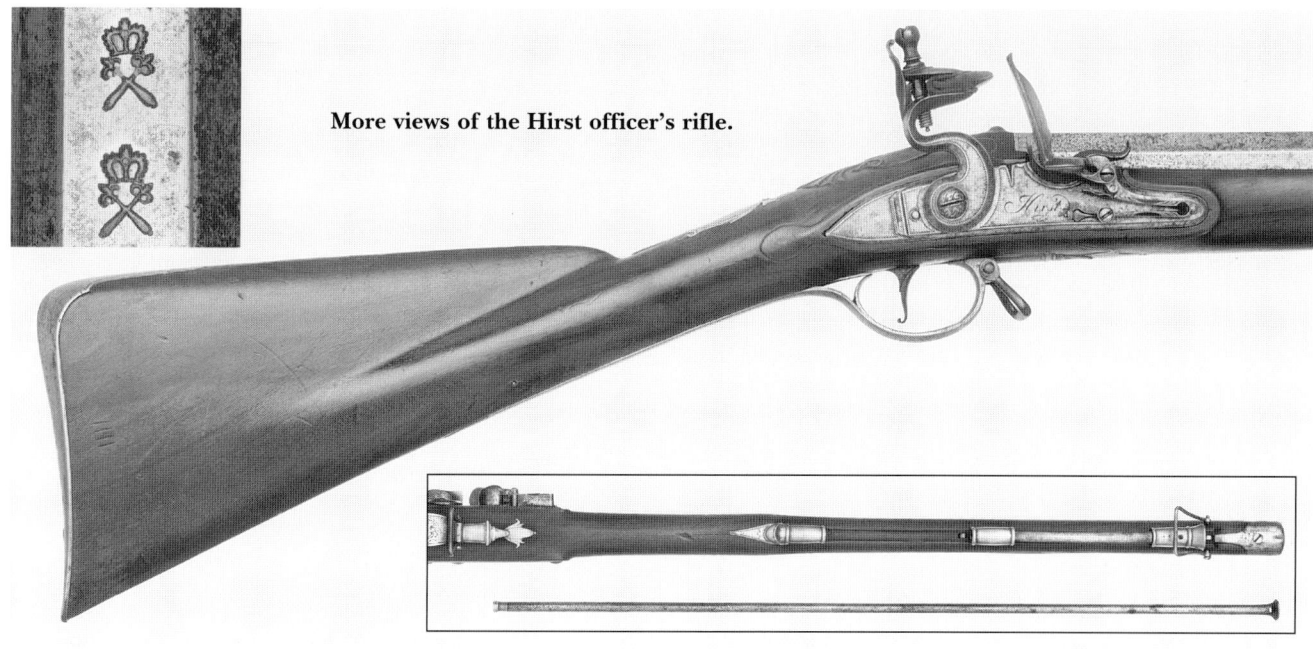

More views of the Hirst officer's rifle.

resembling the Pattern 1776 in overall design, the fitting of a steel fore-end cap and swivel rammer attachment apparently identical to that of the service rifle, and a heavy iron rammer identical even to the removable brass tip, as well as in the bore size, rifling twist, sights, rod pipes and rod-retaining spring between them, suggests that it was made for an officer who had seen the Pattern 1776, and had need of a similar rifle. Prior knowledge would suggest that the officer belonged to one of the regiments early promised rifles, e.g. the dismounted Light Dragoons or a Highland regiment.

The carrying of fusils by officers, in place of spontoons, was a controversial activity whose fortunes waxed and wained with the Commanders-in-Chief and regimental colonels. On colonial service they were decidedly popular, but rifled examples are extremely rare. The fine example shown in the plates on the following page, by John Twigg of London, is the only one reported at the time of writing.

ISSUES
a. Initial Issues
Master General of the Ordnance Lord Townshend's letter of 31 December 1775 to the Secretary of State for America, Lord George Germain, clearly states that the Highlanders (which at that date refers to the 42d Regiment and the newly raising two-battalion 71st Regiment) would like to have five rifles per company, i.e. about one hundred and fifty rifles. Since this interest is stated as the reason for production of the Pattern 1776 rifles, we must assume that these units received rifles. He further states that Col. Harcourt (commanding Burgoyne's 16th or Queen's Light Dragoons) wants a similar proportion, and we know that he did receive 54 government rifles. Being the earliest requests it seems likely that a part of those issued will have been of Hanoverian manufacture.

In his letter to Howe of 12 March 1776, Germain confirms that the rifles are being manufactured, "applications having been made by one and the other for many officers according to their fancy," and firmly places their disposal in Howe's hands with a single qualification:

...but his Majesty has thought it best that they should be sent to you to dispose of as you shall judge best for the Service – Burgoyne's and the Highlanders were promised some before I received these Orders.[45]

He confirms this situation in a letter to Howe of 28 April:

...nor has there been any Distribution of Rifled Barrel'd Guns any more than Light Artillery. ...It [the rifle] is a nasty weapon but since the Enemy will teach us the use of them I shall send you the best I can produce both from Germany and here as soon as possible.[46]

There is an interesting intimation in a letter of Col. Harcourt to his father the Earl, of 23 May 1776:

...the Dismounted part of the Regiment, which I have vanity enough to think are at least as well trained and much better armed *[my emphasis] and appointed than any Light Infantry in the army, are now in the neighbourhood of London, and will be seen by H.M. on their march on Saturday next...*[47]

Since no rifles had yet been delivered to the Ordnance either from Hanover or Birmingham, it is assumed that Harcourt was anticipating the improved armament of his dismounted dragoons, representing a confirmation that he had received assent to the issue of the rifles, without actually having them in the hands of the men. That this was the situation is supported by an order of the very next day, 24 May, by the Board of Ordnance:

Ordered that Messrs Bridges Eade & Wilton send to the Tower 10 Barrels of Double Strong Fine Powder as soon as possible to be kept in Store & that Colo Harcourt be Supplied with a proper Proportion for his Rifled Barrel Guns of Genl Burgoyne's Regiment.[48]

and with further details of the bill of 28 May:

Messrs Alexander Bridges, Jonathan Eades & William Wilton, Superfine powder marked S D S whole Barrels of 100·lb each, 10 @ £7.10.0 each. Whole Barrels for do. 10 Bags for do. 10[49]

The 16th Light Dragoons landed at New York in September 1776 after a thirteen-week voyage during which they lost 58 horses. Major Baurmeister reported that with each troop were forty dismounted dragoons, whose accoutrements were the same as those of the mounted men's, except that they wore leather boots and carried pistols and rifled guns instead of their regular side arms.[50]

This eyewitness account suggests that all of the dismounted men were rifle-armed, but this is corrected by Harcourt's own later request for a replacement of only 54, or one company's-worth, of rifles. After the 16th Light Dragoons had returned from America early in 1779, leaving their arms in the Ordnance Stores at New York, a warrant was issued 8 March for 420 carbines and 420 pairs of pistols to replace these arms. On 30 March, Harcourt applied for rifles as well, and the Board responded:

Rifled Officer's Fusil by John Twigg, London, c.1775. In outline characteristic of a conventional officer's fusil, but the rifled barrel is the only one reported at the time of writing. Length O.A. 58½", 42" half-octagonal barrel, calibre .695" rifled with eight square grooves approx. ⅔ the width of the lands, making 1 turn in 54". This would probably have taken the regulation .693" musket ball and a thin patch. False breech, the barrel secured by one key, the other three securing the separated fore-end. Tower private proofmarks. Flat lockplate 5¾"x¹⁵⁄₁₆", with faceted pan, signed in script, "Twigg". Brass mounted with the acorn finial to the triggerguard characteristic of the 1770s, and a spring-button release on the top of the buttplate tang for the cover of the butt-trap, which holds a short-bladed socket bayonet (an idea copied from Continental sporting arms of the period). Wrist chequered in the diamond-and-dot pattern perhaps introduced by Twigg and later adopted and refined by Durs Egg. Although containing a number of early Twigg features such as the lock and its style of marking, the furniture and stock suggest a mid-1770s date for the manufacture of this fusil.
Courtesy of the late Kit Ravenshear.

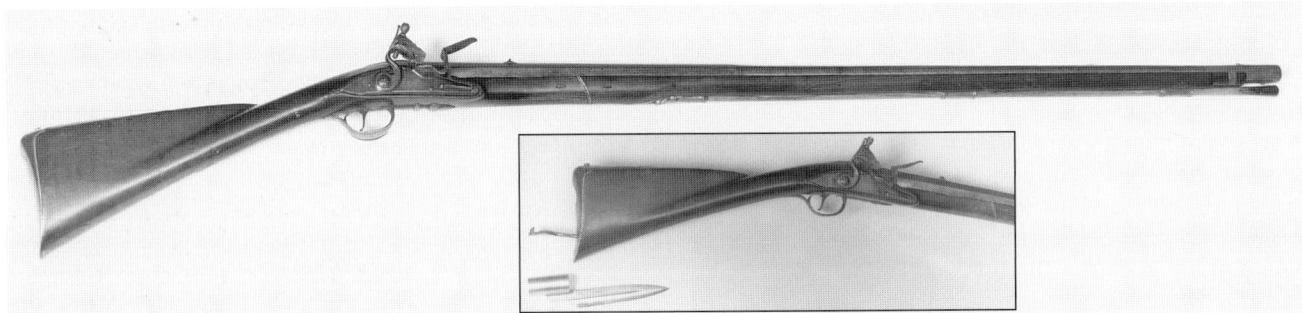

That Col. Harcourt be acquainted in return to his Letter of 30ᵗʰ ulto. desiring 54 Rifle Barrel Carbines for the 16th Regiment of Dragoons, that no other arms can be issued than what are mentioned in the King's Warrant: and that Lord Amherst [then Commander-in-Chief] is pleased to observe that as the 16th is reduced to the same number as the other Light Dragoons They can have no men to serve on foot.[51]

This may also clarify that the rifles were carried only by the dismounted men, despite being fitted with swivel ramrods. But no accounts of the 16th have been found to corroborate either possibility.

b. Subsequent Issues

The presence of Pattern 1776 rifles with the light infantry companies in the two Battalions of Light

Infantry is confirmed by the following diary entry relating to the Battle of Paoli on 20 September 1777:

The most effectual precaution being taken by the General [Sir Charles "No Flint" Grey] to prevent his detachment [2/L.I., a troop of light dragoons, 42d and 44th Regiments] from firing, by ordering the men's Pieces to be drawn, not a man to load, and the Flints to be taken out of the Riflemen's Pieces that could not be drawn.[52]

Since the Ferguson rifle could easily be unloaded without having to fire it off, this reference clearly indicates that the Light Infantry companies of the 2d Light Infantry were carrying Pattern 1776 rifles, as well as Ferguson rifles. That the 1st Battalion was similarly equipped is confirmed by an orderly book entry of 4 December 1778:

...the Riffle men of the Battn are to be Under the Command of Lt French and thoes Men Who have Givin in their Riffels are to be Cuontinued With that Corps as Ushal those Men to be Posted in the Bow of the Boats as the First to Land but not to Fire Ought of the Boats.[53]

In November 1778, an expeditionary force sailed from New York with the intention of retaking the Province of Georgia for the Crown. Eight battalions of infantry were commanded by Lieutenant Colonel Archibald Campbell of the 71st Foot. The troops included both battalions of the 71st as well as two battalions of Hessians and three New York Provincial and one New Jersey Provincial battalions. There was therefore a high potential for previous rifle experience. The four Provincial battalions furnished a corps of light infantry of just over 200 men. Early in January 1779, after the troops had moved inland to Tuckassee King plantation, Campbell formed what he called a corps of "Royal Rifle Dragoons" commanded by Captain William Fleming. This body acted with the light infantry corps, and there is little doubt but that they were armed with Pattern 1776 Rifles. They made a valuable contribution to the British success at the fight at Briar Creek, 3 March 1779.[54]

When the expedition under Sir Henry Clinton sailed for Charleston, their armament included rifles: perhaps a few Ferguson's breechloaders still in the hands of the Light Infantry companies, but primarily the Pattern 1776 muzzleloaders. Capt. De Peyster noted in his Orderly Book on 14 January 1780, while the troops were still at sea:

One half of the Non Comd Off and Privates of each Detacht who are the most active and best Marksmen, to be fixed upon today by the Officers Comd in order the Inst we land to act as rangers, the front Rank of whom are to have Firelocks; the rear Rifles.[55]

We know from local Ordnance returns that several hundred Pattern 1776 rifles were in circulation in the South during the next two years, but exactly in whose hands remains unclear. There are no surviving recorded issues of rifles after the troops reached the South; all issues appear to have been made prior to departure from New York. New York Ordnance returns show that they had received into Store from the administrative custody of the Royal Artillery 16 serviceable and 210 repairable rifles on 1 January 1780 (after the Charleston force had sailed).[56] This suggests that a force amounting to about four companies had handed in their rifles. On 10 March 1780, there were recorded 167 serviceable rifles as well as the 210 repairable,[57] suggesting that this number had been turned in from various corps. It was from this group that the Queen's Rangers received their second issue of 14 (discussed elsewhere in this book), but by 9 May 1781 there were in Ordnance Store at New York only 2 serviceable and the 210 repairable rifles, indicating a considerable re-issue and the continued active use of rifles.[58]

On 1 April 1780 there were in Ordnance Stores at Savannah 21 "Rifles - common British" and another 50 rifles in Store elsewhere in Georgia.[59]

c. *Emmerich's Chasseurs (see Chapter 5)*
d. *New York Volunteer Rifle Company (see Chapter 5)*
e. *Queen's Rangers (see Chapter 5)*

Summing up, there is documentary evidence for the sending of 1,000 rifles to North America (the total number of muzzle-loading rifles manufactured for the Ordnance) and for the specific shipping of fifty Hanover-made rifles to General Burgoyne's forces in Canada and another fifty of the same to General Howe at New York; and for the issue of the Pattern 1776 rifles to several loyalist units including Emmerich's Chasseurs and the New York Volunteer Rifle Company formed from them on disbandment, and the Queen's Rangers. There is inferential documentation for the issue of some 50-odd rifles each to the dismounted men of the 16th and 17th Light Dragoons, for the carrying of rifles by members of the Light Infantry companies, including those of the three companies of the Guards Brigade, and for their issue at company level to the 42d Royal Highland Regiment and the 71st, and possibly to other late-arriving Highland Regiments such as the 76th, 80th and 82nd.

At the time the Pattern 1776 rifles arrived in North America during the winter of 1776–7, there were thirty-one line regiments (310 companies), the composite Guards Brigade in the American colonies and twelve (120 companies) in Canada, and depending upon the views of their commanding officers, any of these could have received an issue of rifles, probably centred on their light infantry companies (46 companies including the 3 of the Guards). Seven of the Canadian regiments surrendered at Saratoga, but not all their light companies were included, and one regiment was drafted. In the colonies two regiments were drafted and the Volunteers of Ireland was raised during 1778. In November 1778, ten regiments then serving in North America were sent to the West Indies. Any rifles held by them would have been turned in to Artillery or Ordnance Stores. Six companies, including two light infantry arrived from two regiments in 1778, and two regiments arrived in 1779 (both Highlanders and perhaps therefore particularly eligible for rifles). In June 1779, the 33rd Foot requested and received permission to be employed as a Light Corps, to which Emmerich's Chasseurs were attached.[60] It may be that the 33rd received more than the usual number of rifles while serving as light infantry, since their own light company would have been detached to serve with the 1st Light Infantry Battalion. This brief survey suggests that an initial issue of rifles at the time of their arrival would more than account for the entire production of 1,000 rifles. If only the 46 light infantry companies received rifles, a minimum of 230 would have been issued. All this is speculation, and since the entire issue was left to the discretion of the commander-in-chief, and since Howe's papers were burnt in the 1790s, we may never know the complete story.

After the close of hostilities, a General Remain of Ordnance Stores at New York City of 10 March 1783 shows 234 serviceable, 141 repairable, and 2 unserviceable English rifles,[61] while at St. Augustine, East Florida, on 8 January 1783, there remained 38 rifles in the garrison stores, but whether these were Pattern 1776 or private rifles is not stated.[62]

Ammunition

Although there are frequent references to the Pattern 1776 rifles using standard carbine-bore (.615-in.) ball, superfine double-strength powder, and carbine flints, there are no official statements regarding the charge of powder, and no surviving authenticated powder of this description from which to judge its grain size. From the fact that cartridge-formers, cartridge paper and twine are specified as part of the equipment to be sent with the rifles, it is clear that they were intended to be loaded using paper cartridges, and since no other qualifications are made, it may be assumed that these were of carbine size throughout. The barrels of all the existing Pattern 1776 rifles have the muzzle area of their bores deliberately and evenly (not muzzle-wear) coned and relieved to aid in loading cartridges or patched ball. The fit of the cartridge or patched ball had to be such that it could be easily rammed down the barrel without the use of a starter.

The carbine cartridge-former was a cylinder of wood .59-in. in diameter, the parallel section being 5.9-in. in length, with a semi-hemispherical hollow at the end opposite the handle. The cartridge paper was shaped and measured as shown in the sketch, with sixteen cartridges being made up from one sheet of cartridge paper. The charge for the regulation smoothbore carbines was 4 drams (110 grains) including priming. In view of the stronger and finer-grained powder issued for rifles it is very likely that this was reduced to the next standard loading of the time, the pistol charge of 3 drams (82½ grains). There is no indication of the manufacture of special rifle-sized tin powder chargers (which were produced in quantity for the Ordnance in loading wall piece, musket, carbine and pistol size cartridges). Modern test-firing with reproduction Pattern 1776 rifles suggests that the 3 dram charge was the most accurate, larger charges being less so.

As of now, no details have come to light as to whether the patched ball was enclosed in the cartridge — as was later done with the Baker rifle (see Chapter 13) or possibly carried separately with the paper cartridges containing only the powder charge — as was done with the Brunswick percussion service rifle. This degree of technology was almost certainly handled at company level. It is probable that powder was carried in powder horns as well as paper cartridges, since the light infantry companies were issued with powder horns as part of their equipment in addition to their 18-hole Ordnance-supplied cartridge boxes or "bellyboxes" with either a shoulder- or a waistbelt, and there is every reason why these accoutrements, including the ball-bag ("small bag" or "shott bag") and small hatchet or "tommy hawk," would have been used by riflemen who were normally drawn or recruited from these very companies. Whether the light infantry companies also carried the larger battalion cartridge box on their hips is open to question and may have varied with the regiment. They may have been carried on some campaigns and used as a magazine. The Queen's Ranger rifleman shown elsewhere in this book is certainly carrying a powder horn as well as a second strap over his right shoulder.

Cartridge paper for .66 calibre (carbine-bore) British military carbines, almost certainly used with the Pattern 1776 muzzle-loading and Ferguson rifles, carried in the Light Infantry 18-hole cartridge boxes which formed a part of the special accoutrements with which they were issued. *Courtesy of the late Capt. A.B. Caruana, R.A. (ret'd.).*

CHAPTER 3

The Ferguson Rifle

From Manufacture to the Battle of Monmouth Court House, 1776–1778

The screwplug design that Patrick Ferguson adopted for his breech-loading rifle was by no means an innovation in 1776. The basic idea dates back at least to the last quarter of the 17th century, when it was utilized by Daniel Lagatz of Danzig, and it was produced, in a version extremely close to what Ferguson later used, by French engineer Isaac de la Chaumette in 1700 and 1704.[1] De la Chaumette actually received English Patent No. 434 of 12 August 1721 for this and related mechanisms,[2] and various English gunmakers including Lewis and James Barbar, Joseph Clarkson and James Freeman produced "Ferguson" rifles during the first half of the 18th century, as did Penterman the elder in Utrecht. The fact that Ferguson was allowed a patent can only serve to illustrate the ignorance of those who granted it.

Documentary evidence for military interest in Captain Patrick Ferguson's screwplug breech-loading rifle first appears in a letter of 18 March 1776 from the Adjutant General of the Army, Edward Harvey, to Ferguson himself, in reply to a previous application:

I have received the favour of your Letter relative to the Improvement of the Rifle Barrel. Any alteration for the arms of the British Troops that may be proposed is always referred to the Board of Ordnance for their consideration. I will take an opportunity, as soon as I am able, to speak either to the Master General, of Lieut. General, to endeavor to get their opinions, but I imagine that there is such a multiplicity of

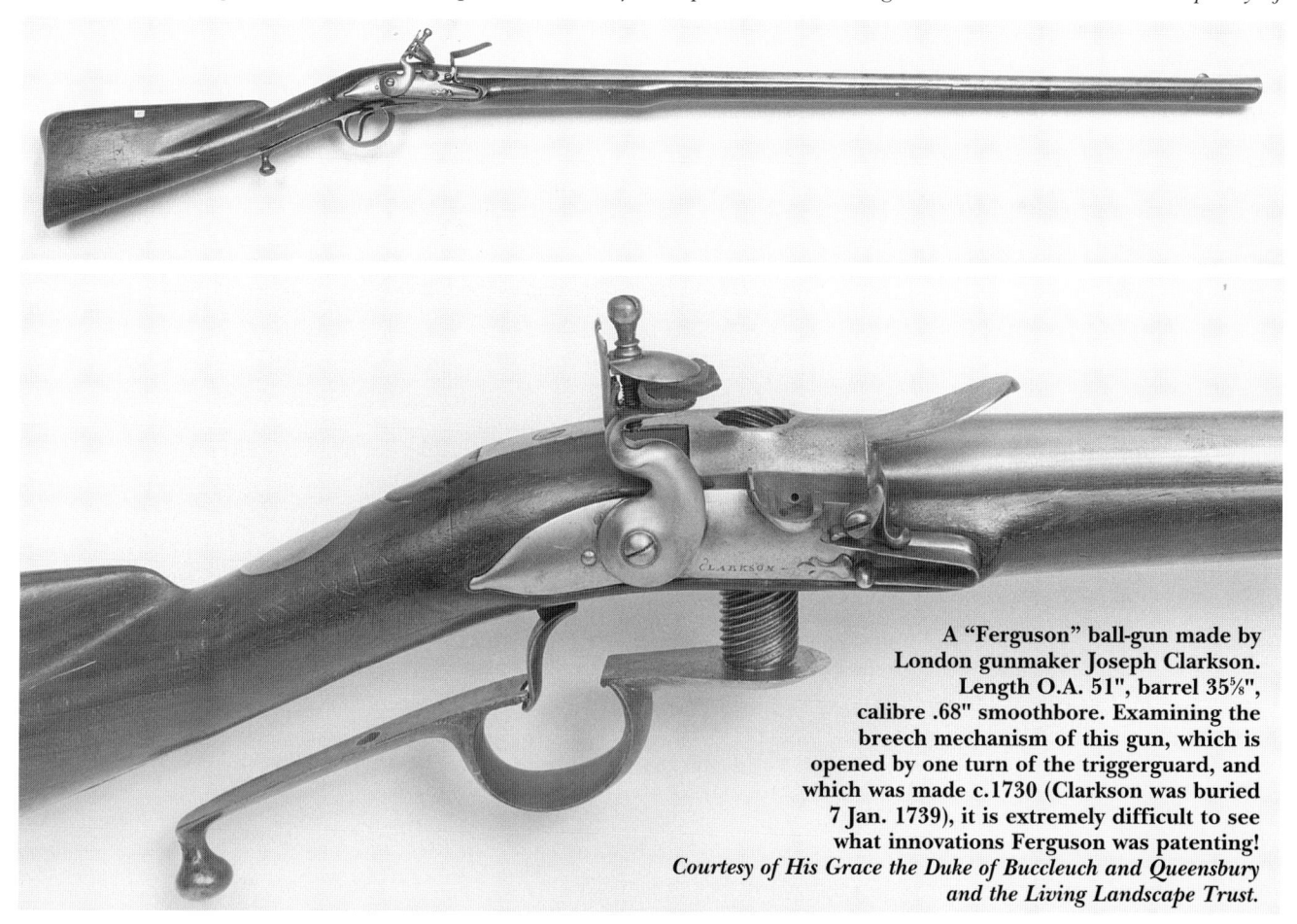

A "Ferguson" ball-gun made by London gunmaker Joseph Clarkson. Length O.A. 51", barrel 35⅝", calibre .68" smoothbore. Examining the breech mechanism of this gun, which is opened by one turn of the triggerguard, and which was made c.1730 (Clarkson was buried 7 Jan. 1739), it is extremely difficult to see what innovations Ferguson was patenting!
Courtesy of His Grace the Duke of Buccleuch and Queensbury and the Living Landscape Trust.

— 35 —

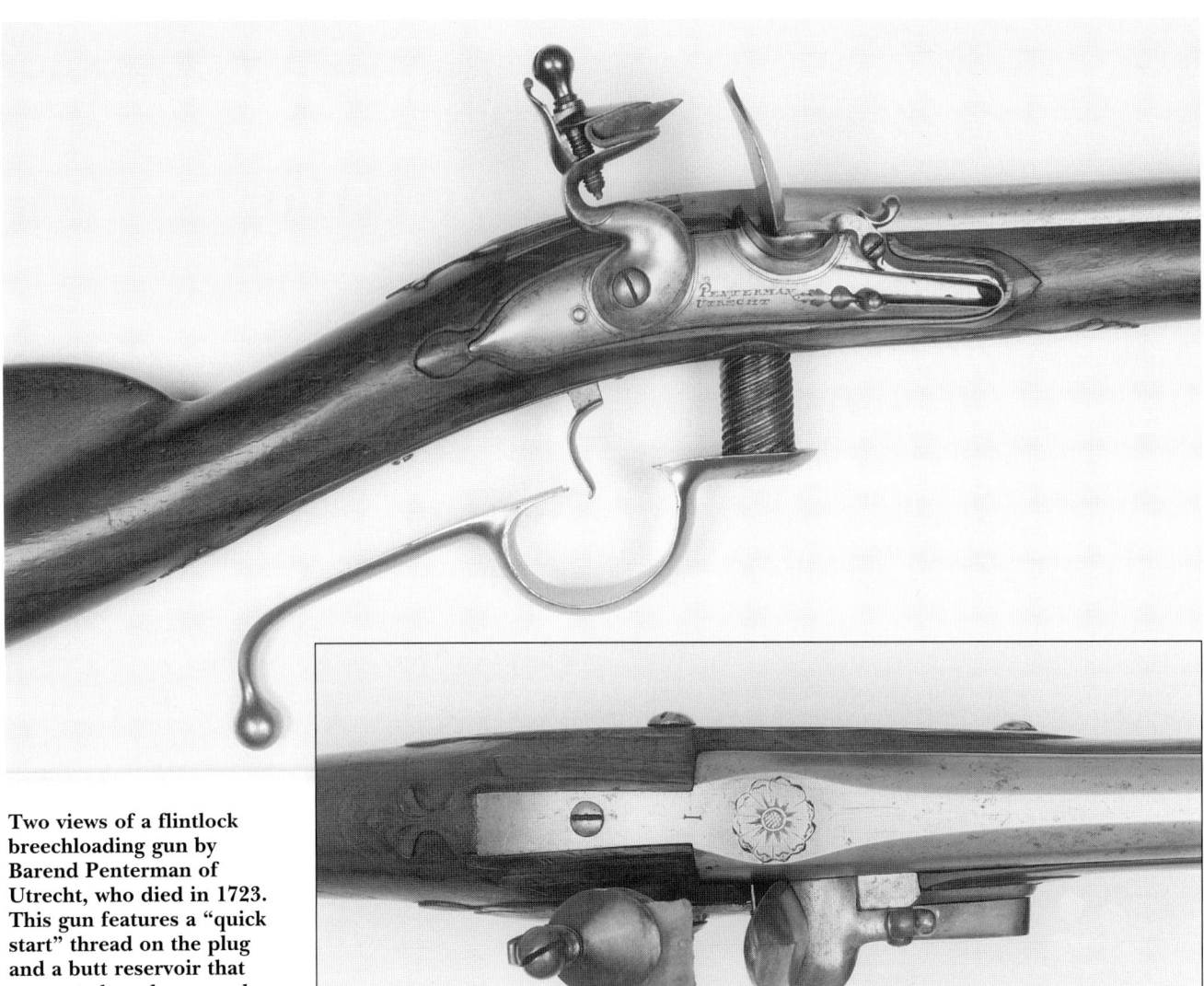

Two views of a flintlock breechloading gun by Barend Penterman of Utrecht, who died in 1723. This gun features a "quick start" thread on the plug and a butt reservoir that seems to have been used to hold a spare bullet.

Penterman's gun used slightly oversized bullets, as the chamber is a little larger than the remainder of the barrel's bore. This presumably aided in compression, and can be compared to the use of oversized bullets seen in other breechloading systems, such as the "Queen Anne" screw-barrels.

Overall, this gun measures 46.75". The barrel measures 31.75" and it has a .675" caliber. The vertical plug at the breech's flat top is engraved as a flower calyx. The lock is inscribed "PENTERMAN/UTRECHT", and bears a struck mark "LL" on the inside.

Courtesy the H.L. Visser collection, Cat. 485, HV-674.

business at present, that delay may be occasioned.

I am very sensible of your Zeal for the Service, and hope that it may meet with proper attention. I am...[3]

Interest was followed by action, at the very time when orders had already been placed in Hanover for 200 muzzle-loading rifles; on 27 April the *Scots Magazine* reported:

On Saturday, April 27, there was an experiment tried at Woolwhich warren before Lord Townshend and several officers, of two pieces of rifle-barrel guns and two muskets, to see which did the most execution, and carried farthest. The rifle-guns were approved of, and fired six times a minute on a new construction, and were the invention of Captain Ferguson, of the 70th regiment.[4]

Another report of the same trials printed in the *Annual Register* and the *Gentleman's Magazine* on 1 June contain further details:

Some experiments were tried at Woolwich before Lord Viscount Townshend, Lord Amherst, Generals Harvey and Desaguilier and a number of other officers with a rifle gun upon a new

— 36 —

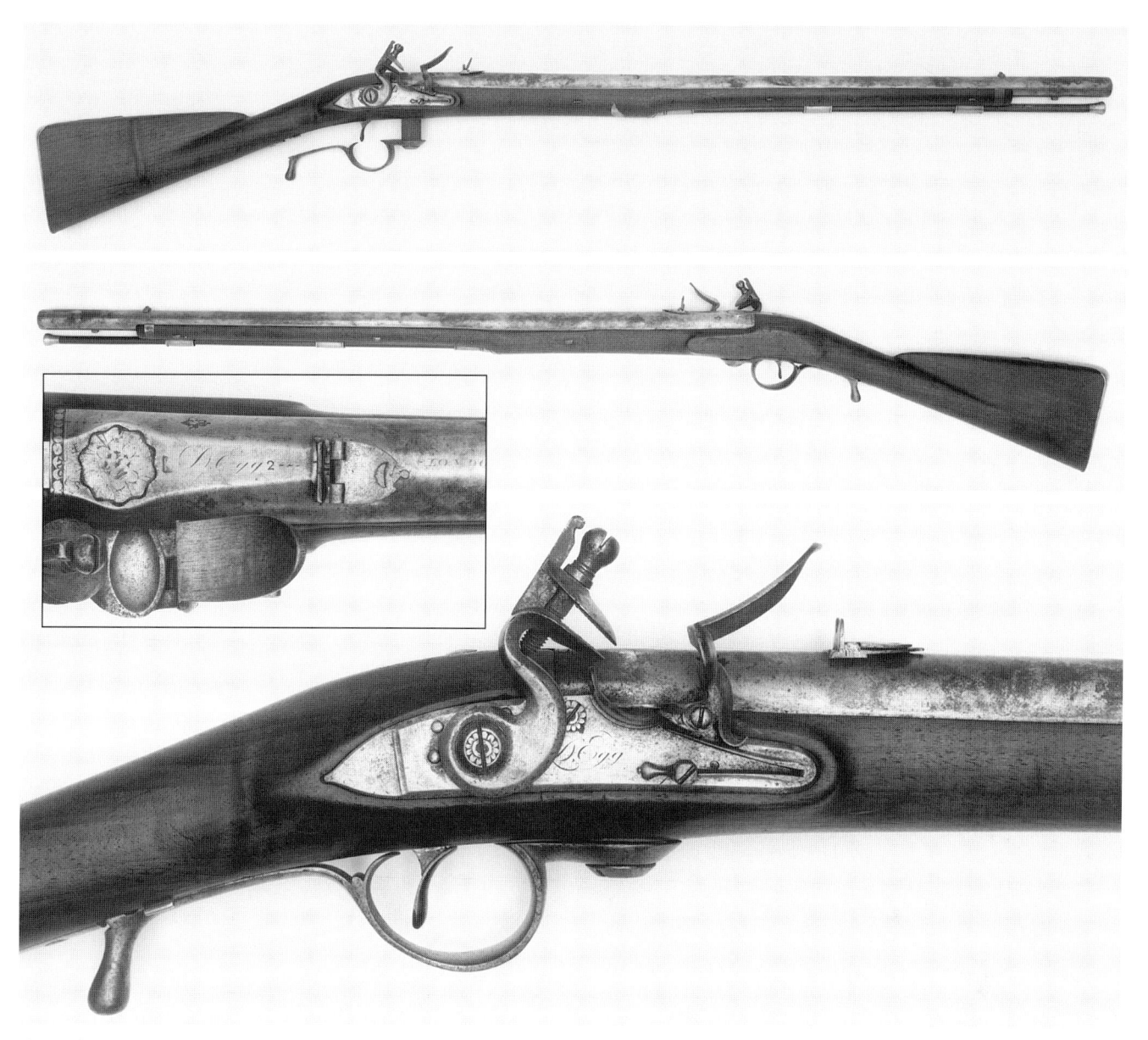

One of the two pattern Ferguson rifles supplied by London gunmaker Durs Egg to the Board of Ordnance in 1776. Note the King's Proof on each side of the barrel and the number "2" struck on the breech after the name, and "FERGUS" in a semi-circle behind the breechplug and over the breech decoration, all on an otherwise clearly civilian-marked piece. Note the form of backsight leaf, missing from the issue example.
Courtesy Messrs. Sotheby's.

construction, by Capt. Ferguson of the 70th Regt.; when that gentleman under the disadvantages of a heavy rain and a high wind performed the following four things, none of which had ever before been accomplished with any other small arms. 1. He fired during 4 or 5 minutes at a target at 200 yards distance at the rate of 4 shots each minute. 2. He fired 6 shots in one minute. 3. He fired four times per minute advancing at the same time at the rate of 4 miles in the hour. 4. He poured a bottle of water into the pan and the barrel of the piece when loaded so as to wet every grain of the powder and in less than half a minute fired with her as well as ever without extracting the ball. He also hit the bulls-eye at 100 yards, lying with his back on the ground and notwithstanding the unequalness of the wind and wetness of the weather, he only missed the target three times during the course of the experiments.

Whatever the exact date of these trials, a decision had been taken by the Board of Ordnance before 3 June 1776, by which time the original pattern rifle apparently used by Ferguson in the trials, made by Durs Egg, was to be paid for with public funds, as well as a second pattern also to be made by Egg. The rifle illustrated has been tentatively identified as one of the pattern pieces on the basis of having both commercial and Ordnance proofmarks, the small "2" ahead of the breech opening being probably a 19th-century inventory stamp. A second identical rifle bearing similar markings but numbered "15" instead of "2", has recently appeared, but has only London commercial proofmarks. Both rifles bear a small mark of what has been identified as the Ferguson family crest stamped ahead of the breech opening, the significance of which is currently not established.

The Secretary to the Master General wrote to the Chief Clerk of the Board:

The Master Genl also desires that the new Rifle piece of Capt Fergusons be paid for, as well as one more which Mr. Egg is to make upon the same Construction, which is to be left at the Tower as a pattern.[5]

The Ordnance Bill Books show that "William Egg" was paid £31.10.0. for these two rifles on 3 June 1776.[6]

At this point a confusing document appears in the series which some people have construed as meaning that the manufacture of the 800 muzzle-loading rifles then in progress in Birmingham should be brought to a halt, since Ferguson's breech-loader was to supersede them. The Ordnance Minutes record on 24 June 1776 that:

John Courtney Esqr having represented in his Letter of 22d Inst that the Master General desires that Orders may be given to the Contractors at Birmingham that no more Rifles be made according to the present Pattern & that the number wanted to Compleat those already bespoke must be finished immediately as a new Construction of Capt. Ferguson's is approved and who is authorized by his Lordship to give directions to the Workmen which must be implicitly followed.

The same was Ordered accordingly.[7]

What the minute clearly states, however, is that the current order should be completed as quickly as possible, and no more made, so that Ferguson's can be made thereafter. In fact, all 800 rifles were completed as ordered, and then production of Ferguson's commenced. By the end of August 1776 considerable progress had been made, as it was the

...Master General's directions that a proper Person be immediately sent to Birmingham to Prove the Riffle barrels making there under the direction of Capt Ferguson he had therefore sent down Mr. King the Master Viewer & Furbisher who is a very proper Person for that Service... Approved.[8]

By 1 October, at least some of the 100 rifles must have been completed and put to use, for the *Scots Magazine* was able to report on that date:

Windsor, Oct. 1. An officer belonging to the 70th regiment has been down at this place for some weeks past, teaching several men (belonging to Lord George Lennox's regiment) [the 25th Foot] the use of the rifle-gun. He takes a party of men out every morning and evening: they fire at a target from one hundred to three hundred yards distance. The officer is so expert, that he hits the bull's eye at one hundred yards every time he fires, and always hits some part of the board at the greatest distance. Their Majesties attended a review of the rifle-men yesterday afternoon, and were much pleased at the dexterity of the officer, who loaded and fired seven times in a minute, and hit the mark each time. He lies upon his back when he discharges his piece.[9]

Further detail was added to the report of this demonstration in 1817 by Adam Ferguson (no relation of Patrick's):[10]

Ferguson then took a rifle himself; and of nine shots which he fired at the distance of one hundred yards, put five balls into the bull's-eye of the target, and four within as many inches of it. Three of these shots were fired as he lay on his back, the other six standing erect. Being asked how often he could load and fire in a minute, he said seven times.

Adam Ferguson had been secretary to the ill-fated Carlisle Peace Commission and had spent several months in America in 1778, when he undoubtedly met, and probably became friendly with Patrick Ferguson. His biographical sketch will be referred to again.

On 12 Novemeber 1776, Ferguson received his first payment for his supervision of the rifle manufacture, £100, significantly for "Riffle Barrel Guns to be delivered to the Tower."[11] (Either the rifles were still in the hands of the trainees, or had not yet left the hands of the manufacturers in Birmingham.)

At this point the question of Ferguson's patent arises (see illustration on the next page). On 2 November, Ferguson had written to the Board of Ordnance saying that he wished to patent his mechanism,

...as he is of Opinion it will be the only means of Securing for the service of the Government the few hands who by 4 months Constant attention have with difficulty been brought to make arms upon that Consruction, & prevent those arms from falling into bad hands by the manufacturng of them which he submitted to the Board.

Ordered to be acquainted the Board have no Objection to a Patent for the Riffle arms in Case the Clauses proposed be inserted and a copy of such Clauses first laid before the Board.[12]

Apparently the workmen of the four Birmingham contractors were not amongst those who had made screwplug breech-loaders for more than fifty years previously in the English gun trade. It is, likewise, curious that of the several features in the patent, none but the screwplug itself (not really patentable at all) were used

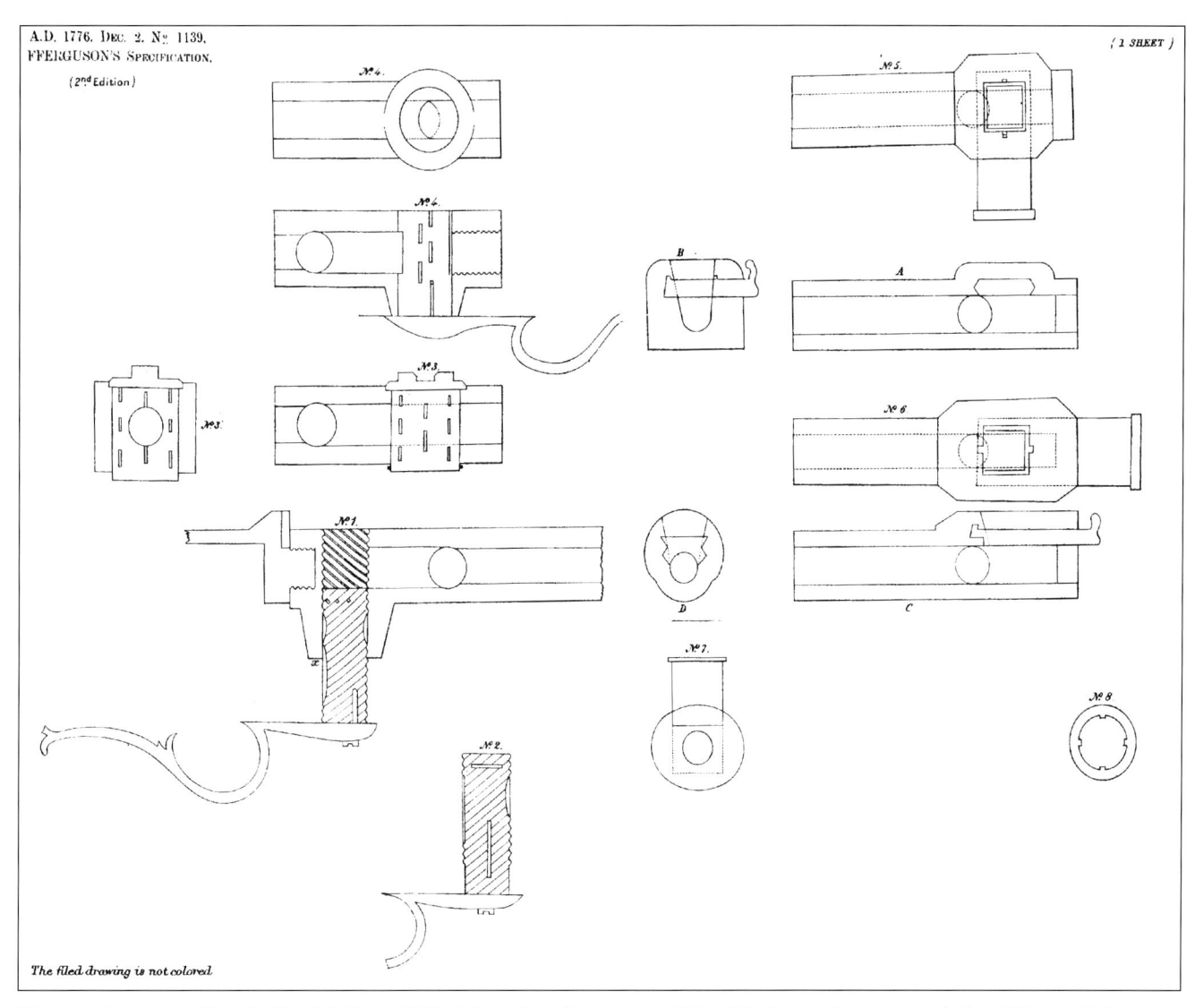

Ferguson's patent No. 1139 of 2 Dec. 1776. Note the alternative sliding-block mechanism, and the rifling which never appears to have been used. *Patent Office Library.*

on the military rifles, and only the anti-fouling grooves and the delicate and impractical backsight on a few of the other known civilian examples.

Nevertheless, Patent No. 1139 of 2 December 1776, was duly issued, as noted in the *Gentleman's Magazine*:

Wednesday 4 [December]. A patent passes the seal to Capt. Ferguson, for an invention in fire-arms, whereby they are rendered more sure in execution, and more quickly charged, than those in common use.[13]

From the above reports it is clear that the rifles had been completed by some time in September 1776. On 10 December Ferguson wrote the Board "that he will do eveything lays in is power to render the new Invention Riffle Gun as useful as possible agreeable to the Patent."[14] The Ordnance paid for them all on 31 December 1776, £100 each to Matthias Barker, Samuel Galton & Son, William Grice & Son, and Benjamin Willetts, for "25 Rifled Guns with Plugs & Bayonets" at £4 each (see several illustrations starting on the next page).[15] As late as March 1777, Grice and Son were attempting, unsuccessfully, to be paid another 4/- each for their Ferguson rifles.

The training program had apparently been completed and the rifles turned into Store in the Tower by January 1777, for on the 38th of that month their outward journey towards America began, with an order of the Board of Ordnance:

That what Rifle Guns there are in Store at the Tower of Capt. Ferguson's be sent to the Commanding Officer at Chatham who will give a Receipt for them.

Ordered that £100 be Imprested to Capt. Ferguson.[16]

Ferguson was already at Chatham waiting to train

— 39 —

British Military Flintlock Rifles

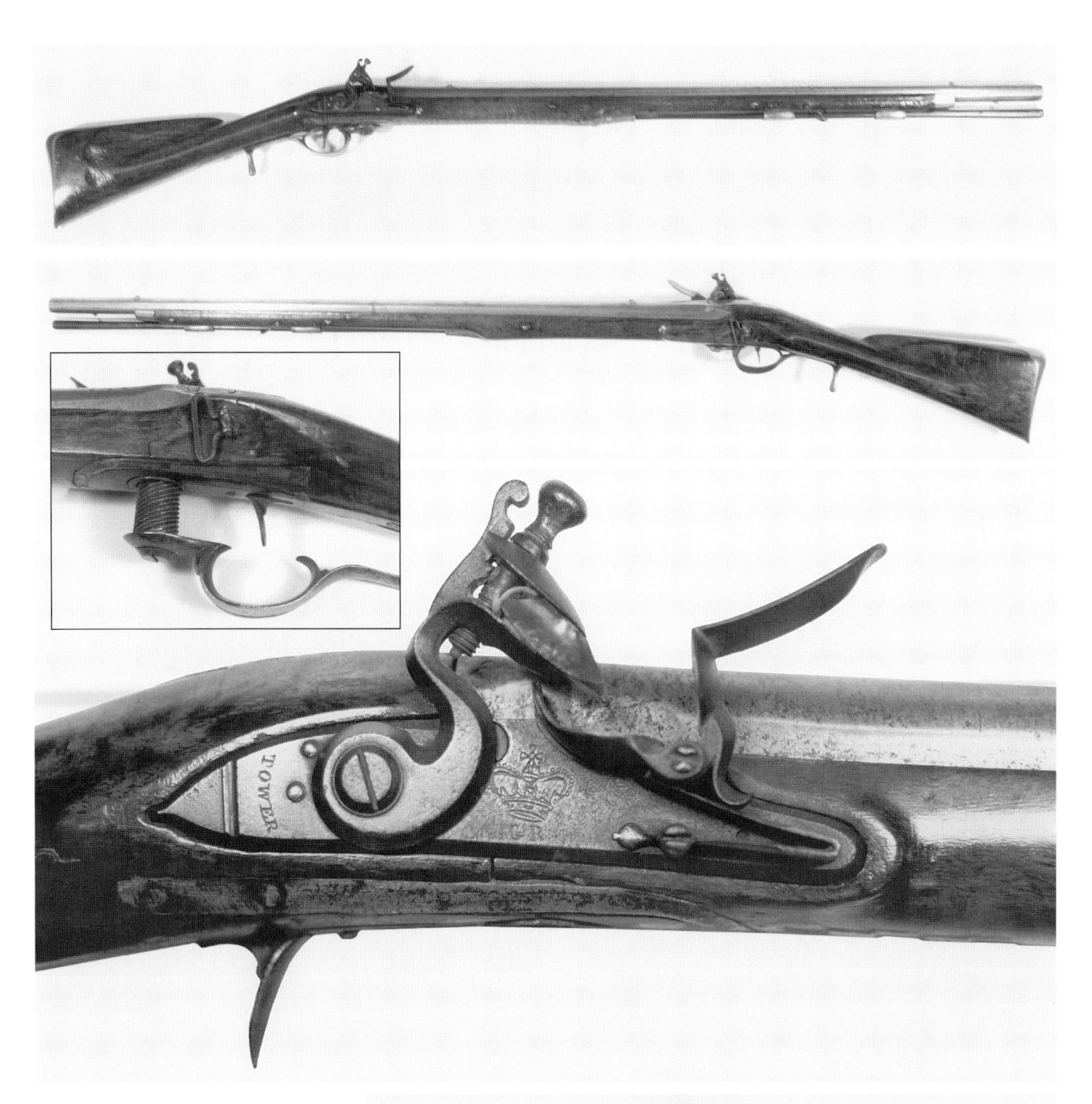

The military-issue Ferguson rifle of which 100 were manufactured in the summer of 1776, closely following the pattern rifle shown earlier. Issue number "2" is engraved on the breech tang and triggerguard bow. Ferguson's inspection mark of a crowned "PF" struck behind the breech orifice. Note the contemporary horseshoe-shaped strap-iron repair around the triggerguard finial and the break through the sideplate flat.

Courtesy of Morristown National Historical Park, Morristown, New Jersey

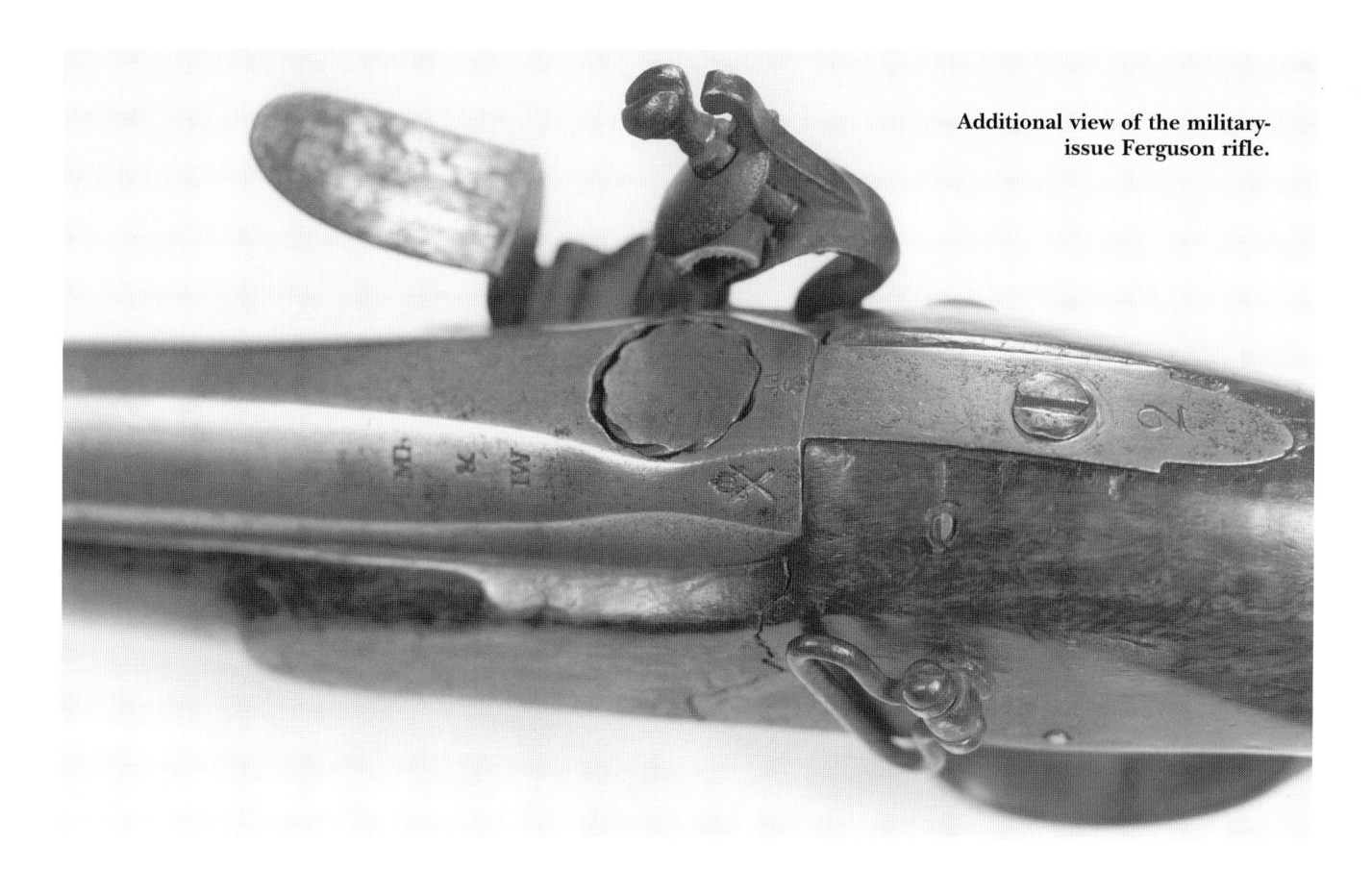

Additional view of the military-issue Ferguson rifle.

recruits, and requested various details to be attended to by the Ordnance:

Capt. Ferguson having requested that the Barrels Slings and Bayonets by him desired may be numbered & Scabbards made for the Bayonets also the Slings and Bayonet Belts may be of Tann'd Leather and 2 Cags of Powder for the Rifles & Carbine Ball in Proportion sent to Fire at Marks at Chatham.
The same was Ordered accordingly.[17]
Capt. Ferguson having requested to be Supplied with 200 Tann'd Leather Bayonet Belts and 200 Slings &c. for the new Constructed Rifle Guns.[18]

This is the first of several clear references to the Ferguson rifles being made to use carbine-bore (.615") ball.

The Board's contractor for accoutrements, Sir Peter & James Esdaile, supplied the required accessories with great speed, as shown by their quote for the scabbards of 25 February and their bill of 29 March 1777:[19]

scabbards for Rifled Gun bayonets	100 at 1/4 each
slings for Rifled Guns	200 at 1/4 each
belts for Rifled Guns	200 at 1/4 each
Tann'd leather	

The numbering of the rifles and accessories, so far as the metal parts were concerned, was completed by the Board's official engraver, William Sharp, and appears in his bill for work completed between 1 January And 31 December 1777:[20]

Numbered only Rifled Guns thrice numbered	100	£3.1.5.
Numbd only Belt Plates for Rifled Men	200	16.8.
Do. Bullet Moulds	12	1.

The thrice numbering refers to having the number of the rifle engraved on the triggerguard bow, buttplate tang and bayonet socket. The bullet moulds are assumed to be of the multi-ball "gang mould" type. This also confirms that the accoutrements were numbered to the guns, and that Ferguson was mindful of the necessity for spares on expendable accoutrements. While waiting at Chatham, Ferguson received a further installment of £100 "on acct of Riffle Barrels."[21]

Late in February the higher echelons of the army began to recognize the existence of the new corps, and to formally advise those officers who would be affected by its operations. On 19 February 1777 the Secretary at War informed the Commanding Officer at Chatham Barracks (the principal recruit depot for troops going to North America):

War Office, 19 Feby 1777
Sir, I have the honor to acquaint you, His Majesty has been pleased to direct that a Detachment of one hundred Men besides commissioned and non commissioned officers...shall be

The bills for the 100 Ferguson rifles and the 800 muzzle-loading Pattern 1776 rifles from the Ordnance Bill Books.
Public Record Office, WO/51.

formed from the Recruits in Chatham Barracks, and...be put under the command of Capt Ferguson of the 70th Regiment.

The intention of this measure is to make Experiments in America of the new Rifle Arms invented by Capt Ferguson, which it is apprehended will be found of considerable use to His Majesty's Service.

As the 6th and 14th Regiments may possibly arrive soon in Great Britain [from the West Indies and North America respectively], it would be most eligible that the Detachment should consist of men who should be transferr'd from those

Corps in order to serve in North America.

I am therefore to signify to you, His mjesty's Pleasure that you do cause the above Plan to be made known to the Parties of the 6th and 14th Regiments, and report to m the number of those who shall offer as Volunteers on this occasion.

I have the honr to be Sir, &c.

Barrington

Officer Commanding
His Majesty's Forces
at Chatham Barracks.[22]

And two days later the superintendent of the recruiting service was notified:

His Majesty having been pleased to direct that a Detachment of 100 Men besides Commissioned and Non Commissioned Officers, shall be formed from the Recruits belonging to the Regiments now in North America, serving under...Sir William Howe and beput under the Command of Capt Ferguson of the 70th Regiment, I have the honor to signify to you His Majesty's Pleasure, that you do repair to Chatham, and see the same carried into Execution.

These Men, notwithstanding their being under this temporary Command, while on board Ship, and until Sir William Howe shall dispose of them, otherwise are to continue to be considered as part of the Strength of their respective Corps.

I have the... Barrington.

Lieut. Col. Townsend.[23]

In order to carry out the necessary training at Chatham, as well as for the actual service to follow, an essential ingredient was a quantity of superior quality gunpowder. On 21 February 1777 the Board ordered from their principal powder contractor Bridges, Eade & Wilton five whole barrels (of 100 lbs. each) of glazed gunpowder (described elsewhere as Superfine Double Strength) at a cost of £7.10.0. per barrel (as opposed to £1.5.0. for the same quantity of ordinary musket powder) which was paid for on 24 February.[24] At the rate of 3 drams (82½ grains) this afforded the trainees some 42,424 rounds.

Another timely payment to Ferguson of £259.4.2. "on acct of Riffle Guns" was ordered by the Board on 4 March.[25] Secretray at War Lord Barrington had a busy day on 6 March 1777, when he formally notified Ferguson's regimental commanding officer, Ferguson himself, and the Commander-in-Chief North America of the King's intentions for Ferguson and his unit during the campaign of 1777:

Sir, I have the honor to acquaint you that the King has been pleased to appoint Captain Ferguson, of your Regt to the Command of a Detachment of One hundred Rifle Men with proper Commissioned & Non Com'd Officers, formed for the purpose of making experiments of some rifles barrel pieces of a new Construction, & to proceed with them immediately to No. America.

Barrington

P.S. Capt. Ferguson is to return to the Regt at the end of the Campaign, unless Sir Wm Howe should have a further Occasion for his Service.

Lieut. Genl Trapaud.[26]

Sir, The King having been pleased to order a Detachment of One hundred Men with proper Comd & Non Comd Officers to be formed for the purpose of making experiment of some Rifle barrel pieces of a new Construction, I am to signify to you H:M:P: that you do take the Command of the said Detachmt & proceed with them to No America.

On your Arrival there you are to follow such orders as you hall receive from Sir William Howe.

I am, Sir, &c. Barrington

Capt Ferguson
of the 70th Regt of Foot.[27]

I have the honor to acquaint you that Capt Ferguson of the 70th Regt of Foot, having by Directions from the Board of Ordnance superintended the making of some Riffle Barrel pieces of a new Construction, the King has thought it proper to order that experiment should be made in the most proper manner as to their Utility. For this purpose Captain Ferguson has been appointed to the Command of a Detachment of one hundred Men with proper Commissioned and Non Comd Officers selected from the recruits belonging to the several Corps under your Command, and is embarked with the aid Command on board the Transport with leave to serve this Campaign in No. America. On the arrival of Captain Ferguson you will be pleased to give him such directions as you may think most proper for carrying H:M: Intentions into Execution.

The Non Commissioned Officers and Recruits are to be continued as effective Men in their respective Corps and be subsisted accordingly.

A Quantity of Green Cloth &c is sent over for the use of this Detachment, in case you should think it advisable to Direct a particular Cloathing for them. [see page 00]

It is H:M: P that as soon as the Campaign is over Captain Ferguson should return to England, and join his Regiment, unless you should judge it expedient to continue him on this Service in No America; in which H:M: is pleased to give leave to Captain Ferguson for such further absence as you may desire.[28]

Not only was Ferguson to be seconded from his regiment, but they were to pay for his expenses in arranging the secondment, as Barrington informed the regimental Agent, James Meyrick, on 10 March 1777, who was:

...to direct that the Sum of One hundred Pounds be given to Capt Ferguson for his trouble and attention in his Service, and the Expence he has been put to in embarking for No America, I am therefore to desire that you will be pleased to pay to the said Capt Ferguson the Sum of One hundred Pounds as above mentioned, and charge the same in your next Contingent Bill for the 70th Regt.[29]

On 3 March 1777, the Board wrote to their outport officers at Portsmouth:

On the Rifle Barrel Guns for Captain Ferguson arriving at Portsmouth, you immediately View the said guns and certify their numbers as also the numbers of all other articles relative to them and to send the said Certificate thereof signed to you by the Board.[30]

By the third week in March, Ferguson and his men had reached Portsmouth, their point of embarkation for North America, and Ferguson, ever mindful of the health of his men, had written to the Secretary at War for a supply of portable soup (an early example of desiccated food much used in 18th-century military diets), only to be informed by the Secretary that he should apply for this commodity to the Storekeeper at Portsmouth.[31] On 23 March, Ferguson wrote to Richard Veale, Portsmouth Storekeeper:

Portsmouth, March 23, 1777
As the Compleat Number of the Powder Flasks are not yet arrived, & as we have got a Signal to sail, I must beg the favour of you to send me the box of Powder flasks and those that are loose by the Bearer. I shall take measures for having them examined by the Officers belonging to the Board at new York and shall write to Lord Townsend's Secretary on the Subject.   Pat Ferguson Capt 70th Regt.[32]

Ferguson had brought his rifles with him to Portsmouth and taken them on board the transport in which he was to cross the Atlantic. On 26 March 1777 the Ordnance Storekeeper at Portsmouth sent a:

Ltr to the Board with a Certificate of the Number of Rifle Guns produced here by Captn Ferguson of the 70th Regiment together with a copy of his Letter of the 23rd Inst respecting the Powder Flasks.
Rifle Guns 67 Bayonets 33[33]

The Board recorded their receipt of this correspondence:

Read a Letter from the Respective Officers [of the Ordnance] at Portsmouth of 25 Ultimo inclosing their Certificate of Rifle Guns produced by Mr Ferguson who carried them on board the ship Christopher *in which he takes his passage to New York & a Copy of is Letter to them of 23d signifying that the Compleat Number of Powder Flasks was not yet arrived & that he should write to Lord Townshend's Secretary on the subject.*[34]

Regrettably, Ferguson's letter to John Courtney about the missing powder flasks has not come to light; however, this reference does confirm that flasks were supplied, and that they were not supplied by the Ordnance but brought in, probably as part of a "petty-cash" purchase by a lesser officer of the Board, since no itemized bill appears in the records. It is reasonable to assume that, as the Ferguson rifle was designed with a distinct powder chamber, the flasks would have been fitted with a non-adjustable charger and spring cut-off, typical of the conventional flask of the period, and presumably not the same as the ordinary powder horns issued to the light infantry companies. There follows a period of almost two months' silence on the subject of Ferguson's rifles.

As late as 5 June 1777, the Master General's secretary was informed:

That he has got 33 Rifles ready to be delivered to his Orders & also 40 Bayonets and expects the remainder very soon and desires to know where they are to be sent.
Ordered to be received at the Tower and sent by land to Portsmouth to go on board the Lord Howe *or any other ship.*[35]

The Board wrote their Storekeeper at Portsmouth on 12 June,

Inclosed I send you an Account of Rifle Barrel Guns and Bayonets delivered to Mr Clark, Carrier to be by him conveyed to Portsmouth and there delivered to Richard Veale Esqr Ordnance Storekeeper to be disposed of as therein mentioned.[36]

and he acknowledged it on the 14th; on 16 June he informed the Board that,

The Chest of Rifle Guns rec'd on Saturday Evening by Clark's Waggon was this day put on bd the Ld Howe.[37]

On 22 June the Storekeeper informed the Board that the New York Fleet had sailed that afternoon at 5 p.m.[38] It thus appears that the second batch of 33 rifles and 40 bayonets did not leave England until 22 June 1777; whether this second batch arrived in time to reach Ferguson's men prior to their sailing from New York on 20 July, or whether by some means they followed the troops to Head of Elk are unanswered questions. There is no further mention of the balance of the powder flasks.

The next news we have of Ferguson and his men is of their arrival at New York. A Hessian Aide de Camp of General Howe's notes in his diary for 26 May 1777:

Fourteen transports arrived from England under a cover of two ships of the line. They had aboard 1,200 English recruits and 150 English chasseurs.[39]

Three days later orders were issued that "The Barrack Master General will provide Quarters for Captain Ferguson's Corps."[40] The army as a whole was informed of the new arrivals and their status in the army on 30 May:

His Majesty having been pleased to form a Corps of Rifle-Men under the Temporary Command of Capn Ferguson 70th Regt composed of Recruits raised for different Regiments serving in North America and that those Men shall notwithstanding be considered as part of the Strength of the regts for whom they were inlisted.[41]

Detailed instructions affecting both the men and their arms followed on 1 June:

All Arms & Accoutrements brought out by Drafts or Recruits are to be delivered to Brigadr Genl Cleveland and lodg'd in the Ordnance Store, taking receipts for the same.

Capn Ferguson of the 70th Regimt will collect from the different Officers who have had Charge of Recruits on board Ship, an Exact list of their names, Regts they belong to, in order to their being transmitted to their respective Regimts. Those belonging to the 6th, 14th & 16th regts are to be turned over to the weakest Regts, the Commanding officers of which will send Certificates according to the Agents of 6th, 14th and 16th Regts.[42]

It was standard practice for arms brought over by recruits to be turned in to the local Ordnance Store, as these arms were intended for the temporary use of the recruits in helping to defend their ship if attacked during the voyage, and that the full complement of arms had been taken with the regiment when it went to America in the first place. The special arms of Ferguson's men may have also been turned in, and subsequently re-issued as needed, or they may have been retained by the men; evidence on this point is lacking.

General Howe had by now received Lord Barrington's letter of 6 March informing him of the King's intention for Ferguson and his corps, and replied to it:

I am to acknowledge the receipt of your Lordship's Letter of 6th March by the Sandwich Packet and have the Honor to acquaint you of the arrival of Captain Ferguson with the Detachment of the Rifle Men under his command the 24th May; from the Experience of so intelligent an Officer I am hopeful this Corps may be essentially Serviceable.

Your Lordship's Directions shall be observed respecting the Payment and Cloathing of this Detachment. I have the honor...[43]

The new corps were not long in getting into the field, forming a part of the force sent into New Jersey on 12 June:

This Morning the 2d Division of the Troops Left Amboy, consisting of One Company Anspach Jagers, Queen's Rangers, Ferguson's Rifflemen, Dismounted and Mounted 17th Light Dragoons..., and were encamped between Brunswick and Pisscatawa...[44]

A map of the situation on 21 June shows the location of Ferguson's riflemen along the Brunswick-Bonhamtown Road, camped between the Guards brigade and the 71st Foot.[45] On that day they were ordered "to march tomorrow morning at daybreak to Amboy... Capt. Ferguson's Corps of Rifle Men to join Brig.-Gen. Leslie at some time and place [Bonham Town]."[46] A series of sharp skirmishes took place during the march towards Amboy, and these and a severe fight at Short Hills on the 23rd were undoubtedly the rifleman's baptism of fire. At the time they were part of Leslie's corps which included Ewald's Hessian *jäger* company and the 71st, both of whom would be frequent companions in arms of Ferguson's men.[47] As the British returned towards their bases and prepared to embark for Staten Island and New York, Ferguson's corps formed part of the reserve.[48] "The Army, when put in motion will march in two Columns from the Right by half Companies. Ferguson's Corps, one Amusette, after the Artillery and with Ewald's Jagers, light infantry and others."[49] It seems likely that Ferguson's corps, as part of the reserves was a part of a two-pronged advance from Amboy on the 26th to prevent rebel interference with British embarkation; the left-hand column under General Vaughn included the British light infantry, and the Kemble entry for 25 June suggests that Ferguson was in the action.[50] At any rate they did not embark until the 29th with the 5th Brigade, and the Queen's Rangers (another future constant companion) at 10 a.m.[51]

Early in July preparations began for the Philadelphia campaign in which Ferguson's corps was to win its finest and final laurels. As is well known, the departure of the troops was delayed and postponed a number of times. Orders for 7 July called for "The Battalion of Loos, Queen's Rangers, Ferguson's Corps...to embark on Wednesday with the Light Infantry and Grenadiers" on the 3rd embarkation.[52] Ten days later an indication of the strength of Ferguson's corps at this time was recorded, along with some other significant units, by the Hessian ADC of Gen. Howe:[53]

A few days ago I had an opportunity to copy the following list of our embarked regiments and their strengths, including servants, laborers, and some washer-women with each company.
 ENGLISH
 Chasseurs (5th Brigade) 130
 Provincials [Queen's Rangers, unbrigaded] 278
 HESSIANS
 Hessian and Anspach jaegers 594

Adjutant General Major Andre's "Distribution of Transports" for the Pennsylvania expedition shows "Ferguson's Rifflers" 130 men, on the *Juno* 234 [tons] with distinguishing vanes Red three blue (Fore). And the Queen's American Rangers in *Eagle* 344 t. At the embarkation of the troops on Staten Island the regiments were brigaded as follows: "Reserve...Ferguson's Rifle Corps."[54] On 20 July Captain Ewald records the fleet as sailing, with Ferguson's in the 1st Division, whose ships had red and white pennants for signals.[55]

The expedition eventually arrived off Turkey Point and on 23 August "...In the afternoon the English light infantry, the grenadiers, and the Hessian jaegers received orders to prepare for disembarkment."[56] On the following day,

On Board the Eagle,*...off Turkey Point, Chesapeake Bay, Sunday, 24th August 1777. Ferguson's Riflemen and the Corps of Pioneers to land in their own Transport's boats along with the first Debarkation.*

This included the 1st & 2nd Light Infantry, 1st and 2nd Grenadiers, and Hessian and Ansbach Jagers.[57] "The second disembarkation, under General Agnew, consisted of the Hessian grenadiers, the Queen's Rangers, Ferguson's sharpshooters, and the 4th and 23rd regiments."[58] They barely got a night's rest when:

August 25. At three o'clock in the morning the light infantry, the English grenadiers, and the Hessian jaegers were put into boats...we proceeded very slowly until we reached [Elk Ferry], eight good miles from the mouth of the river, where we landed at 10 o'clock in the morning without the slightest interference.

[Howe] advanced with the jaegers and light infantry for three miles and then made a halt. ...Disembarking of troops and of the light artillery continued the whole day.[59]
25th. The transports and the Roebuck sailed up the Elk River and lay opposite Cecil Court House, excepting the Roebuck which could not come so far. The Troops landed on the West side of the Elk River in five Disembarkations.

The Light Infantry were advanced about four miles in front towards the head of Elk.[60]

General orders for the 26th showed Ferguson's corps in the van of the advancing army:

H.Q. at Elk Ferry. "The following Corps to be in readiness to March by the right by half Companies, without beat of Drum, to-morrow morning at three o'Clock, in the following order:

Infantry jagers with an Officer and 12 Mounted. The two Battalions of Light Infantry with the Queen's Rangers and Ferguson's Corps.[61]

At Day Break [28 Aug.] Part of the Army consisting of the Jagers, Rangers, Ferguson's Corps, 2 Battalions of Light Infantry, 2 Battalions British Grenadiers, Hessian Granadier Guards, 1st and 2d Brigades, march'd towards the Head of Elk which we took possession of as well as Grey's hill about 1 ½ miles farther.[62]

September opened with an attack on the Queen's Rangers' post, and on the 2nd Ferguson's men were ordered to the post of the 1st Light Infantry.[63] On 3 September occurred the fight at Iron Hill, the first serious engagement of the campaign.

On 5 September "Two battalions of English light infantry under General Erskine advanced three miles in the direction of Christiana Bridge. They were on patrol...returned without...seeing an enemy..."[64] However, "Some men of Ferguson's Corps fired by mistake on a patrol of Light Dragoons and wounded a man and a horse."[65]

By 7 September, the army had been brigaded into the form which it was to retain through the Battle of Brandywine five days later, and "Towards the evening the army set out in three divisions...Third Division Under General Knyphausen, [in order of march] The Queen's Rangers and seventh (rear) Ferguson's Corps."[66]

Before presenting an account of the Battle of Brandywine, it will be of some interest to read Ferguson's own account of his activities since landing at Turkey Point:

We landed in Pensylvania on the 27th August. The Light Infantry Grenadiers and my detachment formed the first disembarkation but we were not molested. Two days after we advanced three Leagues into the country and when near our ground some troops appear'd in front upon which whilst the heads of the Column were forming the Line my detachment pushed forwards 1/2 a mile after some Rebell Light horse who avoided us but we discovered a Column of troops about 1/2 a mile further on and as the inclosed and woody nature of the Country secured a retreat I disencumbered 40 men and advanced to them in hopes of detaining or picking some of them up but they were going off and were very shy; however we exchanged a few Shots broke the Jaw of a Lieut. Colonel of

Militia and took one of their Light horse. The army had by this time arrived at the place from whence we had discovered this Column and did us the honor of pointing 2 field pieces at which we begd leave to decline. I was afraid the Genl would have disapproved of the Liberty I had taken but meeting him at my return was agreeably disappointed and therefore was encouraged to push more out &c untill I was wounded I did not suffer a day to pass without ranging 3 or 4 miles in fron with such partys as could be spared without exposing my Post.

In one of my excursions (Sept. 5), I learnt that a body of 600 militia were assembled within 9 miles of us and applyd to Sir William Erskine to procure the Generals leave and a reinforcement of 100 men to the 50 that I could spare from my post to attack them that night engaging to lose all character as a soldier if we lost 20 Men. In fact, with proper Caution there was no danger in the attempt for we could not faill to drive in and follow their out posts and unless they were closely posted and more alert than is their custom I must have destroy'd most of them with little loss and had I thought it prudent only to give them a rouse without engaging too deep the night secured our retreat. But the General had rode out that evening and I got no leave. Next day this militia divided into Companys to hang upon the skirts of our army; one of 30 men took post at an Inn on a road five miles on my front and whilst I was considering whether I might not pay it a night visit with a few men without troubling the General one of his aids de camp Came to me with orders to push out a strong Patrole to feel for a Rebell General Sulivan, who was supposed to be turning our Right flank with 1200 men. It was then Eight at night so I immediately set out 24 men and after having satisfyed myself that Mr. Sulivan was not on that side pushed on for our militia friends, at the inn all was quiet without, leaving some men to receive those tht might escape by the windows we forced the Doors but our friends had set out on a Scout (as they call it) towards out army 6 hours before. The people mistaking us by our Green Cloathing very readyly directed us how we should meet them and we lay in wait upon their track untill day but they heard of us changed their route and having no relish for night] visitts very quietly dispersed next day every man to his own home. Their militia and Light horse are well mounted and equiped but diffident to an Extreme my Lads were brought to among many. This morning before Brandywine we dvanced within 6 miles of the Rebells and while the army was taking its ground Sir Wm Erskine and other General Officers came to my Post which was on the road to their Camp. In my front was an open wood along the skirts of which the Rebell Horse were showing themselves in different bodys, as I imagined the Generals wished to know what was in he wood. I took 6 men and advanced to it and as the Rebells immediately made way for us we searched it unmolested. I was desired to take a larger party but I had enought and wanted to show how much my Lads body of horse and a number of Officers I believe Mr. Washington reconoitring.[67]

A number of points emerge from this personal account, apart from the fact that Ferguson's men had indeed been clothed with the green cloth sent over by Lord Barrington. The riflemen were in action within three days of landing, and were active in scouting during the entire period of the advance to Brandywine. Ferguson also notes that operational groups of about two dozen of his men were usual, not larger numbers.

On September 11, 1777, the day of the Battle of Brandywine,

At Daybreak the Army marched in two Divisions Lieutenant General Knyphausen with Major General Grant having Stirn's Brigade, 71st Regiments, 1st and 2d Brigades British, Wemyss's and Ferguson's Corps with all the Baggage, march'd by Welch's Tavern straight to Chad's Ford,...[68] *The approaches there ran through a marshy wood to the crossing...General Knyphausen had hardly set out on his march to Welch's Tavern when the Queen's Rangers and Ferguson's sharpshooters, which formed the advance guard, fell into an enemy ambuscade concealed in a marshy wood on the right and left of the highway, through which nearly half of the two corps was either killed or wounded... [my emphasis]. General Knyphausen ordered [the army] to attack the enemy in the wood as soon as the advanced guard had recovered somewht from its shock. ...the Stirn Brigade moved into the defile to the marsh. The enemy then put more troops across the Brandywine to support the troops on the wounded heights, and to make passage across the marsh more difficult. In order to prevent this, General Knyphausen ordered the Queen's Rangers to cross the marsh. ...almost impenetrable morass, fell upon the enemy's left flank with his handful of sharpshooters, whereupon the enemy abandoned his position on this side of the Brandywine.*[69]

This is an illuminating and objective account of the struggle described above by Ferguson. Major Baurmeister clarifies the action at Welch's Tavern, but gives no impession of surprise or ambuscade of the Rangers and Ferguson as described by Ewald:

When our vanguard, i.e., the Riflemen and the Queen's Rangers, arrived at Welch's Tavern, it encountered the first enemy troops. It drove them back and became master of the defile without delaying the march of the column. The skirmishing continued to the last hills of Chad's Ford. ...The van had arrived at a place where the road passes through some swampy land. On both sides of this lowland are hills and woods, and beyond it a road turns off to the left from the main road and runs through this lowland for about a half a mile. This road, which leads to a ford on Brandywine Creek, was enfiladed by an enemy battery situated beyond the creek. ...Captain Ferguson posted his Riflemen behind a house beyond the lowland and was supported by a hundred men under Captain Le Long from Stirn's brigade. [The 49th, with 4 guns] were detached to the right of the column and occupied an elevation directly above the Riflemen. ...Meanwhile the Riflemen and the Queen's Rangers had also advanced towards the left flank of the enemy, who were constantly yielding ground. ...We pushed out light troops and outposts close to the creek...Then we straightened our line, posted one battalion of the 71st Regiment and the Queen's [16th Light] Dragoons on the height of our right flank where the enemy troops had held a fleche...These improvements were completed by half past ten...[70]

Another participant, Serjeant Thomas Sullivan of the 49th Foot, elaborates on this period of the battle in his journal:

September 11th. At daybreak the Army marched in two columns; the Right commanded by Lieut. General Knyphausen, consisting of four Hessian battalions under Major General Sterne; the first and second Brigades of the British, three battalions of 71st Regiment, the Queen's American Rangers and one Squadron of the 16th Light Dragoons, with Ferguson's Corps of Riflemen, under Major General Grant, having with them six medium twelve pounders, four Howitzers, and the Light Artillery belonging to the Brigades. This column took ye direct road toward Chad's Ford, 7 miles from Kennett's Square.

We were not above half a mile on the march, when Ferguson's Riflemen and the Queen's Rangers, commanded by Captain Weyms, of the 40th Regiment, attacked the advance picquets of the enemys Light Infantry and Riflemen, which kept up a running fire, mixed with regular vollies for 5 miles, and they still retreating to their main posts, until they got almost in gun shot of the Ford...

The Queen's Rangers and Rifle Corps at the head of Liet. general Knyphausen's column, avancing to the foot of a hill, saw the enemy formed behind the fence, were deceived by the Rebels telling them, that they would deliver up their arms; but upon advancing they fired a volley upon our men and took to their heels, killed and wounded about thirty of the Corps; by that and the preceding skirmishes they were much disabled...[71]

Continuing his account with the early part of the battle, Ferguson describes his since-oft-related encounter with George Washington, but perhaps the most important point in his account (since he did not pull the trigger) is the statement that he had only twenty men with him, "a few having been disabled by the enemy [perhaps in the ambuscade?] the rest from fatigue." Ferguson relates:

I have been the more particular as I know these little anecdotes will give you and they may serve by way of sketches to give you some idea of our Enemys here as they happened under my eye they are rawn from the Life. The following one is more interesting and there are twenty witnesses to the truth of it. General Howe made a Circuit with the Gross of the army while General Knyphausen with whom we were led a Column by the direct road to attack the Rebells at Brandywine and the Rebells who were ignorant of General Howes movement employed all their Light Troops to the amount of some thousands to retard the Progress of our Column (see Washingtons Letters to Congress) & as the Country was very strong they would have found no difficulty in interrupting our march had they shown firmness equal to the ingenuity of their dispositions. But if their theory was good heir Practice was the reverse for they seemed capable but of two motions discharging their pieces in the air and running in a direct line behind them for they remained planted like Cabbages whilst our parties divided gained their flanks turned their breastworkd and then after throwing away their fire would run off leaving arms hatts blankets &c and when we were once necessitated to advance to their breast work in front altho they kept a good Countenance untill within 12 yards they gave an ineffectual fire and turned their backs to the tenth part of their own numbers, wherefore I will make bold to say that Genl Maxwell who commanded them had better begin his prenticeship as a corperall and that their Light troops (who by the by have seen three times the service of the rest of their army) have learnt to rely upon their heels.

Whilst Knyphausen was forming the Line within amile of the Rebells Camp to wait for G Howes attack, their Rifle men were picking off our men very fast by random shots from a wood some hundred yards in front as it is easy to do execution upon such large objects **I had only 20 men with me (a few having been disabled by the Enemy the rest from fatigue)** *[my emphasis] who however proved sufficient for my lads first dislodged them from the skirts of the wood then drove them from a breast work within it after which our purpose being answered we lay down at the further skirt of the wood not unnessarily to provock an attack being so few without support. We had not lyn long when a Rebell Officer remarkable y a huzzar Dress passed towards our army within 100 yards of my right flank, not perceiving us – he was followed by another in Dark Green or blue mounted on a very good bay horse with a remarkable large high cocked hat. I ordered three good shots to steal near them and fire at them but the idea disgusted me and I recalled them. The Huzzar in returning made a circuit but the other passed within 100 yards of us upon which I advanced from the wood towards him, upon my calling he stopd but after looking at me proceeded. I again drew his attentionm, and made signs to him to stop levelling my piece at him, but he slowly continued his way. As I was within that distance at which in the quickest firing I have seldom missed a sheet of paper and could have lodged a half a dozen balls in or about him before he was out of my reach I had only to determine but it was not pleasant to fire at the back of an unoffending individual who was acquitting himself very cooly of hi duty so I let him alone.The day after I had just been telling this story to some wounded officers who lay in the same room with me when one of our surgeons who had been dressing the wounded Rebell Officers came in and told us* that they had been informing him that Genl Washington was all morning with the Light Troops generally in their front and only attended by a French Officer in huzzar Dress he himself mounted and dressed as above described, the oddness of their dress had puzzled me and made me take notice of it – I am not sorry that I did not know all the time who it was.

further this deponent saith not, as his bones were broke a few minutes after–

I am yr most

p. F.

Philadelphia
Jan: 31: 1778 [all but the closing and initials, place and date are in another hand. Ferguson finished it.]⁷²

What is also clear from the above is that Ferguson was wounded before any crossing of the Brandywine was made late in the afternoon. In his first surviving letter written after the battle, to his brother George on 8 October, Ferguson gives a more general account of the battle as well as his part in it:

My Dr George
I am Sorry to inform you, because I know it will give you pain, that I had the misfortune to receive an ugly wound through the joint of my right elbow on the 11th of last month, when we gave the rebels a general defeat with very little loss (about 40 killed and 380 wounded) posted in the strongest ground they could pic out in a very strong country, Strengthened by entrenchments and a numerous artillery and their whole force was assembled and given to understand by Washington in public that the fate of America depended upon the Success of the Battle.

– our Grenadiers light Infantry four Battalions of the line, 250 American Rangers and my little corps was only engaged, in all about 3500 men. Washington's army consisted by his account of 30,000 men including militia- but in fact not above 24,000 as is said. We were in the heart of the country and our fleet sent 200 miles from us, so that we had every disadvantage, and only to trust in a good cause and our conscious superiority and to do them justice they did no [illegible]... and in the course of two hours my lads underwent the fire of 2000 men who were kind enough to fire in general in the air and run away. The Queen's Rangers Americans commanded by Rachael Wymess' husband seconded us with Spirit and the line will do us the justice to allow that we kept them undisturbed and clear'd the way for them as fast as they could follow us. – My Lads were so fatigued with dashing after the Rebels over all surfaces that I found it necessary to leave one half by turns in the rear with the column of march and work my way with the other- *[my emphasis]* which as my whole detachment was under 90 men was no great command: however by avoiding the road, gaining their flanks, or keeping up a rattling fire from the ground or by bullying them we still got on:– amongst other feats the troops behind us were witnesses when my 30 Lads *[my emphasis]* advanced to a breast work of 100 yards in extent well lined with men whose fire they received at twelve yards and when every body thought they were all destroy'd they Scrambled into the breast work and the Dogs ran away leaving even their Hatts and Shoes by the way:– we were Stop'd from following them by a heavy flanking fire from a very extensive breast work at 80 yards distance I threw my party immediately on the ground, but Wemyss's [illegible] who [illegible] to a severe trial: for such a set of bare runaways never before presumed to disgrace a Gentlemans profession.

The army march'd to the attack in two Columns, one under G: Howe (at the head of which was all the light Infantry of the army follow'd by all the Grenadiers) attack'd the right of the Rebels: The other under General Knyphausen (Hessian) at the head of which my little corps had the Honour to be) attack'd in front. Gen: Knyphausen when I ask'd his orders was pleased to desire me to take my own way and you will see by the inclosed letter that our proceedings have been honour'd by his best report and Gen: How's approbation. - As our Column took the direct road and had only four miles to march whilst Gen: How made a circuit of 15 M We had the whole body of their light troops (riflemen light infantry &c) on hand who occupied every Strength and had erected various breast works to Stop us in front and annoy us in flank in the course of our march.

The first party we had to do with was an advanced Post of 150 men and some light horse who threw away their fire and ran off, with the loss of three or four men and a horse whom we shot flying; their numbers encreased as we [illegible] advanced had kept the road being close to my rear came under a part of it and had a fourth part of his men and officers killed and wounded – this fire continued for some minutes very heavy untill we Sicken'd it after which upon the Signal to rise my Lads like Bay's dead men Sprung up and not one hurt such is the great advantage of an arm that will admit of being loaded and fired on the ground *[my emphasis]* without exposing the men that I threw my people on the ground under pretty Smart firing six times that morning without losing a man, although I had 1/4 part of those afterward kill'd or wounded before I was disabled. [The casualty returns show two men killed, Ferguson and five men wounded – total 8, supporting Ferguson's indication of only some 30 men in action.] When we came in view of the Rebel army, our Column formed the line in readiness to advance whenever General Howes attack begun: The line was much harrassed by a fire from a wood 200 yards in front to which my Lads advanced unsupported and drove the Rebels first from the Skirts of the wood then from a breast work within it and then out of it entirely after which they maintained themselves at the farther Skirt of it for half an hour without any assistance 1/4 of a mile in front of any other troops [see Ferguson's earlier account of this fight above] – The Rebels attempted to flank us and collect a powerful fire round us but they Scarse could discover us but by the smoke and when they came to show themselves our balls rattled among them so quick

— 49 —

and with so good a meaning that they mostly withdrew at last however they lined a fence on our left flank which made it necessary to change our ground to an opposite fence from whence we amused them for Some time untill being outflank'd on that side too from their great Superiority in numbers I got wounded, after which I gave my party orders to break and run untill they were a little under cover of a swell of the ground when to their eternal honour upon the first Signal they rally'd again and threw themselves upon the ground – they were soon after supported, – and without further loss they finished the day by killing or taking in conjunction with part of Wemyss' Rangers their own number of Rebels – of one half of these adventures Wemyss Corps were witnesses and of the other the whole line, particularly I refer you to Captn Burns of Wemyss's Corps son to a tenant of the Duke of B[uccleuch]: at Dalkeith, and to Capt Shand of the artillery a Scotsman in case of any accident to me I wish you to have Vouchers that we did our best to do justice to the experiment for which we were sent out. [my emphasis]

This is wrote with my left hand, a man must not tell his own Story but to his friends of course this need not be shown.

My good Mother and Father will be unhappy to see me in the wounded list whereas if my safety be their object it puts me out of the way of Broken bones for the campaign, you will regret it on another it was indeed hard to be brought up in the beginning of my career, after too that Genl How (who had refused me any addition at first) had been pleased to promise me a very flattering reinforcement in consequence I flatter myself, of having approved of the little diligence and attention I had shown to the Service. [my emphasis]

It will do my father much pleasure to read the first of the two inclosed letters as he will see thereby that the virtue of humanity may be exersized in our Profession, as well as those of courage and conduct and that it will equally meet with the approbation of a General such as we have the happiness of being under.

Our soldiers irritated by the duplicity, treachery and the base cruelty of the Inhabitants of the Jerseys who have been repeatedly detected in firing at our centrys with the Generls Protections in their pockets &c) had taken liberties there which the General was always averse to and had it particularly at heart to put a stop to upon our entering a new country: and as every man of common humanity must be happy in exherting himself for so virtuous a purpose, you may believe I obey'd his commands with diligence and alacrity and I have the satisfaction of knowing that I have protected a number of innocent familys from outrage of other corps and that not a soldier of my detatchment has been detected in marauding whilst under my command – and by God I will never suffer it or Serve in an army where it is allow'd.– Sir James Murray is wounded in the leg but recovered, his only complaint at present a slight fever we are on board the same Hospital Ship in the river Delaware and expect soon to be in Philadelphia which is in possession of our troops – who have given the Rebels a very bloody Drubbing Since we were wounded. –

You may show this to John Hume nobody else I can trust to his candour.

Farewell my Dear George for a month or two I shall have little to do but think of your Troubles.– Remember me to my Uncle most affectly and sincerely Yours ever Pat: Ferguson off Newcastle Octr 18th 1777

Janry 21 1778. It is hard that I am obliged still to have recourse to my left hand– The Doctors still doubt whether my right will belong to me or to the Worms, for my own part I think I shall keep it, for I have fought a long & painfull Battle for it & have held out well. I wrote my cousin a month ago by a bristol ship. farewell my Dear George may you be reliv'd from your present Troubles–

yours most affectionately Pat: Ferguson.[73]

This long letter gives us a clear account of the part played by Ferguson's corps in the Battle of Brandywine, irrefutable evidence of the use of his breech-loading rifles, and of the sequence of events as he saw them, as well as a clear statement of his motives for setting down the detailed account. Although Ferguson himself was removed from the battle by his arm wound, it is clear from several accounts of the afternoon's fighting that his men continued in action, and crossed Brandywine Creek with the Queen's Rangers and others with whom they had fought during the morning.

Toward four o'clock...General Knyphausen immediately formed again for his attack. General Cleveland quickly brought down his guns from the heights to the shore to cover the crossing. The 4th and 5th regiments formed the van, followed by the two battalions of the 71st Highland Regiment, Ferguson's Corps, the Queen's Rangers, the 23rd Regiment... The 4th and 5th regiments, along with the 71st Highland Regiment, Ferguson's, and the Queen's Rangers, waded through the creek at Chad's Ford, which is about fifty paces wide and a half-man deep, under grapeshot and small-arms fire from the enemy's first [the enemy had a battery of heavy guns on the road from Chad's Ford,] battery. They continued their march on the aforesaid road in the best order without firing a shot, deployed with complete composure, attacked the battery and the escort with the bayonet, stabbed down all who offered resistance, and captured four cannon and a howitzer.[74]

Finally, towards four o'clock... Knyphausen gave orders to advance;... the 1st Battalion of the 71st Regiment pushed towards the ford and crossed the stream; it was followed by the Riflemen and the Queen's Rangers, the 4th English Regiment led by His Excellency General von Knyphausen himself,... The crossing was effected on our right wing, about 250 paces from the enemy's battery, which lay a little to the left of the ford. After crossing the troops attacked them furiously, partly with the bayonet.[75]

To date no indication of who commanded Ferguson's corps after his wounding for the remainder of the battle has come to light, but it may well have been the commanding officer of the Queen's Rangers.

If we accept Ferguson's statement regarding General Howe's attitude towards a reinforcement of his force, apparently a change of mind occurring as the result of Ferguson's accomplishments since landing at Turkey Point, then the sudden disbandment of his corps on the day following the battle must be largely attributed not to the malice exposed by Adam Ferguson's statement (see below) but rather to Howe's conviction that Ferguson's corps was of real value only under Ferguson's personal leadership: that it was the man and his dedication to the service, rather than any unique advantages gained by the use of his breech-loading rifle which made the corps useful to the service.

For whatever reason, Ferguson received the following letter from the Adjutant General of the army:

Head-Quarters, 12th
September 1777
Sir,
The Commander-in-Chief has received from Lieutenant-general Knyphausen the most honourable report of your gallant and spirited behaviour in the engagement of the 11th, on which his Excellency has commanded me to express his acknowledgements to you, and to acquaint you, Sir, that he shall, with great satisfaction, adopt any plan that can be effected to put you in a situation of remaining with the army under his command.

For the present, he has thought proper to incorporate the rifle corps into the light companies of the respective regiments. I am very happy to be even the channel of so honourable a testimony of spirited conduct, and of that of your late corps. And I am, Sir, with perfect esteem and regard
Your most obedient humble Servant,
J. Paterson, Adjt Genl.

Captain Ferguson,
commanding
the Rifle Corps[76]

And on the following day the army was officially informed:

H.Q. Camp on the Heights of Brandywine, 13th Sept. After Orders, Evening Gun firing. The British Riflemen are to join the Light Companies of the Regiments to which they respectively belong.[77]

Thus vanishes from the historical record Ferguson's Corps of British Riflemen, but neither the men nor their breech-loading rifles disappeared just yet.

Although General Howe failed to mention Ferguson's unit in his report of the Battle of Brandywine (perhaps not through any ill-feeling but simply because so few men of the company took part), there were other, favourable assessments of the rifle company's largest and last engagement.

General Knyphausen's advanced corps soon fell in with large parties of the rebels, that occupied a wood between us and the Creek. A very severe skirmish ensued in which the British rifle Men and Queen's rangers distinguished themselves much to their honour; and dislodged the rebels with the points of their bayonets. The troops then took post upon the heights along the Creek,... In this situation we waited some hours, but were by no means idle during that time...upon the right the rebels had still a post, which was very troublesome to us; till the 10th Regiment charged and drove them entirely over.[78]

In his report to the Secretary of State for America, General von Knyphausen certainly includes Ferguson's unit in his detailed account of the day's action:

My Lord, The Commander in Chief Sir W Howe having honored me with the Command of the right Column of the Army in the Attack upon the Ennemy on Brandywine Hills on the 11th Septr., I look upon it as my Duty to relate to Your Lordship the Particulars thereof, which are as follows:

At V o'Clock in the Morning I mouved the Column from Kennets Square in the following Order:

An Officer & 15 Men of the Queen's Light Dragoons, Captain Ferguson's Rifflemen, & the Queen's Rangers. The 1st & 2d Brigade British Infantry under Major General Grant.

Major General Stirn's Hessian Brigade

The Remainder of the Queen's Light Dragoons, The 1st & 2d Brigade of Artillery, which was followed by The Baggage, Provision Train & Cattle of the whole Army covered by the 71st Regt.

Advancing on the Road to Chad's Ford, I had hardly come up to Welche's Tavern, when the advanced Corps, viz: Captain Ferguson's Rifflemen & the Queen's Rangers fell in with about 300 Rifflemen of the Ennemy, who were posted in the Wood to the Eastward of the Tavern. These were driven back by my advanced Party from one advantageous Post to the other behind the Defilee to the westward Side of Brandywine Creek, before which was a strong Morass.

The Column, which continued to march on, having reach'd this Defilee, I ordered the Queen's Rangers into the Wood on the left of the Morass, in order to dislodge the Ennemy there – The 2d Brigade with the 4th Regt were sent to occupy the Height on the Left – The Remainder of the 1st Brigade to take possession of a Height to the Right, & Major Genl Stirn's Brigade to proceed in the Defilee towards the Morass, which Captn Ferguson's Rifflemen were ordered to pass, supported by a Detachment of a Captn & 100 Men from the above Brigade.

The Ennemy drew more Troops from their Right over to this Side of the Brandywine Creek, & encreased their Force on the Hills on the opposite Side, commanding the Heights on our Side of the Creek.

Their advanced Troops posted in the Woods at the Foot of the Hills likewise were augmented to render more difficult our Passage over the Morass.

To prevent which the Queens Rangers were ordered to pass the Morass immediately & attack them without Loss of Time, which they did with a Spirit & Steadiness I can not too highly commend — Notwithstanding the strong Fire to oppose them, they rush'd upon the Ennemy with Charged Bayonets; Captn Ferguson attacking at the same Time, their left Flank, Whereupon they ran off into the Wood near the Creek on the Road to Chad's Ford. ...[79]

Yet despite these official plaudits, another man on the scene who almost certainly knew Ferguson personally from about the time of his own arrival in America in the Spring of 1778 as Secretary to the Carlisle Peace Commission, was able to write that:

It was well known in the army that the Commander-in-Chief, Sir William Howe, had taken umbrage at the rifle corps having been formed without his being consulted. It was therefore perhaps not to be expected that he would exert himself to support it. The use of which it had proved, to the great satisfaction of the army, seems to have prevented him from taking active steps to its prejudice, until Captain Ferguson was wounded at Brandywine; of which Sir William took advantage, and reduced the corps without consulting him.

...what mortified him [Ferguson] most was, that during his confinement the rifle corps, deprived of its leader, was broke up, ...the rifles lodged in the store of spare arms, [in the Artillery Park, Walnut Street, Philadelphia] and the men returned to their respective regiments.[80]

Subsequent evidence suggests that while Adam Ferguson was correct about the men of the rifle corps being returned to the light infantry companies of their parent regiments, he was wrong about the breech-loading rifles being sent into Store at this time, unless of course they were subsequently re-issued to the men for the march to New York. What had created the sudden change in General Howe's feelings about Ferguson (if indeed there had been a change) is not known, but his failure to employ Ferguson again must surely have been primarily due to Ferguson's physical condition during the remainder of Howe's time in North America.

Only nine days after Brandywine, during the night of 20–21 September 1777, occurred the "bloody drubbing" referred to by Ferguson, the so-called "Paoli massacre" in which a British force inflicted 150 casualties on rebel General Anthony Wayne's sleeping army. A participating officer of the 2d Light Infantry wrote:

We then marched on briskly still silent — our Company was advanced immediately preceding a Company of Riflemen who always are in front- a picquet fired upon us at the distance of fifteen yards miraculously without effect – This unfortunate Guard was instantly dispatched by the Riflemens Swords.[81]

Two points in this brief reference, first that a company of riflemen was indeed present (these could have been armed either with Ferguson's or Pattern 1776 rifles) and second, that the pickets were dispatched "by the Riflemen's Swords." So far as we know at the time of writing, this can only refer to the 24-inch triangular-bladed socket bayonets furnished with Ferguson's rifles. Blades of such length would not have been familiar as bayonets, but common as sidearms carried by German rifle-armed units. It might, of course, refer to the Hessian jägers who were with the army, except that they are not listed as participating at Paoli. Furthermore, a 1783 painting of this event (see the facing page), commissioned by two participant officers, clearly shows a small group of green-clad men, whose weapons have much-longer-than-usual bayonets, the blades of which extend forward from the underside of the barrels — the only pictorial evidence we have of Ferguson's men, even though after their official disbandment.

Captain Thomas Armstrong, 64th Foot, then serving in the 2d Light Infantry with the light infantry company of his regiment, adds further details. He confirms that on 19 Sept. the 2d Light Infantry were indeed on the right of the line in rear of the jägers and adds:

The men of Fargusen Corps now are atasht to this Battl to join the Riffel-Men under Lt Shaw till further Orders – Lt Matthews to Act with the Riffel-men till further Orders.[82]

At the end of this Orderly Book is a return for the 64th Light Infantry company which includes three "Riffle men,"[83] but these were probably not from Ferguson's corps.

Ferguson's personal fortunes during early 1778 continued uncertain; a letter written by him (with his left hand) to an unknown party sometime in January, describes his situation:

Dear Sir

My Letter from Chesapeak in August with my right hand was scarcely legible & being now obliged to have recourse to my left I have no hopes of yr decyphering this which however you will receive as a mark of my good will at least.

I refer you to my Brother George for an account of the action at Brandywine (Sepr 11) where I got a wound in the joint of my right elbow which has proved very painful & troublesome & it is still doubtful whether my arm can be saved The Dors [doctors] are divided in opinion one half for amputation the other agt it – an attempt to save it will be attended

The Battle of Paoli, 20 Sept. 1777, by Xavier della Gatta, dated 1782. Commissioned by two British officer participants who supplied and corrected the details. A close-up showing five men in green light infantry tunics with gaiter trousers and plumed hats pinned up on the left side. The bayonets of their arms are much longer (compare with redcoats in the foreground) and mounted below rather than alongside the barrels. These cannot be other than former Ferguson's Riflemen acting with the regular light infantry at Paoli. Shown in color on the back cover. *Courtesy of The Valley Forge Historical Society.*

with a lengthy course of pain & a little hazard of my life, but without it I am disabled for service and helpless in every respect & have suffered much for four months to little purpose – appearances are within these few days becoming more favourable & my own opinion which in this instance is worth that of half the faculty it will be saved & at any rate I doubt not to come well through, as I thank heaven it has always furnish'd me with strength of mind & body equal to the trials I have been put to, the sons of Esculapius judging from themselves think every man whose countenance is of the same cadaverous hue with their own is made of stuff only fit to hang wigs upon. They however here allow that I am made of tougher materials altho I put a bad face upon this & most other matters & the partisans of my arm conceive great hopes from a virtue which it seems they have discovered in me & which am sure was neither born nor bred with me namely patience which I put up with from hard necessity being married to her agt my consent, & therefor God willing shall kick her out a doors as soon as I can wield my limbs.

My mother & sisters think I am near buried & must not be undeceived was it not hard to be thus brought up in the beginning of my Career when the difficulties too with regard to my Command were disappearing for altho I could at first scarce keep the 100 men I brought out yet about ten days before I was wounded Sir William Howe himself assured me he meant immediately to increase my Corps & I understand from Sir William Erskine with numbers beyond what I could pretend to expect. [My emphasis] since that I received the two inclosed letters so that the augmentation would assuredly have taken place & I flatter myself the change in the Generals disposition proceeded solely from the Diligence & attention to the Service which it had been my Endeavour to shew [letter ends].[84]

This does seem to suggest that whatever animosity Howe might have felt towards him, Ferguson was under the impression at the time of the battle that his corps was to be usefully augmented and continued in service. It was not until 25 Aug. 1778 that Ferguson was paid His Majesty's Bounty of £182.10.0. "for the loss of the use of his right arm from a wound rec'd at Brandywine."[85]

Although his specially trained rifle corps ceased to exist, his rifles appear to have continued in service, presumably in the hands of the men to whom they had originally been issued, in the light companies of the var-

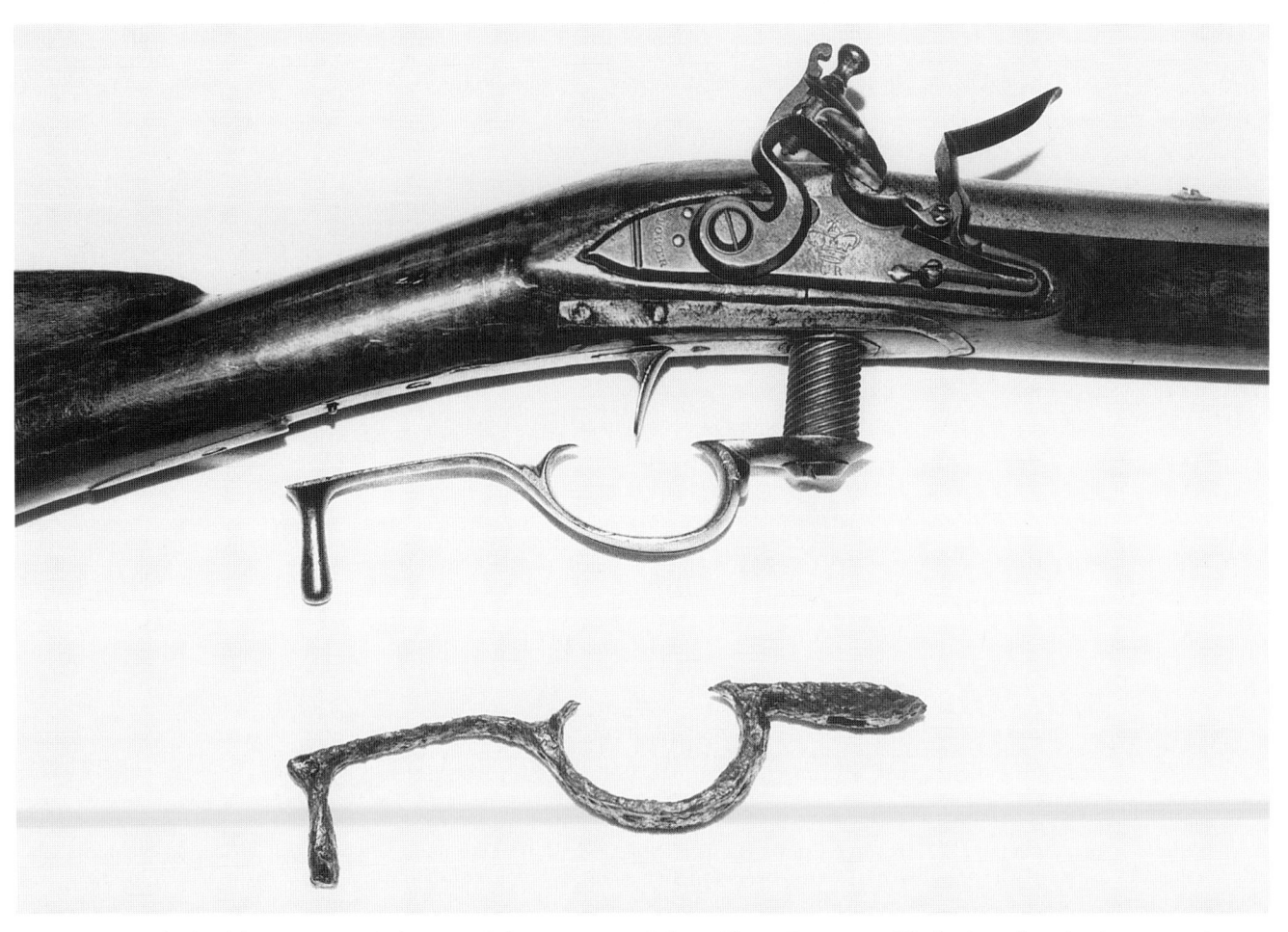

The only physical evidence currently known of the presence of the military Ferguson rifle in America. A triggerguard excavated at a British campsite area near New York City in 1986, shown alongside the Morristown example. It is clearly of identical design and measurement.
Courtesy of Charles Salerno.

ious regiments, brigaded in the 1st and 2d Light Infantry Battalions, and in company with the Pattern 1776 rifles. At the time of writing, however, there is no documentary evidence for the re-issue of Ferguson's breech-loaders, or that they were ever issued to other than regular light infantry of British line regiments. One of the two most conclusive pieces of evidence regarding the withdrawal of the Ferguson rifle from service is an army order of 21 Feb. 1778 (while the army was still in winter quarters in Philadelphia) which calls for a return "to be given in...of the Number of Rifles belonging to Captain Ferguson's late Corps now in the Possession of the Different Regiments."[86] This directly contradicts the statement of Adam Ferguson that the rifles had been delivered into Ordnance Stores in Philadelphia.

Ferguson rifles were probably in action at Monmouth Court House in the hands of the light infantry companies, since it is not until the British army had returned to New York City that the final piece of evidence appears which mentions the rifles in army records:

Memorandum. 24 July 1778. Any Officer or Corps, having in Possession any of Capn Ferguson's Rifle Guns, Bayonets or Powder-Flasks, are requested to send them to Mr Wood at the Ordnance Office, that they may be immediately repaired.[87]

If repairs were indeed what was intended, it seems strange that not only the rifles, but the bayonets and powder-flasks, in short all of the items peculiar to the rifles, should have been specifically called in. It seems more likely that a clean-sweep was being made to completely remove this special apparatus and all that pertained to it. There is no evidence either of the response to this memorandum, or of the Ferguson rifle's re-issue.

The subsequent history of Patrick Ferguson was not concerned with his breech-loading rifles. It may be stated here, however, that the several detachments that he commanded, chiefly of Loyalists and detachments of the 71st Foot and local militias, did on occasion probably contain some rifles, and that there is clear evidence that muzzle-loading rifles of the Pattern 1776, were carried by Ferguson's own very small all-Loyalist unit, the American Volunteers, at King's Mountain. (See Appen-

— 54 —

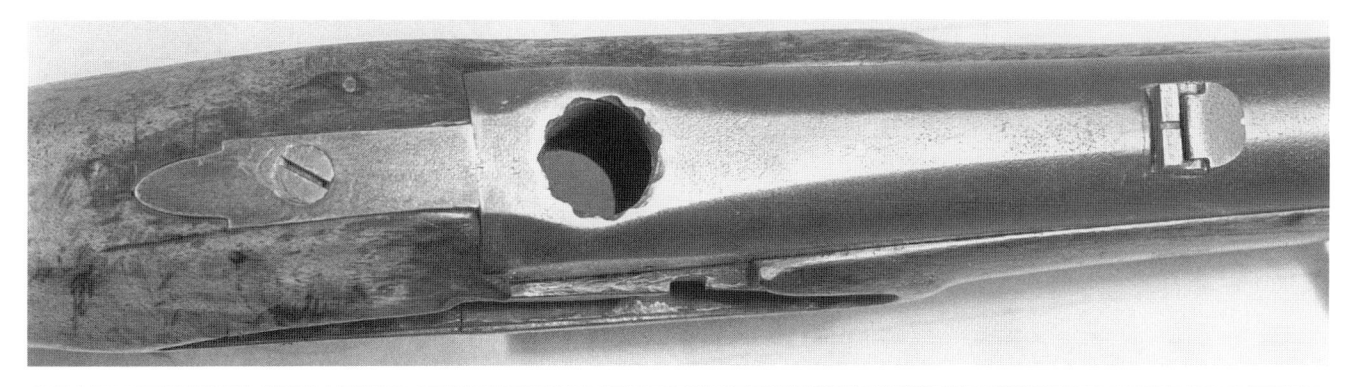

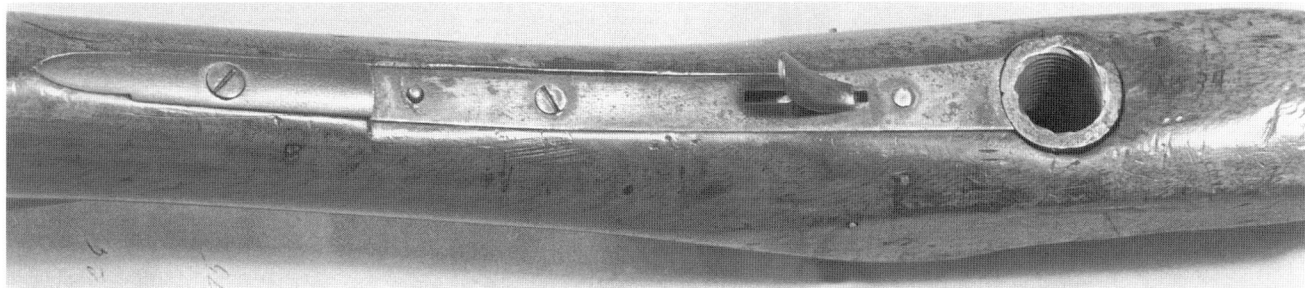

The Ferguson Rifle, From Manufacture to the Battle of Monmouth Court House, 1776–1778

dix 3). Amongst the detailed accounts of the personal effects taken from Ferguson's corpse on the Mountain, there is mention of a pistol and a knife, but no rifle or other longarm; no mention of rifles amongst the statement of 1,500 stands of arms captured; and there is overwhelming evidence from participants on both sides of the battle as to the musket armament of the vast majority of the Loyalist forces: indeed, during May 1780 at Charleston, South Carolina, there had been "Issued to Maj. Ferguson's Corps" from Ordnance Stores in that city, 300 serviceable French muskets and bayonets, and 50 Sea Service swords.[88] While some of the men in the several companies of North Carolina militia serving under Ferguson at King's Mountain undoubtedly carried their own longrifles, it is beyond reasonable doubt that the only Ferguson at King's Mountain was Patrick.

After the close of hostilities, a General Return of arms in Ordnance Store at New York, dated 10 Mar. 1783, includes: "7 Ferguson rifles Unserviceable."[89] The state of these surviving rifles is not surprising, for the greatest weakness of the Ferguson as a military weapon was its extreme weakness of the stock around the breech, where so much wood was removed to contain the breech mechanism, the lock and trigger mechanism, that the remaining wood had little chance of surviving field service unbroken. Both military rifle survivors (see the next paragraph for a discussion of the second example) have extensive damage and in one case contemporary repair around their breech areas, and several of the known officers' rifles are similarly damaged. It is perhaps significant that the only physical evidence thus far discovered which confirms the presence of the Ferguson rifle in North America is a triggerguard (shown on facing page) found at a British camp-

The newly discovered second example of a military Pattern 1776 Ordnance Ferguson.

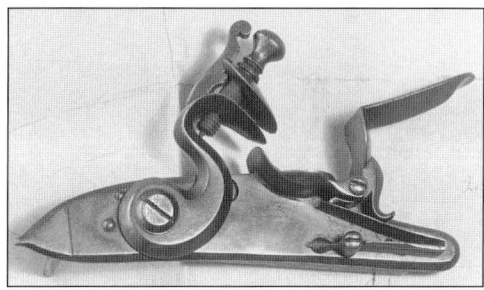

site in the New York City area, the loss of which would have rendered the rifle useless.

In recent years a second Pattern 1776 Ordnance Ferguson rifle has been identified in a public museum where it has lain unrecognized as a military piece since 1904. Thanks to the external markings having been erased and the barrel slightly shortened the catalogue entry failed to give any indication of its true identity. It was not until Jesse Melot visited the museum and, with the cooperation of the museum staff, had the rifle taken to pieces and examined in detail, that it was correctly identified from the undisturbed internal markings. The rifle itself is in excellent condition, but appears to have undergone some modifications, particularly in its stock. Some details of this rifle are shown in this chapter.

An accurate replica has recently been created with which serious experiments have been conducted to determine the functioning and accuracy of the Ferguson rifles. This subject is discussed in detail by the builders in Appendix Six.

Ammunition

The light infantrymen from whom Ferguson's trainees were selected would have already been

— 55 —

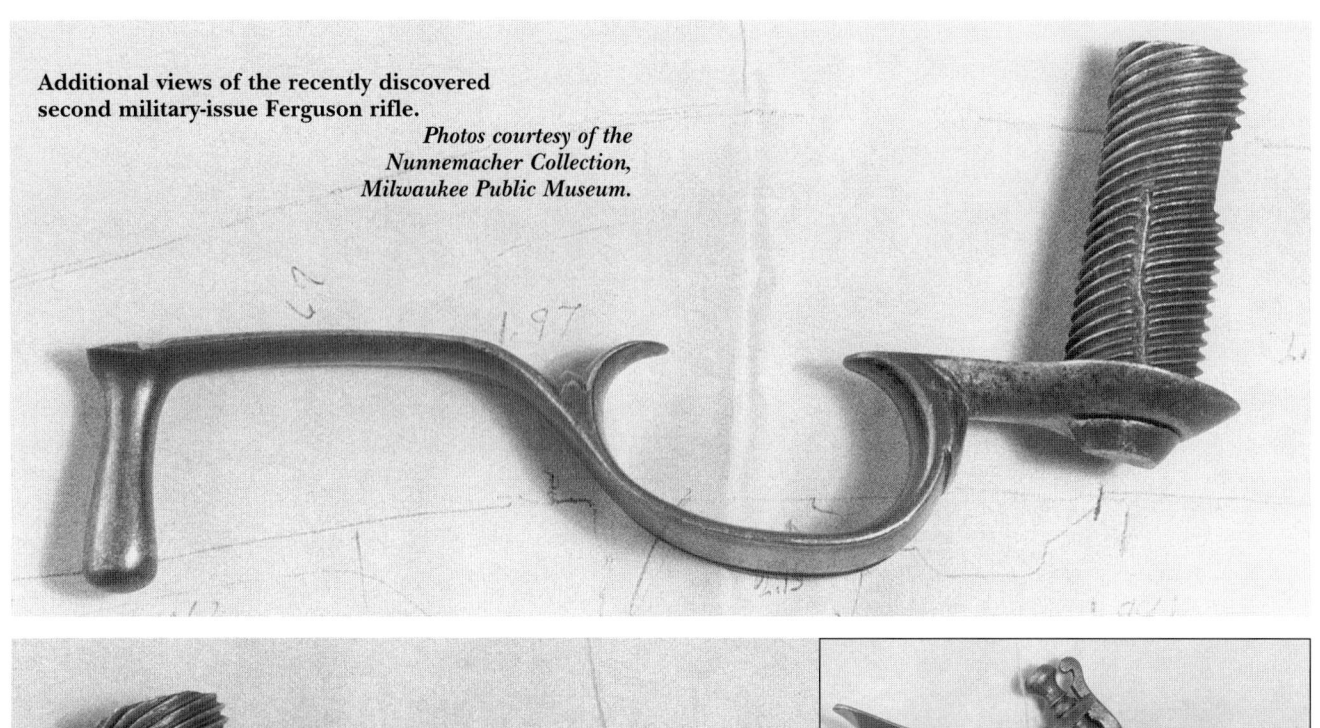

Additional views of the recently discovered second military-issue Ferguson rifle.
Photos courtesy of the Nunnemacher Collection, Milwaukee Public Museum.

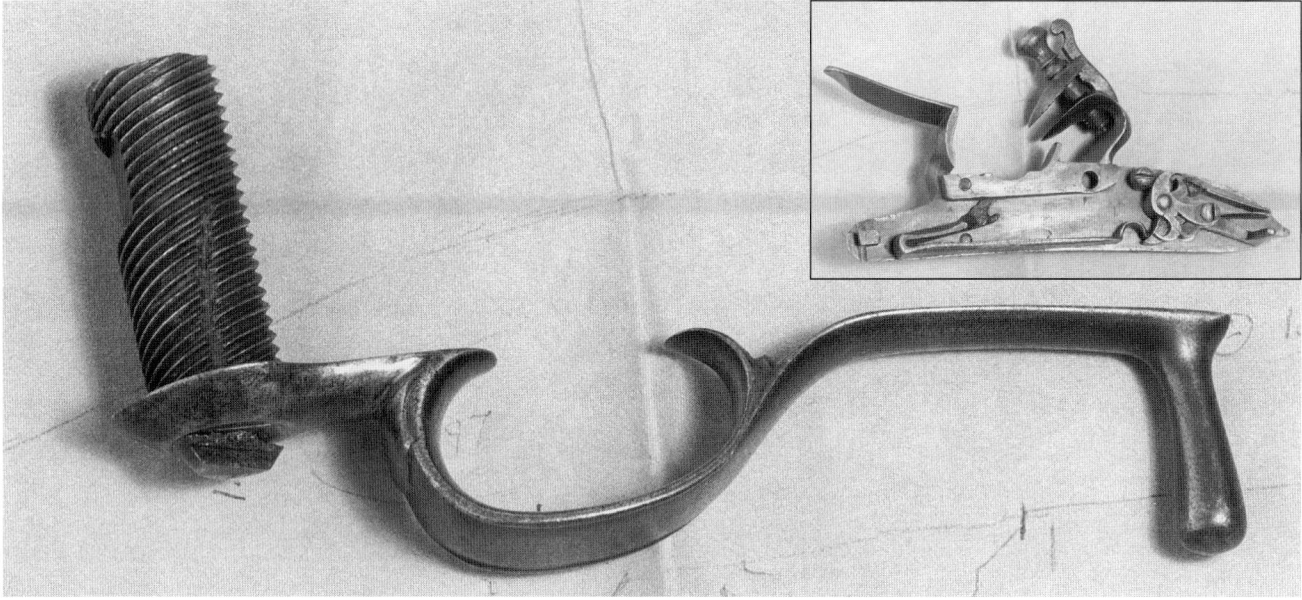

equipped with an 18-hole carbine-bore cartridge box, or "belly-box" as issued by the Ordnance, along with a waist or shoulder belt, a powder horn, ball-bag ("small bag," "shott bag") and small hatchet ("tommy hawk"). It must be presumed that the light infantry powder horns would have been replaced with the powder flasks obtained for Ferguson's use.

The records clearly show that the Ferguson rifle used the same basic components as the Pattern 1776 muzzle-loading rifles: the standard carbine-bore (.615-in.) ball and superfine double-strength powder, and carbine flints; the records are equally clear that a special powder flask was obtained by the Ordnance for use with these rifles. Some idea of the correct powder charge has been gained through the construction and firing of an accurately made replica (see Appendix Six).

Before the late-1790s, powder flasks were very rarely made of copper or other metal; shaped horn or leather, or leather-covered horn, were the common materials used in making powder flasks. Presumably the Ferguson flasks, which were bought-in from the commercial market and not made specifically for the Ordnance, will have been fitted with a non-adjustable brass charger with cut-off throwing the exact charge suitable for the rifle, and some form of carrying rings or loops. They may well have resembled the Light Infantry powder horns which had been issued since 1771 (which also remain unidentified at the time of writing). There is no evidence that the flasks, unlike the other rifle accessories prepared for the Ferguson, were marked in any way, possibly because they appear to have arrived at the very last minute. In field use the Ferguson may well

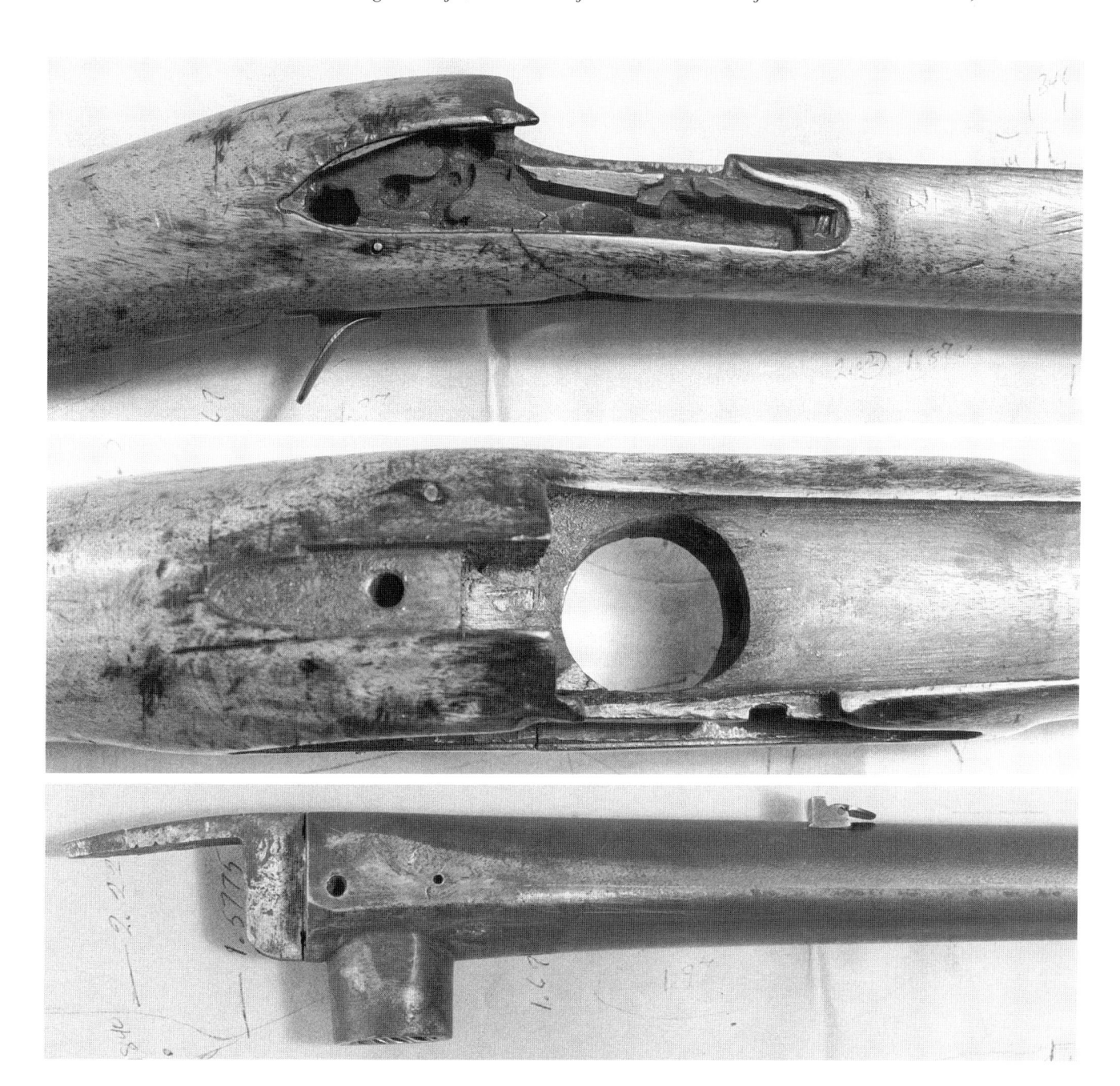

More close-up views of the second example of a military Ferguson rifle. The many photographs of this rifle that are shown in this chapter were taken when the rifle was disassembled for measurement and identification. The rifle's external markings have all been erased, but the internal markings survive undisturbed, making a positive identification possible.

Photos courtesy of the Nunnemacher Collection, Milwaukee Public Museum.

have been loaded using conventional paper cartridges holding only the powder, with the flasks used when cartridges ran out, and for making up new cartridges. It is also possible that a system of dual management such as was later adopted with the Baker rifles was used. This would have meant that paper cartridges would have been used for skirmishing and rapid fire, while loading from the ball-bag and powder flask was reserved for careful sniping and sharpshooting. There is no documentary evidence for any form of lubricant for the ball or cartridge, nor of any special tools used to seat the balls uniformly at the front of the chamber, although the modern evidence in shooting these rifles strongly suggests that both would have been essential to sustained accuracy and continued functioning. See Appendix Six.

The materials printed in this chapter make clear a number of points concerning the military history of the Ferguson rifle. The most important of these is the insignificance of the rifle both in tactical and strategic terms. The idea has often been put forward that had the British army been entirely armed with the Ferguson rifle it would probably have won the war. The structural weaknesses of the design and the properties of gunpowder as a propellant make this virtually impossible. But in addition to these factors it would have required a complete and virtually overnight change in the thinking of British military leaders and those politicians who voted the money for military expenditure. Many thousands of men drawn from the least educated stratas of contemporary society would have had to be screened, selected and given a lengthy training quite beyond the thinking of the time. This would certainly have been an absolute impossibility, given that Britain's situation in the world demanded that she be able to confront her peers in terms mutually acceptable. Any possible *raison d'etre* for the widespread issue of the Ferguson would have applied solely to what was perceived at the time as at best a Colonial uprising of no major significance. The entry of the French and others after 1778 made it even less likely that a major alteration in the principal weapons of the army would be even thought about. Tactically the part the Ferguson played in the hands of around only two dozen men at Brandywine was not seen then or since as contributing to the British success on that day, and there is no evidence to suggest that its effectiveness from the time of first use in June 1777 until it fades from clear view in July 1778 marked it out from the majority of the (muzzle-loading) rifles in use by the army. Strategically it never made any impression at all; launched as a company-level experimental field trial it lasted for one campaign and was then downgraded to the level of all other rifles then in service with light infantry. The concept of breech-loading rifles for military service had been examined in the 1760s and been found wanting, and this was confirmed by the insignificance of the Ferguson's performance despite being in the hands of an active skilled and intelligent officer. Experiments continued after the war but even with the increased appreciation of troop-mobility which developed from the 1790s, factors such as the rapid accumulation of fouling from the combustion of the gunpowder, the weakness, complicated design and consequent cost of both manufacture of breech machanisms in quantity and the lengthy special training of men in their use, rendered the whole idea unacceptable. No basic change in the battlefield deployment of troops occurred to bring into greater demand the potential of a rapid-loading rifle until the problems surrounding the manufacture of the metallic cartridge were solved, forcing a military re-assessment from the late 1860s.

Any idea that the British might have won the American War had they been largely armed with Ferguson rifles, as has been sometimes confidently asserted, could not be more wrong. It is much more likely that the British army would have been tactically crippled after the first major engagement and obliged to withdraw from all contact with the enemy until re-equipped with conventional muzzle-loading arms.

For the history of the Ferguson rifles made in 1776 by Henry Nock for the Honourable East India Company and their service in India, the reader is referred to David F. Harding's *Smallarms of the East India Company 1600–1856*, vol. 2, 429–41; vol. 4, 124, 197–200. It may be noted here that the surviving example of the EICO's Ferguson rifles is also broken through the stock in the same area as the Ordnance examples.

CHAPTER 4

German Riflemen

and Their Rifles in the American War

A note on terminology is appropriate before proceeding to examine German riflemen and their rifles. The term *jägerbüchse* which means literally "hunting rifle" was seldom used by the Germans to describe a civilian sporting rifle, but normally referred to a military rifle. The term most used to describe a civilian sporting rifle was *Birsch* (*Bursch* or *Pirsch*)-*büchse*, literally stalking or hunting-rifle. Therefore, to avoid confusion the term *jäger* (or jaeger to avoid the umlaut) rifle should only be used to describe the military version of the German short rifle. Since most British officers and government officials, as well as German nobility and officials, spoke French, this was normally the language used in correspondence and conversation between them. The German term *jäger* referring to military riflemen and not civilian huntsmen was therefore rarely used, but instead the French equivalent word, *chasseur*. The equivalency of the term is sometimes suspect, since in French military service both before and after the period of the American War, *chasseurs* were often not armed with rifles; their German equivalents in North America always were.

Because so little is known about either the German units or their arms, the emphasis in this chapter will be upon the composition and numbers of the several *jäger/chasseur* units sent to America, and to a lesser extent, on the few rifles which can be reasonably identified as having been carried by them.

The largest rifle-armed unit of the German auxiliary troops that served in North America under British command was the *Feldjägercorps* of the Landgrave of Hesse-Cassel. These included both foot soldiers and a company of mounted riflemen. There was also a *jäger* regiment from the province of Hesse-Hanau, ruled by the son of the Landgrave of Hesse-Cassel, and a second, mixed light infantry and rifle regiment from Hesse-Hanau, which arrived in America in 1781. Much smaller *jäger* companies were supplied by Ansbach-Brandenburg (often called Ansbach-Bayreuth), Brunswick and Anhalt-Zerbst. The Brunswickers and Anhalters and most of the Hanauers served almost entirely in Canada and on the Burgoyne campaign, and the Ansbachers were normally brigaded with the Hesse-Cassel *jägers*.

Considering the number of men who served in these units, there is no doubt that, as far as regular troops are concerned, between the 1,100 rifles carried by British regulars and the more than 4,000 of their German allies, there were far more rifles in British service at any one time during the war than on the American side where, after 1777, rifle companies were *ad hoc* and short-lived, and where rifles were largely in the hands of the numerous rebel militia units, and, with the exception of Boston, largely in the South.[1]

In addition to these regular units contracted for directly with the several ruling princes in Germany, a number of ad hoc units were formed in America from the troops already serving there. These include a company ordered to be formed at New York on 21 July 1778 from one subaltern officer and two volunteer privates from each company of the Hessian infantry. This unit, commanded by Captain George Hanger, was disbanded on 15 November 1778.[2] Hanger's second *jäger* company of 124 men, raised for the South Carolina campaign late in 1779, was blown across the Atlantic en route, (along with Althause's New York Volunteer Rifle Co.) and was returned to New York and disbanded without seeing service. Hanger in the meantime, was attached to Tarleton's British Legion.

The *jäger* companies that served in North America will now be examined by country of origin, listed in order of their numerical importance. It is not the intention, nor within the scope of this chapter to deal with the activities or the performance of the various *jäger* companies in America, but only to establish their numbers, quality and some idea of their armament. They were active in virtually every action of the war, often playing a crucial role in the success of the British forces. Detailed accounts of their operations may be found in a number of contemporary works.[3]

Hesse-Cassel. Ruler: Frederick II, Landgrave.
The initial treaty for the hiring of troops was signed on 15 January 1776 and included two companies of chasseurs, one of which was to be ready to march on 15 February. Three days after the signing, Col. William Faucitt, Britain's agent for hiring troops in Germany,

wrote to the Secretary of State Lord Suffolk:

...a corps of Hessian Chasseurs, that was of great use during the late War [the Seven Years' War]; and finding that a certain Establishment of them, is still kept up in this country, in such a manner that a Body of three or four Hundred of them, regularly train'd up to the Service, & arm'd with Rifle-Barrel-Guns, might be assembled, and formed, in time to embark with the 2nd Division, in the month of March.[4]

Suffolk's reply of 2 February 1776 accepted the offer of these 400 *jägers*. In inspecting these troops (von Donop's corps) on embarkation, Faucitt wrote that:

The Chasseurs are a stout, active Body of Men, arm'd with Rifle-Barrel-Guns, to the use of which they are thoroughly inur'd, being all, without exception, Chasseurs by profession; and as they are commanded by Skilfull, experienced Officers, They cannot fail of being very serviceable. They are cloth'd in Green, with red Facings & Cuffs.[5]

Technical details were not neglected, and on 9 April Faucitt informed the Secretary of State (see also Chapter 2)

it will be necessary for a quantity of Gun-powder, of a finer & better sort, than that usually furnish'd for our Infantry, to be sent over for the particular use of the Chasseurs, whose Pieces, having all Rifle-Barrels, & of quite a different construction from the Firelocks, will otherwise, as They assure me, be in a great measure useless: Having had occasion to write to the Board of Ordnance lately, I took the advantage of that opportunity to mention this to Them; but a word from your Lordship to the Master General upon the subject, will ensure the making such a provision...[6]

As we have seen in Chapter 2, such a provision was indeed made. On 3 June, Faucitt noted of Capt. von Ewald's embarking *jäger* company, apart from their crimson facings and cuffs, that they "appeared to be a very serviceable, good Body; & as General Knyphausen, as well as their Captain, assur'd me, are all excellent Marksmen." The company's establishment, a typical example, was 1 captain, 1 lieutenant, 2 second lieutenants, 4 serjeants, 6 corporals, 105 riflemen, with 1 quartermaster, 1 captain d'armes [armourer], 1 surgeon, 3 cors de Chasse [bugle-horns] and 4 officers' servants.[7] A description of the clothing of the second division of Hessian troops (von Knyphausen's) includes reference to the chasseurs having green coats with scarlet (not merely red) facings and cuffs, buff breeches and waistcoats, black stocks and hats rather than caps.[8]

On 21 November 1776, Faucitt received instructions to raise an augmentation for the Hesse-Cassel *jägers* of 800 men, bringing the new establishment of the *feldjägercorps* to 1,067 riflemen from 10 December 1776 until the end of the war.[9] Faucitt informed Suffolk a month later that:

The Chasseurs are to be assembled at this Place [Cassel], after having been first tried, with regard to their Expertness in firing with the Rifle-Barrel-Gun, by an officer appointed for that purpose; Who, having served constantly with the Chasseurs during the late War, is thoroughly conversant with the use of this Piece.[10]

Reinforcements for the year 1777 were not so easy to come by as during the first year of recruiting. It was noted that "chasseurs, when they are really such by profession, are become exceedingly difficult to meet with."[11] The new units included two companies of Hessian *jägers* of 150 men each, departing from Cassel 8 March for embarkation at Bremerlehe.

In May 1777, a general assessment of the 412 *jägers* (363 actual riflemen) which had arrived at Bremerlehe for embarkation indicates that there was a falling-off in the quality of the recruits. These men were the companies of von Wurmb and von Lohrey, and augmentations for von Ewald's and von Wreden's already in America. Of the entire group Faucitt wrote:

I cannot say, that I was altogether so well pleased with these Chasseurs, as I was with Those, I had seen on former occasions; nevertheless They are in general, a robust hardy-looking Sett of People, and certainly very fit for active Service.[12]

In July, the Muster Master General to the Foreign Troops in His Majesty's Service (Sir George Osborn), writing from Staten Island, noted that the 300 Hessian *jägers* who had just arrived with other German reinforcements "are better clothed than last Year, their Arms & Boots are in good order. The Chasseurs for the Reinforcement are chiefly Hessians..."[13] These two companies brought the Hessian *feldjägercorps* up to its official Establishment of 1,067 of whom 900 were riflemen.[14] Of these, the mounted company consisted of 3 officers, 10 NCOs, 3 musicians, 1 surgeon and 91 mounted *jägers* armed with a pair of holster pistols of the pattern used by Hessian light cavalry. In December 1777, a further 70 Hessian chasseurs embarked at Bremerlehe.[15]

The *jäger* reinforcements for 1778 embarked at Bremerlehe on 5 April included 25 for Hesse Cassel, and it was noted in October that the *feldjägercorps* needed 117 men to complete to their Establishment.[16]

The 1779 reinforcements were mustered at Bremerlehe on 1 May, and of the Hesse-Cassel contingent consisting of 1 first lieutenant, 1 second lieutenant, 4 NCOs and 223 riflemen, it was noted that the clothing:

...which the Chasseurs wore, was very good; as well as the rest of their Appointments; though there were only 100 of them arm'd, it being intended that the arms & Accoutrements for the rest, as also for the Infantry Recruits, shou'd be supplied out of the Landgrave's Depot in America.[17]

Unfortunately, no documents relating to the Landgrave's American depot (presumably in New York City) have come to light. This comment is particularly interesting in view of a letter written by the Deputy Commissary to Foreign Troops (Mr. Porter) at New York, to Lord George Germain, in which he mentions "that the Cloathing of some Companies of Hessian Chasseurs is very bad."[18] It may have been spoiled during the ocean crossing, but one wonders at the discrepancy in reporting.

A partial arming of the 131 recruits occurred again in 1780 with a different reason attached:

but their Arms & Accoutrements, excepting a certain proportion of Rifle-Barrel-Guns, deliver'd to some of the most steady amongst the Chasseurs, by way of guard over the Recruits, were packed up with the Heavy Bagage.[19]

A letter of 26 May 1780 notes that a total of 72 men from eight Hessian regiments were on duty as chasseurs with Clinton's force in Carolina.[20] It is not clear whether these men were of Hanger's ad hoc company which had been blown across the Atlantic to England.

The *jäger* recruits for 1781, 67 of them for Hesse-Cassel, were described as "excellent throughout, clothing new &c."[21]

The last *jäger* recruits sent to America embarked at Bremerlehe on 31 May 1782, the Hesse-Cassel contingent consisting of 92 men.[22] [1,752 men sent over]

Among the Hessian accounts rendered at Cassel in 1786, the items listed below were recorded as "delivered out of the Armory belonging to the Landgrave of Hesse Cassel to conduct the Recruits sent from 1776 to the Year 1783, Delivered to the Corps of Field Huntsmen":

81 lb of Musket Powder filled into 3340, nine ounce Pistol charges, for the Huntsmen Mounted the 100 weight at 30 Dollars [Reichstalers] amounts to   £ 22.16. 0.
178 lb nine ounce[s] Pistol Balls the Lead at 7 Rd [Rixdollars = Reichstalers] per 100w   12. 1. 0.
1 Ream of Cartridge Paper   1.16. 0.
4 Forms [moulds] for Casting Bullets, each to cast 12, at 5 Rd   20. 0. 0.
800 weight of polished Powder at 36 Dollars the 100 weight   288. 0. 0.
4700 weight of Leaden Balls for Rifle Guns at 7 Rd the 100 weight   329. 0. 0.
1968 Flints at 3/2 Rd the 1000   6.18. 0.

Re-equipment of Hessian Jäger zu Pferde [mounted jägers] 14 Nov. 1777 including 167 pairs of pistols at 4.21.4
     57. 0. 0.23

It should be noted that these issues related only to those items issued from the Cassel stores, and not to any issues made in North America.

Hesse-Hanau. Ruler: Wilhelm, Hereditary Prince (heir to Hesse-Cassel).

The Hereditary Prince of Hesse-Hanau was apparently the first of the German princes to offer soldiers to the British Government in August 1775.[24] On 4 December 1776, he offered a corps of *jägers* to the British Government.[25]

The Establishment of the regiment of Hesse-Hanau *jägers* from 10 February 1777 included 412 of which 318 were riflemen:

1 lieutenant-colonel & captain, 3 captains, 1 captain-lieutenant, 4 first lieutenants, 4 second lieutenants, 1 adjutant, 1 auditor, 1 quartermaster, 1 surgeon major, 4 surgeon's mates, 4 serjeant majors, 4 serjeants, 4 quartermasters, 4 captains d'armes, 1 armourer and 1 assistant, 12 horns, 24 corporals, 318 riflemen, 13 officers' servants, 1 valet for the Chest, 1 provost, 4 valets for waggons.[26]

Agent Rainsford wrote to Lord Suffolk:

I have great reason, my Lord, to think the Hanau Chasseurs will be a most select Corps. Col. Creutzberg who commands the Corps writes me the whole would have been embarked by the 8th if their Arquebuses had been ready, they being at that time 460 men.[27]

A few days later he added, "The Company of Chasseurs is in excellent order for service, both from their Completeness Health & Goodness of the Men, their arms & accoutrements are also good."[28] Von Creutzberg's additional companies (382 men) arrived at Nimuegen in April, and were described as "still a better Body of Men than the Company that preceded them, very compleat, well-armed and appointed...most of them are very expert with their Arquebuses."[29] Major General Charles Rainsford used a fairly commonly used French term to refer to the rifles.

In November 1777, 54 Chasseur recruits embarked at Hanau.[30]

Chasseur recruits for 1778 included 1 officer, 1 serjeant, 5 corporals and 68 riflemen for the Hanau company, described as "as fine a body of men absolutely fit for any active service,"[31] who embarked at Bremerlehe on 5 April.

In March 1779, the recruits mustered at Dort included 1 captain, 1 first lieutenant, 10 NCOs, 1 surgeon's mate, 3 *cors de Chasse* [bugle-horns] and 111 riflemen of a new Hesse-Hanau chasseur company for Canada.[32]

A year later the quality of the Hanau chasseur recruits appeared to be up to standard. Of the 3 NCOs and 60 men Faucitt wrote that they

made a very good appearance, being completely cloth'd, accoutred, & arm'd with Rifle-Barrel-Guns; to which, moreover, I can take upon me to add, from having attended Their Dayly Exercises, that They use them with great skill & dexterity: They are likewise a sett of stout, well-made young Fellows, capable of supporting Fatigue, & very fit for the Service.[33]

In 1781 it was much the same story, with 48 of the 251 chasseur recruits intended for the Hanau company:

The Hanau Chasseurs, fifty only in number, and destined...for Canada, are a stout, well-looking Sett of men, many [note: not all] of whom are Chasseurs by profession & the Rest, having been diligently exercis'd in firing Ball, for some time past, at Hanau, are reported to be equally proficient with the others, in the use of the Rifle-Barrel-Gun.[34]

The 1782 recruits embarked at Bremerlehe on 31 May, and included 58 men for the Hanau *jägers*.[35]

The Hanau *jägers* were based in Canada for the duration of the war. They formed the largest part of the force under St. Leger (342 men on paper) which ultimately withdrew from the Mohawk Valley after the unsuccessful siege of Fort Stanwix during the Burgoyne campaign in 1777.

Early in 1781, it was announced that a new corps of Light Infantry was to be raised by Hesse-Hanau, to consist of one company of "Grenadiers Arquebusiers" of 165 men with 142 arquebusiers, "*sur le pied de Chasseurs*" and four companies of light infantry of the same strength, 830 men in all.[36] In April Faucitt was able to say of them

The Hanau new Corps of Light Infantry...are a much better Corps, than I expected to see, & surprisingly set up, & dress'd – Their Clothing is Green, with a red Cape & Cuffs upon the Coat; the Breeches reaching down to the ancles [overalls or gaiter-trousers], & there entering into Half Boots, which They wear instead of Shoes. Their Arms & accoutrements were compleat & good; one Company out of the five, of which the Corps consists, wear leather caps & carry Rifle-Barrel Guns, with Bayonets to them; [my emphasis] the other four have Hats, & are arm'd with the common Firelock. The Lieut. Colonel (Janecke) who commands it, has served in the Prussian Army & seems to be an experienc'd good officer... all the Captains, First Lieutenants and the greatest part of the 2nd Lieutenants & Ensigns, have also been employ'd upon real Service & shew'd much steadiness & attention.[37]

The Establishment of the Light Infantry Corps consisted of 1 lieutenant colonel, 5 captains, 4 first lieutenants, 10 second lieutenants, 1 auditor, 1 surgeon, 5 surgeon's mates, 1 gunmaker, 60 NCOs, 10 hautboys, drummers and fifers, 710 men, 1 driver, 1 provost and 21 officers' servants. Of this total 142 carried rifles.[38]

On 15 August 1781, Frederick McKenzie of the 23rd Foot, then stationed at New York, noted in his diary

Part of the troops lately arrived from Germany, is a Free Battalion of Hesse Hanau. It consists of 5 Companies of 5 Officers, 12 NCOs and 142 men each. One company is armed with a Rifle, with a bayonet on it. The others with Short Musquets and bayonets, and pouches with white belts. The whole in Green with Red Cuffs & Collar, and half boots, with lace before. The Rifle Company have leather Caps with their Princes Cypher in front; the others hats. The Rifle Company is a very fine one, and well appointed.[39]

It is this corps with which a rifle shown later is identified, as being the only Hanau-signed rifle of appropriate design for the period to carry a bayonet bar. [1,264 *jägers* sent over, + 165 light infantry *jägers*]

Ansbach-Bayreuth [sometimes referred to as Brandenburg-Ansbach]. Ruler: [Christian Friedrich Carl] Alexander, Margrave.

The Ansbach Chasseur company had an establishment of 101, consisting of 1 captain, 1 first lieutenant, 2 second lieutenants, 2 serjeants, 5 corporals, 87 riflemen, 1 quartermaster, 1 surgeon, and 1 servant for the tents.[40] A troop return in America of 24 June 1777 shows them slightly over Establishment with 95 riflemen.[41]

Early in 1777 Suffolk was informed that:

His Highness was very desirous of adding another Company of Chasseurs, which wou'd have made out nearly the 6th Part of the whole Corps, according to your Lordship's instructions; but, making it a point, not to give any, but real Chasseurs, who were actually such by profession, He wou'd not undertake to furnish more than one Company, in so short a time as that which was only allowed, before their march.[42]

At the end of the month Rainsford noted that the Ansbach Chasseurs were "a most complete and excellent body of men...being picked men & very expert in the arms they use, & make a very fine appearance."[43]

The second company of *jägers* appears to have been achieved, for by October 1777 there were 3 officers, 4 NCOs, 1 serjeant and 96 riflemen of the augmentation as well as 10 recruits for the original company.[44] As from 1 November 1777, the Ansbach *jäger* Establishment was 3 serjeants, 11 corporals and 181 riflemen, totaling 206 men.[44a] By September 1778, there were 166

Ansbach riflemen, usually brigaded and operating with the Hesse-Cassel *feldjägercorps*. The corps was originally commanded by Captain Christoph von Cramon, who was replaced in July 1778 by Captain Christoph Friedrich Joseph von Waldenfels.

Recruits for the Ansbach chasseurs in 1778 included 3 second lieutenants, 1 surgeon's mate, 1 serjeant, 5 corporals, and 103 riflemen, described as "a fine body of men absolutely fit for any active service."[45] The entire 113 embarked at Bremerlehe on 5 April.

The Ansbach *jäger* recruits for 1779, 30 men, were described as a very fine corps of men "but especially the Anspackers — Their Clothing & every other part of Their Equipment is perfectly good & complete."[46]

The 2 NCOs and 24 riflemen of the 1780 *jäger* recruits are praised by Faucitt as

an exceedingly fine body of men, both with regard to stature & strength. They are likewise very completely equip'd, &, to all appearance, thoroughly well disciplin'd.[47]

Leslie's expedition to Virginia in 1780 included a detachment of Ansbach *jägers* commanded by Captain Friedrich Wilhelm von Roder. They served with the Hessian riflemen.

In February 1781, a new corps of Ansbach *jägers* was to be raised, consisting of 340 men, 3 companies of 95 riflemen each, pay to commence on 2 March 1781. The Ansbach recruits for 1781 amounted to 109 riflemen, who embarked in April.[49]

Two of the new *jäger* companies formed the whole of the Ansbach contingent for 1782, 197 men embarking at Bremerlehe on 31 May 1782, the last Ansbachers to be sent to America.[50] By the time the Ansbachers were returned to Europe in 1783, a total of four *jäger* companies was embarked. [698 *jägers* sent over.]

Brunswick-Wolfenbuttel.
Ruler: until 1780 Carl I; then Carl Wilhelm Ferdinand, Dukes.

The first treaty of 9 January 1776 contains no reference to *jägers* but they were apparently included shortly afterwards; Faucitt noted at their embarkation at Stade, 28 May 1776

The Chasseur Company, cloth'd in Green, with red Facings & Cuffs, were all arm'd with Rifle-Barrel-Guns, and made a good appearance. The Arms, accoutrements & Clothing of the entire Battalion, were complete & good...[51]

These were the company of von Bärner, 147 strong with 123 riflemen, who served throughout the Burgoyne campaign. At Hubbardton on 7 July 1777, they lost 43 "Arquebuses *rayees*" valued at 8 reichstalers 6 silbergroschen each.[52] The survivors after Bennington and Saratoga remained part of the Canadian garrison forces.

As an interesting footnote to the activities of the Brunswick *jägers* at Saratoga, William L. Stone in his edition of the *Journal of Captain Pausch* (of the Hanau artillery) published in 1886, noted that at Freeman's Farm "not a year passes that...short carbines used by the German Yagers...are not plowed up by the husbandmen."[53]

There were no *jägers* listed amongst the Brunswick prisoners with von Riedesel at Cambridge[54] and there are no references to any recruits for the Brunswick *jägercorps* being sent to America. [147 *jägers*?]

Anhalt-Zerbst. Ruler: Friedrich August, Prince.

In October 1777, after a lengthy period of contentious negotiations, Anhalt-Zerbst became the last of the German principalities to sign a treaty for sending troops to North America. At the time of writing I have been unable to locate an Establishment for the *jäger* company, but it was probably between 90 and 100 men. They served in Canada throughout the war.

Recruits for the Anhalt-Zerbst *jäger* company at Stade on 3 March 1778 amounted to 1 officer and 10 men, which increased to 1 NCO and 12 men by 21 March. A month later they were described as having "Clothing chiefly new, stout well-made Body of Men, very fit for service. Their arms & accoutrements chiefly new and in good condition."[55]

In the Spring of 1779 the annual contingent of recruits mustered at Stade, consisting of 1 second lieutenant, 1 NCO and 30 men:

The Zerbst Recruits are a remarkably stout body of men, young, & very fit for the Service; especially the Chasseurs, who, I am assur'd, are all really such by profession; of which, to do Them justice, They had much the appearance. The Clothing of the whole was new & perfectly good & complete: The Chasseurs were arm'd with Rifle-Barrel-Guns, & Hangers.[56]

Note the reference to hangers — not bayonets.

In April 1781, the annual reinforcements included 251 *jägers*, of whom 27 were for the Anhalt-Zerbst Corps; they were described as having new clothing with arms complete and good.[57] [72 *jägers* sent over.]

Summary

A review of the information in the Faucitt Papers shows a total of 4,098 *jägers* sent to North America between 1776 and 1782, a minimum figure considering gaps in the Anhalt-Zerbst returns and possible omissions for the Brunswick corps. Additional men obviously served as *jägers*, being raised from the German infantry regiments as needed, and subsequently

British Military Flintlock Rifles

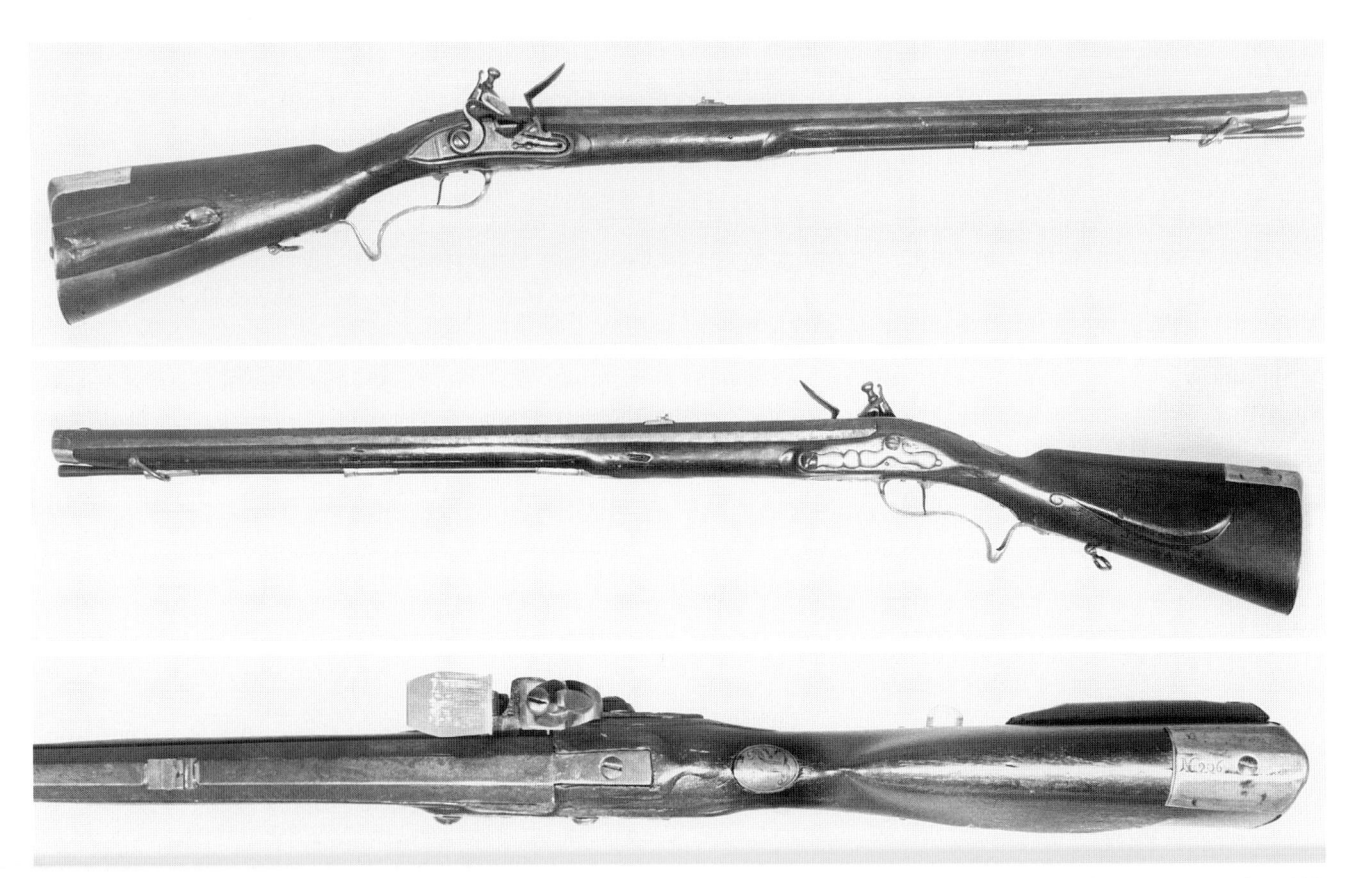

Hesse-Cassel jäger rifle by T.W. Pistor. This was the most commonly used jäger rifle during the American War; nearly 2,000 men carried them in America between 1776 and 1783. Note that there is no provision for a bayonet.
Courtesy of West Point Museum, United States Military Academy, West Point, New York.

returned to these regiments. With only superficial reservations, all of the recruits are spoken of throughout the war as leaving Germany well and completely clothed and equipped, and almost entirely as being well armed and skilled in the use of the rifle, despite the fact that after 1778 professional huntsmen were difficult to recruit.

RIFLES

Very little detailed information on the actual rifles carried by German troops in North America has yet been located. This is chiefly because no one specifically interested in these arms has spent time in the German archives, and also because very few military short rifles of the period bearing distinguishing marks either of the ruler or of the manufacturer have been identified. There is too often little difference between a plainly finished civilian rifle and a military one, and the outbreak of the French Revolutionary Wars only nine years after the close of the American War created a much larger number of rifles in which there were few identified stylistic changes. Fortunately, there are a few exceptions but too few to be able to identify all of the rifles used by the German forces. While examples of rifles from the Ansbach, Hesse-Cassel forces and Hesse-Hanau Freicorps have been tentatively identified by their markings and design, no rifles from the Canada-based main body of Hesse-Hanau *jägers*, the Brunswick *jägers* or the short rifled-carbines of the Brunswick dismounted dragoons, or from the Anhalt-Zerbst *jägercorps*, have been clearly identified at the time of writing.

There are, however, a few details available. All contemporary sources agree that the only *jäger* rifles used during the American War that were equipped with bayonets were those of the rifle company of the Hesse-Hanau Freicorps which arrived at New York in August 1781. All others were without bayonets and carried short-swords (*hirschfänger*), to whose use Ewald makes frequent references in his diary. This situation leads one to identify the Hanau-signed rifle by A. Schwalbach (worked c.1730–1780) shown on the following page as one of the rifles carried by the rifle company of this late-arrived unit. Its very close resemblance to the design of the T.W. Pistor rifle shown above supports this identification and it probably represents a down-market modification of the earlier rifles supplied to the government, since Pistor had supplied more than 700 rifles to them during 1777, and possibly others in following years. It is also possible that this rifle illustrates a possible difference between the rifles supplied for the Hanau *jägers*

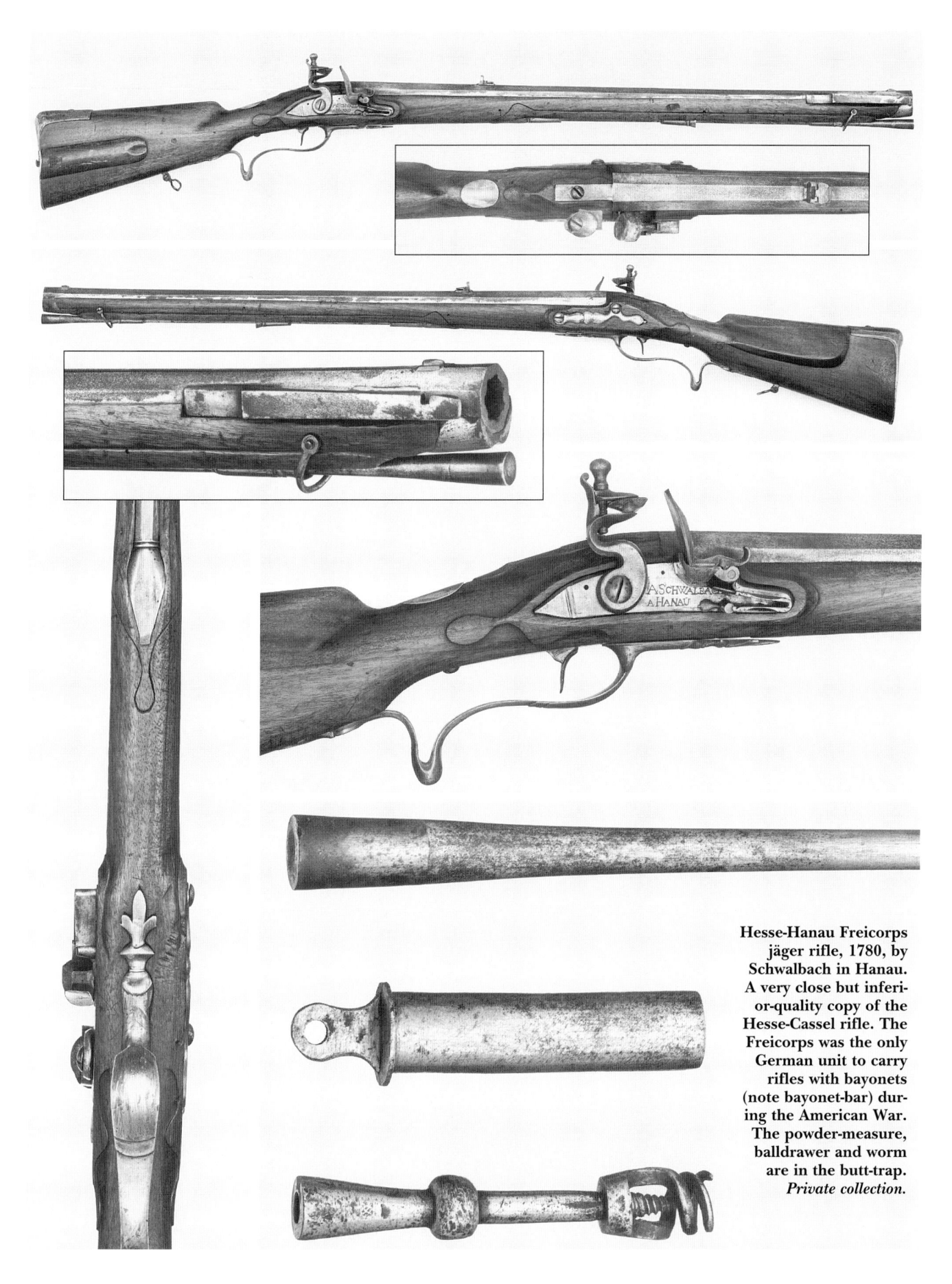

Hesse-Hanau Freicorps jäger rifle, 1780, by Schwalbach in Hanau. A very close but inferior-quality copy of the Hesse-Cassel rifle. The Freicorps was the only German unit to carry rifles with bayonets (note bayonet-bar) during the American War. The powder-measure, balldrawer and worm are in the butt-trap. *Private collection.*

British Military Flintlock Rifles

Ansbach-Bayreuth jäger rifle, unsigned. A very high-quality rifle closely following the Hesse-Cassel example.
Courtesy of the Blücher Museum, Kaub, and Dr. phil. A. Wirtgen.

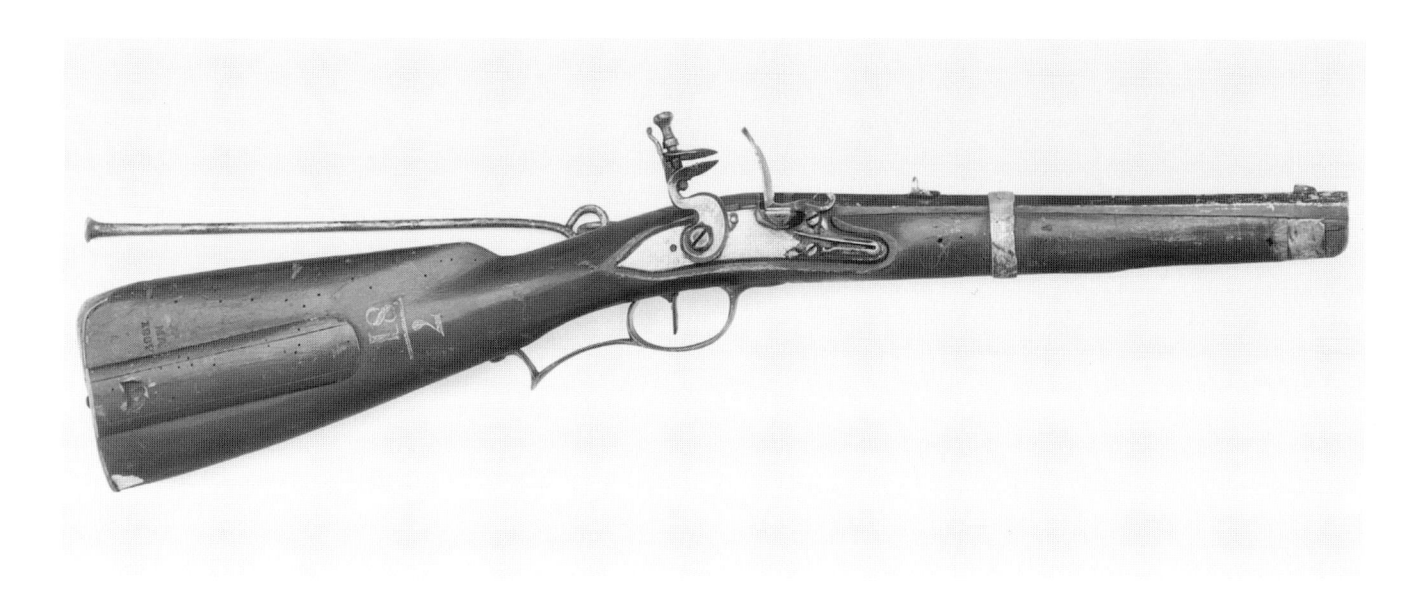

German Riflemen and Their Rifles in the American War

Austrian Model 1789/98 Cavalry Short Rifle. O.A. 27⅝-in., swamped octagonal barrel 12¾-in., .62 calibre rifled with 8 rounded grooves half the width of the lands, with a twist of a quarter-turn in the barrel or one turn in 51 inches. Black painted beech stock, iron furniture. The separately carried iron rammer has been attached to the sling-bar on the left side to avoid loss. This is very similar to the engraving of a Brunswick dragoon rifled carbines ploughed-up in the late 19th century on the Saratoga battlefields.

Courtesy of The Trustees of the Royal Armouries Museum.

and those for the 1781 Freicorps.

The Pistor rifle itself was made by Thomas Wilhelm Pistor of the gunmaking family of Schmalkalden, who died in 1787. On the thumbpiece is the crowned cypher "FL", for "Friedrich Landgraf" of Hesse-Cassel. Rodney Atwood, the only published English-speaking scholar of recent vintage who has actually worked with the German archives of this period says that the Hessians bought their muskets and bayonets from Schmalkalden.[58] In addition to the rifles for Hesse-Cassel and those noted above for Hesse-Hanau, Pistor is also recorded as having supplied what was possibly the initial order of 100 rifles for the Anhalt-Zerbst riflemen early in 1778. The fragmentary evidence strongly suggests that the Pistor firm was probably responsible for a high percentage of the *jäger* rifles sent to the German auxiliary riflemen who served in North America. Further archival investigation might well produce additional details.

The rifle shown at left, originally bearing the monogram cypher of Christian Friedrich Carl Alexander, Margrave of Brandenburg-Ansbach (1757–91) is almost certainly of American War issue. Although the original monogram has now been erased and replaced with civilian initials, the rifle itself is identical to one lost during World War II which bore the original monogram, "CFCAMzB".

The very short rifled carbine shown above bears a close superficial resemblance to the weapon believed to have been carried by some of the Brunswick dismounted dragoons of the Prinz Ludwig Regiment on the Burgoyne Campaign. With only archeological evidence (and that second-hand) to go on, whether Brunswick small arms bore distinctive markings, and whether their carbines had integral ramrods, is yet to be determined. The example illustrated is the Austrian Model 1789/98 Cavalry Short Rifle; very similar patterns were adopted in the Prussian and Russian cavalry.

The fact that two of the rifles from three of the five principalities supplying rifle corps for American service are fitted with thumbpieces carrying the monogram of the ruler, suggests that those of Brunswick, Anhalt-Zerbst and the regular Hanau corps (as opposed to the Freicorps which was not raised directly by the Hanau government), may be similarly distinguished. It is perhaps significant that two of the three rifles illustrated are of the same nominal calibre, just under .65", which would accept regulation British carbine-bore ball of .615", as did both the Pattern 1776 and Ferguson rifles. It may also be in keeping that the 1781 Freicorps rifle is of a smaller calibre (which could have used British pistol-ball), having been raised much later, outside the initial framework of the other units and probably not in direct consultation with British technical authorities. It is certainly significant that all three tentatively identified rifles have a virtually identical pattern of brass furniture and a very similar stock outline and carving based on the Prussian military arms of the period. However, these features also appear on rifles which cannot with any conviction be associated with the American War, but rather with the 1790s. The locks, probably purchased from a variety of local lockmakers, are the most variant feature of the three rifles, the Schwalbach rifle having the very unusual features for Germanic locks of the period, a pan-bridle and steel and feather-spring screws mounted internally.

— 67 —

AMMUNITION

On 19 April 1776, a supply of 150 pounds powder, 3 hundredweight of musket ball and 2 reams of paper were ordered to be issued to the Brunswick *chasseurs* en route to America. On 3 May 1776, the Board of Ordnance informed its Portsmouth office that 48 barrels (4,800 lbs.) of Fine Powder for the Hessian *chasseurs* was being sent down. A similar pattern was followed each succeeding year at the time the annual reinforcements were sent to America. In the Spring of 1777, the Hessian *chasseurs* were to be issued from Portsmouth Ordnance stores with:

Powder	*50 lbs.*
Flints, musket	*4704*
Carbine	*300*
Shot, musket 1 ton, 1 cwt 10 quarters	
Fine paper	*6 quires*
Thread	*1 lb.*

as well as a supplementary issue of 200 lbs. of powder and 1,640 pistol flints for Lieut. Prueschenk's two companies.

The Hanau *chasseurs* commanded by Lieut. Hillebrand were to receive:

Lbs. of lead in musquet ball or otherwise	*381*
Lbs. powder	*150*
Pistol Flints	*550*
Lead to cast Ball for Rifle Barrels	*224*
Fine Paper Quires	*60*
Thread, lbs.	*4*

From the above lists it is clear that the riflemen's rifles were intended to be loaded from conventional paper cartridges, and that lead was not furnished to order, but in whatever form was most readily available, using the moulds belonging to the rifles to cast the correct size ball.[59]

Throughout the late-war British Ordnance records there are references to the *jägers* being issued with "fine," "glazed" or "Chasseur" powder, often in half- or quarter-barrels, carbine ball and/or lead for casting, fine cartridge paper and twine, so there is no question but that they used cartridges to load from. There is a single reference in one of the ammunition issues made from Charleston in April 1780 to "linnen Yards 6", indicating the substance and weave but not the thickness of cloth used for patching.[60] But whether the cartridges were blanks containing only the charge, or whether they contained the patched ball, the records do not tell us. This is one of many questions of detail which may possibly be answered through future research in the German archives. The .57 calibre Hanau Freicorps rifle of 1781 with its rifling of three-quarter turn in the barrel, retains its original powder measure in the butt-trap; this measure holds 98.76 grains of fine-grain powder, rather more than one-third of the ball's weight in powder.

From documents relating to ammunition we know that the Brunswick rifles were not capable of being used with British .615" ball, but were of smaller calibre, being described in 1780 by a captain in von Bärner's *jägers* as taking balls of 36 to the pound (or .506 calibre) and using one-third the weight of the ball in powder (or 108 grains).[61] If there was any relationship between the windage allowed in British rifles (.65 bore an .615 ball), then we might expect to find Brunswick *jäger* rifles to be about .54 calibre and could therefore be used with British pistol ball-.510 calibre-but this is pure speculation. Given the geographical distance of Brunswick from the other participating principalities, it is likely that their *jäger* rifle would be of a pattern distinct from the others, probably produced in Brunswick, Hanover or Herzberg. Anhalt-Zerbst's rifles may well have originated from the same centre as the Brunswick rifles, or entirely from the workshops of T.W. Pistor.

CHAPTER 5
Loyalist Riflemen

If it is accepted that the British wished to place their supply of rifles in the hands of those best able to use them effectively, then it should not be surprising that American loyalists familiar with rifle use and woodland fighting should have been prominent amongst those documented as having received rifles from British official sources.

The use of rifles by loyalists must be divided into two categories: those in regular Provincial units and those used by loyalist militias. The loyalist militia suffered considerably from numerous dis-arming campaigns carried out by the generally more numerous and better organized rebel militias, but it is also true that the loyalist militias carried out dis-arming activities of their own. So, while it is clear that the same American-made longrifles were carried by men on both sides of the political divide, it is much less clear to what extent the loyalist militias were equipped with their own rifles somehow preserved, with captured or surrendered rebel longrifles, or, in the South and Northwest, with British-made rifles primarily intended for their Indian allies.

The use of the rifle in America before the war was confined almost entirely to the colonies south of Pennsylvania, which continued to be the case during the war except by those few rebel units who brought them temporarily into several of the northern colonies, e.g. Morgan's and Cresap's Rifle Companies. The civil war in the southern colonies was of a much more serious and active nature than further north, but it remains unclear what the percentages of rifles were in the hands of the militias of the two factions. The habit of too many writers in referring to any longarm as a rifle greatly confuses any attempt to untangle existing evidence on this area of the conflict.

There are numerous references during 1775 and 1776 (when organized companies of riflemen were prominent in the rebel army) to riflemen coming over to the British with their weapons, and as most recorded instances occurred at Boston and New York, these must have come from the Virginia, Pennsylvania and Maryland rifle companies. The majority are referred to as "Irish," meaning Scotch-Irish. A few examples will suffice:

25 July 1775. Deserters from Virginia riflemen: John Johnson, Turner, no name.[1]

9 Aug. 1775, Charles Town Heights. The enemy desert in numbers, scarcely a night passes but some come to our advanced post here, and also to that at Boston; they are mostly Irish, and bring in their rifled barrel guns.[2]

10 Sept. 1775. These frequent desertions have occasioned the Rebel General to remove the Rifle Men to Cambridge.

Gravesend, 1 July 1776. Several Rifle Men have Deserted to us, and may expect more daily.

15 July. Two Rifle Men came in..., the Rifle Men Desert every day;...[3] Some People come in from Long Island and 3 Riflemen [an English, Scotch and Irishman] with 5 Riffle Guns.[4]

From this constant dribble of rifle-armed deserters there must have built up a fair number of American longrifles in British Stores. How they were disposed of remains an unanswered question, although it may be reasonably asserted that they were not issued to other than militia troops, if at all. They may also have been distributed to allied Indians from 1777, (the most likely place for individual rifles to go) but once again documentary evidence is lacking.

It is recorded that the loyalists who were defeated at Moores Creek Bridge on 27 February 1775 lost "1,500 excellent rifles" as well as 3000 muskets (totals collected from combatants and in the region after the battle).[5] These Highlanders either carried or possessed a large number of rifles. This booty was doubtless distributed amongst the rebel militia in the region, and perhaps used to arm some of the short-term rebel rifle companies which saw service further north. But it is well-nigh impossible to plot any useful concentration of rifle-armed loyalist militia after Moores Creek Bridge, with two notable exceptions, both in the South.

The first occurred during the first Battle of Ninety-Six, South Carolina, 19–21 Nov. 1775, when a rebel described "a Party of about 200 disaffected People...headed by Robert and Patrick Cunningham and Major [Joseph] Robinson...came to Ninety-Six all armed with Rifles..."[6]

The second occurred at the Battle of Briar Creek 3 March 1779, during which "Fifty riflemen were placed in ambuscade at a pass to prevent the Americans from

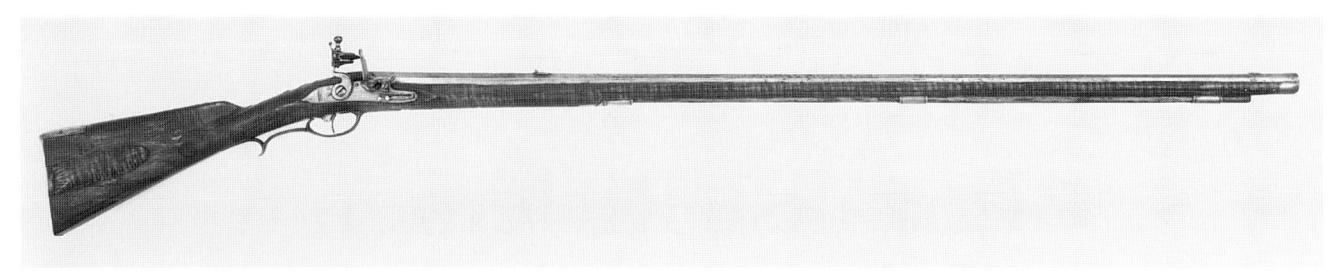

American long rifle, c.1760, place of manufacture uncertain, but probably in the Southern colonies. Rifles of this general style would have been carried by riflemen of the American War period whether loyalist or rebel.
Courtesy of The Trustees of the Royal Armouries Museum.

turning their left and attacking their rear."[7] But it is not clear whether these riflemen were part of Brown's East Florida Rangers, the British regulars of either the 60th or 71st, or of the militia. A part of them were Fleming's Royal Rifle Dragoons. Because of the great difficulty in locating similar references this chapter must be confined to those regular Provincial units who are known to have been issued rifles during the war.

The rifles carried by these loyalist militias will be of the same types as those carried by many Pennsylvania and Virginia troops during the Forbes campaign against Fort Duquesne in 1758, and succeeding campaigns through Pontiac's Rebellion of 1763–4. An example from the period is shown above. Unless perhaps fitted with sling swivels, there is no way of determining whether such privately made rifles ever saw military use, and particularly as to whether any such service was in rebel or British service.

The rifles with which we are chiefly concerned in this chapter are the Pattern 1776 infantry rifle, and captured rebel longrifles about which there is no information beyond the fact that fair numbers were either surrendered by riflemen, or captured, such as the 1500 riflemen taken prisoners at Long Island in August 1776. There is no reference to any captured rifles in surviving British Ordnance records. One such rifle which was very probably owned by Major Peter Traille, commanding the Royal Artillery during the Southern Campaign, is shown on the next page.

In January 1776, Capt. Neill of McArthur's North Carolina Highlanders, paid out on H.M. Service in that colony, £60. for 20 muskets at £3 each, and an equal amount for "12 Rifled Guns" at £5. each,[8] the standard price for locally supplied rifles at that time. These were probably lost at Moores Creek Bridge the following month.

a. East Florida Rangers

The earliest suggestion of equipping a unit in America with rifles probably came from East Florida Governor Patrick Tonyn, who wrote to General Clinton (then in North Carolina en route to the unsuccessful attack on Charleston, and the closest British general officer as well as a personal friend and military colleague) on 15 February 1776, outlining plans for a ranger unit which would include two companies of riflemen. Clinton, in his reply of 20 March, although typically hedged about with qualifications as to their immediate usefulness to his campaign, wrote,

if Mr Brown can raise two or even four companies of rifle men of 50 men each to serve for the term of six months or during the present Rebellion, I think he will do well to raise them.[9]

This unit, Lieut. Col. Thomas Brown's East Florida Rangers, (later re-named the King's Carolina Rangers and finally the King's Rangers) was operational by June 1776, including the riflemen. These men were equipped, at least partially, with imported rifles supplied by Panton, Forbes & Co., whose bill indicates:

To Panton Forbes & Co. for Riffle Guns for the use of the Rangers as per their account   *84.0.0.*[10]

There is no reason to believe that the basic source for the Rangers' rifles, i.e. the merchants supplying both the Government and private Indian trade at St. Augustine and Pensacola, changed in the course of the war. Battle and dis-arming losses would most probably have been made good from this plentiful supply. (See Chapter 6).

The local area British commander, General Augustine Prevost, did not like military units existing outside his direct control, and he wrote to General Howe from St. Augustine on 14 June 1777, suggesting a replacement unit virtually duplicating the successful but Tonyn-controlled East Florida Rangers:

I take the Liberty to submit to your Excellency that if a Troop of 50 good Rangers on Horse Back were allowed to be raised who being armed with their Rifles or Carabines and a good Sword fixed to the Saddle could occasionally either engage on horseback or on foot, it might contribute greatly to the Safety of this Province.[11]

Prevost's wish for a separate and additional ranger

Loyalist Riflemen

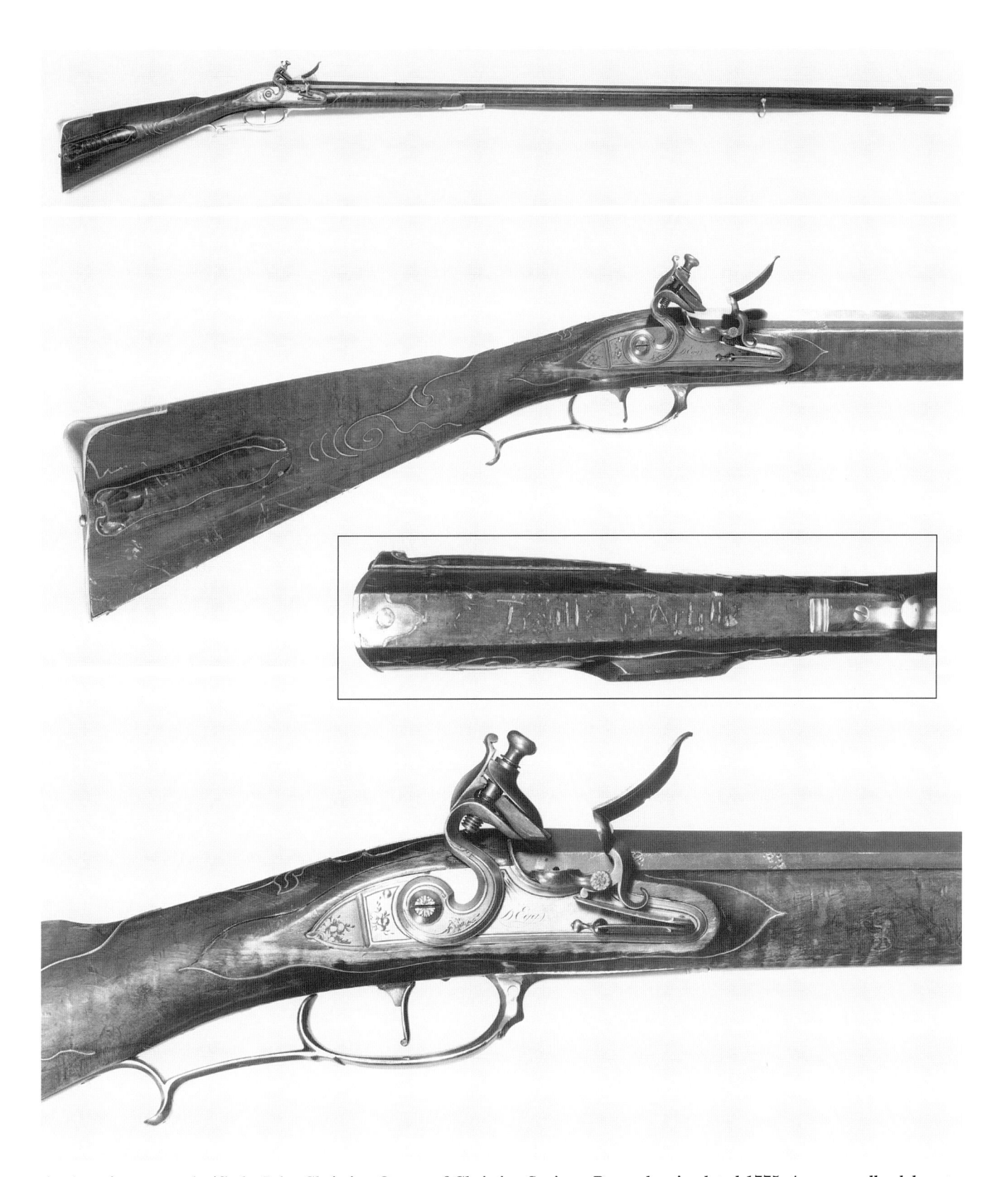

An American smooth-rifle by John Christian Oerter of Christian Springs, Pennsylvania, dated 1775. An unusually elaborate rifle for the time, this may have influenced Captain Peter Traille (who commanded the Royal Artillery – and small arms issues – on the Southern campaigns from 1780) to acquire it; he subsequently carved his name on the underside of the butt. Col. George Hanger presumably obtained it from Traille, for it is he who gave it to the Prince of Wales, later King George IV; it is included as an example of what British officers might have chosen to carry, or perhaps simply as a souvenir of the campaign. (See George Shumway, *Rifles of Colonial America*, vol. 1, pp. 192–6, for further details and illustrations of this rifle.
Royal Collection, Windsor Castle, reproduced by gracious permission of Her Majesty The Queen.

— 71 —

unit was not granted, but he did eventually gain command over Brown's unit.

b. Emmerich's Chasseurs

The earliest recorded issue of British rifles to a loyalist unit occurred in August 1777, when Sir Henry Clinton caused fifty Pattern 1776 rifles to be issued to a company of recently formed light dragoons and riflemen under Col. Andreas Emmerich.

As the Rebels have of late visited the Environs of our Camp and disturbed the inhabitants of W. Chester, I have thought it for the good of the service to collect from the Provincial Corps 100 good Rifle Men, 50 of which I have given rifles to and appointed Capt Emmerich their chief, to which if I have yr approbation I may probably add 100 hussars. they will protect the County of W. Chester and prevent desertion, which I am sorry to say is too frequent in the Provincial & Hessian Corps. – G. Tryon spares us a Capt & 2 Subalterns & I have appointed a Mr Bonafacio (whom Lord Rawdon had the honour of recommending to yr Excelly) to act as Lieut in this Corps till your pleasure is known.[12]

Emmerich's Chasseurs served for exactly two years in the greater New York City area, before being disbanded in August 1779, when its rifle company commanded by Capt. John Althause was transferred to Turnbull's New York Volunteers. Emmerich's corps generally acted with the Queen's Rangers, German jäger detachments, and Ferguson's corps of 71st light infantry, and other light troops.

Another shadowy company described as the Westchester Chasseurs was probably identical to the better known West Chester Refugees. The Refugees' commander, Capt. James Delancey, was paid for the subsistence of the Light Troop of that unit, which is probably what is meant by the Chasseur designation, stated to be 36 men, for the month of October 1777.[13] The use of the term chasseur suggests that rifles may have formed a part of their armament.

c. New York Volunteer Rifle Company

Captain John Althause (senior, his son John was an Ensign in the unit) and his rifle company in Emmerich's Chasseurs were transferred to Turnbull's New York Volunteers at the disbandment of Emmerich's in August 1779, at which time there were 3 serjeants, 3 corporals and 40 privates with 3 contingent men. They were attached to Captain George Hanger's Hessian jäger company (124 men) when the forces sailed for Charleston. The transport *Anna* in which they and Hanger's company were embarked was dismasted during the great storm which struck the southbound fleet, and they fetched up in February 1780, on the west coast of England. Returning to New York in September 1780, the New York Volunteer Rifle Company, still commanded by Althause, was attached to the Provincial Light Infantry Corps for the Leslie expedition to Virginia, but apparently did not actually sail with them. The unit remained encamped on Staten Island until ordered to accompany the Benedict Arnold expedition, during which they served with the Queen's Rangers, continuing with them until being assigned to act with Captain Ewald's Hessian jägers shortly before the surrender at Yorktown.[14] At Spencer's Ordinary

Captain Althause, whose rifle company had been mounted, [was directed] to dismount and to check [the enemy] if they sallied from the wood in pursuit of the cavalry, or for the purpose of reconnoitering; and this he executed very efficiently.[15]

A muster roll of Althause's company covering 24 Dec. 1780–23 Feb. 1781 (Appendix 5) shows large-scale desertions from the unit in January and March of 1781. Of the 44 privates listed, 3 were prisoners, 2 died, 22 deserted of whom 1 rejoined later, and 5 were new enlisted.[16] Throughout 1781 the New York Volunteer Rifle Company operated at about half its Establishment.

d. Queen's Rangers

Although originally raised and generally remembered as a Loyalist regiment, the Queen's Rangers was placed on the regular American Establishment of the British Army on 2 May 1779, so that by the time it acquired a rifle company that autumn, it was technically a regular line regiment. In August 1779, at about the time the New York Volunteers acquired Captain John Althause's rifle company from Emmerich's disbanded Chasseurs, Colonel-Commandant John Graves Simcoe of the Queen's Rangers established a Rifle Company. Initially commanded by Lieutenant Aeneas Shaw who was shortly after gazetted captain:

Serjeant M'Pherson, a corporal, and twelve men, were selected, and placed under the command of Lieutenant Shaw: they were armed with swords and rifles; and, being daily exercised in firing at objects, soon became most admirable and useful marksmen.[17]

By March 1780, the final group of rifles was issued to the company, totalling thirty-three:

Nineteen Rifles will be issued to your Order by Mr. Stephens, Ordnance Store Keeper, which with the fourteen you have at present will make thirty three, and the General [Williamson] desires you will deliver Thirty Three Muskets to the Storekeeper in lieu of them, agreeable to the inclosed Order to Mr. Stephens,...

New York, March 30 1780

Sir, Be pleased to issue out of His Majesty's Stores to Lieut. Colo Simcoe or Order, Nineteen Rifle Pieces, upon his delivering to you, Thirty Three Muskets.

By Order of M Gen Pattison
E. Williams
Major of Brigade

Francis Stephens Esqr.
Ordnance Storekeeper[18]

A muster roll of Shaw's company (Appendix 4) dated 25 October 1780[19] shows exactly thirty three privates, as well as the captain, 1 lieutenant, 1 ensign, 3 serjeants, 3 corporals and a drummer. Interestingly, Serjt. McPherson who is frequently mentioned by Simcoe as acting with the riflemen, and who was killed at Spencer's Ordinary leading the riflemen, was never officially in Shaw's company: he was always carried on the rolls of McKay's Highland company, from whence Capt. Shaw also came. This was not an unusual situation and often creates problems in tracing the identity and location of individual officers.

The infantry (some 400 rank and file including Shaw's Rifle Company) of the Rangers sailed from New York on 4 April 1780 and landed at Stono Inlet South Carolina on the 18th of that month. Simcoe mentions mounting "his riflemen" early in May. They re-embarked for New York on 31 May, landing on Staten Island on 21 June. The riflemen were part of the advance guard in the attack on Springfield later that month, Lieut. Shaw being slightly wounded and Serjt M'Pherson taking the command. The riflemen (as well as Althause's N.Y.V. riflemen and Ewald's jägers) accompanied Arnold's expedition against Virginia in January 1781. Moving against Petersburg, this combination, with the Queen's Rangers huzzars and infantry, formed the advance guard. In the action at Point of Forks Althause's and the Queen's Rangers riflemen served together. Simcoe had evolved his own common-sense approach to dealing with enemy riflemen:

The principle...was to rush upon them; when, if each separate company kept itself compact, there was little danger, even should it be surrounded, from troops who were without bayonets, and whose object it was to fire a single shot with effect: the position of an advancing soldier was calculated to lessen the true aim of the first shot, and his rapidity to prevent the rifleman, who requires some time to load, from giving a second; or at least to render his aim uncertain, and his fire by no means formidable.[20]

This attitude may well sum up the view of the usefulness of riflemen current in the British army, and explain why so little independent comment is made upon their services. Simcoe later noted that:

Queen's Ranger rifleman. One of a series of watercolours painted by Captain Murray of the corps c.1780. The Pattern 1776 and a powder horn are clearly depicted. Some, form of pouch is presumably concealed on the right side.
Courtesy of the Metropolitan Toronto Reference Library MTL 2387.

The Riflemen, however dexterous in the use of their arms, were by no means the most formidable of the rebel troops; their not being armed with bayonets, permitted their opponents to take liberties with them which otherwise would have been highly improper.[21]

It is worth noting in assessing Simcoe's views that he was one of the group of British officers who frequently extolled and encouraged the use of the bayonet as opposed to firepower.

By the time of the battle at Spencer's Ordinary, 26 June 1781, both the Queen's Rangers riflemen and those of the N.Y. Volunteers had been mounted for greater mobility, but generally fought dismounted, being in fact dragoons. However, during the hard-fought encounter on 26 June, "the mounted riflemen of the Queen's Rangers charged with Captain Shank: the gallant Serjeant M'Pherson, who led them, was mortally wounded."[22] When the British occupied Yorktown, Captain Shaw commanded the outpost on the extreme left of the British lines overlooking a cove on the York River. The portrait of a Queen's Ranger rifleman (see above) clearly shows a short-barrelled rifle with sling and no bayonet and there is little doubt that it represents a Pattern 1776 rifle. It also shows a powder horn with no clear indication of a metallic charger, but neither pouch nor cartridge box, athough one of these may be attached to the second strap across the rifleman's chest. By the time this painting was executed by Captain Murray of the Queen's Rangers, the rifleman's sword seems to have been abandoned, if indeed it had ever been issued.

Two of the known surviving examples of the Pattern 1776 rifle have company markings engraved on the buttplate tang, identical in form and style, with R over No. and a number, 23 and 33. It is reasonable to assume that the R refers to "Rifle Company," and that such markings would only be required where there was a distinct rifle company; unfortunately this would include all three of the units documented as having received rifles, and the numbers on the surviving examples come well within the numbers issued to each of them, only just with the Queen's Rangers who are known to have received a total of 33.

e. American Volunteers

When the British expedition under Sir Henry Clinton sailed for Charleston in December 1779, there were several rifle-armed units including the German jägers, the light infantry companies, and a special loyalist unit composed of volunteers from several of the provincial regiments on the expedition, the American Volunteers, commanded by Patrick Ferguson. Captain Abraham DePeyster, Ferguson's ultimate second in command at King's Mountain, in his description of the unit, clearly indicated that the rear rank of the unit when deployed for battle were to be armed with rifles, and since the front rank was made up of firelocks with bayonets, there is no doubt that the rear rank carried the Pattern 1776 rifles. (see Appendix 3)

f. Provincial Light Infantry Battalions

In the same manner as the light infantry companies of the regular line regiments, the light infantry companies of the provincial battalions were brigaded together into a two-battalion Provincial Light Infantry, during 1778. The northern battalion was commanded by Lieut. Col. John Watson of the Guards, and the southern battalion (which formed part of the Charleston expedition) was commanded by Major Thomas Barclay of the Loyal American Regiment. Barclay's unit was at Savannah as part of Campbell's force and mustered 17 officers and 318 men in January 1779. Campbell also raised a company of "Royal Rifle Dragoons" from the troops under his command in January 1779, and placed them under the command of Captain Thomas Fleming. From the mixed composition of his force, and the fact that Fleming's name has not yet been discovered in British Army Lists of the period, it is not possible to say whether the Rifle Dragoons should be classified as a British or Provincial unit. It may be reasonably accepted that the Pattern 1776 rifle was in the hands of a proportion of these companies in line with the practice in the two regular Light Infantry Battalions, and given the presumed familiarity with rifles of some loyalists. It seems at least likely that the "'Rifles, common British, 21" in Store at Savannah on 1 April 1780[23] were intended for use by these troops and others in the area.

g. Detroit Volunteer Chasseurs

At the end of August 1778 Lieutenant Governor Henry Hamilton organized two companies of "volunteer chasseurs" from the Detroit Militia.[24] Given that the population of the area was largely French, it is not entirely clear whether this indicated two companies of riflemen, as implied by English/German usage of the term, or simply elite light troops not necessarily armed entirely with rifles, as implied by the French understanding of chasseur. By this date rifles were certainly in extensive circulation amongst both Indians and whites in the Great Lakes region (see Chapter 6).

As a group within British service, the Loyalists probably carried a larger number of rifles than either the regulars or the Germans. The difficulty comes in discovering which units, and the percentage of men within units, actually had rifles, when, and for how long. The British approach to the military use of rifles was entirely pragmatic and tactical, and in some cases temporary, as is evidenced by the widely varying numbers found in Store during the war. There were undoubtedly other organized groups of Loyalist riflemen, and Loyalists who carried rifles in more than one temporary grouping, especially in the South and on the frontiers. The entire area of Loyalist militia is one ripe for serious research, and the actual composition of the better-known Loyalist Provincial companies and regiments needs further examination from a weapons-oriented viewpoint.

CHAPTER 6

Indian Rifles

in British Service to 1783

"Last summer I raised 500 foot, fifty riflemen, 800 Indians wch is a vast Charge..."

Governor Dongan of New York to the Governor of Pennsylvania, 30 March 1688

During the late colonial period the North American Indians east of the Mississippi River acquired rifles by three means: from their late frontier settler owners (certainly the initial and most frequent means), from trade with the whites, and as gifts from several colonial and the British governments. It is with this latter source that we will be primarily concerned in this chapter.

Authorities on early American rifles vary in their opinions as to both when and where rifles were first manufactured. The quotation from New York Governor Thomas Dongan referring to forces raised by him in the summer of 1687 against the invasion forces from French Canada is the earliest reference to the use of rifles in any number in America known to this writer; the presence of fifty riflemen in mid-western New York would certainly have been noted by the accompanying allied Indians. Equally certain is that these rifles would have been imported from Europe. With regard to American-made rifles, it is clear that they were present in reasonable numbers, generally in the hands of frontier settlers, by the early 1740s in Pennsylvania and the colonies to the south and areas west of Pennsylvania. It is generally agreed that they were very little known or used by the colonists north of Pennsylvania, and that conditions northeast of Pennsylvania did not encourage the spread of rifle use there until the last years of the eighteenth century and the early decades of the nineteenth century.

Given this basic outline it is not surprising that rifles begin to be mentioned in Indian hands by the early 1740s, and in tribes associated with Pennsylvania and further south, most notably the Shawnee and Delaware. Pastor Spangenberg noted in his description of a journey to the Six Nations headquarters at Onondaga in 1745:

On our route we passed the Shawanese towns [in western Pennsylvania], and the place where two years ago [i.e. 1743],

when Conrad [Weiser] was travelling to Onondaga, he was met by twenty Shawanese, each with a rifle, two pistols and a sabre.[1]

and in April 1744 a Delaware Indian,

John Mussemeelin owing some skins to John Armstrong, the said Armstrong Seiz'd a Horse of the said Mussemeelin and a riffled Gun...[2]

A list of goods taken by the French and Indians from the well-known frontier gunsmith John Fraser at Great Meadow, Pennsylvania, on 3 July 1754 included "7 Riffled Guns @ £6.0.0." and another Rifle Gun lost by Joseph Campbel, an employee of Indian traders Taafe & Callendar, a little earlier, was valued at "20 bucks, £7.10.0."[3]

An eyewitness of the Braddock expedition described the Indians with Braddock (what few there were) as "tall, well made, and active, but not strong, but very dexterous with a rifle barrelled gun, and their tomahawk..."[4]

The naturalist John Bartram describing the Indians in a letter of 4 Feb. 1756 noted that "...they commonly now shoot with rifles with which they will at a great distance from behind a tree...take such sure aim as seldom miseth their mark."[5]

Writing from Lancaster to the Governor of Pennsylvania in April 1756, Edward Shippen confirmed that "The Indians make use of rifled guns for the most part..."[6] In November 1756 Pennsylvania's Indian Agent Conrad Weiser recorded that "A Certain Indian, called Armstrong, had a rifled Gun taken or stolen from him in Easton..."[7] Whatever the actual numbers of rifles amongst them, it is clear that the whites were very much aware of their possession by the Indians before the outbreak of the French & Indian War.

Two views on the utility of the rifle at this date are recorded; Edward Shippen's letter quoted above also says:

...if I was in an Engagement with the Savages, I would rather Stand my chance with one of the former Sort [a rifle], which

might require a minute to clean, load and discharge, than be possessed with a Smooth bored gun which I could discharge three times in ye same space, for at 150 yards distance, with the one, I can put a ball within a foot or Six Inches of ye mark, whereas with the other, I can Seldom or ever hit the board of two feet wide & six feet long.[8]

From Shippens' comments we learn some "given" assumptions of the time: that a rifle took a minute to reload and that a musket had three times the celerity of fire of a rifle; that 150 yards was a common shooting distance, and that a musket practice target was two feet by six feet.

But there was another side to the story, as Conrad Weiser advised (based on advice received from the Indians) in October 1756: that in arming themselves to help defend friendly Indians at Shamokin against the French the whites should be "well armed with smooth Guns, no rifled Guns which require too much cleaning..."[9] Those characteristics of the rifle which came to be so familiar in later years were thus early recognised.

Two references from the Upper Creek Nation indicate the growing presence of rifles amongst the southern Indians. South Carolina agent Daniel Pepper wrote Governor Lyttelton on 30 Nov. 1756:

I think it is highly necessary to inform your Excellency that the Indians are daily getting in to the Method of useing Riffle Guns instead of Traders which they purchase where ever they can at monstrous Price, as they can kill point Blank at two hundred Yards Distance. ...As the people who sell them to the Indians are generally very poor, their Gun being the greatest Part of their Estate, a Fine would be of little or no Effect. Imprisonment or something of corporal Punishment would create a greater Dread.[10]

and again on 30 March 1757:

I am highly pleased your Excellency has taken into Consideration the Use of Riffle Guns in this Nation [the Creeks]. I shall restrain the Practice of vending them here in this Nation all in my Power, till a Method is fallen upon to prevent them.[11]

That rifles were reaching the Indians through private trade further north as well is made clear by a reference to a 1757 List of Indian Goods at Rock Creek belonging to the Ohio Company with their prices at first cost in London [indicating their point of origin:]

abt 1 dozn 4 ft square [octagonal; a common mistake] barrel'd Guns very small Bores- best Iron mounted & stock'd like Rifhells, a Bullet Mould to each 27/6

abt 1 dozn Rifhells 4 ft Barrels, best iron – Bullet mould to each 41/6[12]

The smooth-rifles (often called a Ball or Bullet Gun- as opposed to the Rifled Bullet Gun) and the iron-mounted rifles, both of English manufacture, are listed here as items with whose description the frontier was already familiar by 1757.

The involvement of colonial governments, followed by the Crown, in the giving of rifles as gifts to significant Indians seems to have begun only when there was a specific need to gain these influential warriors to the English side in the French & Indian War, but this was still not viewed as a broad policy of equipping numbers of Indians with rifles, only chosen individuals from whom something particular in the way of services rendered might be expected. Records of gifts prior to 1756 refer only to smoothbore fowling pieces and trade guns. A few examples will suffice. Col. John Armstrong, writing to Pennsylvania Governor Denny from Fort Morris, 23 May 1757 as a postscript:

The Five Rifle Guns, agreed by the Commissioners to be given the Cherokees [by George Croghan], I cou'd not conveniently get, but purchased Three [at Fort Frederick][13]

Southern Indian Superintendent Edmond Atkin, in his account of cash paid out at Winchester on behalf of the colony of Virginia in August 1757 noted:

2 Aug. for a Rifle Gun given Outeyreky as per C. Gist's receipt   £4.10.0.
10 Aug. for a Rifle Gun given the Swallow's Nephew as per Rich'd Smith's receipt   5. 0.0.[14]

James Burd supplied the famous Delaware spokesman Teedyuscung with a full set of clothing and equipment including "1 Riffle Gun £5 and 1 English pipe Tomahawk 12/-" in Oct. 1757.[15]

In the Cherokee account of agent Edward Ward, from Fort Lyttelton, dated 14 May 1758, we find "To 1 Rifle Gun delivered to a Chief £4.10.0."[16]

James Kenny, trader at Fort Pitt, noted that "We sold an old rifle gun to an Indian called Simon" on 4 June 1758. It is perhaps significant that he thought this sale worth recording in his narrative journal. It may perhaps have been the rifle bought from "one Donnelson, that came as Packhorse Master" the previous month.[17]

Thomas King, on behalf of himself & two other Indians who were at Easton, mentioned y't at that treaty they were promised three Rifle Guns by the Governours of Penna & New Jersey, they have been here a long time & have not seen these Guns, ...the General [Jeffrey Amherst]...assurances y't they should have the Guns if to be got in Town, or else y't S'r Wm. Johnson should deliver them ye Guns...[18]

One of the most informative early records of the

delivery of rifles to presumed British-allied Indians during the French & Indian War is to be found in the records of the Pennsylvania Indian Stores operated at the Indian town of Shamokin and Fort Augusta, controlled by the Pennsylvania Assembly. These records show the following rifles delivered to the Indian Commissioners:

17 Aug. 1758	*6 Riffle Guns @ £4 each*
10 Nov. 1758	*6 Riffle Guns @ 80/- for Fort Augusta*
	1 Riffle Gun £4.10.0.
19 Apr. 1759	*1 Riffle Gun £5. 0. 0. for Fort Allen*
21 Oct. 1760	*16 Riffle Barrels @ 19/-*
	16 Riffle Locks @ 8/- to Fort Augusta from D. Deshler
16 Apr. 1762	*12 Riffle Guns w/moulds @ 66/8 each*
11 Sept. 1762	*18 Rifled Guns @ £4.10.0. to be taken in at Lancaster from William Henry.[19]*

The above listing contains two of only four probable riflemaker's names noted in records seen by this writer, William Henry of Lancaster [*1729–1786+] being a prolific and well-known maker.

Another Shamokin ledger covering the period 2 June–15 Dec. 1759 records rifles supplied at £5. each to the following:

Molley, John Hatson, Thomas Hatson, John Toporneek, Cobus, 2 Indians no names, John Davis, Nepenose 2 rifles, George Haes 1 at £5 and one at £4.16.0., Phillip, [as well as £1. for stocking his rifle, and a britch screw for 6d], William Davis 2 rifles, French Margaret's relation, Aholand, Peggey's Husband, Captain Peter, Isaac Nutimus for bushing his Rifle 1/-, and William Taylor: twenty-one rifle-armed Indians.

Two extremely interesting bills for repairing rifles for Indians also appear:

Peter	*John Logan*
new stock 12/-	*casehardening the Steel 9d*
mounting 12/-	*new main Spring 2/6*
gunlock 8/6	*mending a Lock 6d*
New Rifling 10/-	*Steel screw 6d*
bullet mowl, wiper & charger 6/-	*a new Britch for his Gun 3/-*
a new Britch 3/	
Trigger & Trigger Plate & cleaning the Barrel 5/-	
mending his Gun 6/- [20]	

The Indian Commissioner's Day Book for Shamokin during 1760 includes a wide variety of repair bills for rifles of various Indians, eight Indians having their barrels newly rifled for 10/-; with most other prices as shown above; a new triggerguard was 4/- and sights 1/- each; powder horns selling for from 1/- to 2/-, mostly 1/6, bullet moulds for 3/-, and William Patterson, John Logan, Nepenose, Molley, Nicholas, John Petty, Seeshackaphee and Weysolikon each purchasing rifles for £5. each.[21] The volume for 1760–61 includes rifles for Weysolikon, Indian no name (at £4.2.6.) and Telinemat (from smith Baltser Geere (several spellings), who also supplied tomahawks) for £6.[22]

Similar records for most of 1762 show the following Indians receiving rifles from the store at Fort Augusta, all at a cost of £5 each unless otherwise noted: Indian no name, Wahshawhose, Woskenew, Isaac, Cuwaywack, Tuccayyou (£4), Keesquapeequon (£6), and Mingo.[23] For most of 1763 there were only three rifles to Mingo, John Longtown's Son and French Moll, and gunstocks varying from 2/6 to 7/6, one rifle barrel for £1.6.0. and powder horns.[24] Also in 1763, there were delivered to the Indian Commissioners at Philadelphia from James Irvine "Three Riffles (stocked) Twelve New & One old Riffle Barrel."[25] What is particularly interesting about these official Pennsylvania store records is that neither trade-gun nor fowling piece appears to have crossed the counters.

Once war and Indian rebellion was ended, officialdom could turn their attention to tightening-up the entire Indian trade. The two imperial Indian Superintendents, Sir William Johnson (northern) and John Stuart (southern) co-operated in the drafting of a set of regulations to govern the trade in 1764. Commenting on the Board of Trade's Plan in October 1764, Johnson wrote of Article 38:

Rifled Barrelled Guns should certainly be prohibited; the Shawanese and Delawares, with many of their neighbours are become very fond of them, and use them with such dexterity, that they are capable of doing infinite damage, and as they are made in some of the frontier Towns, where the Indians will procure them at any Price, I am of opinion, all white persons should be restricted on a very severe penalty from selling them to any Indians, or for their use.[26]

and on the same theme Col. John Bradstreet of 'armed Batteaumen' renown, wrote on 4 Dec. 1764:

Here I must take notice, that from the Governt of Pennsylvania all the Shawnees and Delawar Indians are furnished with rifle barrel Guns, of an excellent kind, and that the upper Nations [i.e. Great Lakes Indians] are getting into them fast, by which, they will be much less dependent upon us, on account of the great saving of powder, this Gun taking much less, and the shot much more certain, than any other gun, and in their way of carrying on war, by far more prejudicial to us, than any other sort. It is submitted if it would not be a public benefit to stop the making and vending of any more of them in the Colonies, nor suffering any to be imported.[27]

The situation was briefly clarified by Guy Johnson, Sir William's secretary, in July 1764 when he noted from Niagara that the Delawares "have many Rifles..."[28]

The much-desired anti-rifle clause was duly included in the regulations promulgated in all of the important Indian-trading colonies, but it had little or no effect from lack of enforcement, and in any case it did not interfere with giving of rifles as gifts by local or imperial governments. A curious note from Southern Superintendent John Stuart to John Pownall at the Board of Trade in London in August 1765, doubtless aimed at economizing, said that

Common trading guns are the most esteemed by, and the best calculated for all the Indians, so that Fuzees [i.e. fowling pieces at about double the price of trading guns] or fine Arms may be entirely saved.[29]

How untrue this was, events would soon prove.

Rifles at Fort Pitt were increasing in numbers in the immediate postwar years. The Province of Pennsylvania bought 14 rifles at the usual £5. each in February 1764. Six rifle guns costing £4.10.0 were sent to the fort by Simons & Henry on 15 Sept. 1766, and a further half dozen at the same price to the Indian trader Richard Callendar at the end of that month. The Fort Pitt (gun?)smith Baltzer Geere was paid £3.10.0 each for 15 rifles in October 1767. In the same month 'for the use of the Crown' at Fort Pitt, 12 rifles were ordered, with a further request that 20 rifles with bullet moulds were wanted "for the Trading Store at Fort Pitt."[30] The Crown paid Moses Henry (working as Indian gunsmith at the fort) £25 (Pennsylvania currency) for 3 rifle guns for the Indian Dept. in October 1767, and for another one the following month costing £8.[31] In April 1768 at George Croghan's order, the Crown again paid £8 each for 5 Riffled Guns for the Indians.[32] During 1771 seven more rifles including one for a chief at a conference in the Lower Shawnee Towns in June, were delivered by the Indian Department.[33] The fact of the Government paying £3 more for their rifles makes one wonder whether they were rifles of a higher quality or simply the Government being charged more for the same product — not a new procedure even in the 18th-century wilderness!

To the north of New York City rifles were also beginning to appear in merchants records, generally those associated with the Indian trade, but the distinctions are unclear. Schenectady merchant Daniel Campbell listed "1 box Riffel guns with boxes in the but Meld & Measure" in an order to the New York merchants George Folliott & Co. in August 1772.[34] In March 1773 he was ordering "10 rifles from Pennsylvania" from merchant William Backhouse,[35] and one year later in March 1774 Campbell ordered another "8 riffle guns from Backhouse."[36] Campbell was involved in trade with Detroit and it is probable that these rifles were heading west.

Rifles were already circulating in Indian hands as far west as the Mississippi and the Illinois country by the mid-1760s. George Croghan ordered a brass-barrelled rifle costing £11.5.0. (Pennsylvania currency) delivered by express to the Miamis "for the use of the Crown" (i.e. as a gift) in March 1765. Two more rifles were delivered to Indians in the Illinois region during 1765. Nine rifles with moulds at £4.15.0. each were delivered to Capt. William Long at the Illinois in May 1767. The officers at Fort de Chartres purchased a rifle for £8. (Pennsylvania currency) for Silver Heels in the Spring of 1769, on the Indian Department account.[37] Remaining unsold in the store at Cahokia on 9 Jan. 1771 was 1 rifle.[38] As elsewhere, rifles were also obtained more casually: "Taken out of a pirogue...at Cahokia, 20 Aug. 1771, 2 guns, one of them a rifle."[39]

Governor Tryon of North Carolina paid £9. for a rifle and £5. for a smoothbore gun for two Cherokee Indians in November 1769.[40] After a congress held at Pensacola from August to November 1771, 116 trading guns and 8 "Riffle Guns" were given to deserving Creeks. Later the same year at Mobile two Medal Chiefs of the Choctaw and Red King of the Chickasaws each received a Riffle Gun.[41]

The Northern Indian Superintendent, Sir William Johnson, wrote his deputy agent George Croghan, then at Philadelphia, on 11 June 1772:

If Mr [Alexander] McKee, or You could procure me a Rifle that is proved & shoots verry exact, (otherwise it would be needless to Send it, as there are Several here but none that will Shoot so nice or exact as I hear they do that way). [my emphasis] You would much oblidge me by Sending it pr any good opertunity, the Amt of it shall be paid to Mr McKee when known by Yrs. WJ. I don't care how plain it is, if it shoots true or exact.[42]

One wonders whether this was not a case of cultural reversal, with Sir William getting the idea of a rifle from his Indian friends. It is very interesting to note that Pennsylvania rifles had already acquired a reputation for accurate shooting over rifles from other areas; one wonders where the inferior-shooting rifles in Johnson's area (just west of Albany) were made. The inventory of Johnson Hall taken on Sir William's death in 1774 shows two rifles valued at £6 and £3.

William Bartram, another of the travelling naturalist family, recorded in 1773 seeing a Seminole Indian on the St. Mary's River two days from Savannah who "was armed with a rifle." He notes three other instances of Seminoles similarly armed.[43] In September 1773, David

Taitt, Deputy Agent and Commissary to the Creeks, gave the influential Upper Creek leader The Mortar "a Riffle."[44] At Pittsburgh in April 1774, the famous Seneca chief Kayashuta was presented with a rifle costing £7.10.0. (Pennsylvania currency) by the Deputy Agent for Indian Affairs in the Western District of the Northern Department, Alexander McKee, the second rifle he is known to have owned,[45] and George Croghan bought a £10. rifle for the White Mingo.[46]

Just how many of the rifles indicated in the preceding pages were actually used in British Service, as opposed to in the British interest, is unknown. The assumption of those colonists delivering them to the Indians must have been, at the very least, that they would not be used against themselves, and governments must have considered that such gifts would bind Indians in the British interest. But whether the frontier settlers who parted with their rifles for a favourable equivalent in cash or kind gave this aspect much thought is doubtful: if they had, they would have kept their rifles.

It seems clear that the great majority of the rifles that came into Indian possession prior to 1776 by whatever means, were of American manufacture, and were probably indistinguishable from the rifles carried by white men. A standard price of around £5. might suggest a particular type or pattern, but this remains to be demonstrated. Indian-British ties between 1755 and the American War were at best temporary and tenuous, and it is clear that the distribution of rifles at governmental level was done on an entirely different basis than during the coming American War. However, since so few facts have been printed about the early possession of rifles by the Indians, this material has been included to indicate how prevalent they were, how familiar the Indians were with their use and their worth, and how aware colonial officials were of the significance of rifles in Indian hands by the time rifles began to be distributed to the Indians and their white leaders in British Service during the American War.

༄ ༄ ༄ ༄ ༄ ༄ ༄ ༄

Mobilization of Indian manpower by the British got off to a very slow start during the early years of the American War, in the north due to administrative chaos and power struggles following the death in July 1774 of all-powerful Sir William Johnson, and in the south by the strong views held by John Stuart against using the Indians against the settlers, particularly without adequate numbers of skilled white leaders. In the west it was largely a question of anti-British, or at least strong pro-French, leanings on the part of many tribes who did not wish to get involved in a white man's war which, in their vast wilderness homelands, did not affect them. There is little documentary evidence for the importation and distribution of rifles amongst the Indians before the middle years of the war, probably because in most theatres there was little official British-Indian activity during that period.

With the prohibition of the export of arms and ammunition from Great Britain without a license, proclaimed in October 1774, and the closing of most American ports with the growing rebellion, Indian supplies of all kinds were routed primarily to Montreal and Quebec in the north and Pensacola and St. Augustine in the south. Occasional shipments went to Halifax and New York.

On 17 Dec. 1775 John Stuart, Superintendent of Indian Affairs for the Southern Department, wrote to Secretary for America Lord Dartmouth, asking him to stop all shipments of Indian goods to the Carolinas and Georgia, and instead to send all such goods to West Florida. Amongst the goods affected by this request were 100 rifles ordered in October 1775 through merchant John Pinman, along with 3500 Indian trading guns.[47] These are the only British Indian rifles noted at the time of writing as being shipped before 1778, in which year rifles began to appear in most theatres of British-Indian activity.

Future white leaders of Indians were already equipping themselves for the coming hostilities: in November 1775 George and John Girty purchased rifles, George's costing £6. and John's £7.10.0., while a third brother James, had a rifle costing £8.10.0. purchased for him by George Croghan in May 1776.[48]

During a visit to London in company with Guy Johnson and other members of the Northern Indian Department who had gone there to complain of their treatment by Canada's Governor Carleton, Mohawk warriors Joseph Brant and John Deserontyon had been presented with rifles by the Master General of the Ordnance, Viscount Townshend. On the return journey they came in useful when the packet in which they were travelling was attacked by a rebel privateer off Bermuda in the summer of 1776. The two Indians

...having brass Rifle Guns made a present by my Lord Townshend were so dextrous & good Marksmen, as to pick off those on Board the Rebel Ship...[49]

To date, no record of the manufacture of these rifles has been found either in Ordnance or Townshend papers. The statement itself poses another question: are the rifles fitted with brass mounts, or are they brass barrelled?

General Sir William Howe's letter to John Stuart of 3 May 1777 describes the white men who were intended to act with and lead Indians, and who were in many cases armed with rifles:

The Directions you received in my Letter of the 13 January for forming, arming & paying such of His Majestys faithful Subjects as may have taken Refuge among the Indians from the Persecution of the Rebels, or who may hereafter be compelled to do it, will I hope furnish a sufficient Number of good Men, accustomed to their [i.e. the Indian's] Methods of making War, to reside among & act with them upon all occasions. Companies formed of Persons well acquainted with the back Parts of Carolina & Georgia, if put under the Conduct of proper Officers, may be of infinite Use in directing the Indians to any object you may have in View for them to execute.[50]

Initially these men would have brought their own rifles with them, but subsequent losses may have been made good from government stores of imported rifles as well as from captured rebel equipment.

Indian rifles exported from England by the private trade begin to appear in March, 1778, when one dozen were shipped from London to Quebec. Further shipments were made each succeeding February: 320 in 1779, 400 in 1780, 300 in 1781 and 250 in 1782, a total of 1282 rifles sent to Quebec. To the southward 1778 is also the date for the first appearance of Indian rifles, when 65 were shipped from London, 50 of them in March, to Pensacola. A further 30 followed in 1779, after which the records end. Only 12 rifles were sent by the trade to East Florida in May 1775 and these are described as "for the Planters."[51] The export trade in arms and ammunition was closely controlled by government both in England and in the colonies: all exports were under carefully scrutinized license, and on arrival in North America were accounted for by government inspectors and allotted to specific purposes; almost all of the rifles mentioned in this paragraph will have ended up in Indian or Indian Department hands.

The above records do not include rifles sent over for Indian use by the Board of Trade as annual gifts. In some cases the descriptions of these shipments are lacking in details, e.g. "25 chests of arms" not specifying the contents. That there was a gradual increase in the percentage of rifles included with each annual shipment is clear from documents later in the war when types of arms are specified, but it is impossible to be specific about the number of Indian rifles sent over for the whole period of the war.

In October 1779, General Campbell obtained 15 rifles for the Indians serving with him from merchant John Falconer & Co.[52]

William Johnston junior, a lieutenant in the Indian Department, reported in September 1780 from Wyalusing, Pennsylvania, that as the result of a successful attack on a rebel encampment "we have all got Rifles."[53]

Leonard Wisner, the Government gunsmith working for the Indians at Pensacola, repaired 80 rifled guns for them during April–June 1780.[54]

At Detroit during the period March–September 1780, Indian Department accounts with Macomb, Edgar & Macomb (merchants from whom they had been regularly purchasing since 1776 in lieu of timely supplies from the Government in London), show 32 rifles being purchased at £18. currency each (a common fuzee was £5. currency). For Detroit and its dependencies (chiefly Michilimackinac) Indian goods requirements for the year 1781 includes "200 Riffle Guns small bore."[55] This is the earliest reference to "small bore" and would refer to a calibre less than .58-inch. There were remaining in the King's Store at Detroit on 17 July 1781, "83 Riffles."[56]

In the closing years of the war rifles became more noticeable. Northern Superintendent Guy Johnson's estimate of annual consumption by the Six Nations, written in July 1780, included 100 rifles and 1,000 lbs. of fine rifle powder.[57] The Board of Ordnance Stores at Quebec contained "96 Riffles for Indians" on 1 Jan. 1782.[58] Detroit's requirements for 1782 included 120 rifles, small bore.[59] For the following year 200 of the same were required.[60] There were sent to Oswego, New York, with a party commanded by Joseph Brant in June 1782, 9 rifles of which two were given to the party.[61] Fifteen rifles at 50/- (£2.10.0.) each, delivered into Store at Niagara since 1 Oct. 1782 had all been issued by 20 December.[62] Guy Johnson's estimate of Indian goods required for 1783 included 600 rifles.[63] In the several Indian Storehouses in Canada in October 1784 there remained 663 rifles.[64]

THE RIFLES

As mentioned earlier, most of the rifles carried by the American Indians in the period 1755–1778, whether or not in British Service, were of local American manufacture, and will be indistinguishable from those made for the ordinary commercial trade. That some rifles were imported from England for the Indian trade prior to 1775 is also clear, but the only details thus far to come to light are those concerning the Ohio Company's dozen rifles at Rock Creek in 1757, with 48-inch barrels and iron furniture. Four foot barrels also remained the most popular length with the Indians for their smoothbore trade guns until after 1783. Between 1778 and 1783, it is equally clear that the origin of the rifles carried by the Indians shifted from America to England.

Probably from 1756, and certainly from 1775, the London gunmaking firm of Richard & William (William from 1766) Wilson & Co. enjoyed a monopoly for the British Government's supply of Indian guns. Invoices and/or references for every year of the war confirm this. Located in the gunmaking district called the Minories, just north of the Tower of London, Richard Wilson began work in 1730, taking his son William into

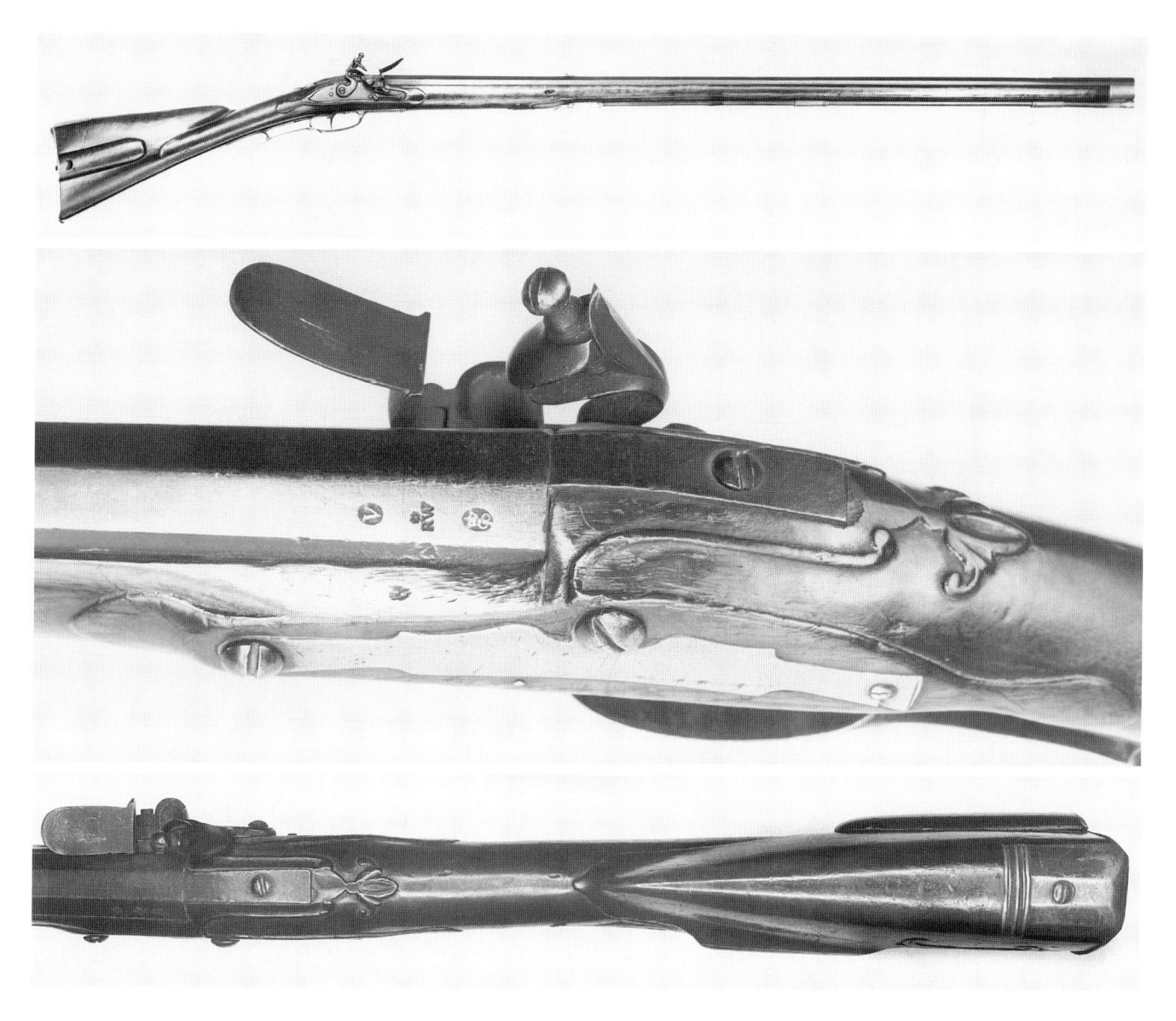

American-style longrifle by William Wilson & Co. of London, supplied for the use of British-allied Indians. All examples known closely follow a pattern also used by gunmakers Robert Barnett and William Grice. Note the "broken" front lower scroll behind the cheekpiece of the butt, a feature found on the rifles of all three makers. Note the spurious imitation London proofmarks with Wilson's mark on the breech. The re-conversion uses an incorrect cock of much later style, and the pan should not have a bridle.

Photographs courtesy of George Shumway.

partnership in 1755, and died in 1766. William carried on and expanded the business, taking his son William as a partner in 1787 and working until two years before his death in 1808. The younger William carried on with markedly less success until his own death in 1832, when the business was sold up. Throughout their 102 years' existence the several Wilson firms continued to use the maker's mark granted in 1730 to Richard by the gunmakers' guild, the Worshipful Company of Gunmakers of London, of an asterisk over the initials "RW" (this mark can be seen on the barrels of guns illustrated in this chapter, including the one above), making the precise dating of many Wilson pieces extremely difficult, since they manufactured very much for a traditional, rather than a fashionable, up-to-date market.

With regard to the rifles supplied by Wilson for the Indians during the American War, we are extraordinarily fortunate in having three Wilson invoices to William Knox, responsible for Indian present-purchasing, comprising the annual Indian gun order for 1781, and certainly typical of what was being supplied. It describes 312 rifles of three different types:

156 Best Rifle Guns wood boxes moulds & cases   52/6
108 Best Rifle Guns with brass boxes moulds & cases   53/6
48 Rifle Guns wood boxes moulds & Cases   50/-

— 81 —

British Military Flintlock Rifles

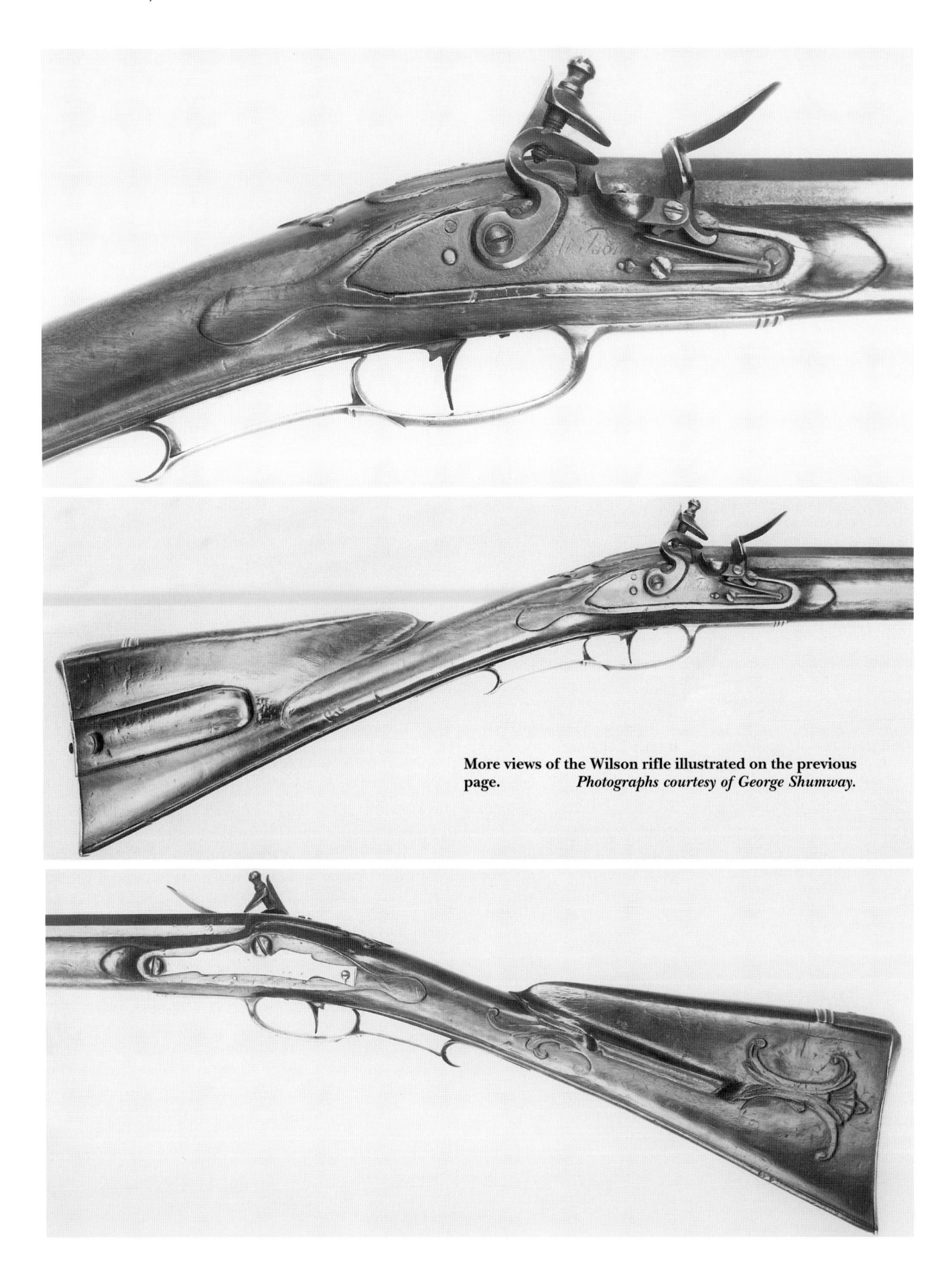

More views of the Wilson rifle illustrated on the previous page. *Photographs courtesy of George Shumway.*

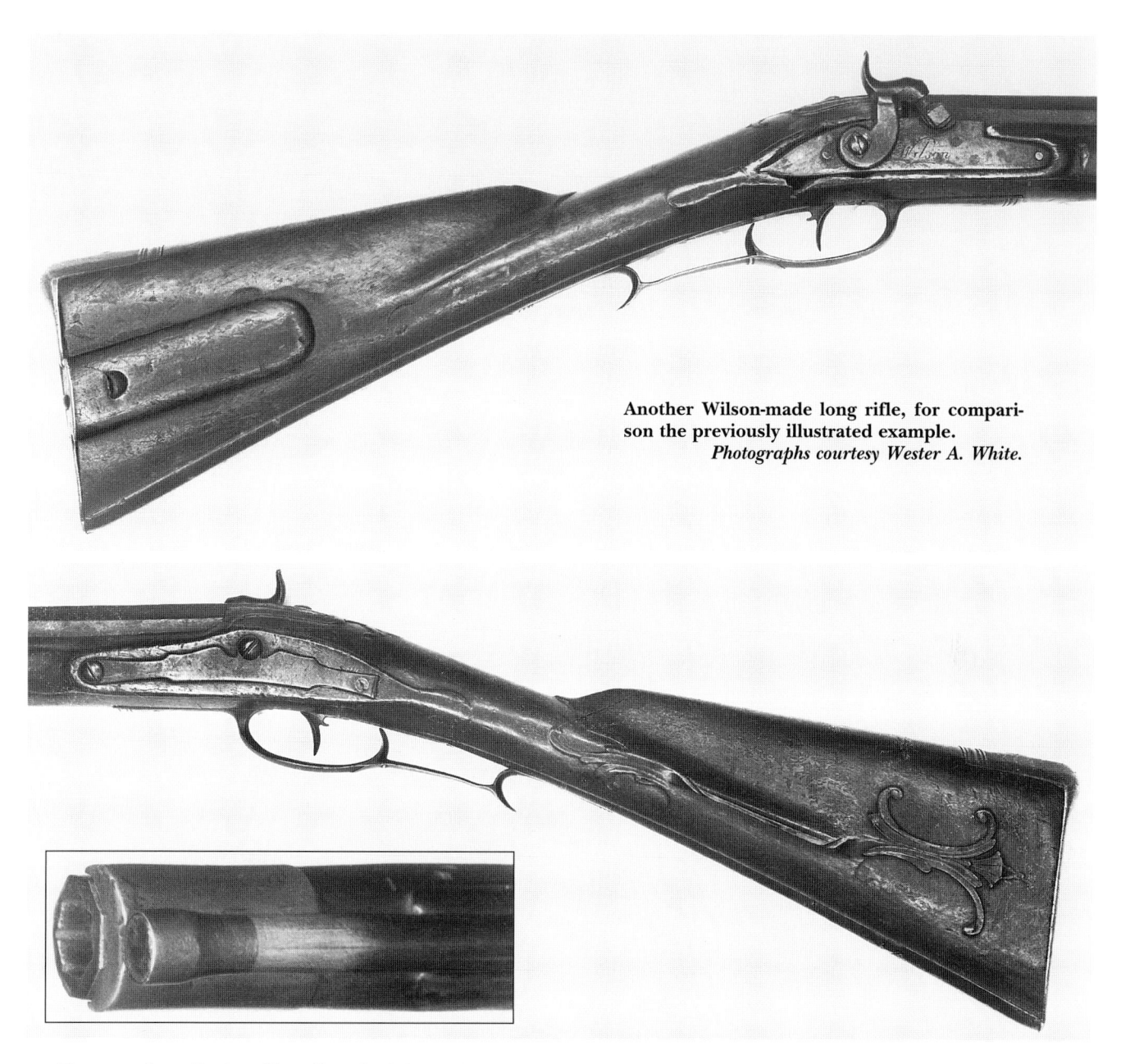

Another Wilson-made long rifle, for comparison the previously illustrated example.
Photographs courtesy Wester A. White.

Two are described as "best," and of these the more expensive by a shilling are the ones with brass butt-traps. It is curious that the cheapest variety at just £2.10.0. are also the least popular. The same invoices also include 4,000 fusils, 145 fowling pieces of two grades (what by the 1790s came to be called "Chiefs' Guns"), and 200 pistols of two grades. All were included in the order being sent to Quebec.[65] Because of their prices, none of the rifles can be mistaken for any of the smoothbore guns in this or other invoices, the most expensive fowling piece typically costing 40/-.

How does this single piece of documentary evidence compare with known examples of rifles considered to be Indian rifles? If we accept, and there is no reason not to do so, the Wilson rifles shown in this chapter as an example of either the 52/6 or the 50/- rifles listed above, we have one of three possible types of Wilson-signed rifles. William Wilson himself wrote to the Board of Trade about his weapons in 1781 that a shilling difference in price was all in the finishing, and not such that an ordinary person outside the guntrade would be able to detect it. This means that the qualities of the wood- and brass-lidded butt-trap rifles will probably be indistinguishable to the modern student, but still leaving a cheaper OR a more expensively finished rifle to identify. All Wilson-signed rifles of this pattern thus far located have the wooden butt-trap cover, as do other rifles of identical design signed by Robert Barnett. Rifles of identical stock pattern, signed by William Grice of Birmingham, have a two-piece brass butt-trap cover (see photos), and this writer believes that what is missing is the cheapest Wilson-signed rifle representing

British Military Flintlock Rifles

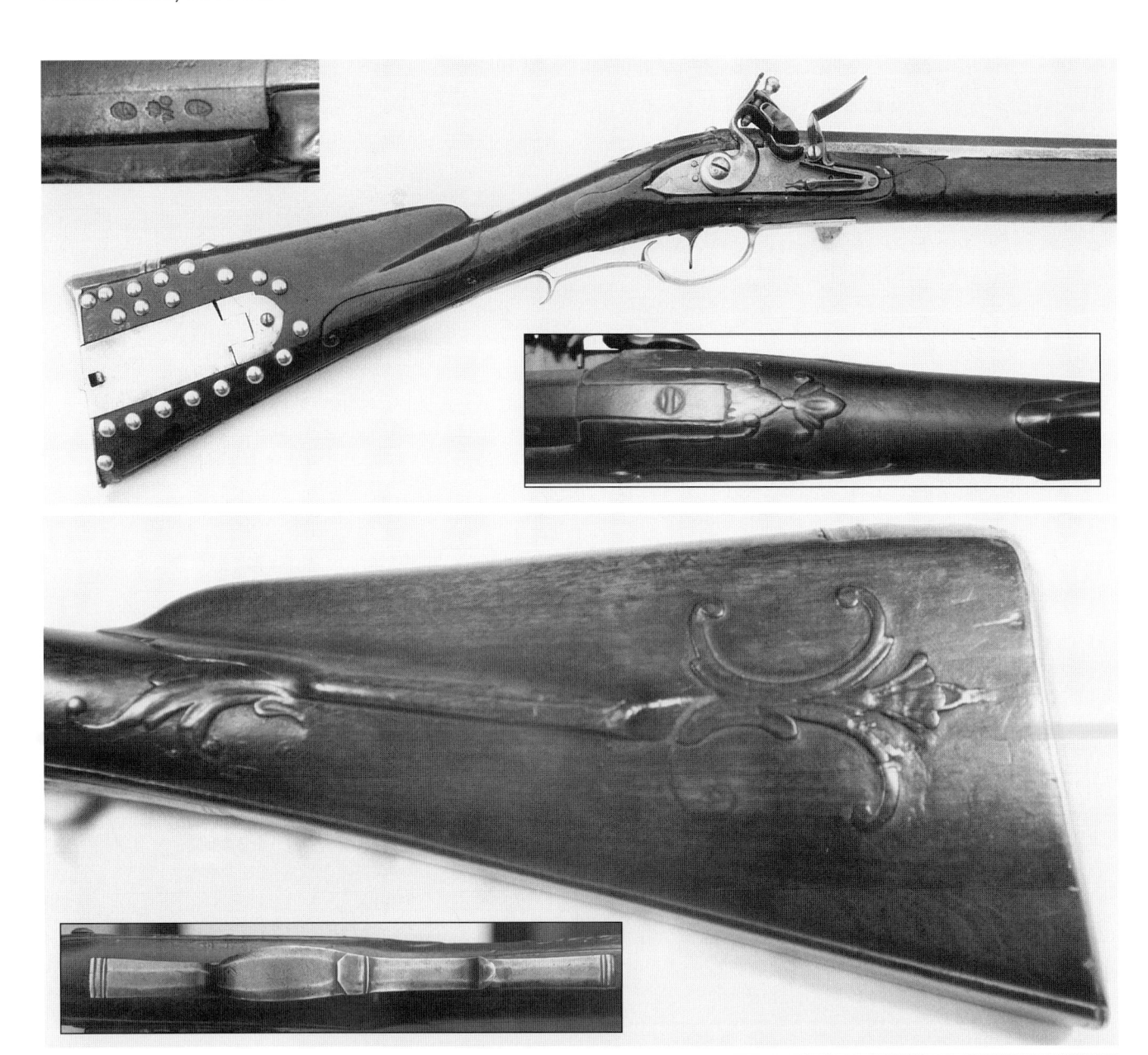

(overall top) American-style longrifle by William Grice of Birmingham. Note the style of the lock, which is the original. All known examples by Grice have the heavy two-piece brass butt-trap lid.
Courtesy Fort Ticonderoga Museum.

(All other views) Details of another Grice longrifle, confirming the carving design used on all known examples of these rifles.
Courtesy of the Benninghoff Collection.

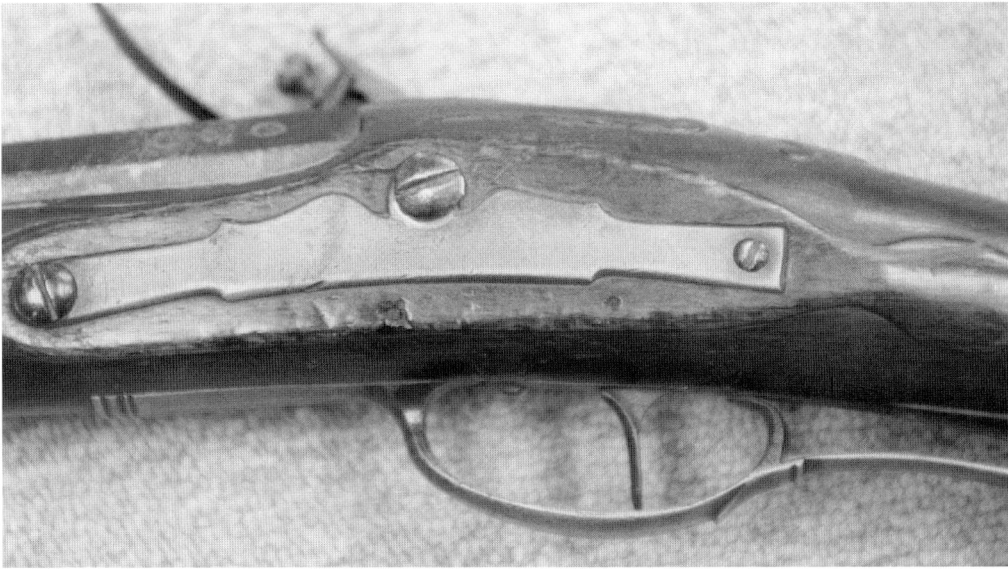

— 84 —

Indian Rifles in British Service to 1783

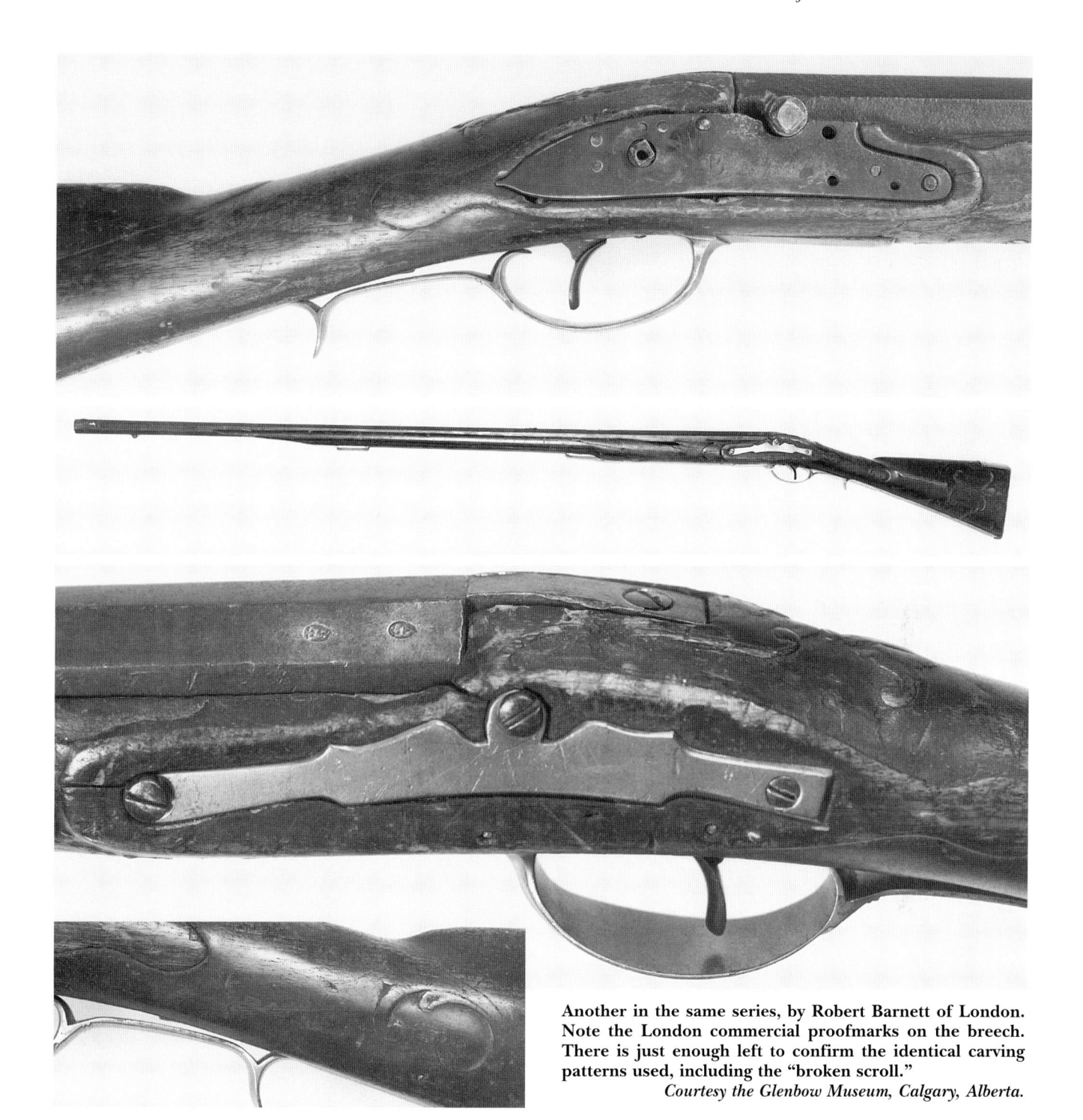

Another in the same series, by Robert Barnett of London. Note the London commercial proofmarks on the breech. There is just enough left to confirm the identical carving patterns used, including the "broken scroll."
Courtesy the Glenbow Museum, Calgary, Alberta.

the 50/- rifle of the invoice. The Grice rifle might have originated for the private trade of the same date, unless Wilson was supplying rifles made by Grice, a proceeding by no means unknown in the guntrade. We do not know who the "& Co." of "Wilson & Co." were at this time (but probably included one of the Barnett family and the younger William Wilson), and given that so much of Wilson's output came from Birmingham, there is no reason why he and Grice may not have teamed-up for this particular venture, Grice having the workforce and Wilson the official contract. It would be extremely unusual for two makers to be producing exactly the same pattern of specialist piece unless there was some connection between them. Neither piece would have been made in Wilson's Minories shops, all known barrels bearing Birmingham proofmarks in imitation of the London ones, and not the correct London commercial proofmarks normally found on Wilson barrels. The view of this writer is, in conclusion, that the Wilson, Barnett and Grice rifles, differing only in the type of butt-trap cover and perhaps in their calibre, represent two grades of the three listed in the invoice. The cheapest of the three types remains to be identified.

Another British Government Indian rifle is mentioned in the records, which remains to be identified, those termed "small bore." The Quebec Board of Ordnance return mentioning 96 rifles for Indians in January 1782 refers to their calibre as taking 25 balls to the pound of lead, or .571" ball (using the table given in Smith's *An Universal Military Dictionary* of 1779). This refers, therefore, to a calibre larger than .58", which the known Wilson and Barnett rifles are (up to about .62"), and therefore may provide a possible identity for the Grice rifles all of which now measure somewhere between about .55 and .58 calibre. There would be every reason not to vary the overall design of a contract rifle if a reduction in bore size were the only requirement. The bore condition of most of the surviving Wilson, Grice and Barnett rifles is such that precise measurement is either difficult or meaningless.

Where did the design for such rifles made in London and Birmingham originate? The popular version has it that an officer returning to Britain from the French & Indian War brought with him a souvenir piece which somehow found its way into the hands of the guntrade. However, it seems far more probable that one of the many merchants dealing in firearms and anxious to get rifles at a lower price than was prevailing locally, most likely at Philadelphia, sent an example to his merchant contacts in London, who would have taken it straight to their arms supplier, very probably the most popular supplier of trade and Indian Department arms, Richard, or his son, William, Wilson. The design itself is extremely close to that of a Lancaster County rifle by John Newcomer shown in drawings by L.H. Harrison and retailed by Dixie Gun Works. Newcomer is recorded from 1767 to 1782. It is therefore at least probable that the design used by the English originated from the most populous rifle-making area in the colonies.

CHAPTER 7

Rifle Development

in the Interwar Years, 1783–1793

The interwar years were, as always, characterized by economies in the military infrastructure, and production of small arms by or for the Board of Ordnance was carefully limited to filling actual requirements. Policies pursued during the American War had left the Ordnance storehouses bulging with a variety of good, mediocre and poor arms, and large quantities of these were disposed of at semi-annual public auctions from 1784. Most of the work done by the Ordnance in the field of small arms during this decade related to attempts by the Master General of the Ordnance to improve on the standard infantry musket. The rifled barrel entered into these experiments only to a limited extent, but two weapons, both for mounted troops, one at field-trials level and the other for regimental issue, were produced.

As with production, so with military thinking. With the end of the fighting in the peculiar and un-typical conditions of North America, British military thinking reverted almost totally to Continental European conditions and requirements with which senior officers were most familiar. It was not until the outbreak of another war, albeit on the familiar Continent, that the younger officers, veterans of the American War, called back into military thinking the advantages and benefits of the rifle for military use.

From the development of successful hand-held firearms until the invention of the tank, the question of the best personal armament for mounted troops bedevilled strategists and tacticians the world over. In every army every commander in chief of cavalry and dragoons or artillery had his own pet theories of the best weapons for the trooper: sword, lance, pistol, carbine, and often combinations of several at once. The pistol-carbine and the breech-loading carbine are but two small chapters in a long saga to which no satisfactory finish was ever achieved. The weapons discussed in this chapter are included because they incorporated the additional contentious feature of rifled barrels.

The Pattern 1785 Crespi-Egg
breech-loading Light Dragoon Carbines

The Austrian Government had issued a breech-loading carbine to its cavalry units between 1771 and 1781 from which date they were gradually withdrawn. Designed by Milanese gunmaker Joseph Crespi, its salient feature is a chambered breechblock hinged at the rear to lift upwards, exposing the mouth of the chamber for loading a paper cartridge; it was the first, and until the issue of the Hall breech-loading rifle and carbines to the United States army in the mid-1820s, the longest-serving military flintlock breech-loading small arm.

Given the experimental turn of mind of the new (1782) Master General of the Ordnance, the third Duke of Richmond, it is highly probable that he was the origin for the idea of putting this system to a field trial with British troops. Given Durs Egg's reputation as a gunmaker and his pre-eminence in the construction of breech-loading systems, most notably the Ferguson, it is not surprising that Richmond turned to him to provide first the patterns and subsequently all but the locks of the Crespi-system carbines.

Two features recommended the Crespi system for British military service: firstly it had already been tried in service for a decade and the results could be evaluated; secondly, it was so designed that a standard pattern paper cartridge could be used in loading it. In order to further advance the basic idea, two new features were appended to the breech design: a screwless lock (i.e. a lock in which all screws with the exception of the jaw- and tumbler-screws of the cock, were replaced by pins or lugs), and a rifled barrel for half of the production.

The London gunmaker Durs Egg (who had not previously worked for the Board of Ordnance apart from supplying two pattern Ferguson rifles in 1776, and who was currently involved in work on a rifled cannon at Woolwich) was given an order on 25 Dec. 1782 for two pattern carbines. On 2 July 1784, he requested payment of £31.10.0. for two breech-loading carbines he had made for Maj. Gen. Ainslie (lieut.-colonel commandant of the 15th King's Light Dragoons), agreeable to the orders of the Master General.[1] At the end of the month Ainslie was given one of the two carbines by the King, and the other was handed over to the Board.[2]

The breech frames of both these pattern carbines

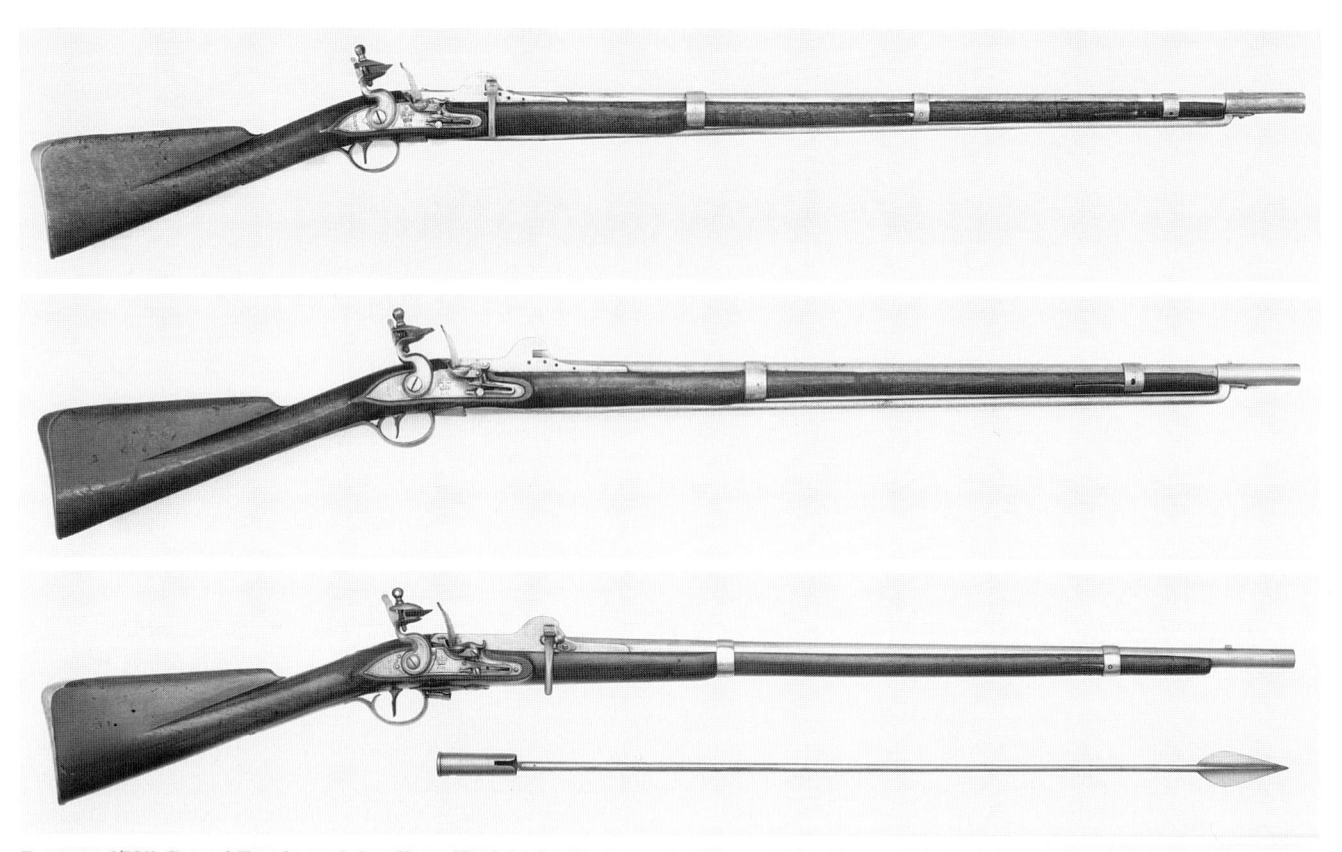

Pattern 1785 Crespi-Egg breech-loading rifled Light Dragoon Carbines with their socket-spearpoint bayonets, two examples with the bayonet in the carrying position. Note that the longest example with the bayonet separated does not have Hennem's screwless lock. *Courtesy of the Trustees of the Royal Armouries Museum, Leeds.*

broke on the second proof, and Egg supplied two new frames. In February 1785 Egg was given an order to make thirty breech-loading carbines with long spear bayonets, half of each of three lengths to be rifled, and all fitted with locks designed and manufactured by Jonathan Hennem.[3] The lengths related to barrel lengths and were 28", 33" and 38".[4] Hennem delivered his locks into Store on 18 April.[5]

A Board of General Officers was convened to consider carbines for light dragoons in general, and specifically whether a breech-loader and a long bayonet would be appropriate, and how many carbines per troop should be rifled. The brief of the Board clearly suggests the Austrian Crespi carbine as rendered into English by Durs Egg as the focal point.[6] The carbines approved by the Board after two inspections and meetings on 2 July 1784 and 27 Jan. 1785 were anglicised versions of the Crespi design, even to the long shanked spear-bayonet, and were destined for issue to five regiments of light dragoons. They were reported ready to be issued from the Tower for troop trials on 1 March 1785. Each regiment was to receive six carbines of the three differing lengths, with one of each length issued to a regiment being rifled.[7] By 6 March Lt. Gen. William Fawcett had notified the colonels of the intended light dragoon regiments to apply for the carbines.[8]

Each of the five light dragoon regiments (the 7th, 10th, 11th, 15th and 16th) received:

	Feet	Inches
1. Shortest Barrel	2	4
2. Rifled do.	2	4
3. Next Length	2	9
4. Rifled do.	2	9
5. Longest Barrel	3	1
6. Rifled do.	3	1[9]

After a trial period lasting less than a year during 1786, the carbines were reported on by the several regiments.

The 7th Light Dragoons reported that the longest carbines were much too heavy to be used with facility by light dragoons, with the middle size subject to the same complaint in a lesser degree. The shortest, 28-inch, were the best, and

from the facility & expedition of loading, is certainly an improvement on the old Carbine [the Eliott]; and of these the Rifle-Barrel is to be preferred, from the truer direction of the shot.

From their construction, they are all liable to be much injured by the common Movements of Cavalry...they are more

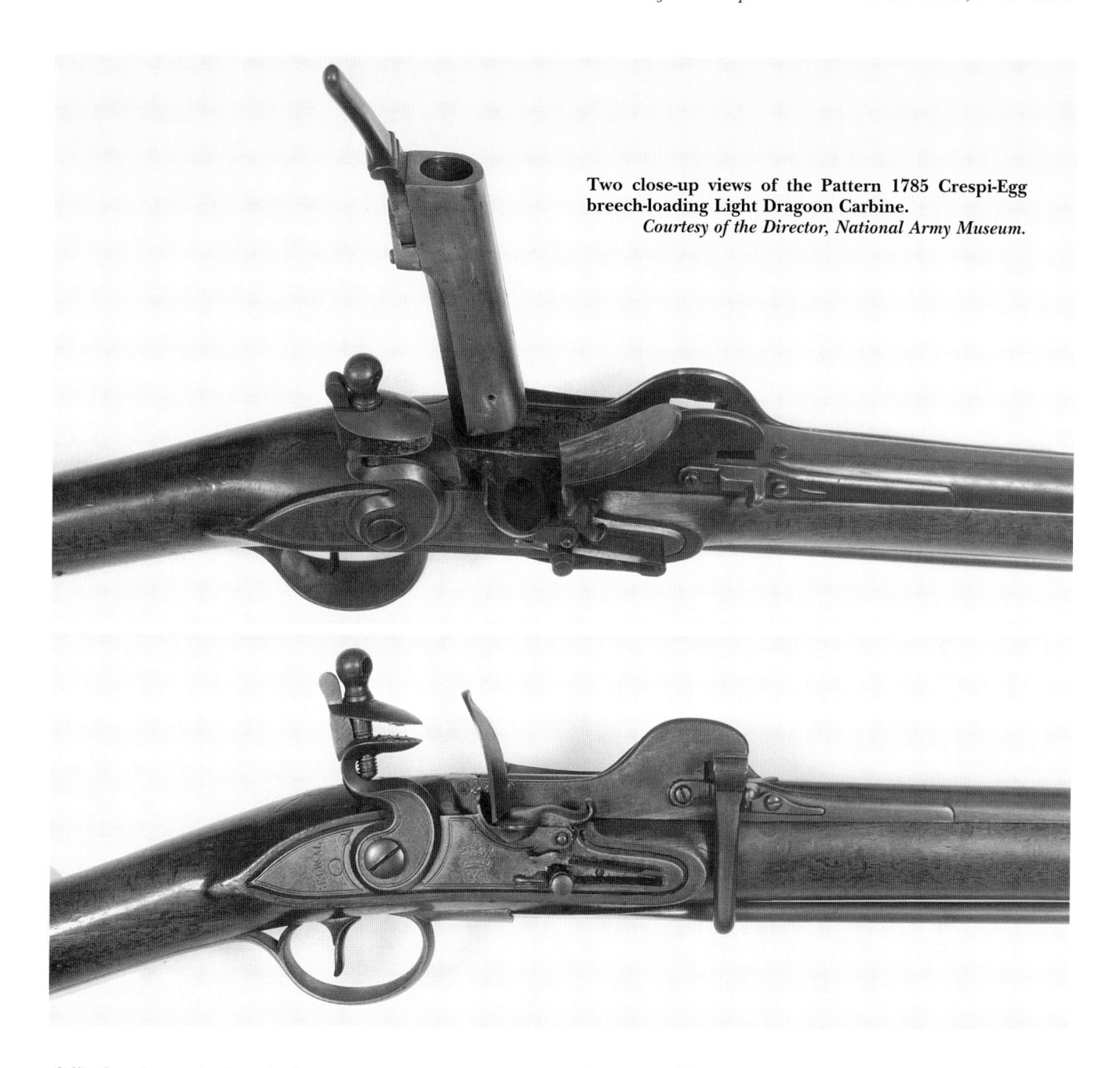

Two close-up views of the Pattern 1785 Crespi-Egg breech-loading Light Dragoon Carbine.
Courtesy of the Director, National Army Museum.

difficult to be repaired on the Spot.

The 10th Light Dragoons found the two middle length carbines with 33-inch barrels weighing 7 lbs. 14½ ozs. (the rifled one a half-ounce less) to be the best adapted for light dragoon service, specifying that "a preference is to be given to the Rifle Barrel, as upon Trial it carried much truer, and the best Shots were made from it."

The 11th Light Dragoons voted for the shortest rifled version:

Nothing can be better adapted for a Lt Dr than this Carbine, provided the Spear, which is a weight of 1 lb. 1 oz. was taken from it; it carries & will, with exactness do Execution at the distance of 500 Yards; and is to be preferred to any of the Plain Barrels, as 'tis impossible to lose the Ball...

General George Ainslie, who had the advantage of owning one of the two original pattern carbines and was obviously in favour of the whole idea, reported for his 15th Light Dragoons:

I find them in all respects a Superior Fire Arm to those of the old Construction.

The longest Size [virtually the same as a musket!] appears to me preferable because it is equally, easily & expeditiously loaded on Horse-back, & a very superior arm when on Foot.

The advantage of having them Rifled cannot be doubted, provided this be done with care & exactness...

The 16th Light Dragoons considered

...the construction of them is preferable to that of those now in use, & that the shortest is the only proper length to be carried compactly and used with ease by Lt Drs on Horse-back.

All of them will carry Ball extremely well, & the shortest are capable of doing Execution at the distance of 500 yards, but they cannot be fired with certainty at so great a distance. I am of opinion that the shortest Plain Carbine is the best calculated for a Lt Dr, as I have seen it throw Ball with great exactness at the distance of 147 Yards, & it is much easier kept clean than the Rifle one.[10]

Four out of five regiments favoured the rifled barrel but there was no consensus with regard to length. The Board of General Officers, having digested all the reports in 1788, came down in favour of the 28-inch rifled version, concurring with the 7th and 11th, and with all but one regiment as regards the rifled barrel.[11] So far as the military were concerned, then, the Crespi system as rendered by Egg, was approved. As is generally the case, the surviving records do not tell us precisely why, in the face of such generally favourable practical experience, the carbine was not adopted. The element of initial cost undoubtedly entered in, and the realities of field maintenance would have posed many problems in training and armourer's skills. The reference to keeping the rifled version clean when compared with the smoothbore version must also have given pause for thought.

That the more general concept of a rifle for military use had not disappeared from British official minds is evidenced by a series of comparative trials carried out in the Autumn of 1791.

Account of some Experiments carried on by the late Honorable Lieut. Genl. Parker on the 2nd August 1791 to ascertain the Comparative Execution of three Rifled Barrels of equal Weights and Dimensions but differing in Obliquity [i.e. twist] of their Rifles. They were fired at the Distance of 200 Yards into a Target of 6 feet square of 2 Inch Elm Plank with 2 drams of Powder.

Experiments continued by Major Blomefield, August 4, 1791 with three Rifled and a smooth one at 200 yards. Half Turn One Turn 1½ Turn Smooth Barrel.

Experiments Continued by Major Blomefield August 5th, 9th September 7th, 15th & 17th with the Three Riffled Barrels. Distance of Target 300 Yards, Charge of Powder 3 drams.

Description of Barrels.
Length Exterior:		2' 6" 0
	Bore:	2' 5" 44
Diameter:	*Breech, in decimals:*	1.2
	Muzzle	.93
	Bore [lands]	.61
	[grooves]	.66
Weight	*Smooth Barrell*	3 lbs 15 oz 8 dr
	½ Turn	3 15 8
	Rifle 1 Turn	3 15 8
	1 ½ Turn	3 15 12
Balls	*Weight 21 to the lb*	
	Diameter 0.6[12]	

From the details of these 1791 trials, it is clear that another milestone along the long and hesitant path leading to the future British service rifle had been reached: the length, dimensions and approximate calibre of the barrel were determined at this time, leaving Ezekiel Baker to make the final contribution in 1800 of the rifling twist — the quarter-turn in the length of the barrel, or one full turn in ten feet.

Pattern 1793 Royal Horse Artillery double-barrelled Pistol-Carbine

Since we are dealing with the rifled barrel in all the forms in which it was used in actual service by the British forces, it is appropriate to end this chapter of experiments with a brief discussion of one of the last of the largely unsuccessful efforts devised by the Master General of the Ordnance the Duke of Richmond and his favourite gunmaker, Henry Nock — the Pattern 1793 Royal Horse Artillery Pistol-Carbine.

Although generally described as a pistol, its removeable, shifting, or detachable butt was an integral part of its design and intended use, so that it is more accurate-

---

(facing page, top) "Account of some Experiments carried on by the late Honorable Lieut. Gen. Parker on the 2nd August 1791 to ascertain the Comparative Execution of three rifled Barrels of same weights and Dimensions but differing in Obliquity of their rifles. They were fired at the Distance of 200 Yards into a Target of 4 ft 6 square of 2 Inch Elm Plank with 2 drams [55 grains] of Powder." Four shots were fired from each barrel, and penetration was also noted.

(facing page, center) "Experiments continued by Major Blomefield, August 4, 1791 with three Rifled and a smooth one at 200 Yards." This is the only surviving trial of a "smooth rifle" (often called a "ball gun" in the late 17th and 18th centuries in England) in British military records. Only two shots out of six fired, 7 and 12, struck the target from the smooth barrel.

(facing page, bottom) "Experiments continued by Major Blomefield August 5th, 9th, September 7th, 15th & 17th [1791] with the Three Riffled Barrels. Distance of Target 300 Yards, Charge of Powder 3 drams" [82½ grains]. At left the half-turn barrel made 38 hits; centre the whole turn barrel also made 38 hits; right the 1½ turn barrel made only 3 hits.

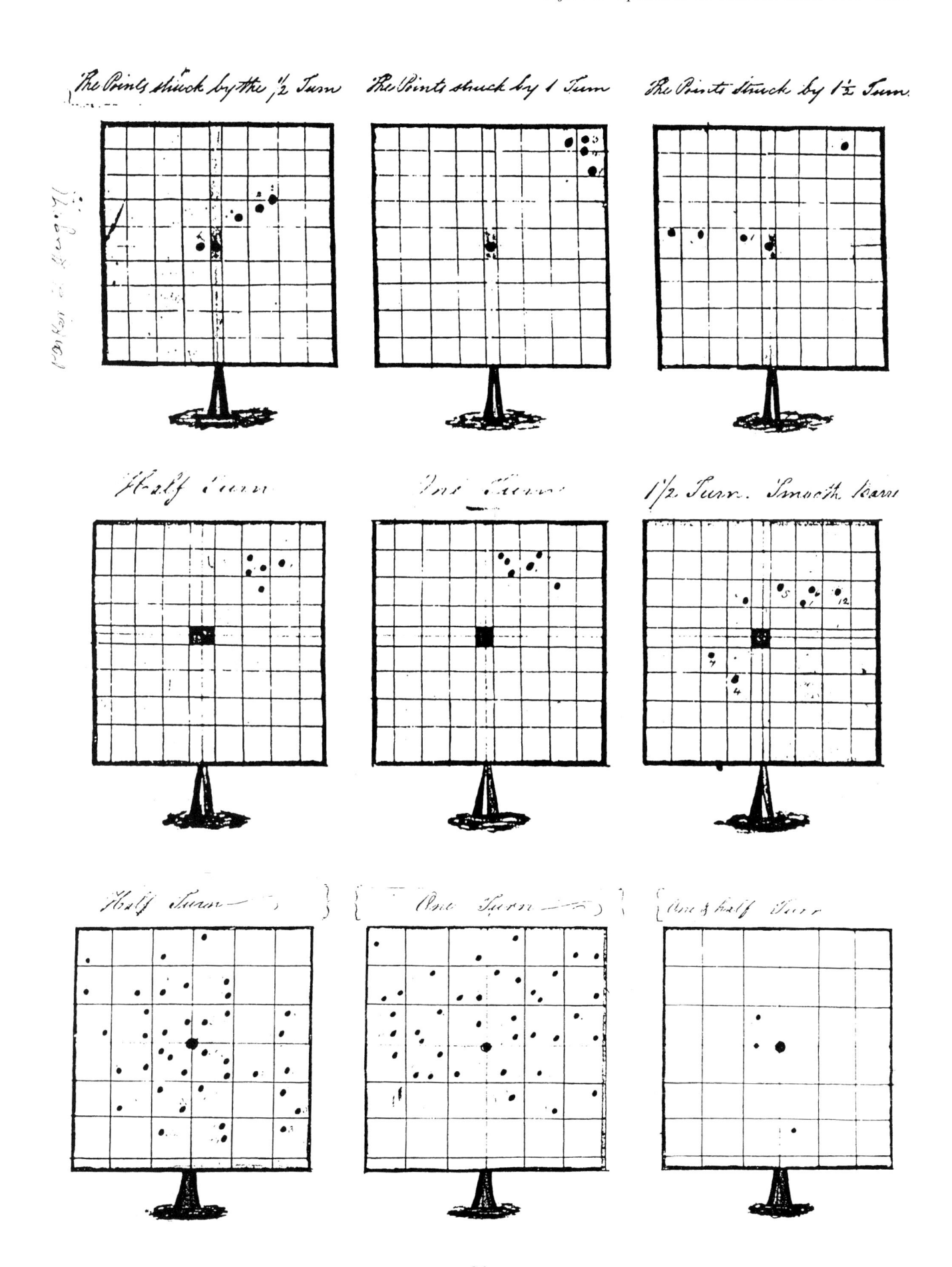

Rifle Development in the Interwar Years, 1783–1793

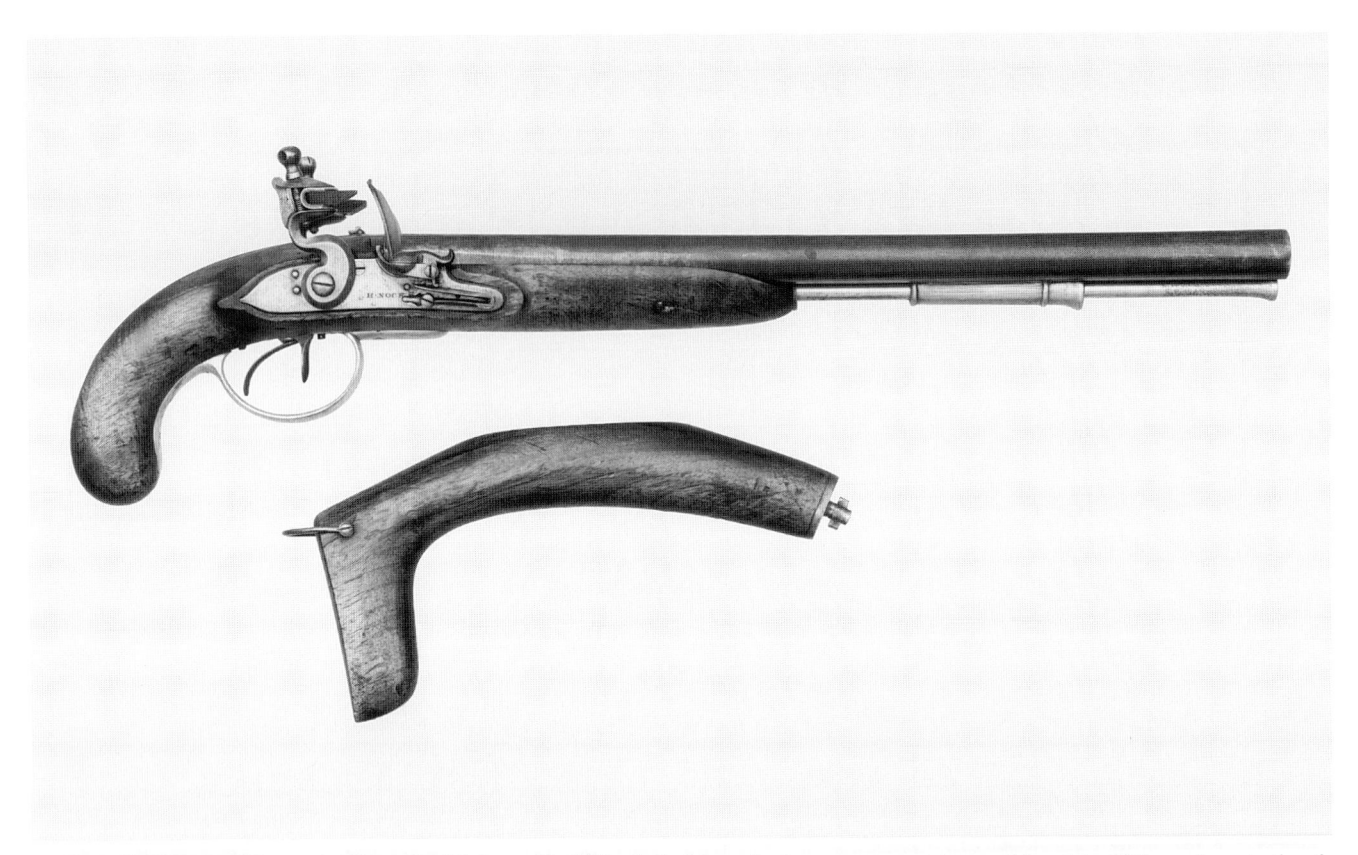

Pattern 1793 Royal Horse Artillery double-barrelled Pistol-Carbine. A clumsy attempt to combine late-18th-century technology all into one weapon for an elite unit, these unsuccessful carbines incorporated side-by-side barrels, the left one being rifled, with a detented lock and set-trigger, and a detachable or "shifting" butt for longer range use of the rifled barrel.
Courtesy of the Trustees of the Royal Armouries, Leeds.

ly described by the term pistol-carbine. They were designed to be carried in the saddle holsters of the newly raised (January 1793) regiment of Royal Horse Artillery, the pistol in one holster and the butt in the other. Nock's bill for their manufacture, dated 30 Sept. 1793, gives a tolerably detailed description of these highly sophisticated but awkward and ungainly combination weapons:

Pistols for the Horse Artilly. Double barreled one of the Barrels Rifled 18 In: long 13 Ball to the lb. one detant Trigger[,] a Slide in the left Hand Tumbler[,] folding elevating Sights [,] a Shifting Butt & a Steel Rammer & the Barrels browned.[13]

As with virtually all weapons of this description, it was too long and much too heavy (7 lbs., 12 ozs) to be effectively handled as a pistol, and not sufficiently strong or balanced as a carbine. Although a spring is mounted inside, the single trumpet-pipe was intended to retain the rammer in position, the later adoption of a swivel-rammer suggests that it was not entirely efficient. The fitting of a single-set, or hair-trigger, as the left, rear, to the left-hand lock for the rifled barrel (rifled with 9 grooves, see Appendix 1) represented a civilian refinement which must have caused difficulties given the level of weapons training and the perils of field maintenance. Apart from the overall design, it did introduce two features which were subsequently much more widely adopted on British service arms (with varying degrees of success): the bolted lock (i.e. fitted with a sliding safety-catch) and the browned barrel which became standard for infantry arms from 1815.

CHAPTER 8

The British Rifle and

Rifle-Armed Units During the French Revolutionary Wars, 1793–1802

...it had always been the practice of this Country, in time of war or upon any extraordinary occasion, to draw very large supplies of arms (and particularly our Rifles) from the Continent and which source is now cut off.[1]

After almost a decade of peace, on 1 February 1793 the French Republic declared war on Great Britain.

As is suggested by the above quote, the period of the French Revolutionary Wars (as opposed to the period of the Napoleonic Wars which followed it) was dominated so far as rifles in the British service is concerned, by rifles of foreign origin and manufacture. As if to confirm this general situation a Home Office report of 7 June 1794 unequivocally states: "there are no Rifled Musquets in Store."[2] It should be noted that the term "rifled musquets" was frequently applied to all types of rifles, even the Baker rifle, throughout this period.

There can be no question that whatever rifles were obtained through various means by British Government agencies during the 1793–1802 period, the majority of those in use by British forces and forces in British pay were of foreign manufacture, and of those the majority were made in one of the German firearms-producing centres such as Suhl, Zella-Mehlis, Potsdam, Cassel, Hanau or Hanover; arms made in more recent years but before the French occupation, in the Netherlands and Liège, equipped many allied units in the field during the 1790s. Older arms still in serviceable condition were pressed into service, and many an officer raising his own small unit for service obtained what arms he could in the commercial marketplace, only later discovering that he had not achieved a bargain. With very few exceptions the rifles used by foreign troops in British pay were brought with them into British service and not supplied from British sources. When Britain did supply rifles before 1802, they were of foreign fabrication, and even after Baker rifle production commenced, foreign-made rifles were sometimes issued to foreign troops in British pay.

In February 1795, ammunition was being sent to the British Commissary in Holland, George Williamson, to be made up for the "Hessian Yagers and other Corps whose Calibre the British Musquet Ball Cartridge will not fit."[3] This is the earliest clear reference to the presence of foreign auxiliary riflemen with British forces after the outbreak of war in 1793. These would have included two chasseur companies of 212 men each in the service of the Landgrave Ludwig X of Hesse-Darmstadt and two companies totalling 202 men serving George III as Elector of Hanover, both in British pay.[4]

In August 1795, Sir Ralph Abercromby, commanding an expedition to the West Indies, wrote requesting a "Corps of Riflemen" and suggested they might be obtained from Hesse-Darmstadt.[5] In the Spring of 1796 Abercromby's troops, then at Barbadoes, included "a good battalion of German riflemen, designated Löwenstein's Chasseurs (see below), who subsequently became a part of the 60th Regiment.[6]

The London gunmaker and contractor to the Board of Ordnance, Durs Egg, told the Board in May 1796 that he could not afford to make rifled muskets of the pattern he had recently supplied to the Board for as little as £3.10.0., that he would have to get £4 each for them. But, if he was paid ready money he could supply them for £3.15.0. Egg was allowed this price but on the normal payment plan, and there are no numbers mentioned nor any reference to this payment in the Bill Books.[7] This mid-'90s aborted effort was the only attempt by the Ordnance to enter into rifle production during the period under discussion. The Egg rifle-musket shown in H.L. Blackmore's *British Military Firearms 1650–1850* [Plate 39 (right), page 146], is probably of the type submitted by Egg, but this ex-Weller Collection example is a purely commercial product bearing no Ordnance or other Government markings. The design is basically a lengthened Pattern 1796 Heavy Dragoon Carbine, with the heavy iron rammer and large pipes, no swell where the ramrod enters the normally closed lower portion of the stock, and a triggerguard with the front finial acting as a tailpipe and containing a rod-retaining spring. The lock is India Pattern with the sole exception of the cockspur, which retains the Land Pattern curl and notch design. The 39-inch externally India Pattern barrel is fitted with a plain block backsight; the bore is .704 calibre and rifled with nine deep narrow angular grooves.

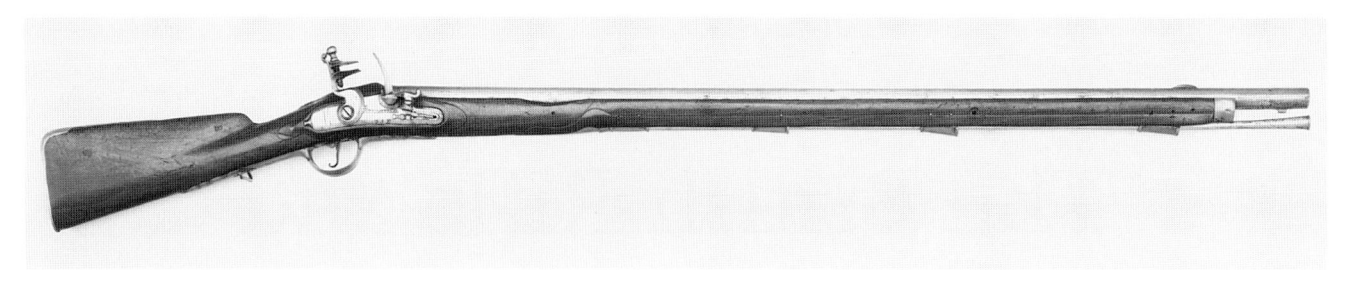

The Prussian light infantry rifle musket of 1798–1800 purchased for the Ordnance via the City merchants Paul and Haviland Le Mesurier. They are a mixture of components from several earlier Prussian service arms, put together by the Schickler brothers, entrepreneurs of the Potsdam Arsenal, for commercial sale, to use up these supplies of older parts.
Courtesy of the Trustees of the Royal Armouries Museum, Leeds.

The Prussian Rifle Muskets

A ready-made rifle basically similar to the Egg pattern of 1796 soon made its appearance and was accepted by the Ordnance. On 12 May 1798,

The Rifle Barrel Musquet of Foreign Fabric...has been examined by the Master Furbisher at the Tower and he reports that he finds the Barrel good and well rifled but that the Lock Stock and Furniture are very coarse Workmanship but that on the whole the Arm is Serviceable. The Opinion of its Value is £1.16.[8]

Shortly afterwards, on 20 May 1798 it was confirmed that the Secretary to the Board of Ordnance, R.H. Crew, had approved a "Rifle Barrel Musquet of Foreign Fabric approved by the Master Furbisher, immediate steps to be taken to procure either of this or any other Pattern, that may appear preferable, at least 2000 stand"[9] which were intended for the new Volunteer regiments. These were part of a much larger operation.

Between 21 Feb. 1797 when a contract was signed with London merchants Paul and Haviland Le Mesurier, and 31 August 1800 this firm supplied 6,691 Prussian rifle muskets to the Board of Ordnance, as well as many more thousands of smoothbore Prussian muskets; the first deliveries did not occur until November 1798 with the arrival of 1,986 rifle muskets with steel rammers, bayonets and scabbards for 35/- each. The above-quoted examinations relate to the pattern pieces for this first batch of arms. The examination appears to have resulted in a reduction in price, for by the time of the next delivery of 1,777 in October 1799, the price stabilized at 33/-. Remaining deliveries of 2,119 (January–April 1800) and 809 (July–August 1800) completed the recorded deliveries of the Prussian rifle muskets.[10]

Like Britain, Prussia was caught largely unprepared by the outbreak of the French Revolutionary Wars, and her arsenals were full of old arms left over from the wars of Frederick the Great. Unlike Britain, the Prussian authorities decided on a large-scale programme of repair and reconstruction using a combination of old but re-usable parts with new stocking and replacements where required to create a new serviceable weapon. The rifle muskets sold to Britain were one of the results of this programme. The new weapon (see above) was based on the Model 1787 Fusilier-Schützengewehr, or light infantry marksman's gun, and the lock, stock and furniture are of this pattern. The thin-walled 41-inch tapered round barrel is .68 calibre and rifled with eight rounded grooves making one turn in the length of the barrel; the backsight consists of a groove along the "humped" tang of the barrel. Between the docks and the Ordnance stores, most of these weapons passed through the hands of the principal London contractors whose workshops cleaned and repaired them and blacked their barrels. This is the first instance of a blacked finish being applied to other than Sea Service muskets, and it was still being carried out in 1804. Most, but apparently not all, of these rifle muskets were submitted to either the King's Proof, or private Tower proof (both processes being carried out in the same Tower shops) before entering Ordnance Stores. The majority of these Prussian rifle muskets were probably issued to troops serving outside of the British Isles, perhaps to the early detachments of the 60th Regiment; they are also known to have been issued to the Duke of Northumberland's Percy Tenantry.[11] It is also likely that they were issued to units proposed to be armed "like the Prussian Schutzen" e.g. Löwenstein's Fusiliers and Hompesch's Fusiliers (see later in chapter). Dr Arnold Wirtgen, in his excellent scholarly study of Prussian arms of this period, describes and illustrates this pattern in detail, although he mistakenly says the barrels were of English fabrication.[12]

It is clear that most of the rifle muskets, rifles and rifled carbines which were in the hands of British-allied troops were of Germanic, or in the parlance of the time "Dutch," fabrication, some examples of which are shown in this chapter, and some captured in Dutch colonies, may have been of actual Netherlands manufacture.

Captured Foreign Rifles

The majority of Britain's enemies during the period 1793–1802 were not rifle-oriented, the single notable

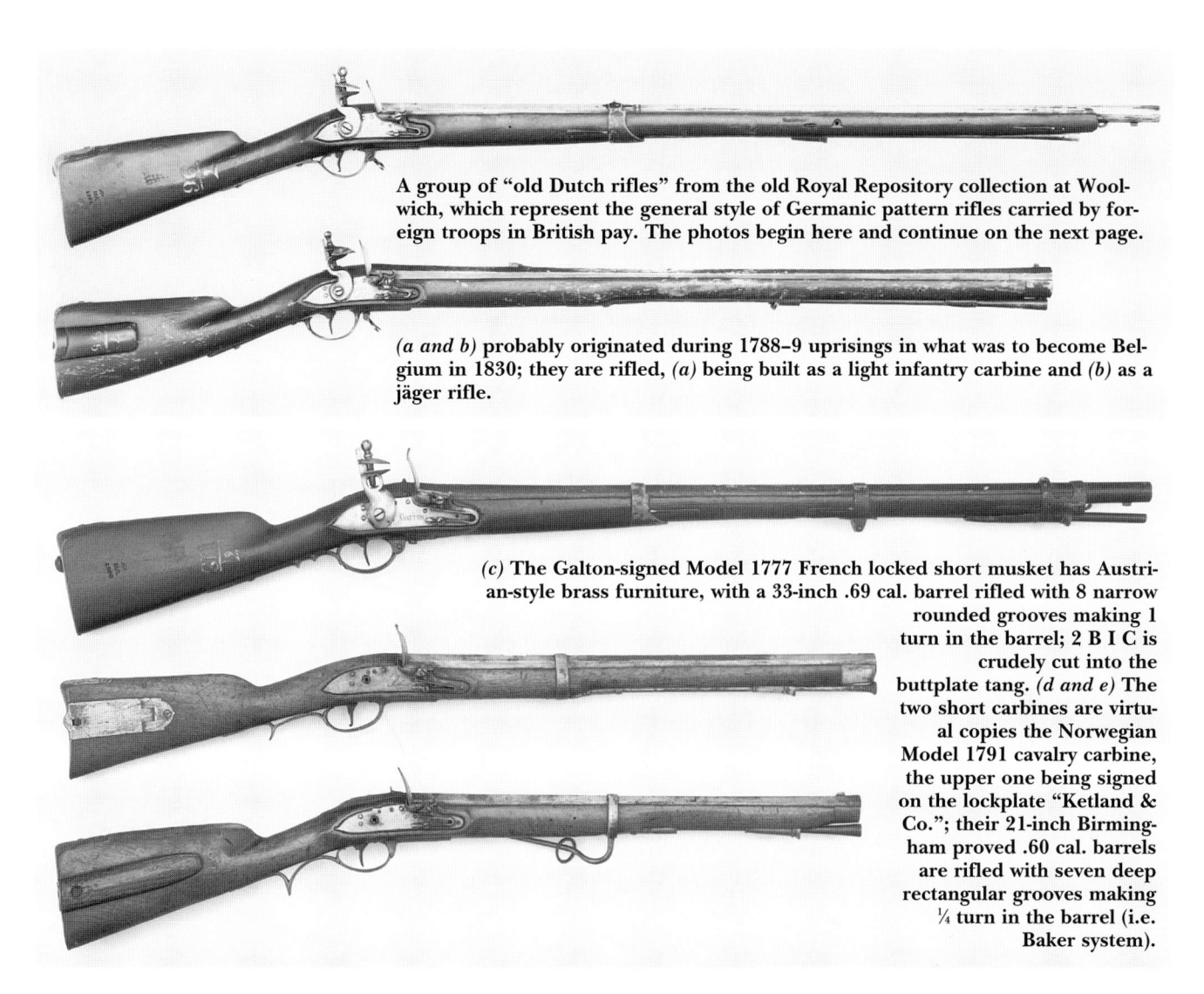

A group of "old Dutch rifles" from the old Royal Repository collection at Woolwich, which represent the general style of Germanic pattern rifles carried by foreign troops in British pay. The photos begin here and continue on the next page.

(a and b) probably originated during 1788–9 uprisings in what was to become Belgium in 1830; they are rifled, *(a)* being built as a light infantry carbine and *(b)* as a jäger rifle.

(c) The Galton-signed Model 1777 French locked short musket has Austrian-style brass furniture, with a 33-inch .69 cal. barrel rifled with 8 narrow rounded grooves making 1 turn in the barrel; 2 B I C is crudely cut into the buttplate tang. *(d and e)* The two short carbines are virtual copies the Norwegian Model 1791 cavalry carbine, the upper one being signed on the lockplate "Ketland & Co."; their 21-inch Birmingham proved .60 cal. barrels are rifled with seven deep rectangular grooves making ¼ turn in the barrel (i.e. Baker system).

exception being the newly created French puppet regime which, in 1795, declared itself the Batavian Republic (formerly the United Provinces of the Netherlands), and its colonies. It is significant that Orangist (royalist) Dutch emigres formed the largest percentage of men in rifle-armed units raised for British service during this period. Between September 1796 and September 1800 the Ordnance acquired control over at least 730 rifles of which 223 can be confirmed as of Low Countries origin (200 from Ceylon and 23 from Surinam) and the remaining 507 being of uncertain origin captured in the stores on the island of Malta in September 1800.[13] An order for 150 rifles for Löwenstein's Jägers on Malta as part of Abercromby's Egyptian expedition, was approved in July 1801, and was probably filled from the rifles captured on the island.[14]

The 200 rifles taken at Ceylon were valued by the Ordnance for prize-money purposes at 26/-, a good price for a captured weapon suggesting reasonable condition and quality; half of these may have comprised the armament of the Regiment de Meuron's rifle company and remained with those troops when they transferred to British service in October 1795 (see below). Of the remaining 23 Dutch rifles, they were described as "short rifles" and valued at a much lower price of 15/-, possibly suggesting poor condition.[15] Ceylon was handed over to the East India Company for administration between 1796 and 1802, and 100 of the 200 captured rifles may have been taken into their service. Indeed, they may have already belonged to a Malay Battalion which had been in Dutch service, and who transferred their allegiance to the British in 1796. There had been a Dutch Malay jägercorps raised in Ceylon as early as 1764, so the arms in question may well have been exactly as described, "old Dutch rifles."[16] As late as June 1808, the 4/60th stationed at Antigua reported that their rifles were "worn out old Dutch arms very bad, received at the Cape." A year later, the "old Dutch Rifles in possession of the Rifle Company" were in the local Ordnance stores and the men were armed with Dutch muskets.[17]

British Military Flintlock Rifles

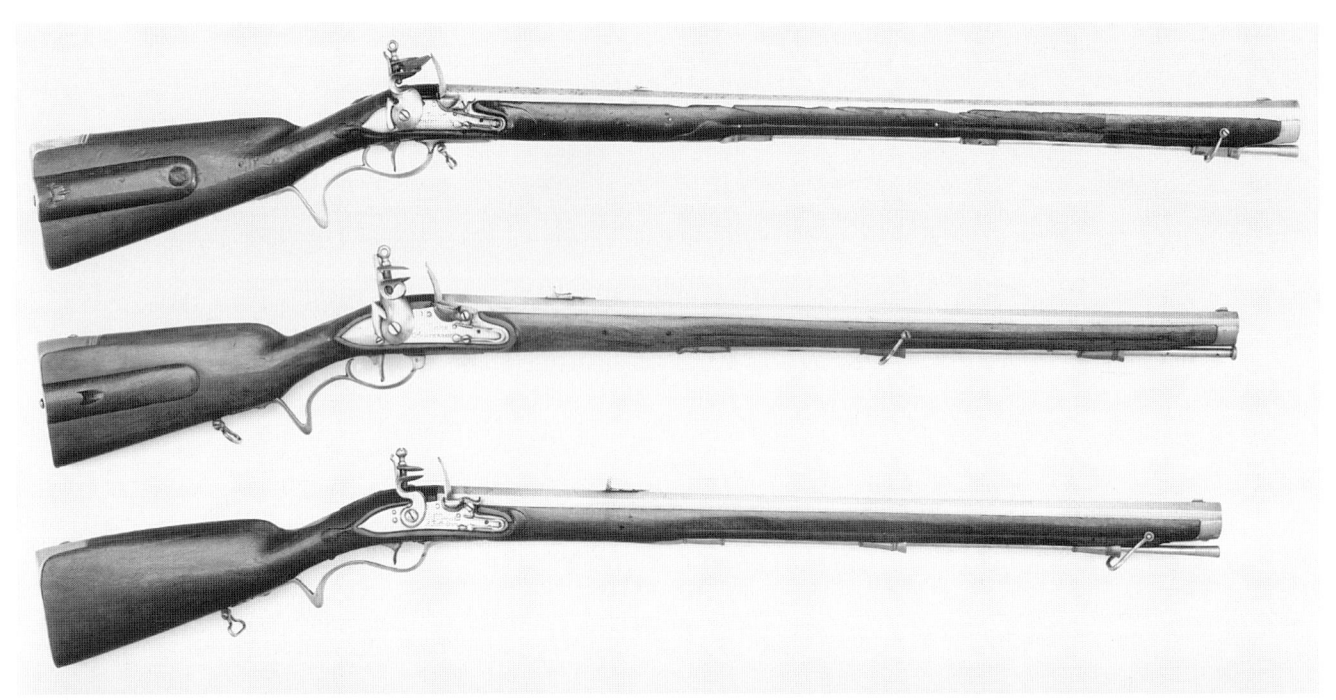

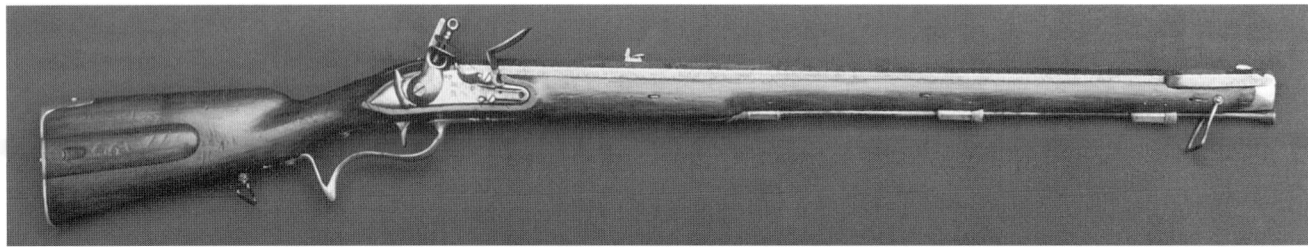

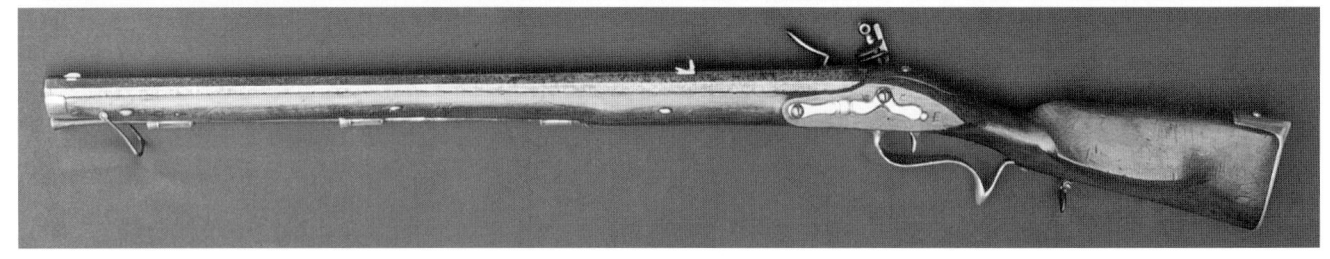

(f,g,h) **Three rifles of Dutch fabrication by Thone of Amsterdam, J. Tomson and J.N. Pisvisse, both of Rotterdam, respectively. In design they represent pre-Model 1798 Batavian jäger rifles of the types most likely to have come into British service with their contracted or captured owners.** *Courtesy of the Trustees of the Royal Armouries Museum, Leeds. (i, two views)* **The Batavian Model 1798 Jäger Rifle, some of which may have come into "British" use.** *W.A. Dreschler.*

If, as shown above, it is true that the rifles in British service during the 1790s were almost entirely of foreign manufacture, it is equally true that they were used by foreign troops, whether with or without some British officers, and whether "in British pay" or on the British Establishment.

From the records it appears that in point of seniority Captain George W. Ramsay's York Rangers (sometimes referred to as the York Chasseurs) was the first rifle unit to be raised after the declarations of war, in May 1793. Ramsay gained field experience with light troops when he commanded the Light Company of the 30th Foot in the "last war in America." The unit landed at Charles Town, South Carolina, 3 June 1781, and a battalion of flank companies commanded by Major Marjoribanks served in Lord Rawdon's relief of Ninety Six.[18] Ramsay, who had been a captain since March 1780, initially offered a unit of 5 officers and 100 riflemen,[19] but this was increased to two companies of 4 officers and 108 riflemen each on 26 June 1793. On 30 Jan. 1794, a sixth company was added and the rank & file now totalled 600. In April 1795 a further increase was made to 800 rank & file and Ramsay was gazetted Lieut. Col. Commanding with effect from 25 May 1795. The first companies were active in the Low Countries by late 1793, when they were described as an "active and useful

— 96 —

force." In Jan. 1796, the corps, with 47 officers and 729 effectives, and an artillery company of 49 men, was readied for St. Domingo along with Hardy's Royal York Fusiliers (see below), but was diverted to St. Lucia, and thence to St. Vincent. On 3 Oct. 1797, the unit was ordered drafted to the 60th Regiment, and Ramsay and most of his men were transferred to the 3/60th.[20]

In July 1793 an augmentation of two rifle companies was ordered for the Comte de Chartre's Loyal Emigrant Regiment, and both saw much active and hard service through 1795.[21]

The next rifle unit to appear was that of Thomas Carteret Hardy previously a major in the 86th Foot, who agreed, on 26 Sept. 1794, to raise a corps of ten companies of riflemen with 4 officers and 112 men each, to be called the Royal York Fusiliers. H.R.H. Frederick, Duke of York, being the current Commander-in-Chief of the British Army, and in the field with his troops, accounts for the frequent use of "York" in unit titles of the period. By 25 April 1795 only seven companies with 491 men had been raised, well short of their 784 Establishment. By July there were eight companies awaiting embarkation for England, their number rising to 844 by September. The *St. James's Chronicle* mentions the unit as "Hardy's corps of German riflemen" on 6 February 1796. The unit sailed from the Isle of Wight in February 1796 with 33 officers and 672 riflemen. They remained at St. Lucia until April 1797, when they were ordered to be reduced, and most of the men had gone to the 3/60th by June 1797.[22]

A far less successful unit, Power's Chasseurs, was raised in September 1794, and consisted of two companies of 10 officers and 214 men; there were only 100 men present by early 1795, and shortly after that the unit disappears, probably drafted into the York Fusiliers.[23]

The York Hussars originated in June 1793, but was not a cohesive unit until the following year; it was present at the Battle of Boxtel as "Irwine's British Hussars" and it is not even clear when it acquired the title of York Hussars. By September 1795, the 714-man unit was at Stade awaiting transports for England. It was placed on the British Establishment with 27 serjeants, 36 corporals and 564 men, with nearly half of the officers being British. They re-embarked at Southampton at the end of February 1796 as part of Gen. Perryn's brigade for St. Domingo with 42 officers and 646 men. They were in constant action until mid-1797, when they went to Jamaica with 30 officers and 200 men. The Hussars were the only foreign regiment for which recruiting continued after early 1797, when many of the others were drafted into various battalions of the 60th Foot. The Hussars were at the Isle of Wight from October 1799 to February 1800 when they went to Weymouth. Shortly after arriving in Weymouth, the unit was authorized to be issued 600 carbines and 608 pistols, representing a complete re-armament. In July, a further issue of 331 carbines and 441 pairs of pistols was authorized.[24] Whether any of the carbines were rifled is not indicated but in October 1800, Lieut.-Col. Long, commanding the regiment, reported to the Adjutant General that he had in his possession at Weymouth "106 old Rifle Carbines (part unserviceable and of different Calibres)," and wanting to know if he could turn them in to Ordnance Stores; permission was given the following month.[25] From this it would appear that the unit had carried rifled carbines during its earlier service. In November 1800, the unit was authorized to be issued 60 carbines and 441 pistols (suggesting that the previous authorization had not been fulfilled and correcting the issue from pairs to single pistols). The Hussars were disbanded at Weymouth 24 July 1802.[26]

Waldstein's Regiment of Waldeckers was raised on a capitulation of 27 July 1795 with a chasseur company. It was in England by May 1796, with 12 officers and 267 men, but by April 1797 it was over 800 strong. It was in the West Indies by August 1797 with 30 officers and 789 men and while in Martinique was drafted into the 4/60th in April 1798.[27]

Colonel de la Tour's Regiment of Royal Foreigners (Etranger) originally included three chasseur companies of 106 men each. In December 1795 they were with Abercromby's forces at St. Lucia, and then at Grenada in June 1796. By Jan. 1797 the regiment was down to 707 effectives thanks to hard fighting and disease, and a year later most of the unit was drafted to the 3/60th.[28]

The second battalion of the Swiss Regiment de Meuron which transferred to British service from that of the United Provinces (for which it had been raised in 1781 serving at the Cape of Good Hope and at Ceylon where the transfer took place) in October 1795, included a rifle company of 104 rank & file.[29]

The brothers von Hompesch and Prince Löwenstein-Wertheim: the nucleus of future rifle corps

Baron Carl von Hompesch and his younger brother Ferdinand were, between them, responsible for the raising of four units for British service during the mid-1790s, which were either entirely or partially armed with rifles. Like the two earlier York units described above, all were subsequently absorbed by other regiments before the peace of 1802, mostly into battalions of the 60th Foot.

By a capitulation of 27 February 1794, Carl von Hompesch undertook to raise within three months three squadrons of hussars, each squadron comprised of three troops of 3 officers and 81 men each. By Sept. 1794, Hompesch's Hussars amounted to only 13 officers and 215 men, still 400 short of their Establishment. Nevertheless, they were at the Battle of Boxtel, and suf-

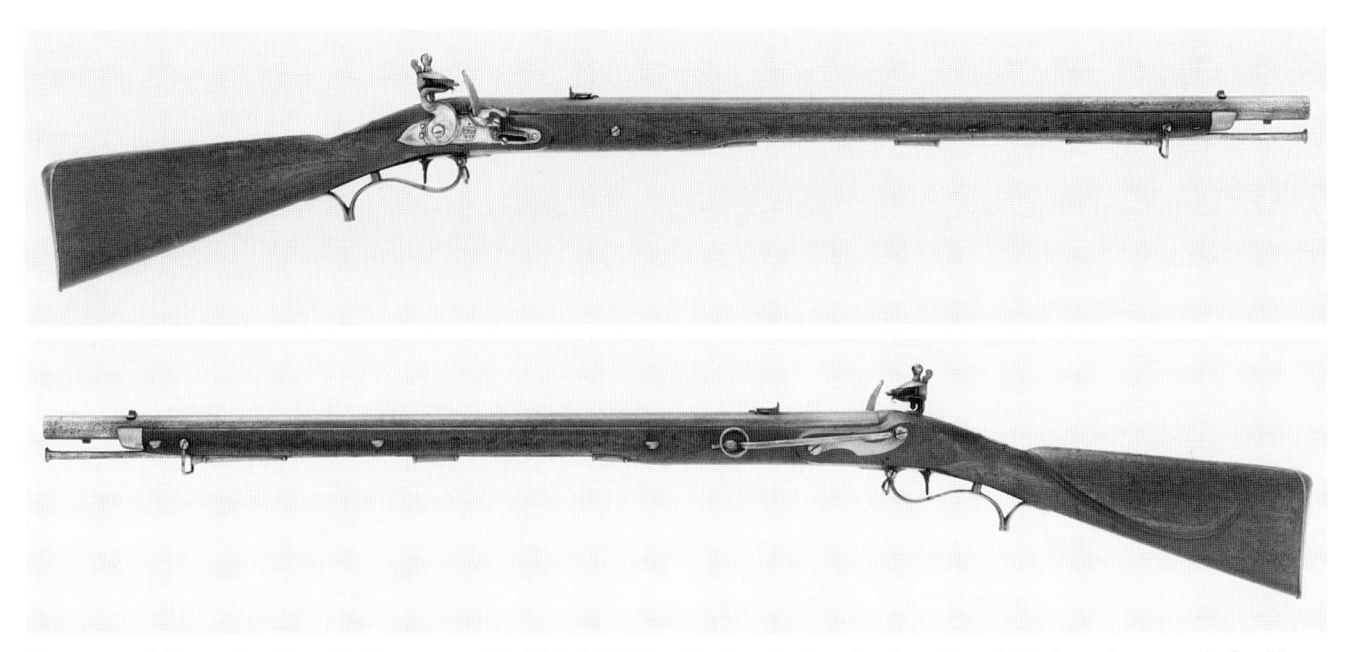

A commercially made rifle with the engraved initials "H H" on its thumbpiece is often thought to have been made for Hompesch's Hussars, but a variety of circumstances and timing make this a virtual impossibility, as will be described later in this chapter. See also Chapter 17. *Courtesy of the Trustees of the Royal Armouries Museum, Leeds.*

fered severely at Oldenzaal in February 1795. Although what happened next is not entirely clear from the records, the unit was probably re-raised early in 1795, and by October it numbered 39 officers and 774 men who were at Stade awaiting embarkation for England. They were on the Isle of Wight by early 1796 where they were referred to as the "Prince of Wales's Hussars" with a total of 1,070 men. They sailed for the West Indies on 18 Mar. 1796, arriving at St. Domingo where they remained from July 1796 to July 1797, at which date they mustered only 318 men. It appears that they were then drafted to the York Hussars, with the officers returning to England in November 1797.[30] There is no record of the Hussars being equipped with rifles, but the unit has been mentioned because of the rifle (see photos) which is often associated with the unit. The design features of this rifle being largely post-1800 coupled with the fact that the Hussars were in England for so short a time militates strongly against their being armed with an English-made weapon of this specialist nature. If any of the several Hompesch units had ever been styled "Hompesch's Horse" it might explain the initials on the thumbpiece of these rifles, but there is again no evidence of such a designation.

Under the terms of the same capitulation of 27 February 1794 Carl von Hompesch also committed himself to the raising of a two-company unit of foot chasseurs, Hompesch's Chasseurs à pied, which enjoyed but a very short existence. Each company was to consist of 3 officers and 102 men. Both companies were completed by August 1794, totalling 7 officers and 221 riflemen. Of the 160 men engaged at Boxtel on 15 September, three-quarters were casualties. After February 1795, records of the unit fail, and their remnant numbers were either disbanded or drafted into the Hussars.[31]

Carl von Hompesch's younger brother Ferdinand (who was Lieut. Col. of Hompesch's Hussars) undertook by a capitulation of 3 March 1796 to raise a mixed unit of light infantry and chasseurs. Known as Hompesch's Fusiliers (or Light Infantry), it consisted originally of eight companies of 4 officers and 115 men each. This was shortly increased to ten companies organized as six companies of fusiliers and four companies of chasseurs. Originally, the entire corps was to be armed "like the Prussian Schutzen" with ten men of each company carrying a rifled carbine of a special pattern. This suggests that the fusiliers carried the long-barrelled Prussian rifle muskets described above, while the rifled carbines were short barrelled possibly with a sword-bayonet. The men were all recruited in Germany, but the unit itself was formed on the Isle of Wight; by 23 July 1796, they mustered 6 officers and 292 men, but by October they were over Establishment. Two companies were armed with rifles and swords (sword-bayonets?) "like Lowenstein's." By February 1797, there were 33 officers and 900 men of the unit at Martinique, and thereafter at Trinidad and finally at Antigua from Dec. 1797. Their last muster, at Antigua on 1 April 1798, shows 17 officers and 528 men; by 1 May most of these had been absorbed into 2/60th. Additional men of Hompesch's infantry companies still on the Isle of Wight went into the 5/60th.[32]

On 21 July 1796, Ferdinand von Hompesch further offered to raise two companies of chasseurs a cheval,

— 98 —

mounted riflemen. By 1797, 244 such men were attached to Hompesch's Fusiliers, with whom they appear to have operated throughout their short existence. In February 1797, Col. Nesbitt noted that Hompesch's chasseurs à cheval, 230 men, were "totally unprovided" with arms or equipment — an apparent opportunity for the supply of English-made weapons?[33] Most of the men from this mounted chasseur unit went into Hompesch's Mounted Rifle unit (with which these two companies should not be confused) in 1798.[34]

A letter concerning the foreign corps written by Col. Nesbitt, commissary of foreign troops, in 1797 states that

Hompesch's Corps has at present 3 Companies of Riflemen and three companies of mounted riflemen, both which being a kind of troop we never can possess by any other means it would perhaps be adviseable to keep up...

Regiments of Infantry having each a company of riflemen and one of artillery – with an Engineer attached to each: 1. York Rangers 2. Royal Foreigners 3. Waldstein 4. Wittgenstein. Chasseurs 1300.[35]

The last of the von Hompesch corps, Hompesch's Mounted Riflemen, was raised on an order of 9 January 1798. It consisted of four troops with 114 non-commissioned officers and men each, with Ferdinand von Hompesch as its colonel. By April 1797, three companies of mounted riflemen had been collected, probably for the mounted chasseurs attached to Hompesch's Fusiliers, who did not go to the West Indies. A return of an augmentation to the "Regiment de Hompesch" dated 10 May 1797 and signed by Lieut. Col. de Rottenburg shows three companies of chasseurs à cheval: Capt. Muller 124 R&F, Capt. Kayser 124 R&F and Capt. D'Avangour 120 R&F; as well as one company of chasseurs à pied of 126 men commanded by Capt. D'Orb.[36] It seems likely these formed the nucleus of the unit officially created in January 1798. The Mounted Riflemen went to Ireland in April and served during "the '98" where it co-operated with companies of 5/60th. It next went on the Ferrol expedition in August 1800, was at Cadiz in September, and then went on to Egypt as part of General Finch's cavalry brigade. It was back in Ireland by August 1802, 72 men short of its Establishment of 461. Hompesch's Mounted Riflemen was disbanded at Portsmouth on 28 September 1802.[37]

The first of three units raised by Constantin, Prince Löwenstein-Wertheim, was Löwenstein's Chasseurs which were in fact a pre-existing unit in the service of the United Provinces which was taken into British service in April 1795. It was organized into seven companies with four officers and 85 men each, the men coming initially mostly from Alsace and Switzerland. The unit was soon increased to twelve companies organized in two battalions with 100 men to a company. By July 1795, 600 men were at Stade on the Elbe River in northern Germany, awaiting embarkation for England; by September their number had increased to 800. They arrived at Portsmouth in November 1795, 1,190 strong. Their numbers had decreased by desertion and disease to 67 officers and 996 men with Major General Sir Ralph Abercromby's forces at St. Lucia in May 1796. The General described Löwenstein's as "a good battalion of German riflemen." The 1st Battalion went to Grenada and the 2nd to St. Vincent, but were re-united on Martinique by November 1796. They served together at Trinidad and then at Puerto Rico — their last active service — and were back at Martinique by June 1797. From there, six companies, 43 officers and 530 men, were drafted into the new-forming battalion of the 60th Foot in December 1797.[38]

The second unit raised by Prince Löwenstein was to consist of eight companies of infantry and a single company of artillery, and was known as Löwenstein's Fusiliers. The original agreement of 22 Aug. 1795 was superceded by a second capitulation of 23 Feb. 1796, which called for the eight companies to consist of 4 officers and 137 men each, "to be armed with rifles like the Prussian Schutzen." By July 1796, 8 officers and 425 men had been assembled on the Isle of Wight and the 1797 Establishment called for 1,318 of all ranks including 51 artillerymen. When the unit was inspected on 4 Nov. 1797, it was considered to be "much inferior to Löwenstein's Chasseurs (or Jägers)," and two companies carried rifles with sword bayonets. Whether this means the others carried longer rifles (like the Prussian Schützen) without sword bayonets, or whether only two companies had rifles of any sort, is not clear. The Fusiliers embarked for the West Indies in December 1797 and mustered 35 officers and 932 men at Martinique the following April. The unit suffered heavy losses at Puerto Rico and then went to Barbados, from where most of the men were transferred to the newly forming fifth battalion of the 60th Regiment.[39]

A State of the Establishments for foreign corps of 1796 includes the following:[40]

	serjeants	corporals	chasseurs
York Rangers	3	5	75
Löwenstein's Chasseurs	60	108	1020
Löwenstein's Fusiliers	5	8	100
Hompesch's Infantry & Chasseurs	20	32	400
Hompesch's Chasseurs à cheval	10	16	200

Löwenstein's last unit was also the most short-lived, and had no connexion with the earlier units except their common founder. Löwenstein's Jägers (or Light Infantry) was created by a capitulation of 14 January 1800, and one company was already in service by June of that year. By December, there were six companies with 21 officers and 453 men. They served with Austrian and Bavarian troops during 1801, and increased by a further three companies before the Peace of Luneville (9 Feb. 1801). On Malta in June 1801, they mustered 24 officers and 575 men before accompanying Abercromby's forces to Egypt. At Alexandria in July they had 18 officers and 520 men who were commended for their performance during the siege. They returned to the Isle of Wight in April 1802, and were disbanded on 14 May 1802. Of the remaining 450 men two-thirds went to the 5/60th and the remaining 75 to other battalions of this regiment.[41]

A number of rifles (see earlier photos) survive bearing on their oval thumbpieces the initials "H H" in what appears to be correct original shaded engraving. These have long been considered to be rifles provided for Hompesch's Hussars. There are, however, a number of serious problems with this attribution. In the first place, there are a great many design features identical to the Baker rifle adopted in 1800, *even to the quarter-turn rifling of the barrel*, the most notable exception being the rounded lock which most closely resembles the Pattern 1798 Heavy Dragoon Carbine lock. Most of these features are new to the Baker rifle on an English product, although the barrel dimensions can be dated at least as early as the Woolwich trials of 1791. For a light-cavalry regiment these rifles have very long barrels, the full thirty inches of the Baker Infantry rifle. While there is no question that these rifles are of English fabrication, there is considerable question whether Hompesch's Hussars were positioned appropriately either in time or location to have received arms of this description.

The 5th battalion of the 60th Regiment of Foot was raised from early 1798 from foreign regiments in British pay which did not reach sufficient numbers to be embodied, most of which have been described above. The rifles with which this unit was initially armed were reported to have six groove rifling, but beyond this detail no further information has yet come to light.[42]

An Indenture dated 25 January 1798 accounts for 1,538 lbs. of lead and 2,000 carbine flints delivered from Portsmouth Ordnance Stores to the Board's Order of 16 January "for the use of Riflemen ordered to St. Domingo on their way to Jamaica." These were probably the riflemen of the 4/60th.[43]

In May 1798 Colonel John Money published a 27-page pamphlet entitled *Observations on the use of Chasseurs and Irregulars with an Army in an Inclosed Country* in which he argued for the creation of large numbers of rifle-armed troops both for the defense of England and use in any "inclosed country." Money had served with rifle-armed German troops in 1760–2, and as Adjutant in the 63rd Foot with Burgoyne during the American War, and was thoroughly convinced by his personal experiences that light troops trained and equipped as closely as possible like American Indians "with nothing to carry when action is expected, but a powder-horn and a bag of loose balls." Of the rifle for military use, Money wrote:

Irregulars in most services in Europe are furnished with a rifle, either long or short, with which they are taught to fire with great exactness, insomuch that some of them are expert enough to hit a dollar [approx. 1½" diameter] at a considerable distance. Will any British officer, who knows the use of fire-arms, say, that, with one of the muskets used by our light infantry, he could fire as accurately at a mark as with a park-keeper's rifle? Would any park-keeper use one in preference to his own rifle? Certainly not. But rifles, it may be said, have no bayonets. No: – not indeed to kill deer with; but in the Austrian service the Regiment des Loups *has bayonets, as well as several corps in the French service, but not those regiments which use the short rifle, of which there are some amongst the Germans.*

Objections to chasseurs, merely on account of the original cost of the rifle, to obviate such a reason (which indeed can have but little weight where old prejudices are got the better of) deduct the price of the soldier's firelock, the difference of expence in the cloathing, and of the accoutrements, the balance will not be found great against the rifleman.[44]

The extent to which rifle consciousness had permeated British military thinking by 1798, and possibly as a partial response to the nudge given by Money's argument earlier in the year, is reflected in the publication by the War Office, in August 1798, of the first manual for riflemen. Originally written in German by Baron Francis de Rottenburg, often known as "the father of British riflemen," it was translated by the current Adjutant General, Sir William Fawcett. Fawcett it will be recalled, was active in recruiting German jägers during the American War and had contracted for the manufacture of the first Pattern 1776 Rifles in Hanover in 1776. De Rottenburg was born in Danzig in 1757; from 1782 to July 1791 he served in the French army, and then in the Polish service until November 1794. He was a major in Hompesch's Hussars, rising to Lieut.-Col. before becoming Lieut. Col. commanding of 5/60th from its formation until 1809. The basic firing drill in his riflemen's manual was performed using conventional paper cartridges, but it was noted that this was only applicable "when a corps of riflemen is required to act in close order," otherwise the principal instruction for recruits was "to load with the powder measure and loose ball...and to fire at the target; the loading with car-

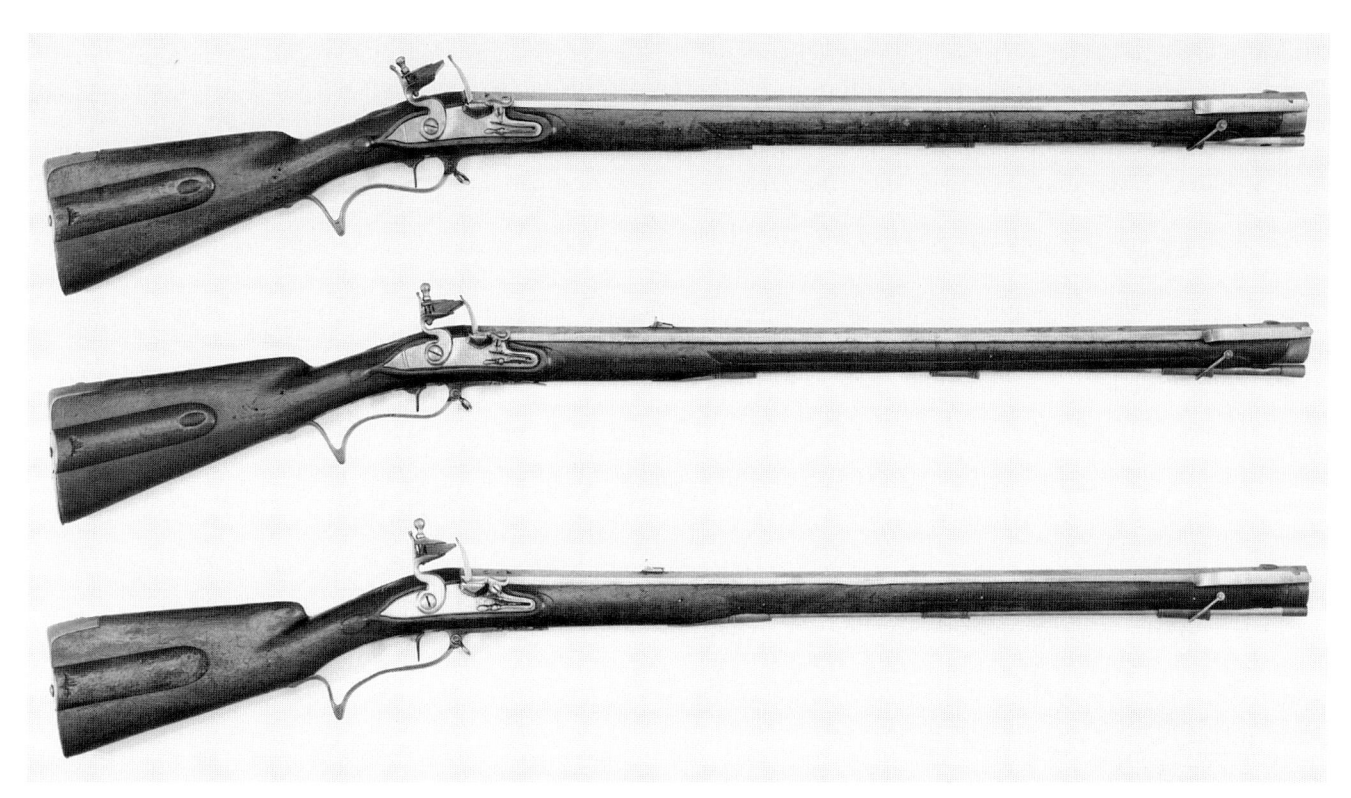

A trio of rifles of German manufacture very probably part of an order completed in 1800 in Hesse-Cassel for the 1,000-man Prince of Orange's Rifle Regiment, the first clearly identified rifle unit of regimental size in the British service.
Courtesy of the Trustees of the Royal Armouries Museum, Leeds.

tridge is a secondary object." The arms-related text of this first British rifleman's manual is found in Appendix 10.

On 14 Nov. 1799, William Bolts offered a group of Prussian arms to the Board which included 6,000 cavalry carbines with rifled barrels and a sabre to each so constructed as to fit on the carbine and serve as a Bayonet at 40/-.[45] There is no evidence of their being either purchased or taken into British service.

Although there are no rifles listed amongst the Dutch stores taken when the British occupied the Cape Colony in September 1795, there are a number of references indicating that Dutch rifles taken here were later used by regiments in British service. Indeed it is almost certain that the first *ad hoc* rifle company formed from regular British regiments since 1793 were armed with captured Dutch rifles. At some point during 1799, the local Kaffir tribesmen were murdering and robbing the "upcountry" Boer farmers, and as part of their response to these depredations, the British formed a rifle company at Wynberg near Capetown, from men of the 8th Dragoons, and the 22nd, 34th, 65th, 81st and 91st Regiments of Foot. The company was placed under the command of Captain Effingham Lindsay of the 22nd Foot. A member of the company recalled that they were uniformed in green and that the barrels of their rifles were browned "to prevent them being seen in the woods." This company operated for "upwards of two years" in the area of South West Africa, and when the Cape Colony was returned to the Dutch in 1801, they were sent to India.[46] There is another brief reference to a Dutch-service rifle corps serving in South Africa as part of the Dutch forces to whom the British handed over the Cape Colony in February 1803: "The Rifle Corps are a few French and the rest Poles, near 1000 men."[47] These men had come out from Europe as part of the new garrison, and it is highly likely that the "old Dutch" rifles subsequently carried by several units in British service may have originated with this Dutch Franco/Polish unit at the Cape. Given the timing, it is possible that these rifles were the Batavian Republic's Model 1798 Jäger Rifle (see image "i" in the Dutch guns illustration shown earlier). The design of this Dutch rifle is suggestively close to that of the Baker rifle adopted two years later by the British Board of Ordnance.

Late in 1799, a regiment of riflemen was authorized to be raised by the exiled Dutch Prince of Orange as part of the Dutch Emigrant Brigade; this appears to be the first recognizable rifle regiment in British service, as well as the largest at the time. There were no suitable rifles available from Ordnance stores for this regiment, so an agreement was signed in June 1800 for 1,012 rifles with sword bayonets and cleaning implements to be made by the Hesse-Cassel gunmaker And. Herman

Thornbeck. Several rifles, some with their cleaning tools and powder measure still in the butt-trap, which are probably part of this production, remain in the Royal Armouries Museum collection. The Board said it had no objection to His Serene Highness the Hereditary Prince of Orange purchasing rifles in Germany for the Corps of Riflemen under his command, and a sum of £1000 towards their cost was approved by the Board.[48] A further £1600 was paid by the Board in October 1800.[49] (See Appendix 7.) All of these were finished, delivered and paid for by October 1800, by which time the regiment was stationed at Lymington.[50] It seems likely that the raising and equipping of this 1,000-man regiment by the Prince of Orange aided the War Office in its decision to raise a purely British rifle regiment. It may even have served as a pattern for the new regiment.

By September 1801, this Dutch corps was stationed on Jersey from where the Inspector of the First Battalion of Dutch Light Infantry, H. Power, reported that "there is amongst them a number of good Marksmen, and almost one Half are sure of their Man at the distance of Two Hundred Yards."[51]

Despite moves towards the adoption of a British-made military rifle, the Baker rifle, the purchase of foreign-made rifles continued. On 31 July 1800, the Board ordered £756.2.7. paid to Col. J.C. Bentinck for 374 serviceable rifled musquets "of foreign manufacture" which he had purchased and delivered to the Tower.[52]

In November 1800, with the six battalions of the 60th Foot already formed and Manningham's new Rifle Corps having already received its baptism of fire, the Horse Guards sent to the Secretary to the Board of Ordnance "...a Return of the number of men in the British Service for whom Rifle Arms are required, agreeable to the tenor of your letter of yesterday."[53] As so often happens, the return with its invaluable statement of numbers, has not survived.

The Treaty of Amiens, signed on 27 March 1802, brought not so much a peace as a mutually welcome armistice, rather like that of 1748, to Britain and France. There was a large-scale disbanding and reduction of British regiments, and most of the small units of foreign riflemen were disbanded, some of them to be incorporated into units again raised with the outbreak of war with Napoleon's French Empire in May 1803.

Although no rifle production had been initiated by the Board of Ordnance, by the end of the French Revolutionary Wars they had acquired, through purchase and capture, a minimum of 8,800 foreign-made rifles which can be accounted for if not always identified, plus many hundreds more such rifles which had come with rifle units raised for British service on the Continent, chiefly before 1796. Many of these were probably lost on service, especially in the West Indies, which saw the highest concentration of rifle use after the withdrawal of British and allied forces from the Continent at the end of 1795. By the end of 1797 a decision had been taken to incorporate as many foreign troops as possible into new battalions of the 60th (Royal American) Regiment of Foot, a multi-battalion regiment formed in 1755–6 deliberately to attract foreigners into British service. Virtually all of the rifle-armed troops which had survived West Indian service were taken into the all-rifle 5th battalion of the 60th established at the end of December 1797.

If much of the above narrative seems disconnected and vague, it must be admitted, in conclusion, that much too little is known about the specific details of rifle use by British-allied troops during the French Revolutionary Wars. Careless, undated, ambiguous and imprecise use of terminology, nomenclature and unit designations in primary source material of the period makes it extremely difficult and sometimes impossible to clearly identify rifle-armed units during the 1790s. The frequent use of the term "chasseur" interchangeably to mean either light infantry or riflemen greatly complicates the separation of the latter from the former. There were also many small rifle-armed units scattered amongst European armies, some of them for a very short period of time; it was common practice to arm a few men of each company in a regiment with rifles, sometimes in addition to a rifle company, and "chasseur" companies were variously armed with light muskets and/or rifles in varying proportions which often cannot be established. Countries, rulers, commanders and units changed their allegiances and names with bewildering rapidly during the period. From the date of their first introduction during the first half of the 18th century, most military rifles were closely patterned on the Germanic sporting rifle. The same pattern of rifle was sometimes adopted as a standard for more than one unit, possibly supplying the units of more than one country. While there is, on the one hand, considerable documentary evidence, and on the other, a large selection of rifles which can be dated to the period, efforts at linking the documents to the rifles have, to date, been fairly unsuccessful.

"Not a has-been, just a never-was"

In addition to the heterogenous groups of rifles which were actually used by a few British troops and a far larger number of foreign troops in British pay during the period of the French Revolutionary Wars, the Board of Ordnance considered a number of designs for military rifles, all of which were quickly rejected. A number of these hopefuls survive today with Ordnance markings on them, and must thus be accounted for.

In 1801, the Covent Garden sword cutler and gunmaker James Wilkes submitted a breech-loading rifle to *(top view)* **The 1801 experimental screwplug breech-loading rifle by James Wilkes, which received unusually detailed attention from Manningham's new rifle corps for four years before being rejected.** *Courtesy of the Trustees of the Royal Armouries Museum, Leeds.*

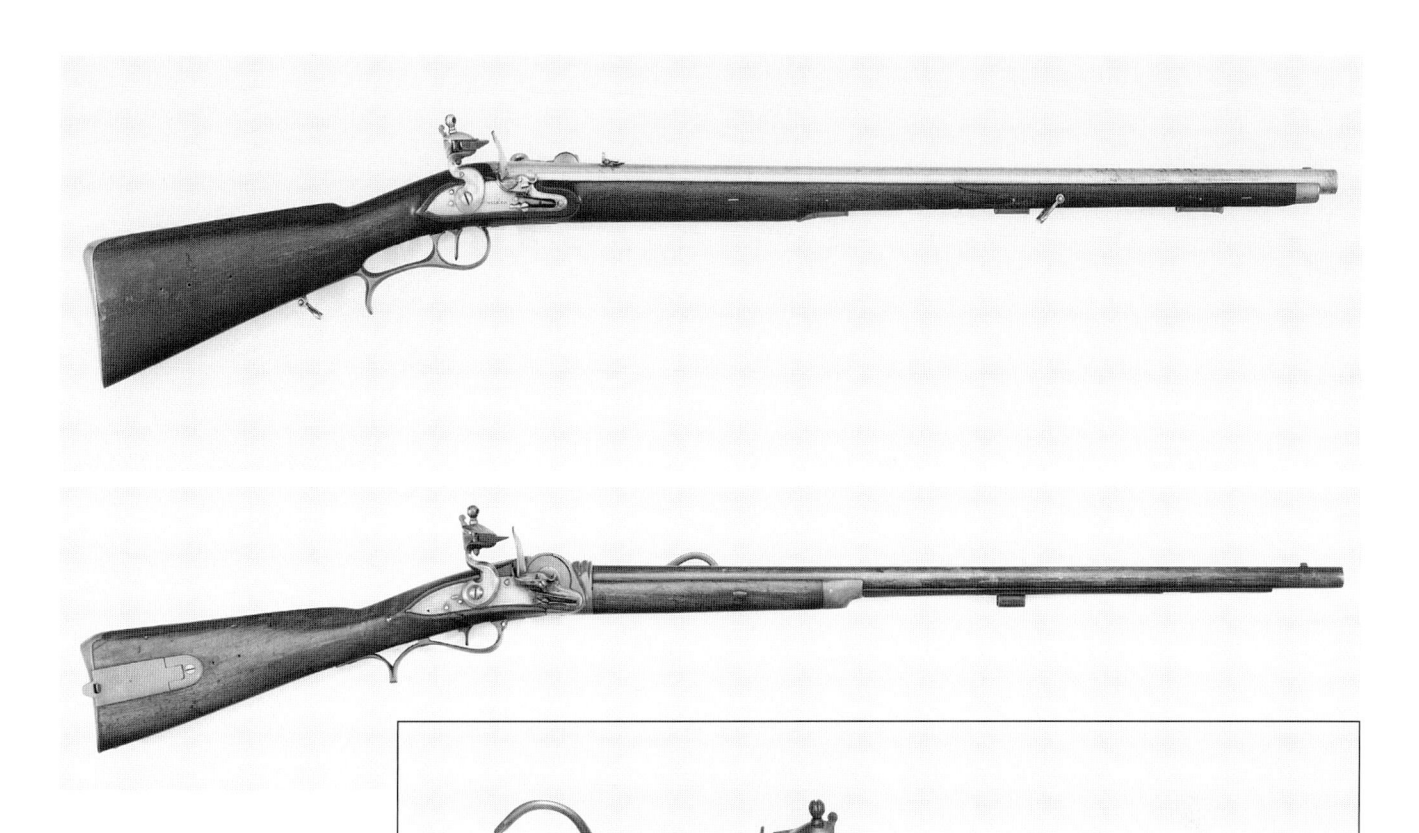

(bottom two views) **An adaptation of the long-established Lorenzoni system of breech-loading by a Mr. Hulme or Helme was sanctioned by a Committee of Field Officers in 1807. Despite twenty examples being purchased, there is no further record of trials or even of rejection by the Ordnance or the army. The frame or receiver is of bronze.** *Courtesy of the Trustees of the Royal Armouries Museum, Leeds.*

the Ordnance (see photo above) and it was unusually given the opportunity of trials, fairly extensive trials, by the new Rifle Corps under Coote Manningham at Caesar's Camp, Bagshot. After Manningham's initial trial, the Board requested Wilkes on 21 June to supply two more rifles with the sights adjusted to prevent the rifles shooting too much to the right, and with the diameter of the loading orifice at the breech made the same as that of the bore.[54] Consideration of the rifles dragged on for four years, until May 1805, when they were rejected, and Wilkes received eleven guineas for his trouble.

None of the structural features of the Wilkes rifle owes anything to the Baker rifle then being produced for the Ordnance. The breech mechanism was basically an old idea: a screwplug linked to the gun, in this case located so that the powder was loaded first, followed by the ball, the same sequence as followed with the conventional muzzle-loader; the innovation was in locating the opening on the left side of the breech, and in the design of the link and its base.

The impetus for the consideration of another breech-loading design came from a Committee of Field Officers rather than the Ordnance. In May 1807, this Committee ordered twenty examples of a pattern submitted by a Mr. Hulme or Helme, at a cost of five guineas each. Having apparently received the rifles, strangely there is no further reference to them in surviving records. Hulme's system (see above) was simply an adaptation, really a simplification, of the seventeenth-century mechanism designed by Lorenzoni (and a number of others), but eliminating the elaborate and delicate magazines for powder and ball, and the self-priming device often included. This single-shot version was loaded by revolving the lever along the left side, which turned a cylinder or drum set across the breech of the barrel, exposing the breech and a loading cutaway on the drum. The ball was loaded first, followed by the powder, a poor system, since the fouling forced a change in the exact seating of the ball after a few shots and thereby increasingly altered the point of impact of the ball.

CHAPTER 9
The Baker Infantry Rifle, 1800–1814

What came to be known as "the Baker Rifle" was created and developed in an atmosphere of "rifle consciousness" within the Board of Ordnance and increasing use of rifles by British armed forces. As we have seen in Chapter Eight, many thousands of rifles were already in Ordnance Stores and in the hands of various companies on active service from the Caribbean to the Mediterranean. Throughout its operational life "the Baker Rifle" was always referred to, when it was necessary to be specific, simply as "the Infantry Rifle" to distinguish it from "the Cavalry Rifle." Baker's name was not used until after the introduction of "Lovell's Improved Brunswick percussion rifle" in the early 1840s. Even today there is no clear indication of how much of the finished weapons' design was contributed by Ezekiel Baker; even the use of the twist of a quarter-turn in the rifling in British military rifle barrels may not have originated with Baker.

The first indications that the Board of Ordnance was once again considering the manufacture of a rifle of its own (as opposed to purchasing new or second-hand foreign imports) appear in late 1799, when Ezekiel Baker delivered seven different types of rifle barrels fitted with various designs of sights. These formed the basis for a series of trials before a Committee of Field Officers at Woolwich in January and February 1800, which included various other rifling systems and barrel designs.

Woolwich 14 Feby 1800
Report of Experiments carried on at Woolwich in consequence of the Honble Boards order of the 4 Inst with two Rifled Barrels to ascertain their Comparative Execution, by firing them at the Distance of 300 Yards into a Target of Fir Plank of 2 Inches in Thickness, its height was 11 Feet and breadth 9 Feet, Twelve Rounds were fired from the Barrels, when fixed into a Mortar Bed Weighing about 25 cwt in such a manner as to be perfectly immoveable and afterwards Twelve Rounds were fired when mounted in their Stocks from the Shoulder; The Wind blew rather Strong forming an Angle of nearly 45°. The Balls were placed in a greased Leather Patch the Charges of Powder and Description of Barrells are as follows.
Description of Mr Egg's Barrel

			Ins. D
Length	Exterior		39.08
	Bore		38.55
Diameter	Breech		1.7
	Muzzle		0.9
	Bore		0.65
Depth of Rifles			0.015
Weight			4.15 ozs
No of Rifles			8

Obliquity in Length of Bore Turn ¾ 18 out of 24 hits[1]

Durs Egg Target, February 1800

Woolwich Trials targets of February 1800 which led to the adoption by the Board of Ordnance of Ezekiel Baker's design of rifling for infantry rifles. Eight barrels were fired at 300 yards, 12 rounds each from a fixed mortar bed and from the shoulder (except Baker's where only 12 were fired from the mortar bed), in the order illustrated: Durs Egg, Ezekiel Baker, Samuel Galton, Mr. German, numbers 3, 4 and 5, and Henry Nock. The first target, Egg's, is shown here, others are on the next page.

— 105 —

Ezekiel Baker | **Samuel Galton, #1** | **Mr. German, #2** | **Barrel #3**

Barrel #4 | **Barrel #5** | **Henry Nock, #6**

More targets from the Woolwich Trials targets of February 1800 which led to the adoption by the Board of Ordnance of Ezekiel Baker's design of rifling for infantry rifles. The first two targets (Egg's, shown on the previous page, and Baker's) may have been fired separately, seeing as they are not included in the numbered sequence or the table of results below.

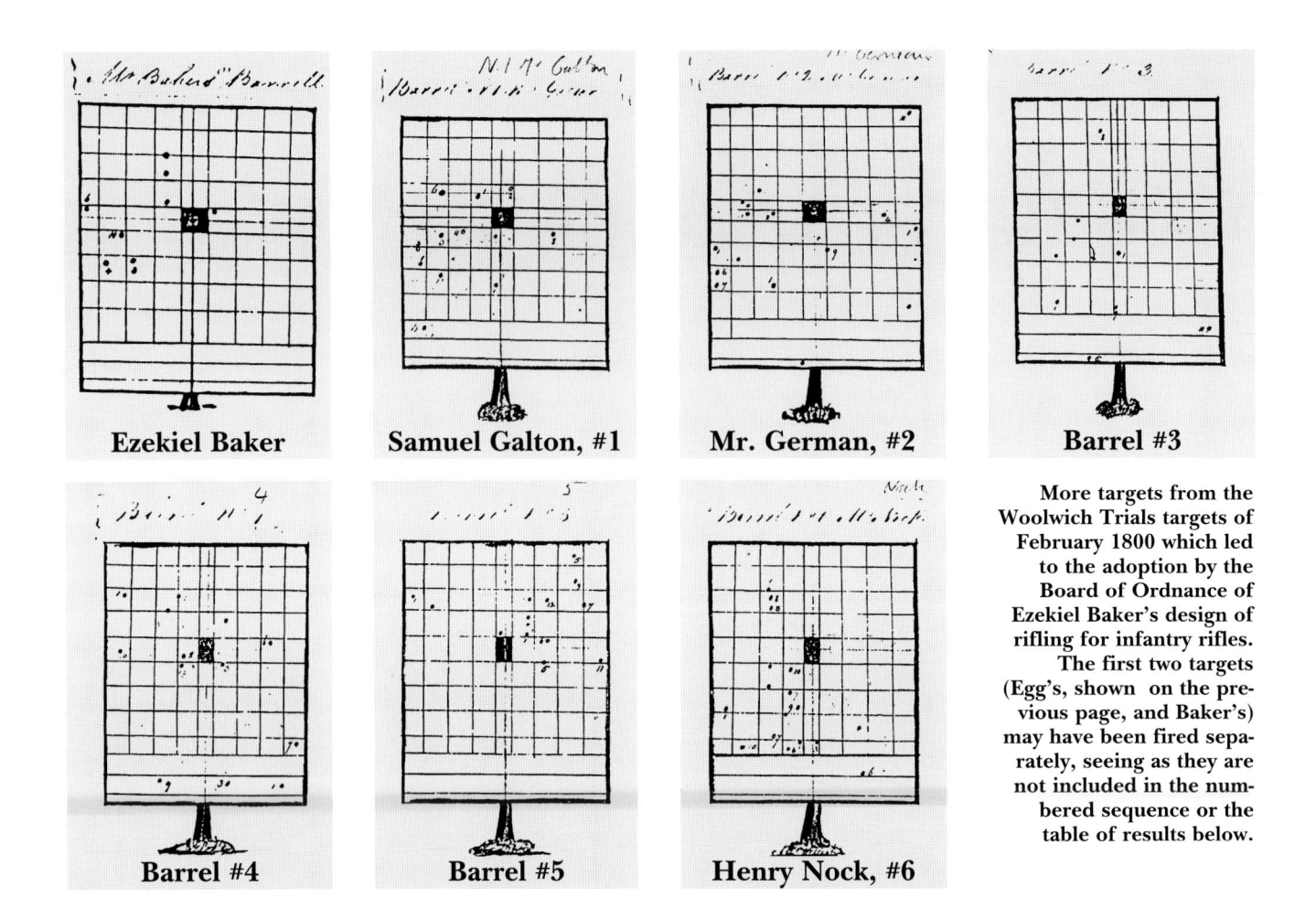

Baker's barrel is not described. The target shows only 8 hits and no second round of 12.

Experiments with Six Rifle Barrels conditions as above. No 1 from Galton, No. 2 from 'Mr. German' and No. 6 from Mr Nock.

No.	Length	Weight	Diameter Br	Diameter Muz	Diameter Bore	Depth Rifl	No. Grvs	Twist	Charge drams	No.Balls /lb
1	27.9	3.8.9	1.15	1.0	.63	.015	8	½	3	19
2	28.50	4.12.12	1.25	1.06	.61	.015	7	1	3	22
3	27.95	4.8.0	1.27	1.07	.76	.01	8	¾	5	11
4	29.5	3.12.11	1.16	0.87	.68	.015	8	¾	4	17
5	28.1	3.7.2	1.16	1.2	.64	.01	8	½	3	19
6	38.9	4.4.12	1.17	0.9	.74	.015	8	¾	4½	13½

Hits (target diagrams and tables, see illus)

1. 11 hits, 1 out low
2. 15 hits, 1 out low
3. 8 hits, 2 out low
4. 10 hits, 3 out low
5. 13 hits
6. 16 hits, 1 out low. Vertical stringing, best grouping.[2]

Baker himself, in his usual modest way, described the trials of 1800 in the eleven editions of his self-laudatory book *Remarks on Rifle-Guns*:

In 1800, the Government being about to raise a rifle regiment, a Committee of Field Officers was appointed by the Board of Ordnance to fix on the best kind of arms for their use, and several gunmakers were desired to send in specimens. There were barrels of French, German, Spanish, Dutch, American, and all nations, brought forward in competition: but mine beat them all, in a trial at Woolwich before the Committee – the distance three hundred yards. My barrel was two feet six inches, with a twenty to the pound bore ball, rifled one quarter turn in the angle of the barrel; and so highly was it approved of, that I afterwards mounted it as a pattern for military use.[3]

EARLY BAKER PRODUCTION

Pattern 1800 Rifles

Ezekiel Baker supplied two pattern rifles and two each of barrels at 24/- each and locks on 12 March 1800.[4] A month later, presumably using the original patterns supplied by Baker, contractor Joseph Grice of Birmingham supplied 20 "Rifled Musquets, Musquet Proof Bore, for Patterns" and a further 10 in Carbine Proof bore "for Patterns" and Birmingham gunmaker Robert Wheeler junior supplied 11 musket proof bore and 20 carbine proof bore "rifled musquets" all as patterns, and all priced at 48/- each.[5] There were therefore at least 31 musket-bore rifles and 30 carbine-bore patterns in addition to the two Baker examples (one in each bore size?) for distribution amongst the contractors who would manufacture the new rifle. Baker's own early deliveries included 59 musket-bore rifles, but the carbine bore was settled on for future production before the end of 1800.

The officially defined components of the new Infantry Rifle were listed as the Barrel, Steel Rammer, Lock, Stock and

Brasswork	*Small Work*
Heelplate	*Spring for rammer*
Trigger Guard (Handle)	*Trigger*
Sidepiece	*Breech Nail (tang screw)*
Trigger Plate	*Side Nails (lock screws) 2*
Thumb Piece	*Thumbpiece Nail*
Long Pipe	*Swivels, pair*
Short Pipe	*Woodscrews, large, 2*
Nose Cap	*Breakoff (False breech)*
Joint for Box	*Bolts (slides, keys) 3*
Plate for Box	*Spring for Box*
	Elevating Sight
	Small Nail for breakoff
	Foresight, brass
	Iron pinning wire in 6" lengths

In addition to the indecision about the most useful bore size there was some question about the utility of the buttbox (butt-trap, patchbox) with its heavy brass lid, used for holding tools and patches. At first, rifles were made with and without buttboxes, but by 1802 the utility of the compartment had been accepted. Most of the rifles already made without buttboxes were altered by the gunmakers to include them.

As indicated in Chapter 8, certain components which ended up in the early Baker rifles may have been designed and ordered as early as 1798.

Rifle barrels were originally supplied in two materials: best iron forged from skelp at 13/- each and best iron twisted the whole length at 20/- each. The initial barrel order was for 3,000, 1,500 of each type.[6] Thanks to a general lack of rifling benches in the gun-trade the barrels were supplied smoothbored and then issued to contractors who possessed the necessary equipment. Durs Egg was the first contractor apart from Baker himself to sign on for this work, which included rifling the bore, fitting the sights and bayonet-bar, and browning the barrel, for which he received 22/- each.[7] Henry Nock was the third gunmaker to carry out this function, and during 1800 a total of 578 barrels were finished in this manner by these three contractors. In 1801, a further 1,054 barrels were completed in this way, indicating that many barrels did come from the rifle fabricators in a complete state.

During the production period of the Pattern 1800 rifle, barrels were supplied by Joseph Bayliss, Thomas Gill, John & Samuel Heely & Co., Gad Parsons, William Rock, Thomas Russell, John Simes, Thomas Stokes, Taylor & Davis, John Tru(e)man, Robert Wheeler junior, and Mary Willetts. Only 101 musket-bore barrels were supplied (all in plain iron), not including the pattern rifles, the balance of the 2,458 barrels being carbine-bore, of which only 88 were in plain iron. During 1801, the method of supply changed and barrels came in as part of completed arms, although generally still requiring to be finished by rifling, sighting, fixing the bayonet bar and browning. The first rifle barrels were delivered (by Thomas Russell) in June 1800.[8]

Locks for the Pattern 1800 were supplied by James Negus, Joseph Sherwood, Peter Spittle (in 1801 only) James Wilkes, Mary Willetts and Joseph Wood. Locks without detents were paid for at the rate of 8/-, while those with detents brought 8/6. In the autumn of 1801, Ezekiel Baker (500) and Henry Nock (275) fitted detents to 775 locks originally supplied without them, receiving 6d. each for the work. The total of locks delivered in 1800–01 amounts to 1,710 of which 1,446 were originally without detents and 264 with detents; 775 were subsequently fitted, indicating that 671 locks may have survived without flies.

Smallwork when supplied directly to the Small Gun Office Stores in the Tower came from James Bailey, but during this period the contractors often supplied their own (possibly purchased directly from Bailey). The same holds true for brasswork: most was furnished by the contractors along with the stocks, but Jane Mayor did supply some sets of rifle brasswork to the Ordnance.

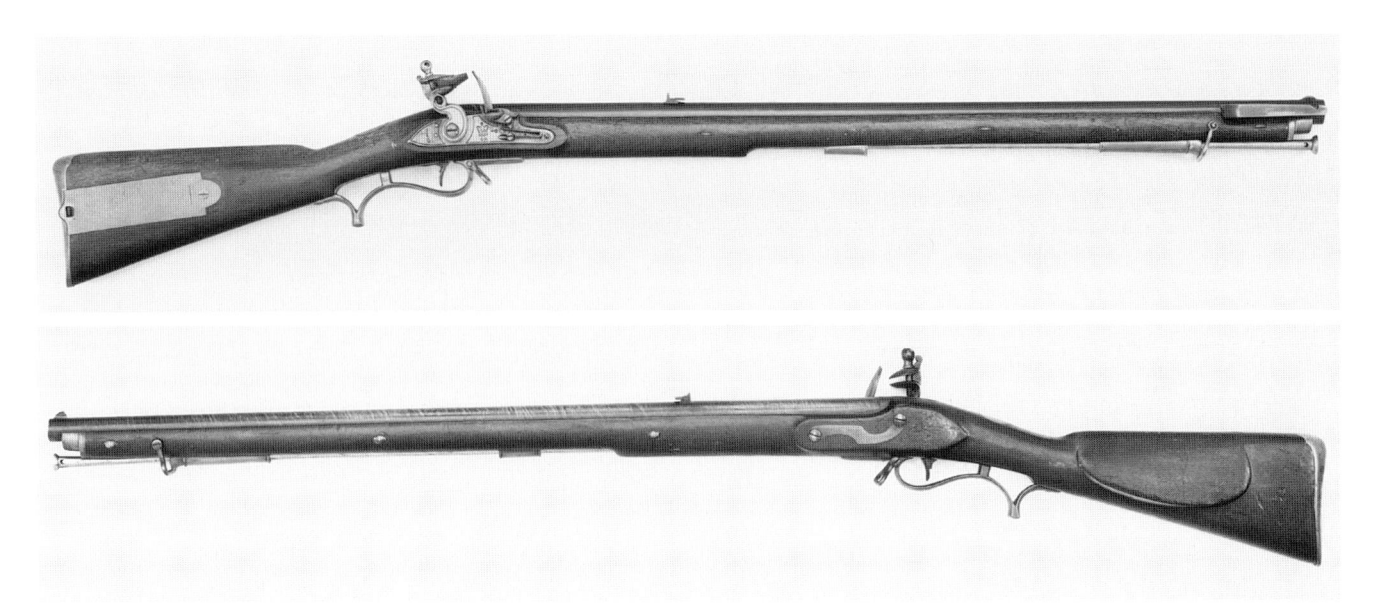

The Pattern 1800 Infantry Rifle. Usually referred to during its working life as "the Infantry Rifle" or "rifled musquet" or "rifled carbine" — the latter because of not only its shorter than musket barrel but also its calibre, and only later in the 19th century called "the Baker rifle." *Courtesy of the Trustees of the Royal Armouries Museum, Leeds.*

The specially designed sword bayonet for the Baker rifle (see illustration in Chapter 12) was designed by the Birmingham sword cutler Henry Osborn, who also supplied 502 of the 990 bayonets delivered during 1800, and 2,473 of the 3,043 supplied during 1801. Joshua Johnstone supplied 200 sword bayonets in autumn 1800.[9] James Woolley supplied the balance, 288 in 1800 and 570 in 1801.

The first complete Baker rifles to be turned into Ordnance Stores arrived during September; contractors billed at the end of September 1800 include Ezekiel Baker, Thomas Barnett, Martin Brander, Durs Egg, Harrison & Thompson, Samuel Pritchett, Thomas Reynolds, James Wilkes and Robert Wright. David Blair, Ketland & Walker, Henry Nock, Robert Wheeler junior and Mary Willetts all appeared as suppliers before the close of 1800. In the course of 1801 contractors Samuel Galton, Joseph Grice and Henry & John Whately joined the list of contractors supplying Baker rifles. Most of the rifles turned into Store during these two years came from the contractors 'without barrels, locks and bayonets, to be rifled' and either with or without buttboxes. Those without boxes (the majority) were priced at 32/-, while those fitted with buttboxes were allowed at 36/-. This means that the Ordnance supplied to the contractors the items listed as "without," the contractors supplying the remaining components and the labour of rough-stocking, setting up and finishing the rifles.

During 1800, 741 rifles were supplied without buttboxes and 272 with boxes. These figures include all the 59 musket-bore examples (not patterns) of which 43 did not have boxes. For a complete Infantry Rifle with buttbox, rifled, sighted and browned, with sword bayonet, Baker was allowed 97/-.

Deliveries of Infantry Rifles for the first half of 1801 totalled 1,240, of which 726 were made with boxes and without boxes 514. In July 1801, Nock and Baker were ordered to fit buttboxes into the stocks of the remaining finished rifles in the Tower, in the Engraving Room.[10] Baker was billed for completing 400 such jobs, and Nock 344. Deliveries for the second half of 1801 amounted to 92 to the end of September, all with buttboxes, when production of a new pattern, really a "subspecies" commenced, the "Rifle for West India Regiments" discussed below.

Deliveries of Pattern 1800 Baker Infantry Rifles from September 1800 to September 1802, totaled 59 musket-bore and 960 carbine-bore, (excluding 31 patterns for the former and 60 patterns for the latter) in 1800 and 1,382 in 1801, for a grand total of 2,342 of this pattern. Government records whose sources are not identified claim that 44 rifles were turned in during 1803 and a further 345 in 1804, but no information supporting these deliveries has been found in the Ordnance records for that period. It is possible that they were made by the workforce in the Small Gun Office in 1803, or possibly by the newly organized Royal Manufactory of Small Arms in the Tower of London in 1804, but at the time of writing this cannot be confirmed.

In February 1802, Baker billed the Ordnance for fitting buttboxes to 635 rifles in the hands of the Rifle Corps at Weymouth and Blatchington Barracks, charging 4/- each including travelling expenses for his workmen.[11]

The first colonel of the Rifle Corps, Coote Manningham, was reimbursed £23.2.10. by the Board of Ordnance for having his rifles regimentally marked in July 1801.

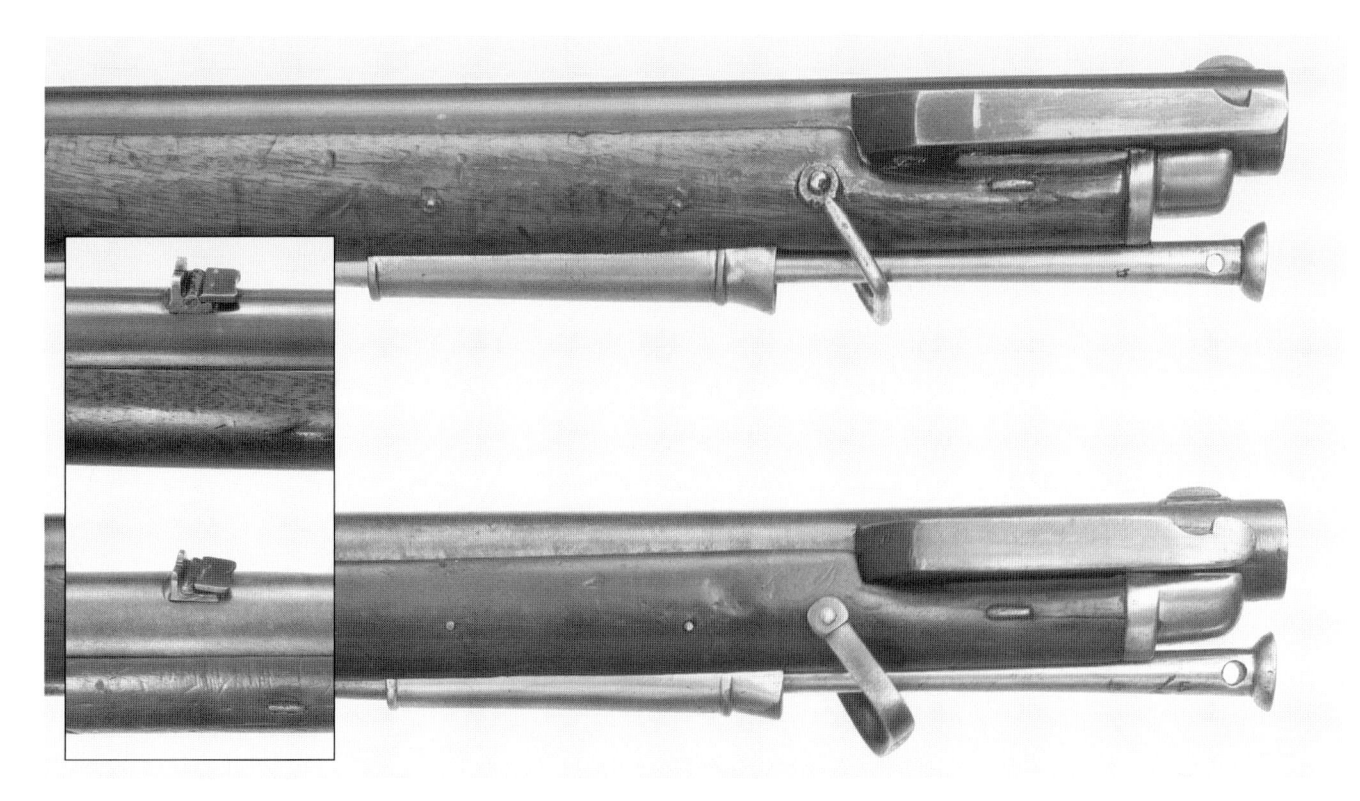

Sets of tools intended to be carried in the buttbox along with cut patches were supplied by Ezekiel Baker, Henry Nock and Joseph Sherwood during this first production period. A set consisted of "ball drawer, wiping eye and lever" for which the suppliers were allowed 1/6 per set (see photo in Chapter 13).

The Pattern 1800 Baker Infantry Rifle was frequently referred to during its working life, particular by the military, as a "rifled carbine" and its overall length of about 46 inches certainly agrees with eighteenth-century definitions of carbine length. By the mid-nineteenth century it would have been considered a "Short Rifle." (See Appendix 1 for a detailed technical description of this and subsequent Baker rifle patterns).

The usually twist-iron but occasionally plain iron barrel is 30¼" in length, round and tapered overall from just over one inch at the breech to about .870" to .890" at the muzzle. The breechplug is formed externally as a hook, and the stock is inlet with a false breech secured by a wood screw, into which the "hut" hooks to secure the barrel at the breech. There are three rectangular tenons or loops on the underside of the barrel, through which three flat slides or keys pass from the left side of the forestock to the right; in addition the heavy loop for the upper sling-swivel screw also acts to hold the barrel in the stock. The brass foresight is a rounded blade about one-half inch long, formed as one piece with a baseplate about ³⁄₃₂" wide, which is brazed into a shallow

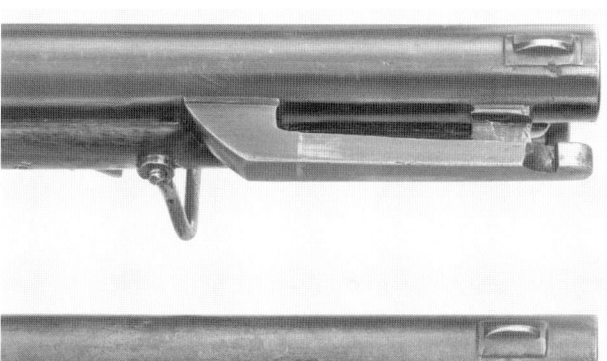

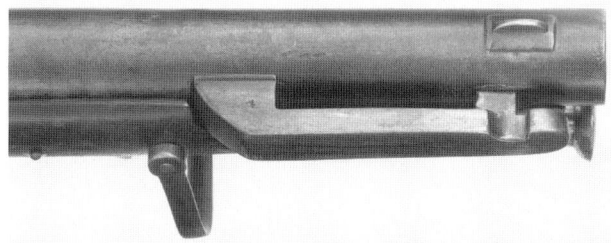

Early Infantry Rifle sights and bayonet-bars. The bayonet-bar was dovetailed and brazed to the right side of the muzzle on all but one sub-pattern of this rifle. Note also the form and size of the steel-blade foresight, and the New Land Pattern nosecap. The block backsight with a single hinged leaf was dovetailed into the barrel on the Pattern 1800 and 1805 rifles. *Courtesy of the Trustees of the Royal Armouries Museum, Leeds.*

dovetail in the barrel one-quarter inch from the muzzle. The notched block backsight has one hinged leaf about ⁷⁄₁₆" long lying to the front, and is dovetailed into the barrel about 6¹¹⁄₁₆" from the breech. A bayonet- or "sword"-bar (see photos) is located on the right side of the barrel, dovetailed and brazed in position. It mea-

The standard pattern lock for the Infantry Rifle used on all patterns of the rifle until the final one of 1823 when a change was made to a rounded carbine virtually indistinguishable from that of the Pattern 1798 Heavy Dragoon Carbine. The lockmaker's name or initials are sometimes stamped externally as shown.
Courtesy of the Trustees of the Royal Armouries Museum, Leeds.

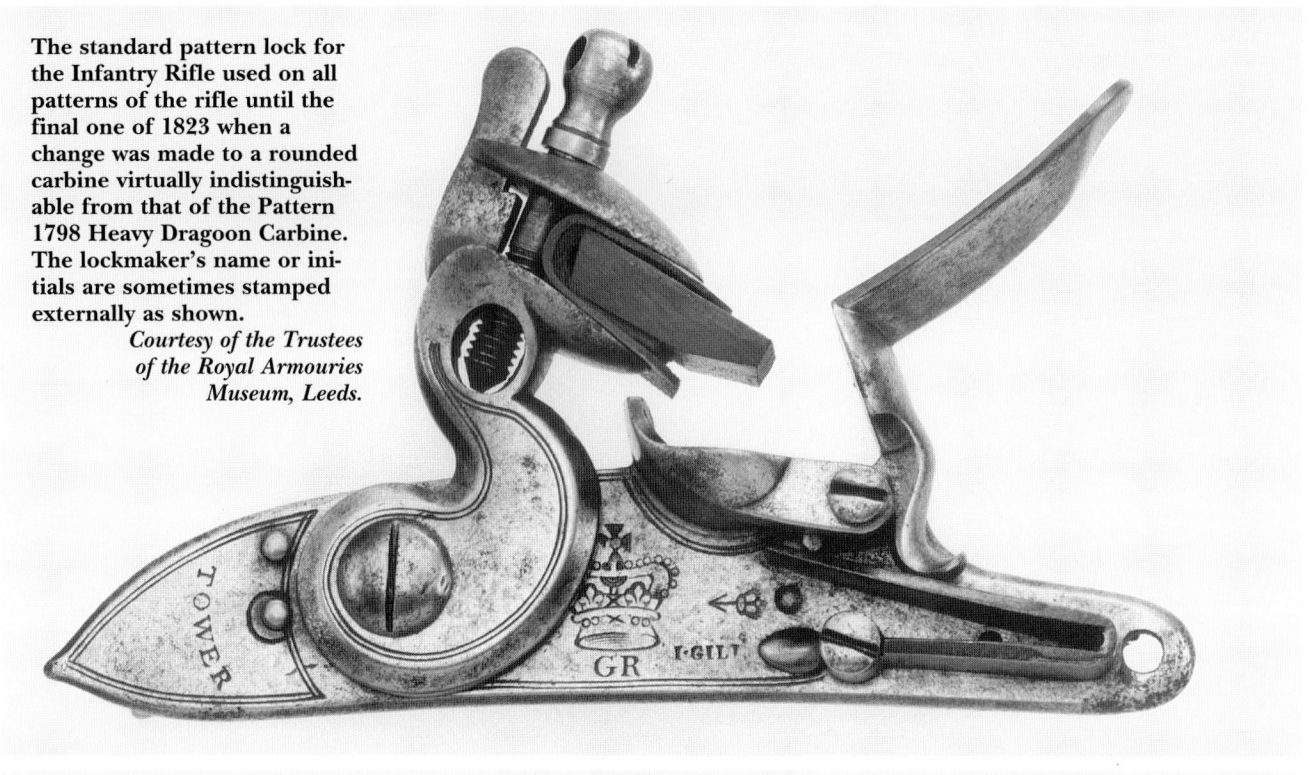

sures about 3¹¹⁄₁₆" long x ⁷⁄₁₆" wide, with a notch cut into the upper edge about ⅜" from the front. The left side of the breech is stamped with the King's Proofmarks (the Proof and View marks) and occasionally with a barrel maker's mark. This latter is more often found (when present at all) on the underside of the barrel.

The bore was described as "carbine-bore" interpreted in this case as .625" taking a ball of 20 to the pound of lead or .615". It is rifled with seven rectangular grooves of uniform depth, just slightly narrower than the lands, making one-quarter turn in the length of the barrel, or one complete turn in 120 inches. The muzzle is slightly counterbored or "crowned" to protect the ends of the grooves, but there is no relieving or funneling of the bore itself to aid in the seating of patched balls as there is with the Pattern 1776 Rifle barrels.

The Baker Infantry Rifle, 1800–1814

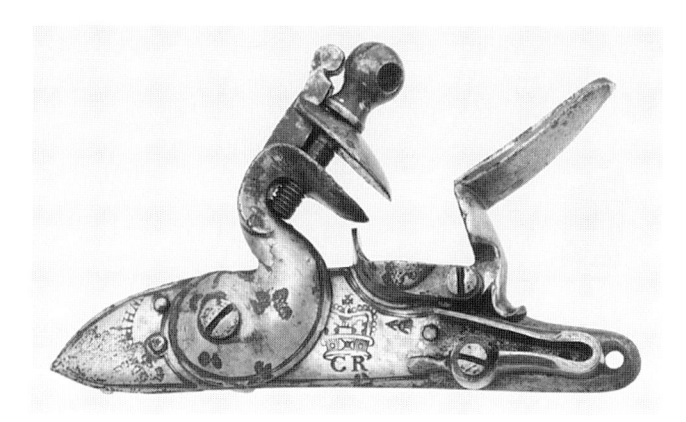

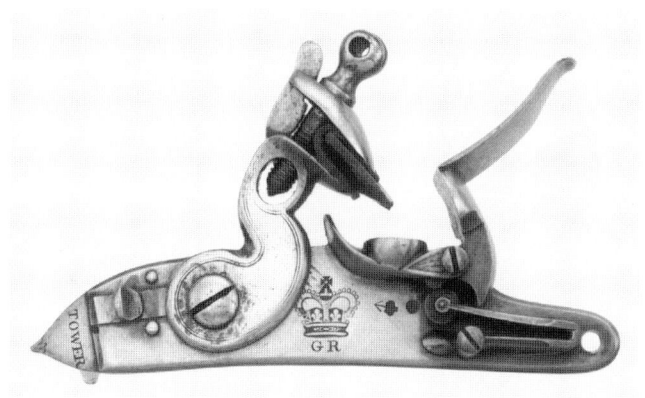

Two lock variations found on examples in the Royal Armouries collection. (top) is a privately produced lock incorrectly applied to a Pattern 1800 rifle. (bottom) appears on a single example of the Pattern 1805, and may be an "improved" pattern which, for the sake of economy and speed of delivery, never went beyond this prototype.
Courtesy of the Trustees of the Royal Armouries Museum, Leeds.

Until the production of the Pattern 1823 the Baker rifle lock was of one basic pattern (see photos on previous page). The lockplate is flat with a narrow bevelled edge and measures about 5⅜" long x 1 1/16" wide. It has a plain pan whose cavity is teaspoon-shaped. The ring-neck or throat-hole cock is also flat with a bevelled edge and the comb has a slight curve at the rear similar to that on the India Pattern. The top jaw is oval and slotted to act vertically along the comb. The tumbler is frequently but not invariably fitted with a detent or "fly." The markings and decoration are all stamped rather than engraved, including the double border lines on lockplate and cock body. The government ownership mark of a Crowned Broad Arrow is stamped beneath the pan, and ahead of the cock the lockplate is stamped with a Crowned GR. Across the tail is stamped the word TOWER. The lockmaker's initials are normally stamped on the inner surface of the lockplate along with the crowned numeral of an Ordnance lock inspector. There is one variant that has been seen on a few rifles, which might best be described as the "New Land Pattern rifle lock." This has a raised or semi-waterproof pan with a parallel-sided cavity, and the lockplate and cock lack any decorative borderline engraving or stamping. It would appear that this more expensive lock was briefly put into production, but then dropped in favour of the cheaper conventional pattern previously described. To confuse the issue, the collection in the Royal Armouries Museum, Leeds, contains two examples, one a Pattern 1800 and the other a Pattern 1805, with differing lock patterns which are now believed to be unique examples either as suggested patterns or unsuccessful experiments. The rounded lock with swan-neck cock (photo this page) is a privately produced example, and the so-called "Paget" lock on the Pattern 1805 (see photo) with its raised pan, roller-equipped feather-spring, stepped lockplate tail and sliding safety bolt was almost certainly considered as too costly for the job. A third variant, also unique at the time of writing, is identical to the standard Baker lock but has a raised or "semi-waterproof" pan in the manner of the New Land Pattern.

The walnut stock of the Pattern 1800 Baker Rifle is full length to about ⅜" of the muzzle. The ⅜"-diameter ramrod channel is fairly shallow and open for most of its length, with the rammer not well protected by the wood. At the grip or wrist the stock is shaped with a semi-pistol grip in the Continental manner, and there is a raised cheekrest on the left side of the butt which is oval in outline along all but the comb area where it is straight. There are individual variations in the measurements, but they are approximately 6"x3" and about a half-inch wide, or 'high' along the bottom or outer edge. The cavity of the buttbox on the right side of the butt is formed in two sections, the one closest to the hinge being a 1⅜" diameter circular compartment, and the rear a rectangular compartment which varies in size from about 2⅛" to 1 15/16" long by 1⅜" to 1½" wide; the depth of both compartments varies from ⅝" to 15/16".

Stock markings include crowned numeral inspector's stamps towards the upper end of the ramrod channel and occasionally a stocker's initials or stockmaker's name to the rear of the second pipe. The sidepiece flat often has the initials of the stocker and an as yet uniden-

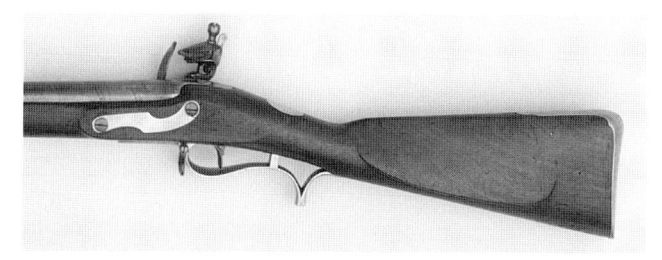

The raised cheekrest (cheekpiece) on the left butt of all Ordnance Baker rifles shows considerable minor variations in thickness and the outline of its edge largely due to the relaxation of inspection standards.
Courtesy of the Director, National Army Museum, London.

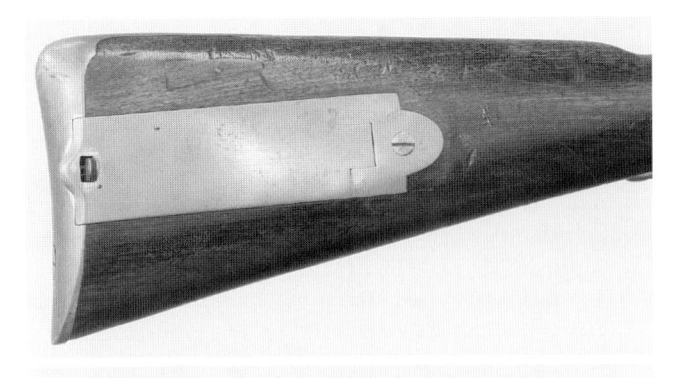

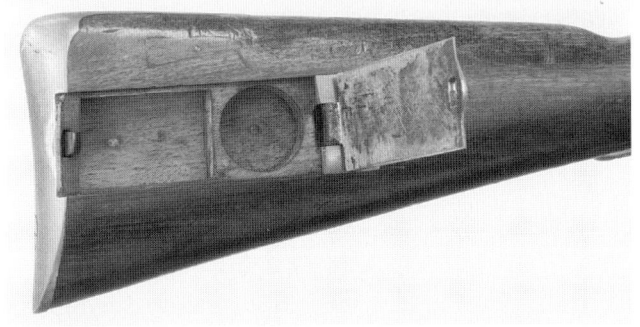

The salient feature of the Pattern 1800 Infantry Rifle is the single-stepped hingeplate of the butt-trap, with a two-compartment cavity in the butt for both cut greased patches and tools. *Courtesy of the Trustees of the Royal Armouries Museum, Leeds.*

tified "P" topped with three feathers. While this can be associated with the Prince of Wales's crest, its widespread use on most types of Ordnance small arms of this period is not yet explained. Two stock inspector's crowned numerals are usually stamped just below the rear triggerguard finial, and the Storekeeper's stamp is on the butt's right side, with or without a date beneath it. The conventional mark is sometimes replaced with a "View" mark of crowned crossed sceptres.

The brass furniture of the Baker rifle is of heavy construction throughout. The nosecap is of New Land Pattern with a pronounced lower lip to help retain the swelled steel rammer in its channel. There are two rammer pipes, the upper or long-trumpet pipe which is about 3⅝" in length and is secured by two cross-pins with the mouth about four inches from the tip of the forestock; the second pipe is of Pratt design, that is, a straight taper from front to rear with a narrow collar at each end. It is secured by a single cross-pin and is 1⅝" in length, located with its mouth about 2¾" below the rear of the trumpet-pipe. There is no tailpipe. The sidepiece is flat and flush with the surface of the stock, and is of a design which might be loosely described as reversed "C"s, a design first used by the Ordnance on the Pattern 1756 Light Dragoon Pistol and later on some Eliott carbines. The triggerguard is formed with a curved grip for the hand to the rear of the bow, which is supported by a pillar beneath its central section; there

is a screw through this pillar which serves to fasten the plain oval thumbpiece inlet into the upper surface of the grip. The front finial of the guard is heavily rounded on its surface and flat at the front. A ramrod-retaining spring is inlet into the inner surface of this finial and secured by the front guard screw. The lower finial is a plain rounded taper. In addition to the screw through the pillar, a woodscrew through the front and rear finials fix the guard to the stock. The cover or lid of the buttbox is one of the distinguishing features of the Pattern 1800 Baker Rifle: the hinge-plate with its centrally located woodscrew for fastening the plate to the stock, has a step in its curved outline which is absent on subsequent Baker buttbox covers. The cover is larger than on subsequent patterns, measuring just under six inches in overall length (the cover plate itself being five inches long) by about 1⅝" in width. The rear edge of the cover is formed with a protruding tab just forward of which there is a small rectangular slot in the body of the cover through which the fastening spring passes. The spring itself is embedded in the stock to the rear of the rectangular compartment. This cover is the only piece of Baker Infantry Rifle furniture which varies in its design. The buttplate is slightly rounded, or convex, and is secured to the stock by screws at the heel and near the toe of the plate, and by a cross-pin through a tenon on the underside of the tang. The tang has a step near the heel, a long parallel section and then a stepped 5/16" tapering finial to the tip.

The heavy steel rammer has a flared head terminating in a flattened button not much larger than the flared section beneath it. There is a hole through the flared head to take the "lever" or torque bar used in

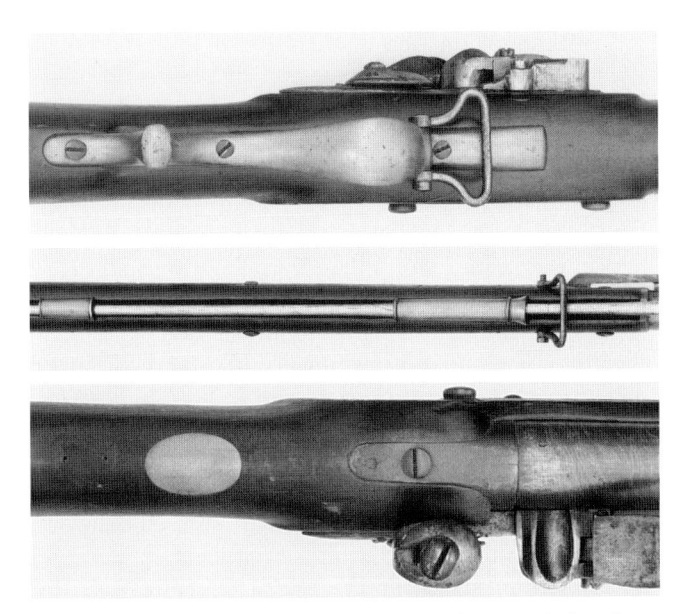

Baker Brass Furniture. Only the sidepiece and the short pipe resemble earlier furniture patterns. *Courtesy of the Trustees of the Royal Armouries Museum, Leeds.*

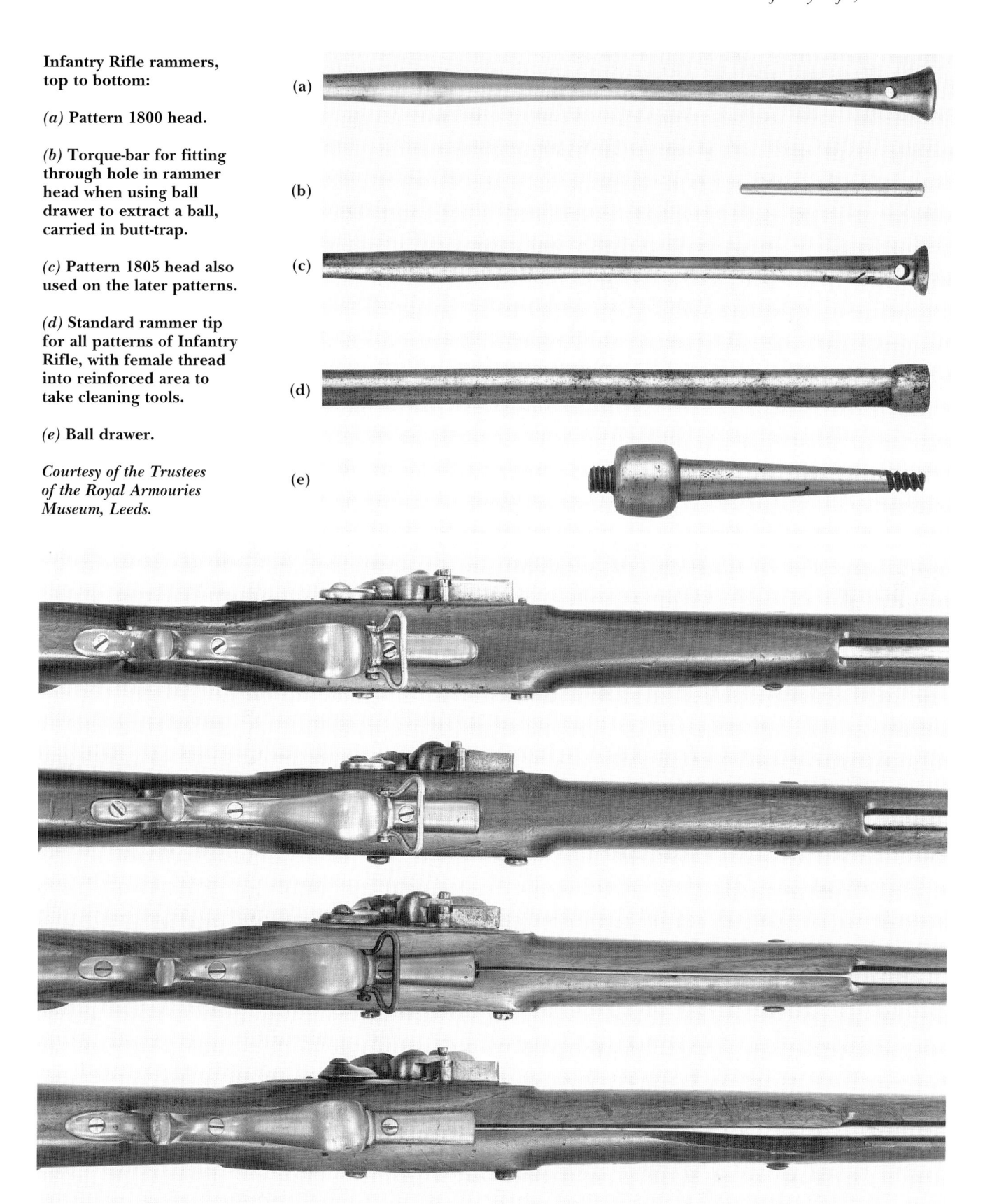

The Baker Infantry Rifle, 1800–1814

Infantry Rifle rammers, top to bottom:

(a) Pattern 1800 head.

(b) Torque-bar for fitting through hole in rammer head when using ball drawer to extract a ball, carried in butt-trap.

(c) Pattern 1805 head also used on the later patterns.

(d) Standard rammer tip for all patterns of Infantry Rifle, with female thread into reinforced area to take cleaning tools.

(e) Ball drawer.

Courtesy of the Trustees of the Royal Armouries Museum, Leeds.

Infantry Rifle forestocks. Pattern 1800 *(second from top)* and Pattern 1810 *(top, with rounded front finial to triggerguard)* stocks have no slit, but Pattern 1805 and latter patterns *(Pattern 1823 shown at bottom)* all have a slit to avoid the rammer becoming jammed in the stock from dirt or swelling from dampness.

Courtesy of the Trustees of the Royal Armouries Museum, Leeds.

– 113 –

withdrawing a ball from the barrel. There is a half-inch diameter symmetrical swell in the body of the rod about seven inches from the head. The tip of the rod is enlarged in diameter, slightly cupped on its surface (as it is used to seat the ball) and threaded for the tools which are carried in the buttbox.

Pattern 1801 Rifle For West India Regiments

The experiences of several rifle companies serving in the West Indies during the later 1790s apparently suggested to the Ordnance the wisdom of designing a "down-market" version of the new Infantry Rifle which would take into consideration the very primitive conditions, harsh climate, problematical storage facilities and degree of training of the troops most likely to be sent to that area. The result was the Infantry Rifle for West India Regiments which featured a plain iron carbine-bore barrel and "plain locks" (i.e. without detents) on all rifles, with half the production made without either sword-bar or buttbox.[12]

On 29 Sept. 1801, 800 rifles for regiments in the West Indies were ordered to be supplied complete except for the bayonets. Production was apportioned amongst eight contractors:

Nock	200	Barnett	75
Baker	100	Brander	75
Egg	100	Wright	75
Pritchett	100	Thomson	75

Those with buttboxes and sword-bars were allowed at £3.6.0. and those without either at £2.19.0.[13] The first deliveries were made during December 1801, when Baker, Barnett, Brander, Harrison & Thompson and Wright turned in a total of 400, 198 of which were of the cheaper version. Between January and the end of March 1802, a further 1,623 West India Infantry Rifles were delivered by David Blair, Durs Egg, Samuel Galton, Joseph Grice, Ketland & Walker, Henry Nock, Samuel Pritchett, Robert Wheeler junior, and Mary Willetts. Of these, 827 were without buttboxes and sword-bars. The total production of Pattern 1801 West India Regiments Infantry Rifles was 2,023 of which 1,025 did not have buttboxes or sword-bars.

At the time of writing, none of this pattern has been identified. It may be assumed that in its major design features it closely resembles the Pattern 1800 Rifle except for the items omitted on a proportion of the production. It is very likely that most or all which survived their original period of service in serviceable condition were subsequently fitted with sword-bars and buttboxes, making their positive identification impossible since it is not certain, because of the nature of later records, how many other plain, as opposed to twisted, barrels were supplied.

Pattern 1805 Infantry Rifle

Most unfortunately it is impossible to detail the production of components for the Pattern 1805 rifles in the same manner that the Pattern 1800 was described: with the organization of the Royal Manufactory in the Tower of London and the adoption of "open contracts" for the London and Birmingham contractors, in late 1805 the Board of Ordnance changed its system of record keeping, and the relevant ledgers no longer list deliveries of component parts. All that is described is the delivery of completed arms and the state in which they were delivered for payment purposes, i.e. completely supplied by the contractor in all its parts or "without" a number of parts, which were supplied to the contractors, their price being deducted from the final figure allowed the contractor.

On 28 June 1805, the Assistant Inspector of Small Arms, Thomas Alsop, informed the Board

that there were a considerable number of Rifles for Infantry under orders more than the Stores could supply, he therefore recommended that the 2000 Musquets of that description ordered to be Set up in the Rl Manufactory at the Tower should be distributed among the London Gunmakers in the following proportions, Viz:

Baker	300	Ashton	200
Marwood	250	Egg	150
Peake	250	Barnett	150
Brander	200	Wright	150
Thompson	200	Fearnley	150

Rifled barrels, soft-state locks, rammers and sword-bayonets should be delivered from Stores and that a price of £2 should be paid to the contractors for finding all the remaining components, rough stocking and setting up the rifles. This program was approved by the Board on 1 July.[14]

In November 1805, the Board issued an order for the open delivery of as many Infantry and Cavalry Rifle barrels as the makers could deliver for a period of six months. This order was revoked in mid-February 1806, but the Board received those either completed or in process under the order, as well as rifle rammers.[15] The following month the Board said they did not require more than 3,000 rifles of each type from the Birmingham trade; the Superintendant was therefore to ensure that no greater number of barrels was sighted, looped or rifled. Superintendent Miller's reply showed roughly 4,500 of each type on hand with the makers; he said there were totals of 12,911 Infantry and 10,772 Cavalry Rifle barrels in various stages of manufacture. The ceiling of 3,000 each to be completed was adhered to and the balances ordered to be completed excepting the rifling, looping and sighting and were to be kept in Store.[16]

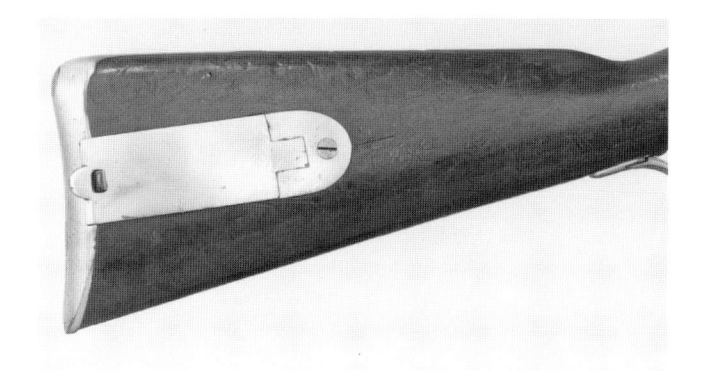

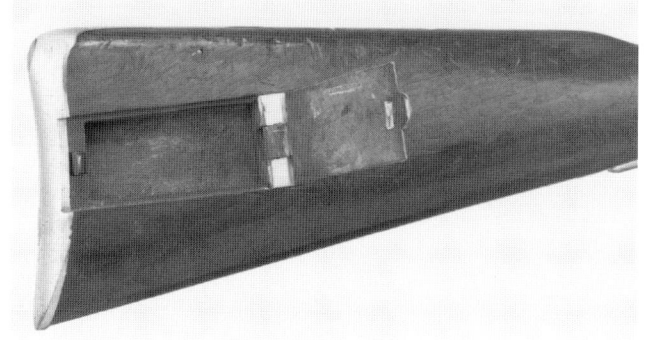

Pattern 1805 Infantry Rifle butt-trap cover with plain rounded outline hingeplate and single compartment cavity.
Courtesy of the Trustees of the Royal Armouries Museum, Leeds.

During May 1806, Miller agreed with the contractors for the prices of rifled barrels: 20/- for the Infantry and 14/3 for the Cavalry.[17]

In December 1810, the Board ordered that Ezekiel Baker was to rifle the Infantry Rifle barrels in Store in the Tower at the same price as paid for rifling in Birmingham[18] where it was done chiefly by Francis Arnold and John Gill. These names are sometimes found stamped on the underside of Baker rifle barrels.

In August 1811, Superintendent Miller informed the Board that 200 rifles per week could be set up in Birmingham, to which the Board replied by ordering 2,500 Infantry rifles set up.[19]

In its physical features, the Pattern 1805 Infantry Rifle differs in several cosmetic particulars from the Pattern 1800, some more obvious than others. The most obvious of these are the design and size of the buttbox cover (see photo) and the presence of a slit in the underside of the forestock of the Pattern 1805.

The twist-iron barrel is 30¼" in length, round and tapered overall from just over one inch at the breech to about .870" to .890" at the muzzle. It conforms in all other particulars to the Pattern 1800 barrel except that the backsight is mounted closer to seven inches (i.e. further) from the breech and the foresight, especially the base plate, is rather larger, as well as the blade being heavier. The breechplug is formed with a false breech the same as on the Pattern 1800. There is a reference to a change in the form of the false breech in June 1806,[20] but the exact nature of this change has not yet been identified. The barrel is secured to the stock in the same manner as the Pattern 1800, and the sword-bar is of the same design and measurements. Barrel markings are also the same. The particulars of the bore are the same as for the Pattern 1800.

There were no changes to the design of the Baker rifle lock used on the Pattern 1805, although as noted above there was at least one piece made with a much improved "Paget" pattern lock (see illustration earlier in this chapter), which probably proved too time-consuming and expensive to manufacture under the circumstances then existing. There is also at least one Pattern 1805 rifle with an otherwise standard lock which has a raised pan with the later parallel or U-shaped cavity. This probably represents an attempt at improvement which once again proved inexpedient from factors of time and cost.

The walnut stock of the Pattern 1805 Baker Rifle is in general of the same design as the Pattern 1800, but is made somewhat lighter overall — a difficult feature to quantify, but somehow "thinner" to the feel. The ⅜"-diameter ramrod channel is the same as on the previous pattern, but in the area from the entry point to the front finial of the triggerguard there is now found a ¹⁄₁₆" to ³⁄₃₂"-wide by 7½" to 7⁹⁄₁₆"-long slit down the forestock. This was intended to enable the soldier to keep the ramrod from being jammed by either dirt or swelled wood. The cheekrest on the left side of the butt is of the same general design as the Pattern 1800 but varies more in dimensions, with measurements from 6⁷⁄₁₆" to 7⅛" in length by 2¾" to 3" in width.

These and other variations within a given dimension are accounted for by the methods of manufacture and inspection forced on the Ordnance by the expansion of its manufacturing base to meet the greatly increased demands of both British and allied forces. The buttbox in both cavity and cover differs from the Pattern 1800 in being smaller and simpler in design. The cavity is now formed of a single rectangular space measuring about 2⁷⁄₁₆" to 2¾" long x 1³⁄₁₆" to 1⁵⁄₁₆" wide. Stock markings are the same as those noted for the Pattern 1800.

The brass furniture of the Pattern 1805, with the single exception of the buttbox cover, is of the same design and dimensions at the Pattern 1800. The buttbox cover has a plain curved outline to the hinge-plate and measures 4⁹⁄₁₆" to 4¾" long x 1⅜" to 1½" wide.

The heavy steel rammer (see earlier photo) differs from the Pattern 1800 in having a less pronounced flare to the head, and a wider, flatter and thicker button head. The rod itself is slightly thinner in diameter, and the swell is as small as ⁷⁄₁₆" diameter on some examples.

— 115 —

British Military Flintlock Rifles

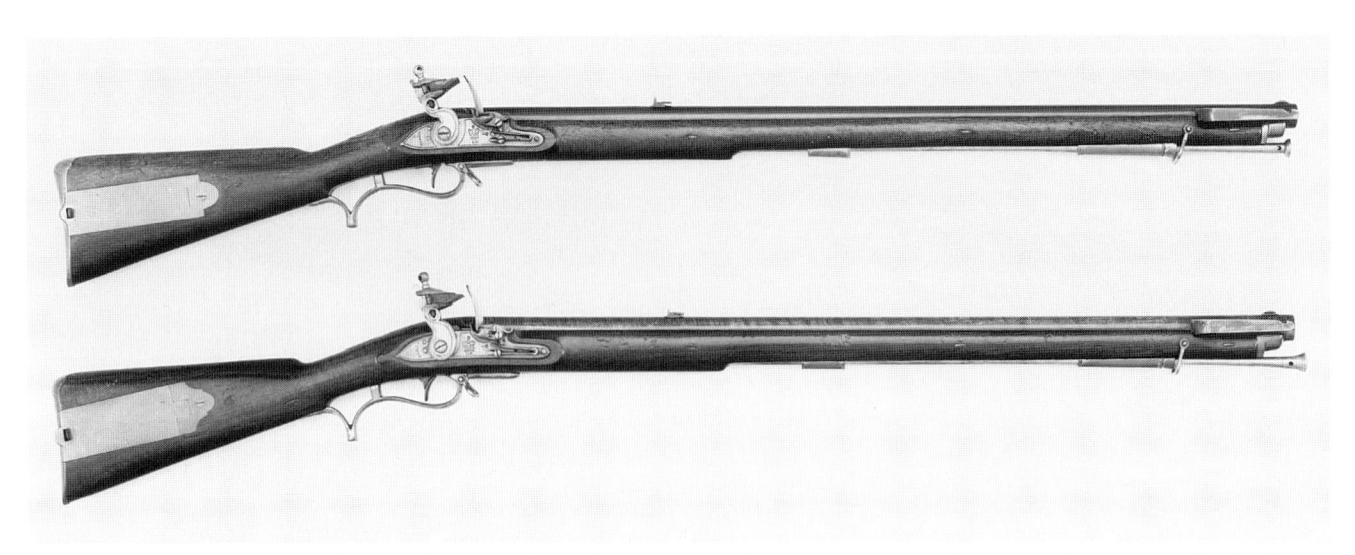

Pattern 1810 musket-bore Infantry Rifle. Note the unique pattern of butt-trap cover and large semi-waterproof lock. Shown alongside a Pattern 1800 rifle, where the overall larger size of the Pattern 1810 is clear.
Courtesy of the Trustees of the Royal Armouries Museum, Leeds.

Pattern 1810 Musket-bore Infantry Rifle

The Pattern 1810 Musket-bore Infantry Rifle is certainly the most mysterious of the Baker series. Only 100 examples were produced in April (20), May (60) and June (20), 1810[21] all by Ramsay & Richard Sutherland of Birmingham, and of these only the example in the Royal Armouries Museum collection is known to survive. They were produced following the standard practice of the period, i.e. "without barrels, locks, bayonets & rammers" which were supplied by the Ordnance, and were priced the same as the standard carbine-bore versions then being made, £2. On the one surviving example the lock is itself by R.&R. Sutherland. No clue as to the intended use for what was obviously by this date a special-purpose weapon, has been discovered at the time of writing.

The browned twist-iron 30½" barrel measures 1.20" across the breech and .955" across the muzzle. The .70" calibre bore with seven-groove rectangular rifling is of the standard pattern with the usual quarter-turn in the length of the barrel. The backsight is dovetailed 7¼" from the breech. The foresight and sword-bar are similar to previous patterns.

The lock (see photo that is shown below), while similar to the conventional Baker rifle lock, has contours somewhat closer to the New Land Pattern Musket lock and has a raised pan with a parallel-sided pan cavity (like the just-introduced Pattern 1810 India Pattern and the New Land Pattern musket locks) shaped in the same way as the musket lock. The lockplate measures 5$\frac{13}{16}$" x 1$\frac{1}{16}$", making it about a half-inch longer than the standard pattern.

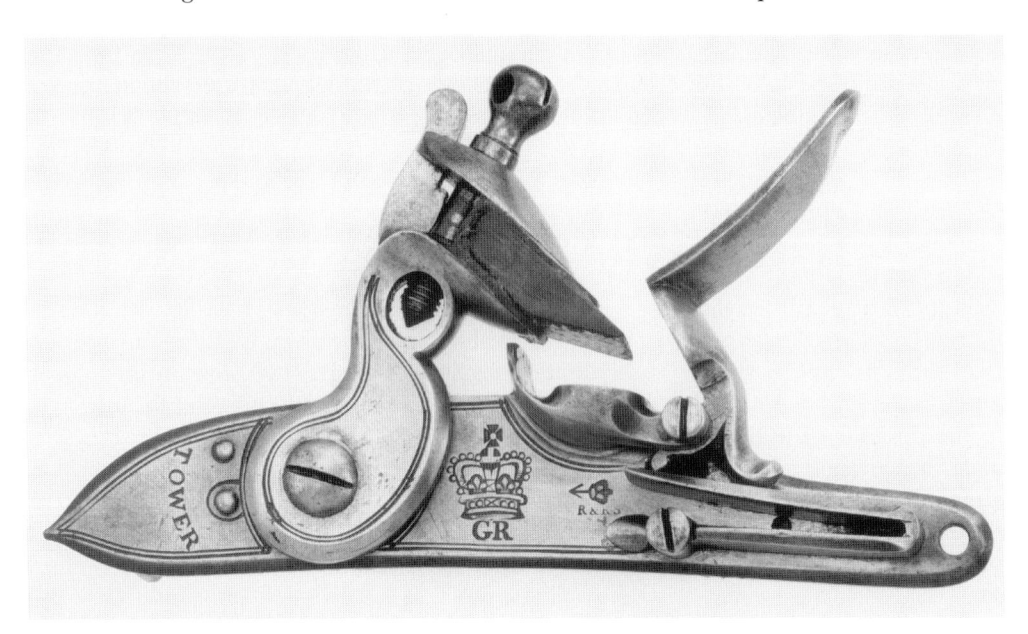

Pattern 1810 musket-bore Infantry Rifle lock. Note the raised pan and the initials of the lock (and entire rifle) makers, R. & R. Sutherland of Birmingham.
Courtesy of the Trustees of the Royal Armouries Museum, Leeds.

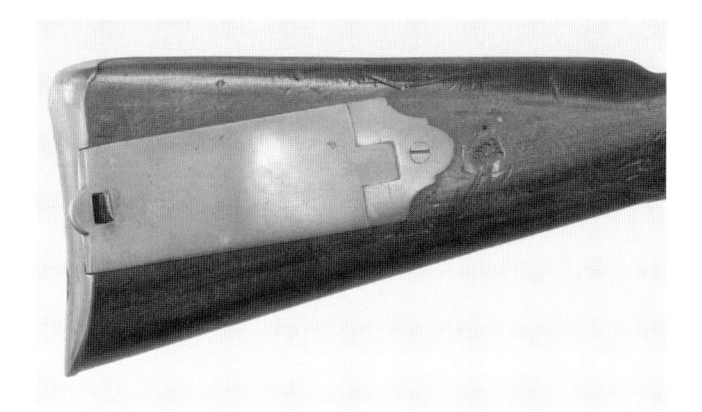

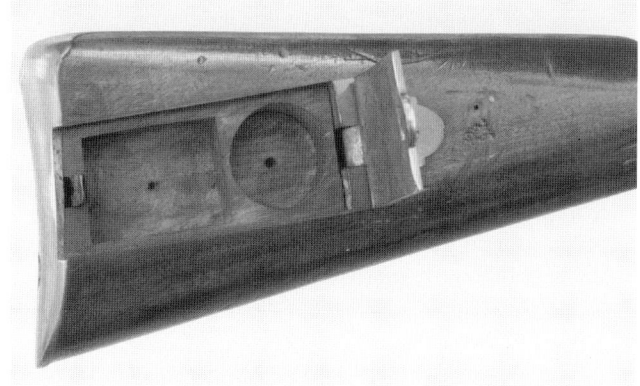

Pattern 1810 musket-bore Infantry Rifle butt-trap cover and two-compartment cavity for both patches and tools. The outline of the hingeplate is perhaps the most obvious difference, apart from the overall size of the rifle, from the earlier patterns.
Courtesy of the Trustees of the Royal Armouries Museum, Leeds.

The stock is essentially that of the Pattern 1800, without a slit in the forestock, but is made slightly heavier to accommodate the larger barrel. The buttbox cavities are larger to accomodate musket-bore patches: 1⅜" diameter by 9/16" in depth and 2" x 1½" and 13/16" in depth.

The brass furniture differs from the previous patterns in two components: the triggerguard and buttbox cover. The triggerguard has a rounded rather than a flat front finial but is otherwise the same as on other patterns. Apart from the calibre and size of the barrel the greatest change from the norm comes in the buttbox cover, which is not only larger overall (6" x 1⅞") but of a design found to date only on the Pattern 1810.

Dublin-made Baker Rifles?

The status, extent and distinguishing features (if any) of Dublin-made small arms after the dissolution of the Irish Board of Ordnance, and its replacement by the Dublin Small Gun Department, as a result of the Great Rebellion of 1798, are virtually unknown to modern researchers. That they were actually producing Ordnance small arms is suggested from the nature of the staff of this Department and the presence of and payments to a Master Furbisher (Mr. Cooke) and viewers who were to be paid by the Dublin office. There are a number of references in the surviving Board of Ordnance records but these relate not to production figures but to comparative costs of producing in Dublin and London. Thus, we have a comparison of costs for producing the Infantry Rifle between London and Dublin in April 1811:

	London	Dublin
Barrel	1. 8.6.	1. 4.0. plus rifling 6/-
Lock	8.9.	2.2. forging + 6/10 filing
Setting up complete except for bayonet	2. 0.0.	3. 1.9.
Infantry Rifle	£3.17.3.	£5. 0.9.[22]

An earlier part of this same letter states that

...the prices paid in Dublin were much greater than those in London and which he [Thomas Alsop, Assistant Inspector of Small Arms, who made the report] was of opinion should be suffered to continue.

The Board in London then ordered

That a Statement of the prices paid for setting up these Arms in England be transmitted to the Respective Officers in Dublin and that they be informed they are not to authorise the payment of greater prices for setting up arms of the same description in Ireland in future *and that if they anticipate any difficulty in carrying this Order into Execution The Board desire they will report fully thereon for their determination.*

My emphasis on "continue" and "in future" suggest that whatever happened after this letter was received in Dublin, it does suggest that some arms (beyond patterns to determine prices) were produced in Dublin earlier, very likely from components sent from England. The statement quoted in the next chapter with reference to Cavalry Rifles in 1806 supports this belief. Another supporting piece of evidence is the pair of silver cups presented to Dublin gunmaker John Rigby in 1816 "by the contractors in Dublin 'As an acknowledgment of his exertions in the interests of the trade.'"[23] We do not know what these exertions were, or whether they relate to the manufacture of small arms for the Ordnance in Dublin, but the suggestion is positive rather than negative. Opposed to this is the fact that there is no indication in any of the Government reports on small arms production during the period to 1815 that Dublin-made weapons are included in the numbers. Since the system had been unified from 1801 and there was no longer a separate Irish Parliament to whom such reports of expenditure could be made, there is every reason to believe that Dublin production, if it occurred, should be included in the overall figures, and accounted for whether or not the prices differed, but especially if they did differ. On balance, given the physical lack of evidence of production and the very considerable increased cost of production in Dublin, the writer thinks it most unlikely that Infantry Rifles were produced by the Dublin trade, even if other types of arms may have been produced there for a short time.

Possible Modifications

The design of the Baker rifle was challenged throughout its long service, but unfortunately the records do not give details of any of the many "improvements" which were tried and apparently rejected. Judging from the surviving examples, the first significant change to the overall design came in 1815 when earlier patterns were modified to take a socket bayonet. But occasional correspondence clearly indicates that changes and modifications were being suggested by those who used the rifles. The following reply to Colonel Manningham from the Adjutant General's Office in July 1802 (the earliest suggestion of changes to the Baker rifle being requested by those using them) is typical of the sort of vague yet verbose correspondence with which the researcher has to contend:

I have laid your letters of the 23rd and 30th June [not located] before the Commander in Chief; as HRH does not appear perfectly satisfied with respect to the Expediency of the alteration you propose in your Rifles, I should recommend your postponing any further steps in the business until you have an opportunity of personally explaining to HRH the advantages with which you conceive that it will be attended.[24]

In June 1806 it is indicated that there had been a change in the pattern of the false breech on rifles.[25]

Perhaps the strangest modification which appears to have been carried out was "the removing the Sights of the Rifles lately received by the 2nd Bn of the King's German Legion from the Tower" in June 1807.[26]

The men of the 95th (Rifles) Foot seem to have been dissatisfied with the stocks of their rifles; the complaint seems to have centred on the straightness of the butt, its lack of "bend." In June 1809 (by which time many of the regiment were already in the Peninsula) Col. Manningham wrote to the Commander-in-Chief about "a defect in the construction of the Rifles recently supplied to the 95th Regt" and requested that it receive "immediate consideration."[27] Later the same month Manningham requested that the NCOs of 2/95th "be supplied with Rifles having bent Stocks" and that this be done as soon as possible since these men were about to march from Hythe for embarkation for foreign service. He indicated that 60 serjeants and 58 corporals were affected by the request.[28] On the 29th of June, the Adjutant General told Manningham that:

Having referred to the Board of Ordnance your letter of the 25th Inst requesting that Rifles with bent stocks might be issued to the Non Commissioned Officers of the 2nd Battalion of the 95th Regt, I have the honor to annex for your information the copy of a Letter from the Acting Secretary to the Board on the subject.[29]

A request made two years later, in June 1811, from 3/95th also requesting bent stocks for 105 rifles and swords to be supplied suggests that perhaps this modification was carried out. If so, it is unlikely that they will be identifiable today, since the method normally employed to change the bend of a stock was to steam it, bend it and dry it. This method, depending on the direction of the grain and the skill of the craftsman, was only temporary, and the stocks tended to gradually return to their original position over a period of months or a few years.

In May 1810, the second and third battalions of the Rifle Corps were ordered to test some rifles which had been altered by a Mr. Outridge of the Isle of Wight; three went to the second battalion at Hythe and two to the third battalion at Braeburne Leas.[30] They were reported on in June, but as too often, the reports do not survive.[31]

In February 1812 a Captain Gasser, described as "an excellent Marksman" submitted a rifle which "is represented to be in some respects superior to those at present in the Service, which he is anxious to prove by trial." The Duke of York wrote to the Master General indicating that "he trusts your Lordship will be pleased to afford him [Gasser] an opportunity of doing so."[32] In October (suggesting a certain lack of immediacy) a trial was held between a Baker rifle and a Tyrolean rifle; the Commander-in-Chief was not convinced about Mr. Gasser's improvement but thought enough of it to submit it to the Master General and Board for their views — which were not recorded.[33]

In March 1813, Capt. Bartleman, Royal Marines, sent a pattern rifle to the Commander-in-Chief, who sent it to the Ordnance for their comments.[34] As usual, the response from Ordnance, if any, has not survived.

It is significant that these improvements or challenges to the Baker design all appear at a time when there had been several years field experience with the Baker which suggested these ideas.

Pattern 1807 Rifled Wall Piece

Although it is not a Baker rifle in any sense except for, perhaps, the form and twist of the rifling, the rifled wall piece is placed here as the least inappropriate location for a wartime limited production rifled arm.

Because these arms, although probably pre-existing, contain two major changes from the basic pattern, the backsight and the rifling, they are accorded a distinct designation.

The first reference to these wall pieces comes in September 1806, when James Bailey, smallwork contractor to the Board, was billed for supplying seventeen "elevating sights for wall pieces" at a cost of 3 1/2d. each.[35] These were of the same design as those for the Infantry Rifle, only larger, with a notched block and one or more hinged leaves. In November, the Inspector of Small Arms, Lieut. Col. James Miller, Royal Artillery, informed the Board of Ordnance that the total price of rifling and finishing "the wall pieces" was 19/11 each. "They not being of an equal calibre to a sufficient exactness for Rifles he had them all bored up and fine board to an equal size."[36] In February 1807, the Birmingham barrel rifler, Francis Arnold, was paid £11.4.0. for rifling the barrels of sixteen wall pieces,[37] and during the same month, Joseph Sherwood supplied the Ordnance with one "pair of Bullet Moulds" for a Rifled Wall Piece at a cost of £1.16.0.[38] suggesting that all sixteen pieces were intended to be supplied with ammunition from one source.

There are no other references to components for wall pieces during this period, which suggests two possibilities for the origin of these arms, none of which has been identified at the time of writing: either the guns already existed in Store and were simply rifled and fitted with the appropriate backsights, or they were assembled by the workmen in the Royal Manufactory in the Tower from components already in Store. If the complete arms were taken from Store and rifled, it is highly likely that they came from the most recently made wall pieces, the one hundred supplied by Henry Nock in 1788 and 1791, or from amongst the three hundred East India Company wall pieces which had been manufactured in 1793 and purchased from the Company by the Ordnance in May and July 1794. Col. Miller's remarks could apply equally well to already existing guns or to newly set up pieces. Obviously intended for some specific purpose, unfortunately no references have been found to what this might have been.

🙢 🙢 🙢 🙢 🙢 🙢 🙢 🙢

From its introduction in 1800, until the end of the Napoleonic Wars in 1815, the Baker Infantry Rifle was produced in three significant patterns: the Pattern 1800, Pattern 1801 West Indies, and the Pattern 1805. Of the first, some 2,400 were set up between September 1800 and May 1801, of the second just over 2,000 were delivered between December 1801 and March 1802 and of the third almost 19,000 were made. No rifles were delivered between March 1802 and late 1804, and this latter is questionable since it relates to the new manufactory in the Tower of London. Contractor deliveries of the Pattern 1805 began generally in October 1805, although one contractor, John Gill, was for some reason able to begin his deliveries in July.

The two sets of production figures for rifled arms which conclude this chapter are both taken from official sources, and while both appear to be correct within themselves, there is no obvious reason for the disparities in their totals, illustrating the difficulties in having to rely on original documents when reaching conclusions. At almost five pounds per piece, Infantry Rifles were the second most costly of the many patterns of small arms produced for the Ordnance on a regular basis (after the Cavalry Rifle which was made in much smaller numbers), and it is not therefore surprising to find that their production was tied to a particular need. Production peaked in 1808 with the requirement to arm or rearm rifle units going to Portugal and Spain.

For the period 1805–1815, during which the Pattern 1805 rifles were produced, thirty-one contractors (thirteen in London, eighteen in Birmingham) produced almost 19,000 rifles. The "top ten" rifle producers, all located in Birmingham, were: Ketland & Walker (including their several firm styles) 1503; Ketland & Alport 1391; Samuel Galton 1242; Robert Wheeler 1144; Willetts & Holden 1087; W. & S. Dawes 983; John Gill 971; Blair & Sutherland 948; H. & J. Whately 921; and Henry Morris 783. Ezekiel Baker, perhaps appropriately, was the largest London producer of Infantry Rifles, supplying 712.

Rifle Production according to the General Returns of Arms produced 1804–1815

	Tower	London trade	Birmingham trade	Totals
1803[39]	-	-	-	44
1804	325	-	-	325
1805	190	359	804	1353
1806	1281	571	1527	3379
1807	348	724	1630	2702
1808	-	127	3932	4059
1809	96	400	490	986
1810	no detailed returns this year			*1239
1811	-	-	1924	1924
1812	1525	365	1487	3377
1813	497	1139	643	2279
1814	721	475	-	1196
1815	-	32	727	759
	4,983	**4,192**	**13,164**	**22,339**

Includes 100 musket-bore rifles.
These figures include both Infantry and Cavalry Rifles.

Baker Infantry Rifle Production according to the Ordnance Bill Books, 1805–1815
(London and Birmingham contractors only)

	London	Birmingham	Total
1805	350	764	1114
1806	620	1586	2207
1807	724	1605	2329
1808	77	3513	3590
1809	400	506	906
1810	400	*1035	1435
1811	1019	1981	3000
1812	365	1486	1851
1813	1353	600	1953
1814	497	5	502
1815	32		32
	5,837	**12,982**	**18,819**

* Includes 100 musket-bore.

CHAPTER 10
Cavalry Rifles, 1790s–1828

The cavalry rifles which were issued to various mounted units of and in British service from the 1790s to the 1820s were all part of the never-ending search for the ideal weaponry for mounted troops. The question was first raised with the invention of the self-contained wheellock lock mechanism in the sixteenth century and remained unsolved until the adoption of motorised units in place of horse-mounted soldiers. The very role mounted troops should play was at the heart of the question and, beginning in 1756, this was resolved into two basic categories: heavy and light. The proliferation of varieties of mounted troops striving to achieve both force and mobility, and the fluctuations in opinions of regimental and commanding officers and in relevant government officials created a vast variety of muskets, carbines and pistols as well as edged weapons and polearms to delight the student and collector.

During the period under discussion, British mounted troops were divided into Heavy and Light Dragoons, and Cavalry or "Horse," all armed with smoothbore firearms. At the beginning of the period, the Heavy Dragoons were armed with the Pattern 1770 Heavy Dragoon Carbine and the Pattern 1738/56 pistol, while the Light Dragoons and Cavalry carried the Pattern 1773 Eliott Carbine and Pistol. During the 1790s, two varieties of Heavy Dragoon Carbine began to replace the earlier pattern, the musket-bore Carbine of 1797 with the Nock screwless lock, (called by the Ordnance the "swivel lock") and the same carbine fitted with a conventional carbine (or "Office pattern") lock, the Pattern 1798; the Patterns 1797 and 1798 musket-bore pistols accompanied the carbines. Not until 1808 did a new carbine begin to be issued for the Cavalry, the 16-inch Carbine, christened in the 1840s as the "Paget" carbine. At the time of the adoption of a new pattern of Eliott carbine in 1773, Generals Eliott (15th L.D.) and Burgoyne (16th L.D.) had both expressed a wish for the adoption of a rifled carbine for light dragoons, but nothing further came of it at that time.

BRITISH CAVALRY RIFLES 1793–1802

The first appearance of the rifled carbine in British service occurred during the confused period of the French Revolutionary Wars, when a number of small units of refugee foreign troops were taken into British service. Generally speaking, it has thus far proved impossible to firmly identify any of these rifled carbines. Most were of Continental fabrication and were not purpose-built for the units which carried them, but rather arms which were available in the commercial market. A few were of English manufacture but foreign (generally Germanic, occasionally French) design, and a smaller number still of both English design and manufacture. The weapons and the documentation are there, what is lacking is a clear link between the two.

One rifled carbine for which there is at least a tenuous link is shown in Chapter 8 and has been suggested to be that carried by Hompesch's Hussars, a unit raised in 1793 and ultimately incorporated into the 60th Regiment in 1798. The sole reason for this attribution is the shaded initials "HH" engraved on the thumbpiece, which engraving appears to be of the correct date; the triggerguard bow on this example is engraved "40", suggesting that there were at least thirty-nine others. This is a well-made quality piece with a detented lock and roller feather-spring. The lock design is very close to the Pattern 1796 Carbine lock, while the rifling characteristics are those of the Baker rifle. Despite having Infantry Rifle dimensions, it is fitted with a sling-bar on the left side.

PATTERN 1801 LIFE GUARDS RIFLE

The first British regular service cavalry rifle was supplied to the Life Guards in 1801. There is a reference of 1680 which states that the Life Guards were issued with eight rifled carbines per troop. Unfortunately, this appears in a work which is a verbatim translation from a French volume of 1678; there is no evidence that English troopers were armed in the same manner as their French counterparts.[1]

The first clear evidence for the manufacture of rifles specifically for the Life Guards occurs in 1801, when Ezekiel Baker, amongst the first arms he supplied to the British Government with barrels rifled to his specifications, delivered 48 rifles for this regiment.[2] At the time of writing, no example of this small order has been identified, although it is possible that the Baker-made rifle described and illustrated in Chapter 17 may be one of these rifles or the later pattern of 1812.

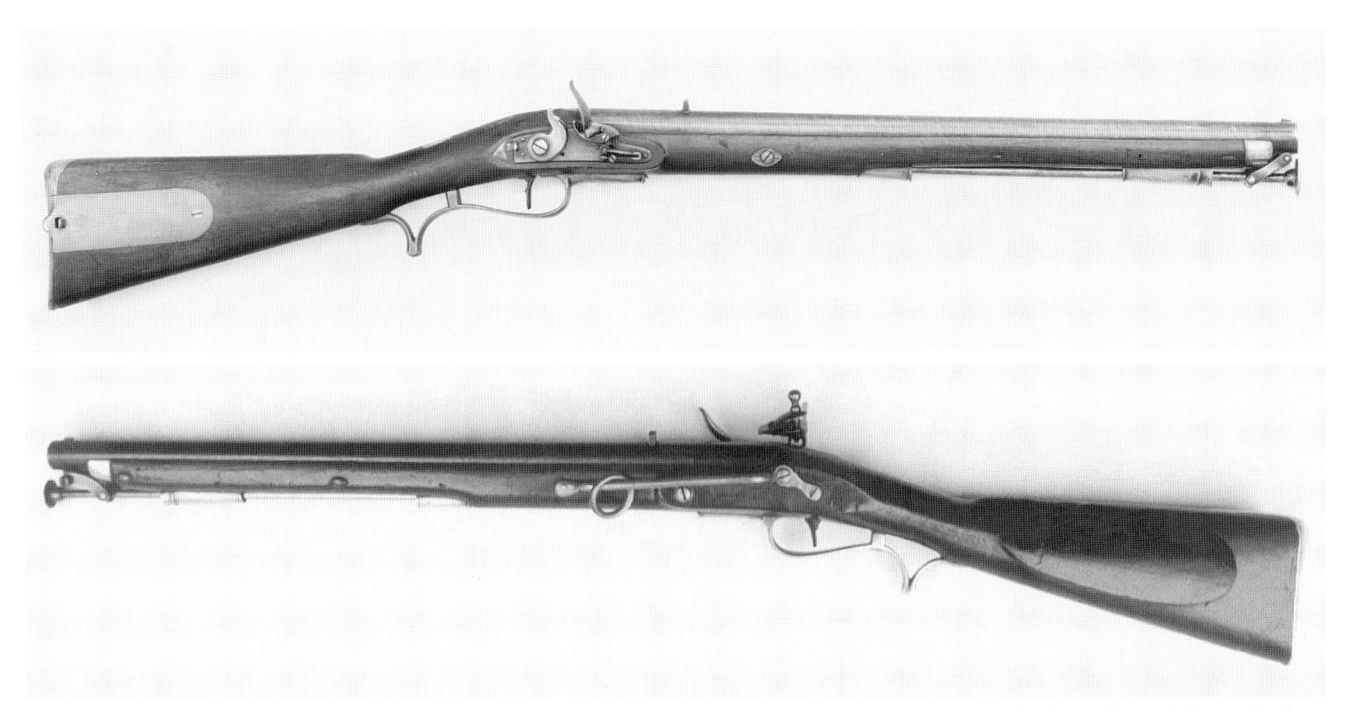

Pattern 1803 Cavalry Rifle. A shortened version of the Infantry Rifle with a swivel rammer, plain block backsight, and sling-bar adapted for mounted use. The 20-inch browned twist barrel is rifled in the same manner as the Infantry Rifle. Note that by 1803 the outline of the butt-trap cover has already been simplified, and that a tailpipe has been added to protect the entry-point of the rammer into the stock. *Right side courtesy of the Trustees of the Royal Armouries Museum, Leeds; left side courtesy of David Evans, photography by W.S. Curtis.*

PATTERN 1803 CAVALRY RIFLE

Since at least 1773, certain officers in the British cavalry had wanted a rifle for a part of their troopers. Charles James, in his 1802 *Military Dictionary*, includes a one sentence entry under "Mounted Rifle" which reads: "a corps of riflemen in the British service, dressed like hussars, and mounted on horseback"[3] suggesting that the use of rifles on horseback by the British did not originate with the Baker carbine or the 10th Light Dragoons. Baron Ferdinand von Hompesch was appointed colonel of a regiment of Mounted Riflemen in June 1798 along with 7 captains and 6 subalterns, but they were disbanded in 1802.[4] In 1803 the rifle fanciers within the mounted arm of the service achieved a significant forward step with the official adoption for the first time of the Cavalry Rifle (shown above). The successful competitor for the new rifled carbine was the designer of the current infantry rifle, Ezekiel Baker, who tells us in his book

In 1803, I tried a rifle-barrel for cavalry, twenty inches in length, before the same Committee [of Field Officers as in 1800] at Woolwich, in competition with other makers; when a decided preference was given to mine, which I afterwards mounted as a pattern for the Tenth Regiment of Light Dragoons, under the command of His late Majesty George the Fourth when Prince of Wales.[5]

The official report contains some interesting details and reveals Henry Nock, soon to be dead, as the principal opposition.

Expt with 4 Rifle Barrels 20 Inches long. Woolwich 1 June 1803

1 Bar¹ Nocks /Ball 16 to lb 1/2 Turn in 2 ft. Charge 105 Grains.

		Ball 20 to lb	
		Charge 84 Grains	
Mr Baker	2	One Bar ¼ Turn in 2 ft	
	3	One ⅜ nearly	
	4	One ½ Turn	
B¹ 1	perforated	9	Elm Boards of ½ In.
2		8	
3		8	
4		9	

Balls in 6ft Target at 200 yds

N 1	½ Turn	4	Balls
2	Bare ¼ Turn	8	
3	⅜ Turn nearly	6	In 12 Rds.
4	½ Turn	5	

The Rifle No. 2 (¼ Turn) fired by Mr. Baker 18 Rds in

— 122 —

Details of the Pattern 1803 Cavalry Rifle. Note the bolted semi-waterproof lock, very similar to the subsequent "Paget" pattern lock adopted for smoothbore cavalry carbines in 1805. Note also the method of securing the front of the sling-bar through the fore-end.
Courtesy David Evans, photos by W.S. Curtis.

less than 7 Minutes. 15 of these Rounds hit the 6 Feet Target at 100 yards.[6]

On 18 June 1803, the Master General requested Ezekiel Baker to make 40 rifled carbines exactly similar to the pattern he had made to the Master General's order, for 4 guineas each. These were for a trial at Woolwich to be carried out by Col. Blomefield and Capt. Blomefield of the Artillery.[7]

On 15 July 1803, the Horse Guards ordered that ten men of each troop of the 14th and 15th Light Dragoons were to be "forthwith armed with Carbines having Rifle Barrels"[8] which amounted to 80 rifled carbines per regiment. A supplementary order of 26 July increased this total to 100 per regiment.[9] On 9 August, the Commander-in-Chief ordered that "rifle carbines to be supplied, one hundred to a regiment, to the several regiments of Light Dragoons."[10] There were, as yet, no such carbines with which to implement this order, and it was some years before this was, to some extent, achieved. The first 40 rifled carbines produced by Baker were delivered to the 10th Light Dragoons, whose Colonel happened to be H.R.H. The Prince of Wales.

By September 1804, the Commander-in-Chief had indicated that he wanted "Ten Men pr Troop of each Regiment of Light Dragoons in Great Britain [to be] furnished with Rifles of the same Pattern as those used by the 10th Light Dragoons" and he wanted to know at "how early a period this request on the part of HRH [the Duke of York, CinC] can be complied with."[11]

In February 1805, the Inspector of Small Arms, James Miller, agreed a price of 14/- each at Birmingham and 15/- at London for Baker's rifled carbine twist-iron barrels ready to be rifled, with a finished price per barrel of 21/-.[12] Between March and July, 1,000 sets of brasswork for Cavalry Rifles was delivered into Store by Joseph Mayor, and in July, James Bailey delivered 1,000 sets of smallwork for Cavalry Rifles. Barrel contractors J. & S. Heely, Joseph Oughton, Gad Parsons, Thomas Portlock and Elizabeth Trueman delivered 906 Cavalry Rifle barrels between February and October. During 1805, a total of 725 cavalry rifles were completed by the Royal Manufactory in the Tower of London, but there is no other recorded activity on this weapon either by Baker or the contractors even though there was a surplus of 440 cavalry rifle barrels in store. That there was additional manufacture of Cavalry Rifles between 1805 and 1815, apart from those supplied by Baker, is confirmed by the issues of these arms to various regiments (see Chapter 14).

Baker's new cavalry rifle was not unchallenged, and eighteen months after the first trials, a second series was held with barrels submitted by three other makers. Arnold later becoming a barrel rifling contractor for the Ordnance. It is curious that the other three makers used the quarter-turn twist standard in the Infantry Rifle while Baker used a half-turn and achieved poorer results at long range. Durs Egg, with the heaviest barrel, achieved the best results throughout.

Expt^t Rifle Barrels of 20 Ins at Target 9 Feet Square. Woolwich, Feb. 1805

Barrels	lbs.	ozs.	
1. Arnold	2	11¼	¼ Turn
2. Gill	2	11	¼ Turn
			in the Whole Barrel
3. Egg	2	11½	¼ do.
4. Baker	2	7½	½ Turn

Shots Struck Target 12 Rounds

	100 yds	200 yds	300 yds
N 1 Arnold	11	11	4
2 Gill	12	8	4
3 Egg	12	12	6
4 Baker	12	8	3[13]

In March 1806, the Board advised the Inspector of Small Arms that they did not require more than 3,000 Cavalry Rifle barrels, and he was to prevent any greater number than that being finished up (i.e. rifled, sighted, looped and browned); 3,000 were to be set up of the 10,772 barrels then in various stages of manufacture.[14] Although there are no further references to the manufacture of cavalry rifles, it is assumed from the general lack of records relating to the Royal Manufactory in the Tower, that they were fabricated during 1806–7.

A Dublin-made Cavalry Rifle?

Apart from Ezekiel Baker and the Royal Manufactory in the Tower after 1804, a third source of Cavalry Rifles (as well as Infantry Rifles and other arms) may have been the Ordnance workshops in Dublin. Unfortunately, there is even less information on their production than on that of the Tower establishment. But a letter from the Horse Guards to the Secretary to the Board in September 1806 suggests that Dublin was indeed producing at least some Cavalry Rifles:

...from the progress making in Dublin with manufacture of Cavalry Rifles and short Carbines [the so-called "Paget" with a 16-inch barrel], it is expected that a sufficient number will be prepared by the end of the present month to supply a Regiment of Light Dragoons...[15]

An 1811 comparison of prices for producing the Cavalry Rifle in the two centres revealed a significant difference:

	London	Dublin
Barrel	£ 1. 1.0.	£ 17.0. plus 5/ for rifling
Lock	15.0.	2.2. forging + 14/1 filing
Rammer	2.9.	–
Setting up complete	1.15.0.	3. 4.0.
	3.13.9.	5. 2.3.[15]

Why the iron swivel rammer was omitted from the Dublin pricing is unknown. This comparison was made five years after the indication that some production was under way; whether the 1806 production formed the basis for the pricing carried out later cannot be confirmed from the surviving records. But given this extreme difference in cost, it is very unlikely that many Cavalry Rifles were produced in Dublin for the Ordnance.

PATTERN 1812 LIFE GUARDS RIFLED CARBINE

The Horse Guards informed the Ordnance on 15 August 1812 that the arms of the 2nd Life Guards were to be changed; 320 carbines of the same design as those used by the Heavy Dragoons [i.e. the Pattern 1798] were wanted, as well as 48 rifled carbines and 382 swords of a pattern submitted.[17] Only five days later, on 18 August, the Board were warned that the regiment was ordered for foreign service and that the arms were wanted as quickly as possible. The same armament was also ordered for the 1st Life Guards.[18]

By the Board's Order of 21 Aug. 1812, 100 rifles "such as used by Heavy Cavalry with rifled Barrels to be prepared for the Life Guards." Miller asked for a pat-

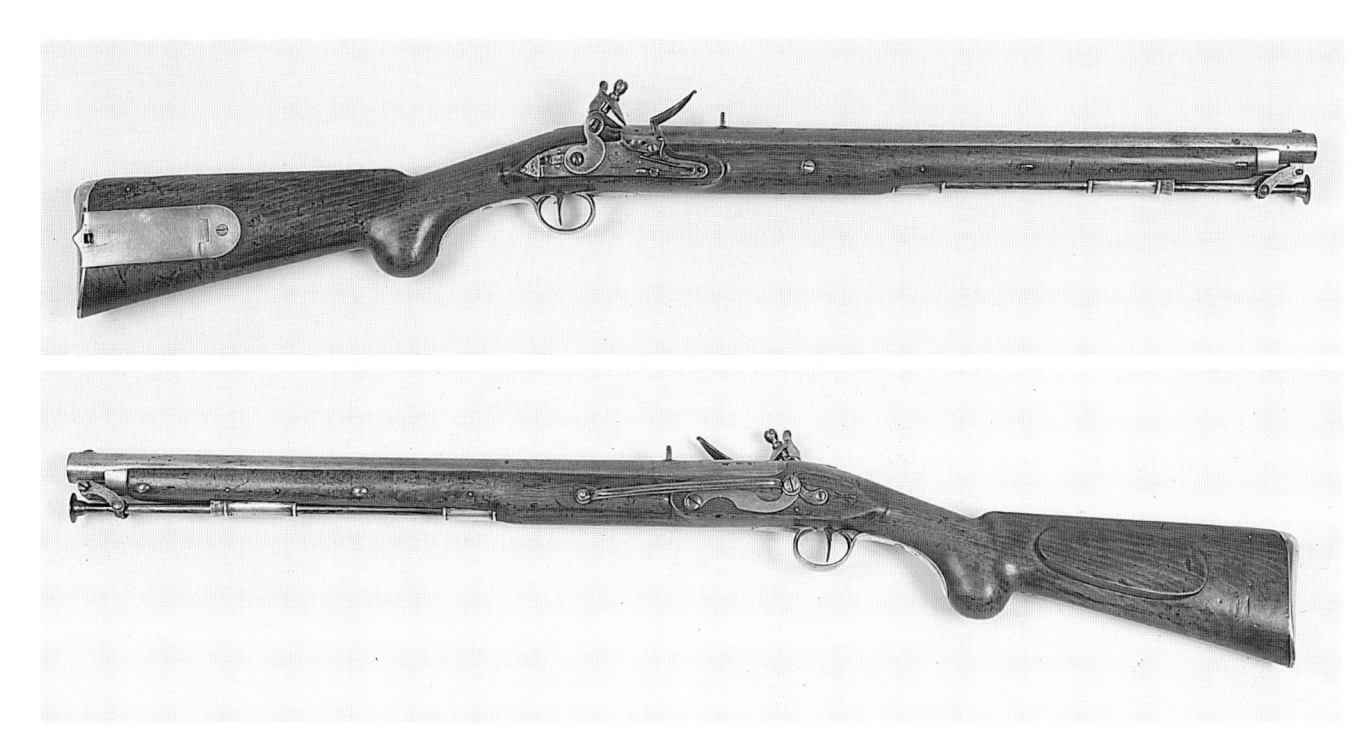

Pattern 1813 Cavalry Rifle, incorporating Col. Palmer's all-wood pistol grip in place of the earlier Baker-style grip-guard. This new feature is generally referred to as the "swell on the stock." It is normally fabricated in two pieces with the lower part or ball of the grip glued and screwed to the butt, but this example has been set up with a rare one-piece stock.
Courtesy of T.A. Edwards.

tern carbine to be sent.[19]

The contract for the Life Guards Rifled Musket-bore Carbine set prices at

Setting Up	£1.4.0.	*Bayonet*	2/9
Lock	7.11.	*Ramrod*	2/-
Barrel (twisted)	17.0.	*Rifling*	7/-
		to be made same as the	
		Infantry rifle, the rifling 6d less.	
Implements 1/2 per set.[20]			

The rifling was done by the same two contractors who rifled the Infantry Rifle barrels, Gill and Arnold.

The contractors (Blair, Dawes, Galton, Gill, Hollis, Ketland & Allport, Ketland, Walker & Co., Morris & Grice, Moxham, Rolfe, Sutherlands, Whately and Wheeler & Son — all in Birmingham) are recorded as delivering 102 of the 100 carbines ordered, with the two regiments receiving their proportion of forty-eight carbines each.

In December 1814, an inquiry into the price of 24/- for setting up this carbine was ordered.[21]

At the time of writing, no example of this carbine has been identified. It is assumed to closely resemble the Pattern 1798 Heavy Dragoon Carbine, but with a Baker-rifled twist-iron barrel fitted with a backsight.

It is, however, possible that a rifle described and illustrated in Chapter 17 may be the Life Guards rifle, even though its length and general configuration do not accord with contemporary dimensions of carbines. The cost of the barrel at 17/- is more than either the Infantry Rifle or the Cavalry Rifle, suggesting additional length to be rifled.

PATTERN 1813 CAVALRY RIFLE

In August 1811, Baker delivered 500 cavalry rifle barrels which he had rifled, at 6/- each. The grip-guard used on the Infantry Rifles and for the Pattern 1803 Cavalry Rifle apparently did not find favour with the cavalry. It was apparently a Lieut. Col. Palmer who proposed an alteration to the stock of the Cavalry Rifle, which was approved by the Commander-in-Chief in December 1812, provided the Ordnance also approved. It is assumed that this alteration was the pistol-grip, since no other alteration to the basic design of the Cavalry Rifle stock is known.[22]

In January 1813, Baker offered to set up 500 Cavalry Rifles for the 10th Light Dragoons at 40/-, which was approved, and he was ordered to proceed.[23] In April, Baker was billed for "Rifles Cavalry with swell on the stocks for the 10th Regt of Light Dragoons, 502 @ 40/'" along with 500 sets of box implements for cavalry rifles.[24] In December 1813, there were none in Store of the pattern at present in the hands of the troops (presumably the Pattern 1803 with the grip-guard). They wanted only the new pattern, and materials for making them were in Store, Baker would set them up.[25] Later that month, Baker delivered two pattern rifles for six

British Military Flintlock Rifles

Details of the Pattern 1813 Cavalry Rifle. The lock is the new Pattern 1813 Bolt lock also used on Light Cavalry pistols. Note the curled or teardrop finial at the rear of the sling-bar, and the simplified design in securing it to the fore-end. Note also the straight-sided swivel bars of the swivel rammer when compared with the earlier Pattern 1803 design.
Courtesy T.A. Edwards.

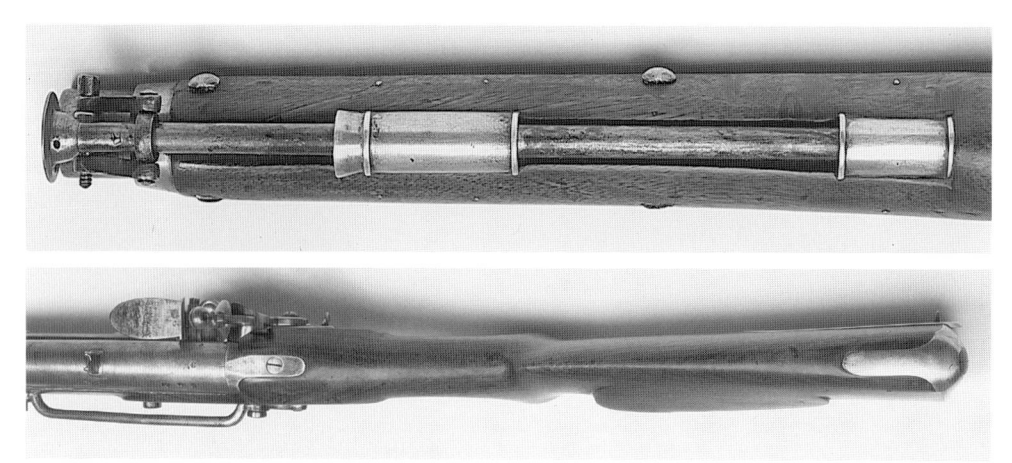

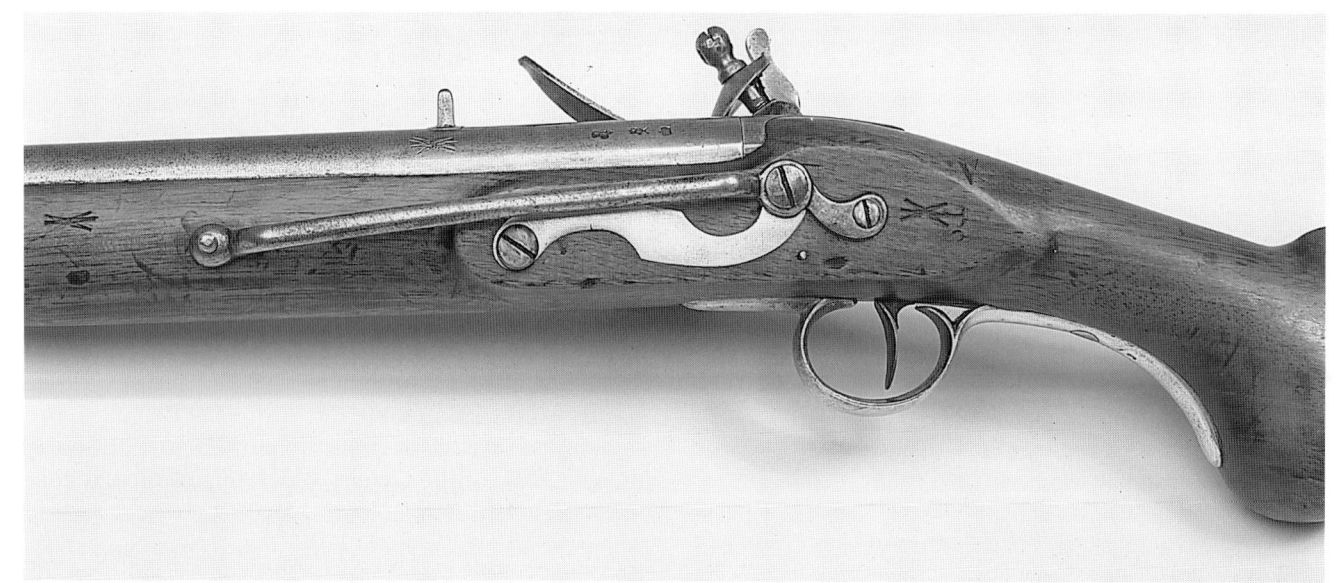

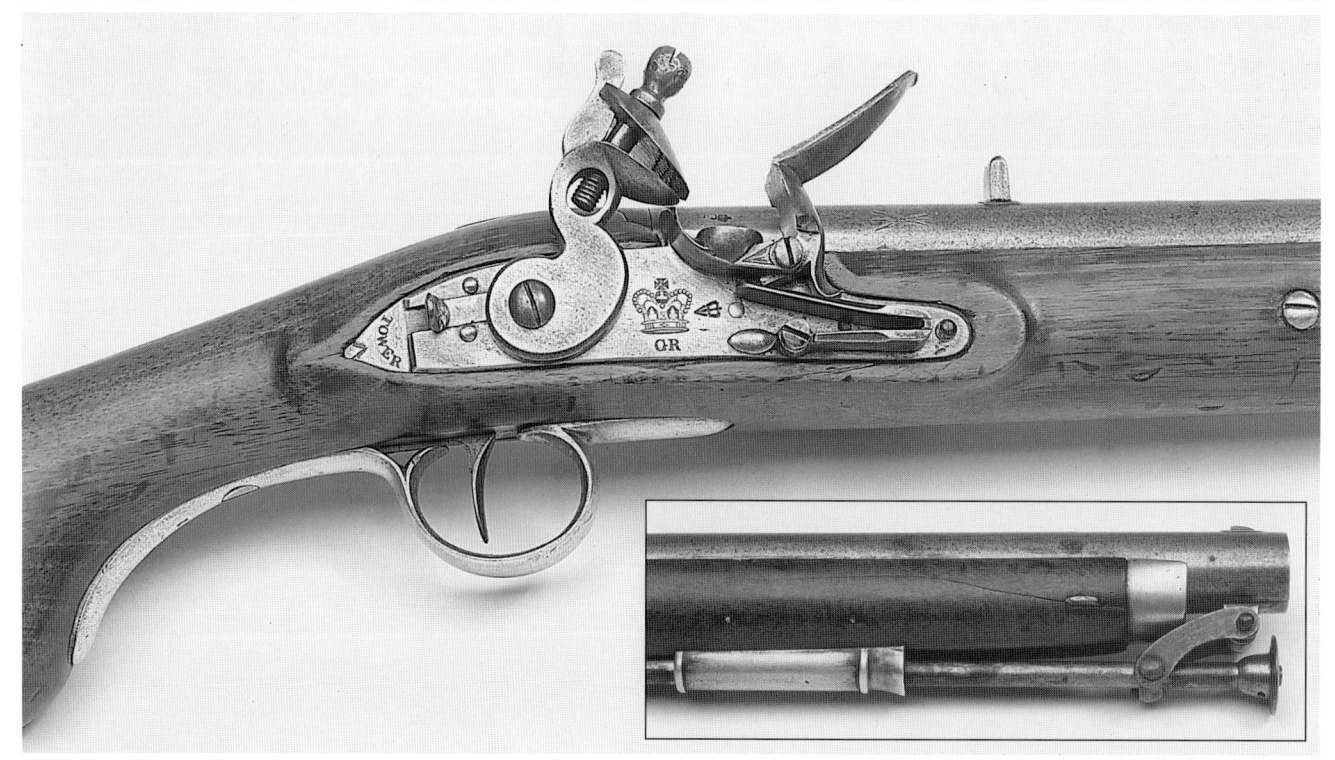

— 126 —

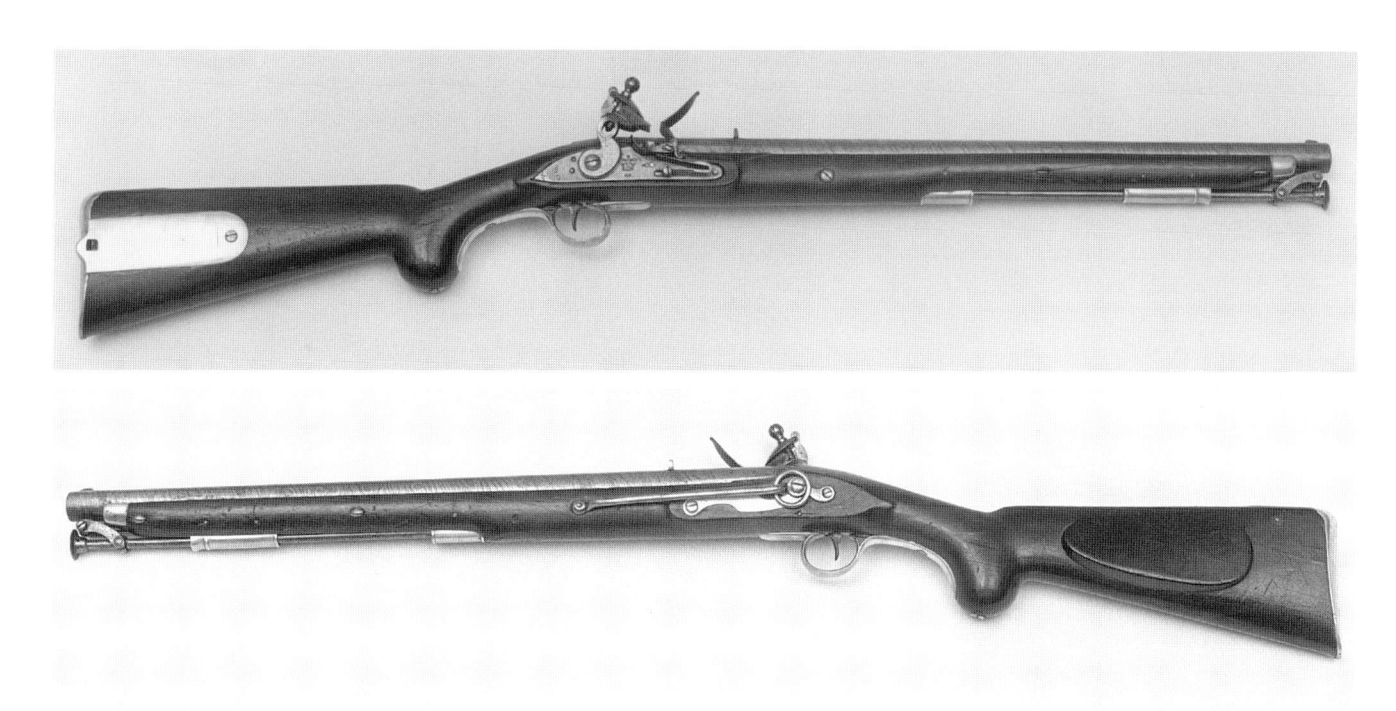

Pattern 1813/27 Cavalry Rifle. Although some of this pattern may have been newly set up, it is clear that the great majority were no more than restocked Pattern 1813s also fitted with a new simplified lock which eliminated the safety bolt.
Courtesy the Director of the National Army Museum.

guineas each.

On 2 Nov. 1813, the Commander-in-Chief authorized the Ordnance to issue the 10th Light Dragoons, then at Brighton, with 508 rifled carbines being a "special armament, by way of experiment."[26] It is assumed that these were the pistol-gripped carbines Baker had delivered in April 1813. Baker rifled a further 502 cavalry rifle barrels, and delivered a second order of 500 Cavalry Rifles for the 10th Light Dragoons "with swells on the stocks" at 40/- each in May 1814, and 391 sets of butt-box implements at 1/8 each.[27] These are assumed to be of the Pattern 1813.

PATTERN 1813/27 CAVALRY RIFLE

Since the records indicate that all of this pattern were re-stocked from the 1813–14 production, with some new components, the composite designation has been adopted.

The 10th Royal Hussars had last received an issue of their special rifled carbines in July 1815, and by the late 1820s these had become well worn and damaged from prolonged, if not arduous, service. The records indicate that Baker & Son (1823–36) supplied all of this pattern, with 112 being new stocked with his own wood and set up for 30/- each by September 1827 and a further 220 similarly described by November 1828, for two shillings less. Other contractors involved included:[28]

Reynolds, ironwork for 114 Cavalry Rifles, 24 July 27 10th H.
Glascott brasswork for 114 Cavalry Rifles, 9 Aug. 27
   do.   220   14 Aug. 28 for 10th Hussars.

17 Sept. 1827– Baker & Son delvd. 112 CR @ 30/- w/implements @ 1/6
8 Nov. 1828 – do.   217 do. 28/- new stocked

Most of the pistol-grips on the stocks of these carbines are made in two pieces, the lower rounded knob area being glued and also held by a screw from the centre of the underside of the knob into the stock.

Details of the Pattern 1813/27 Cavalry Rifle. *(top)* New simplified lock with no safety bolt and typical New Land Pattern design, small neat markings and decoration, with notable exception of curled toe of the steel. *(bottom)* 10th Royal Hussars marking on the New Land style buttplate tang. *Courtesy the Director of the National Army Museum.*

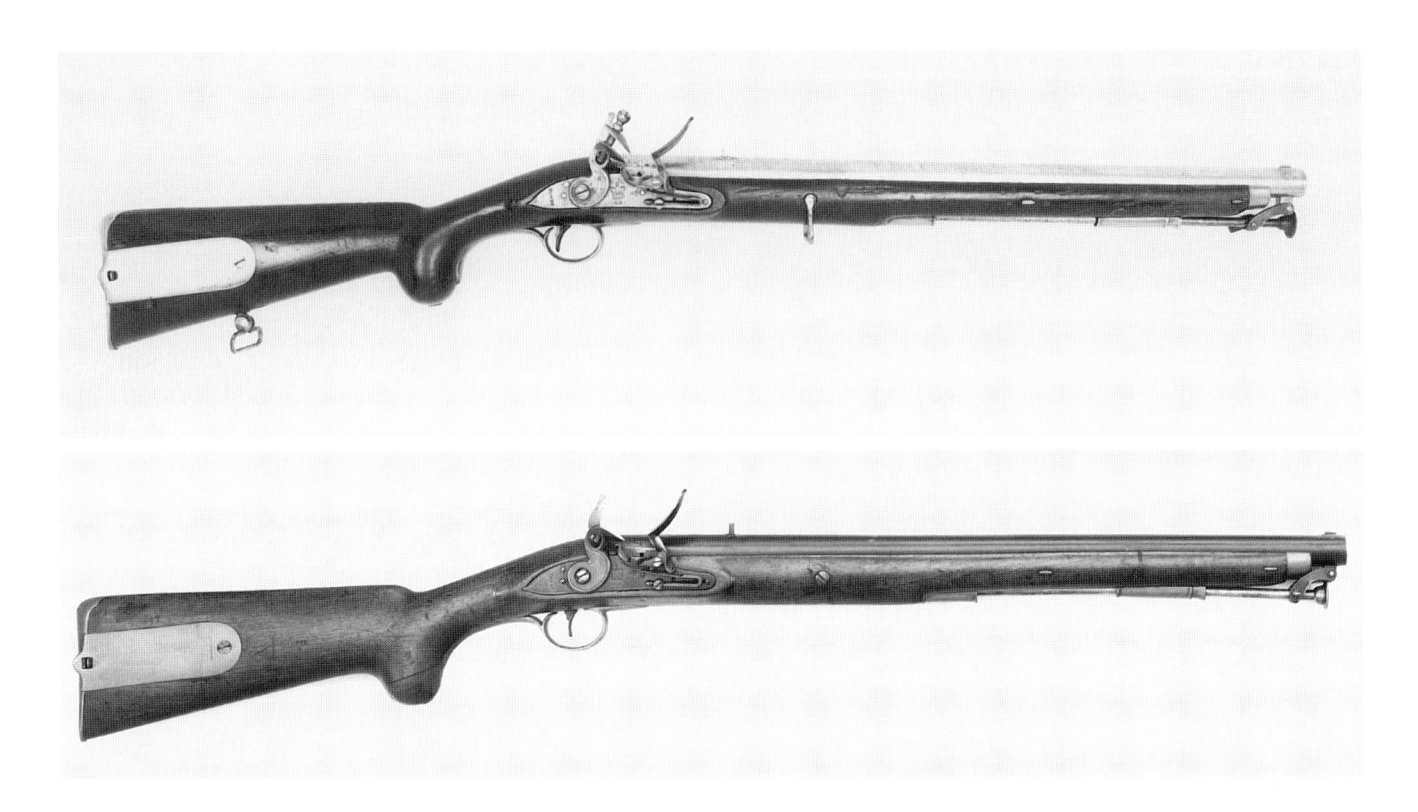

(top) **Pattern 1813/27 Cavalry Rifle with the sling bar removed and fitted with sling swivels. A regimental variation generally associated with dragoon use.** *Courtesy of the Musée Royal de l'Armée, Brussels.*

(bottom) **Pattern 1813/27 Cavalry Rifle, the stock dated 1827 and the lock with single border line decoration on the plate and cock body.** *Courtesy of the Trustees of the Royal Armouries Museum, Leeds.*

Given their long years of service and wide distribution amongst the mounted forces, it is not surprising to find occasion "in service" alterations to suit the needs of particular units. An example of this practice is shown on this page, where the carrying method has been altered from sling bar to conventional sling swivels, probably for dragoon or dismounted use.

Despite the wide circulation of rifled cavalry carbines on active service during the Napoleonic Wars (see Chapter 14), the concept underwent a distinct downgrading with the return of peace. This was doubtless due to a combination of factors including peacetime economy in expenditure on the armed forces, the broad question of the most efficient armament for cavalry and dragoons and the narrower question of what individual commanding officers wanted for their regiments. The fact that the smoothbore Pattern 1798 Heavy Dragoon Carbines and so-called "Paget" carbines remained in service until replaced with (smoothbore) percussion arms suggests that the above factors combined to create an atmosphere in which the concept of precision small arms for cavalry possessed little appeal. Not until the ease of loading afforded by first the Minie bullet and then breech-loading, did rifling become a standard feature of small arms for mounted troops.

CHAPTER 11

Postwar Baker Rifles

With what they thought at the time was the end of the war with the signing of the Treaty of Paris on 30 May 1814, the thoughts of the British Government, very much including the Board of Ordnance, turned to the immediate implementation of peacetime economies on the broadest possible scale. However, in the run-up to the peace which was obviously pending, the Board did take cognizance of several problems which had become apparent with its arms in the course of more than a decade's combat and field use, but which it had been impractical to deal with while the war continued. Amongst these was the practical utility of the sword-bayonet which had been issued with the Baker rifle since its adoption in 1800.

The basic idea of combining a long-bladed bayonet-like edged weapon with a short-barrelled rifle dated back to the eighteenth century, when it had sometimes been adapted to fix on the rifle barrel, and at other times to be used separately as a shortsword (hirschfänger in the original German concept). Mounting a bayonet of any sort on the muzzle of a firearm badly impaired its accuracy (whether rifled or smoothbore) so that the idea of a bayonet fixed to a sharpshooting instrument was inherently counter-productive. But history shows us that there are other considerations to be taken into account in a military situation, such as the feelings of personal security and individuality amongst troops considered, and considering themselves, elite, and the elimination of duplication of uses of equipment to be carried in the field, amongst others. So it took fifteen years of warfare on several continents to establish that the sword-bayonet issued with the Baker required improvement. That these improvements would all too soon be superceded by requirements of peacetime economy was also predictable.

THE PATTERN 1800/15 BAKER RIFLE ALTERED FOR SOCKET-BAYONET

The Board's Order of 8 May 1815 for 500 Infantry Rifle swords opened a discussion which led to the temporary replacement of the sword-bayonet with a conventional socket bayonet for the Baker rifle. So far as the records and existing examples indicate, all of the rifles for socket bayonets were altered from earlier production; there was no new production of this type. All but two examples either examined or reported at the time of writing are of Pattern 1800 design, suggesting a deliberate plan to begin conversion with the oldest suitable rifles in Store or in the hands of the troops. It may also suggest that the majority of the altered rifles of Pattern 1805 were subsequently used up in service prior to the replacement with the Brunswick Rifle from 1839.

On 19 May 1815, the Adjutant General of the Army wrote the Board:

...that the Troops who were armed with Rifles when on actual Service and in presence of the Enemy had experienced much disadvantage from the want of Bayonets [,] the Sword at present attached to the Rifle being on various accounts by no means so efficacious a Weapon as the Bayonet, and stated that His Royal Highness the Commander in Chief requested that a Pattern Rifle and Bayonet might be prepared for Inspection leaving the sight of the rifle in its present state, and totally unconnected with the Bayonet, the Holder or Hitch of which should be on the lower side of the Barrel, and also stated that His Royal Highness was of opinion the Sword should still form a part of the Equipment of Rifle Men, but that one of a more convenient and eligible description than the one now in use should be adopted.

Ordered, Dundas to prepare and submit pattern, and to send along Patterns of Swords in Store he thinks suitable for Rifle-men, and did the Adj. Gen. have any particular ideas about design?[1]

By 31 May, Dundas had submitted a pattern rifle and bayonet as well as a rifleman's sword "agreeable to the form proposed by the Adjutant General" and the Board ordered that the patterns be sent to the Commander-in-Chief and that he be informed that the Board feel the best of the sword patterns is the one already in use by the 52nd Regiment.[2]

On 12 June, the Adjutant General informed the Board that the Commander-in-Chief agreed with the Board about the sword of the 52nd Regiment being the most suitable pattern for the Rifle Corps, and that he also entirely approved of the pattern rifle and bayonet. There remained the questions of how the new pattern arm could be got into the hands of the Rifle Corps "with the least inconvenience and the smallest expence to the Public." The Duke of York suggested that the

British Military Flintlock Rifles

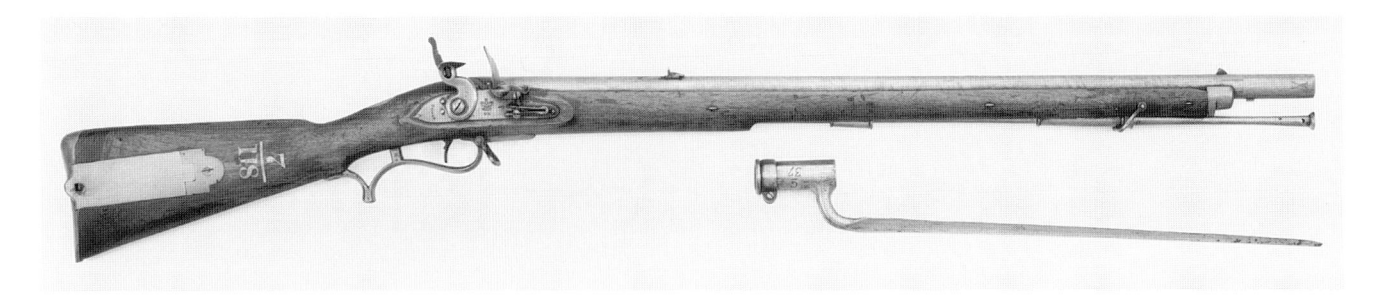

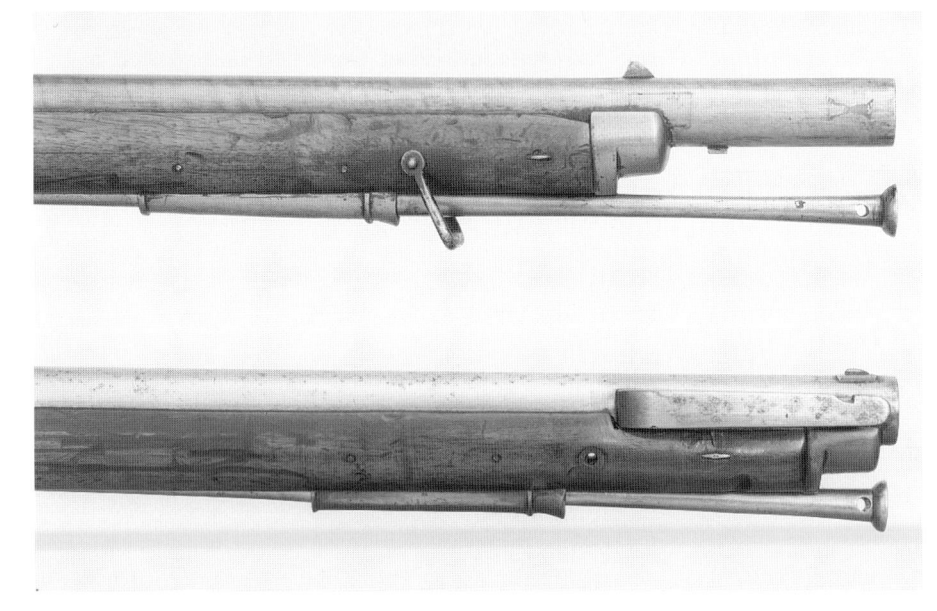

(top) **Pattern 1800/15 Infantry Rifle.** The muzzle area has been modified to take the socket bayonet shown. Note that the high blade foresight has been moved back to a point even with the front of the fore-end, and a bayonet stud dovetailed and brazed on the underside of the barrel. No border engraving on lock.

(left) Postwar Infantry Rifle muzzles (above) Pattern 1800/15 showing the fillers for the fixing points of the removed bayonet bar, the new high-blade foresight and bayonet stud. (below) Pattern 1823 showing the return to the bayonet bar for the hand-bayonet.
Courtesy of the Trustees of the Royal Armouries Museum, Leeds.

process begin with the officer commanding that portion of the Corps stationed in England ordering part of their rifles sent to the Ordnance to have new sights and bayonet studs fitted along with the other alterations required as well as a separate sword, and that these be returned to the appropriate depot for these troops before a second part of their arms were sent in. This would continue until all the rifles of the Corps in England were altered. At that point, the best method of getting the rifles of the Rifle Corps on foreign service altered would be decided.[3]

On 28 June, the planned alteration of the rifles of 3/95th had to be postponed: the battalion was ordered for immediate embarkation for service with Wellington; the 200 rifles ordered sent to the Tower on 22 June should be returned to Shorncliffe as quickly as possible.[4]

On 10 July 1815, the Inspector of Small Arms, Col. Miller, reported that 5,000 Rifle Bayonets suitable to the new pattern would be supplied by fifteen Birmingham contractors persuant to the Board's Order of 28 June, at a price of 2/11 each including the collar [locking ring] and spring. For further details on this socket bayonet see Chapter 12.[5]

On 19 July, the rifles at the depot of the 3/95th were ordered sent to the Tower for their alteration.[6]

On 26 July, Miller was ordered to send 1000 of the new bayonets to Dublin as soon as possible, for altering the rifles of the 5/60th.[7] On the following day the Adjutant General in Ireland was informed that the rifles of the 5/60th were to be altered at Dublin to the approved pattern.[8]

As late as February 1816, the rifles at the Shorncliffe depot of 1/95th had not been altered.[9]

Two official returns from this period indicate rifles in Store and the rifles recently manufactured:

17 May 1816. A Return of Small Arms & Materials now in Store at the Tower and others Depots or Manufactories, belonging to the Board of Ordnance:
      Rifles 6,449 in UK and at foreign stations

Weekly Return of Small Arms manufactured for Government during the last six months:
Rifles, Infantry	247
Do. North West Infantry	40 [for Indians][10]

In appearance, the Pattern 1800/15 Baker is recognized by the length of barrel extending beyond the termination of the fore-end, by the absence of a bayonet-bar on the right side of the barrel at the muzzle, and by the location of the high blade front sight in position level with the front of the nose cap. The alteration consisted of:

— 130 —

1. Cutting-back the fore-end, re-inletting the trumpet ramrod pipe.
2. Fitting either a new, rounded, New Land Pattern nose cap, or refitting the original cap.
3. Replacing the foresight with a high triangular-blade dovetailed into the barrel level with the front of the nose cap (and therefore behind and clear of the socket of the bayonet when fixed).
4. Brazing in fillers for the original foresight dovetail and points of attachment for the bayonet bar and re-browning either the affected muzzle area or the entire barrel.

For technical details of this conversion see Appendix I. The remainder of the rifle will be of either Pattern 1800 or Pattern 1805, and unchanged. All but two of those examined or reported at the time of writing are of Pattern 1800.

THE PATTERN 1820 BAKER RIFLE

Under the Board's Orders of 12 and 19 January 1820, a total of 450 rifles were manufactured by eleven contractors for 26/- each. They were described as:

Rifles, Infantry, with Steel Rammers & Bayonets, rough stocked out of the Contractor's own well seasoned Walnut tree heart Stocks – made off cleansed and Set Up, the Office finding all other materials.[11]

This indicates that these new-production rifles were of the same design around the fore-end and muzzle as the Pattern 1800/15 Rifles to take a socket bayonet, but using other parts of the by-now standard Pattern 1805 design. There is no associated contractor production relating to this production, so the "Office" was obviously able to supply all components from Stores. Whether the barrels required removal of the sword-bayonet bar, or were supplied in the semi-finished state (with no bayonet bar fitted) is not clear, and at the time of writing no example of this contract has been identified.

Production was as follows:

Ezekiel Baker*	45	Ann Marwood	20
Thomas Barnett	45	John Peake*	45
Brander & Potts	45	William Parker*	45
Durs Egg*	45	Thomson & Son*	45
Joseph Egg*	25	Robert Wright	45[12]
Ann Fearnley	45		

Joseph Egg was not billed until 31 Dec. 1820; Baker, Peake and James Thomson & Son on 31 Jan. 1821, and Durs Egg and Parker on 28 Feb. 1821.

From the fact that all components except the stocks were provided from Ordnance Stores for this production, it must be assumed that the locks used were of the traditional flat form adopted in 1800, and not of the new, cheaper, rounded form adopted and produced for the Pattern 1823 rifles.

The socket bayonets for this small group of 450 rifles were probably the Duke of Richmond's Musket bayonets, 565 of which were altered at this time to fit the Baker rifle (see Chapter 12).

THE ROYAL MANUFACTORY ENFIELD — BACKGROUND

Although proposed as far back as 1794, the new Royal Manufactory of Small Arms at Enfield Lock (on the Lea Navigation Canal) in Middlesex, north of London and near the Royal Gunpowder Factory at Waltham Abbey did not commence operations before 1816, and was never, prior to the 1850s, a large-scale production centre. The interest for this work lies in the fact that the Pattern 1823 Baker Rifle was the first small arm produced in quantity at the new establishment. Prior to this production, Enfield was concerned chiefly with refurbishing and reworking existing arms as a training exercise for the various specialist areas of gun-making. Patchy records indicate barrel forgers working by mid-1816, with the former Superintendent at Lewisham, John Colgate, in charge of the Barrel Branch and John Noble from the discontinued Royal Manufactory at the Tower in charge of the Stocking & Finishing (i.e. fabricating) Branch, which now incorporated lock-making as well. Not until 25 Oct. 1818 was Enfield designated as a small arms manufactory in all its branches, albeit on a much reduced scale.[13]

One of the few statements which can be made with certainty is that Enfield was involved in the alteration and repair of Baker rifles prior to its contribution to the fabrication of the Pattern 1823 Rifles which is well known. It is equally clear that whatever may have been the total of its rifle work prior to 1824, the Pattern 1823 Rifles represent the first significant small arms fabrication undertaken at Enfield.

During 1821 and 1822, before the production of the Pattern 1823 was mentioned, the Ordnance engraver John Gyde, repaired the engraving on 115 rifle locks, and newly engraved 123 for the Royal Manufactory Enfield,[14] suggesting at the very least, the fitting of new and repaired locks to existing Baker rifles.

THE PATTERN 1823 BAKER RIFLE

On 3 April 1823, the Surveyor General of the Board of Ordnance wrote to the Master General suggesting the production of ten thousand new Infantry Rifles; the Master General approved on 14 May. Production was to be divided between the Royal Manufactory Enfield and the London gun trade, with components coming from the Birmingham trade, Enfield and Ordnance Stores. It was further specified:

That the 5000 Rifles which are to be rough stocked and set up by the Trade be finished gradually, viz. a certain number every 6 Months till they are all finished – for which payment will be made at the reduced Peace Prices.

This resulted in deliveries being spaced out until 1827. The rifles produced by the trade were to be rough stocked and set up for 26/- each, the same as for the Pattern 1820 rifles.

Five thousand rifles were to be rough stocked and set up at Enfield, for which 2,200 barrels in Store at the Tower and 600 skelps at Enfield were to be used; a further 2,800 skelps of twisted stub iron were to be provided by the Birmingham trade to complete the number for Enfield. The locks were made at Enfield. Brasswork for these 5,000 rifles was to be re-cast at Enfield from old brasswork in Tower Stores.

The second five thousand rifles were to be rough stocked and set up by the London contractors. For these, 5,000 locks were to be supplied by the trade, and 5,000 barrels would be made in Birmingham.

Ten thousand sets of iron smallwork (break-offs, triggers, swivels, screws, barrel slides or keys and pinning wire) — excepting 500 break-offs from Tower Stores- and 4,500 ramrods were to be furnished by the trade. Five thousand sets of brasswork were to be re-cast by the trade from old brass in Tower Stores.

Ten thousand good sound heart stocks were to be selected from the Ordnance Stores at Woolwich by a Viewer from Enfield, and sent respectively to Enfield and to the Tower for the London trade.

The 10,000 Bayonets with Brass Handles were to be prepared at Enfield from Musquet Bayonets and materials in Store at the Tower.

The sighting, rifling and browning was to be confined to two or three London gunmakers as was the case in 1800.[15]

Ezekiel Baker, although appearing most often as one amongst many contractors, continued to exercise a degree of control over the design and production of the rifle which today bears his name. On 10 July 1823, a bill recorded that Baker had delivered to the Small Gun Office in the Tower:[16]

A Lock as a Pattern for Rifle Guns in soft state	£ 10. 0. 0
2 New plug gauges for Rifle Barrels	1. 0. 0
a pr of Brass Cramps to hold Barrels in vise	
to turn out [breech] pins [plugs]	3. 0.
3 New Gauges and Plates of Iron for Musket Fuzie	
and Rifle Flints, engraved, case hardened &c	1. 1. 0
1 Gauge for Rifle do.	3. 6.
35 Barrels Rifled before they were discovered	
to be too wide for the gauge, 7/6	13. 2. 6

In August 1823, components began to arrive at the Tower. Mary & G.M. Glascott delivered 2,000 sets of brasswork plus an additional 620 long forepipes, re-cast from HM old brass between July and October; skelps of best twisted stub iron came from Richard Adams by December.

BARRELS. Infantry Rifle, made from "the best twisted Stubb Iron" in the plain state, "and strictly kept to weight, Gauge, &c. according to the Pattern, to be 2 feet 7 in. in length and from 4 lbs. 2 oz. to 4 lbs. 4 oz. in weight, to be delivered in the plain unrifled state and to be very carefully bored to the inside Gauge sent," price 15/- each to the Board's Order of 16 July 1823. The price was increased to 16/- by the Board's Order of 25 July 1823. Deliveries were as follows:[17]

Deliveries for 1823–1825

Bayliss & Son	1 Apr. 1824	160		
Jane H. Blair	8 Dec. 1823	150		
Thos. Bulleis	1 Dec. 1823	150		
John Clive	22 Sept. 1825	50		
Thos. Clive	15 Dec. 1823	150		
Clive & Turton	31 Aug. 1823	150	1 Dec. 1825	150
S. & J. Dawes	8 Dec. 1823	150		
F. Deakin & Son	16 Oct. 1823	150		
Mary Deakin	5 Jan. 1824	150		
Samuel Deakin	15 Dec. 1823	150		
Wm. Deakin	22 Sept. 1823	150	17 Aug. 1825	50
Eliz. Gill	3 Nov. 1823	150		
Joseph Greaves	12 Jan. 1824	150		
John Gunby	22 Dec. 1823	150		
Thos. Hadley	13 Oct. 1823	150		
Joseph Harris	10 Apr. 1824	150		
J. Heely & Co.	10 Nov. 1823	150		
Fras. Johnson	15 Dec. 1823	150		
Meredith & Moxham	24 Nov. 1823	150		
Morris & Grice	1 Dec. 1823	150		
Muntz & Co.	17 Nov. 1823	150	18 Nov. 1825	50
J. & C. Oughton	21 Oct. 1823	150	4 Apr. 1826	50
Henry Osborn	13 Oct. 1823	150	21 Dec. 1825	50
Benj. Parsons	7 Oct. 1823	150	6 July 1825	50
Gad Parsons & Sons	8 Dec. 1823	150		
John Parsons	3 Nov. 1823	150		
Phineas Parsons	16 Oct. 1823	150		
Martha Plant	24 Nov. 1823	150		
Theodore Price	8 Dec. 1823	150		
Ann Priest	10 Nov. 1823	150		
Jos. H. Reddell	15 Dec. 1823	150		
J. & S. Rock	5 Jan. 1824	150		
Benj. Round	19 Apr. 1824	150		
John Russell	22 Dec. 1823	150		
Thos. Stokes	13 Oct. 1823	150		

R. & R. Sutherland	24 Nov. 1823	150	
Eliz. Trueman	29 Jan. 1824	150	
Joseph Turner	17 Nov. 1823	150	
Joseph Turton	11 Aug. 1823	50	
John Whately	29 Dec. 1823	150	
John Wheeler	29 Dec. 1823	150	
Robt Wheeler	22 Dec. 1823	150	
Willetts & Co.	1 Mar. 1824	150	
Woolley & Serjeant	10 Nov. 1823	150	

Barrels 1823-5 = 6,810

Of the earliest deliveries, Baker and Durs Egg each sighted, rifled, fixed hand bayonets and browned the barrels for 1,000 rifles by March 1824.[18]

LOCKS supplied under the Board's Orders of 4 July and 23 Nov. 1823; price generally 5/8, but 5/9 and 5/10 very occasionally. Price variations are believed to be based on the longevity and "standing" of the individual contractor, a traditional policy with the Ordnance, not on any difference in lock design or construction.

— LOCKS SUPPLIED, MAKERS, QUANTITIES AND DATES —

	1823		1824		1825		1826	
John Adams					15 Dec.	50		
Wm. Allport	17 Nov.	50						
Lewis Bayliss			19 Feb.	150				
Richard Bills	29 Sept	50			9 July	50	31 Aug	150
Samuel Bills	27 Sept	50			9 July	50	7 Sep	150
Jane H. Blair	24 Nov.	50						
J.P. Blakemore	4 Oct.	50			30 Nov.	50	5 Dec	150
Mary Blakemore	18 Sept	50			18 Oct.	50	5 Dec	150
Thos. Bulleis	24 Nov.	50						
John Clive jun.			19 Feb.	150				
F. Deakin & Son	30 Oct.	50						
Mary Deakin			5 Jan.	50				
Samuel Deakin	15 Dec.	50						
Wm. Deakin	24 Nov.	50						
Mary & John Duce					5 Apr.	100	13 Oct	150
					6 July	50		
Fletcher & Co	15 Oct.	50						
Eliz. Gill & Sons	17 Nov.	50						
John Gunby	15 Dec.	50						
Thos. Hadley	3 Nov.	50						
Wm. Howell	7 Oct.	50	1 Mar.	150	6 July	50		
Fras. Johnson	24 Nov.	50						
Eliz. Ketland	10 Nov.	50						
Ketland Walker & Co.	13 Oct.	50						
Thos. Ketland	27 Oct.	50						
Wm. Leonard	25 Oct.	50						
Morris & Grice	27 Oct.	50						
Deborah Negus	30 Oct.	50						
J. & C. Oughton			12 Jan.	50				
Hy. Osborn	13 Nov.	50					13 Jan	50
							7 Apr.	50
							2 Aug	50
John Partridge	29 Sept.	50			9 July	50	29 Aug	150
Michael Peters	13 Nov.	50						
Theodore Price							18 Jan	50
Jos. H. Reddell	17 Nov.	50						
Samuel Rock	17 Nov.	50						
Joseph Round	8 Dec.	50						

Hannah Shenstone	29 Sept.	50						
J. & W. Sherwood	25 Sept.	50	2 Feb.	150	14 Mar	50	21 Jul	300
Siddons & Co.	8 Dec.	50						
John Slater	13 Oct.	50	2 July	50			31 Aug.	150
James Smith	23 Sept.	50			13 June	50	7 Sep	150
M. & F. Spittle	29 Sept.	50	23 Feb.	250				
Peter Spittle	27 Oct.	50						
Thos. Stone	29 Sept.	50			2 May	50	24 Aug.	150
	5 Nov.	50						
R.&R. Sutherland	15 Oct.	50						
Chas. Thornhill	15 Oct.	50			11 July	50	9 Sep	150
Job Wilks	16 Sept.	50			13 June	50	31 Aug	150
John Wheeler	30 Oct.	50						
Wheeler & Son	25 Oct.	50					6 Jan	50
Whitehead & Co	27 Sept.	50			18 May	50	13 Oct	150
					13 Dec.	50		
Willetts & Co	25 Sept.	50						
Woolley & Price	18 Nov.	50						
Woolley & Serjeant	18 Oct.	50						
		2300		**1000**		**850**		**2350**

Locks 1823–6 = 6500.[19]

Two thousand bayonet scabbards were supplied by Hawkes, Moseley & Co. at 1/- each.

James Bailey provided two thousand sets of rough-forged ironwork, consisting of:

Break-off breech	4 1/2d
Back Sight	1 d
Trigger	1 d
Springs, Rammer	1 d
Nails, Breech & Side	1/2d each
Box	3/4d
Woodscrews, lg & sm	1/2 & 3/4d each
Bolts (6,000)	1/2d
Swivels	2 1/2d pair
Nails, small for Handles	1/4d
Iron Wire, large for Box joints,	20 3/4 lbs. at 10d pr lb.
pinning	26 lbs. at 10d pr lb.

Sets of implements (ball drawer, wiping eye and lever) were supplied by Baker (1,000 sets) and Sherwood (1,000 sets).

RIFLES. "Rifle Infantry with hand Bayonet & Rammers Rough Stocked out of the Contractors own well seasoned Walnut tree Stocks made off cleansed and set up - the Office finding all other Materials 26/-" was how the finished production of these rifles from the various components listed below appeared in the official records.

Bill	Contractor	Number
16 Feb. 1824	T. & C. Ashton	133
26 Jan. 1824	E. Baker	183
1 Mar. 1824	Barnett & Son	183
23 Feb. 1824	Brander & Potts	183
26 Jan. 1824	D. Egg	183
23 Feb. 1824	J. Egg	183
1 Mar. 1824	A. Fearnley	151
23 Feb. 1824	A. Marwood	133
23 Feb. 1824	W. Parker	183
2 Feb. 1824	R.E. Pritchett	151
23 Feb. 1824	Thomson & Son	183
2 Feb. 1824	R. Wright	183
		2032[20]

From amongst the first Pattern 1823 rifles to be completed, 600 were issued to the First Battalion the Rifle Brigade in September 1823. From the timing these were almost certainly rifles fabricated at Enfield.

1825–7 PRODUCTION

In June 1825, a second delivery of components began. In addition to the barrels and locks noted above,

William Reynolds	*2000 sets of rough-forged ironwork, 2000 sets (April 1826)*
Glascott	*2000 sets of brass furniture re-cast from old brass in the Tower (June 1825) 2000 sets (May 1826)*
Hawkes, Moseley & Co.	*2000 bayonet scabbards*

Ezekiel Baker   *4000 sets of implements*
Sherwood   *3000 sets (June & September)*
     1000 sets (December)

Baker and Egg once again each carried out the rifling, sighting, fitting of hand bayonets and browning the barrels of 1,000 rifles, and a second and final 1,000 each in May 1827.

Locks furnished at this time increased in price to 7/6 each for all contractors.

RIFLES WERE SUPPLIED AND PRICED TWO WAYS
26/- = rough stocked and set up, all materials supplied except stock
42/6 = compleat with Hand Bayonets, except barrels and locks.

— RIFLES SUPPLIED, MAKERS, QUANTITIES AND DATES —

	1825	*Number*	*1827*	*Number*
J. Adams	26 July	50 @ 42/6		
T. & C. Ashton	4 Nov	136 @ 26/-	9 Apr.	200
E. Baker	"	184 "		
Baker & Son	13 Oct [this one is in 1826]	200 "		
Barnett & Son	6 Jan.	184 "	30 Jan	200
Brander & Potts	23 Jan	184 "	3 Mar.	200
D. Egg	4 Nov	184 "	19 Mar	200
J. Egg	8 Mar	150 "	9 May	150
T. Hampton	30 June	50 @ 42/6		
R. & W. Hollis	29 July	50 "		
W. Ketland & Co	"	50 "		
A. Marwood	16 Mar.	136 @ 26/-		
T. Moxham	29 July	50 @ 42/6		
W. Parker	23 Jan.	184 @ 26/-	15 Feb.	200
R.E. Pritchett	"	150 "	9 May	160
T. Reynolds	8 Mar	140 "	"	140
R. & R. Sutherland	10 July	50 @ 42/6		
Thomson & Son	28 Dec.	184 @ 26/-	7 May	200
Wheeler & Son	29 July	50 @ 42/6		
R. Wright	3 Feb.	184 @ 26/-	14 May	200
		2550		**1850**

The above lists show a total of 6,432 rifles being delivered by the trade between 1824 and 1827; assuming that the entire 5,000 to be fabricated at Enfield were delivered, a grand total of 11,432 examples of the Pattern 1823 Baker rifle were produced. During 1826 Enfield is recorded as producing 1,486 rifle barrels, 1,003 rifle locks, rifling, sighting and fitting hand bayonets to 882 barrels, and setting up complete 774 rifles.[21]

The Pattern 1823 Baker Rifle (see photos on the next page) is quickly distinguished from other patterns of the Infantry Rifle by its having a "round lock" with a swan-neck cock, and a plain, non-adjustable high block backsight. The design of the patchbox is unchanged from the Pattern 1805 but it is slightly smaller in size. There are no other changes in design from the Pattern 1805. For technical data see Appendix I. Those manufactured at Enfield will display a higher degree of finish than those made by the trade, and will be stamped across the lockplate tail "R^L M^Y ENFIELD" in two lines.

During 1829, a variety of work connected with Baker Infantry Rifles was carried out at Enfield. This included boring and filing 477 rifle barrels, of which 221 were finished off by being rifled, sighted, bayonets fitted and the barrels browned. A total of 556 Infantry Rifle barrels were "twice proved." Enfield also made up 485 Hand Bayonets out of old materials and manufactured 404 rifle locks with steel sears and tumblers in the soft state (i.e. not case-hardened). Presumably using the above materials, Enfield rough stocked and set up complete 336 Infantry Rifles during 1829, the last recorded production of flintlock rifles at the Royal Manufactory.[22]

In the Baker series the design of the Pattern 1823 is best characterised as an "economy model." Whether the simpler cheaper components (the India Pattern Car-

British Military Flintlock Rifles

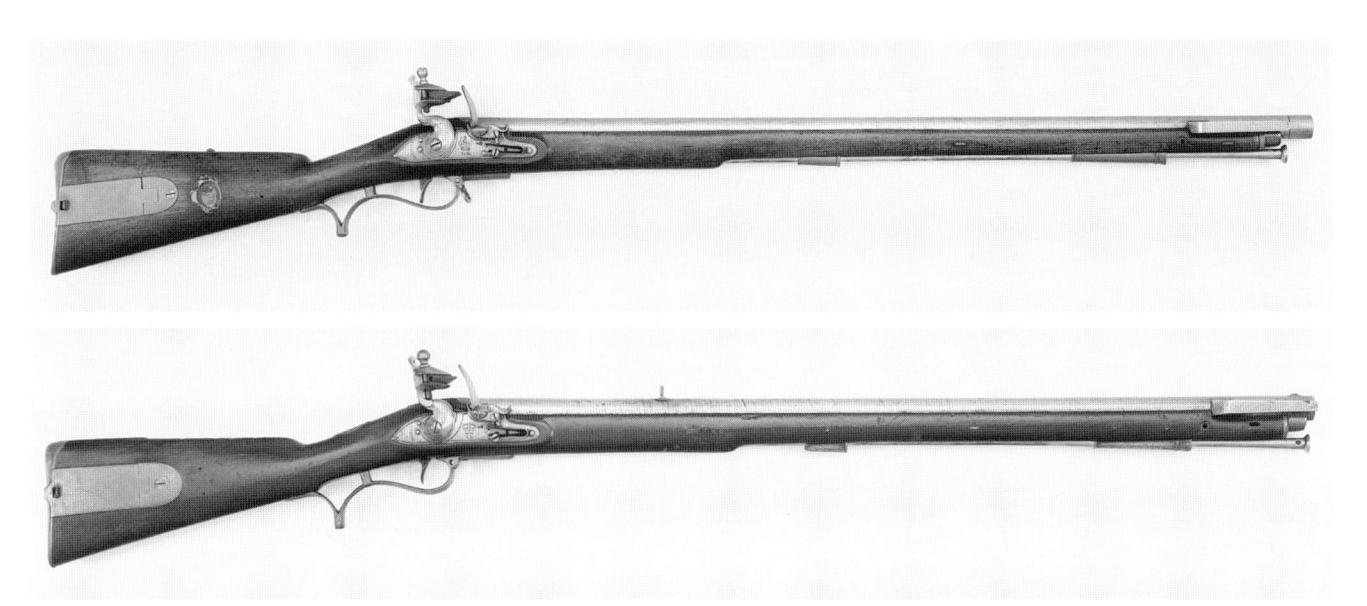

Pattern 1823 Infantry Rifle. *(top)* An unfinished Sealed Pattern showing the barrel not yet trimmed at the muzzle, without sights or finish filing on the bayonet-bar, in the state as supplied for "rifling, sighting, fitting bayonets and browning," functions most frequently carried out by Durs Egg and Ezekiel Baker. *(bottom)* A standard London/Birmingham contract Pattern 1823 Infantry Rifle. Note the rounded lock with swan-neck cock and the high block backsight, the salient features of this pattern. *Courtesy of the Trustees of the Royal Armouries Museum, Leeds.*

Pattern 1823 Infantry Rifle with its hand bayonet, as made by the Royal Manufactory Enfield. Apart from the lock markings and some of the barrel contractor's markings there is no difference between this and the contractor made examples. *Courtesy of the Trustees of the Royal Armouries Museum, Leeds.*

(left) Pattern 1823 Infantry Rifle lock. This design represents a return to the "office pattern" lock used on the Pattern 1798 Heavy Dragoon Carbines, and the India Pattern Carbine lock, and is the only rounded lock used on the Infantry Rifle throughout its long period of manufacture. Contractor locks will have initials or name stamped on the inner surface of the plate, and "TOWER" stamped across the tail of the plate where this example shows Enfield markings. Note also the return to the older double-border line engraving of the plate and cock body and some decorative lines on the pan-bridle. *Courtesy of the Trustees of the Royal Armouries Museum, Leeds.*

— 136 —

(right) **Pattern 1823 Infantry Rifle sights.** The foresight is cast brass incorporating a small blade with a baseplate which is dovetailed and brazed into a raised platform on the barrel. Earlier patterns almost always have steel blades and baseplates dovetailed and brazed to the barrel. The plain block backsight with a U cut out at the top with a small notch filed in the base of the U, sighted for 200 yards. Earlier types had been more complicated and less soldier-proof, with a hinged leaf lying forward of the block, the block being sighted for 100 and the leaf for 200 yards.
Courtesy of the Trustees of the Royal Armouries Museum, Leeds.

bine lock, plain block backsight, re-cast brasswork and simpler bayonet using surplus musket bayonet blades) were actually adopted for their cheapness or from reasons of experience and usage cannot now be clearly established, but the end result, when compared with the earlier patterns, is clear.

PATTERN 1823 SHAH OF PERSIA BAKER RIFLES, 1836

Shah Mohammed (1835–48) ascended the throne of Persia with the backing of both Russia and Britain, although his policy in general was less friendly towards the latter. A British military mission was resident in the country from 1834 until 1838. As a part of this mission, early in 1836 Lieut. Richard Wilbraham, Adjutant of 1/95th and four serjeants of each battalion of The Rifle Brigade were to go to Persia in charge of 2,000 stand of rifles, intended by the Foreign Office as a present to Shah Mohammed.[23] For nearly three years the mission modernized, organized and instructed Persian troops. But then the Shah advanced on and besieged Herat and only pressure from the British Government forced him to abandon the operation; the end result was a break with the British Government. The mission was obliged to depart, and being unable because of their weight and bulk, to take the rifles with them, the Rifle Brigade officers rendered them useless by taking the locks only. If Cope is correct about there being 2,000 rifles, then half of the number taken to Persia must have come from existing Stores with the other half only being newly manufactured.

The rifles, standard Pattern 1823 with Hand Bayonets, were manufactured to the Board's Order of 9 March 1836. All were billed during August and all but four on 1 Aug. The price was 27/9 for rough stocking and setting up, with barrels, locks, rammers, bayonets, and brasswork all supplied from Stores.

Since the locks for these rifles were supplied from Stores, it is an unresolved point whether the royal cyphers engraved on the lockplates ahead of the cocks had been modified from GR to WR, William IV having ascended the throne in 1830. It is possible that the originally engraved GR has been overstamped with WR, as was done with some late musket locks. One new-condition example examined by the writer was a virtual duplicate of the Pattern 1823, except that the block backsight was perhaps 1/8" higher, and the lock was engraved with the WR cypher of William IV.

Rifling, Sighting, Smoothing & Browning barrels, and fitting Hand Bayonets @ 13/-:

E.J. Baker	*26 Aug.*	*472*
W.A. Beckwith	*26 Aug.*	*168*
R.E. Pritchett	*11 Aug.*	*160*
J. Squires	*26 Aug.*	*40*
		840

The remaining 160 barrels were presumably taken

from existing Stores.

Rifles:

Thomas Ashton	60	
Ezekiel John Baker	110	25 Aug.
John Edward Barnett	160	
William James Bond	40	
Joseph Egg	40	
Lacy & Reynolds	150	
William Mills & Son	40	25 Aug.
William Parker	60	
Thomas Potts	160	
Richard Ellis Pritchett	60	
Thomas Reynolds	40	25 Aug.
James Thompson & Son	40	13 Aug.
James Yeomans	40	
	1000	

Hand Bayonets compleat: John & Robert Mole, 29 Aug. 1000 @ 2/3

Hand Bayonet Scabbards, brass chaped: W. Learmonth & Co., 840

THE VICTORIAN BAKER RIFLE

The production of Baker rifles during the early years of Queen Victoria's reign (1837–39) is clear enough as regards numbers, but not at all clear with regard to possible identifying markings: were repaired rifles from Store re-proved with current VR proofmarks, and was the lockplate engraving corrected to reflect the new monarch? Infantry Rifles taken from Store and repaired only, for 12/- each, mostly with sword bayonets, some with hand bayonets, during 1838 totalled 696. These may or may not carry the original Georgian cypher on the lock and GR barrel proofmarks.

New production components may be safely assumed to bear up-to-date markings. Five hundred seventy-two flint Infantry Rifle locks at 5/6 each, were produced by eleven contractors to the Board's Order of 2 Feb. 1838, 52 from each contractor, are presumed to be engraved with a Crown over VR ahead of the cock.
572 locks total, from:

R. Ashmore	14 Feb.
J. Ashton	21 Feb.
J. Corbett	4 June
J. Duce	23 July
W. Partridge	25 Apr.
J. Rubery	25 Apr.
S. Sansom	23 July
B. Turner	7 Mar.
J. Whitehead	7 Mar.
C. Wilson	22 May
J. Yates	21 Feb.

Eighty new barrels at 16/- each, to the Board's Order of 27 July 1838, (John Clive 40 billed 27 Sept. and Joseph Turner 40 billed 27 Oct.) will carry Victorian proof marks.

Other ancillary operations carried out during 1838 include Boring, rifling, sighting, smoothing & browning barrels, & fitting hand bayonets at 13/- each, by:

E.J. Baker	19 July	344
J.E. Barnett	"	80
W.A. Beckwith	"	250
J. Leigh	"	40
T. Potts	"	80
R.E. Pritchett	21 June	120
J. Squires	19 July	200
		1114

Grips for Rifle Hand Bayonets, by Glasscott Bros., billed 14 Apr. 1838: 184
Hand Bayonets compleat: J & R Mole, 5 May 1838: 960
Implements, sets @ 6d ea: Joseph Aston, 14 July: 1800
Leather Accessories, sets, Learmonth & Co., 31 Oct.: 316

All of which led to the completion of the following rifles, Pattern 1823, rough stocked and set up under the Board's Orders of 3 January and 16 February 1838, price 27/9 each:

— PATTERN 1823 RIFLES COMPLETED, 1838 AND 1839 —

	1838		1839	
Thomas Ashton	58	21 June	2	29 Jan.
Ezekiel John Baker	97	14 July	1	4 Mar.
	12	21 Aug.		
John Edward Barnett	143	20 July	17	4 May
	10	17 Oct		
William Thomas	38	19 Sept	2	27 Feb.
William Heptinstall	38	20 July	2	6 Apr.
Lacy & Co.	150	24 July		
James Brooks Leigh	40	24 July		

William Mills	34	6 Apr.		
William Parker	60	24 July		
Thomas Potts	137	14 July	22	6 Apr.
	9	17 Oct.	1	18 Apr.
Richard E. Pritchett	59	21 June	1	29 Jan.
Reynolds & Son	40	24 July		
James Yeoman & Son	39	14 July	1	5 Feb.
	930		**83**	

While the 572 new rifle locks manufactured for this contract may be assumed to have the Crowned VR cypher engraved ahead of the cock on their lockplates, the balance of the 1,013 rifles set up may have had the GR of the cypher overstamped, or (much less likely) they may have been fully erased and re-engraved.

By the Board's Order of 12 Mar. 1838, the first BRUNSWICK Rifles were set up, by Barnett, billed 5 Feb. 1839.

British Military Flintlock Rifles

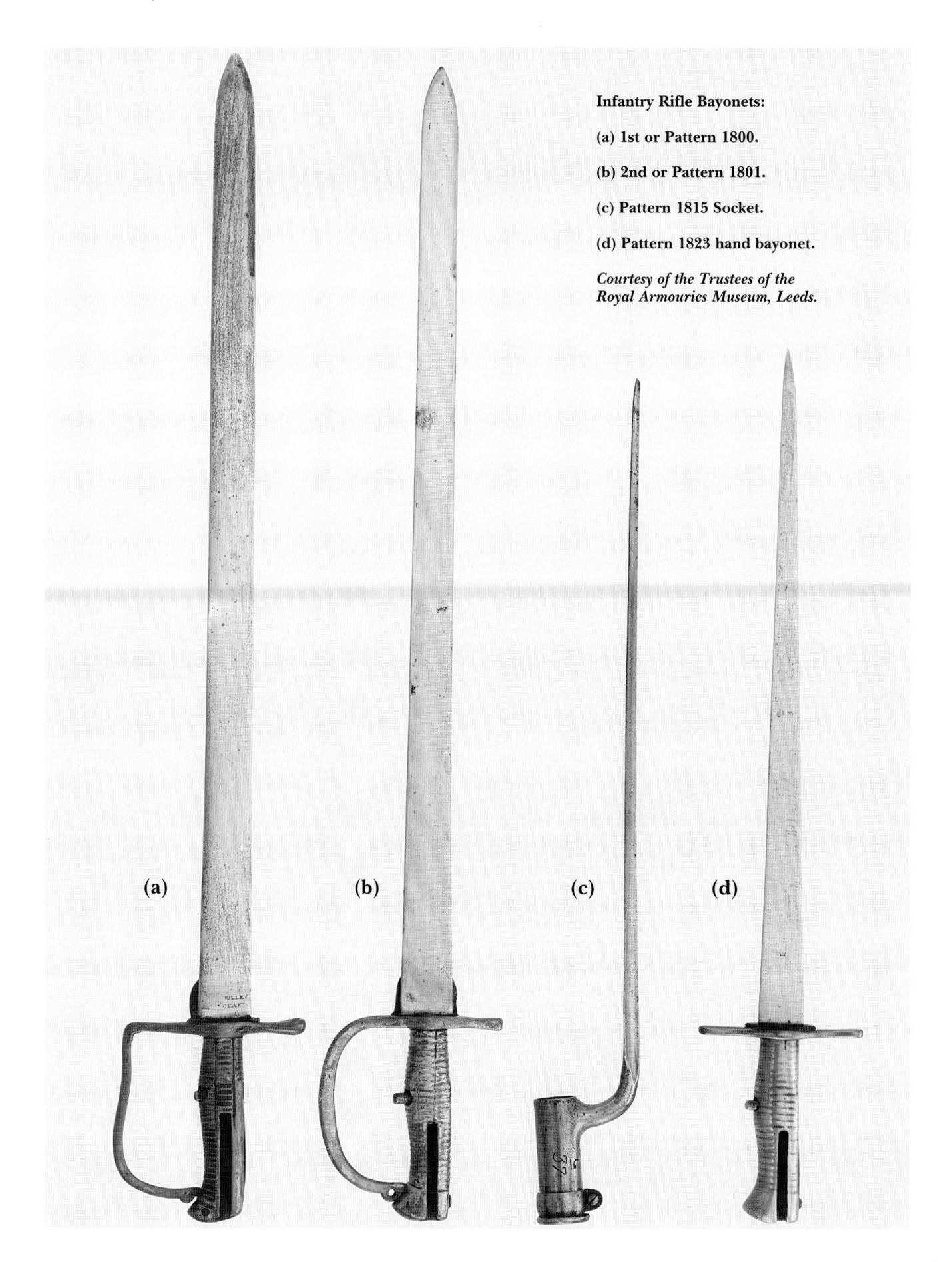

Infantry Rifle Bayonets:

(a) 1st or Pattern 1800.

(b) 2nd or Pattern 1801.

(c) Pattern 1815 Socket.

(d) Pattern 1823 hand bayonet.

Courtesy of the Trustees of the Royal Armouries Museum, Leeds.

(a)   (b)   (c)   (d)

CHAPTER 12
Baker Rifle Bayonets, 1800–1838

There are four basic patterns of Ordnance Baker bayonet. Two of these are so-called sword-bayonets or rifle-swords which were used from the first introduction of the Baker rifle until 1816. As a result of fifteen years' campaign experiences the sword-bayonet was abolished in favour of a conventional socket bayonet which combined a standard triangular blade with a short collared socket and two-motion fixing with a locking ring like that used for the earlier Duke of Richmond's muskets. There was no new production of rifles for the Pattern 1815 socket bayonet with the possible exception of the Pattern 1820, actual examples of which remain to be identified; all were converted from earlier patterns, and at the time of writing all but two have been of the earliest patterns with stepped butt-trap covers. The final pattern was a crude expedient, combining modified hilts of the sword bayonets with a cut-down triangular blade from an India Pattern musket socket bayonet. It is not clear why a return was made to the more expensive form of bayonet-bar fitting on the barrel.

**THE SWORD BAYONET,
OR "RIFLE SWORD" 1800–1815
PATTERN 1800 (FIRST PATTERN)**

What is generally accepted as the First Pattern (1800) Baker sword bayonet, designed for use with the Pattern 1800 Baker Infantry Rifles, has long been known to have been designed by Birmingham manufacturer Henry Osborn, operator of the Bordesley Mills, Deritend, who had supplied bayonets to the Board of Ordnance since 1791. Osborn's first warrant for rifle bayonets is dated 11 March 1800, and his first delivery in June was for 111 "sword bayonets with scabbards for rifled musquets @ 11/- each."[1] He delivered 502 examples during this period, but in December it was noted that the rifle bayonets did not suit the purpose, and Osborn was paid £50.11.10. plus 15 guineas travelling expenses to "travel up [to London] to Establish the pattern."[2] From this it would appear that the initial deliveries of Baker bayonets were unsatisfactory and that a second design was produced after December 1800.

In the meantime, Joshua Johnstone began delivering sword bayonets with scabbards in July, for a total of 200 during the year, and James Woolley shortly afterwards for a total of 288. Woolley, Deakin & Co. also delivered 56 sword bayonets during 1800. There were, therefore, 1,046 sword bayonets delivered during 1800 which appear to have been unsatisfactory, and which may not have been issued, or else issued and later withdrawn.

The First Pattern Baker sword bayonet (see photo on previous page) is identified chiefly by the broad straight blade and the "square" shape of the knuckleguard on the hilt. The overall length of this pattern is 27½ inches, with the blade measuring 22⅞ inches. There is a false edge to the front of the blade measuring 6 inches, and at the base the blade is from 1¼ to 1⅜ inches in width and ⅜-inch thick. The contractor's name is generally but not invariably stamped on the back edge of the blade just above the crossguard. The end of the knuckleguard nearest the pommel is thickened to allow for boring and rigging a sword-knot. A slot is milled into the brass hilt on the side opposite the knuckleguard, and a flat leaf-spring is dovetailed into the "inner" side of the pommel and hilt with a button protruding through the inside of the grip acting as a release. The hilt itself is horizontally grooved and slightly swelled near the middle to fit the hand, with two or three vertical lines along the length of the hilt through the grooving. The quillon is straight.

The scabbard, which is the same for both patterns of sword bayonet, is of blackened leather sometimes supported internally with thin slats of wood on each side, and mounted with brass throat and chape, the former incorporating an oval frog stud on its "outer" side.

PATTERN 1801 (SECOND PATTERN)

The Second Pattern sword bayonet, which is presumed to originate with the design developed by Henry Osborn in December 1800, was produced during 1801 by Osborn, James Wooley and Woolley, Deakin & Co.. Osborn delivered by far the largest number, 2,149, James Wooley 570 and Woolley, Deakin & Co. 534. Osborn also delivered six pattern bayonets: "skeleton sword bayonets as Patterns for fitting the sword bayonets to Rifle Musquets" at 21/- each.[3] Excluding the patterns, there was a total of 3,253 Pattern 1801 bayonets delivered during 1801.

The Second Pattern Baker bayonet is distinguished from the First Pattern by the rounded or "D" shape to the handguard of the hilt. The overall length is 28½ inches and the length of the blade is 23¾ inches. As with the First Pattern, the contractor's name is stamped on the back edge of the blade just above the crossguard. The design of the blade is altered only by the elimination of the false edge on the Second Pattern.

There are no further records of sword bayonet deliveries until 1805. By this time several changes had been made in the design of the Infantry Rifle, but there is no indication of any change in the bayonet design or price of 11/- each including scabbard, and it is therefore assumed that the Pattern 1801 continued to be produced until temporarily superceded by the socket bayonet in 1815. Unfortunately, the method of supply changed with the outbreak of the Napoleonic Wars in 1804 and the establishment of the Royal Manufactory of Small Arms in the Tower of London. From 1807 record-keeping methods changed as well, and there are no further records of the supply of components until the end of the war in 1815.

With the resumption of bayonet production in 1805, several new contractors appear as suppliers of sword bayonets. William & Samuel Dawes, John Gill, Thomas Hadley and Reddell & Bate. A further number of contractors became suppliers of sword bayonets after 1807 and were still supplying in 1815 when components re-merge in the records; these include Thomas Bate (of Reddell & Bate), Craven & Cooper, Osborn, Gunby & Co. (from 1808) and Joseph Reddell (of Reddell & Bate). All of these firms had previously supplied other types of bayonets and/or edged weapons.

Sword bayonet production for 1805–15, so far as it is recorded in the Ordnance records, amounted to:[4]

Bate, Thomas	1815	65
Craven & Cooper	1815	61
Dawes, S. & J.	1815	66
Dawes, W. & S.	1805	438
	1806	238
	1807	27
Gill, John	1805	300
	1806	204
	1815	64
Hadley, Thomas	1806	345
	1815	66
Osborn, Henry	1805	400
	1806	257
	1807	49
Osborn, Gunby & Co.	1815	66
Reddell, Joseph	1815	65
Reddell & Bate	1805	366
	1806	246
Woolley, Deakin & Co.	1805	428
	1806	161
	1807	112
Wooley, James.	1815	66

The figures for 1807 given above are incomplete, since the accounting system changed during that year. Totals for any one year can be approximated by using the number of rifles produced, bayonet production normally equalling or exceeding gun production.

The final order for Infantry Rifle sword-bayonets of the Second Pattern was placed on 8 May 1815 for 500 pieces divided amongst eight contractors:

Dawes	66	*Osborn & Gunby*	66
Reddell	65	*Bate*	65
Woolley	66	*Gill*	64
Craven & Cooper	61	*Hadley*	66

for a total of 519.[5]

PATTERN 1806 SAW-BACK SWORD BAYONET

A number of Baker sword bayonets with saw-back edges are in museum and private collections. The pattern for this variant sword bayonet was supplied by Ezekiel Baker and billed on 24 September 1806 as "A Rifle Sword, saw-cut on the back for Riflemen as a Pattern £1.1.0. and another ditto."[6] By the Board's order of 22 Sept. 1806, it was priced at 14/-, as opposed to the plain-bladed version at 11/-.[7] It is impossible to say how many saw-back sword bayonets were produced: the period during which they would have been made was one in which rifle bayonets were not listed. They are certainly found with far less frequency than the Pattern 1801.

In design the Pattern 1806 saw-back Sword Bayonet is identical to the Pattern 1801 Baker bayonet, except for having the back edge of the blade cut with saw teeth, and is therefore considered as a variant. At the time of writing, the Pattern 1806 is the earliest known attempt to combine a saw-blade with the soldier's bayonet.

PATTERN 1815 SOCKET BAYONET

On 19 May 1815, the Commander-in-Chief, H.R.H. Frederick, Duke of York, requested the Board of Ordnance to submit a pattern rifle and bayonet. He specified that the foresight of the rifle be kept entirely separate from the bayonet (as on the current rifle) but that "The Holder of Hitch [i.e. the bayonet stud] of the Bayonet should be placed on the opposite side, that is the lower side of the barrel"[8] in the current French manner.

The Pattern 1815 Baker Socket Bayonet measures 20.8 inches overall; the triangular blade is the standard musket length of 17 inches, and the short socket is 2.9 inches long with a wide, slightly rounded locking ring at the base. There are three shapes of shoulder found on these bayonets which may be described as well rounded with a very short shank, smoothly tapering with almost no shank, and angled with a short shank. The new-production bayonets have the smoothly tapering shoulders and will bear the contractor's name on the inside base *(top)* **Pattern 1806 Saw-Back Sword Bayonet.** Blade lengths on these bayonets can vary slightly, but are about 23.2".

(bottom) **Pattern 1816 Rifleman's saw-back Sword.** Although the army abandoned the combined sword-bayonet, they could not bring themselves to relieve the rifleman of having to carry both a bayonet and a sword — a return to the mid-18th-century infantry practice of carrying a socket bayonet and a hanger. The example shown is the most recent of candidates to be identified as this anachronistic sidearm. *Both images Courtesy of the Trustees of the Royal Armouries Museum, Leeds.*

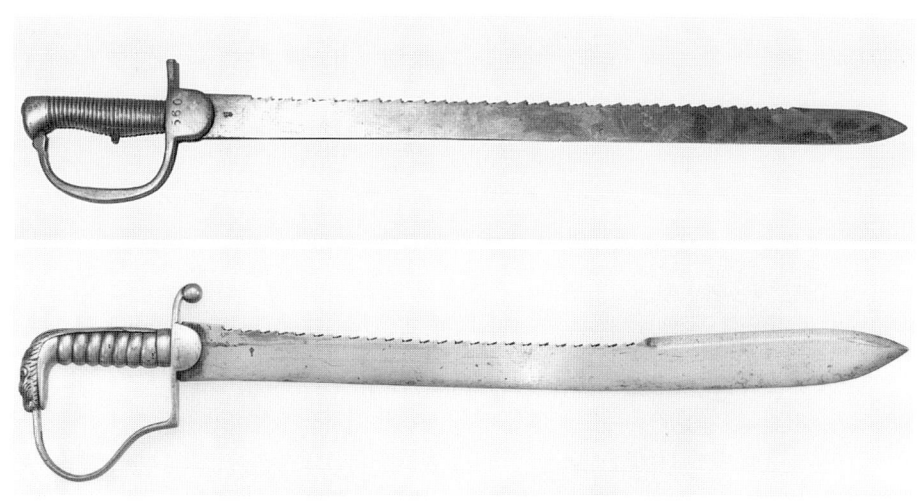

of the blade. The other two are converted examples, and the differences may represent work done by contractors and at Enfield.

On 10 July 1815, Miller reported that 5,000 Rifle Bayonets would be supplied to the Board's Order of 28 June at 2/11 each including the collar and spring. Fifteen contractors would provide the bayonets:[9]

Dawes	350	Hill	350
Osborn & Gunby	350	Galton	350
Allport	268	Woolley	350
Gill	350	G. Salter	350
Wheeler	350	Hadley	350
J. Salter	350	J. Rock	266
Chambers	350	Oughton	350
M. Rock	266		

The blade is the conventional triangular form and the socket made with a two-motion slot and a locking ring identical to that on the Duke of Richmond's muskets and the Pattern 1797–8 Heavy Dragoon Carbines.

PATTERN 1816 SAW-BACK RIFLEMAN'S SWORD

Thanks to the adoption of a short-sword by Light Infantry regiments, and consequent upon the adoption of a socket bayonet in place of a sword bayonet for the Baker rifle, it was felt necessary to give the riflemen a sidearm in addition to the bayonet. The Assistant Inspector of Small Arms, Captain Dundas, submitted to the Board on 22 May 1815 a pattern sword for riflemen "made agreeably to the form proposed by the Adjutant General," and the Board sent it along with a pattern rifle and another sword requesting "that HRH be acquainted the Board are of the opinion the sword which has the number of the 52d Regt on it is the best adapted to the purpose."[10] On 12 June, HRH (the Duke of York, Commander-in-Chief) approved the new pattern rifle and the 52d Regiment pattern sword, and directed that the Inspector of Small Arms, Colonel Miller, make enquires about the price at which the sword could be supplied.[11] There then arose an "innovation." On 23 June 1815 the Adjutant General opined:

...that the Sword...proposed to be adopted for the service of Rifle Corps, would be rendered still more eligible, by being made applicable to the purposes of a Saw in the same manner as the Swords of Light Infantry Serjeants of the Coldstream Guards.[12]

On 29 June the Adjutant General sent a sword of this description to the Board of Ordnance and requested that one be prepared and sent to the Commander-in-Chief for his inspection.[13] The price for the saw-backed swords was agreed at 13/6 each, and production was in progress by March 1816.[14]

Of this new saw-backed sidearm, Colonel Norcott of the Rifle Brigade wrote in 1816:

As the bayonet has been lately substituted to fix on the rifle in place of the sword, I would suggest that it be abolished altogether; the soldier has no use for both. It was always a preventative to his easy marching from the manner in which it was slung, and is very heavy. If it be said that it must be of use upon service in order to cut wood, or to hut, I can testify that the Light Division in Spain carried small felling axes, purchased by the captains for their men at the particular request of the latter, ...and used them in preference to either sword or bill hook. ...indeed, I scarcely ever knew the soldier use his sword, but for the purpose of dividing the meat, or for clearing ground to lay on.[15]

Under a contract dated 31 Mar. 1816 for swords with saw-backs for Infantry Riflemen @ 13/6 each, 5,000 were to be supplied by:

Thomas Hadley	*560 (548)*
Cooper & Craven	*560 (650)*
Gill	*560 (607)*

Osborn & Gunby	640 (640)
Dawes	560 (544)
Wooley	1000 (1102)
Reddell	560 (549)
Bate	560 (544) = (5194)

The numbers in parentheses are those actually delivered.[16] A further 28 of these swords were delivered in March 1818, 12 by Hadley and 16 by Dawes.

At the time of writing, speculation continues as to the physical identity of this rifleman's saw-backed sword. The sidearm shown here is suggested by the late Howard L. Blackmore in a recent article as being the most likely candidate, and his evidence strongly supports his case.[17]

MODIFIED DUKE OF RICHMOND'S MUSKET BAYONETS FOR PATTERN 1800/15 BAKER RIFLES, AND PATTERN 1820 BAKER RIFLES

In January 1819, Col. Miller, Inspector of Small Arms, reported that there were a number of rifles in the Tower Stores that required "common" bayonets instead of sword-bayonets. Of these, 500 had been sent to the Royal Manufactory Enfield for conversion. On 27 December, George Lovell reported that there had been a dispute between the barrel men and the stock men as to who should carry out the conversion work. By mid-1820, the Master Furbisher at the Tower, Jonathan Bellis, reported that there were 565 bayonets made under the orders of the Duke of Richmond in the 1780s "which with a very little alteration could be made applicable to the Infantry Rifles now setting up in the R M Enfield." This modification was approved.[18]

The timing of these remarks indicates that the conversion of earlier rifles to socket bayonets, as adopted in 1815, was still continuing; but by mid-1820 the modified bayonets were probably intended for the new rifles being set up under the Board's orders of January 1820.

Bayonet work was also carried out by the Birmingham contractors during July 1820 amounting to £62.10.0. between twelve contractors: William Allport, Samuel Chambers, S.&J. Dawes, Elizabeth Gill, John Hill, Elizabeth Ketland, J.&C. Oughton, Henry Osborn, John Salter, George Salter, Wheeler & Son and James Wooley. But it is not clear whether this relates to the above-approved modification or to other work.[19] These converted Baker socket bayonets can be recognized by the filled-in front sight slot beneath the locking ring on the socket and by the longer shank joining the blade to the socket, with either angled or rounded shoulders.

PATTERN 1823 HAND BAYONET

The reasons behind the adoption of a combination of the worst of both features of the previous two types of Baker rifle bayonet are unknown. The result (and perhaps also the reason) is an "economy" product, and the presence in Store of large numbers of India Pattern bayonets may go far towards an explanation for the design of this instrument.

These bayonets were supplied with the rifles by the rifle contractors and were made up with blades from India Pattern socket bayonets then in Store and issued to the contractors along with the brass grips supplied by Mary Glasscott & Sons.

The first order of 2,000 of these bayonets was placed with the Royal Manufactory Enfield on 4 June 1823.

Hawkes, Moseley & Co. of Piccadilly supplied bayonet scabbards with brass chapes for the Hand Bayonet at 1/- each, 1,000 in December 1823, and a second thousand in May 1824.

PATTERN 1825 HAND BAYONET

In April 1825, complaints about the excessive weight of the Hand Bayonet issued to them in 1823 were received from the Rifle Brigade. The enthusiastic Lt. Col. Brown had designed a lighter version with a buckhorn handle. This was ultimately rejected, but the brass hilt and the blade of the Hand Bayonet were reduced, thus achieving a reduction in weight from as much as 1 lb. 9 ozs. for some Enfield examples and 1 lb., 5 ozs. for the original standard, to 15½ ozs. This new pattern was approved on 7 October 1825.

The Pattern 1825 Hand Bayonet uses the same basic blade as the Pattern 1823 but slimmed down. Both crossguard and hilt are much reduced in thickness and diameter respectively. The pommel has much more of a bird's-head appearance. Enfield made 2,234 of these Hand Bayonets during 1826, but there are no records for production during 1824–5.[20]

Hawkes, Moseley & Co. supplied narrower scabbards for the Pattern 1825 Hand Bayonet, 1,000 in 1825, 3,000 in 1826 and another 1,100 for the Dublin demand in December 1826. Mary Glasscott & Sons supplied a second order of 8,000 brass grips with crossguards for Hand Bayonets, of re-cast brass, in the summer of 1830, undoubtedly of the 1825 pattern.

For the Pattern 1823 rifles supplied to the Shah of Persia in 1836, John & Robert Mole, were billed for 1,000 hand bayonets @ 2/3 each on 29 Aug. 1836. W. Learmonth & Co. supplied 840 brass chaped hand bayonet scabbards.

The final deliveries for Baker bayonets occurred in 1838, when the Moles were billed for 960 hand bayonets on 15 May, and the Glasscott Brothers were billed for 184 brass grips for rifle hand bayonets on 14 April.

There are many minor variations and modifications found on Baker bayonets, which is beyond the scope of this rifle-oriented study to delineate. Readers are recommended to *British and Commonwealth Bayonets* by Ian D. Skennerton and Robert Richardson, pages 64–79.

CHAPTER 13

Accoutrements & Ammunition

for the Baker Rifles

RIFLE TOOLS AND MAINTENANCE

The standard tools issued with each Baker Infantry and Cavalry rifle consisted of a ball drawer, a wiping eye and a lever which was used as a torque-bar through the hole in the head of the steel ramrod when drawing a ball (see below). These implements were to be carried in the butt-box of the rifle and cost one shilling and sixpence per set. Of the latter device the designer, Ezekiel Baker, says

Under the head of the rammer is a small hole, to put in a lever, which makes the rammer similar to a carpenter's gimlet, and forms a purchase to screw into the ball, and by that means the ball is easily drawn out of the barrel.[1]

Thanks to lessons learned under combat conditions, a powder charger was added to the "box implements" on all rifles delivered beginning in April 1810[2] and ceasing in 1814. No example of this implement has been identified at the time of writing.

Keeping the rifle in a clean and serviceable condition was given top priority in the Regulations for the Rifle Corps published in 1801:

The care of rifled arms is of such serious importance, both from the expence of the workmanship, and the superior nicety of their construction, that Captains of companies are made particularly responsible for their own. Each Captain will have as many complete stands of arms and sets of accoutrements in his possession, as he has men able to bear arms in his company, all of which he will mark, number, and distinguish: no arms or accoutrements are ever to be changed from man to man, as long as a Soldier is in the same company...

Every company will therefore have an arm-chest, which is to be made so as to contain twenty-five stands of arms, accoutrements and appointments complete; ...Every Rifleman going on furlough, on pass for more than forty-eight hours, or into hospital, is to have his arms and accoutrements carefully deposited in the arm-chest. As Riflemen are supposed to be Soldiers of the greatest attention towards arms, no lenity will

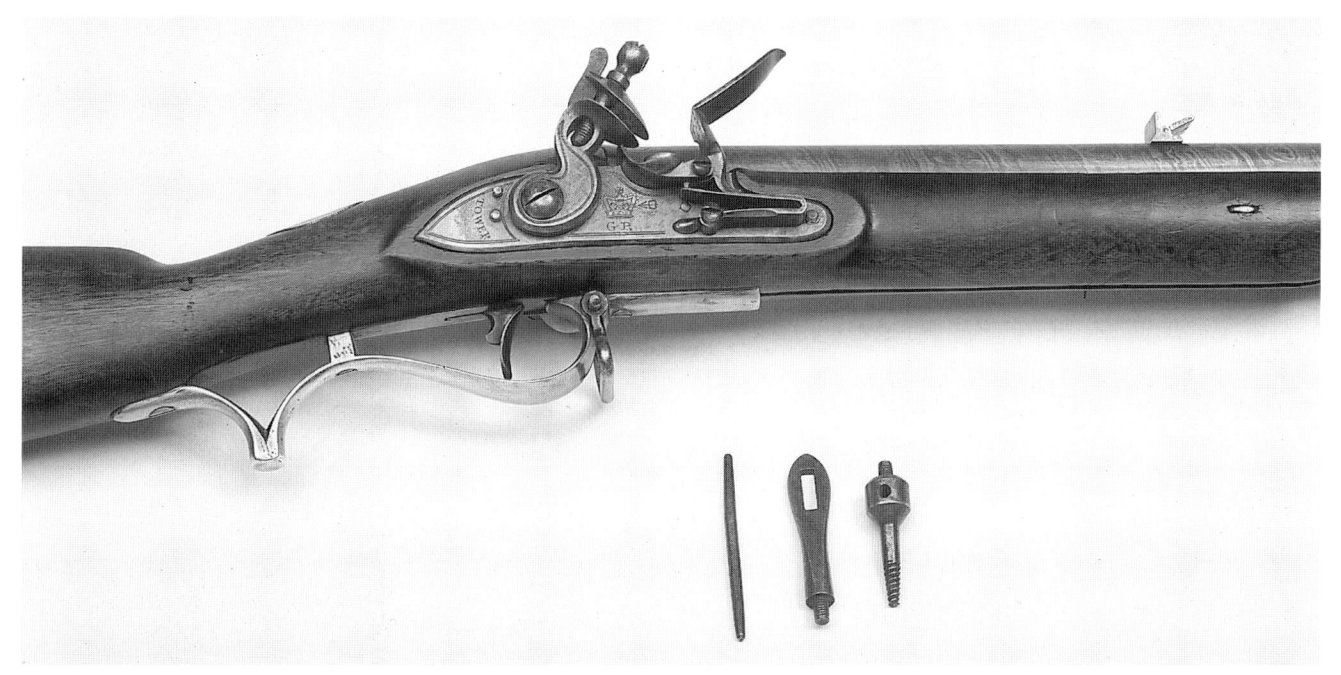

"Box implements" for the Infantry Rifle 1800–1840, consisting of a torque bar, wiping eye and ball drawer. Shown here with a Pattern 1805 Infantry Rifle. *Courtesy T.A. Edwards.*

— 145 —

be shewn to those who injure or spoil them. No locks are to be taken off, on pain of punishment, by any man who is not one of those who are permitted men by their Captain. If a Soldier be not what is to be called a Trusty man, and wishes to repair or clean anything within the lock of his rifle, he must go to the Armourer or the Serjeant of his squad, take it off, and repair the injury, or clean it in his presence...

The browned barrels are never to be rubbed with any rough substance; the lock-caps are to be at all times worn, excepting on guard. When an Officer wishes to inspect, he will order them off for the time, for if a Soldier's lock cannot be trusted out of the sight of his Officer at all parades, he is totally unfit for the rifle service;...

Each company...will have an armourer...The Armourer Major will establish his forge and work shop as near to the corps as possible; his price of work, as also the wages which he is to give to the journeymen armourers will be yearly settled by the Board of Works.

ACCOUTREMENTS

The various accoutrements carried by the rifleman appear to have been deliberately designed to afford both ready access and magazine storage capacity for both loose powder and ball and for cartridge loading. Thus the powder horn and tin box of the pouch served as magazines, while the copper powder flask, the ball-bag, and the wooden box of the pouch served as ready access points.

Writing from Horsham Barracks on 15 April 1800, Col. Coote Manningham sent a list of "Appointments required for the Establishment of the Rifle Corps" as follows:

For 35 Serjeants, each   One Sword Belt
One Pouch
One Pouch Belt
One Rifle sack
One Powder Horn
One Ball Bag
One Rifle Sling
One Lock Cover

The same articles were also for each of 435 rank and file. "The Serjeants Pouch Belts to have affixed in front, across the Brest, a socket for a small whistle, three Inches long, with a chain six Inches long affixed as pr pattern." For the fourteen Buglers, there were to be:

One Pistol Pouch
One Pistol Pouch Belt
One Sword Belt
One Bugle
One Bugle Case[3]

To date, neither a special pistol nor its holster has been identified for the bugle-horn men of the Rifle Corps. A subsequent letter suggests that contractors Adams & Welford may have supplied this initial proportion of accoutrements. Another early listing specifies:

Articles usually furnished to the Rifle Corps, 11 June 1803
   Rifles, Carbine bore with Sword Bayonets and Scabbards, Ramrods, Boxes, Wiping Eyes, Ball Drawers and Levers
   Lead for Balls cast by the Corps
   Gunpowder FG in Qr Barrels of 22 lbs each
   3½ drams is the quantity of powder used for each ball.[4]

The first inspection return for the Rifle Corps thus far located (Shorncliffe, 23 Dec. 1803) describes the accoutrements then held by the rank and file as:[5]

> *Pouches and Belts*
> *Sword Belts*
> *Slings*
> *Lock Caps (340)*
> *Powder Horns (336)*
> *Powder Flasks (329)*
> *Ball Bags (330)*

A Return of Arms of the 5th/60th at Halifax N.S. 20 Sept. 1804 showed 783 Rifles, Pouches & Belts, and Powder Horns.[6] A third return dated 1 Oct. 1805 shows 780 horns, wanting 65.

An Inspection Return of 8 Apr. 1806 for 2/95th at Hailsham shows 820 Rifles with: Pouches & Belts, Sword Belts, Slings, Lock Caps 804, Powder Horns 691, Powder Flasks 880, Tin and Wood Boxes 819, Ball Bags 825, Bullet Moulds 882.[7]

From 1807 a printed return form is used for Arms and Accoutrements and no provision is made for listing the special accoutrements of Rifle companies; only a few hand-written forms in the field show these, e.g.

Alameda, 3 Feb. 1813, 1/95: 643 rifles, Powder Flasks 239 good, 99 bad, 104 wanting.[8]

Ospeya, 6 Feb. 1813, 3/95: 382 rifles, Powder Flasks 191 good, 15 bad, 176 wanting; lock covers 305.[9]

Rifleman Costello in his memoirs of service in the Napoleonic Wars describes in detail what a rifleman on campaign carried in 1809:

Regulation Heavy-Marching Order Kit at the time of the forced march on Talavera [1809]:
1 knapsack & straps
1 powder-flask, filled
2 shirts
1 ball-bag containing 30 loose balls
2 pr stockings
1 small mallet (to hammer ball into muzzle of rifle)
1 pr shoes

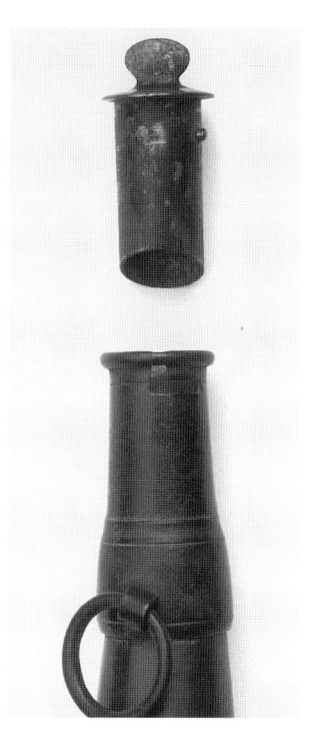

Powder horns and chargers of the period 1800–20. At the time of writing no horns which can be authenticated as used by the 95th, 60th or other rifle-carrying regular army unit have been identified. The descriptions in the text suggest a removable scoop-type charger as a general type. The charger tops shown here are of this type, giving some idea of the possible variations.

Courtesy D.F. Harding and T.A. Edwards.

1 belt & pouch containing 50 rds ammo
1 pr spare soles & heels
1 sword-belt and sword
3 brushes
1 rifle
1 box of blacking
1 razor, 1 soap-box, 1 strop
1 extra pr trowsers
1 mess-tin, centre-tin and lid
1 haversack
1 canteen (used as a water bottle)[10]

A slightly later listing in a Warrant of 15 July 1812 gives rifle corps accessories as:

sword belt, pouch and belt, sling, lock cover, powder horn with lace or strap, copper flask, bullet bag.[11]

POWDER HORNS

The powder horn was "a large cow horn slung from two rings by a green cord... The bottom...was made of wood, covered, and mounted with brass; the mouthpiece was fitted with a spring such as is usually fitted to a shot belt." The horns varied slightly in size but were intended to hold from forty to sixty rounds (4,400 to 6,600 grains) of powder. Serjeants carried horns of a slightly smaller size to contain about twenty-five rounds (2,750 grains) of powder.[12] There are 7,000 grains to one pound.

The way in which such items reached the hands of the troops in indicated in this letter of 1803 to the regimental agents of the 5/60th:

...as Powder Horns in addition to Pouches appear to be absolutely necessary for a Corps of Rifle Men, the Secretary at War approves of Lt. Gen. Stanwix's causing a complete set to be provided for the present Establishment of the 5th Battalion of the 60th Regt taking especial care that they be provided at the most reasonable Rates: and the cost of the same will be defrayed by the Public.[13]

Lt. Gen. Thomas S. Stanwix was Colonel of the 5/60th.

The military outfitters Learmouth & Beazley in Parliament St. supplied powder horns to the 5/60th in 1805 (presumably replacements or additions to those obtained by Stanwix in 1803), and doubtless to other regiments as well.[14]

The design of the horns in possession of the 5/60th when they went to Portugal was found to be unsatisfactory on campaign:

Guarda D'Abrantes,
June 14th, 1809
Sir,
I beg leave to state to you, for the information of His Royal Highness the Commander-in-Chief, that the powder-horns with which the 5th battalion 60th regiment is supplied, have, by experience, been found to be ill-adapted to the service, and

by their construction have not only occasioned much loss of powder, and subjected the colonel to great expenses in repairs, but have proved after all to be entirely useless, being too large and having no measure fitted to them.

They have been furnished by Messrs Beseley and Reise of Parliament Street, London, after patterns delivered to them, but experience having now shown their inutility, I beg leave to suggest the propriety of providing the battalion with powder-flasks of same description as those in possession of the 95th regiment, large enough to contain forty rounds of fine-grain powder at five drachms each round, including the priming, with proper measures adapted to them for different distances...
To the Adjt-General of Forces
Horse Guards, London.[15]

This reference indicates that there were at least two different patterns of powder horn in use by rifle regiments in Portugal, and that the type used until then by the 5/60th was not fitted with an integral powder measure. A "flask" holding 5,500 grains, or about three-quarters of a pound of powder, is recommended. Note also the preference for a larger charge of powder, five drams (137 grains) as opposed to the regulation 3½ (96¼ grains, normally expressed as 96).

Curiously, as late as July 1811 the Adjutant General's office was writing to the Board of Ordnance enquiring whether the "Magazine Horns, used by Rifle Regiments, are supplied by the Board of Ordnance."[16]

An Inspection Return of the 4/60th stationed in Surinam, dated 12 May 1814 shows 107 Powder Horns in the hands of the riflemen.

A general review of the accoutrements of the Rifle Corps was held in 1816, which reveals a number of adaptations made as the result of campaign experiences. Col. Norcott of the 1/95th, the reporting officer, said that as a result of the various expeditions on which the Rifle Corps had been sent, and the first campaign in the Peninsular (1808) it was clearly proved that the horns could not be maintained in serviceable condition. They were "rendered incomplete by the loss of the mouthpiece, and spring, or by damage, and could not be repaired." He said that:

...men who had them in an incomplete state, were perfectly useless to the Service, and that accidents were continually liable to happen from the quantity of loose powder about the person of the soldier with the mouthpiece of his horn lost, or damaged... Under every circumstance that then existed it was found advisable to discontinue their use, and supply the Corps with ball cartridge ammunition.[17]

For the men under his command he adopted a modification which he now recommended for general adoption: the fitting of a cork stopper with a string-fastening to the mouth of the flint horn, and covering the body with (presumably heavy) black leather. He commented that this system worked well and had been used by most of the Second Battalion during the campaign in Spain under Sir John Moore.

POWDER FLASKS

It is curious that while powder horns are mentioned in the initial outfitting, the powder flask does not appear until more than two and a half years later. It may be that this was a subsequent refinement suggested by training or the whim of Manningham or one of his officers, or it may have been present from the first equipping of the 95th and not mentioned because Manningham knew the Ordnance would not supply such an item. It is worth noting in this context that all of the accoutrements he lists were normal Light Infantry accoutrements as far back as the establishment of light infantry companies in line regiments in 1771.

The "small copper powder flask" is described as holding thirty rounds (3,300 grains or just under a half-pound) of powder, "with the mouthpiece screwed on the orifice," so that the measure of powder was "supplied by pulling back the spring and tilting the flask. The soldier loaded from this flask and it was replenish'd from the magazine horn as required." The flask was fitted with two rings at the neck, and was carried on a green cord around the soldier's neck. It was sometimes carried in a pocket on the left breast of the jacket, and sometimes hung down at the side.[18] At the time of writing no example of this flask has been identified.

In his review of the accoutrements of the Rifle Corps in 1816, Colonel Norcott found the flask itself useful but that the mounting (top and collar) should be made stronger and that the method of carriage should be stronger and afford more protection to the flask. He recommended a leather case fitted on the right side of the waistbelt.

That the powder flask remained a part of a rifleman's accoutrements as late as 1820 is clearly shown by two orders for sets of accoutrements placed with T.M. Keats in the Spring of that year. The first was for 1,044 sets of rifle accoutrements consisting of a waist belt, pouch belt, gun sling, ball bag, lock cover, pouch and powder flask at 23/- per set; these were for the Glasgow Volunteer Infantry Sharpshooters and for Stores in the Tower. The second order for 256 identical sets adds the detail that they were to be of black leather, and states that they were for Tower stores.[19]

It appears from a letter written in 1826 (see discussion later in chapter) that the powder flask was discontinued sometime between 1820 and the date of the letter; the reasons put forward in the letter rejecting their re-introduction probably explain the motives behind the move, in addition to which peacetime economy cannot be disregarded.

Accoutrements and Ammunition for the Baker Rifle

A powder flask non-adjustable spring-charger of the early 1800s throwing the correct charge for the Infantry Rifle. A copper flask holding just under a half-pound of powder would look very ungainly fitted with a charger of this size. To date no flask has been authenticated to any of the regular army rifle-carrying units of the 1800–20 period.
Courtesy D.F. Harding.

POWDER CHARGERS

From April 1810, until the end of their production in 1814, the Birmingham contractors supplied Infantry Rifles which included amongst the "box implements" — the tools carried in the butt-box — a powder charger. A total of 5,099 powder chargers were thus supplied with the Baker rifles from the Birmingham contractors. This new device was first included with the tools for the one hundred musket-bore rifles delivered in 1810 by the Sutherlands, and it is assumed that these will be for a larger charge than those for the standard carbine-bore rifles. The inference must be that the devices previously employed for measuring powder charges for the Infantry Rifle - the scoop charger on the top of the horn and the nozzle of the copper flask - were inadequate or unsatisfactory: there can have been no other reason for the Ordnance to suddenly, in the midst of a wartime production programme, introduce a new implement when two others designed to perform this function were already standard issue. There was no corresponding increase in the price of the box implements. The orders for box implements supplied by the Sherwoods of London, for use with rifles made by the London trade and presumably the Royal Manufactory in the Tower, make no mention of a charger. At the time of writing none of these chargers has been identified.

BALL BAGS

The ball-bag was intended to carry 30 (according to Rifleman Costello) loose patched balls, serving as a ready-access supply. It was described in 1816 as having a leather running-string or thong to close it at the mouth, and an outer cover or flap which extended about an inch over the mouth all around, fastened by a round leather button on the body of the bag. It was carried on the right side of the waist-belt almost in front of the body, secured by two loops. The ball-bag was replenished from the pouch. In 1816 Col. Norcott pronounced the ball-bag "so perfect that it is impossible to improve upon it."[20]

MALLETS

Although not mentioned in any of the contemporary lists of riflemen's equipment, small wooden mallets

— 149 —

were supplied with which to seat the tightly patched ball in the muzzle of the barrel. Baker supplied 169 of these during 1800[21] and a further 250 by July 1801[22] all priced at 2 1/2d each. It has long been considered that, because there are no references in the Ordnance records to mallets after the initial orders from Baker, the use of the mallet was discontinued. The following letters indicate that their use survived at least into the early years of the Peninsular campaign. After the initial 419 mallets, a second delivery appears in the War Office records in March 1804:

Three hundred and fifty wooden mallets being wanted for the service of that part of the 95th or Rifle Corps which is stationed in the district under the command of Lt. Gen. Sir J.H. Craig, I have the honor to request you will receive and transmit H.M. Commands to the Master General and Board of Ordnance that the said mallets may be issued out of H.M. Stores for the use of the said Service and the Expense thereof charged to the Estimate of Ordnance for Parliament.[23]

It would appear that these mallets were supplied at the rate of one for every two men, and since the Regulations make it clear that riflemen generally acted in pairs and in bodies of even numbers, it is an early example of the "buddy" system.

New Barracks, Cork,
June 11th 1808
Sir,
The 5th battalion, 60th regiment, never having been provided with small wooden mallets for the purpose of driving the forced rifle-balls into the barrel, and this instrument being absolutely necessary in the field, I feel it my duty to represent that one mallet for every two men should, if possible, be furnished. They should be made of hard wood with a handle about six inches long, pierced with a hole at the extremity of the handle for fastening a string to it.
I annex a requisition for the same, and have the honour to be, etc. etc. W.G. Davy
To the Assistant Adjt.-General, Cork.[24]

Davy commanded the 5/60th under Wellington in the Peninsular; [another quoting of this letter gives the number of 450 mallets] Davy later asked for "powder-flasks of the same description as those of the 95th Regt."[25]

From the above, it will be noted that a carrying cord for the mallet was to be fitted through "the extremity of the handle" which would preclude its use as a "long starter" to put the ball down the barrel sufficiently to give the rammer better guidance. This arrangement is confirmed by the mallet shown as part of the rifleman's equipment on the monument to Colonel Manningham.

CARTRIDGE POUCHES

The accoutrements thus far discussed have all related to the use of loose powder and ball. There is ample evidence to suggest, however, that by far the most typical form of ammunition utilised by all British rifle units was the paper cartridge. These were carried in a leather pouch or cartridge box. A *circa* 1802 description of this leather accoutrement states:

The Pouch for a Rifle Corps to have a wooden box bored for 12 rounds and another [box] of tin capable of holding 24 rounds.

The second pouch was undoubtedly an adaptation of the "magazine pouch" which had been adopted for line infantry in 1784.

The First Pattern Pouch was described in 1816 as being:

...an oblong with the top perfectly flat, side leathers united with the front, thus forming a complete case as a guard against weather. The spare flints were carried in a small leather bag with a running string, and this was attached to the body of the pouch under the cover of it.
The interior consisted of a tin case divided into two equal parts, and a wooden frame with holes for twelve cartridges. The loose balls covered with greased rags were kept in the tin compartments, and the ball cartridges in the wooden ones.[26]

The Second Pattern Pouch (there is no indication when this came into use) "differs from the former one in no respect as to interior" but was curved like the conventional Ordnance cartridge box to fit the body. There were no side leathers and the flint pocket was smaller and without a string to close it, being inadequate to hold the flints securely. Col. Norcott reported that the new pouch "cannot contain, without the risk of bruising the cartridges in the paper packages as now made up, more than four parcels of ten each; and the wooden holes, twelve, this making in the whole, fifty-two rounds, a number infinitely too small for Riflemen to have in their possession." This was clearly an economy version that did not meet service requirements. Rifleman Costello, writing in 1852, says the pouch held 50 rounds rather than 36, probably referring to the Second Pattern. He felt rather over-burdened with ammunition.

LOCK CAPS [COVERS]

This standard and essential protection for a flint lock against wet weather is not generally mentioned amongst accoutrements because, like the muzzle-stopper or tompion, it was supplied at regimental level and not by the Ordnance. They were usually made of oiled cloth or leather. There were two patterns used by the Rifle Corps, the second type utilizing pieces of sponge at top and bottom to deter water seeping along the barrel and into the lock. This was found to absorb and concentrate the water and was considered distinctly inferior to the original simpler variety.[27]

In a General Order to the army dated at Quinta, 11 June 1811, the troops were informed that:

The Commander in Chief having sent to this country a new invented cover for musket and rifle locks, of which he has directed the experiment might be tried by the troops in this country, ten of them will be deliverd to each of the following regiments upon application to the Commissary General; and the Adjutant General will send to those regiments a paper describing the mode in which the soldier will be enabled to prime and fire his musket when it may be desirable to keep the lock covered from the weather.

List of regiments: Coldstream Guards, 3rd Guards, 92d, 95th for rifles, 43d, 45th 40th, 61st, Chasseurs Britannique.[28]

No mention of a special lock cover has been found in surviving documents of the 95th Regiment.

BAYONET SCABBARDS

The brass-mounted black leather scabbards for the two basic patterns of sword-bayonet and the triangular-bladed Pattern 1815 socket and Pattern 1823 hand-bayonets, came with the bayonet from the makers, but the leather frog by which the scabbard was attached to the sword-belt was supplied by the regiments. See Chapter 12.

TOOLS AND ACCOUTREMENTS FOR THE SHAH OF PERSIA'S BAKER RIFLES, 1836

When 2,000 Baker rifles were prepared for the Shah of Persia in mid-1836 (see Chapter 11), they were accompanied by the usual assortment of maintenance tools and accoutrements. The Birmingham firm of Robert Wheeler & Son supplied 2,000 sets of implements in June. In the same month, Edward Curtis supplied 1,906 sets of accoutrements consisting of pouches, pouch belts, slings, waist belts, brown lock covers, and ball bags at 9/8 per set.[29]

BULLET MOULDS

There were two sizes of ball used with the Infantry Rifle, one of them being the standard carbine-bore ball of .615" diameter. Since this was a commonly available ball used in the cavalry, artillery and infantry arms of any British field army, it is unlikely that moulds casting balls of this size were in issue to individual units or riflemen. However, the second size of 22 to the pound or .596" diameter was peculiar to the rifle regiments, and if moulds were issued it is far more likely they will be for this size. Colonel Francis de Rottenburg of the 5/60th purchased bullet moulds for his men amounting to £6 at the same time that he paid for having regimental markings engraved on their rifles at a cost of £12.10.0.[30]

As noted below, the Colonel of the 95th included a knowledge of casting ball as amongst the skills to be acquired by individual riflemen as early as 1803.

BAKER RIFLE AMMUNITION

Concerning powder charges for the Baker rifle, the "inventor" himself had this to say:

In apportioning the quantity of powder for a rifle, one charge for all distances should be carefully attended to; and if the powder be good, I have ascertained that nearly one third of the weight of the ball, priming included, is the best estimate.[31]

Baker's estimate, with the weight of the 20 to the pound ball at 355 grains, gives 118 grains or between 4¼ and 4½ drams. The Ordnance settled for somewhat less at 3½ drams (96 grains), which apparently increased to 4 drams (110 grains) after the end of the war.

Ammunition for the Baker rifle in British service was divided into two broad types: loose powder and patched ball for precision shooting, and conventional paper cartridges for skirmishing or more rapid firing. At some point later in the war, all rifle ammunition supplied from Government sources was in the form of paper cartridges, with either patched or naked ball. It is not clear whether this was based on combat experience or a need to simplify logistic requirements, or both. Balls intended to be patched, usually referred to as "forced balls" were of 22 to the pound diameter (about .596-inch), while those for use in paper cartridges, "running ball" were of 20 to the pound (about .615-inch) diameter. The Regulations for the Exercise of Riflemen of 1798 (see Appendix 10) clearly identified the circumstances under which cartridges were to be used:

The above regulations for firing with cartridges, will only be applicable when a corps of riflemen is required to act in close order, an instance which will very seldom occur, provided this arm is put to its proper use, and officers will observe in all cases, where riflemen act as such, and whenever it is practicable, their men are to load with the powder measure and loose ball; the principle instructions therefore for recruits will be how to load with the loose ball, and to fire at the target; the loading with cartridge is a secondary object...[32]

On 23 Sept. 1800, the contractor Charles Smith billed the Ordnance for 40 tin powder measures delivered at the Tower for the use of the Rifle Corps: 20 were to hold 3 drams of powder for balls 17 to the lb., and 20 to hold 3½ drams of powder for balls 16 to the lb.[33] These were intended for loading cartridges for the carbine-bore and musket-bore rifles respectively.

In his *Military Lectures* published in 1803, Col. Coote

Manningham of the Rifle Corps stated that:

Every individual [in the Rifle Corps] must be instructed in the method of making up his ammunition, of casting balls, of covering them with rag or leather, and greasing them; and the commanding officers should take care that he has along with his company, bullet moulds sufficient for this purpose. The quantity of powder each rifleman carries will suffice for a long time, and they may frequently, when detached, be able to meet with lead.[34]

Jonathan Bellis the Master Furbisher at the Tower of London, received travelling expenses for attending some trials at Woolwich in May 1801 "with long Rifle Balls" and the following month further experiments "with Rifles Manufactured at Birmingham."[35] One can only speculate whether the "long Rifle Balls" were of the egg-shaped hollow-based variety first described by J.G. Leutmann in 1728, and mentioned in Scloppetaria in 1808, before being claimed by William Greener in 1835.

A voucher for Ordnance Stores issued to Captain Sidney Beckwith at Portsmouth on 28 Feb. 1801, just prior to a detachment of the 95th embarking for the Copenhagen expedition, lists the following items in addition to armourer's tools:[36]

Carbine Ball, Cwt	7
Formers, Carbine	6
Linen for do. Yds	25
Funnels	6
Pistol Flints	800
Melting Ladles for lead	6
Tallow, lbs.	9

This seems to settle the point that, at least officially, the patching used for Baker rifle balls in the early years was of linen, even though "rag or leather" or "fustian," is mentioned in un-official although contemporary accounts. The chief difficulty is in determining accurately just what was meant at the time by each of these terms.

An Admiralty reference of 1803 sheds some light on the quantity and granulation of powder considered standard for rifle cartridges of that date, and also substantiates other references with regard to the regiment casting its own ball. "FG" stood for "fine glazed" at this period:

Articles usually furnished to the Rifle Corps, 11 June 1803
  Rifles, Carbine bore with Sword Bayonets and Scabbards
Ramrods, Boxes, Wiping Eyes, Ball Drawers and Levers
Lead for Balls cast by the Corps
Gunpowder FG in Qr Barrels of 22½ lbs each
 3½ drams is the quantity of powder used for each ball.[37]

By September 1805, it appears from a Board of Ordnance statement, that white fustian was used in making Rifle Ball Cartridges. This indicates that by this date paper cartridges included ready-patched balls.[38] Tallow appears as the official lubricant for the patching.

A letter from Col. de Rottenburg to the Adjutant General's office dated 5 Nov. 1806 sheds good authoritative light on both the lubricant and patching material then in use. De Rottenburg had written the manual for riflemen in the late 1790s, and at the date of this letter was commanding the 5/60th rifle regiment; there is unlikely to have been a better informed or more-up-to-date individual associated with the current military use of the rifle. He wants a supply of "Ticking and Tallow for Patches, which are required by Rifle Regiments when loading with forced Ball..."[39] This substantiates the use of tallow and somewhat clarifies the thickness and weave of the cloth then used for patching. However, the order for ammunition for the expedition to Portugal in 1808 given below indicates fustian patching and wax as a lubricant: a deliberate coarsening and cheapening of the components, an appreciation that the deep rifling of the Baker required a heavier patching material and less volatile lubricant, or absence of expertise on the part of the recording clerk? It also indicates that initially, pistol-size flints rather than the later carbine-size flints were issued for the Baker rifle. Given that the rank and file for this expedition numbered 101, this gives just over 150 rounds and eight flints per man.

An undated list of proportions required to make up 1,000 Small Arms Cartridges includes:

Nature	Powder			No. Lead	Powder			No. in each Barrel	
	lbs.	ozs	drachms	Balls/lb	lbs	ozs	drams	Ball Qtr	Blank Half
Rifle	15	11	4	20	-	-	-	750	-

As part of the Ordnance Stores sent to Montevideo, 4 Apr. 1807 there were: "Rifles of different Patterns 500, with 280,000 Lead Balls and 195 Quarter Barrels of Powder for Rifles."[40] A Return of Ammunition required by two companies of 2/95th going to Gibraltar in April 1808 specified:

Ball Cartridges of 22/lb	10,500
Lead Balls 20/lb.	84,000
Lbs fine grain powder	1,420
Carbine Flints: 2,520.[41]	

The Adjutant General was informed in July 1808 that the Light Brigade of the King's German Legion required rifle ammunition, as it was about to go on service with Sir John Moore's expedition to Portugal; they had been issued with carbine ammunition for the previous expedition to the Baltic![42]

As part of a depot for the King's German Legion on the Continent, 280 rounds of ammunition for each of 2,000 Rifles was to be kept, as well as 5,000 spare muskets and 200 Cavalry Carbines.[43]

A Battalion Order of 17 June 1808, issued on the eve of their departure for Portugal, expresses an approach which actual combat experience soon altered:

The true "Rifleman" will never fire without being sure of his man; he should if possible make use of forced balls, and only load with cartridges in case of necessity, as when a brisk fire is to be kept up. And he will recollect that a few direct shots that tell will occasion greater confusion than thousands fired at random and without effect...[44]

This bias towards precision shooting was backed by the shipment of 500,000 rifle cartridges with balls of 22 to the pound[45] with waxed fustian patches to Lisbon in December 1808.[46] Note that the cartridges incorporate the waxed patched balls. This quantity was soon seen to be inadequate:

As it appears that the 95th Regt embarked for Portugal under the orders of Brigadier General Crawfurd is only provided with 120 Rounds of Rifle ammunition: I am desired by Lord Castlereagh to suggest to you for the information of the Master General of the Ordnance the propriety of forwarding by the first Store ship a further supply in loose Powder & Balls at 20 to the Pound and in Cartridges the Balls 22 to the Pound.[47]

Lord Wellesley wrote to the officer commanding the Royal Artillery on the expedition that at the artillery depot established at Almeida, 24 June 1809, there were to be 1,200,000 rounds of musket ammunition and 200,000 of rifle ammunition.[48]

At the same period, but in another theatre of the worldwide conflict, ammunition as part of Ordnance Stores for the British forces in Sicily and the Ionian Islands, as at 30 May 1810, included:

Ball cartridges for musquets, common		2,000,000
	buckshot	50,000
	rifle, 22 to lb.	60,000 + 10,000 rifle flints[49]

Inspection Returns for the depot companies of the first and second battalions of the 95th at Shorncliffe Barracks in October 1813, mention having loose powder and ball, and loose powder & ball and cartridges.[50]

That there were differences of opinion amongst field officers of the rifle regiments as to the best type of ammunition for use by riflemen during the Peninsular campaigns is evidenced by a report of 1821:

Both the species of Rifle ammunition...are for [the same] arm; but the different Rifle corps did not fully accord as to their use, some preferring the cartridges of 20 to the lb. and of others those of 22 to the lb. covered with fustian.[51]

This report also makes it clear that of the two types of ammunition available, both were in cartridge form.

During the expedition to North America in 1814–15 which resulted in the Battle of New Orleans, "Major Munro had made arrangements for bringing up with the Army 300,000 musket ball cartridges and 50,000 Rifle ditto." He then sent a further 600,000 musket and 60,000 rifle cartridges.[52] Ammunition returns at the British headquarters depot at the Villere's House on the same date show:

Rifle Ball Cartridges	22 to the lb.	10,800
Do.	20 to the lb.	107,250
and since arrived do.		750

When the army was being evacuated after the battle, on 12 Jan. 1815, it was ordered that all small arms ammunition be brought on board the ships except 200,000 musket cartridges and 30,000 Rifle ball cartridges. On 18 Jan. 1815 the rear-guard boat would have 25,000 musket cartridges and 10,000 Rifle cartridges.[53]

Back at Woolwich in the Spring of 1815, perhaps thinking in terms of making up a basic stock of peacetime ammunition, the Ordnance recorded that "Col. Congreve of the Artillery wants 5000 yards of fustian and 1000 quarter-barrels of Rifle Gunpowder for making up 500,000 Rifle Ball Cartridges."[54]

From the rather jumbled mass of often contradictory information given above, certain basic features of Baker rifle ammunition appear. Ammunition was initially available as either loose powder, patches and balls, or as paper cartridges made up with and without ready-patched balls. Whether all rifle companies always had a supply of all three types of ammunition available it is impossible to say; it is clear that prepared cartridge ammunition dominated throughout the service. Practical experience on a large scale in the field brought the abandonment of loading with loose powder from a flask in the early years of the Peninsular Campaign.

With a fading of wartime memories and a hankering after a higher degree of precision, some officers in the much-reduced peacetime Rifle Brigade attempted to bring back the system of loading from a flask with loose powder and ball. Eleven years after Waterloo one of them wrote to the Commander-in-Chief and received the following reply:

Horse Guards
Sir   26th June 1826
Your letter of the 18th November last has been laid before

the Commander in Chief, recommending the re-issue of loose Powder and Copper Flasks to the Corps under your command, with a proportion of Bullets of Twenty to the Pound, for the purpose of arriving at more accuracy in Rifle practice than is attainable from the present Cartridge Ammunition made up with Bullets at Twenty-two to the Pound; and I have His Royal Highness' commands to acquaint you, that, in concurrence with His Grace the Master General of the Ordnance, His Royal Highness has recently authorized an Investigation into this subject, from which He has come to the conclusion, that however important it may be to arrive at the accuracy in Rifle Firing which is the object of your representation, yet He is persuaded that such advantage could not be gained in the mode you suggest without being subject to the inconvenience which has already been experienced, and which has caused the discontinuance of the equipment that you now seek to re-establish.

In the first place it has appeared from the oldest practical soldiers in the Rifle Brigade that the Copper Flasks were discontinued on service in the peninsular in consequence of the Accidents, and the Personal injuries thereby sustained, from their constant liability to blow up in Action.

2ndly it appears that after the Barrel of the Rifle has been soiled by Firing, it becomes almost impracticable to drive home the loose Ball with the greased Rag; and the prospect of this difficulty together with the apprehension that the loose powder in the Flask may blow up in action appears practically to have induced the soldiers to expend all their loose ammunition first - and hence the advantage of having a reserve for Rifle practice is lost to the soldier.

It is quite evident, from the testimony afforded on this subject, that the above are the primary causes which have led to the discontinuance of loose ammunition in the Rifleman's equipment; and His Royal Highness is of opinion that it could be highly inexpedient to load the soldier with an additional weight of equipment in time of Peace, which during the course of active operations in the field, has been found cumbrous, and ineffective for general purposes against an enemy.

His Royal Highness is quite aware that the accuracy of Rifle firing is in some measure lost by Balls being made up in Cartridges which are much smaller than the Calibre of the Rifle- though He cannot concur in the notion generally and erroneously entertained, that in such a case, a Rifle is no more effective for accuracy of firing than a common musket!

It appears, however, to His Royal Highness, that the measure of reducing the Ball to Twenty-two to the Pound, for the purpose of increasing the celerity of loading in Rank and File, has been most un-necessarily adopted; and that this object will be sufficiently attained by issuing all Cartridge Rifle Ammunition at Twenty Balls to the pound- while this increase in size will contribute to gain the advantage of accuracy of Firing which is aimed at by your proposal of having loose ammunition; and while both objects are thus in a great measure attained, the difficulties which might arise from having two sizes of Bullets in the Rifleman's equipment will be avoided.

Under all these circumstances His Royal Highness cannot concur in the expediency of your recommendation, that the Copper Flasks should be re-issued to the Rifle Brigade. But His Royal Highness will recommend to the Master General of the Ordnance that all the Cartridge Ammunition for the Rifle Brigade in future be made up in Paper with Bullets of Twenty to the Pound.[55]

One wonders whether the new uniformly large-size ball cartridges gave problems with loading when the barrels became foul.

J.M. Spearman's *The British Gunner* under date of 23 April 1828 reported both the service charge and the exercise charge for the rifle to be 4 drams (110 grains). Ball size was stated both as 20 to the pound and .60-inch, remaining identical with "common carbine" but apparently somewhat increased in size (or perhaps rounded-up for convenience?) from the earlier .596-inch. The difficulty in defining the rifle ball continues to lie in locating sufficient accurate official statements of what 20 to the pound represents at specific dates. Rifle cartridges were made both with and without fustian patches. In order to prepare 1,000 rifle cartridges, the following raw materials were required:[56]

Powder, F.G.*	15 lbs.	11 ozs
Paper, fine white	2 quires	21 sheets
whited-brown	1	22
Thread, Dutch	3 lbs.	14 ozs.
Twine, packing	1	13
Fustian, patches of 1000		
Shot-lead	45	7½ with patches
	50	without patches

*Although not specified in the above table, powder for "Rifle Arms" was to be marked on the heads of powder barrels "R.A." as opposed to "F.G." which meant fine glazed.

The cartridge paper was cut in the form of a "right-angled trapezoid," the longest side being 6", the short side 2.6" and the width 5.15" (identical to the carbine and carbine-bore pistol). The wooden former for rolling the cartridges was .59" in diameter and 5.9" long, with a hollow in the end for the ball .18" deep. Sixteen rifle cartridge papers could be cut from a single sheet of cartridge paper, and it was computed that 400 complete cartridges could be made by one worker in a day's work. A box of rifle cartridges contained 1,300 rounds weighing 85 lbs., 10 ozs., exactly the same as the common carbine.[57]

That cartridges were the norm for use with the Baker rifle in the years leading up to the adoption of the percussion Brunswick rifle is confirmed by both official and quasi-official published works, including the Horse Guards' *Manual and Platoon Exercise of Riflemen* of 1 March 1834 and Royal Artillery Captain F.A. Griffiths' "pocket" aide memoire, *The Artillerist's Manual and British Soldiers Compendium*, the fourth edition of which appeared in 1847 specifying cartridges with a 4 dram charge for the Baker rifle.

CHAPTER 14

Rifle Corps and Companies

in the British Army, 1798–1841

THE 60TH REGIMENT OF FOOT

Rifles had first been issued to men of the 60th in 1757 but these and other subsequent issues had been at the discretion either of the local Commander-in-Chief or regimental officers reacting to local conditions. Rifles from various foreign sources had been carried by a miscellany of foreign troops taken into British pay during the 1794–7 period but at no more than company strength. Rifles are reported to have been delivered to a battalion in 1794, possibly 1/60 or 4/60, but clear evidence is lacking.[1] It is also claimed by the same source and equally without supporting evidence, that "about 1794" a rifle company was formed in each of the then existing four battalions of the 60th. The raising of the 5th Battalion of the 60th Foot in 1798 was the first deliberate all-rifle unit of battalion size regularly established in the British army.

An Act of Parliament dated 30 Dec. 1797 called for the addition of a fifth battalion to the 60th Regiment of Foot; the actual raising order was dated 12 January 1798. The core of the new battalion was four companies formed on the Isle of Wight by drafting 300 men of Hompesch's Chasseurs (see Chapter 8) and six companies amounting to 600 men of Löwenstein's Chasseurs on Martinique "bringing their own foreign rifles with them."[2] Butler says the rifle with which the 5/60th was first equipped had six grooves and was therefore "certainly not the Baker rifle"[3] as indeed it could not have been in 1798.

A rifle company was added to the 2/60th in Sept. 1801,[4] at which time they were issued with 105 rifles and 107 sword bayonets, and the Ordnance were supplying them with rifle ball by March 1802.[5]

The York Rangers were drafted into the 2/60th,[6] and a second rifle-carrying unit, the Royal York Rangers was subsequently raised. Waldstein's Chasseurs were drafted into 4/60.[7]

The first clear evidence we have for an issue of rifles to a battalion of the 60th comes in the Spring of 1803 when the 5/60th was en route to Nova Scotia:

Delivered out of His Majesty's Stores at the Tower to Mr. Clark, Carrier, the undermentioned Arms to be by him conveyed to Portsmouth, and there delivered to William Spencer, Esq., Ordnance Storekeeper, who is to apply to Admiral Gambier to forward them to Nova Scotia, being for service of the 5th Battalion of the 60th Regiment of Foot

Nos. 1–35	*Rifle Musquets with Sword Bayonets, Scabbards, Boxes, Ball Drawers, Wiping Eyes and Leavers*	350
	Rifle Musquets without do.	350
	in 35 chests	

W. Weaver

Office of Ordnance
30th May 1803   receipt signed 6 June as delivered.[8]

The reference "without ditto" for half of the above seven hundred rifles indicates that these were part of the rifles for the West India regiments of which half were not to have buttboxes or bayonets. Whatever their structural details, it does appear that this was the point at which the 5/60th received Baker rifles to replace their earlier foreign rifles – but see below!

On 6 April 1804, two bugles were issued to the Rifle Company of 3/60th, and 78 rifles & swords were ordered to the battalion 13 July 1804.

While stationed on Antigua in June 1808, it was noted that the eighty rifles of the 4/60 were old Dutch arms received at the Cape of Good Hope, did not carry the English ball cartridge, and were worn out; there were 60 repairable and 20 wanting.[9] By October 1809, all 84 rifles were in bad condition and "deposited in the Ordnance Store."[10]

The 5/60th was inspected at Halifax, Nova Scotia, 20 Sept. 1804, at which time it was noted that:

This Battalion is armed with Rifles and Swords to fix to them; at present the former are not alike being of a different make, but the Commanding Officer has receiv'd notice from the Secretary to the Board of Ordnance that the number wanting, 280, to arm the Battalion uniformly, will soon be sent out.[11]

There were 783 rifles in the battalion, of which 351 were good, 432 bad. "Amongst these 432 bad Rifles are 351 new ones, set down as unserviceable for having no Swords."[12] These latter are obviously part of the half of the Pattern 1802 West India Rifles which did not give satisfaction on service. There were still problems with the 845 rifles present in October 1805, when it was noted that among these, 351 had come from the Tower and 273 from Ordnance Stores at Halifax, all without sword bayonets, "but being in all other respects perfectly adapted for the Service have been retained by the Battalion."[13]

By a raising order of 12 July 1799 the 6th Battalion was added to the 60th Foot with an Establishment of 1,159 of all ranks. A company of riflemen had already been raised from this battalion in February 1799 and sent to the army in Holland where, at the attack on Egmont-op-Zee it lost 6 killed, 7 wounded and 4 missing.[14] Two companies of riflemen from this battalion were sent with the forces to Holland on 24 Sept. 1799.[15] The 6/60th received 75 rifles and swords 6 Dec. 1804.

During May 1809, Sir George Beckwith ordered the rifle company of the 4/60th to be supplied with new rifles corresponding in length and calibre to those of 3/60, suggesting that the 4th had been operating with rifles other than the Baker rifle up to this late date.[16]

The 7/60th was raised at Guernsey by an order of 1 Sept. 1813, and included 200 riflemen. The final, 8th, battalion was raised at Gibraltar late in 1813. Although established with two companies of riflemen there is no evidence for their being issued anything but Light Infantry muskets and serjeant's fusils.[17] From 15 Dec. 1815, the 60th Regiment was re-organized as a rifle battalion and 7 light infantry battalions each with a rifle company.[18]

Reductions of the 8th, 7th, 6th and 5th battalions by mid-1818 left only four battalions of the 60th. The 2nd was created a rifle battalion on 16 July 1818, and the 1/60, 3/60 and 4/60 became Light Infantry battalions.

When 1/60 and 4/60 were disbanded in 1819, 2/60 became 1/60 and 3/60 became 2/60, and by an order of 12 May 1820 they were authorized to wear the rifle dress of the old 1st Battalion. The regiment's original title "The Royal American Regiment" was officially changed to "The Duke of York's Own Rifle Corps & Light Infantry" on 25 June 1824, and again changed in Dec. 1830 to "The King's Royal Rifle Corps."

On Service

Three companies of the 5/60th were active during the Great Rebellion in Ireland in 1798.[19]

In Feb. 1799 the 5/60th was sent to Martinique, where, at Fort Royal, Löwenstein's Chasseurs of 78 serjeants, 81 corporals and 891 men were incorporated into the battalion.[20]

A Monthly Return of what is apparently the 5/60th at the Isle of Wight for 30 June 1800 shows 700 rank & file present and fit for duty. They sailed for Jamaica in October.[21]

The strength of the rifle flank companies in four battalions of the 60th are shown in the inspection returns of May and June 1808:

	Muskets & Bayonets	*Rifles & Swords*
1st Battalion, at Jamaica	740	80
2nd Battalion, at Jersey	360	40
3rd Battalion, at Antigua	727	103
4th Battalion, at Antigua	720	80

Wartime rifle issues to the battalions of the 60th Regiment of Foot as taken from the War Office records are as follows:

— WARTIME RIFLE ISSUES TO THE 60TH REGIMENT OF FOOT —

Date	1st Bn.	2nd Bn.	3rd Bn.	4th Bn.	5th Bn.	6th Bn.	7th Bn.	8th Bn.
24 Sept 1801		105						
6 June 1803					700			
13 July 1804			78					
6 Dec. 1804						75		
15 Apr. 1805			6					
6 June 1805	80			80		80		
26 May 1806					49			
3 July 1806					322			
7 July 1806			6					
17 Dec. 1806			27					
27 May 1809		16						
12 July 1809		21						
22 July 1809				80				
31 Oct. 1809		35						
14 July 1810	105							
29 May 1811					40			
13 Aug. 1811					40			

Date	1st Bn.	2nd Bn.	3rd Bn.	4th Bn.	5th Bn.	6th Bn.	7th Bn.	8th Bn.
4 Oct. 1811					60			
9 Nov. 1811					100			
28 Jan. 1812				66				
7 Feb. 1812					60			
10 Mar. 1812				39				
11 Feb. 1813					50			
7 June 1813	5							
12 July 1813					60			
30 July 1813			33					
14 Sept 1813							200	
Total issues by battalion	**190**	**177**	**150**	**265**	**1,481**	**155**	**200**	**0**

This gives a total of 2,618 rifles accounted for in the administrative records.

The surviving War Office records do not give a complete picture of the number of rifles present in the several battalions, but on-the-spot inspections do give a much clearer view.[22]

— ON-THE-SPOT INSPECTIONS SHOWING RIFLES PRESENT —

Date	1st	2nd	3rd	4th	5th	6th	7th
1804		†			783		
1807	128	23		23	844	84	
1808	80	100	103	60*			
1812	105	126	105	101	274		
1813		124+124**		100	58a, 70b	107	
1814	105	126+124**	128	100+100c		106	200
1815	105	100		100		105	200
1816	105	98	91	90	890	105	199

†*A letter to the Ordnance of March 1802, mentions supplying rifle ball to the 2/60th.*[23]
**These are described as "worn out old Dutch arms, very bad, received at the Cape of Good Hope."*
*** Two companies, one at Barbados and one at Demerera.*
aOne company at Roncesvalles; bMcMahon's company; cTwo companies at different locations on Surinam.

The later careers of the several battalions of the 60th may be summarized as follows: 1/60th served at Grahamstown on the South African frontier from 1811 until the end of the war. At Cape Castle in June 1817, the battalion had 105 rifles and rifle swords, and at the final inspection before re-organization, in October 1818, they possessed 123 rifles and swords (with powder horns) the other companies being armed with 759 muskets and bayonet.[24]

The re-organized 1/60th Rifle Battalion possessed 636 rifles and 659 rifle swords when it was inspected at Quebec in September 1819. In October 1821, the battalion's armament was described as "very good rifles," a year later being described as "in use about 6 years" suggesting an issue date of 1816. When the battalion returned to England in August 1824, its 600 rifles and 596 swords were all described as unserviceable, and they required 776 to complete. One source shows 776 new rifles of the latest Pattern 1823 design being approved for issue to the battalion in September 1826.[25] The depot companies at Coimbra, Portugal, had received a new issue of 540 rifles with bayonets and scabbards by May 1827, and the service companies at Mafra in October 1827 had the same numbers. Not until they had returned to Fermoy Barracks in Ireland in May 1828, is the battalion described as having 775 rifles and 776 bayonets.[26] At Corfu in August 1836, the battalion's accoutrements were all unserviceable, and of 374 rifles fired during inspection, 58 missed fire, but no movement towards replacement occurred until the summer of 1840. Despite the progressive introduction of percussion rifles, the battalion was issued 811 new flintlock rifles while they were stationed at Windsor during early 1840, only to have them replaced by October 1842, (at Manchester) with 840 percussion rifles, rifle swords and new percussion accoutrements; the new ammunition included 60,312 service and 32,100 practice percussion caps.[27]

The Second Battalion of the 60th was at Barbadoes from 1810 until July 1817, and then at Nova Scotia and Quebec. By a War Office letter of 4 Aug. 1818, 2/60th was ordered converted to an all-rifle corps.[28] Thus reorganized, the new 2/60th at Quebec in May 1819, possessed 639 rifles, many of them from the disbanded 7th battalion.[29] This new structure seems to have been modified to a light infantry battalion to include six rifle companies and four with muskets and bayonets. By the time the battalion was inspected at Halifax, Nova Scotia, in November 1819, the unit was armed with 100 rifles and swords, 10 serjeants fusils and 398 muskets and bayonets. There was constant reference by inspecting officers between 1825 and 1829 that four companies were lacking rifles to complete to the new Establishment. The depot companies received new Pattern 1823 Baker rifles with hand bayonets by October 1828, but the service companies did not receive theirs until they returned to Albany Barracks from Berbice in the West Indies, in May 1830. At that time, they were issued with 693 rifles and hand bayonets.[30] From this time also there are no further references to muskets and bayonets in possession of the battalion, indicating a return to a Rifle Battalion structure. By the Spring of 1840 the battalion knew that new arms were to be anticipated. Stationed on Corfu in April 1840, their 507 rifles and bayonets were described as "fit only for Garrison duty with considerable repairs until 1841."[31] At New Castle, Jamaica, in May 1842, a similar statement was made about the 621 rifles and bayonets then in the hands of the battalion: they would be serviceable with considerable repairs, they were old, and many were defective; an issue of Lovell's new rifle was looked for towards the end of the year. In November, new arms were expected, but they were not actually received until mid-1843, at New Castle, Jamaica.[32] The depot companies were receiving their percussion rifles during their inspection of November 1843, at Belturbet.[33]

3/60th served in the West Indies until 1816 and then went to Nova Scotia. The last surviving Inspection Return for the battalion, at Halifax in May 1819, shows them armed with 77 rifles and swords and 263 muskets and bayonets.[34]

4/60th served on Dominica, and on Demerara from 1817 until its final inspection in October 1818, when it was armed with 77 rifles and swords and 653 muskets and bayonets.[35]

At the end of the campaign of 1814, 5/60th was at Bayonne; it had lost all its officers and had about 40 riflemen left. Those with Wellington had only 9 officers and about 250 riflemen. The battalion had sailed from Cork with 33 officers and 1,007 NCOs and men; they had received drafts of 11 officers and 558 men. They returned to England with 18 officers and 232 NCOs and men.[36]

Stationed at Gibraltar in May 1817, the battalion possessed 623 rifles out of an Establishment of 887, with another 264 unserviceable, and 612 powder horns wanting to complete.[37]

6/60th served almost entirely at Jamaica, but was disbanded in Feb. 1818 at Halifax, Nova Scotia.[38] In May 1817, it was inspected at Fort Augusta, Jamaica, where it was armed with 105 rifles with all their swords unserviceable, and 506 muskets and bayonets.[39]

7/60th was sent to Nova Scotia, arrived 28 May 1814 with 811 rank and file, which included two rifle companies.[40]

**THE RIFLE CORPS (1800),
95TH FOOT (1802), RIFLE BRIGADE (1816)**

In the closing months of 1799, Colonel Coote Manningham of the 41st Foot and Lt. Col. William Stewart of the 67th Foot addressed a joint letter to the Commander-in-Chief of the British Army, His Royal Highness the Duke of York, recommending the formation of an established corps of riflemen for the British army. This letter was found to no longer exist as far back as 1870-5, when a careful search for it was made, and it was suggested at that time that it had probably been turned over to the Board of Ordnance and destroyed in the Tower fire of October 1841. Whatever its content, the Commander-in-Chief seems to have approved of the idea of additional rifle training for the army, as indicated by the following letter to Coote Manningham:

(Private)   Horse Guards
                                          Jany 7th 1800
My Dear Sir

I have much Satisfaction in informing you, that HRH the Comr in Chief proposes assembling a Corps under your Command, for the purpose of instructing them in the use of the Rifle, and in the System of Exercise adopted by Soldiers so armed.

I shall be very glad to have the pleasure of seeing you upon this Subject, and for that purpose I beg the favor of you to call at the Horse Guards as soon as you conveniently can. I have the honor to be &c

                                                Harry Calvert
                                        Adjutant General.[41]

Ten days later, the proposal was put into practical effect:

                          CIRCULAR
                                    Horse Guards
                                    17 January 1800
Sir

I have the honour to inform you that it is His Royal Highness the Commander in Chief's intention to form a corps of detachments from the different regiments of the line for the purpose of its being instructed in the use of the rifle and in the system of exercise adopted by soldiers so armed. It is His Royal Highness's pleasure that you shall select from the regiment under your command, 2 sergeants, 2 corporals and 30 private men for this duty, all of them being such men as appear most capable of receiving the above instructions, and most competent to the performance of the duty of Riflemen. These non-commissioned officers and privates are not to be considered as being drafted from their regiments but merely as detached for the purpose above recited; they will continue to be borne on the strength of their regiments, and will be clothed by their respective colonels.

His Royal Highness desires you will recommend 1 captain, 1 lieutenant, and 1 ensign of the regiment under your command who volunteer to serve in the corps of riflemen in order that His Royal Highness may select from the officers recommended from the regiments which furnish their quota on this occasion a sufficient number of officers for the Rifle Corps. These officers are to be considered as detached on duty from their respective regiments, and will share in all the promotion that occurs in them during their absence.

Eight drummers will be required to act as bugle-horns, and I request you will acquaint me, for the information of his Royal Highness, whether you have any in the Regiment qualified to act or of a capacity to be easily instructed.

I have the honour &c &

Harry Calvert, Adjutant General.[42]

The above circular (with dates of both 9 and 17 January) was addressed to the commanding officers of the second battalions of the Royal (1st) Regiment of Foot, the 21st, 23d, 25th, 27th, 29th, 49th, 55th, 69th, 71st, 72d, 79th, 85th and 92d Regiments of Foot. These fourteen regiments were to supply a body of 14 captains, 14 lieutenants and 14 ensigns with 28 sergeants, 28 corporals and 420 men to form the core of an instruction battalion.[43] Of the above group, the 23d, 25th, 27th, 29th, 49th, 55th, 69th and 85th were to send a recruiting party to Dublin to recruit men for the new unit "for life and unlimited service" from the Irish Militia.[44]

As usual, when any new unit was to be formed from existing regiments, an opportunity was presented to commanding officers to rid themselves of their least useful men, and the new rifle corps was no exception. Six of the regiments applied to send their unserviceable men, one sending 22 such out of the 30.

Initially, this was intended to be merely an enlarged version of the "Corps of Experiment and Instruction" which Patrick Ferguson had commanded in America from the Spring to the Autumn of 1777 (see Chapter 3). Manningham obviously wanted a permanently established unit, but as the following letter shows, this had not yet been accepted by the authorities:

Horse Guards
May 9, 1800

Sir,

I have laid your Letter of the 8th before the Comdr in Chief; HRH agrees perfectly with you on the general principles therein laid down; but reverting to the peculiar Establishment of the Corps under your Command, directs that the detachment of the 92nd Regt shall proceed to join, according to the route you will have received. HRH perceives all the Inconveniences you suggest, and your remarks may possibly furnish the Groundwork of the Establishment of a Corps hereafter; but the present is rather a Corps of Experiment & Instruction, and I trust its utility, and the progress it cannot fail to make, under your and Col. Stewarts Superintendance will insure a similar one being formed on a permanent footing.[45]

After much discussion, it was finally agreed in October 1800, to establish the new unit as a regular regiment with effect from 25 August 1800. It was to have a strength of eight companies and be entirely armed with rifles. Initially, the unit would consist of:

1 Colonel	*2 assistant surgeons*
2 Lieut. Colonels	*1 serjeant major*
2 Majors	*1 quartermaster serjeant*
8 Captains of companies	*1 paymaster serjeant*
16 1st Lieutenants	*40 serjeants*
8 2nd Lieutenants	*40 corporals*
1 Adjutant	*1 bugle major*
1 Quartermaster	*16 bugles*
1 Paymaster	*1 armourer major*
1 Surgeon	*8 armourers*
760 privates[46]	

In March 1801, a new Establishment was laid down for the Rifle Corps with effect from 25 Dec. 1800, with the following changes from that of 25 August:

1 Colonel Commandant	*50 serjeants*
7 Captains of companies and 1 Captain-Lieutenant	
20 1st Lieutenants	*50 corporals*
10 2nd Lieutenants	*20 bugles*
	10 armourers
740 privates, organized in ten, vice eight, companies.[47]	

Manningham was replaced as colonel of the 95th Regiment on 31 Aug. 1809 by Gen. Sir David Dundas, GCB, who was at the time Commander-in-Chief. Dundas was replaced by the Duke of Wellington on 19 Feb. 1820, who held the colonelcy until his death in 1852.

There was considerable opposition to the idea of an entirely rifle-armed regiment apart from those which could be hired from abroad. General Lord Charles Cornwallis, with his considerable experience of rifle use by both sides during the Southern Campaigns in America in 1780-1, was particularly vocal in his criticism of such an innovation, although the objection seems to have been to a large single corps of riflemen rather than to rifle companies or to riflemen dispersed amongst light infantry companies:

I am glad to find the Duke of York has given up the idea of having corps of riflemen,...[48]

The Duke of York has, through Brownrigg, asked my opinion on the formation of a corps of riflemen of 600 to 1800 in this country, to be taken either from the Line or the Fencibles. Unwilling to weaken the regiments of the Line, I have proposed that 15 or 20 men should be enlisted for general service from each regiment of Fencibles, and have submitted my opinion, with the utmost deference, that only a tenth part of the corps should be armed with rifles, and that the others should be trained as light infantry, and brigaded for the present with the light companies of the Irish militia. I quoted the instance of Colonel Wormb in America, who solicited that the rifles should be taken from a great proportion of his Yaghers, and that they should receive firelocks instead.[49]

Even after Cornwallis' recommendations had been over-ridden, he took the opportunity to belittle the new unit to his obviously sympathetic correspondent:

...and Colonel Manningham's rifle corps – which last is a very amusing plaything.[50]

Charles James in his article on "Rifle" in his military dictionary published in 1802 says that:

They [riflemen] formed the most formidable enemies during the last war in America, being posted along the American ranks [flanks?], and behind hedges, &c. for the purpose of picking off the British officers; many of whom fell by the rifle in our contest with that country. They have proved equally fatal in the hands of the French during the present war, and they have been wisely added to our establishment. Considerable improvements are daily made; and we shall not despair to see not only additional corps of riflemen, but light infantry battalions, like the chasseurs of the French, form a considerable portion of the British army. This has been called a murderous practice, and some persons have questioned how far it ought to be admitted in civilised warfare.[51]

The first parade of the new unit occurred at Horsham, Sussex, on 1 April 1800, at which 443 men were present of the Establishment of 448.

This group of detachments was trained at Swinley Camp in Windsor Forest by its lieutenant colonel, William Stewart.

This original group of men, after serving on the Ferrol expedition in July 1800, was subsequently broken up at Malta some weeks later, 357 out of the 482 NCOs and men returning to their regiments. The corps was re-established in the autumn of 1800 with a regular establishment of ten companies under its former officers but with the men drawn chiefly from the disembodied Irish Fencible regiments. A letter of service was belatedly granted on 31 March 1801.[52]

Between August 1800 and April 1801, the corps was at Blatchington Barracks near Seaford, Sussex. By 24 Jan. 1801, the unit strength was 442 privates of the Establishment of 760, wanting 318 to compleat.

In Feb. 1802, Ezekiel Baker billed the Ordnance for "boxing" (i.e. fitting butt-boxes to) 635 rifles of Manningham's Corps, then stationed at Weymouth and Blatchington, including all transportation expenses of sending the rifles to and from these points.[53]

On 12 June 1802, in line with a general reduction of the army at the Peace of Amiens, the Rifle Corps was reduced to an Establishment of 30 serjeants, 40 corporals and 710 privates.[54]

On 8 January 1803, the Rifle Corps was officially numbered in the regiments of the line as the 95th Foot[55] with Manningham as Colonel and Major Sidney Beckwith as Lieutenant Colonel. It continued to be generally referred to as either the Rifle Corps or the Rifle Regiment.[56] On this same date, the 52nd Foot was officially converted to a Light Infantry battalion, which would work closely with the Rifle Corps as musket-armed back-up until the close of the war.[57]

On 6 May 1805, a second battalion to the 95th Foot was ordered to be formed, at Canterbury, by the transfer of 21 sergeants, 20 corporals, 7 bugle-horns and 250 men from the first battalion, to be commanded by Lieut. Col. Hamlet Wade. The balance of the men were to come from volunteers from the militia.[58]

The following was the strength of both battalions of the 95th as of 10 May 1809:[59]

	1 Apr. effective	Left in Portugal	left in Spain from militia	Volunteers	Totals
1st Battalion	799	8	88	641	1,536
2nd Battalion	863	37	38	641	1,579
Totals	1,662	45	126	1,282	3,115

On 4 May 1809, a third battalion was added to the 95th by using the excess of over 1,000 recruits obtained in a recruiting drive for 1/95 and 2/95, whose Establishments at the time were both for 1,008 rank and file. The Hon. (Sir 1813) William Stewart was Colonel of the 3/95th from 31 Aug. 1809 until 1816.

On 23 Feb. 1816, the Prince Regent ordered the 95th taken out of the numbered line regiments, and re-designated The Rifle Brigade.

The 3/95th was disbanded as of 25 Dec. 1818.

On 11 Jan. 1819, 2/95th received a draft of 213 men from the disbanded third battalion.

On Service

In July 1800, at Stewart's urgent request, all three then existing companies of the experimental Rifle Corps accompanied the expedition to Ferrol. In this context it is interesting to note that in an inspection of the corps held at Blatchington Barracks on 23 Sept. 1800, Manningham noted that the "Corps is not yet formed, but consists partly of Detachments that are borne on the strength of their several Regiments and partly of Volunteers from Ireland" and their ammunition is described as "not made up." There is no mention of arms, and indeed no Baker rifles were delivered into Store at the Tower until September, 1800, raising the question of what rifles the Rifle Corps carried to Ferrol.[60]

Nine officers and 200 men from the Ferrol group of the Rifle Corps took part in the Battle of Mandora during Abercromby's expedition to Egypt on 13 Mar. 1801, and at Alexandria on 21 March.

In April 1801, a detachment under Stewart went to Copenhagen with the Parker/Nelson expedition. One hundred and one rank and file were on board Nelson's *Elephant* (74), with the remainder embarked in the *Isis* (50).[61] The Corps of Riflemen at the first British attack on Copenhagen consisted of 8 officers and 107 men under Lt. Col. William Stewart and Captain Sidney T. Beckwith.[62]

In November 1805, a British/Hanoverian force of 25,000 men under Lt. Gen. Lord Cathcart was sent to co-operate with the Swedes and Russians to clear the French out of Holland and Hanover. Five companies of the 1/95th, 400 men, disembarked at Cuxhaven on 18 Nov. 1805 and re-embarked there on 15 Feb. 1806 without seeing action.[63]

Three companies of the 2/95th embarked for South America. They joined 5 companies of the 1/95th at Montevideo 14 June 1807, after eleven months on board ship. These attacked the French at Passa Chico, near Montevideo on 2 July 1807, and also participated in the second attack on Montevideo three days later. Also present were three other companies of the 2/95th commanded by Major Gardner who had first gone to Buenos Ayres as part of the expedition launched from South Africa under Sir Samuel Auchmuty.[64]

Five companies of the 1/95th under Beckwith embarked for Denmark 9 July 1807. At the second attack on Copenhagen in 1807, the Rifle Corps was represented by ten companies, five each from 1/95 (29 sgts, 27 cpls and 488 men) and 2/95 (40 sgts., 39 cpls., and 467 men).[65] During the battle at Kjoge (19 Aug. 1807) the 95th cleared the woods and made a successful attack on the churchyard at Herfolge.[66] All ten companies of the 95th embarked at Copenhagen for England on 21 Oct. 1807, those of 2/95 landing at Deal on 13 November and those of 1/95 landing three days later.

Colonel Robert Craufurd's expedition to re-capture Buenos Ayres included five companies of the 1/95th, 25 sergeants and 376 men. This group sailed from Montevideo for England 8 Aug. 1807.[67]

Sir John Moore's abortive expedition to Gottenburg in April 1808 included three companies of 1/95.

Four companies of 2/95 commanded by Major Travers and consisting of 20 sergeants and 399 men embarked with Wellesley's force for the Peninsula on 12 July 1808, landing at Douro on 24 July. With them came the 5/60th nearly 1,000 strong, this being the first time the two rifle units had operated together.[68]

The first action of the Peninsular Campaign in which the Rifle Corps served was the skirmish at Obidos on 15 Aug. 1808. In this outpost action Major Travers commanded one company of 2/95th and two from 5/60th.

Two additional companies of 1/95 arrived with reinforcements on 20 Aug. 1808.[69]

By a General Order of 21 Aug. 1808, a rifle company was to be attached to each of the newly arrived 7th and 8th Brigades, leaving three with Headquarters Light Brigade.[70]

With the arrival of five companies of the 1/95th and four companies of the 2/95th on 26 Oct. 1808, eighteen out of the twenty companies in the two battalions of the regiment were operating in Spain during the Corunna campaign. Moore's Reserve Division included all ten companies of the 1/95th, 700 strong, with Craufurd's 1st Light Division including eight companies of the 2/95th with 750 of all ranks.[71]

In April 1809, Wellesley's nine brigades received riflemen. He broke up a half-battalion of 5/60th and put one company to each of five of the brigades, retaining the other half-battalion intact with the 3rd Brigade. The two brigades composed of the King's German Legion had their own riflemen, so that eight of the nine brigades had one company of German riflemen. The 6th Brigade had a party of the 95th from the 1st Battalion of Detachments (of which two battalions were formed 25 Jan. 1809).

The ill-fated Walcheren Expedition of 1809 included eight companies, 988 corporals and men of the 2/95th, who embarked at Dover on 20 July 1809, landing at South Beveland on 1 August.[72] The 2/95th returned from Walcheren and landed at Dover 14 Sept. 1809 with a loss of 300 men from fever in six weeks, with a further loss of 133 within three months.

Two companies of the 2/95th, 215 men, under Major Amos Norcott, were on independent duty in Spain and Portugal from 1809 until they rejoined at Almeida in the autumn of 1812.[73]

Returns of 25 Dec. 1812 show the following numbers of the Rifle Corps on service in Spain, and the reserves remaining in England:[74]

	Companies	Officers	Sgts.	Buglers	Riflemen
1st Battalion	6	29	39	18	620
2nd Battalion	6	25	35	9	516
3rd Battalion	5	23	27	11	484
	17	77	101	38	1620

Reserves and Depots in England

1st Battalion	2	42
2nd Battalion	4	213
3rd Battalion	5	274
	11	529

The fighting strength of the 95th when they crossed the Spanish border and invaded France on 20 May 1813 amounted to:

	Companies	Officers	Sgts.	Buglers	Riflemen
1st Battalion	6	40	38	17	573
2nd Battalion	6	25	39	11	411
3rd Battalion	5	21	26	10	347
	17	86	103	38	1331

This represented a loss of 289 men since the beginning of the year.

At the Battle of Tarbes, 20 Mar. 1814, all three battalions of the 95th were the sole British participants against the French, and won the battle.

On 12 Sept. 1814, the Ordnance was ordered to pack up a list of Ordnance and Stores which included 500 Rifles and 200,000 rounds of rifle ammunition for the expedition to North America of 1814–15, which culminated in the Battle of New Orleans. The Rifle Corps was represented by five companies, 488 men, from the left wing of the Third Battalion under Colonel William Thornton. They embarked at Plymouth on 18 Sept. 1814, only two months after returning from the Peninsular campaigns. At the commencement of the Battle of New Orleans, this unit was part of the right flank of Pakenham's line of battle, between the 93d Foot and the light infantry companies of the 7th, 43d, 93d and 1st West India Regiments. On 7 January 1815, 300 of the 95th were to occupy the "old batteries" as part of the army's general advance. The Rifles embarked for England 4 April 1815, and arrived at Plymouth 2 June.

Rifle issues to the three battalions of the Rifle Corps recorded in the War Office records are as follows:

Date	1st Battalion	2nd Battalion	3rd Battalion
1 Sept 1803	5 [or 51?]		
6 June 1805	251	634	
21 Dec. 1807	618	397	
26 Feb. 1809		272	
24 Mar. 1809	665		
2 May 1809	111		
15 June 1809			1054
23 June 1809		64	
29 May 1811			105 left w.
24 July 1811		18	
25 July 1811	60		
10 June 1812	40		151
24 Oct. 1812	394		
7 June 1813		44	
12 July 1813			87
25 Oct. 1813	28	9	17
30 Apr. 1814		134	
10 Aug. 1814			25
22 Oct. 1814		239	
5 Feb. 1816			106

In connexion with the re-arming of the rifle corps with a bayonet and short-sword in 1815, a list was submitted to the War Office giving the current effective strength of those units which were to be equipped according to the new mode. It is of particular interest as indicating those units currently rifle-armed which were not to be included for the future:[75]

(see table below)

"Return of the Corps which are armed with Rifles shewing their effective Strength & Establishment" [22 June 1815]

		Effective Strength			Establishment		
		Serjts.	Buglers	R&F	Serjts.	Buglers	R&F
60th Foot	5th Bn	44	9	211	45	22	610
95th Foot	1st Bn	69	16	760	65	22	1010
	2nd Bn	71	18	670	65	22	1010
	3rd Bn	63	18	676	65	22	1010
		247	61	2317	240	88	3640

Thus the "regular rifle corps" were 1,323 men below Establishment just a few days after Waterloo; these figures do not represent casualties suffered in that fight.

The alteration of earlier patterns of Baker Rifle to take a socket bayonet remains a shadowy operation in terms of documentary evidence (See Chapter 11). From postwar Inspection Returns it appears that the First Battalion was not equipped entirely with bayonet-fitted rifles, as opposed to rifle sword-fitted rifles, until the Spring of 1819, while stationed at Cambrai in northern France.[76] Figures for a mixed armament during 1817–18 show the following:[77]

	Rifles	*Rifle-swords*	*Rifle Bayonets & Scabbards*
May, 1817	*583*	*472*	*168*
May, 1818	*508*	*400*	*158*
Nov. 1818	*517*	*381*	*169*
May, 1819	*680*	*22*	*680*

By December 1823, these altered arms were being described as "old, general bad construction and materials. They were originally furnished by contractors. New arms are daily expected."[78] While this comment has a distinctly biased tone to it in favour of the new largely Royal Manufactory Enfield-made rifles, it has to be said that all but two of the Baker rifles converted to socket bayonet in 1815 known to the present writer are of the Pattern 1800, and that therefore they must have been at least old. The majority of the arms made for the Ordnance throughout the period were of contractor origin in components if not final assembly. By May 1824, the First Battalion had received their 600 Pattern 1823 Baker rifles with hand bayonets and scabbards, "All new. Rifles of the very best description."[79] This euphoric welcome did long endure: by the time of the next inspection at Belfast in October 1824, it was noted that:

The locks are not equal in point of excellent workmanship. The Hammers are reported soft as is generally the case with Arms newly issued.[80]

The First Battalion was stationed in Canada, chiefly Halifax, from July 1825 until returning to England in the Summer of 1836, and during this time there were no further comments about their arms. An inspection held in March 1839, while the battalion was stationed at Windsor, found all 700 rifles and bayonets unserviceable, but no details of their condition survive. By August 1840, the battalion had received a complete new set of 840 percussion rifles, rifle swords and accoutrements.[81] The Second Battalion was subjected to the same mixed armament as its sister battalion between 1815 and its re-armament in May 1824. The figures are as follows:[82]

	Rifles	*Rifle-swords*	*Rifle Bayonets & Scabbards*
May, 1817	*598*	*384*	*175*
May, 1818	*584*	*584*	*200*
Nov. 1818	*564*	*384*	*180*

At Kinsale, in May 1823, the battalion possessed 110 serviceable rifles with bayonets and scabbards, and 490 of the same unserviceable. It was noted that "a general change is shortly expected for a Rifle of a better description." At Limerick in October of the same year, it was recorded that the rifles had been received in 1805 "and are in general indefferent."[83] This supports the evidence of surviving altered examples being almost all of the Pattern 1800. The Second Battalion received a complete new set of 600 Pattern 1823 Baker rifles in May, 1824, and they too quickly noted their "inferior locks."[84] A further 176 had been issued for a battalion augmentation in the Summer of 1825. In June 1835, while the battalion was stationed at Argostoli in the Ionian Islands, it was noted that their rifles "will need renewing." By October 1837, when the battalion was inspected on its return to Portsmouth, their arms, although serviceable, were described as being "14 years in use." There is a gap in the Inspection Returns for the battalion from October 1838 when they had their 696 rifles, bayonets and scabbards, until June 1840, by which time they had received a complete new set of 840 percussion rifles, rifle swords & scabbards and new percussion accoutrements.[85]

THE 7TH, 9TH, 10TH, 14TH, 15TH, 18TH AND 23D LIGHT DRAGOONS

In July 1813, H.R.H. the Commander-in-Chief approved the issue of rifled carbines to the 7th Light Dragoons if there were a sufficient number in Store.[86] On 12 Aug. 1813, the eight troops of the regiment in Spain were authorized to receive 610 rifled carbines.[87] In September 1813, a statement of the arms in the regiment showed: with 8 troops in Spain 610 rifled carbines, 82 carbines and 1,384 single pistols; with 4 troops at Arundel 15 rifled carbines, 122 carbines and 176 pistols; and wanting to complete to Establishment 405 rifled carbines and 573 pistols. On 11 Oct. 1813, orders were given to supply the 405 rifled carbines and the 573 pistols. This indicates that 1,030 Cavalry Rifles were in the hands of this one regiment of light dragoons.

The 8th Light Dragoons received at least 82 Cavalry Rifles at some as yet un-determined date, and were still equipped with them while stationed at Cawnpore in 1821-2.[88] In December 1823, at Fort William, while all the regiment's carbines and pistols were unserviceable, their 80 Cavalry Rifles were reported in good order. They disappear after an inspection at Chatham in May 1823.[89]

The 9th Light Dragoons were issued 80 Cavalry Rifles in June 1814.[90]

The 10th (Prince of Wales's Own) Light Dragoons, then under orders for the Peninsular, were ordered to be issued with 500 Cavalry Rifles and 600 pistols on 30 Dec. 1812.[91] In November 1813, the regiment, then at Brighton, was ordered 508 rifled carbines described as "a special armament, by way of experiment." It is unclear as to exactly what was either special or experimental since, by this date, the Prince's regiment had been equipped for some years with rifled carbines.[92]

The 11th Light Dragoons had 80 Cavalry Rifles (10 per troop) in 1820–23 while serving in India.[93] In May 1823, the 11th, then at Meerut, were used to carry out what was probably the first British "troop trials" of the percussion system, but it is not clear whether the carbines altered to the new system were Cavalry Rifles or Paget Carbines:

An experiment has been made by permission upon several of the Carbines, by altering the Lock according to the late approved Invintion for Fowling Pieces, but it is not found, upon trial, to succeed with arms of this description.[94]

The subsequent fate of these percussioned carbines, whether rifled or smoothbored, and indeed of the 80 Cavalry Rifles, the records do not reveal.

An Inspection Return of October 1819, for the 13th Light Dragoons stationed at Arcot, states that "Each Troop has Ten Rifles, perfectly new, not yet served out to the Corps."[95] Their subsequent issue and use does not seem in doubt, for in December 1834, while the regiment was at Bangalore, it was noted that the 80 rifled carbines had not yet been replaced, and by May 1839, they were returned as unserviceable, worn out.[96] They disappear to be replaced by percussion arms by the time the regiment is inspected at Ipswich in September 1842.[97]

The Secretary at War informed the Board of Ordnance on 16 July 1803 that ten men per troop [80 for each regiment] of the 14th and 15th Light Dragoons "shall be forthwith furnished with Carabines having rifle Barrels...as soon as possible."[98] In referring to the 15th (King's) Hussars at Canterbury in October 1823, the Adjutant General states "that Rifles would be issued to replace those [number not specified] that were bad, but none have as yet been received."[99] By June 1824, the regiment had its full complement.

The 18th Light Dragoons received 35 rifles complete on 24 June 1809. Twenty-three of these were lost on service in Portugal and Spain and were replaced in October 1810.[100]

At Cape Town in November 1814, the 21st Light Dragoons had amongst their current ammunition supplies 11,825 "rifle Ball cartridges" suggesting that some of their carbines were in fact Cavalry Rifles.[101]

The 23rd Light Dragoons were initially issued 78 Cavalry Rifles; 54 were received as replacements for those handed over while in Portugal in Nov. 1811, and another 24 in June 1812.[102] An additional 12 pieces were ordered to them the following month, but on 28 Aug. 1812 the Commander-in-Chief ordered that each regiment of light dragoons was to receive five rifled carbines per troop, so that the total required for the 23rd would be 50 and not 78.[103]

THE KING'S GERMAN LEGION

The King's German Legion was the largest and most highly respected foreign regiment in British service during the Napoleonic Wars. Originally formed from refugees from the Kingdom of Hanover when it was occupied by the French in 1803, over the years troops from other nations, still mostly Germans, also joined. On 13 Oct. 1803, the War Office notified the Board of Ordnance that "A Corps formed of H.M. Hanoverian subjects" was to be issued 200 muskets & bayonets and 132 rifles and sword-bayonets.[104]

Each line battalion of the K.G.L. had in each company ten rifle-armed men.

Rifle issues to the companies of the Line Battalions of the King's German Legion as recorded in the War Office records:

Date	1st Bn.	2nd Bn.	3rd Bn.	4th Bn.	5th Bn.	6th Bn.	7th Bn.	8th Bn.
3 May 1804			18					
18 May 1804	68							
27 June 1804			22					
7 Sept. 1804			12					
26 Oct. 1804				28				
23 Nov. 1804				28				
20 May 1805					52			
5 June 1806						52		
16 June 1806							52	52
11 June 1807		98						
8 Dec. 1807								1

Date	1st Bn.	2nd Bn.	3rd Bn.	4th Bn.	5th Bn.	6th Bn.	7th Bn.	8th Bn.
17 Dec. 1807				2				
18 Jan. 1808					5			
19 Jan. 1808	19	15					13	
29 June 1810	44							
27 Sept 1811							52	
15 Apr. 1812		16						
10 June 1812		12			12			
20 July 1812								13
28 Sept 1812	12							
27 Sept 1813			8					9
25 Oct. 1813	2				22			
7 Mar. 1814				7			46	
23 Aug. 1814	52	66			56			
10 Sept 1814				98				
Total issues by battalion	**197**	**207**	**60**	**163**	**147**	**52**	**163**	**75**

giving a total of 1,064 rifles issued to the eight Line Battalions.

As late as the Spring of 1807 the 8th Line Battalion of the K.G.L. reported that the rifles in the hands of its men were of three different calibres. The Commander-in-Chief ordered an investigation and that rifles of the same calibre "as those made use of by other Corps" be issued to the 8th.[105] The Assistant Inspector of Small Arms examined the rifles.

The Light Battalions of the King's German Legion received their initial issue of 132 rifles and swords on 18 Dec. 1804. The 1st battalion received additional issues of 5 sword bayonets on 8 Apr. 1805; 136 and 139 sword-bayonets on 14 Aug. 1806. In April 1808, when the two Light Infantry battalions as well as the 1st, 2d, 5th and 7th Line battalions were under embarkation orders for Portugal, they were ordered to notify the Board without delay of the specific quantities of the several materials required to complete a three-months supply of rifle ammunition for each of these units.[106]

Rifle issues to the two Light Infantry Battalions of the King's German Legion:

	1st Bn	2nd Bn
18 Dec. 1804	132	
14 Aug. 1806	136	129
27 Oct. 1807	60	60
2 Jan. 1808		16
30 Oct. 1811	26	24
15 Apr. 1812	76	76
(augmentation of 2 companies each)		
10 June 1812		12
30 July 1813	11	21
25 Oct. 1813		25
20 Nov. 1813	22	25
23 Aug. 1814	338	
10 Sept 1814		358
Total issues by bn.	801	746

This gives a total of 1,547 rifles issued to the two Light Infantry battalions.

An inspection return of 5 May 1814, at St. Etienne, shows:

1st Light Bn. K.G.L. 392 Rifles & Swords, 253 Muskets & Bayonets

2nd Light Bn. K.G.L. 392 Rifles & Swords, 253 Muskets & Bayonets.[107]

THE CEYLON RIFLE REGIMENT

The 1st Ceylon Regiment was raised in 1801 as light infantry and retained as such until its re-armament with percussion rifles. It is not clear from the early fragmentary records when rifles were first issued to the regiment, but an inspection return of January 1814 shows a rifle company with 60 rifles; they still had them when inspected in Sept. 1816. From 1817 to 1822, inspection returns show the rifles apparently replaced with cut-down muskets — 111 with 1,060 muskets and bayonets in July 1817, and the same number with 1,256 muskets and bayonets in October 1820.[108] By March 1822, the regiment had received 120 new rifles, rifle swords and equipment. In 1822, the regiment was designated as the Ceylon Regiment (Riflemen), by December 1826 the Malay companies were called the Ceylon Rifles, and the title Ceylon Rifle Regiment was awarded 25 June 1827. During this period, the five rifle company serjeants and 115 rank and file riflemen were equipped with powder flasks, powder horns, bullet (or ball) bags and lock covers. In July 1826, it was noted that rifles had recently arrived from England and were to be issued to the nine Malay companies that had not yet received them.[109] This re-equipment was a gradual process: by June 1828, a total of 400 rifles "complete" were in the hands of the rifle companies. The number had increased to 970 rifles and 902 muskets and bayonets by August 1829, when it was also noted that ball drawers, leavers and wiping eyes were also issued to each rifleman and lock covers for both rifles and muskets.[110] By July 1833, the numbers had increased yet again to a total of 1,017 rifles complete, and 706 muskets and bayonets. During the February 1835 inspection, it was noted that the rifles were beginning to show signs of use. By early 1836, the powder horns and powder flasks are no longer listed amongst the riflemen's accoutrements.[111] Replacement accoutrements were issued to the regiment in the autumn of 1836 which included pouches and belts, bayonet waist belts, slings, lock covers and ball bags. A complete set of new accoutrements was issued them late in 1838: 1,043 pouches, 1,203 slings and 988 lock covers.[112]

In May 1840, the rifles of the Ceylon Rifles were described as unserviceable from long use, and an application for new rifles was submitted to London. By May 1841, there were specifically 870 rifles unfit for service and only 180 in a serviceable condition, and all 738 muskets and bayonets were also listed as unserviceable. New rifles were expected from England.[113]

The regiment was issued with new rifles in June 1841. A total of 1,834 Baker rifles, including 50 for the Ordnance Stores at Colombo, were organized by the Inspector of Small Arms at the Royal Manufactory Enfield, George Lovell. He reported to the Board that there were 900 rifle barrels in Store with Hand Bayonets and another 542 with Sword Bayonets. He proposed that 392 with Hand Bayonets be rough stocked and set up at Enfield using available materials and new brasswork where necessary, and asked whether, with regard to the barrels for sword bayonet, the corps might be well advised to have a mixture of the two sorts of bayonet, the sword being useful in cutting through the rough country in which it served. The Commander-in-Chief replied that one pattern was required and that the regiment had previously had the hand bayonet; but he temporized by saying that, if the accoutrements could be altered without undue trouble [expense] to take the sword bayonets, then a mixture could be sent as Lovell proposed.[114] The first inspection return reflecting the receipt and issue of the new rifles is dated January 1843, and shows 1,470 rifles, 1,050 rifle bayonets and scabbards, 420 Rifle Swords and scabbards, and 210 muskets and bayonets.[115] From this it is unclear whether the "Rifle Swords and scabbards" refers to sword-bayonets or to the saw-backed sidearms made in 1816 to accompany the rifles altered for a socket-bayonet. No further information being available in the records we are left to assume that the mixture was probably sent, since it represented the least time and expense to the Board.

By the Spring of 1847, the regiment had 1,365 serviceable rifles and 105 unserviceable, with 630 listed as wanting. A year later, there are 1,730 serviceable rifles and 532 wanting, with all 243 muskets and bayonets unserviceable, with a note that "New Rifles just received and will be issued immediately."[116] The November 1848 inspection shows 1,805 new percussion rifles and sword bayonets, with 507 wanting, along with 570 spare nipples, 190 spring-cramps and nipple keys, and 1,805 brass jags, ball drawers, snap-caps and stoppers. The previous month the service companies stationed at Victoria, Hong Kong, were described as being armed with 630 of the same new rifles with rifles swords and equipment.[117]

THE ROYAL CANADIAN RIFLE REGIMENT

This regiment was raised as two battalions by an order of 16 July 1841 and received 1,050 Baker rifles in the autumn of 1841. Of this total 600 were arms repaired at Enfield and 450 at the "Round Table" in the Small Gun Office at the Tower, i.e. they were all second-hand rifles. No implements being available from Stores, Joseph Aston of Birmingham supplied 1,050 sets at 7d. each.[118] This is very probably the last newly raised regiment to be initially armed with British flintlock service rifles. Their second-hand rifles did not stand the rigours of service for long: by August 1843, with the regiment stationed at Niagara, all 1,050 were listed unserviceable, with a note that new arms were shortly expected.[119] Not until September 1844 does an inspection find the regiment equipped with 840 new percussion rifles with rifle swords, "a beautiful and perfect arm."[120] By February 1845, the regiment had its full complement of 1,050 rifles and rifle swords along with ball drawers, brass jags, nipple keys and snap-caps for each man.[121]

THE PORTUGUESE CAÇADORES

On 15 Jan. 1810, the Secretary at War informed the Board of Ordnance that Lord Wellington had made repeated and urgent requests for arms, without which the Portuguese Force could not be made efficient; these included 30,000 muskets, 6,000 carbines, 2,000 rifles, 4,000 pairs of pistols and 6,000 cavalry swords.[122] The following month it was noted that "our officers are very anxious to have some [rifles] for the Portuguese sharp shooters who are stated to be very expert."[123]

In June 1811, Wellington applied for 2,000 rifles for Beresford's Portuguese army then being formed. Its paper strength was 40,810 including 4,620 Caçadores in six battalions each with 770 rank & file, although actually only about 550 strong on average. Assuming the 2,000 rifles were for these six battalions, this would give 330 rifles and 220 muskets to each. This proportion is very similar to that in the King's German Legion Light Battalions.

The Portuguese already had rifles earlier than this large requisition, since Wellington mentions them on 11 May 1809.[124] These may have been Lisbon-made copies of the Baker rifle.

To the original six regiments of Caçadores were added three more from the Royal Lusitanian Legion, and a further three were raised in 1811, making twelve.[125]

Portuguese Caçadores in the Anglo-Portuguese Army, 16 Jan. 1814:[126]

1st - 421 men   *7th - 265 men*   *11th - 215 men*
2d - 274 men   *8th - 189 men*   *14th - 222 men*
3d - 318 men   *9th - 231 men*
5th - 293 men   *10th - 172 men*   *Total: 2,600 men*

OTHER FOREIGN-BASED RIFLE COMPANIES, POST-1800

Foreign troops in British pay accounted for 10% of the British army in 1804 at the opening of the Napoleonic Wars; by 1808, this had risen to 17%, and by 1813 they represented 27% of the British army's fighting manpower.[127]

The continuing use of the French term "chasseur" to denote both light infantry and rifle-armed units often makes it difficult to accurately identify and distinguish the latter from the former.

There are several "standard" sources for the many small units recruited for British service from foreign personnel during the period 1793–1815; many of them do not agree on dates of raising, or whether they were raised as rifle-armed units. Wherever possible, I have included information on the possession of rifles taken from inspection returns.

The Bourbon Regiment may in fact have been more than one unit, as the early references to it are contradictory; it is mentioned as a two battalion rifle regiment. Both (if there were two) were formed sometime between 1803 and 1810, and in January 1812 the Prince Regent approved of its being "clothed and equipped in a like manner as the 95th or Rifle Corps"; inspection returns of January 1814 and 1815 show a rifle company with 73 rifles.[128]

The Brunswick Light Infantry battalion was supplied with 25 rifles for its recruiting company in November 1812.[129] The Brunswick Corps commanded by the Duke of Brunswick at Waterloo included two rifle companies commanded by Major von Rauschenplatt.[130]

The twelve companies of light infantry designated the **Brunswick Oels Jagers** were placed on the British Establishment effective 25 Sept. 1809, and arrived in Lisbon in Sept. 1810. The extent of their equipment with rifles is unclear. They joined the Light Division 13 Nov. 1810. This unit was attached to the Brunswick Legion in December 1814.

A **Calabrian Free Corps** of sharpshooters was raised in Sicily in 1809 and served around the Mediterranean rim, with detachments in eastern Spain in 1812–13. How many of this corps carried rifles is unknown.

Although the name **Chasseurs Britannique** suggests the use of rifles, the records are contradictory as to whether they actually received or used them. They were raised in May 1801 as a rifle regiment and survived until 1815.

The Corsican Rangers were raised on Minorca in 1799 as a rifle regiment; they were disbanded in 1802. Their actual armament is uncertain.

The Royal Corsican Rangers was raised in September 1803, and by January 1805 they mustered 264 rank and file. In July 1812, they received 113 rifles to complete their two rifle companies (they already had 139), as well as 2,060 [New Land Pattern] Light Infantry muskets.[131]

Count Froberg's Levy were authorized to be issued with 200 rifles and sword bayonets on 31 May 1806,[132] but they had not yet received them on 9 May 1807.

The second battalion of the **Greek Light Infantry** had two rifle companies for which it received 206 rifles in July 1813.[133]

De Roll's Regiment (1795–1816) had two rifle companies, one formed in 1809 and the second from at least 1812. One of the rifle companies suffered 50 casualties out of 97 men engaged at the Battle of Ordal, 13 Sept. 1813.

The Royal York Rangers (successors to the York Rangers) formed on Guernsey in 1808 from ten companies of the Royal African Corps, were issued 210 rifles complete on 1 Sept. 1809. They served throughout the war in the West Indies. Inspection returns of 1815 show 1097 muskets, 202 rifles and 36 fusils; a return of 19 Dec. 1816 shows only 101 rifles all "regularly marked."[134] By July 1817, this number had increased to 188 rifles and rifle swords, 29 serjeant's fusils and 478 muskets and bayonets.[135]

De Watteville's Regiment was formed in 1801 from earlier Swiss levies. Their chasseur company included twelve men with rifled carbines.[136]

The Royal West India Rangers were formed in October 1806 as a "condemned battalion" of British deserters and volunteers from prison hulks, and from the Royal African Corps. They were issued with 210 rifles complete on 29 Dec. 1806, with a supplementary issue of 210 on 30 Sept. 1807. An augmentation to the two rifle companies added a further 40 rifles in June 1813. An 1815 inspection return shows 254 rifles, while a similar return of 24 Oct. 1816 shows 262 rifles of which 50 are unserviceable.[137] By July 1817, the number of serviceable rifles and rifle swords was 212 (of a complement of 262) with 986 muskets and bayonets. The last two returns for the regiment, at Antigua in May and December 1818, both show 94 rifles for a complement of 212, and 224 muskets and bayonets.[138]

AD-HOC RIFLE COMPANIES IN BRITISH REGIMENTS

The 12th Foot, at Mauritius in August 1811, had a rifle company with 94 rifles reported in good condition.[139] These were probably Baker rifles of East India Co. manufacture issued prior to the regiment's embarkation in September 1810; they still had them in January 1814, although by June 1817 their number had shrunk to 46.[140]

The 1/14th Foot formed a rifle company for the Java Expedition of 1811, selecting the best shots from each company, and being armed with East India Co. Baker rifles; they still retained 48 rifles in late 1814.[141]

While it was stationed on Jamaica between the summer of 1827 and the autumn of 1832, the **22nd Foot** had 24 rifles and rifle swords, as well as 4 serjeant's fusils and between 474 and 516 muskets and bayonets.[142]

The 1/23d Foot had a rifle company with 52 rifles out of a complement of 70 in June 1809 while stationed at Halifax, Nova Scotia. The reporting officer said that the 8 unserviceable rifles could be replaced from the local Ordnance Stores.[143]

In November 1820, the **26th Foot** received 5 rifles and rifle swords from the Ordnance Stores at Gibraltar. By December 1821, this number had doubled, and these ten rifles were retained by the regiment during its service at Gibraltar and in Ireland, until 1826. In December 1829, while at Fort St. George, Madras, the regiment had one rifle and rifle sword.[144]

Between July 1825 and May 1831, during which time it was serving on the island of Jamaica, the **33rd Foot** had 24 rifles, without sword or bayonet, in addition to its usual complement of 4 serjeant's fusils and between 482 and 570 muskets and bayonets.[145]

The 1st battalion the **43d Light Infantry** received 194 rifles and sword bayonets on 14 Sept. 1805.[146] It is not clear how long the regiment retained these rifles.

For a brief period covered by a single inspection return, the **50th Foot,** while at Stony Hill, Jamaica, in January 1826, had 24 rifles with bayonets and scabbards in addition to its 370 muskets and bayonets.[147]

The 54th Foot had a single rifleman in its ranks between December 1829 and December 1835, during which period the regiment was stationed at Cannanore (1829–31) and Trichinopoly (1832–35).[148]

The second battalion of the **56th Foot** was issued with 200 East India Co. Baker rifles for its rifle company in 1816 but they were left in India when the regiment returned to England by October.[149]

The 59th Foot formed a rifle company for the Java Expedition of 1811 and, like the 14th and 69th companies in this campaign, it was probably armed with East India Co. Baker rifles, 78 of which they retained as late as May 1817.[150]

On 20 Oct. 1809 the **2/62d Foot** had two rifles.[151] These were not reported in March 1807.

While stationed in Surinam in May 1810, the **64th Foot** was in possession of 4 unserviceable rifles.[152]

In May 1817, the **65th Foot,** then at Bombay, had 179 rifles and rifle swords in addition to 667 muskets and bayonets. Despite the statement that "The Rifles are ordered to be returned into Store as soon as they can be replaced by muskets from the Depots," the rifle company saw action in late 1819 at Ras-ul-Khymah in the Persian Gulf, but the rifles had been turned in by 1821.[153]

A rifle company was formed in the **69th Foot** for the Java Expedition of 1811, and was armed with East India Co. Baker rifles.[154]

For the background to all these issues of East India Company-made Baker rifles, the reader is referred to David F. Harding's *Smallarms of the East India Company 1600–1856,* vol. IV, Chapter 40.

Inspection Returns dating from December 1822 to October 1829 show that the **75th Foot,** during service at Gibraltar, Windsor Barracks and Ireland, had 4 rifles with rifle swords in addition to its 576 to 740 muskets and bayonets.[155]

During its tour of duty on Jamaica between May 1825 and January 1833, the **77th Foot** in common with several other British regiments, had 24 rifles without rifle swords or bayonets, in addition to its 570 to 492 muskets and bayonets. The Return of August 1832 from Spanish Town states that the ammunition totals include rifle ammunition. The final return of the series also includes 24 rifle bayonets and scabbards.[156]

There was a rifle company in the 1st battalion of the **78th Highlanders** as early as April 1803, very probably armed with captured Dutch rifles from the Cape of Good Hope. The 2nd battalion, the 78th Highlanders, were issued 11 rifles complete on 30 Aug. 1808. In connexion with this issue, the regiment was informed by the Ordnance on 26 August that "Powder Horns & Flasks are not supplied to Regiments from that Department."[157] By 28 Oct. 1809, the inspecting officer noted that "29 Rifles are in the Regtl Store, the Rifle Party having been done away. I have directed that on the Regiment moving from the Fort, they shall be delivered to the Ordnance Store."[158] Despite this threat, the regiment still held them on 25 June 1812, perhaps because they had not yet departed Fort George.[159] An inspection return of 14 Dec. 1816 shows the 1st battalion still possessed 78 rifles.[160]

The 1/82d Foot, at Gibraltar in 1810, had 5 rifles.[161] In October 1822, while at Port Louis, Mauritius, the 82d had 30 rifles and rifle swords as part of its arms complement which included 3 serjeant's fusils and 459 muskets and bayonets.[162]

In April 1803, the riflemen of the **84th Foot,** in

camp at Kamaun, are mentioned, and it is probable that these men had captured foreign rifles from the Cape of Good Hope. The 84th once again carried rifles during a tour of duty on Jamaica between June 1827 and September 1832, 24 or 25 rifles without rifle sword or bayonet being listed during this period.[163]

During the Java campaign in August 1811, a five-company detachment of the **89th Foot** was formed into a rifle battalion, almost certainly armed with East India Company Baker rifles.[164]

The 91st Foot while serving on Jamaica between the Spring of 1825 and June 1830, carried between 22 and 24 rifle with rifle swords in addition to 2 serjeant's fusils and between 450 and 559 muskets and bayonets.[165]

During its brief service on Jamaica between May 1825 and March 1826, the **92d Foot** added 24 rifles and rifle swords or bayonets (one report for each type) to its armament in addition to 498 muskets and bayonets.[166]

The 97th Foot serving on Ceylon between Dec. 1832 and July 1835 carried 24 rifles, the July 1835 return only including rifle swords as well; when it moved to the Cape of Good Hope in November 1846, the regimental pioneers were issued with 7 flint rifles and bayonets.[167]

THE BRITISH MILITIA

A number of militia regiments were allowed to convert to light infantry or rifle corps, presumably to encourage the development of a cadre of men trained in these special skills who might subsequently succumb to the blandishments of the recruiting companies and volunteer for service with regular units of this nature.

The Royal Cardigan Militia was approved by the Commander in Chief to be "clothed, equipped and exercised" as a rifle corps with effect from 22 June 1812;[168] it is not clear whether, or when, they received rifles, but they were still described as a rifle corps in 1825.

The Royal Carnarvon Militia was to be armed and equipped as a rifle corps with effect from 31 Mar. 1812.[169] At the time, it consisted of 9 serjeants and 143 men who were to be issued rifles. They were still described as a rifle corps in 1825.

The Royal Denbigh Militia were converted to a rifle regiment in August 1813, and received rifle accoutrements for 19 serjeants and 361 rank & file in March, 1814.[170] The regiment received 84 rifles which had not been previously issued as part of their allowance in August 1815.[171] They were still described as a rifle corps in 1825.

The three-company **Royal Flintshire Militia** was converted to a rifle regiment and received 227 rifles in July 1812.[172] In March 1814, 227 sets of accoutrements were issued to the unit suitable for use with rifles.[173] They were still described as a rifle corps in 1825.

The Militia of the Island of Jersey was probably the earliest militia regiment to receive rifles, 200 being issued for two rifle companies on 30 June 1800.[174] In all likelihood these were not Baker rifles.

The 2d Royal Lancashire Militia received 160 rifles and sword bayonets on 1 July 1805.[175]

The 3d Royal Lancashire Militia had 110 rifles in April 1807.[176] One company of the regiment was ordered to be clothed and exercised as riflemen in September 1812, but there is no mention of them being so armed either then or subsequently: they received 105 Serjeant's Fusils.[177]

The Royal Pembroke Militia were to be armed, equipped and clothed as a rifle corps, and were issued rifles for their 14 sergeants and 278 rank and file in July 1811.[178] They were still a rifle corps in 1825.

Two companies of the **Shropshire Militia** were converted to rifle companies and were issued 212 rifles in October 1810.[179]

The Sussex Regiment of Militia had its new arms engraved and numbered in the autumn of 1803; included were 128 rifles.[180] They still possessed 102 rifles in May 1807.[181]

The North Yorkshire (44th) Militia had 217 rifles in October 1809, with 33 wanting to complete their Establishment.[182]

The West Yorkshire Militia received sufficient "rifles" for two rifle companies on 4 May 1804. The 3rd West Yorks Militia had 132 rifles in April 1807.[183]

BULK, NON-SPECIFIC, RIFLE ISSUES

Apart from issues direct from the Board of Ordnance to specified regiments, during the period from 1793 to 1815 when Britain was supporting the wars against the French and their allies through funding and arming of her own allies, large numbers of arms were ordered by the several Secretaries of State to be shipped for allied governments and for expeditions to be mounted by British and allied troops. Amongst these were a number of rifles, of which some were unquestionably of foreign manufacture, while others were standard-issue Baker pattern.

18 Apr. 1807. To be sent to the Rio de la Plata, an order including 200 rifles, probably as spares for the companies of the Rifle Corps send on the Montevideo campaign.[184]

In April 1808, 200 rifles were ordered to Gibraltar for the garrison.[185]

On 15 Jan. 1810, Wellington wants arms for a unified Portugese Force, including 2,000 rifles; some of these at least may have been foreign-made rifles.[186] Confirmation of the demand for 2,000 rifles was made the following month.[187]

In May 1810, a shipment of ammunition for the British forces in Sicily included 60,000 rounds of rifle ammunition with ball 22 to the pound, and 10,000 rifle flints.[188]

In September 1810, 100 rifles and 200 of the "lightest sort of firelock" were to be sent to Heligoland to arm the merchants.[189]

27 March 1813. To be shipped with the utmost expedition to Prussia an order including 500 rifles & swords with 400 rounds per rifle.[190]

In August and September 1814, an order for ordnance and small arms was prepared, probably to send with the troops for New Orleans, which included 500 rifles and 200,000 rounds of rifle ammunition.[191]

CONCLUSION

The purpose of this chapter is to demonstrate both the large numbers and the wide distribution of rifles in the British Royal service during the French Revolutionary and Napoleonic Wars and the period of peace that followed, until the adoption of the percussion Brunswick Rifle. Those interested in the further wide use of the flintlock military rifle by the East India Company's forces should consult David F. Harding's four-volume history of the Honourable Company's arms, their ammunition, use and performance. No attempt has been made here to give a detailed military history of the units that carried rifles, the intent being only to show the widespread use of the rifle by British forces in all corners of the globe.

There remains much uncertainty as to the actual types of rifle carried by some of the units discussed in this chapter, especially by small foreign units in British pay. Given the numbers of foreign-made rifles captured by British forces after 1793, as well as those purchased abroad, there is no question but that some units will have carried rifles other than the regulation Baker patterns. Determining which units had which rifles, and whether they were ever re-equipped with Baker rifles, requires a unit by unit study, and with the general loss of unit records for the period it is a problem that is likely to remain unsolved.

CHAPTER 15

British Army Rifle Marksmanship

with the Flintlock Rifle

Before discussing the marksmanship training of British riflemen and its effects, some attempt must be made to determine the inherant accuracy of the weapon put into their hands. For the years prior to the issue of the Baker rifle, there is no known contemporary evidence for military rifle accuracy with the exception of a few hearsay comments of little value to a detailed enquiry, and of the 1790s trials described in Chapter 8. Even with the Baker rifle, given its length of service, the extant material dates from the very beginning (1800) and towards the end (1835) of its military career.

The first evidence we have of how well the Baker rifle, or rather the Baker barrel, could shoot, comes from the Woolwich trials of 1800, and appeared as an illustration/advertisement in Baker's own book. Reproduced here, it shows a nine-foot square target into which 11 of 12 balls have been fired at 300 yards, giving a group of approximately five feet square. It must be noted that this was done with a musket-bore barrel, using balls of .693" diameter with 4 drams (110 grains) of powder, and not with the carbine-bore which was shortly afterwards adopted as the standard calibre. The rifling twist is the only feature in common with the standard calibre rifles. This target must represent an ideal level of accuracy, since the barrel was firmly fixed in a mortar-bed for testing, eliminating all "human-error" elements of both gun assembly and factors such as sight-picture and trigger-pull. Later in the nineteenth century it was proven that this method of firmly fixing a barrel separated from its stock in an immoveable bedding did not produce the most accurate results since it prevented or distorted barrel "whip," but during the period of this study it was the accepted norm. Since this result 'had the preference of the whole' group of English as well as foreign rifles tested, we can assume that this degree of accuracy was considered as an acceptable standard. It seems likely that subsequent troop-trials showed the recoil of the musket-bore rifle to be unacceptably severe, resulting in the substitution of a carbine-bore version which presumably had not shown that it was capable of this level of accuracy.

Baker's cavalry rifle 20-inch barrel produced the target shown at right, using a .615" ball and 84 grains of

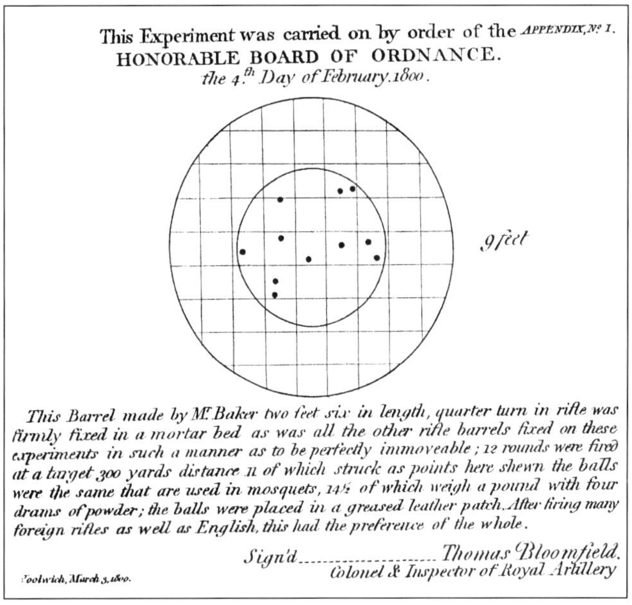

The target shot during Board of Ordnance experiments in 1800 with a musket-bore rifle barrel by Ezekiel Baker, at 300 yards, the barrel being fixed in a mortar-bed.
From Baker's Remarks on Rifle Guns;...

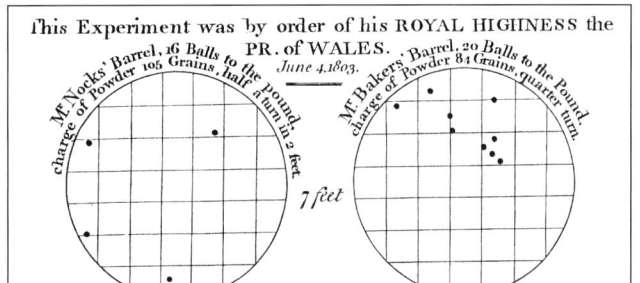

Targets made in 1803 at 200 yards with 20-inch Cavalry Rifle barrels fixed in a mortar-bed. Note that while the twist of Nock's barrel is specified as half a turn in two feet, Baker's is only described as a quarter turn, not specifying in what distance. *From Baker's Remarks on Rifle Guns;...*

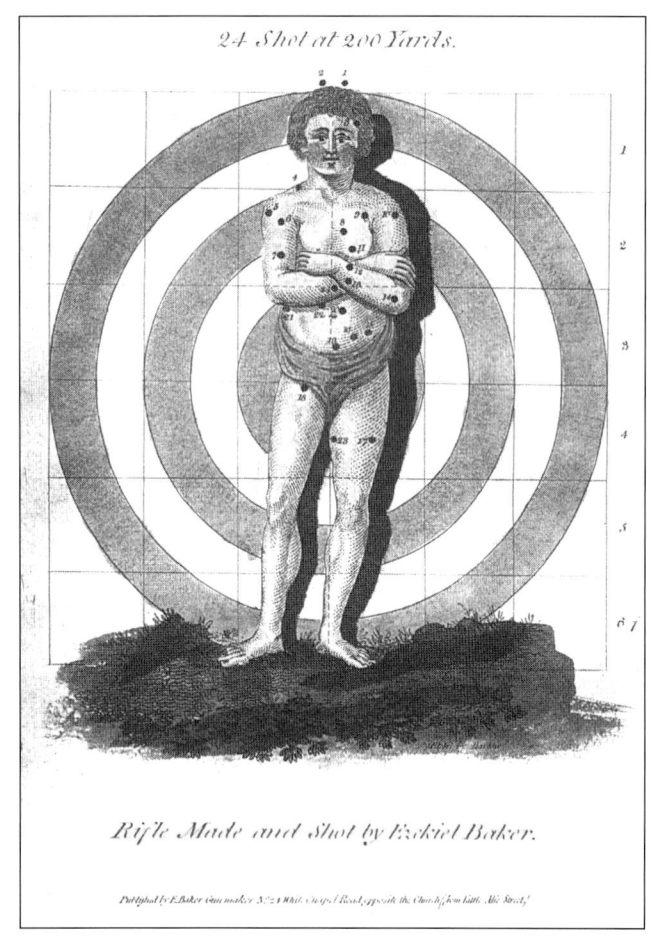

British Military Flintlock Rifles

that a great many factors enter into the final choice which have nothing to do with target accuracy.

The third piece of evidence from this early period is again taken from Baker's book (see this page), and shows the result of two-dozen rounds fired at 200 yards by Baker, presumably with a carbine-bore rifle. The vertically arranged group on a six-foot square target indicates a cold clean barrel for the first two shots, and thereafter very acceptable military accuracy at the "normal" distance for rifles of 200 yards — twice effective musket range. Baker's target fired at 100 yards (not shown here) is remarkably similar in grouping characteristics, including the first two shots being just over the man's head.

A group of targets fired with the issue Baker rifle by George Lovell in 1835 forms the final evidence for the inherent accuracy of the Baker rifle. The targets shown are six feet square, each square measuring six inches and with a six-inch bull's-eye. What is of particular value about these targets is that they show the carbine-bore rifle being used with a plain unpatched cartridge and with loose powder and a patched ball, the two extremes of standard ammunition for skirmishing and precision shooting. The results are about as opposite as one could expect, even given double the distance for the precision shooting. Only the 100-yard target fired with plain ball begins to compare with the results obtained at the beginning of the Baker's career, and makes one suspect that Ezekiel Baker was an extremely fine rifle-shot while

Target shot by Ezekiel Baker with one of his rifles at 200 yards, in the standing position. Out of two dozen shots only the first two from a cold barrel failed to strike the figure. *From Baker's* **Remarks on Rifle Guns;...**

powder, giving a group of about 4½ feet by just under 2½ feet at 200 yards. Baker's description of his own off-hand shooting with a finished cavalry rifle is given in the caption. These results for the short-barrelled carbine must, once again, be taken as an acceptable standard of accuracy, given that this pattern was subsequently adopted and produced. It has always to be remembered when considering the accuracy of military small arms

(three on bottom) Targets shot by the Inspector of Small Arms, George Lovell, in 1835 when the flintlock was being phased out in favour of the percussion ignition system. Left and middle targets are six feet square, right target 12-feet square, with a six-inch bull's-eye, each square being six inches. Originally, these targets also had a male figure 6 feet high by 18 inches wide which has been omitted for clarity. All balls were 20 to the pound. Left: 100 yds., 20 shots from shoulder-rest, loaded without patch, charge 3 drams. Middle: 200 yds., 20 shots as above, loaded with loose ball & patch, wind nearly nil, "perfect conditions." 6 misses. Right: 300 yds., 40 shots, 19 misses. The black outline shows the area of the normal six-foot square target.

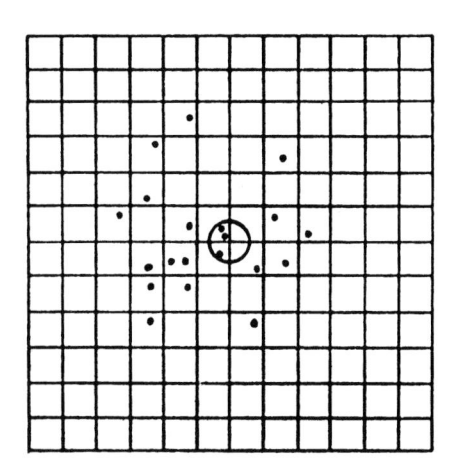

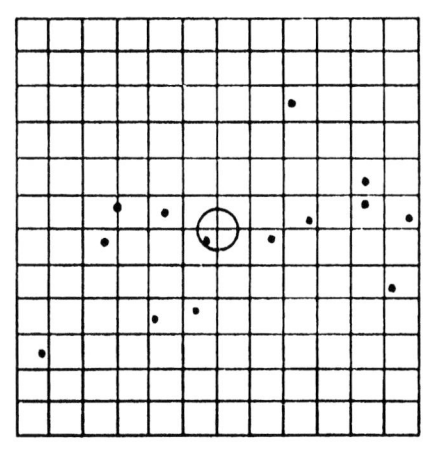

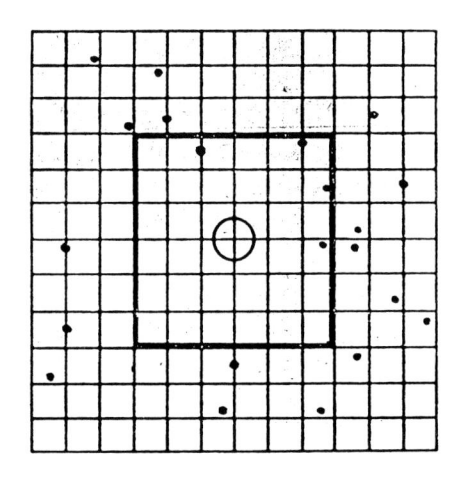

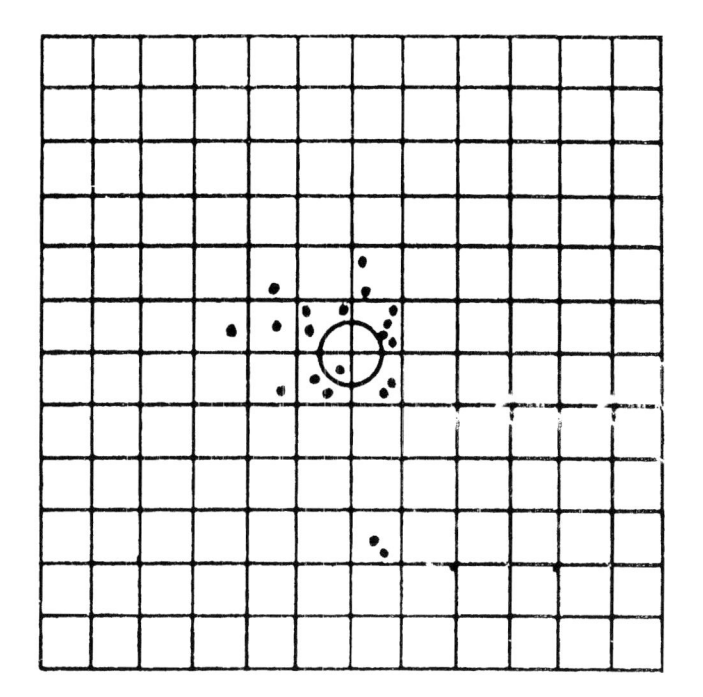

(above) **Just how much difference there was between the flintlock and percussion ignition systems as they affected rifle accuracy is suggested by this 20-shot, 100-yard target fired with a percussion Baker rifle using balls 18½ to the pound and only 1½ drams (42 grains) of powder. This and the previous plate are taken from War Office records of 1835 (PRO,WO44/677).**

George Lovell was not.

Lovell's 1835–6 trials which led to the adoption of the two-groove percussion Brunswick Rifle should perhaps be seen in the light of the intention to adopt a new system, as shown in the illustration above, just as the 1800–03 trials may be viewed in the light of an intention to adopt a military compromise, preferably of "English" origin.[1]

MARKSMANSHIP TRAINING

Prior to the publication of De Rottenburg's Regulations in 1798, there was no official manual for rifle training. Prior to the raising of the 5th battalion of the 60th Regiment there had been only company-strength rifle units, and these of a temporary for-the-war nature; what there was of training had been on a regimental or even company level.

The regulations for the Rifle Corps laid down in 1800 describe in detail how marksmanship was to be inculcated into the riflemen of the newly-organized unit of which Coote Manningham was colonel. Whether anything of a similar nature was adopted by the older units of the 60th Foot is not known.

According to the Regulations, target practice was carried out at four distances: 90 yards, 140 yards, 200 yards (generally described as "the usual distance") and 300 yards "beyond which no established practice is to go." The shortest distance of 90 yards was intended primarily for recruit training. Surtees (a participant) claims that firing was first done "from a horse" (i.e. a rest) at 50 yards.[2]

There were two patterns of target: a round wooden target with concentric rings, and a human-figure target painted on canvas. The wooden target was four feet in diameter and painted white; on it were painted three black circles. The first circle was four inches from the centre of the 1½-inch bull's-eye; the second circle was nine inches from the centre, and the outer circle at fifteen inches from the centre. Each circle was two inches thick with the inner edge reckoned as the measured distance. It was to be set in the ground at a height of from 3 feet 4 inches to 4 feet two inches, and these heights were to be marked on the "leg" of the target as this was considered to be important. The screen or figure target was achieved through the use of a wooden "mould" or silhouette whose outline was traced on the canvas and then painted in. The frame was to be made seven feet high by three feet wide, and facing figure, never more than six feet by two feet, to be standing with his arms either crossed across the chest, or in the position of "ordered arms." In the exact centre of the figure an eight-inch diameter circle was to be inscribed. The Quartermaster or Master Carpenter of the unit was to keep two wooden figure moulds, one of a man of six foot and the other five-foot five inches. A marked distance cord was issued with these targets on demand by the company captain.

Target practice was to consist of six rounds per man per day, all to be fired at one distance on the day. Serjeants fired four rounds per session once a week, and not with the men. Recruit firing was used to establish three classes: 1st Class or bad shots; 2nd Class of tolerably good shots; and 3rd Class of marksmen. A company was to be divided into three squads according to these classes before proceeding to the firing range. Target rolls were to be kept and the classes re-graded every two months according to the men's progress.

The 1st Class were always to be exercised at 90 and 140 yards. The 2nd Class fired "occasionally" at these distances but normally at 200 yards; while the marksmen comprising the 3rd Class were to fire occasionally at 200 yards but generally at 300. It was recommended that companies fire alternately at the two types of target and that they be placed in a sheet of smooth water the better to observe the fall of shot.

Grading into the three classes of marksmanship was based on the following levels of achievement:

Marksman or 3rd class – 4 shots in the round target or 3 in the figure target at 200 yards or 300 yards, for two days out of three, for two months after the receipt of his rifle. Failure to achieve this level for a subsequent two months demoted him to the 2nd class.

2nd class – *2 shots in the round target or the figure target at 140 yards or more, for two days out of three. Failure to achieve this level at any subsequent period resulted in demotion to 1st class.*

1st class – *all companies were initially in this class and were promoted by results. Each man was individually marked, shot for shot. A "hit" was reckoned as being "one full inch within the extreme edge of the whole of the round target, and one half inch within the whole of the figure above the knee, which is to be lined across by the Quarter Master..."*

Incentives to improvement in marksmanship were, initially, premiums offered by company captains to the best shots; these often took the form of cash payments, or of small medals of which some survive. Those who achieved the 3rd class or marksman level were regimentally rewarded by the wearing of a small green cockade above the regulation black leather one on the front of the soldier's cap.

In addition to the "standard" form of target practice described above, the Regulations also suggested "tactical" variations. These included men running about for the shooters to level at with blank cartridges, and the use of moving targets. "A target may be constructed on wheels, and drawn from side to side during the practice, by ropes affixed for the purpose. In all target practice, the ground cannot be too much varied; woods, heights, hollows, plains, brush-wood, water, and every other description of surface, should be fired over occasionally. ...Firing on the ground [i.e. prone] to be frequently practiced." A light infantry manual elaborates:

The kneeling position should always be adopted by skirmishers in firing whenever the ground and other circumstances admit of it. The position is easily and readily taken, and affords considerable facility in taking a steady aim. The Soldier is less exposed kneeling than standing- and the loading is effected with as much ease in the one posture as in the other.

In rocky and uneven ground, or when stones or other objects offer by which the men can cover themselves, they may sometimes with advantage fire lying.

The caution to lie down is passed along the rear of the line, (or the Bugle sound may be used) and the whole drop on both knees and throw themselves on their bellies- every man taking advantage of any stone, bank, or other cover that may happen to be near him. The firing proceeds as before, but the loading will in general be performed in a kneeling position. The Soldier may however if the kneeling position should expose him very much, load lying, as follows.

After priming he will roll over on his back, and placing the butt of the [rifle] between his legs, the lock uppermost and the muzzle a little raised, carefully insert the cartridge – draw his ramrod and finish his loading – rolling over again on his breast when ready to fire.[3]

A trial of marksmanship between the 95th Rifles and the 43rd and 52nd Light Infantry took place about 1808. Unfortunately, it was not reported until 1831 and most of the detail is lacking. The targets of the Rifle Corps were placed at 200 yards "the usual distance" and those of the Light Infantry between 80 and 90 yards. A group of about 80 men from each regiment fired six rounds per man. The riflemen's target "was so riddled and cut to pieces that it was with difficulty brought home, whilst the target of the Light Infantry was, comparatively, in a good state of repair."[4]

A moving target was set up on Hythe beach, but the pulling ropes were often shot to pieces.[5] William Surtees mentions that recruits first fired "from a horse" (of the gymnasium rather than the stable variety) at 50 yards. He fired ten rounds of which all were on the target with two bull's-eyes, which, for a recruit was considered "a wonderful exhibition." Surtees further tells a story reminiscent of the target-between-the-knees tale of the Lancaster riflemen of the 1770s, wherein Major Wade and a rifleman named Smeaton often held a target for each other at a range of 150 yards.[6] In June 1804, Gen. Moore issued orders "that the 95th should be practised in the mode of firing from the edge of the cliff to a target placed at the water edge."[7]

In March 1810, a force of 200 men from 2/95 and 300 from 3/95 were about to embark for foreign service, and, having notified the Commander-in-Chief, he wrote to the Board of Ordnance stating that:

...as the season of the Year has not permitted the men of the 2nd & 3rd Battalions of the 95th Regiment to practice firing with Ball for some Months past' he would like to have additional ammunition made available to them for target practice – which was granted.[8]

In the Spring of 1814, the Commander-in-Chief approved the purchase and distribution of 200 "machines made for target practice," also described as "traversing musket rests" "swivel rests for firing Rifles." These were made in May 1814, by the Ordnance contractors James and Joseph Sherwood at a cost of 6/- each[9] and were distributed to thirty depots and garrisons around the country, including Hythe, Shorncliffe and Braeburne Leas.

The greatest single obstacle to forming any accurate opinion on the efficacy of British rifle marksmanship during the period the flintlock rifle was in issue is the lack of clear references to distances involved. While there are many accounts of feats of marksmanship by British riflemen in most theatres of combat around the world, especially during the period of the Baker rifle, they almost never mention the distance or give details which would enable a distance to be even roughly calculated. Short of visiting and precisely identifying the

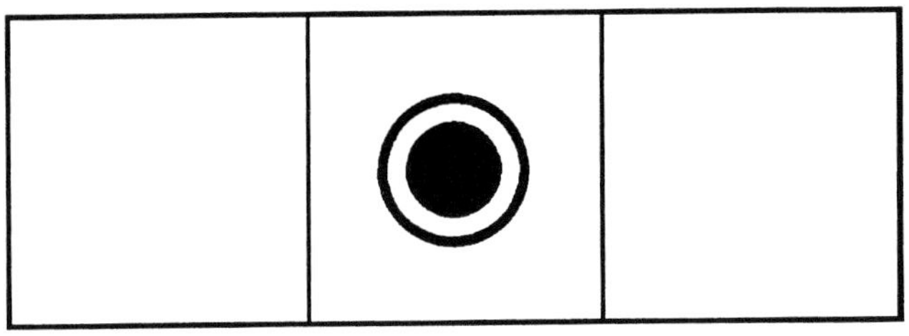

The postwar marksmanship training target for "trained soldiers," which is presumed to have included riflemen. It was used vertically (not as shown), six feet high by two feet wide, the bull's-eye being 8 inches in diameter and ring 12 inches. Drawn from official description by D.F. Harding and taken from his *Smallarms of the East India Company 1600–1856.*

site where a particular incident occurred, there is no way of satisfactorily evaluating the skill of the British flintlock rifleman.

A rare exception occurs with reference to the Siege of Badajoz in 1812. "When, on the 30th the breaching battery (no. 9) opened on La Trinidad the fire of the French sharp-shooters at a range of about 300 yards from the covered way, was so severe and accurate, that it was necessary to send for a party of the 95th Rifles to occupy the trench in front whence at ranges of between 250 and 350 yards they easily kept down the fire of the defenders."[10] This perhaps tells us as much about the possibilities of the musket in the hands of skilled marksmen as about the rifles.

The British riflemen at the Battle of New Orleans in 1815 were about 150 yards from the American breastworks. "An American soldier came within about 150 yards of our line and began to plunder such of the killed and wounded... Corporal Scott asked permission from his captain to take a shot at him. This being granted...he took up his rifle, and taking a steady aim, he fired , and tumbled the plundering villain..."[11]

In the postwar years, semi-annual inspection reports make only occasional references to the abilities of the riflemen in the remaining battalions of the 60th and the two battalions of the Rifle Brigade. Perhaps significantly there is no high praise for marksmanship, but rather "some of the men are good marksmen," "marksmanship has improved greatly since the last inspection," "the men shoot tolerably well."

By a Horse Guards' General Order of 25 October 1824 the target used for practice throughout the army was simplified and standardized on the basis of a six-foot by two-foot surface (see illustration); this was divided into three "divisions," an upper, centre and lower, with an eight-inch black bull's-eye (and aiming mark) in the centre of the centre division, and a heavy ring twelve inches in diameter and one inch thick around the bull's-eye. New recruits were to start their training on an eight-foot square target on which an eight-foot circle was painted. It would be logical to assume that the combat veterans' level of marksmanship would exceed that of postwar recruits, and that as the "old sweats" left the units the newer men, with a lack of motivation typical of a peacetime army, would have achieved lower scores than were achieved by wartime personnel.

The sole reference located by the present writer which describes marksmanship results with the Baker rifle in Royal regiments comes late in the Baker's service history, in March 1832, while the six service companies of the Second Battalion of the Rifle Brigade were stationed at Corfu. As it is the only example known at the time of writing, it is quoted here in full:[12]

(see table below)

Companies Captain	*Bullseyes*	*Upper Div.*	*Centre Div.*	*Lower Div.*	*Total Hits*	*Misses*	*Rounds Fired*
G.M.Stevenson	63	381	545	342	1331	2798	4129
Chas. H. Boileau	41	311	486	470	1308	3368	4676
John Woodford	44	238	481	428	1191	2846	4037
Richard Irlous	54	276	450	480	1260	2997	4257
John Fitzmaurice	59	311	531	411	1312	2065	3377
H.F. Beckwith	56	389	592	346	1383	2157	3540
	317	**1906**	**3085**	**2477**	**7785**	**16231**	**24016**

These figures, for an "elite" specialist unit, show that only 32.4% of the shots fired were hits, and only 1.3% were bull's-eyes; they also indicate that of the non-bull's-eye hits, 12.8%, the largest percentage, were where they were supposed to be, in the two-foot square centre division of the target around the bull's-eye. The only other force with which these figures can be compared are the riflemen of the East India Company forces, specifically rank and file of the rifle companies of eight Madras Native Infantry regiments. Their results show an average of 24% of hits at 200 yards using loose powder and greased patched ball ammunition. Unfortunately, the type of ammunition used by the Rifle Brigade in their firing is not stated, but the probability is that it was patched ball cartridges.[13]

Attempting to form opinions on the basis of modern shooting with these rifles is of some value, but does not greatly enhance the information given in various trials of rifles during their service life. No military paper cartridges from this period survive, so we cannot confirm that the ball diameter and texture of patching is correctly duplicated today. The quality of gunpowder is almost certainly different from that used in the 18th and early 19th centuries. Given these handicaps, it has been found that Baker rifles will easily keep within a thirty-inch circle at 200 yards, a standard size of target in the early nineteenth century. Those who shoot these rifles today do so as a hobby and with no great frequency, and never with the psychological factors inherent in a combat situation which would inevitably detract from the skill of the individual rifleman on a target range.

CHAPTER 16

Rifles for Indians

in British Service, 1783–1840

With the end of the American War in 1783 and the omission of the British-allied Indian tribes from any mention in the peace treaty, the value of the tribes to the British Government and its colonial economic strategy greatly declined. They were now seen chiefly as forming a buffer zone between the new American nation, the section of the United States known as the Old Northwest which contained several posts still occupied by British troops, and British Canada. Whatever attention was paid by the Government to the fur trade and the Indian's part in it was given as a sop to the merchants of London, the west of England and Scotland who were engaged in this trade, and to the interests of the Hudson's Bay Company and the North West Company.

From the time that rifles were first used as gifts from the British Government to the headmen and chief warriors of allied tribes, these rifles had been obtained by the Board of Trade from the private sector, chiefly through the London gunmaker William Wilson of the Minories, as discussed earlier in this book.

During the seven years of the American War the Indians had received more rifles from the British Government than during any previous period of time, and by the end of that war, rifles had become an integral part of the military equipment of war chiefs, head warriors and others of the Indian elite as defined by the Government. It is clear that in addition to the rifles distributed officially through the agents of the Indian Department, some rifles also reached Indian hands via the private traders, although their numbers were not large — there was little profit in them when compared to alcohol, woollen goods and trade guns.

By the close of the war the northern and southern Indian frontiers were awash with firearms. Officially claimed Northern Indian losses during the war (the only area for which figures have been found) amounted to more than £16,500, and listed amongst the lost articles were a total of 23 guns and 8 rifles including one belonging to Joseph Brant valued at £6.[1] When presents to replace these losses were settled upon in November 1786, amongst the goods were 100 guns for chiefs and 200 guns for warriors, but no specific mention of rifles.[2]

On the actual invoice of goods distributed amongst the Mohawks, Six Nations, Delaware and Shawnee, there is no mention even of guns. The Missasaugas received 150 guns for their "wartime fidelity" but again rifles were not mentioned. Ordinary and chiefs guns are mentioned in the annual presents from 1788, but rifles do not appear until 1790, when a statement of presents given to a group of Pottawatamies, Hurons, Chippewas and Ottawas at Detroit includes 20 rifles at 50/- each.[3] A requisition dated 10 October 1792 for presents for the year 1794 includes "50 long Rifles" as well as 50 guns.[4] The next surviving requisition, dated 9 July 1794 for goods and presents for 1796, includes "100 Rifle guns, long" in addition to 300 guns and another 300 guns for chiefs.[5] The rifles were to be packed 20 to a case while guns were 25 to a case. Two present lists dated 7 September 1796 for the Chippewas and the Ottawas, included 11 rifles and 7 rifles respectively.[6]

The first suggestion of any change to the overall specifications of the Indian rifle comes in a requisition dated at La Chine, 3 Aug. 1795 for goods for 1797. This calls for "100 Long Rifle guns, small in the bore." Goods given in exchange for a land cession by the Chippewas in January 1796[7] include 18 rifled barrel guns worth 50/- each as detailed at the end of the last paragraph. The identity of the new "small bore" rifle calibre first appears in a list of goods for the year 1798, dated 3 October 1796,[8] which calls for 60 long Rifles carrying 40 balls to the lb., at 60/- each. By the then current reckoning, 40 to the lb. gave a bore diameter of .494". Another helpful indicator, or perhaps a "red herring" towards identifying Indian rifles of this type is the listing of "Gun locks, double bridle, fit for Rifles and Indian fusees, 50 @ 8/- each." Whether Indian guns and rifles of this period were actually fitted with double-bridle, as opposed to either plain or single-bridle locks, is open to question. Certainly, no actual arms identifiable as intended for Indians have yet been seen with this technologically advanced and expensive form of lock. This requisition may well have been filled with conventional Indian locks. It may also have been a short-lived upgrading of Indian arms allowed by peacetime conditions. Another order for Indian goods for a land cession in

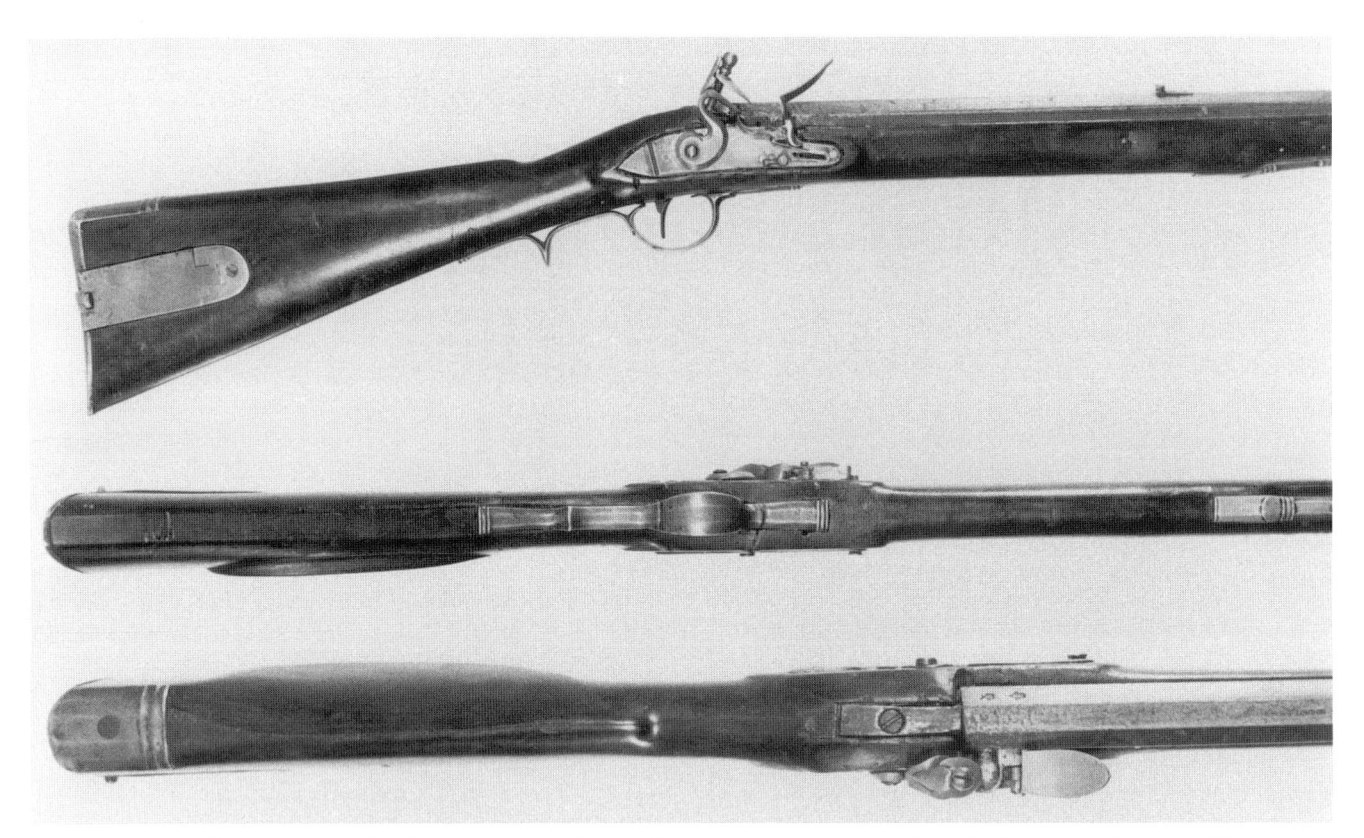

Pattern 1813 Indian Contract Rifle by Ketland & Allport. Given the strong desire of the Ordnance to disrupt military arms production as little as possible, this design, as well as those of the other smoothbore guns of this contract, were kept as close as possible to those that had been supplied to the Indians prior to the general European war. This design of Indian-trade rifle dates from the mid-1790s and will be found with commercial maker's signatures and proofmarks (Wheeler being a good example), in place of the King's Proofs on the barrel of this example. *Courtesy of The Museum of the Fur Trade.*

1796 also specifies 8 rifles of 40 to the lb. calibre. Requisitions dated 4 October 1797, for Indian goods for Upper and Lower Canada for the years 1799 and 1800, again include (for 1800 only) double-bridle locks (60) @ 8/- each, as well as 150 rifles for each year, packed 10 in a case, small bore, at 55/- each.[9] A supplementary requisition based on the fact that the presents for 1799 had not yet (1 Nov. 1797) arrived, called for another 100 rifles, and 60 double-bridle locks.[10]

With the opening of the new century there was a considerable reduction in the number of Indian rifles called for in the annual requisitions. Under date of 9 October 1800 the goods for 1801, which were intended also to form a complete supply for Lower Canada, included only 20 rifles,[11] with no arms at all being called for in 1802 and 1803. A Return of Indian Goods remaining at La Chine and Quebec, dated 24 June 1804, shows 23 rifles in store, all having arrived from England in 1802–3.[12] No rifles were requisitioned in 1804 or 1805, but the combined order for Lower Canada in 1806 and 1807, dated 1 July 1805, called for only 10 rifles at the usual 55/-.[13] The Missasaugas were given 16 rifles (costed at 77/- Quebec currency as opposed to 56/- for chief's guns and 28/- for common guns) in a bill dated 6 September 1806. Indian Goods for Upper Canada for 1808, requisitioned 27 Aug. 1806, included 70 rifles, but none for Lower Canada.[14] For the following year, 20 rifles were demanded for Lower Canada, and for 1810, 10 rifles at a new reduced value of 52/6.[15]

The records for the northern Indian frontier between 1783 and 1811 show that from the time of their first appearance in 1790 until 1810, a total of 866 Indian rifles were ordered sent from England for distribution by the Indian Department agents. In comparison, the number of Department-requisitioned chief's guns between 1789 and 1810 totalled 3,850, while the common fusees for the same period totalled 5,780.

The precise identification of the rifles distributed between the end of the American War and the 1813 Contract rifles is less easily achieved than accounting for their numbers. It seems very likely that since William Wilson of the Minories continued to supply the guns for Government Indian presents through at least 1792, he continued to supply the same sort of rifles which he had furnished during the late war. The introduction of a new smaller calibre, which first appears in 1796, may also signal the point at which a change was made in the overall design, and possibly in the supplier as well, for we know Wilson lost his monopoly sometime during the 1790s. Although no firm evidence has

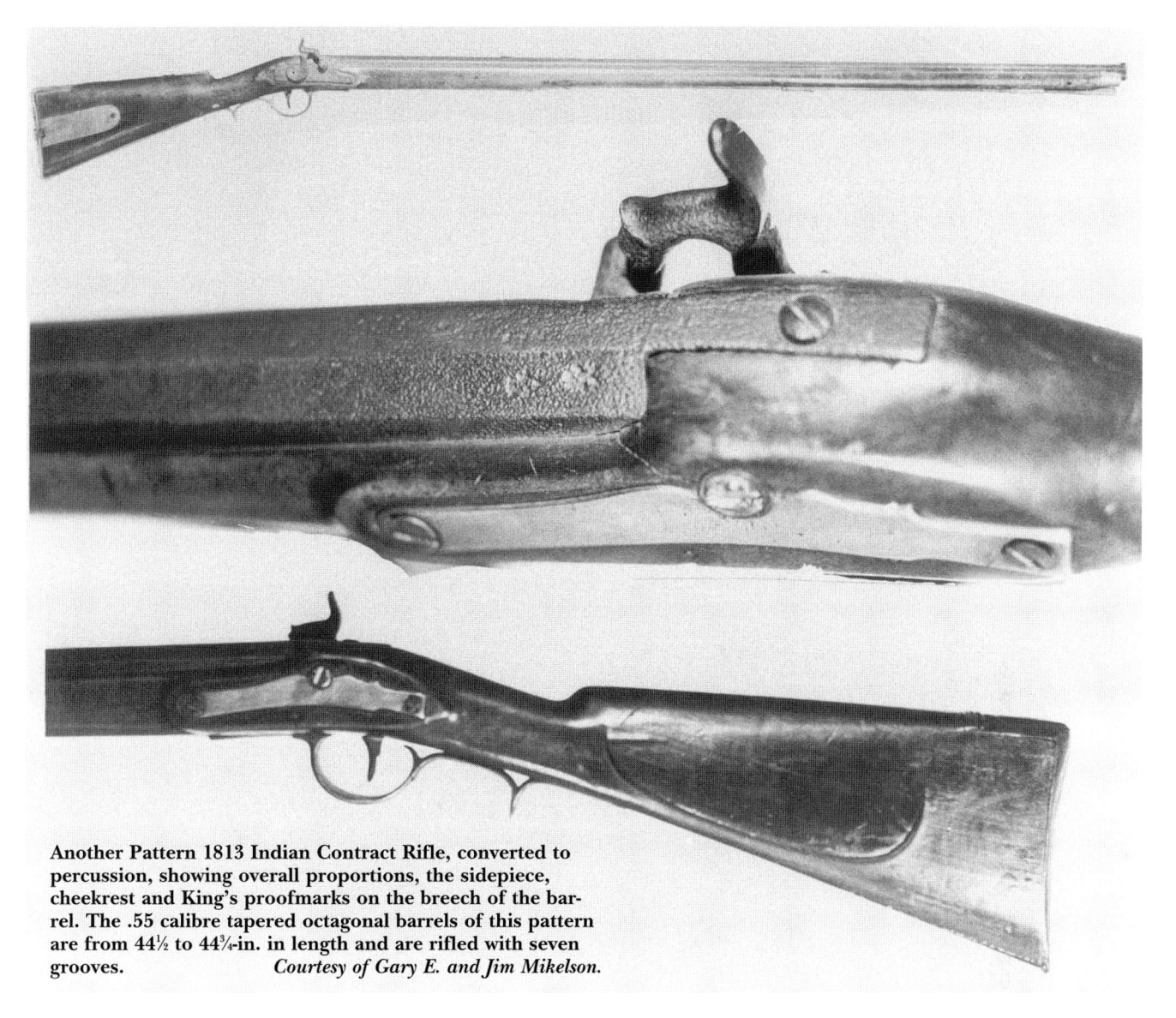

Another Pattern 1813 Indian Contract Rifle, converted to percussion, showing overall proportions, the sidepiece, cheekrest and King's proofmarks on the breech of the barrel. The .55 calibre tapered octagonal barrels of this pattern are from 44½ to 44¾-in. in length and are rifled with seven grooves. *Courtesy of Gary E. and Jim Mikelson.*

come to light at the time of writing, it is probable that the new rifle design was very close to that of the 1813 contract rifles (photo on previous page).

THE BOARD OF ORDNANCE
1813 CONTRACT INDIAN RIFLES

Thanks to the long wars against the French, the Board of Ordnance had been gradually channeling all gunmaking activity into some form of usefulness to the military effort, and choking off whatever could not be adapted. Chiefly for this reason, when the War of 1812 broke out in the United States, it was felt expedient for the Board to arrange for the manufacture of firearms for the allied tribes rather than distract the workforce into the private sector. The result was the 1813 contract for trade guns, chief's guns, rifles and pistols. The patterns selected for these arms varied only in slight details from those being manufactured for the private trade in the 1790s and early 1800s before the Board commenced it restrictive policy. For a detailed survey of this series of arms, the reader is referred to my article in *The Museum of the Fur Trade Quarterly*, (Chadron, Nebraska, USA), vol. 21, numbers 1 and 3, Spring and Fall 1985. The rifles only (see illustrations) will be discussed here. After this one contract and with the end of both the War of 1812 in America and of the general European conflict in 1815, the supply of Indian arms was once again assumed by the Board of Trade.

The early campaigns of the War of 1812 demonstrated to the British Government just how important Indian allies could be, and after an attempt by the Board of Trade in March 1813 to obtain arms for the Indians, the Board of Ordnance entered the picture for the first time since 1753. This was based on the statement that "the Public Supplies are materially deranged by the provision of Arms by individuals." Having taken over the responsibility for supply, the usual delays occurred. It was not until 2 June 1813 that the Inspector of Small Arms at Birmingham, Colonel Miller, was ordered "to report whether any inconvenience would result from Arms of these descriptions being made under his Superintendence; and at what price they could be provided." The fact that, at this stage, the barrels were ready for proof while the balance of the arms were only in the pattern stage, strongly suggests that the barrels were of a design already available in the trade. It is interesting that the initial request for arms sent to the Board at the end of June did not include rifles. It seems that the arms "were taken from the last supply for this Service."

Colonel Miller's report on the several patterns and their prices, dated 12 July 1813, contains the first mention of rifles. Not surprisingly, they are the most expensive arms in the group:[16]

	£	s.	d.
Rifle Gun	2	7	6
Chief's Gun	1	10	0
Common Gun	1	1	6
Pistols, each		11	6

Miller felt that they could be most efficiently produced by having the barrels proved and viewed and then turned into Ordnance Stores from whence they would be issued to the contractors in the long-established method of the Ordnance, the "Ordnance System" of controlled manufacture. The first bills for completed arms appear in September 1813. Although a total of 26,786 Indian arms were delivered between this time and 1816, only 1,538 of them were rifles, all of which were delivered during 1814 and 1815.

Given the delivery dates of the rifles, it is highly unlikely that any of them would have been in the hands of the Indians prior to the opening of the campaign of 1814. Since both the importance of the Indians to the war effort generally and the numbers of them participating had both declined after 1813, the 1813 contract rifles in common with the other arms in this group, cannot be considered to have played a major role in the fighting. It is probable that the 1,000 Indian guns brought with the reinforcements under Major Edward Nicolls of the Royal Marines to Pensacola, Florida in August 1814 were a part of this contract. It is therefore possible that these arms saw more use in the Western and Southern spheres of operation than along the Canadian border.

The 1813 contract Indian rifles were supplied by the following Birmingham Ordnance contractors during 1814 and 1815:[17]

	1814	*1815*	*Total*
Blair, Jane Hannah	40	40	80
Dawes, William & Samuel	30	30	60
Galton, Samuel	60	60	120
Gill & Co., John	30	30	60
Hampton, Thomas	30	40	70
Hollis, Richard & William	30	30	60
Ketland & Allport	90	70	160
Ketland, Walker & Co.	106	74	180
Lowndes, Thomas	40	30	70
Morris & Grice	50	50	100
Moxham, Thomas	46	34	80
Rolfe, William I.	45	45	90
Sutherland, Richard & Ramsay	90	90	180
Whately, Henry & John	40	40	80
Wheeler & Son, Robert	44	44	88
Willetts & Holden	30	30	60
	801	737	1,538

THE TATHAM RIFLES OF CAPTAIN NORTON, 1816

At an entirely different level are the rifles made for distribution amongst the Iroquois chieftains and headmen by the British officer "gone native," Captain John Norton, by the London gunmaker Henry Tatham of Charing Cross Road, business partner of Joseph Egg between 1805 and 1815. Far from being a cheap "trade" item, these rifles represented good quality typical London sporting rifle production of the period.

John Norton (c.1768–c.1831) of the British Indian Department, born a Scotsman, was a colourful and controversial figure on the northern frontier who began his career amongst the Indians after being discharged as a private from the 65th Regiment in Canada. He met Joseph Brant in 1792 and lived at the Grand River lands from this time. By 1800, he had "gone completely Indian" and became an adopted Mohawk chief with the name Teyoninhokarawen. After Brant's death in 1807, he set himself up as the successor to Joseph Brant, and in opposition to William Claus, Deputy Superintendent, and the rest of the established hierarchy of the Indian Department. The problem was that Norton saw himself as independent of the Department, leading his own private band of Indians, while the Department saw him only as a difficult leader of an integral part of their organization. After successful participation in the battles of Detroit, Queenston Heights and the Niagara campaign of 1813, he convinced the new British Commander-in-Chief to detach him from all control by the Department in their management of the Six Nations (Iroquois).

In the meantime, by a "General Order Affecting the Awards of Presents to the Indian Warriors" of October 1813, Norton's position had been enhanced. He had long been recognized by both the army and the Indians as a "Chief of Renown," and as such was now, by the General Order, entitled to requisition Indian presents from the central stores without going through the Indian Department. In March 1814, he was officially commissioned as "Captain and Leader of the Five Nations Grand River Indians" with power to "reward the faithful services of the warriors acting with him." These rewards were to come from "an ample Proportion of Presents" which were to "be put up separately for the Indians of the Five Nations, to be distributed under Captain Norton's directions."[18] Norton's lust for power required the distribution of lavish quantities of presents, and he attempted to bring some of the western (Detroit area) tribes under his control as well as the Six Nations. During 1815, he became so insubordinate and insolent that he lost much support amongst the Indians, and was sacked from all duties involving Indian management. Although he received a Government pension from June 1815, he by no means relinquished his interest in, or activities on behalf of, the Indians.

It is in connexion with his independent organizing of Indian gifts that the Tatham rifles come into Norton's story. Norton left Canada to visit England late in 1815, carrying a letter of recommendation from the Commander-in-Chief and Administrator of Upper Canada, Lieut. Gen. Sir Gordon Drummond to the Secretary for War & the Colonies, the third Earl Bathurst, and was in London by December when he wrote to Major General Sir Henry Torrens (military secretary to the Commander-in-Chief from 1809 and aide-de-camp to the Prince Regent from 1812) on 21 December 1815:

London Dec: 21, 1815
Sir,
I take the liberty to inform you that I have seen three patterns of rifles made by Mr. Tatham, the two first of a very superior quality as might be deemed a peculiar mark of distinction to a few leading Chiefs and warriors, the other plain and complete in every part such as would be peculiarly esteemed by all the faithful warriors both in war and in hunting should you be pleased to examine them I think they would meet your approbation.[19]

In a letter to Henry Goulburn (Under-secretary of State for War and the Colonies 1812–21 and a commissioner for peace with the United States in 1814) of 13 February 1816, Norton included more detail about the Tatham rifles, and included his Indian name, Teyoninhokarawen, in his signature. Norton had sent in a list of deserving chiefs and warriors and then continued:

As it regards the arms for the same Mr. Tatham has made three patterns: the common plain, but useful for every purpose of the hunter or the warrior and at a low price – the other of superior quality single barrelled – those of the first [quality] of exquisite workmanship & double barrelled a few of which might distinguish the first characters.

The rank of Lt. Col. which his Lordship is pleased to order me is highly gratifying[.] I must however observe that had it been executed here immediately from our Great Father my heart would have been more at ease, as none of the Generals under whom I had the honor to serve will remain in America on my return there...[20]

The gunsmith Henry Tatham wrote to Norton on 23 March 1816:

Charing Cross Mar 23: 1816
Sir
Conceiving you would be anxious to hear from me, I write to inform you how matters are with respect to the Rifles. I have through the medium of Sir Henry Bunbury had a sight of Mr. Goulburn, who stated as the reasons he could not proceed that, he had not yet got an answer from the Treasury, and that untill that was the case, he could not give the order.

I think a Letter from you to this effect would expedite matters. That as in the communication received from Mr. Goulburn, His Royal Highness has been pleased to say, you are to present these Rifles, and as the time of your departure is drawing nigh, it is necessary that the order, agreeably to his decision should be in some state of forwardness. That the patterns, names, and number, are all in possession of Mr. Tatham, subject to Mr. Goulburn's final determination. Perhaps you will be in Town soon. I have but little doubt I shall make the whole for you. I do think your perseverance would bring the matter to a decision.   I am Sir
Your respectful &
obliged humble svt
Henry Tatham
P.S. Favor me with advice.[21]

In the lefthand margin of this letter are two columns of figures undoubtedly relating to the division of production amongst the three grades of rifles. These read:

10	10
30	20
90	40
	60

Both columns equal 130, suggesting the total production of the three grades, but the breakdown into four categories in the second column has yet to be identified. Was a fourth style or grade being considered? Since there were at least seventy-six of the middle-grade rifles made, none of these figures appear to fit the final distribution of grades.

While in Scotland in early April 1816, Norton wrote again to Henry Goulburn:

Dunfermline April 4, 1816
Sir
The season fast approaching in which I should prepare to return to Canada, I take the liberty to remind you of the rifles,

which his Royal Highness the Prince Regent has graciously expressed the intention of placing at my disposal for the distinguished chiefs and warriors. In a former letter I mentioned that Mr. Tatham had prepared three patterns, two of a very superior quality, the other plain, and useful at a moderate price...[22]

A further complication entered the proceedings later in April 1816 when the "buck was passed" from the Treasury to the Board of Ordnance:

Treasury Chambers
22d April 1816

Sir,

Having laid before the Lords Commrs of His Majesty's Treasury your further letter of the 12th Instant on the subject of the Rifles to be placed at the disposal of Major Norton the Indian Chief of the five Nations, I have it in command to acquaint you for the information of the Earl Bathurst [Secretary for War & the Colonies 1812–27] that the Board of Ordnance have been desired to prepare the Rifles for this Service and that your letter stating that Mr Tatham had prepared Patterns which had been approved was forwarded to that Department in order that they might obtain them from him in Case they should think it expedient...[23]

The Ordnance records show no signs of the Ordnance either taking over the Tatham patterns, or of assuming responsibility for the supply of rifles for Norton's use. As late as 17 June 1816, the merchant Alexander Davison, a long-time friend of Norton's who had been active in supplying quasi-military and other commercial small arms to the Ordnance since the 1790s on a contract basis, wrote to Norton:

[Mr Goulburn] said the Order for the Guns was proceeding through the Commissary General, but could not tell me who executed it. I presume it went to the Ordnance. I said every thing I could of the very great importance it might be, not only to You, but to this Country to have that Order well executed agreeably to the Patterns which you had selected. Indeed I said all I could with delecacy upon the Subject. His reply to me was "we are not now at war with the Americans." I observed, the greater (in my mind) was the necessity of shewing extraordinary attention to the Indians, and prove to the several Nations, that we were not unmindful of them in peace, and the better to secure their exertions when we required them in War. I felt great disposition to go into a large field connected with the subject, I evidently saw his disinclination to talk upon the subject. The Good people in Office will have their own way, and Individuals have no control over them.

Had I had anything to do with the Order for Guns, they would now have been Half a cross the Atlantic Ocean. I regret I have so little had it in my power to be Useful to You. The Time perhaps may come, when Official Men may not turn a deaf Ear to Information and to Truths...[24]

From this it would appear that the Ordnance passed the buck to the Commissary General's department which, strictly speaking, is where Indian Department resources should have been dispensed since the military re-assumed control of the department early in 1816.

Hugh Percy, second Duke of Northumberland (1742–1817), long-time friend of Joseph Brant, who signed with his Indian name Thorighwayeri, wrote Norton on 23 June 1816 that:

...I hope likewise the Rifles and other Presents are ready to be shipped off to meet you on your arrival at Quebec, that you may not return empty handed into the Presence of the Allied Chiefs.

As I am no minister, and therefore look upon myself as bound to keep my Word, I have the pleasure to inform you, that the Wall Piece with its Stand, is completely finished and has been properly & most carefully proved at Woolwich. I hope you will approve of it when you see it, and that you will find it a most usefull & formidable Weapon against an Enemy. Its great advantage proceeds from its being able to go through the Woods or any where where a man on foot can pass & its carrying its Ball further than a Field Piece of a caliber of three Pounds, or Four Pounds. Not knowing for certain that you will sail from Greenock, I cannot judge whether there will be time for it to arrive there before your Departure, & therefore...doubt whether to send it down by the Waggon, or ship it from London for Quebec. Be kind enough to let me hear, as near what time you expect to sail as possible?[25]

The ultimate fate of the Duke's wall piece remains to be discovered.

Regardless of who finally assumed responsibility for paying Henry Tatham's bill, it is clear from the number of examples still in existence of the three different patterns, all identified by similar decorative motifs and the platinum-inlaid Royal Arms in a dovetailed block on the breech of the barrels, that Tatham did supply three styles of rifles for Norton's Indians.

Henry Tatham senior was born in 1770 at Frith St., Soho. He is not described as a gunmaker until his appointment as Gunmaker to the Prince of Wales in 1799. In an insurance policy dated 21 February 1799 covering £1,000 worth of property, Tatham's address is given as "at the corner of Buckingham Court and Charing Cross" where he is described as a sword cutler and gunsmith.[26] This may well be the same premesis described from 1800 as 37 Charing Cross. In May 1801, prior to his association with Egg, Tatham supplied the Board of Ordnance with 100 Malayan kris (wavy-bladed daggers) for 9/1 each.[27] In 1801, Tatham went into partnership with Joseph Egg, an arrangement that was not dissolved until 1814. Tatham & Egg also had what

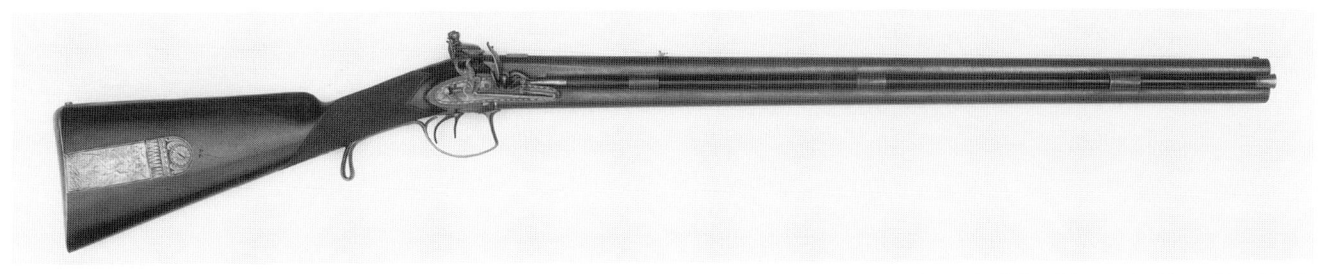

The top grade of Indian presentation rifle made by Henry Tatham senior in 1816 for Captain John Norton's Canadian Indian allies. The over/under tapered round barrels are 29 inches long, .56 cal. rifled and 14 bore smooth. The locks are of the external mainspring design made popular by Joseph Egg. *Courtesy of the Trustees of the Royal Armouries Museum, Leeds.*

were probably workshop premises at 60 Frith St., Soho, from 1805 to 1808 only. There may be some connection with Joseph Egg's premises at 59 Frith St. at the time the partnership was formed. From 1814, Tatham continued in business for himself at 37 Charing Cross until 1824 when his son Henry joined the firm; Henry senior died in 1835 and junior carried the business on until his death in 1860.

Fortunately, examples of all three patterns of the Tatham/Norton Indian rifles have survived. All three types were current production styles offered by the London gun trade, the distinguishing feature being the platinum- or gold-foil poinçon of the Royal Arms mounted in a rectangular block which is dovetailed into the top of the barrel just ahead of the breech. All have browned twist-iron barrels and highly polished blued iron furniture.

Of the top grade, the double-barrelled over-and-under rifle/ball guns only a few examples are known. The example illustrated on the next page is numbered 1520 and is 44¾" overall, with 29" slightly tapering round barrels, the upper barrel with a full-length flat or sighting plane. The upper barrel is .56 calibre, rifled with ten rounded grooves which are just wider than the lands, making one turn in the length of the barrel. The lower barrel is 14 bore, smooth, with thick barrel walls to allow the use of either a patched ball or smallshot. The backsight is dovetailed into the barrel and has one hinged leaf, and a silver-blade foresight is inlaid directly into the barrel. The barrel is stamped with London commercial proofmarks and the "WF" barrel-maker's mark of William Fullerd of Clerkenwell, London (1808–35). A gold ribbon or scroll is inlaid on the top of the upper barrel in which is engraved "TATHAM LONDON" in block letters. There are two gold lines across the breech of the upper barrel and one across that of the lower barrel; each vent is platinum lined. There is a wooden ramrod held in two pipes mounted at the join of the barrels along the right side. The locks are of the external-mainspring design made famous by Joseph Egg on his over-and-under pistols. Both lockplates are engraved in script, "TATHAM", and the waterproof pans are gold-lined. The buttbox cover is engraved with a large stag, and is released by a button in the buttplate tang. The left side of the butt has a raised cheekpiece.

At least two examples of the over-and-under combination gun with very short full-octagonal twist-iron barrels are signed by Joseph Egg, Tatham's partner of fourteen years. These rifles are very similar to the Tatham group, including the platinum Royal Arms in a dovetailed rectangle on the top of the barrel. This may be part of the Tatham group, or ordered separately for presentation to another group of American Indians; their provenance has yet to be identified.

The middle-grade half-stocked rifles appear to have the highest survival rate. All of this type thus far examined or reported carry internal production/serial numbers. A group of twenty-six rifles in the Royal Armouries Museum, Leeds, collection, has made possible a detailed study of this pattern. The gaps in the numbers of this group are partially explained by a few

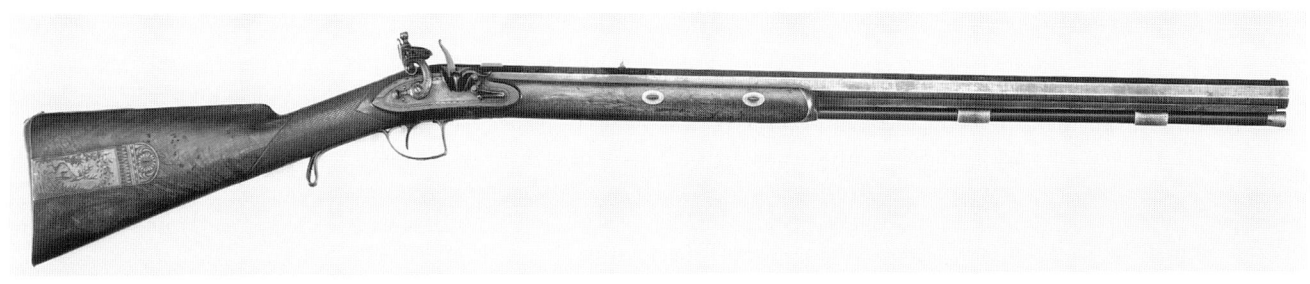

The middle-grade Indian presentation rifle for Norton's Canadian Indian allies by Henry Tatham. The tapered octagonal .56 calibre (26 bore) twist-iron barrel is just over 30 inches in length, rifled with ten grooves making one turn in the barrel. *Courtesy of the Trustees of the Royal Armouries Museum, Leeds.*

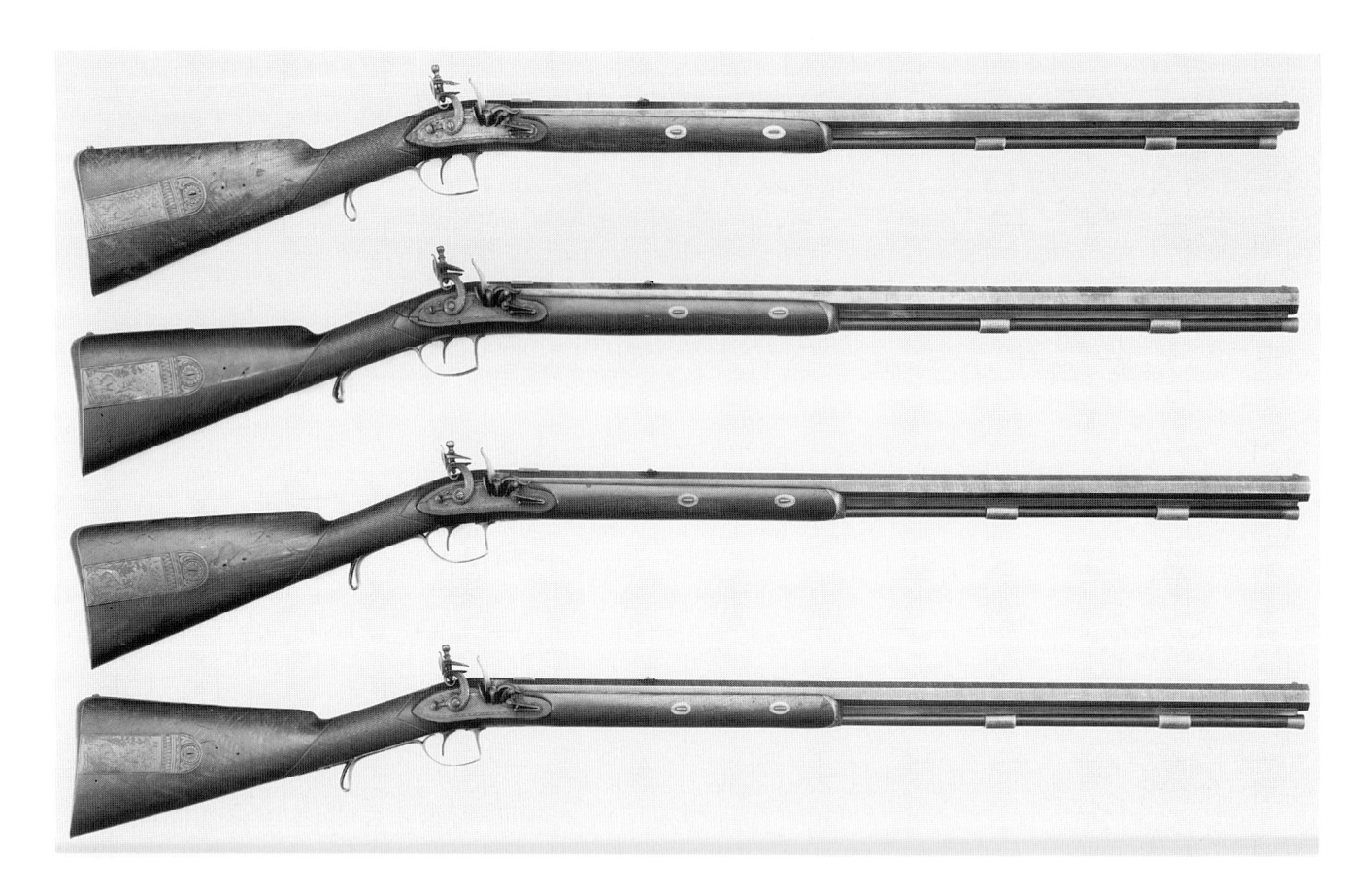

British Military Flintlock Rifles

rifles being disposed of from the collection over the years, but far more of the missing numbers are not documented, suggesting possible original issue. The sealed pattern of this grade is serial numbered 1457, and the highest number in the group is 1533 with a gap between 1457 and 1492. Barrels numbered from 1457 to 1506 bear the initials "WF", while those from 1511 to 1533, with the exception of 1518 which is "WF", have a reversed upper case "S" believed to be the mark of William Smith, gunmaker of Lisle Street, London.

The typical example of the middle-grade half-stocked rifle (see below) is about 46¼" in overall length. While the rifling on all the full-octagonal 30½–30¾" browned twist iron barrels of the middle grade consists of ten grooves with a twist of one turn in the barrel length, those marked "WF" have slightly rounded grooves, and those with the reversed "S" have squared grooves. London Gunmakers Company proofmarks are stamped on the underside, one mark on the left flat and one on the right with the maker's mark and serial number on the bottom flat. The separate break-off patent breeches with gold-lined vents are decorated with a thick and a thin gold line and "TATHAM LONDON" gold-inlaid in two lines. About a third of the distance between the breech and the backsight a raised rectangular block is dovetailed into the barrel, containing a gold-lined poinçon of the Royal Coat of Arms. A notched block backsight with one hinged leaf is dovetailed 6" from the breech, and the silver bead foresight is inlet directly into the barrel. The barrel is fitted with a rib and two plain cylindrical ramrod pipes and is held by two slides with oval silver plates.

The flat locks are inlaid flush with the surface of the wood and are not bevelled. They are fitted with so-called "French" or reversed-C cocks and a double-fenced waterproof gold-lined pan with a roller on the feather-spring. Lockplates are engraved with a sunburst just behind the pan, and "Tatham" in script ahead of the cock. The serial number of the rifle is stamped on the upper surface of the reinforce of the lockplate which receives the sidenail. They are secured by a single sidenail with a plain circular blued sidenail-cup and by an internal hook at the front.

A group of four middle-grade Tatham 1816 Indian presentation rifles showing the minor variations in stocking and finishing of this series. Note the spring-activated butt-trap release-button on the top of the butt tang.

Courtesy of the Trustees of the Royal Armouries Museum, Leeds.

Two examples of the lowest grade of Tatham 1816 Indian presentation rifle. The browned tapered octagonal twist iron barrels are 31¼ in. and 30¾ in. respectively, both are .56 calibre and rifled with ten grooves like the other grades. Note the different patterns of buttbox cover engraving. *Courtesy of the Trustees of the Royal Armouries Museum, Leeds (upper) and of Christie's Images (lower).*

The blued iron furniture of the middle-grade consists of a short flat-fronted fore-end cap acting as a tailpipe; a flat-fronted two-piece triggerguard with a pinched-in scroll grip at the back, lying flush with the stock between bow and grip; a rounded-front buttbox cover engraved with a flower-head around the single screw of the hinge-plate, scrolls and borders on cover and hinge-plate and with a large stag engraved vertically along the cover within an oval of landscaped foliage; and a conventional fowling piece buttplate, with a spring-release button for the buttbox cover at the heel of the tang. There is a rounded-outline cheekrest on the left side of the butt. The group of middle-grade rifles shown on this page illustrates the degree of variation in stocking and furniture found on examples within a single contract at this period in the civilian gun-trade; note particularly the variations in the triggerguards and the angle of the butt on the bottom example.

The lowest grade are full-stocked and much more heavily built than the higher grades, exhibiting more minor variations between individual examples than the middle grade. The example illustrated here (at top) is 46¼" overall with 31¼" octagonal barrel in .56 calibre, rifled with ten rounded grooves just wider than the

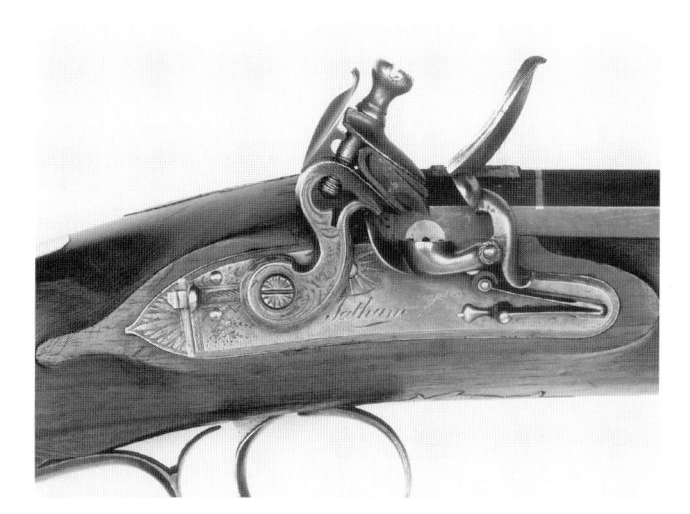

The lock of the full-stocked, lowest grade of Tatham 1816 Indian presentation rifles. The lockplate measures 4¹⁄₁₆ in. x ⅞ in., and the mainspring is fitted with a swivel. In all respects this is a fine (though not "best") quality sporting-gun/rifle lock of its period. Note the location of the dove-tailed block containing a poinçon of the Royal Coat of Arms on the breech of the barrel. The bands inlaid on each side of the block are of platinum (white metal?). The octagonal rectangular thumbpiece on the top of the wrist is inlaid across rather than along the stock. *Christie's Images.*

The trophy of arms display engraved on this buttbox cover of a full-stocked Tatham 1816 Indian presentation rifle is very different from the design usually found on this grade, shown in the lower view. Note that the flags are not engraved as Union Jacks. Curiously, both these rifles have the number 82 stamped in the stock just ahead of the buttbox. The other larger stamps include the Government condemnation mark (the addorsed Rs) and the sold-out-of-Stores mark (the addorsed Broad Arrows).
By courtesy of Christie's Images (upper) and Messrs. Sotheby's (lower).

lands making one turn in the length of the barrel; barrel lengths vary to 30¾". Other examples have more conventional square-cut rifling. The undersides are stamped "WF" for William Fullerd, and some are numbered (e.g. 315) while others are not. There is a break-off or false breech, but no separate patent breech. The backsight is dovetailed into the barrel and has a single hinged leaf; the iron blade foresight is inlaid directly into the barrel. The vent is platinum lined. On this grade the poinçon of the Royal Arms in the dovetailed rectangular block is sometimes gold- and on other examples, platinum- or whitemetal-lined. It is located between two platinum (whitemetal?) lines at the breech virtually above the vent, not further forward on the barrel as on the higher grades. The barrel itself is unmarked except for commercial London proof marks. The barrel is secured to the stock by three slides without surrounding protective plates.

The locks on the lowest grade or full-stocked rifles are smaller and cheaper than on the half-stocked rifles and are flat with a bevelled edge and a stepped tail fitted with a sliding safety bolt. The lockplate has a raised unlined pan with a single fence and conventional pan-bridle, and a roller on the feather-spring; it is fitted with a ring-neck cock on which the throat-hole is roughly of crooked heart shape. The lockplate is engraved with a sunburst around the sidenail tip and TATHAM in script ahead of the cock; The lock is held by a single sidenail with a plain blued sidenail cup.

The furniture, with the exception of a horn fore-end cap and ramrod head, consists of blued iron. There are three cylindrical and collared ramrod pipes for a stout wooden ramrod; a graceful scroll-grip triggerguard is fitted. The rounded-front buttbox cover is engraved with a shield and trophy of arms (the details of this trophy vary between examples as shown above), and opens with a spring thumb-catch as on the Baker rifle, rather than with a button on the buttplate tang of the middle grade. A number agreeing with that on the side or underside of the barrel is often found stamped in the inside of the buttbox cover. The wrist of the stock is checquered and there is a small octagonal silver escutcheon inlaid in the top of the wrist; there is a rounded-outline cheekpiece on the left side of the butt.

While it might be tempting to conclude that the Tatham/Norton rifles were yet another example in a long line of "too little, too late" in British Indian diplomacy, the dating of Norton's correspondence clearly indicates that the idea of a presentation to loyal Indians was not put forward until after the effective end of hostilities, late in 1815. Norton is clearly still not in possession of "the arms for the distinguished Chiefs and warriors" at the end of April 1816.[28] Writing from Dunfermline on 14 May 1816, Norton still hopes to be

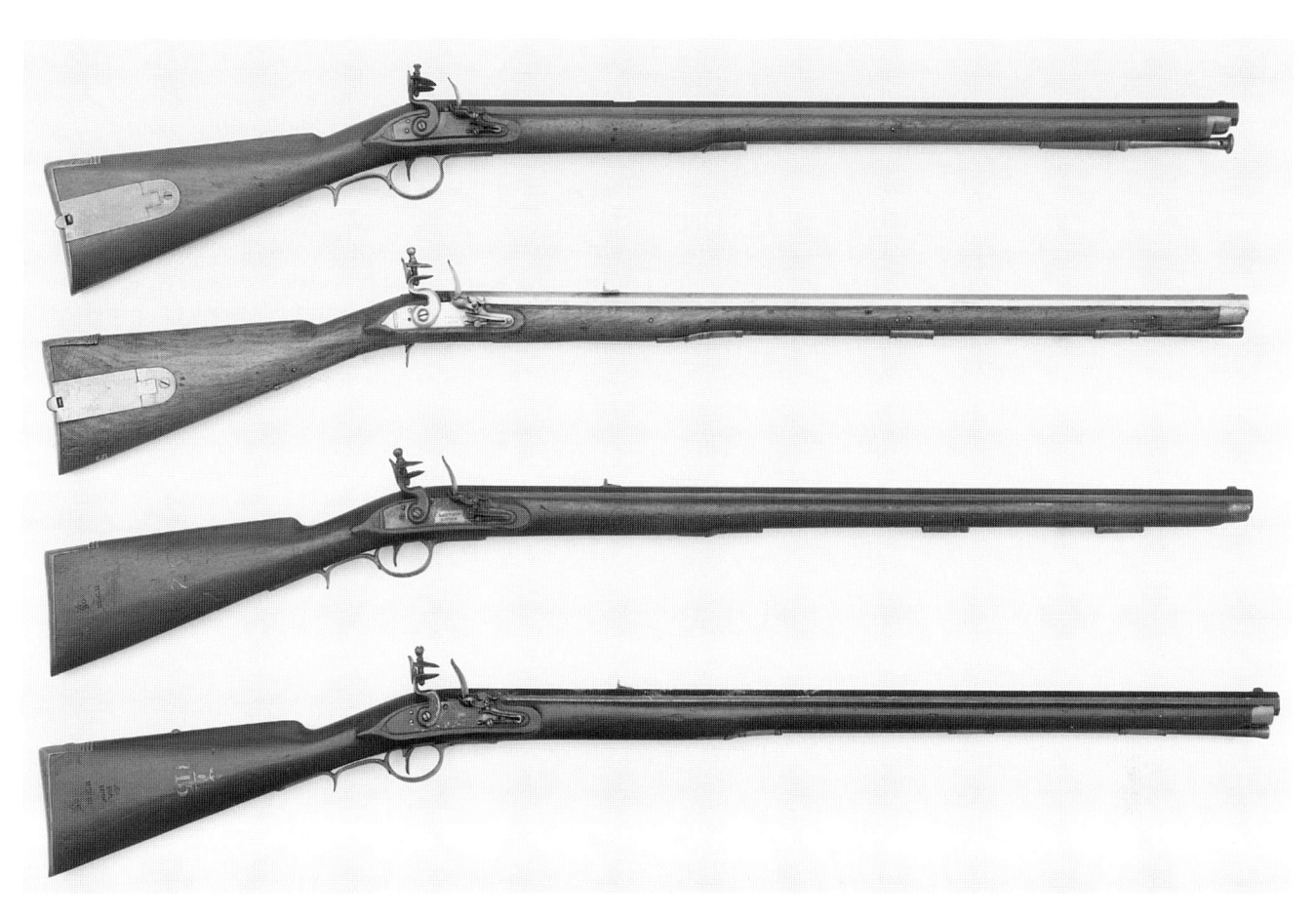

Rifles for Indians in British Service, 1783–1840

The last style of Government-gift flintlock Indian rifles were of purely commercial origin and manufacture and were bought in by the Board of Trade from the end of the War of 1812 until the supercession of the flintlock by the percussion ignition system. All examples have blued octagonal barrels from 30 to 31 in. long, in .53 calibre and all have square American-style buttplate tangs. The top rifle is by Wheeler with brass Baker-pattern furniture. The second rifle is by Wheeler & Son and has a combination of Baker and American-style brass furniture. The third and bottom rifles are signed by Lacy & Co. The third rifle has a roller on the feather-spring and a stepped lockplate, while the bottom has neither.
Courtesy of the Royal Armouries Museum, Leeds.

able to present to the brave and faithful warriors, to whose aid against the enemies of our Beloved Sovereign I am indebted, some token of regard from His Royal Highness, that may cheer and strengthen their hearts in the good cause, and increase the numbers of our adherents, should the horizon be darkened again with the clouds of war.[29] The rifles were clearly intended as a reward for services rendered and to bind for the future.

THE LAST OF THE GOVERNMENT-GIFT FLINTLOCK TRADE RIFLES

With the end of the War of 1812, the value of the North American Indian tribes to the British Government sank to its lowest level. With the complete loss of influence over the Southern tribes and the driving back of British influence in the northern and northwest areas of the frontier, the Indians lost most of their value except as purveyors of furs and the occupiers of land increasingly sought by white settlers. Their use as military and diplomatic pawns had virtually disappeared. Most of the territory still occupied by "British" Indians after 1815 was now under the control of the Hudson's Bay Company and the North West Company, commercial organizations which had their own trading networks and suppliers. It was realized by all those in Government concerned with Indian affairs, that despite the continued needs of the tribes in Canada, who had long been acculturated and dominated by dependence on European material goods, the value of those goods must now be considerably reduced if they were to continue to represent a justifiable return on public expenditure. Although British firms and traders continued to supply many Indian tribes within the territory of the United States, this was a part of the civilian fur trade network, and not the responsibility of the British Government, with whose activities this work is concerned.

The rifles prepared by the Board of Ordnance contractors in 1814 and 1815 were of quite elaborate and refined design, harking back to the earlier period of English rifle design. The rifles which were made in the postwar era were both plainer and cheaper in design and workmanship. They were, in fact, nothing more than the currently available commercial North American export-trade rifles purchased by the Board of Trade as required, the only distinguishing marks being the presence of the Broad Arrow stamp denoting British Government ownership. With regard to those for the commercial trade, there is no reason to consider these rifles as being confined only to the Indian trade; they would have served the general North American export market equally well. All bear Birmingham commercial proof-marks of the 1813 design, and exhibit considerable variation in the details of construction. Thanks to this anonymity in design and to the firm styles used by the most common makers, it is virtually impossible to date these rifles with any degree of accuracy beyond "ca. 1820–40." It is likely that, in common with smoothbore trade guns, they went on being distributed well into the percussion era.

The most noticeable characteristics of the postwar Indian trade rifles are the shorter barrel and overall length and smaller calibre than the 1813 rifles and earlier types. The overall design is more obviously a combination of German/American and English features. In general this series is 46½" to 47¼" in overall length, with octagonal barrels of 31" to 31½" in length. Internally the barrels are .53 calibre, rifled with seven square grooves making one-half turn in the length of the barrel or one turn in 62". Four examples are shown to illustrate the variations in design encountered in this series.

The top example in the illustration (see previous page) is signed WHEELER and can be dated to the mid-1820s. Part of the brass furniture (nosecap, trumpet pipe and buttbox) and the steel ramrod is of Baker rifle pattern, while the sidepiece, buttplate and triggerguard are of typical German/American longrifle pattern, as is the cheekpiece, flat underside of the butt, and the dove-tailed sights. The lock is a standard export-trade lock of 1790s design with no technical improvements.

The second example in the illustration is signed on the lockplate by WHEELER & SON and can be dated from the late 1820s to the early 1840s. The Baker-style buttbox is retained, but the nosecap is plain without a step at the rear to support the rod and the ramrod pipes, of which there are now three instead of two, are now of German/American octagonal style with collars, and what is probably an original style wooden ramrod. The Crowned IR mark on the breech of this and the previous Wheeler rifle may be that of James Russell or a member of the Rock family, both Birmingham barrel-makers of this period.

The third and bottom examples are signed LACY & CO. LONDON on the lockplates. The firm style "Lacy & Co." was used by Lacy & Witton of 63 Fenchurch Street, London, between 1823 and 1829 (and perhaps for a longer period on lower-quality arms such as this type of rifle). Despite the London address, the barrels bear the standard 1813 Birmingham commercial proof marks. The trade lock is fitted with a roller on the feather-spring on the third rifle but not on the lower one. The lower example has a flat lockplate while the other three have a stepped tail to their plates. Note also the absence of a buttbox on both LACY & CO. examples, a further cheapening of the basic pattern. The two lower rifles bear post-1859 "III.C.R." stamps on the butt, indicating they were still in Tower stores when this system of reserve classifications was introduced. The latest reference to Indian rifles in the Ordnance records is on 24 Aug. 1833 when E. Baker & Sons supplied "Moulds, Bullet for Rifles, 50 @ 1/2 for Canada (Presents)."[30]

The history of the rifle in the hands of the North American Indian tribes, so far as the British Government was concerned, was always governed by expediency. The first rifles obtained by the Indians came violently by way of their late frontier owners. When their value became appreciated through circulation and use, white settlers and frontier gunmakers were induced by the profit motive to sell/trade a few rifles to the Indians, but this number can never have been large. Rifles in Indian hands were already perceived as a threat to the white population before the French & Indian (Seven Years') War. Given the nature of Indian warfare and their carelessness with the white man's mechanical innovations, rifles were always more of a prestige possession than a practical tool, and their distribution was always officially confined to the chiefs and head warriors. Nevertheless, they continued to reach Indian hands legally through white traders and gradually in the course of the war, through official British Indian agents in both the Northern and Southern Departments. The American War saw the largest numbers distributed amongst the tribes, but with the end of that war and of much of the Indians' value to the British Government, rifles disappeared from lists of presents for almost a decade before making a small-scale re-appearance early in the 1790s. In keeping with the gradual and general disappearance of elaborate decoration on British small arms and with the decline in the importance of the Indians to the Government, gift rifles became plainer with each succeeding design, the Tatham/Norton presentation rifles forming a special case, culminating in the plainest of the type in the post-1816 period. Once the focus of trade shifted westwards from the Eastern Woodlands and Great Lakes tribes to the Plains Indians, the rifle practically disappeared from official gift lists. What rifles did reach the Indians from this point onwards while often of British or Liège manufacture, came largely from American commercial sources, thus completing the circle begun nearly a century earlier.

CHAPTER 17

A Miscellany of Unexplained

British Military Rifles

Due to the large number and variety of units that equipped themselves with rifles, or were already equipped with rifles, on first entering British service from the early 1790s, and due also to the nature of the record keeping of the Board of Ordnance which did not include detailed accounts of the work done by the workers in the Small Gun Office within the Tower of London, there are a number of rifles in existence which do not fall into easily identifiable places in the history of British military rifle usage. The purpose of this chapter is to illustrate and describe a number of this class of rifle in the hope of discovering further examples for study which may eventually enable researchers to accurately identify their place in the story.

Two categories of rifle pose particular problems in relating the rifle to British military service:

1. Foreign-made rifles brought with foreign troops into British service.
2. British-made rifles made by civilian gunmakers of military or quasi-military pattern with markings indicating British Government ownership or issue.

Foreign-made rifles carried by troops when they were taken into British service generally remained in the hands of those troops until they became so worn out as to require replacement, or until the troops were drafted into another unit already armed with British rifles of a different calibre. What happened to the rifles after they were handed in to Ordnance Stores is a question the answer to which forms the basis for one explanation for foreign-made rifles with British features and/or markings. If the rifles were considered to be repairable, were they, under the stress of wartime demands and the large number of foreign troops in service, repaired by Ordnance gunsmiths? Were the repaired and serviceable rifles then placed in Store for future issue? The *logical* answer to these questions is: Yes. But, is it the *factual* answer?

Although there are few recorded specific instances, we know that the Ordnance on occasion "bought in" various types of weapons for a variety of reasons. Tradeguns were sometimes purchased as Government gifts to native tribes in North America and the Caribbean Islands and Central America, from the same private-sector gunsmiths who made them for the civilian trade. The 1756 rifles purchased in Germany by Colonel Prevost and taken to America by him in 1757 are a specific example of the Government paying for a private purchase of foreign-made rifles, as indeed was the first recorded acquisition of rifles by the Ordnance in 1746. The first 200 of the Pattern 1776 Rifles were made to a pattern but purchased from a Hanoverian gunmaker on Government account. So the precedent was clearly established by the outbreak of the French Revolutionary Wars.

The rifles discussed and described below are listed in the chronological order which the writer feels is appropriate.

1. Rifles by John Probin, probably first half of the 1790s

Several of these rifles exist and have unit markings on the brasswork, suggesting that they were manufactured for some type of military unit, and that they were issued.

In April 1776, Lord Guernsey (Heneage Finch, who succeeded as the fourth Earl of Aylesford in 1777, and lost a younger brother, John, fighting in America in the same year) recommended to the Board that John Probin be allowed to make rifle barrels for the Ordnance. The Board replied by requesting one of his barrels to be sent to the Tower where it would be tested.[1] While there is no follow-up to this reference in the Ordnance records, it does suggest that John Probin may have been equipped and prepared to make rifles of a military pattern at this time. Probin was a Birmingham gunmaker first recorded working in 1769. He died 8 July 1800.[2]

There are several features in the design of these rifles that could suggest a date of manufacture as early as the late 1770s. On the rifle shown on the following page, the lock has two screws showing through the lockplate behind the cock, and the cock itself is of the form popular at this period with Ordnance contractors. The lock engraving is very similar in workmanship to that of the Pattern 1776 Rifle and the Ferguson, i.e. crude.

— 189 —

British Military Flintlock Rifles

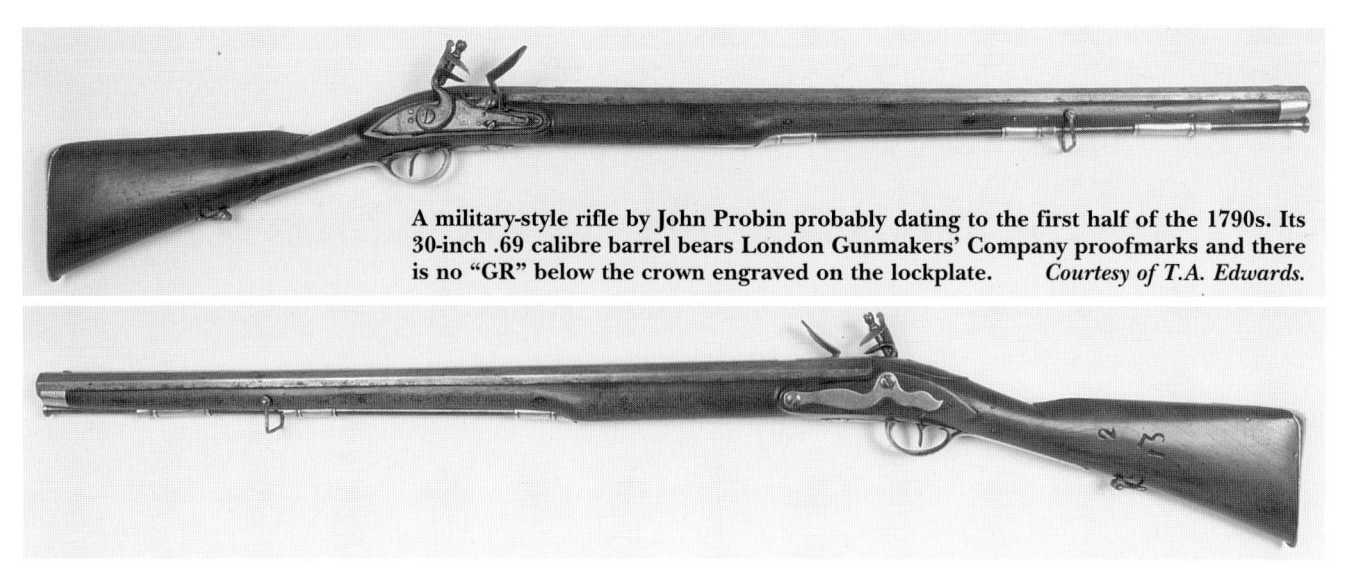

A military-style rifle by John Probin probably dating to the first half of the 1790s. Its 30-inch .69 calibre barrel bears London Gunmakers' Company proofmarks and there is no "GR" below the crown engraved on the lockplate. Courtesy of T.A. Edwards.

There is a raised apron carved around the barrel tang; the sidepiece is a close copy of the current Land Pattern design with the exception of the upswept tail. On another example the lock engraving lacks the initial to Probin's name across the tail of the plate, and the engraving is of much better quality, although having only a single border line. However, on both examples, the termination of the comb of the butt and the use of a flared second ramrod pipe below the trumpet pipe suggest a possible later date of production with older features carried over, as was common in the first half of the 1790s.

The 30-inch octagonal barrel is .69 calibre, with eight deep square grooves half the width of the lands making one-half turn in the length of the barrel. Between the London Gunmakers' Company proofmarks is the maker's stamp in a sunken oval, IB, which initials are repeated on the stock.

A Broad Arrow, indicating Government ownership at some point in its existence, is stamped in the stock just below the lower triggerguard tang.

2. Big-bore "Tower" rifle

The design of this rifle includes several features taken from the Pattern 1776 Rifle, notably the peculiar form of swivel-ramrod (but with an attempt made to reinforce the swivel point and stops), the grip-guard, and the retaining spring mounted between the upper and middle pipes.

The barrel has private Tower proofmarks struck on the top flat at the breech, with a crowned 4 inspection stamp between the two other stamps.

The lock is very close to the Ordnance pattern of the 1780s and has correct pattern Crowned GR and TOWER markings as well as double border line engraving, but without any Government ownership markings or inspection stamps.

Unique to this rifle are the butt-trap cover with its

A musket-bore military-style rifle. Its most noticeable feature is its similarity in pattern of buttbox cover to the Grice Indian rifle shown earlier in the book. Royal Armouries Museum, Leeds.

spring-latch and the straight tapering tang of the buttplate.

3. 60th Regiment Jaeger Rifle

This rifle probably represents a German rifle brought into British service in the 1790s, turned into Store and subsequently restocked by an English gunmaker, possibly an Ordnance worker. There is no other way to explain the fit of the obviously English rifle-style lock in the wood and surrounding carving. The cock is a much later incorrect replacement. The style of the regimental markings is unconventional, but this does not reflect upon their possible authenticity.

4. "HH"-marked dragoon rifles

Several of these rifles are known to exist, each with letters and numbers engraved on their triggerguards (in the manner of cavalry weapons) clearly indicating issue to a military unit. Examples of these rifles with "HH" engraved on their thumbpieces thus far examined or reported do not bear any British Ordnance stamps, but given the number of small foreign-raised units in British service, this rifle is included as an example of what might have been issued to them without ever passing through Ordnance hands from the raising to the disbanding of the unit. But the general styling of these "HH" rifles does appear to be post-1802. See Chapter 8 for details on one example.

5. Nock infantry rifle

In appearance, this rifle is of the same design as a large number of Volunteer Rifles made by Henry Nock using his enclosed screwless lock. The reason for its inclusion here is the presence on lock, stock and barrel

(top three views only) **A German jäger rifle of the 1790s, possibly re-stocked by an English gunmaker.**
Courtesy of R. MacInnes.

A Baker-style rifle by Henry Nock, virtually identical to a series of Volunteer rifles produced by Nock in the mid-1790s, except that all of the principal components bear Ordnance inspection markings which preclude its being a "bought-in" piece of commercial manufacture, and the barrel has King's Proofmarks. *Courtesy of R. MacInnes.*

British Military Flintlock Rifles

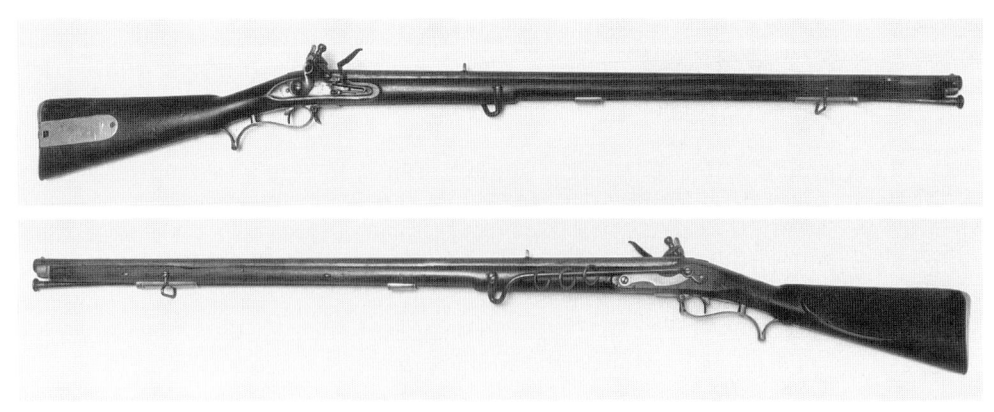

A 36-in. barrelled Baker rifle by Ezekiel Baker probably c.1812, with King's Proofmarks and other correct Ordnance markings as well as regimental company marks on the barrel, thumbpiece, rammer and in the butt-box cavity.
Courtesy D. Cooper.

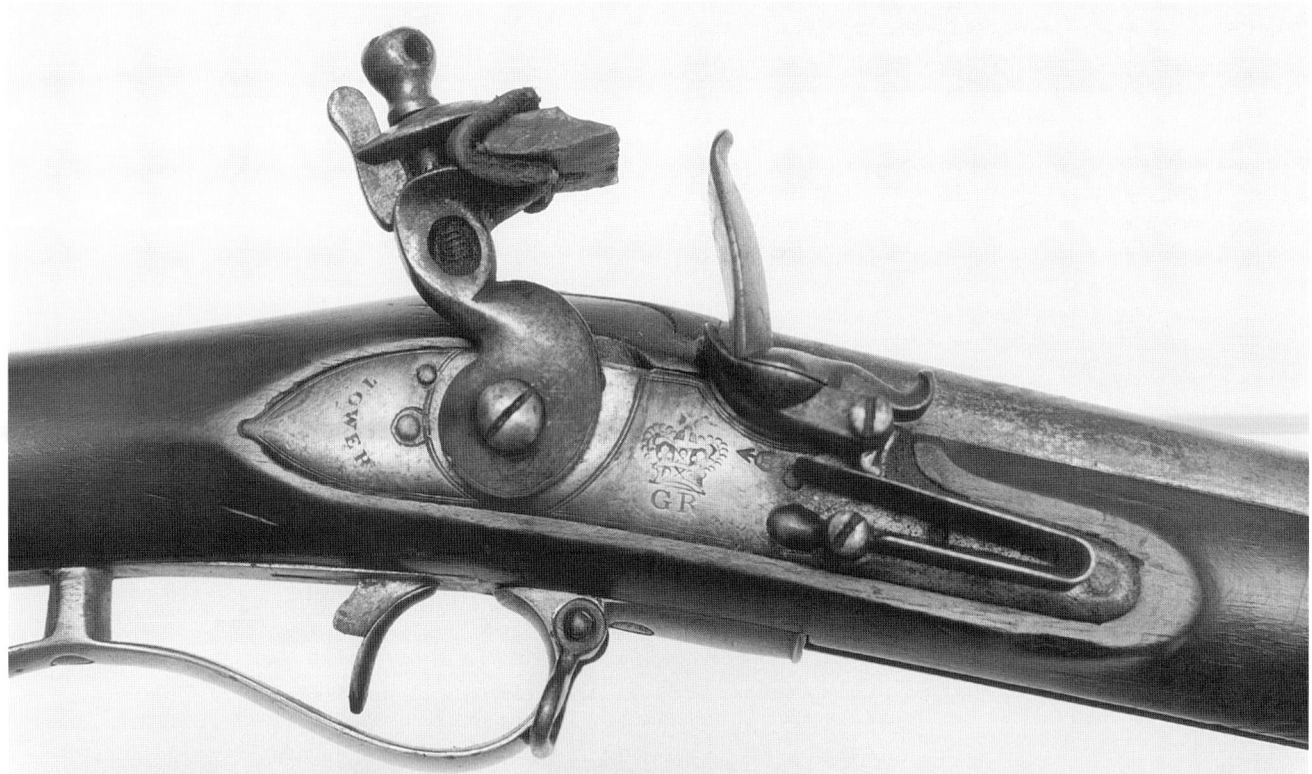

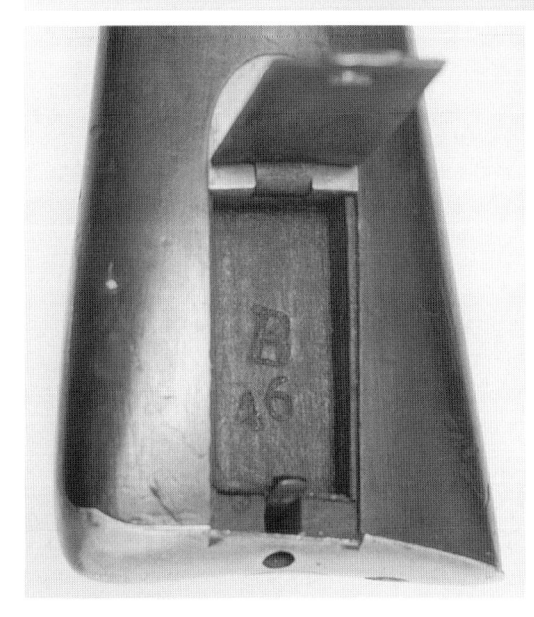

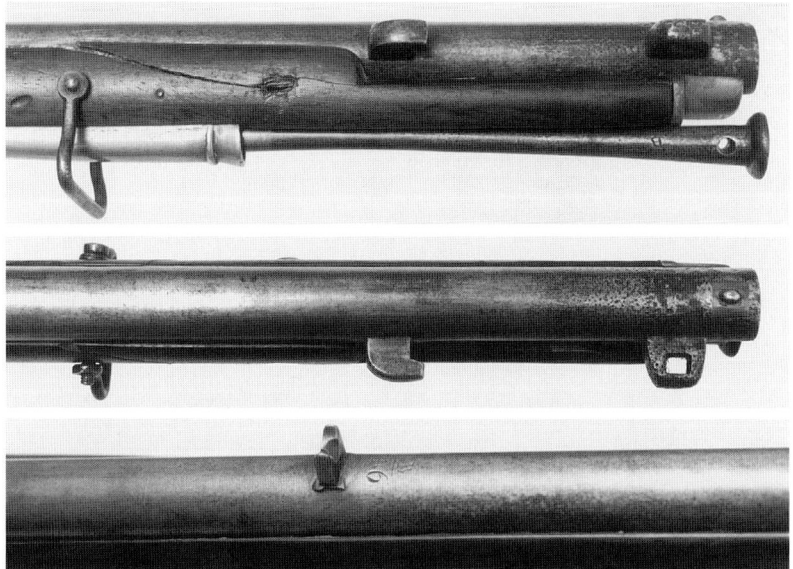

Another view of the 36-in. barrelled Baker rifle by Ezekiel Baker.

of Ordnance markings. Several markings could have been applied to the rifle after its manufacture and on taking it into Ordnance Stores, but the Crowned Broad Arrow mark struck on the case-hardened lockplate would not fit with that explanation, nor would the several inspection and assembler's marks on metal and wood.

The 26-inch barrel is octagonal for 2¾ inches at the breech; it is 16 bore with seven grooves making one turn in the length of the barrel. The left side at the breech is stamped with correct Ordnance proof and view marks, the King's Proof. Engraved on the top flat in two lines is "H. NOCK Patent". The barrel is fitted with a break-off breech and held by three slides and the upper sling swivel screw.

Nock's screwless lock, the plate measuring 4¾ inches, is engraved with the Crowned GR beneath the pan and H. NOCK across the tail, with the Crowned Broad Arrow stamped just to the right of the engraved crown in the cypher.

The walnut stock is slit in the manner of the Pattern 1797 Heavy Dragoon carbine, and there is no integral cheekpiece. The butt-trap cover resembles the Baker design but is larger, measuring 5" x 2¾". The right side of the butt, just ahead of the butt-trap cover, is stamped with a Broad Arrow over BO. Just below the lower trigger-guard tang is stamped a crowned 7, struck twice. In the rammer channel is W.T. and 7, and the channel as well as the inside of the lockplate and the lock recess are each stamped with the assembler's number VIII.

The overall design is not far removed from the Pattern 1794 (Harcourt's) Dragoon Carbine (all made by Nock) and its successor the Pattern 1797 Heavy Dragoon Carbine, with the addition of a Baker-style bayonet bar, ramrod and butt-trap. These features were taken from the Baker design, and these rifles must have been made c.1800–04. The number 62 engraved on the buttplate tang suggests that there were originally at least 61 others made and issued to this unit.

6. Long-barrelled Baker rifle, primarily with Pattern 1805 features

Although bearing no Storekeeper's mark on the butt, this rifle is otherwise fully Ordnance marked, with Ordnance proof marks on the barrel and the Crowned Broad Arrow struck on the lockplate along with the correctly engraved TOWER and Crown GR markings. Internal lock markings include an Ordnance Inspector's crowned 8 and the initials I.B. In addition there are company issue marks (B over 46) on the barrel, thumbpiece and rammer head.

The most noticeable feature of this rifle is its long barrel, 36³⁄₁₆" as opposed to the regulation 30" for Infantry Rifles, giving the rifle overall a length of 52½" as compared to the 46" of the Infantry Rifles. It is fitted with the standard form of break-off breech, and with a standard Infantry Rifle foresight, the plain block backsight being brazed to the barrel 8" from the break-off. The barrel is secured in the stock by the usual three slides or keys and the upper sling-swivel screw. (See Appendix 1 for technical details).

Apart from the extra six inches of length, the most unusual feature of this barrel is the sword-bayonet mounting on the right side of the barrel at the muzzle. The design appears to be similar to the Norwegian Models 1711, 1755 and 1791 rifles,[3] although it is not clear on which of these models the design was first used, thanks to a policy of altering/updating earlier patterns. The two separate blocks occupy a space of four inches front to rear, the front block having a square

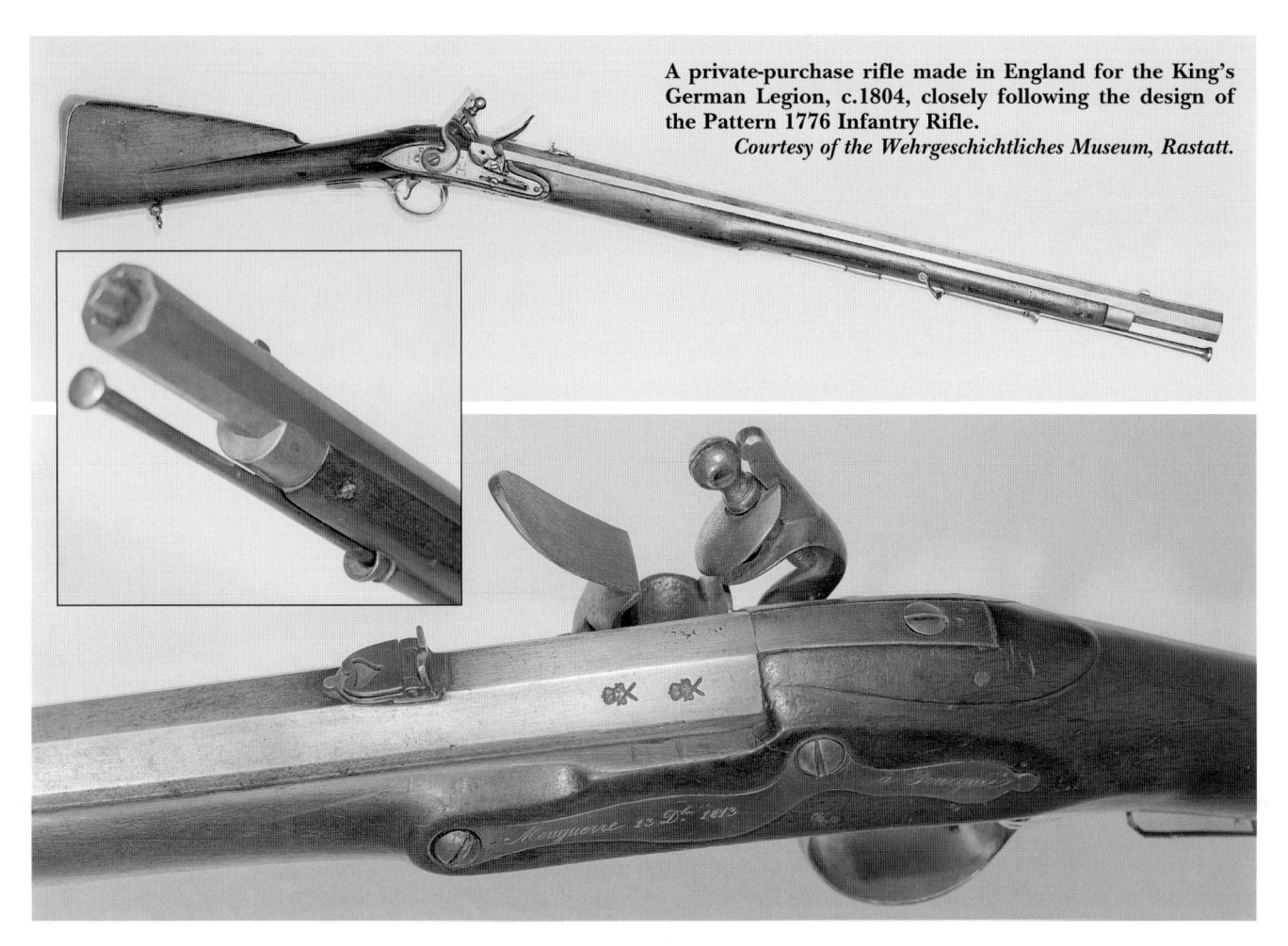

A private-purchase rifle made in England for the King's German Legion, c.1804, closely following the design of the Pattern 1776 Infantry Rifle.
Courtesy of the Wehrgeschichtliches Museum, Rastatt.

hole cut through its centre and the rear block shaped as a catch or hook when seen from above.

The ramrod is a conventional Baker rifle rod with a swell 8" from the head.

The lock is of standard rifle length and width but is unusual in having a rounded surface to the lockplate, not used on regulation Baker rifles until the Pattern 1823. It may have been used as a deliberately distinguishing feature for a Guards weapon.

The stock conforms generally to the standard design for the Pattern 1805, with the slit between the entry-point of the ramrod and the front of the triggerguard, and the brass furniture conforms in all respects to that for the Pattern 1805 Infantry Rifle.

Although it is possible that this rifle is one of the Life Guards rifles delivered by Ezekiel Baker in 1802 (see Chapter 10), the writer feels that there are too many "later" features of standard Baker design to have been made so early — chiefly the slit stock, rounded hinge-piece of the butt-trap cover and single rectangular butt compartment, plain block backsight, and the rounded surface of the lockplate. The other most likely possibility is that it is the Pattern 1812 Life Guards Rifled Carbine (see Chapter 10), although the extra-length barrel would not, by this date, have been considered appropriate for this description. Also, Baker is not listed as one of the suppliers of this pattern.

7. Private purchase rifle for the King's German Legion, c.1804.

The buttplate tang engraving on this rifle, which is clearly Germanic is style, indicates that it was the 17th rifle issued to the 4th Line Battalion of the King's German Legion. Chapter 14 gives an account of the isues of rifles to the various battalions of the King's German Legion, indicating that the first issues of the 4th Battalion, 56 rifles, were made in October and November 1804. Between that time and September 1814, the 4th Battalion received only 9 other rifles. In September 1814, they were issued 98 rifles, presumably a complete new set (of Baker rifles?). This battalion received a total of 163 rifles from their original raising until September 1814. Since there are no Government or Ordnance markings on the rifle described below, and no references to "payment in lieu" of the Ordnance Baker rifle, it must be assumed that some special arrangement existed, as yet undiscovered, between the British authorities and the organizers/officers of the K.G.L. whereby at least some part of their armament was privately supplied and paid for. At the time of writing, this is the only

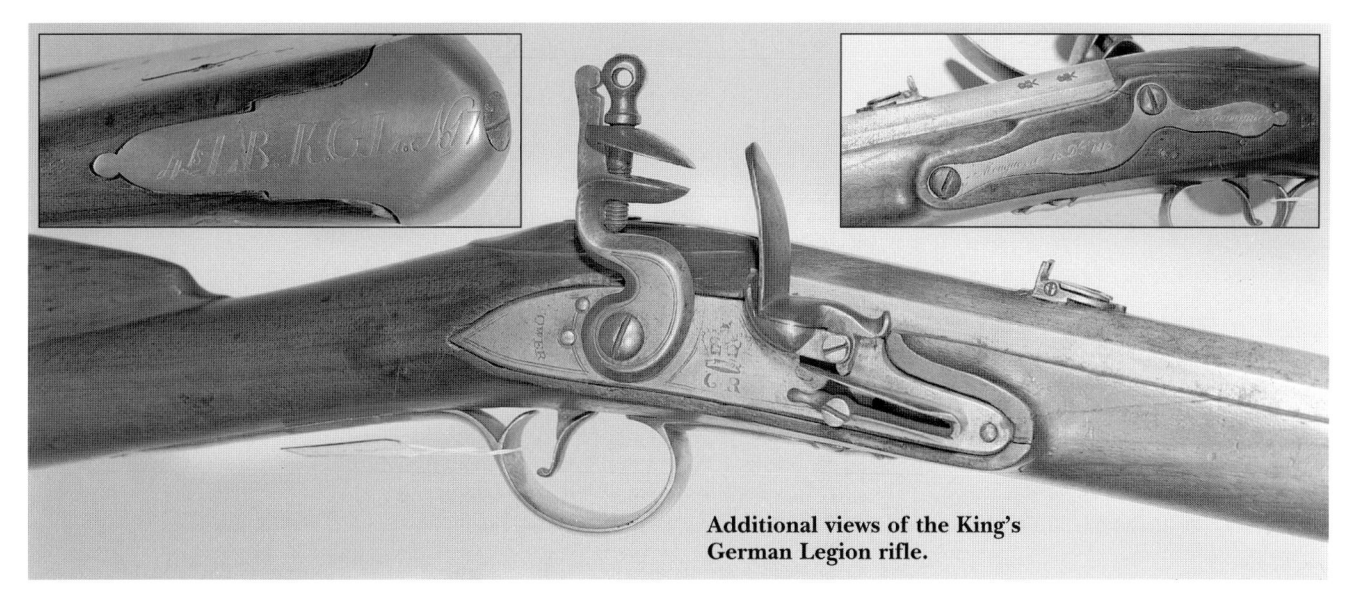

Additional views of the King's German Legion rifle.

example of this pattern rifle known to the author.

Whoever was responsible for the design of this rifle made his decisions at a critical point in the development of the British service rifle, because he (they) chose to follow a design that was, by the early years of the nineteenth century, very much out of date. It is extremely curious that a specially designed weapon for issue to German troops would contain amongst its features no Germanic styling or devices such as a cheekrest, a butt-trap for tools and patches, or a grip-rail triggerguard, all of which had been incorporated into the Baker rifle in 1800, presumably as a result of experience gained during the French Revolutionary Wars. By 1803, the absence of a bayonet on a military rifle was also very old-fashioned, but being part of a unit largely armed with bayonetted muskets may account for this particular omission. A rifle of this design, at the date it must have been produced, suggests that its designer was of an extremely conservative mind, or was simply unaware of design developments.

This rifle bears a striking resemblance to the Pattern 1776 Infantry Rifle throughout its design, with the exceptions of the rammer and its external retaining spring, the sights, and the locations of the two sling swivels in the fore-end and on the underside of the butt. Note also that the triggerguard is of standard Land Pattern for carbines, without a thickening at the front of the bow or piercing for a sling swivel screw. The muzzle configuration, lacking any arrangements for an attached rammer, resembles other standard muzzle loaders except in the placement of the blade front sight, which is set back to a point just ahead of the position of the nosecap, as though leaving space for possible modification in the future to take a bayonet.

The overall length of this rifle is 43.8 inches. The slightly swamped octagonal barrel is 28½ inches long and is rifled with eight rounded grooves slightly narrower than the lands, the land diameter being .657" and across the grooves .692". With these measurements the standard British carbine ball of .615" could have been used with a patch. The breech bears *private Tower* proofmarks. The back sight is dovetailed into the barrel, and consists of a block with one hinged leaf that has a heart-shaped aperture as well as a notch at its top, giving a sighting option of three ranges. The steel rammer is of the pattern used on the Pattern 1800 Baker rifle. The nosecap, long trumpet forepipe, barrel-shaped and collared middle pipe, tailpipe, sidepiece and buttplate are all of Land Pattern as found on the later Eliott Light Dragoon carbines. The lock is the Pattern 1777 Extra Flat Carbine lock with standard engraved markings but *without* the Crowned Broad Arrow government ownership stamped beneath the pan. The English walnut stock is of standard Ordnance pattern with a handrail butt, raised oval tang apron and a swell at the tailpipe. There is no Storekeeper's stamp or any other Ordnance marking on the stock. The condition of this rifle strongly suggests that it saw but little use prior to its capture by the French at the Battle of Mouguerre in December 1813, but at the same time this date does indicate that rifles of this description were still in the hands of some troops of the line battalions of the King's German Legion.[4]

8. A Volunteer rifle

This rifle is by Henry Morris, a Birmingham gunmaker who worked from 1802 until his death on 28 December 1809. The owner's name, Philip Beesley and the date 1813 are engraved on the Short Land Pattern sidepiece. The browned twist iron barrel is fitted with a break-off breech, and a two-leaf backsight is dovetailed just ahead of the break-off. The breech is struck with Private Tower Proofmarks. The most modern features of this rifle are its refined lock with waterproof pan and

British Military Flintlock Rifles

A Volunteer rifle with owner's name and dated 1813. Despite these later engraved markings, the design of the rifle suggests a date of manufacture in the 1790s.

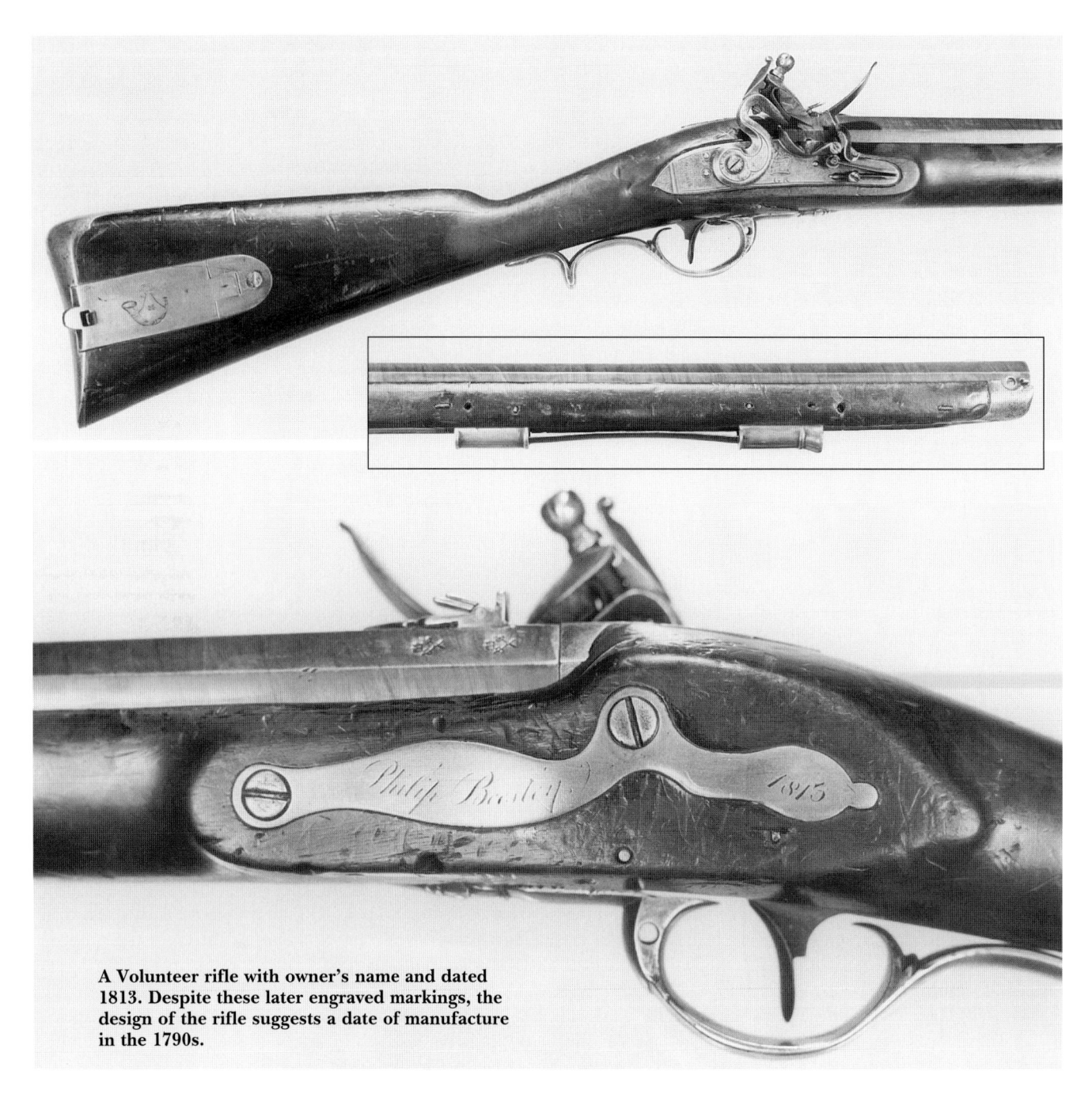

roller on the feather-spring, and the simplified New Land Pattern style of stock which lacks carving apart from the side-flats, and has a plain form of butt which replaced the older handrail style on the latest Ordnance arms shortly after 1800. The buttbox cover is of the Baker Pattern 1805 but most of the other features strongly resemble those on the Pattern 1776 Infantry Rifle, including the method of fixing the swivel-rammer and its nosecap, the rammer pipes and the use of an external rod-retaining spring between the two upper pipes, the Short Land Pattern sidepiece and the style of grip-guard. The rifle is included here as it has too often been mistaken for the Pattern 1776.

9. A possible rifled carbine for infantry serjeants.

It has a 33-inch round blued plain iron barrel in carbine-bore (.625"), rifled with eight square grooves and fitted with a break-off breech, a "light infantry" form of back-sight and a bayonet stud for a socket bayonet serving as a foresight. The barrel is very

(more information about the above rifle) **The lock is fitted with a rainproof pan and a roller on the feather-spring, and has a Crowned GR engraved ahead of the cock and MORRIS across the tail. Several features including the ramrod pipes, the form of swivel-rammer and the external rod-retaining spring between the first and second pipes, strongly resemble the Pattern 1776.**

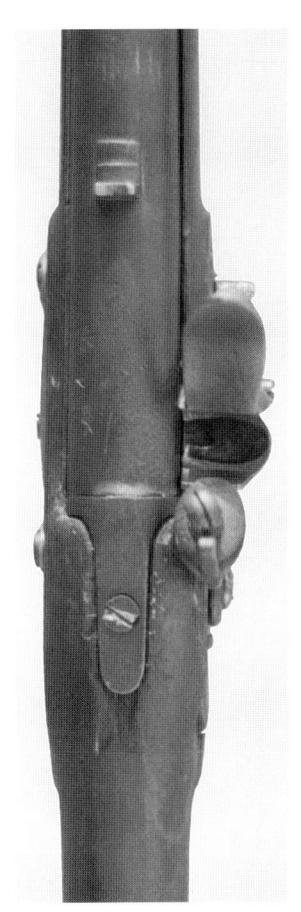

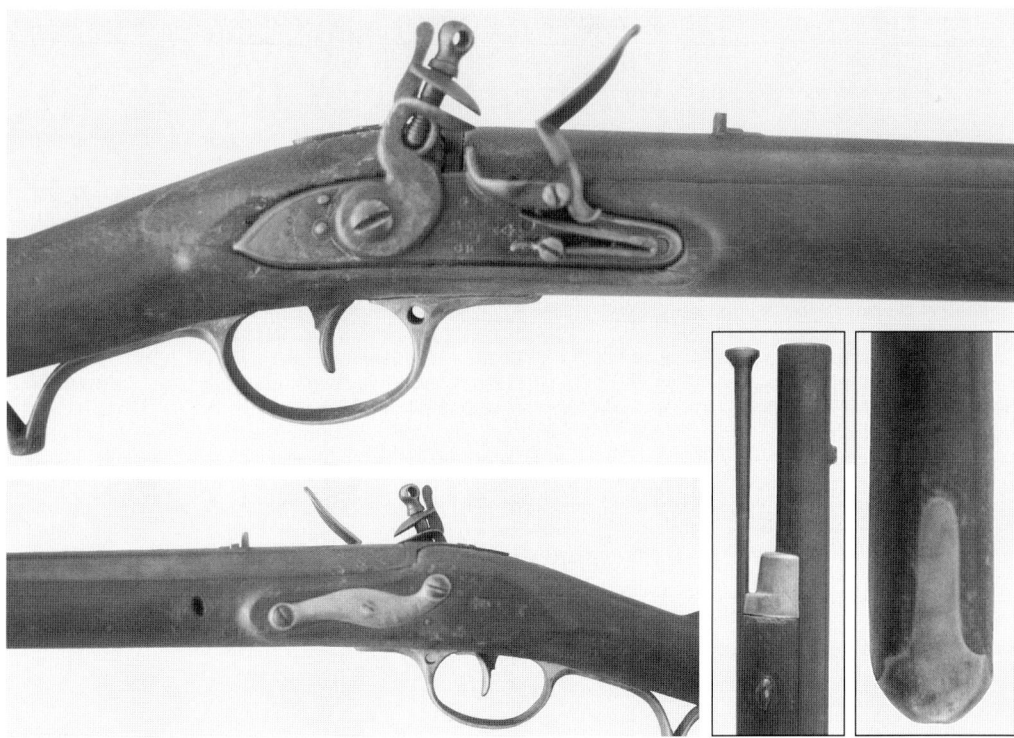

A Miscellany of Unexplained British Military Rifles

A late and unidentified Ordnance Baker rifled carbine. The barrel length of this rifle, 33-in., as well as its general configuration, strongly suggest that it may represent the initial stage of an experimental Serjeant's Carbine under consideration prior to the cheaper final design which involved simply cutting down New Land Pattern Light Infantry carbines and abandoning the idea of rifling.
Courtesy B.C. Knapp

heavy for its calibre, measuring 1.25" across the breech and .900" across the muzzle, which represents a major improvement over the Baker pattern. The barrel is held by two slides and the upper sling swivel-screw (missing). With the exception of the lock, the design features of the piece more closely resemble the Brunswick than the Baker Infantry Rifle, the ramrod pipes being the only feature which might be described as "Baker" as opposed to New Land Pattern. The flat lock measures 5¼" by 1¹⁄₁₆", and has standard Ordnance markings of a Crowned GR stamped ahead of the cock, with TOWER in a curve across the tail; the plate and cock body have double border-line engraving. The plain New Land Pattern stock comes to 3¼" of the muzzle. All parts are fully Ordnance marked and of the Georgian (pre-1830) period, suggesting that this may be an initial stage in the development of a new rifled carbine for infantry serjeants dating from the late 1820s, which was ultimately rejected in favour of cut-down New Land Pattern Light Infantry muskets.

It should be remembered that there are a great many English-made military-style rifles that were produced for civilian use during the period 1793–1840, usually — but not invariably — incorporating one or more features of the Baker rifle in their design. Whether these are Volunteer rifles or "Gentleman's Rifles"[4] they have no direct connexion to rifles made for the Board of Ordnance and British military service. The "HH" rifle included in this study is an example of a rifle which probably falls into this category, but it has been included because of its long popular — though almost certainly erroneous — association with Hompesch's Hussars. There are so many possibilities for the non-Governmental manufacture of military-style small arms that it is virtually impossible to identify them: several levels of militia from regional to local, private-armed tenantry units, Volunteers, Fencibles and Yeomanry Cavalry to name but the most obvious. It is an area of social study that has received far too little attention in the past, and the sources for which having largely vanished, is unlikely to be adequately dealt with in the future. It is likely that in future the greatest increase in our knowledge of flintlock rifles in British service will come in the area of foreign-made (almost always Germanic) rifles with some feature or markings identifying them as having seen service with British or British-allied troops.

The writer would be pleased to learn of any examples which might fall into the category of British service-used flintlock rifles.

— 197 —

APPENDIX 1
Technical Specifications of British Service Rifles

Every effort has been made to obtain full and correct measurements for the rifles described below, but a number of major problems may prevent these measurements from tallying exactly with examples located in future. At the time of writing there are only single examples known in excellent condition from which completely reliable measurements could be taken from several of the rifles discussed. Others either are as yet unknown, or are in poor, worn and/or altered or badly restored condition. It was not always possible to obtain a full range of measurements, and the correct instruments for the job were not always available. The information below, with the exception of the Pattern 1776, Ferguson, and Grice rifles, is offered with these caveats.

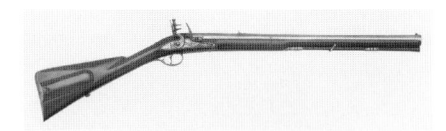

RIFLE BY BENJAMIN GRIFFIN TYPICAL OF EARLY ENGLISH ATTEMPT AT OFFICER'S RIFLE (Page 17)

Overall length: 38-3/4"
Barrel length: 23-7/8"
Calibre: .70, 15 round grooves almost equal to the lands, making one turn in six feet, or 1/3 turn in the length of the barrel.

BARREL is octagonal, swamped, and fitted with break-off. Measures 1.150" across breech, 1.095" across muzzle, with narrowest point .990" 5-3/8" from the muzzle. Held by two slides (keys). Block backsight with one leaf dovetailed 5" from the tang. Steel blade foresight dovetailed at muzzle. London Gunmakers' Company proofmarks with the "foreigner's mark" i.e. not a member of the Gunmakers' Company, stamped on left flat.

LOCK is flat with beveled edge, lockplate measuring 5-5/8" x 1" The pancover is domed.

STOCK is plain English walnut, the handrail butt with a pronounced cast-off to permit aiming with the left eye. The comb measures 9" Butt-trap cover measures 5-3/8" x 1-7/8", and the compartment measures 4-1/2 x 1-5/16" Drop of the butt is 2-1/2" and at heel 4"

STEEL FURNITURE consisting of three balustre-moulded ramrod pipes, sidepiece, trigger guard and buttplate. The pipes are 1-3/8" long and .530" diameter. Buttplate measures 5" x 2" Note the bow & quiver motif engraved on the buttplate tang: the design is of Roman origin and is frequently found on French and English textiles and architectural decoration in the 17th and 18th Centuries.

HIRST 1762 EXPERIMENTAL SCREW-PLUG BREECH-LOADING RIFLES

These two rifles are the survivors of five similar rifles supplied to the Board of Ordnance in April 1762. They were obviously assembled from readily available sporting rifle parts: without close examination these arms would pass for conventional steel-mounted fowling pieces typical of their period in outline and design. Only the heavily-built trigger guard with its knob-grip and the tiny backsight on the barrel indicate their special purpose. Although the design of the breech mechanism is entirely typical of its type, the calibre and rifling twists are probably the only "custom-made" features of the series. Apart from the Board of Ordnance Storekeeper's stamp on the right side of the butts, there is nothing military about the design of these pieces.

Carbine-bore rifle (Page 20)
Overall length: 50".
Weight: 8 lbs. 11 ozs.
Barrel length: 34".
Calibre: .625/.64, intended to take the standard .615" carbine ball, with twelve rounded grooves equal in width to the lands, making one-half turn in the barrel, or one turn in 68 inches or 5-2/3 feet.

BARREL is round, swamped without either proof or maker's marks on it. The backsight block, which is notched almost to its base, is dovetailed 1" ahead of the tang. The tiny steel blade foresight is brazed directly into the barrel at the muzzle. Secured to the stock with three slides, but fitted with a plain breech-tang. Given the total absence of proof and maker's marks, it seems likely that this carbine-bore barrel was specially prepared for this rifle to Ordnance specifications. The barrel is engraved near the breech "HIRST TOWER HILL LONDON". The breechplug is secured to the front of the trigger guard by a large screw. It takes 8-3/4 turns to remove the plug for loading. The lower tang of the guard is undercut to act as a stop, and there is a spring-button to retain the lever in position.

LOCK measures 5.8" x 1", the rounded lockplate terminating in a long tapering point at the tail. The shallow teaspoon-shaped pan with its teardrop-shaped bridle, and long-sear spring (only one screw showing through the lockplate behind the cock) are typical features of the period. The signature is confined to a script "Hirst" ahead of the cock and there is no decorative engraving.

STOCK is full-length English walnut with a conventional hand-rail butt with low straight comb. Breech tang carved with ribbons and shell design.

STEEL FURNITURE includes three ramrod pipes, trigger guard, ornamental rococo cartouch thumbpiece, sideplate and long stepped-tang buttplate. The sideplate is flat with bevelled edges, moulded at the front and stepped at the tail, with a woodscrew through the tail in addition to the two sidenails, and engraved with a horseman and hounds pursuing a stag at which the hunter is firing.

Musket-bore rifle (Page 20)
Overall length: 49-1/4".
Weight: 7 lbs. 2 ozs.
Barrel length: 34".
Calibre: .659", intended to take the standard .693" musket ball, with twelve shallow rectangular grooves equal in width to the lands, making one-quarter turn in the barrel, or one turn in 136 inches or 11-1/3 feet.

BARREL is round, swamped, with London Gunmakers' Company proof and view marks stamped on the left breech, with the Crowned F foreigner's mark between them. Hirst was never made free of the Gunmakers' Company. The backsight block is dovetailed 1-3/4" from the tang, the tiny steel blade being inset and brazed at the muzzle. Secured to the stock by three slides, although fitted with a conventional breech-tang.

The breechplug is secured to the front of the trigger guard with a large screw. It takes 6-1/2 turns to remove the plug for loading. A plain rounded screw in the lower guard tang acts as a retaining stud for the guard-lever.

LOCK measures 5.8" x 1", the rounded lockplate terminating in a long tapering point at the tail. The pan and other features are identical to the previous rifle. Engraved ahead of cock "Jno Hirst", the lockplate, cock, top-jaw and back of steel engraved with a nick & dot border.

STOCK is full-length English walnut, identical in style to the previous rifle, the breech tang relief-carved with a very simi-

— 198 —

lar ribbon and shell design.

STEEL FURNITURE includes three ramrod pipes, trigger guard, ornamental asymmetrical rococo cartouch thumbpiece, sideplate, and long stepped-tang buttplate. The sideplate is rounded with a plainer outline than the previous rifle and lacking the third screw, and is engraved with a sportsman firing at a stag in a park, with a house in the background, with a nick & dot border.

PATTERN 1776 RIFLE, HANOVERIAN-MADE (Page 24)

In overall design this rifle appears to be a "typical" German military rifle of the period with brass furniture of a design found on numbers of other rifles from several countries. Its salient feature is the unique design of the swivel rammer and its swivels, and the attendant nosecap and rammer pipes with external retaining spring, all of which were apparently designed by August Heinrich Huhnstock of Hanover, who made 200 of these rifles for the Board of Ordnance in 1776.

Overall length: 43".
Weight: 7.8 lbs.
Barrel length: 27-11/16"
Calibre: .62" lands .620", grooves .648", turn of 1 in the length of the barrel, or 1 in 27". The muzzle is relieved for about 3/4", with .652" grooves and .628" lands with .120" chamfer at the muzzle. Seven (7) rifling grooves apparently equal to the lands, squared .140" wide.

LOCK measures 5-1/4" x 1-1/32", the flat lockplate with beveled flat edges terminating in a point at the tail. The outer edges of the bridleless pan and pan-cover have three facets and there is a faceted collar where the pan joins the plate. Flat swan-neck cock with beveled edge as on the lockplate, the broad leaf-shaped comb with a bevel up the back and ending in a forward curl at the tip, with a very slight backward curve towards the top. Plain oval jaws. Back of steel is plain. Rounded teardrop feather-spring finial with screw fastening from inside. Lockplate is unmarked, inside and out.

BARREL is swamped octagonal, 1-3/16" across breech, 1.050" across muzzle, tapering to .940" 12-1/2" from muzzle. Front sight dovetail 1" from the muzzle; rear sight dovetail 6-5/8" from breech. Side flats at muzzle mounted with rammer swivels, both screws of which go through into the bore. Steel RAMROD, body .637" thick throughout, broad head is .652" in diameter, .160" thick. Tip has .230" diameter male thread 1.460" long, suggesting a missing brass attachment. Secured to stock by three crosspins and the tang screw. Plain breechplug, the tang with tapered tip crudely numbered 184 across its tip. No external markings. Struck deeply on the underside with a large S in a rectangular poinçon, with a second poinçon whose outline is pear-shaped terminating at the bottom in a trefoil, containing the initials JG over an illegible design.

STOCK is full length, oil-finished European walnut, with swell 1.365" wide at tailpipe. Comb is 9-11/16" long including buttplate; butt is 4-7/8" deep x 2" wide. Centre of trigger to centre of buttplate 13-1/2". Very narrow raised border around tang terminating at rear in a long narrow raised teardrop. Width of stock immediately behind lock tail 1.865" and just ahead 1.590". Stamped with Storekeeper's mark on left butt behind the raised rounded outline cheekpiece which measures 6" long by 2-1/4" wide. The underside of the fore-end alongside the rammer channel is flat, and the underside of the butt curves downwards beneath the grip of the trigger guard and is then straight and flat to the toe of the butt. The [replacement] wooden butt-trap cover has a rounded surface with an ornamental thumbhole at the rear and [the original] measures 6-5/8" long by 1-5/8" wide. The rectangular cavity measures 5-4/8" long x 1-3/8" wide and is 1-1/8" deep.

BRASS FURNITURE includes nosecap, three rammer pipes, grip-rail trigger guard, raised and beveled sideplate and buttplate. The nosecap is held by an external screw and is 1-1/2" long on its underside and each side is 3/4" long with a 1.060" long flat. The front of the cap is finished with three facets about 3/32" wide. The upper ramrod pipe has a flared collar mouth and 1-13/16" long x .615" external diameter, inlet 3-1/16" from the muzzle. The middle pipe is 1-17/32" long by .617" external diameter and is 9-1/16" from the muzzle. The tailpipe, which has a short tapered blunted spearpoint tang, is 3-5/8" long x .615" external diameter, and is 15-5/8" from the muzzle. All pipes are very similar to the English design rather than Germanic. The first three pipes are each secured by two crosspins, and the tailpipe by one. A curved steel rod-retaining spring .425" wide lies between the upper and middle pipes, 4-3/16" between the pipes, secured to the pipe at each end by an iron rivet. The upper sling swivel is held by a screw through a loop dovetailed into the underside of the barrel, 2-3/4" from the muzzle. The lower sling swivel is mounted at the front of the trigger guard bow. The design of the trigger guard and buttplate finials and the sidepiece are similar or identical to a variety of Germanic military rifles of the period and it would be impossible to identify this rifle were it not for the features in the design of the fore-end covered above. The grip-rail trigger guard is 10-1/4" long and secured by a crosspin through the front tang and a woodscrew through the lower finial. The upper finial is in the form of a symmetrical foliated trefoil, and the lower finial is a plainer trefoil design. The grip-rail is much straighter and closer to the stock than on most military guards of this period, with a simple downward at the rear. The sidepiece is of a common design used on several rifles of the period with minor changes in size and proportion to the three elements, e.g. the Danish Model 1791 Rifled Carbine; it is 4-1/2" long, and held by the two sidenails and a woodscrew through its tail. The design might be described as very close to the regular rounded Land Pattern musket sidepiece, but with the forward part interrupted by an oval rounded insert a little ahead of centre between the two sidenails. The buttplate measures 4-5/8" long x 2" at its widest point and is cut to receive the butt-trap cover. It is held by one screw through the lower part of the plate and a second screw through the lower tang. The tang finial is the same as that of the upper trigger guard tang, a symmetrical foliated trefoil on an urn base.

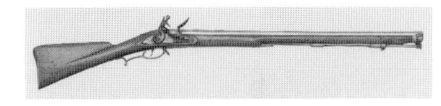

PATTERN 1776 RIFLE (Page 28)

In overall proportions the rifle is based upon the German military rifle of the period, with its swamped octagonal barrel just under thirty inches, and grip-rail trigger guard. The details of the design are a combination of German and English characteristics. Of the former the swamped octagonal barrel, the angular style of rifling,, the two-leaf backsight, and grip-rail guard are the most characteristic, while the swivel ramrod is the most innovative. English features are of a more cosmetic nature and based on current Board of Ordnance designs; they include the calibre (to take standard carbine ball), the handrail style of butt, the lock which is a smaller version of the "Extra Flat Carbine" lock then in use, the raised 'apron' carving around the barrel tang, the swell at the tailpipe and the Land Pattern sideplate. The inclusion of such up-market features as a break-off or false breech and slides rather than barrel-retaining pins indicate an awareness of the need for efficient maintenance of the piece in the field. The functionality of these features is enhanced by replacing the usual brazed loop on the underside of the barrel to take the upper sling swivel with a screw-held plate inlaid in the barrel bed of the stock. The absence of a butt-trap and cheekpiece, typical features of the German rifle of the century, may reflect an effort at economy and simplification of manufacture, failure to appreciate their functional utility, or simply a desire to eliminate unnecessary "foreign" gimmicks.

The following measurements are taken from what is at the time of writing the only known near-mint and apparently unissued example which shows no appreciable wear on wood or metal parts.

Overall length: 44-3/4".
Weight: just under 8 lbs
Barrel length: 28-13/16"
Calibre: "carbine bore": lands .630", grooves .650", turn of 1/2 in the length of the barrel, or 1 in 56-1/2". The muzzle is relieved for about 1", with .690" grooves and .650" lands. Eight (8) rifling grooves apparently equal to the lands, squared .150" wide.

LOCK measures 5-7/8" x 1-1/16", the flat lockplate with bevelled edges terminating in a point at the tail. The outer edges of the pan and pan-cover have three facets. Swan-neck cock, the comb of rectangular section, flat, with very slightly backward curve towards top, flat surface with tapered bevelled edge, double-borderline engraved, as is the top jaw; jaw-screw slotted and pierced. Back of hammer (steel) has double-border line engraving, with heart at top. Spined teardrop featherspring finial. Lockplate is crudely engraved Crowned GR ahead of cock and TOWER across tail, with Crowned Broad Arrow stamped beneath pan.

BARREL is swamped octagonal, 1.22" across breech, 1.05" across muzzle, tapering to .860" 9-5/8" from muzzle. Originally browned. Front sight dovetail 1-1/16" from the muzzle; rear sight dovetail 6-5/16" from breech. Vent diameter .056". Side flats at muzzle mounted with rammer swivels, both screws of which go through into the bore. Steel RAMROD, body .335" thick throughout, broad head is .725" diameter, .250" thick. Tip has slightly cupped-mouth brass collar which screws off to admit tools on male thread. Secured to stock by three flat keys and a hook or false breech. Struck with King's Proof on top flat, 1-1/2" from breech, and maker's mark (either MB/&/IW, SG, WG or BW) on left flat 1-7/16" from breech.

STOCK is full length, oil-finished English walnut, with swell .600" wide at tailpipe. Comb is 8-3/4" long including buttplate, butt is 4-7/8" deep x 1.990" wide. Handrail on sides 6-1/4". Centre of trigger to centre of buttplate 13-3/4". Oval raised apron at tang of typical Government musket pattern. Width of stock immediately behind lock tail 1.840" and just ahead 1.725". Width of stock at front of tailpipe 1.300", at rear of fore-end cap 1.200". Depth of fore-end from top edge to rod channel edge at middle pipe .940". Stamped with Storekeeper's mark on right butt, IC on rear of sideplate flat and Crown over Crowned 6 in rear of trigger guard.

BRASS FURNITURE (except iron fore-end cap) includes three rammer pipes, trigger guard, flat flush sideplate and buttplate. Sideplate is 1775 Land Pattern 5-1/2" long; trigger guard is 9-1/4" long held by forward cross-pin and woodscrew just below rear finial. Lower sling swivel through front of guard bow is 1-3/8" (1.450") wide internally, upper swivel is 1.400" wide internally. Buttplate is 4-7/8" long; the tang is similar to, but not identical to the Pattern 1769 Short Land Pattern, 4-1/4" to centre of heel screwhole.

The iron fore-end cap is held by an internal screw. It measures 2-1/4" from front to tip of under-tang; each side is 1-3/16" front to rear, with a 1/2" wide shallow semi-circle cut out 3/16" from the front edge. Front edge of the cap is finished with three facets approx. 1/8" wide. There is also an iron trigger plate.

The upper rod pipe has a flared collar mouth, is 1-3/4" long x .640" external diameter, inlet 4-3/16" from the muzzle; the middle pipe is 1-7/16" long x .630" external diameter and 11-1/4" from the muzzle; the tailpipe, which has a tapered spearpoint tang is 3" long x .590" external diameter and 17" from the muzzle. The upper pipe is held by one crosspin at its rear, and the two lower pipes by two crosspins each. A curved steel rod-retaining spring .420" wide lies between the upper and middle pipes, 5-1/4" between pipes the iron rivet being visible in the underside of the upper pipe. The upper sling swivel is held by a screw through a loop on a plate inlaid in the barrel bed of the fore-end 3-3/4" from the muzzle.

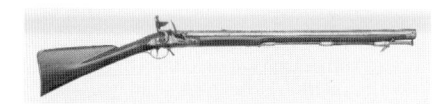

HIRST OFFICERS' RIFLE, 1776
(Page 30)

This may best be described as an up-market version of the Pattern 1776 rifle made by the gunmaker who, until 1776, was responsible for supplying all English-made rifles ordered by the Board of Ordnance. The similarity in style, bore characteristics, and particularly the fitting of the swivel-mounted heavy iron rammer, all point to a close connection with the Government model.

Overall length: 43-1/4".
Weight: 8 lbs. 9 ozs.
Barrel length: 27-7/8"
Calibre: nominal carbine bore .65, with eight rectangular grooves very slightly narrower than the lands making one-half turn in 27-1/4", or virtually in the length of the barrel, or one turn in 54-1/2", extremely close to the twist of the Pattern 1776 rifles.

BARREL is swamped octagonal, 1.235" across the breech and 1.090" across the muzzle, .950" 8-1/2" from the muzzle. The block backsight with two hinged leaves is dovetailed 5-1/2" from the breech, and there is a low open-block backsight forged integral at the front of the breech tang. Secured to the stock by two slides and the upper sling swivel screw. The stops for the swivel rammer on each side of the muzzle have been ground off, although the threaded holes for the swivel-screws remain. Struck on upper left breech flat with private Tower proof and view marks, (Crowned crossed sceptres struck twice).

The heavy iron RAMROD is virtually identical to that of the Pattern 1776 rifle, including the removeable brass tip. The swivel mechanism is missing but was clearly of identical design to the Pattern 1776.

LOCK measures 6" x 1-1/16" with a flat lockplate and swan-neck cock with bevelled edges, the tail of the plate being stepped. The shallow teaspoon-shaped pan with teardrop-shaped bridle, and the long sear-spring are characteristic of the period, and the pan-cover is domed. A roller is fitted to the toe of the steel. Most unusually for the period the mainspring is fitted with a swivel connexion to the tumbler. The plate is stamped inside with the coronet over RW of Richard Welford, but whether the second or third maker of this name is not clear since the second Richard is last recorded in the year this rifle was probably manufactured. The plate is signed in script HIRST, and is engraved on it borders with a single border line and a zig-zag pattern, repeated on the cock, top-jaw and back of steel.

STOCK is full-length English walnut with handrail butt, the breech tang relief-carved with ribbons and shell pattern. The barrel-bed is stamped T.K, possibly indicating that the stock was supplied by/or stocked by Thomas Ketland of Birmingham, or by another unknown gunstocker. The upper sling swivel, which is unusually long, is screwed through the fore-end and a lug on the underside of the barrel. The left side of the butt, just near the buttplate is stamped with a small I0, perhaps suggesting that at least nine others of this type may have been made. The comb is 9-1/8", and trigger pull measures 13-5/8".

BRASS FURNITURE (excepting iron fore-end cap) consisting of three large heavy ramrod pipes, trigger guard, sideplate, thumbpiece and buttplate with broad long stepped tang. The fore-end cap measures 2-1/2" along its underside and has a semi-circular cut-away on each side for the now-missing ramrod swivels. The upper pipe with its 7/8" flared mouth is 1-7/8" long, the middle pipe being 1-1/2" long; between them is rivetted a rod-retaining spring 4-3/4" long. The sideplate is flat with a bevelled edge, engraved with a nick & dot border and with rococo scrolls and a flag & cannon trophy. The unmarked rococo thumbpiece has a central oval cartouch surmounted by a scallop shell and bordered with drapery on sides and bottom. The lower sling swivel is screwed through the front of the trigger guard bow, and the bow is engraved with rocailles. The front finial is the characteristic tulip of the period. The buttplate tang is engraved with rococo scrollwork and segmented nick & dot borders.

PATTERN 1776 FERGUSON BREECH-LOADING RIFLE (Page 40)

The Board of Ordnance military Ferguson rifle closely resembles a typical British officers' fusil or carbine of the period, with its full-length stock with handrail butt and key-fastened barrel. One of its most unusual features is being fitted for a bayonet, and that the bayonet is held in position by a stud on the underside of the barrel; all other British military weapons of the period have a stud on the top of the barrel which served, and was always referred to, as a sight.

Overall length: 49"
Barrel length: 32-7/8" to face of breech-plug, 34-1/16" to tang
Calibre: nominal carbine bore, .65. Measures .607" across lands at muzzle, and .648" across grooves. Eight groove angular rifling, grooves being slightly narrower than the lands with a twist of one-half turn in 30" barrel, or one turn in 58", very close to the turn of 1 in 56 in the Pattern 1776 rifles.

BARREL is round with flats filed on the sides and top at the breech, where it measures 1-5/16" across the side flats. The rear sight is dovetailed into the barrel 4-5/8" from the tang, and was originally fitted with two hinged leaves, now missing, but probably for use to 300 yards. The iron blade foresight is brazed to the barrel at a point even with the termination of the fore-end 4-5/16" from the muzzle. The maker's mark, MB & IW is stamped in three lines on the left flat of the breech (other maker's marks would be WG, SG, BW); the King's proof and view marks are stamped on each side of the barrel to the rear of the loading orifice. Ferguson's inspection/approval mark, a small crowned PF is stamped immediately behind the loading orifice, and the gun-issue number, 2, in engraved at the rear of the barrel tang. The underside of the barrel is stamped WRF, MB [Matthias Barker, the barrel-maker] and a Crowned 8 inspector's mark.

BREECHPLUG is 2-1/16" in length. Its diameter tapers from .910" at its base to .840" at its top, and is made of gunmetal with an eleven-start thread. One complete anti-clockwise turn opens the breech, and two complete turns removes the screw entirely from the barrel and stock. There is no stop on the breechscrew to prevent this removal, and there are no anti-fouling grooves. The fact that the gun-issue number, in this case 2, is engraved on the trigger guard bow, suggests that complete removal of the plug, deliberately or otherwise, may have been foreseen. The plug has a square shank at the bottom which fits into a square hole in the front tang of the trigger guard, and is held in position by a large screw. The rear portion of the trigger-plate is inlet to contain the guard, and there is a small spring-loaded ball to stop over-winding the guard in closing the breech. It is possible that the shank of the plug may originally have been fitted with a leather washer between the trigger guard and the bottom of the stock.

LOCK measures 5-1/4" x 1", the lockplate and cock flat with bevelled edges, a single vertical groove cut across the tail, with the tail surface filed away to leave a very fine ridge along the rear edge of the groove. Two screws showing behind the cock, indicating the use of a short sear-spring. Crudely engraved (apparently by the same hand as the markings on the Pattern 1776 rifles) with a Crowned GR ahead of the cock, and TOWER slightly curved, vertically across the tail. There are no internal markings, and no Government ownership stamp (the small crowned Broad Arrow) on the exterior surface. The design of the lock is that of a very up-to-date civilian sporting lock including such features as the teardrop pan-bridle and feather-spring finial, bevelled tumbler screw and well defined and curved comb to the cock. The lock is secured to the stock by one screw into the side of the barrel on the right side, behind the cock.

STOCK is of English walnut and extends to 4-3/8" of the muzzle. In style it closely resembles the infantry carbines of the period with the characteristic hand-rail butt. The fore-end is fitted with three flat keys which secure the barrel in place, an unusual feature in that there is no break-off breech, generally associated with keys, fitted to facilitate the easy removal of the barrel. Sling swivels are fitted at the conventional point through the fore-end, and on the left side screwed into the sideplate flat. The Ordnance Storekeeper's mark (Crowned addorsed GR) is stamped in the right side of the butt.

Measurements:
From centre of trigger to
centre of butt:	13-3/4"
Comb:	9"
Drop at comb:	1-1/2"
drop at heel:	2-1/2"
Slides (keys) mounted at 1-3/4", 9-7/8" and 19-13/16" from fore-end tip.	

Unquestionably the weakest feature of the Ferguson design was the amount of wood necessary to be removed at the breech of the barrel to accommodate the enlarged barrel, the threaded tube which contains the breechplug, and the lock. This example and many of the privately made officer's rifles which show any signs of use are broken through the stock at the breech. This rifle has a contemporary professional repair of a horseshoe-shaped iron strap inlet and pinned into the wood.

BRASS FURNITURE consists of fore-end cap, three ramrod pipes and buttplate. The trigger-plate is iron. The two collared barrel-shaped ramrod pipes are 1-1/2" in length, and are secured by two crosspins each, 2-7/16" and 8" from the fore-end tip; the tailpipe is of similar design with a conventional short pointed tang, and is mounted 15-3/4" from the fore-end with one cross-pin. The pipes are clearly intended to take a wooden rather than a steel rammer. The buttplate is similar to carbine stepped long-tang buttplates of the period, but is not identical to the Land Pattern; it is secured to the stock in the conventional military style by a cross-pin for the tang and two screws for the plate.

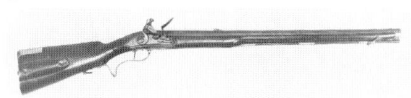

HESSE-CASSEL JÄGER RIFLE (Page 64)

The rifles carried by the largest contingent of German riflemen serving in North American during the American War were not fitted with bayonets, did not have double-set triggers, and were decorated only in having basic military-style stock carving closely following the current Prussian pattern. They also carried the cypher of the ruling prince engraved on the thumbpiece. A military unit issue number is engraved on the buttplate tang. These characteristics should be borne in mind when considering either unmarked examples, or those signed by other makers of the period. Particular care should be taken in evaluating the authenticity of any engraved markings. Whether any rifles were supplied to the Hessian forces by other gunmakers than the one who made this example is at present unknown, but it seems as least possible that other makers may have received contracts for very similar weapons in the course of the war.

Overall length: 43-5/8"
Barrel length: 28-11/16"
Calibre: .62, with 7 groove rifling; the half-round grooves are approximately 1/8" wide, and approximately .020" deep, and make effectively one full turn in the length of the barrel.

LOCK measures 5-5/16" x 1-1/16". The plate and cock are flat with bevelled edges, the plate terminating in a slight teat, and with a single vertical groove filed across the tail. Signed in engraved block letters "T.W. Pistor", The large tumbler-screw is flat with a bevelled edge and the cock-screw is both pierced and slotted. The underside of the pan is faceted and there is no pan-bridle. The feather-spring has a teardrop finial. Only one screw visible through plate behind cock.

BARREL is swamped octagonal, 1-5/16" across the breech, 13/16" across muzzle, and at narrowest point 11-13/16" from muzzle 7/8". Backsight is dovetailed 6-3/4" from breech.

STOCK is full length, and of European walnut. The butt is 4-13/16" deep and 2-3/16" wide. There is full-length moulding along the rod channel, with aprons at both terminals of the lock-and sideplate flats and around the barrel tang all in the current Prussian style. Measurements: from trigger to centre of buttplate: 12-13/16" comb 9-1/4" butt-trap lid 5-7/8" long, and tapers from 2" wide at the base to 1-1/2" at the top.

BRASS FURNITURE. Trigger guard is 10-1/2" long. The upper ramrod pipe is 1-13/16" long, inlet 3-1/8" from fore-end tip; the middle pipe is the same length, inlet 9-15/16" from tip, and the tailpipe including spearpoint finial is 3-7/8" long and inlet 16-11/16" from the fore-end tip. A plain oval thumbpiece is inlet into the top of the wrist, engraved with the crowned cypher F L for Friedrich Landgraf surrounded by a single border line. The slightly convex, flush-fitting sideplate is characteristic of many jäger rifles of this period, closely resembling the British Land Pattern plate with an added oval feature inserted roughly midway between the two sidenails. The grip-rail trigger guard with trefoil front and rear finials is also of a very commonly found pattern, with a large rounded curving grip-rail well away from the stock. It is secured by a cross-pin even with the front of the bow and a screw through the rear finial. The flat-fronted buttplate tang has five ill-defined facets, the central one of which is engraved with the issue-number of the piece.

HESSE-HANAU FREICORPS JÄGER RIFLE (Page 65)

In overall design these are extremely similar to the Hesse Cassel rifles, but in general the stocks are thinner, and with poorer quality inletting of the metal into the stock and overall finishing. Three original tools were found in the butt-trap, including a ball-drawer, worm and powder measure. The powder measures holds 6.4 grammes (98.76 grains) of fine-grain powder.

Overall length: 43.7"
Weight: 9.37 lbs.
Barrel length: 29"
Calibre: .575", the 7-groove rifling making 3/4 turn in the length of the barrel (or one turn in 38.64").

LOCK plate measures 5.31" x .94" and is flat with a narrow bevelled edge, the tail with a single groove across it and terminating in a point. The pan is faceted, and very unusually has a pan bridle; both steel and feather-spring screws enter from the inside, another unusual feature on a Germanic lock of this period. The plate is crudely signed in block letters A. SCHWALBACH/A HANAU.

BARREL is swamped octagonal, 1.29" across the breech and 1.02" across the muzzle. The backsight is dovetailed 7" from the tang. The rectangular bayonet bar on the right side at the muzzle is 3.42" in length of bar itself, not including baseplate.

STOCK is European walnut. The relief carving at barrel tang, lock- and sideplate flats is in the Prussian style, and is quite shallow, very crudely executed and thin or narrow in its dimensions when compared with that of the other German rifles. The step in the underside of the butt at the rear of the trigger guard is pronounced. The comb measures 6.29" in length; from centre of buttplate to trigger is 13.38".

BRASS FURNITURE is almost identical in design to that used on the Hesse-Cassel and Ansbach jäger rifles, but is thinner and not so well finished. The buttplate measures 4.72" x 2.12".

ANSBACH-BAYREUTH JÄGER RIFLE (Page 66)

This rifle shares many characteristics in common with the two previously described Hessian rifles, particularly the design of the furniture, and there is little reason to doubt that it may have been made in the same location if not by the same contractors. It is the best finished of the rifles thus far identified as used by the German jäger corps in America.

Overall length: 43.89"
Barrel length: 28.85"
Calibre: .65", with 7 half-round grooves.

LOCK plate is 5.39" long by 1.06" wide, flat with narrow bevelled edge, the tail with a single groove cut across it, and terminating in a teat. The integral pan is faceted on its underside, and the feather-spring finial is a teardrop with a tiny ball.

BARREL is octagonal, swamped, and secured to the fore-end by two cross-pins and the upper sling-swivel screw. There are no external markings. Brass blade foresight dovetailed, the blade 0.66" long. The rear sight is a dovetailed block with no ornamental finial, with one leaf.

STOCK of European walnut with very pronounced Prussian-style relief carving at the barrel tang, lock- and sideplate flats, all terminating in well-defined large teardrops at the rear. The fore-end has a full-length moulding along the ramrod channel terminating in a well-defined teardrop to the rear of the tailpipe finial. The butt-trap measures 5.27" by 1.33", the wooden lid is missing, but markings in the stock indicate a rounded front of conventional design. The underside of the cheekpiece has a flat surface, the front of the carving terminated by a plain incised curl. The step in the underside of the butt at the rear of the trigger guard is much smoother and less pronounced than on the Hessian rifles.

BRASS FURNITURE. The 1.37" long fore-end cap is identical in design to those of the other two German rifles already described, and is also screwed directly into the underside of the barrel. The three faceted and collared ramrod pipes, of which the upper two have flared mouths, measure 3.83", and the lower two are the same length, 1.75". The flat, bevelled-edge sideplate is 4.86" long, with a convex-surface disc or circle at the mid-point between the two sidenails. The oval thumbpiece, which should have the initials CFCAMzB engraved on it (they have been erased and replaced with civilian initials on this example), is 1.47" long by 1" wide. The trigger guard is 10.78" long with pronounced trefoil finials at each end; secured to the stock by a cross-pin at the front and a screw through the rear finial. The lower sling-swivel screw now passes through the front base of the bow, but a plugged hole in the underside of the butt below the trigger guard suggests that it may previously have been mounted on an eye threaded into the butt. The surface of the bow area has three flats terminated at the back by an ornamental groove curving across the bow. The grip-rail section terminates in a reinforced rounded hollow knob. The buttplate is 4.72" long by 1.92" wide, the flat-fronted tang with five flats on the top one of which a rack number may be engraved.

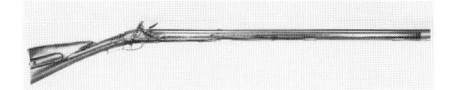

BARNETT, WILSON and GRICE INDIAN RIFLES (Page 81)

These rifles are closely patterned on an American longrifle typical of the early Lancaster rifle made from the 1750s to the 1770s, having a long barrel of large calibre, and a wooden butt-trap cover, but being unusual in the amount and elaboration of the stock-carving. They are heavier in the stock than most contemporary American-made rifles.

A major problem in describing these rifles is that no Barnett or Wilson rifles and only one Grice rifle survive in original condition: bores are worn beyond precise measuring, most of the locks have been converted to percussion and most of them incorrectly re-converted to flintlock using later-style parts. With regard to internal bore characteristics, accuracy has been further jeopardized by the fact that those most interested in these arms have been concerned with external stylistic features rather than internal technical ones.

These rifles were made wholly within the civilian gun trade and to a pattern, but comparative measurements of various dimensions, particularly in the stocks, will vary between makers more than on Ordnance-inspected arms.

Overall length: varies with barrel length, between 59-1/2" and 61-1/2".
Barrel length: 43-1/2" to 45-1/4".
Calibre: reports vary from approximately .55 to a very worn .63. Rifling is 7 angular grooves, with one turn in the length of the barrel; the lands being three times the width of the grooves.

BARREL is swamped octagonal, measuring 1-3/32" across the breech and 1" across the muzzle. The block backsight is dovetailed 8-1/2" from the breech, and the foresight is dovetailed 1-5/8" from the muzzle. The crosspins securing the barrel to the stock are located 9-1/16", 24-5/8" and 40-7/16" from the breech.

BARREL MARKINGS. On Barnett rifles conventional London Gunmakers' Company proof and view marks are struck on the upper left breech flat. Some examples may have Barnett's mark (granted in 1759) of RB beneath an asterisk struck either bet-ween the proof marks, or on the underside of the barrel. On Grice rifles there are two markings in ovals imitating London marks, the upper mark being a Crowned P and the lower one a copy of the Crowned V, with a Crowned WG struck between them. On Wilson barrels the markings are obviously-imitation London markings: the upper oval containing a plain V, and the lower one a Crowned GP, with Wilson's mark of an asterisk over RW struck between them.

LOCK plate is 5-1/8" long by 1", (lengths vary between 5-1/16" and 5-1/4"), flat with a bevelled edge terminating in a teat at the tail. The cock is swan-neck, flat with a bevelled edge and the tip of the comb curls forward. The pan is round, and without either a fence or pan-bridle, only the internal tumbler bridle. All reported examples have a short sear-spring, with two screws showing through the lockplate to the rear of the cock, the upper one only barely, probably a transition from the old habit of a blind-hole or one hidden behind the cock to the new design of piercing the lockplate fully, a feature which supports the later 1770s as the manufacture date. Grice and Barnett rifles are signed with the engraved surname of the maker in block letters, while Wilson examples have the surname in plain copperplate script.

STOCK is English walnut, the length of comb being 8-3/4"; trigger pull is 14-1/8". The lock and sidepiece flats measure 8-1/4". The most curious feature of the stock is the addorsed C-scroll carving at the rear of the cheekpiece: the original from which the English gunstockers copied their stock had been damaged on the front lower arm of the C, and it is present on all reported Barnett, Grice and Wilson rifles as dropping suddenly from a relief scroll to a simple incised line completing the arm. Close comparative examination may well show that the stocking was all done in one workshop.

BRASS FURNITURE is of the same pattern for all three makers, the Grice rifles at present being known only with a hinged brass butt-trap lid measuring 4-7/8" x 1-7/16", the other two having sliding wooden covers. The mounts consist of a cast nosecap 1-9/16" long, three ramrod pipes 2" long (the tailpipe having a 1-3/4" tang), each held by two pins. The front of the top pipe is is 4-3/4" from the muzzle; the distance from the rear of the top pipe to the front of the middle pipe is 10-5/16", and from the rear of the middle pipe to the front of the tailpipe is 12-1/16". The flat sideplate 5-3/8" long with bevelled edges and a tail-screw, and the grip-rail trigger guard is 9-1/2" overall length with the bow 1" at its widest. The buttplate measures 5 to 5-1/8" x 2-1/8", the faceted square-ended tang being 2-1/4" long.

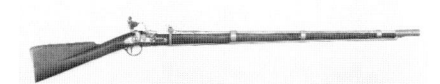

PATTERN 1785 CRESPI-EGG BREECH-LOADING RIFLED LIGHT DRAGOON CARBINES (RA XII-254) (NAM 1995.08.9.1) (RA XII-255) (Page 88)

These trials carbines were produced in three barrel lengths, other features remaining the same. S = short barrel M = mid-length barrel L = long barrel

Overall length:
L (54"); M (53-3/8"); S (48-5/8").
Barrel length:
L = 34-1/8" to face of breechblock.
M = 33-7/16" to face of breechblock. Diameter at muzzle .740", and across breech ahead of tang 1.260".
S = 29-1/16" to face of breechblock.
Iron foresight set 2-5/8" from muzzle. Backsight is a groove along the length of the hingeplate of the breechblock handle. Calibre: .610" across lands, .650 across grooves; 8 square grooves making (long barrel) 1-1/4 turn in the barrel or 1 turn in 28-1/4"; (short barrel) 1-1/8 turn in the length of the barrel, or 1 turn in 29-1/2".

BREECHBLOCK measures 3-3/4" x .960" at front and .980" at rear. Calibre of chamber .66", length of chamber 3" with flat base. London Gunmakers' Company proofmarks stamped on underside. Top flat engraved in block letters, D.EGG LONDON. The block is hinged by a transverse bolt at the rear, and by turning the handle in front of the lock upwards and swinging it to the left, the block is then pulled to the vertical position for loading a conventional paper cartridge. A retaining spring on the left side holds the block in position for loading.

LOCK: flat, bevelled, plate measures 6-1/8" x 1-1/16". Hennem's screwless lock. Engraved ahead of cock with Crowned "GR", and "TOWER" across tail. Double border lines engraved on plate and cock body. Held by a single sidenail which also serves to anchor the rear of the sling bar.

STOCK is English walnut, fore-end comes to 3-1/2" of muzzle, no cap. Comb is 8-3/4" long, and from centre of trigger to centre of buttplate is 13-5/8". Underside is cut away for bayonet, and there is a drainage slot from the underside of the "shoe" in which the breechblock lies.

FURNITURE consists of three flat iron barrel bands each 5/8" wide, brass triggerguard and buttplate.
On the long-barreled carbine the lower band is 11-5/8" from the tang of the barrel; the middle band is 21-3/16" from the same point and the upper band is 30-13/16", measuring to the rear edge of each band.
On the medium-length carbine the lower band is 11-1/2" from the tang of the barrel and is held by the front of the 12-3/8" sling bar mounted along the left side. The two upper bands are each secured by band spring with a pin through the band, mounted to the rear of each band on the right side. The triggerguard is Land Pattern Carbine but has a special sheet-brass hollow fan-shaped front finial 1-1/2" wide to hold the point bayonet when it is not fixed. The buttplate tang is of the Royal Forester's Light Dragoon carbine pattern with a 3-1/2" tang; the plate measures 4-9/16" x 1-15/16"

BAYONET: length of central cylindrical portion varies with the barrel length, measuring 38" overall on the mid-length barrel version. The spearpoint measures 3-3/4" x 1-1/2", and the socket is 3-1/2" long with a small wing — but to hold the socket in place on the barrel either fixed or reversed in carrying position. The socket is slotted to fit around the foresight when in carrying position. There are no markings.

A bayonet for the short-barreled version measures 33-1/2" overall, the point measuring 3-1/2" x 1-9/16", and the socket 3-5/16".

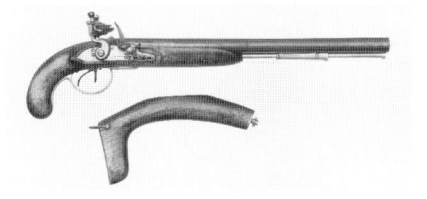

PATTERN 1793 ROYAL HORSE ARTILLERY PISTOL-CARBINE (RA XII-843) (Page 92)

Overall Length: 34-1/2" with stock
Weight: 7 lbs. 12 ozs. 24-1/2" without stock.

BARRELS: 18-1/8" long from break-off; browned iron. A single thick barrel-retaining pin located 5-1/2" from the break-off.

— 203 —

King's Proof struck on top/left side at breech, maker's mark HN on left side at breech. Tapering tang measures 2" long. Front sight iron blade set into central rib 15/16" from the muzzle. Backsight is a notched block with one leaf hinged facing backwards and inlet into the break-off or false-breech 1/2" from the front edge. The left-hand rifled barrel is .70 calibre rifled with 9 angular grooves equal in width to the lands, making one-quarter turn in the length of the barrel. The right-hand smoothbore barrel is .73 calibre. Width of barrels across breech just ahead of break-off is 2-1/16" and across the muzzles 1-15/16". Diameter of a single barrel at the muzzle is .975".

Locks: Flat lockplate 5-1/4" long x 1" wide with a finely beveled edge. Safety bolt fitted to left-hand lock only. Plain teaspoon-shaped pans. Flat swan-neck cocks with beveled edge ring-neck cocks; throw of cocks (from centre of tumbler screw to front tip of lower jaw) is 1-7/16". The cockscrews are pierced and slotted. The combs are of plain pillar form with slightly rearward curving tips. The oval top jaws are slotted. The steels measure 1-5/8" high x 7/8" wide. The locks lack any decorative engraving. Plain feather-springs with teardrop finials. The left-hand lock has a detented tumbler working in conjunction with the single-set left-hand trigger. Each lock is secured by an internal hook at the front and a short screw into the side of the false-breech. Engraved ahead of cock H. NOCK in block letters. Inside lockplate stamped with P N. Left-hand lock with a faint number 51.

STOCK: walnut, fore-end to 9-7/8" of muzzle. Plain curved butt shaped like the Pattern 1797 Heavy Dragoon Pistol. Lock and sidepiece flats 6-1/16" overall. Stamped along left side of trigger-guard: crown, crowned 8. Storekeeper's mark with date 1786 on right upper side of butt. A long iron tang strap is inlaid along the back of the butt with an oval widening at its lower end. This strap abuts the squared-off barrel tang at the front and is held by three screws, two of which are located one on each side of the oval widened area. In the centre of this area is a hole cut in the shape of a bow-tie, to receive the similarly shaped key on the front of the detachable shoulder stock.

BRASS FURNITURE: No nosecap, a brass washer at the entry point serving as both cap and tailpipe.

Ramrod Pipe: Long trumpet forepipe with flared mouth and two collars, 3-1/2" long, 15/16" diameter at mouth, 3/4" at rear, brazed to the under rib, with a rod-retaining spring riveted inside. Internal diameter of pipe 7/16". The mouth of the pipe is 4" from the muzzle and the rear of the pipe is 2-5/16" from the entry point.

Trigger-guard is heavy and plain with rounded surface. Upper finial is parallel-sided with a plain rounded front. Overall length of guard: 7-1/2" secured by a screw 1-3/8" from the tip of front finial and a pin through the stock just above the rear of the guard bow. The bow is 1-3/16" at its widest point.

Thumbpiece: None.
Buttcap: None.

Ramrod: Heavy steel with slightly domed ill-defined button-head, with a central threaded hole for tools. The tip is cupped to fit the ball in loading.

PRUSSIAN LIGHT INFANTRY RIFLED MUSKET (RA XII-3772) (Page 94)
Overall Length: 57-1/8".

BARREL: 41" long, tapered round; calibre .68, rifled with 8 round grooves one-third the width of the lands and making one turn in the length of the barrel; balustre-moulded at breech for 1/2". Barrel-retaining pins located at 8", 17" and 34-15/16" from the breech, and the upper swivel screw 26-11/16" from the breech, just ahead of the second pipe. Proof marks consist of private Tower proof and Prussian proof of a stick-like stylized eagle stamped on top of the breech. Tang measures 2-7/16" long x 1/2" at front x 7/8" at rear. Brass blade front sight measures 1-1/8", and is inlet into the barrel 4-5/8" from the muzzle. The backsight is a rounded hump on barrel tang without a groove on this example. A rectangular bayonet stud is brazed on the under-side of the barrel 3/4" from the muzzle, and measures 5/16" x 1/8".

Diameter of barrel across breech ahead of turning is 1.140" and across muzzle .880".

The barrels were proved and then blued/blacked as a part of refurbishing before being taken into British Ordnance Stores.

LOCK: double-bridle with flat surfaces and widely bevelled edges. Lockplate measures 6-5/16" long x 1-3/16" wide. The comb of the cock is leaf-shaped with a well developed curl at top; the faceted hexagonal top-jaw is not notched to fit the comb. Comb measures 1/2" across its widest part. Throw of cock (from centre of tumbler screw to front tip of lower jaw) is 1-13/16". The steel is hexagonal and measures 1-3/4" high x 1-3/16" wide and the back is faceted. The finial to the feather-spring is a flat-surfaced teardrop.

The lockplate is engraved ahead of the cock POTZDAMMAGAZ in heavy block letters, and along lower bevel of lockplate D S E [Daum Splittgerber's Erben= successors to Daum and Splittgerber, operated 1775–1795].

The two sidenail heads are 1/2" diameter and are recessed into the surface of the sidepiece.

STOCK: walnut, to 3-1/8" of the muzzle. Drop at comb 1-1/4", and at heel 1-3/4". Comb length 9-3/4" from vertical plane of butt-plate. Wavy outline barrel tang apron measures 4-3/4" x 1-3/16". Lock and sidepiece flats have full oval aprons front and rear measuring 8-9/16" overall. The edges of the ramrod channel are reinforced by flat moulding 1/2" in width, terminating in an apron around the tailpipe similar to that around the barrel tang. Diameter of the ramrod channel is 5/16". Distance from centre of trigger to centre of butt-plate is 13-1/2". A rounded-edge cheekpiece on the left side of the butt measures 6-7/8" x 2-7/8".

There are no British stock-markings on this example.

BRASS FURNITURE: Nosecap is flat sheet-brass with open front, 1-1/16" long, secured by a brass rivet.

Ramrod Pipes: All pipes are of the same pattern with an overall tapered outline when seen from the side; each has a flared mouth, five flats and a round collar at front and rear.

Upper pipe is 1-11/16" long; held by two pins 34-1/4" and 35-1/4" from the breech. The mouth of the pipe is 2-3/16" from the tip of the nosecap. Distance from rear of first pipe to front of second pipe is 7-11/16".

Second pipe is 1-11/16" long, held by two pins 24-13/16" and 25-15/16" from the breech. The distance between the rear of the second pipe and the front of the third pipe is 6-3/16".

Third Pipe is 1-5/8", held by two pins 17-1/8" and 18-1/16" from the breech. From the rear of the third pipe to the mouth of the tailpipe measures 4-1/2".

Tailpipe is of the same design as the other pipes with a large flame-shaped tang. Overall length is 4-3/4".

Sidepiece is flat with a bevelled edge proud of the surrounding wood, 6" overall with 3-7/16" between the two sidenail centres. The design is basically serpentine or wavy.

Trigger guard is flat and faceted and although inletted in the wood lies proud of the surface. Length overall 12-3/16"; secured by a pin 3-1/2" from the front finial and by a second pin 5-1/2" from the rear finial. There are two screws through the lower tang just ahead of the lower finial one on either side of the lower sling swivel which passes beneath the tang 3-1/4" forward of the lower finial. The bow is 1" at its widest point.

Thumbpiece: None.

Buttplate has a long ornamental tang measuring 5-1/2" from the vertical plane of the plate, and secured by three flush screws. The Royal Cypher, a crowned FWR, is deeply engraved between the two rearmost screws. The plate measures 4-3/8" from heel to toe and 1-3/4" at its widest point.

Ramrod: heavy tapered steel, the head with a threaded hole for tools.

INFANTRY RIFLE BY GALTON, 1790s (RA XII-1967) (Page 95)
Overall Length: 48-1/2"

BARREL: 33-1/16" tapered round, measuring 1.310" across the breech and .880" across the muzzle; .70" calibre rifled with 8 angular grooves equal in width to the lands, making three-quarters of a turn in the length of the barrel. Fitted with a break-off breech.

The backsight is a notched block on the front of the false-breech.

A bayonet stud is brazed to the underside of the barrel 13/16" from the muzzle; it measures 5/16" x 1/8", and there is an Austrian Laukart-style spring catch protruding from the front of the fore-end which engages in a hole in the socket of the bayonet.

The top flat of the breech is stamped with a small rampant lion facing left within a shield.

LOCK: French Model 1777 design, the lockplate measuring 6-3/8" x 1-1/8". Round ring-necked cock, brass detachable pan. The feather-spring has an oval finial.

The lockplate has a flat surface ahead of the cock and tail has a rounded surface. Ahead of the cock is engraved GALTON in block letters.

STOCK: walnut, to 3" of the muzzle, the butt is plain without handrail, the comb 8-3/4" long with a drop of 1-3/8" at the comb and 1-1/4" at the heel. A plain curved edge cheek-piece on the left side of the butt measures 6-3/4" x 3". There is no raised carving around the barrel tang.

BRASS FURNITURE: consists of three barrel bands, trigger-guard, sidepiece, and buttplate.

The barrel bands are of Austrian Model 1798 design.

The upper band is double-strapped and held in position by a band spring with a pin through the right rear side of the band. The foresight is cast integral on the top of the rear strap.

The middle band is flared at front and rear, with the base for the upper sling swivel cast into the underside. It is also secured by a pin-spring from the rear.

The lower band flares towards the front on its underside to form an entry point for the rammer. It is held in position by a step in the stock at its rear and a spring inlet into the fore-end ahead of the band.

The trigger-guard is of individual design with a well defined tri-lobed flower-head as front and rear finials (not fleurs-de-lys), finger grips in the lower tang, and a large reinforce at the front of the bow for the lower sling swivel screw.

The flat sidepiece has bevelled edges, and is of a common design on Germanic and Scandanavian military rifles of the period.

Thumbpiece: None.

The buttplate has a short faceted and squared-off tang measuring 2-1/8" in length, secured by a screw; there is a bumper-screw fitted below the heel of the plate. From heel to toe the plate measures 4-1/2" and 2" across at its widest point.

The heavy steel ramrod is missing.

– BAKER RIFLES –

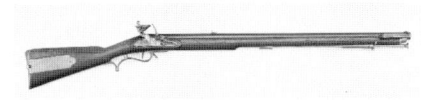

PATTERN 1800 BAKER RIFLE (CARBINE-BORE) (RA XII-147) (Page 108)
Overall Length: 46-1/4"

BARREL: 30-3/8", tapered round, 1.090" across breech and .890" across muzzle; barrel-retaining keys (slides) at 8-1/8", 18-1/8" and 28" from the break-off breech, measuring to the centre of each key; upper sling swivel screws through the fore-end at 26-1/4" from the break-off. The break-off tang is 2-1/8" long and 9/16" across at the rear with inspector's crown stamped at the tail.

The iron blade foresight measures 1/2" x 3/32" and is mounted on a 5/8" x 1/2" baseplate located 1/2" from the muzzle.

The backsight is a block on a baseplate with one hinged leaf 7/16" in height, dovetailed 6-11/16" from the break-off.

A bayonet bar (sword bar) is brazed by two rectangular extensions to the right side of the barrel, with the front of the bar 1/8" to the rear of the muzzle. The bar measures 3-11/16" x 7/16", with a notch cut into the upper edge 3/8" from the front.

LOCK: Flat lockplate measuring 5-3/8" x 1-1/16". Plain teaspoon-shaped pan. Flat ring-necked cock, with the edges and those of the lockplate having a narrow bevel. The comb of the cock is plain and curls very slightly rearwards; the oval top-jaw is notched to move along the comb and the cock-screw is both pierced and slotted. The steel measures 1-5/8" x 15/16", the toe of the steel has an upward curl. The feather-spring has a plain convex-surface oval finial. The tumbler is fitted with a detent.

The markings are stamped, not engraved, and consist of the Crowned GR cypher ahead of the cock, and TOWER across the tail. The borders of the lockplate and cock body have double line decoration. The Crowned Broad Arrow is stamped beneath the pan. Internally the lockplate is stamped with a crowned 3 and the initials WR.

The rounded-head sidenails are 1/2" in diameter.

STOCK: full length walnut, to 3/8" of the muzzle, with a step forming a semi-pistol grip on the underside at the rear of the trigger guard and measuring 10-1/8" to the toe; the butt is plain without handrail, the comb 8-3/4" long with a drop of 1-1/4" at the front and 1-1/2" at the heel. A plain curved edge cheekpiece on the left side of the butt measures 6" x 3" but the measurements vary. Distance from centre of trigger to centre of buttplate is 14-3/16". The flats surrounding the lock and sidepiece are 6-1/4" long, plain rounded at the front with a simple teardrop at the rear. There is no raised carving around the barrel tang. The ramrod channel is 3/8" in diameter. The distance from the nosecap to the entry point of the stock is 20-3/8". There are two separate compartments in the butt-trap: the front one is circular, 1-3/8" diameter, the rear one is rectangular and measures 2-1/8" x 1-3/8"; both are 5/8" deep.

The ramrod channel is struck with crowned 8, crowned 1 and crowned 8. The sidepiece flat is stamped IR, and there is a crown and a crowned number stamped below the rear or lower trigger guard finial.

BRASS FURNITURE: consists of a nosecap, two ramrod pipes, trigger-guard, sidepiece, thumbpiece, butt-trap cover and buttplate.

The nosecap is of the New Land Pattern with a rounded nose and a collar at the rear, 1" long and secured by a single brass rivet.

The upper ramrod pipe is of long trumpet form 3-5/8" long with a flared mouth 3/4" in diameter, being 5/8" diameter at the rear of the pipe, with an internal diameter of 1/2". Secured by two pins 22-7/8" and 25-1/16" from the break-off. From the front of the nosecap to the front of the trumpet pipe measures 4-1/16". The distance between the rear of the trumpet pipe and the mouth of the second pipe is 8-7/16".

The second pipe is straight tapered (Pratt pattern) with a collar at each end, 1-5/8" long x 5/8" widest external diameter, with an internal diameter of 3/8". It is secured by one pin 13-1/8" from the break-off. The distance from the rear of the second pipe to the entry point is 2-3/4".

The trigger-guard is of the characteristic "Baker" grip-guard form, a curved downward extension behind the bow acting as a pistol-grip for the hand; overall length is 8-1/8" and the guard is secured by three screws: a wood screw through the front finial 1-5/8" from the flat tip, a second through the rear finial 1/2" from its rounded tip, and by the screw through the supporting pillar in the centre of the grip extention which secures the thumbpiece. A flat ramrod-retaining spring conforming to the forward tapering outline is fitted into the underside of the front finial and held by its dovetail and the upper guard screw. The lower sling swivel screw is fitted to the upper front of the bow, and the bow is 1" across at its widest point.

The flat sidepiece is flush with the surrounding wood, generally described as "addorsed C-scrolls" in design, also of "light troops" pattern having been used since 1756 on a variety of light dragoon and light infantry arms. The plate is 3-1/2" long, measuring 3" between centres of the sidenail holes, which are not recessed to admit the heads of the sidenails.

The thumbpiece is a plain oval inlet flush with the wood measuring 1-7/16" x 15/16", and secured by a screw into a boss cast into the underside from the pillar in the centre of the trigger-guard grip.

The cover or lid of the butt-trap is flat and flush with the surface of the wood, has a stepped rounded outline at the front of the hinge, and is secured by a single woodscrew through the centre of the hinge-piece. It measures 5-15/16" x 1-9/16". The lid is opened by grasping the finger-tab of the lid at the back pressing or pinching the notched head of the spring which protrudes through a small square hole in the lid just ahead of the tab; this releases the lid to be pulled open.

The buttplate has a two-stage tang secured by a cross-pin; the tang measures 3-5/8" overall, 2-3/16" from the shoulder of the plate to the first step, and 3/4" from the first step to the tip. From heel to toe the plate measures 4-3/4" and 1-7/8" across at its widest point. The right edge of the plate is recessed to receive the butt-trap cover.

The heavy steel ramrod has a wide flat beveled button-head 11/16" in diameter. There is a torque hole 1/16" behind the head to accept the torque bar when using the ball-drawer. There is a swell of 1/2" diameter in the rod 7" from the head. The rod is .300" in diameter along its parallel section. The tip of the rod has a female thread with a protective brass collar.

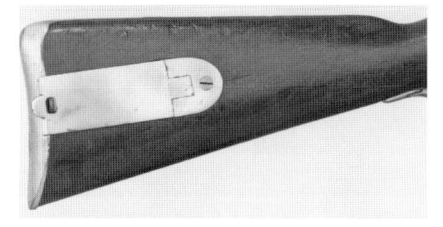

PATTERN 1805 BAKER RIFLE
(RA XII-10431) (Page 115)
Overall Length: 45-3/4"

BARREL: 30-1/2", tapered round, 1.090" across breech and .880" across muzzle; barrel-retaining keys (slides) at 8-3/16", 18-1/8" and 27-7/8" from the break-off breech, measuring to the centre of each key; upper sling swivel screws through the fore-end at 26-1/2" from the break-off.

The break-off tang is 2-1/8" long and 9/16" across at the rear.

The iron blade foresight measures 1/2" x 1/8" and is mounted on a 11/16" x 3/8" baseplate located 3/16" from the muzzle.

The backsight is a block on a baseplate with one hinged leaf, dovetailed 7" from the break-off.

A bayonet bar is brazed by two rectangular extensions to the right side of the barrel, with the front of the bar 1/8" to the rear of the muzzle. The bar measures 3-11/16" x 7/16", with a notch cut into the upper edge 3/8" from the front.

LOCK: Flat lockplate measuring 5-3/8" x 1-1/16". Flat ring-necked cock, with the edges and those of the lockplate having a narrow bevel. The comb of the cock is plain and curls very slightly rearwards as on the India Pattern; the oval top-jaw is notched to move along the comb and the cock-screw is both pierced and slotted. The throw of the cock is 1-5/8". The steel measures 1-5/8+" x 15/16", the toe of the steel with an upward curl. The featherspring has and oval finial.

The markings are stamped, not engraved, and consist of the Crowned GR cypher ahead of the cock, and TOWER in small capitals across the tail. The borders of the lockplate and cock have double line decoration. The Crowned Broad Arrow is stamped beneath the pan. Stamped inside with Crowned 3 and B&S [Blair & Sutherland].

STOCK: full length walnut, to 1/4" of the muzzle, with a step forming a semi-pistol grip on the underside at the rear of the trigger guard; the butt is plain without handrail, the comb 8-3/4" long with a drop of 1-3/8" at the comb and 1-1/4" at the heel. A plain curved edge cheek-piece on the left side of the butt measures 7-1/8" x 3" but the measurements vary. Distance from centre of trigger to centre of buttplate is 13-1/2". The flats surrounding the lock and sidepiece are 6-1/2" long, plain rounded at the front with a simple teardrop at the rear. There is no raised carving around the barrel tang. The ramrod channel is 3/8" in diameter and has a slit through the normally closed lower part of the channel 7-9/16" in length by 3/16" in width. Distance from fore-end tip to entry-point is 20-3/4". The single rectangular compartment of the butt-trap measures 2-5/8" x 1-3/16".

BRASS FURNITURE: consists of a nosecap, two ramrod pipes, trigger-guard, sidepiece, thumbpiece, butt-trap cover and buttplate.

The nosecap is of the New Land Pattern with a rounded nose and a collar at the rear, 1-1/16" long and secured by a single brass rivet.

The upper ramrod pipe is of long trumpet form 3-1/2" long with a flared mouth 11/16" in diameter, with an internal diameter of 7/16". Secured by two pins 23-1/8" and 25-3/16" from the break-off. The distance between the rear of the trumpet pipe and the mouth of the second pipe is 8-5/8".

The second pipe is straight tapered Pratt in design with a collar at each end, 1-9/16" long with an internal diameter of 1/2"; secured by one pin 13-1/8" from the break-off. The distance from the rear of the second pipe to the entry-point (there is no tailpipe) is 3-1/16".

The trigger-guard is of the grip-guard form, a curved extension behind the bow acting as a pistol-grip for the hand; overall length is 8-3/8" and the guard is secured by two screws, through the front finial 2" from the flat tip, and the rear finial 3/4" from its rounded tip, and by the screw through the supporting pillar in the centre of the grip extension which secures the thumbpiece. A flat ramrod-retaining spring conforming to the forward tapering outline is fitted into the underside of the front finial and held by its dovetail and the upper guard screw. The lower sling swivel screw is fitted to the upper front of the bow, and the bow is 15/16" across at its widest point.

The flat sidepiece is flush with the surrounding wood, generally described as "addorsed C-scrolls" in design, also of "light troops" pattern having been used since 1756 on a variety of light dragoon and light infantry arms. The plate is 3-11/16" long, measuring 3-1/8" between centres of the sidenail holes, which are recessed to admit the heads of the sidenails.

The thumbpiece is a plain oval inlet flush with the wood measuring 1-7/16" x 13/16", and secured by a screw into a boss on the underside from the pillar in the centre of the trigger-guard grip.

The butt-trap cover is flat and flush with the surface of the wood, has a rounded outline at the front of the hinge, and is secured by a single woodscrew through the hinge-piece. It measures 4-9/16" x 1-3/8". The lid is opened by grasping the finger-tab of the lid at the back pressing or pinching the notched head of the spring which protrudes through a small square hole in the lid just ahead of the tab; this releases the lid to be pulled open.

The buttplate has a two-stage tang secured by a cross-pin; the tang measures 3-9/16" overall, 2-1/4" from the shoulder of the plate to the first step, and 5/8" from the first step to the tip. From heel to toe the plate measures 4-7/16" and 1-13/16" across at its widest point. The right edge of the plate is recessed to receive the butt-trap cover.

The heavy steel ramrod has a wide flat button-head 11/16" in diameter. There is a torque hole .370" behind the head to accept the torque bar when using the ball-drawer. There is a swell of 7/16" diameter in the rod 7" from the head. The rod is .280" in diameter along its parallel section. The tip of the rod has a female thread with a collar.

— 206 —

PATTERN 1810 BAKER RIFLE (MUSKET-BORE) (RA XII-148) (Page 116)
Overall Length: 46-3/8"

BARREL: 30-3/8", tapered round, 1.200" across breech and .955" across muzzle; barrel-retaining keys (slides) at 8-5/16", 18-3/16" and 28" from the break-off breech, measuring to the centre of each key; upper sling swivel screws through the fore-end at 26-1/4" from the break-off. The break-off tang is 2-1/8" long and 9/16" across at the rear with inspector's crown stamped at the tail.

The iron blade foresight measures 1/2" x 3/32" and is mounted on a 5/8" x 1/4" baseplate located 1/2" from the muzzle.

The backsight is a block on a baseplate with one hinged leaf 7/16" in height, dovetailed 6-11/16" from the break-off.

A bayonet bar is brazed by two rectangular extensions to the right side of the barrel, with the front of the bar 1/8" to the rear of the muzzle. The bar measures 3-11/16" x 7/16", with a notch cut into the upper edge 3/8" from the front.

LOCK: Flat lockplate measuring 5-3/8" x 1-1/16". Plain teaspoon-shaped pan. Flat ring-necked cock, with the edges and those of the lockplate having a narrow bevel. The comb of the cock is plain and curls very slightly rearwards; the oval top-jaw is notched to move along the comb and the cock-screw is both pierced and slotted. The steel measures 1-5/8" x 15/16", the toe of the steel has an upward curl. The feather-spring has a plain convex-surface oval finial. The tumbler is fitted with a detent.

The markings are stamped, not engraved, and consist of the Crowned GR cypher ahead of the cock, and TOWER across the tail. The borders of the lockplate and cock body have double line decoration. The Crowned Broad Arrow is stamped beneath the pan. Internally the lockplate is stamped with a crowned 3 and the initials WR.

The rounded-head sidenails are 1/2" in diameter.

Stock: full length walnut, to 3/8" of the muzzle, with a step forming a semi-pistol grip on the underside at the rear of the trigger guard and measuring 10-1/8" to the toe; the butt is plain without handrail, the comb 8-3/4" long with a drop of 1-1/4" at the front and 1-1/2" at the heel. A plain curved edge cheekpiece on the left side of the butt measures 6" x 3" but the measurements vary. Distance from centre of trigger to centre of buttplate is 14-3/16". The flats surrounding the lock and sidepiece are 6-1/4" long, plain rounded at the front with a simple teardrop at the rear. There is no raised carving around the barrel tang. The ramrod channel is 3/8" in diameter. The distance from the nosecap to the entry point of the stock is 20-3/8". There are two separate compartments in the butt-trap: the front one is circular, 1-3/8" diameter, the rear one is rectangular and measures 2-1/8" x 1-3/8"; both are 5/8" deep.

The ramrod channel is struck with crowned 8, crowned 1 and crowned 8. The sidepiece flat is stamped IR, and there is a crown and a crowned number stamped below the rear or lower trigger guard finial.

BRASS FURNITURE: consists of a nosecap, two ramrod pipes, trigger-guard, sidepiece, thumbpiece, butt-trap cover and buttplate.

The nosecap is of the New Land Pattern with a rounded nose and a collar at the rear, 1" long and secured by a single brass rivet.

The upper ramrod pipe is of long trumpet form 3-5/8" long with a flared mouth 3/4" in diameter, being 5/8" diameter at the rear of the pipe, with an internal diameter of 1/2". Secured by two pins 22-7/8" and 25-1/16" from the break-off. From the front of the nosecap to the front of the trumpet pipe measures 4-1/16". The distance between the rear of the trumpet pipe and the mouth of the second pipe is 8-7/16".

The second pipe is straight tapered (Pratt pattern) with a collar at each end, 1-5/8" long x 5/8" widest external diameter, with an internal diameter of 3/8". It is secured by one pin 13-1/8" from the break-off. The distance from the rear of the second pipe to the entry-point is 2-3/4".

The trigger-guard is of the characteristic "Baker" grip-guard form, a curved downward extension behind the bow acting as a pistol-grip for the hand; overall length is 8-1/8" and the guard is secured by three screws: a wood screw through the front finial 1-5/8" from the flat tip, a second through the rear finial 1/2" from its rounded tip, and by the screw through the supporting pillar in the centre centre of the grip extention which secures the thumbpiece. A flat ramrod-retaining spring conforming to the forward tapering outline is fitted into the underside of the front finial and held by its dovetail and the upper guard screw. The lower sling swivel screw is fitted to the upper front of the bow, and the bow is 1" across at its widest point.

The flat sidepiece is flush with the surrounding wood, generally described as "addorsed C-scrolls" in design, also of "light troops" pattern having been used since 1756 on a variety of light dragoon and light infantry arms. The plate is 3-1/2" long, measuring 3" between centres of the sidenail holes, which are not recessed to admit the heads of the sidenails.

The thumbpiece is a plain oval inlet flush with the wood measuring 1-7/16" x 15/16", and secured by a screw into a boss cast into the underside from the pillar in the centre of the trigger-guard grip.

The butt-trap cover or lid is flat and flush with the surface of the wood, has a stepped rounded outline at the front of the hinge, and is secured by a single woodscrew through the centre of the hinge-piece. It measures 5-15/16" x 1-9/16". The lid is opened by grasping the finger-tab of the lid at the back pressing or pinching the notched head of the spring which protrudes through a small square hole in the lid just ahead of the tab; this releases the lid to be pulled open.

The buttplate has a two-stage tang secured by a cross-pin; the tang measures 3-5/8" overall, 2-3/16" from the shoulder of the plate to the first step, and 3/4" from the first step to the tip. From heel to toe the plate measures 4-3/4" and 1 7/8" across at its widest point. The right edge of the plate is recessed to receive the butt-trap cover.

The heavy steel ramrod has a wide flat beveled button-head 11/16" in diameter. There is a hole 1/16" behind the head to accept the torque bar when using the ball-drawer. There is a swell of 1/2" diameter in the rod the centre of which is 7" from the head. The rod is .300" in diameter along its parallel section. The widened tip of the rod has a female thread.

— CAVALRY RIFLES —

KETLAND & CO. 1790s CAVALRY RIFLE (RA XII-3057)
Overall Length: 35-3/4"

BARREL: 21-1/8" octagonal plain iron, 1-3/16" across breech and 1-1/16" across muzzle. .62 calibre rifled with 7 angular grooves half the width of the lands, making one-quarter turn in the length of the barrel. Barrel retained by two pins and sling bar ring at front.

The sights are missing but were dovetailed to the barrel with broad baseplates; the back-sight was moved from the barrel tang to a point 4-1/2" from the tang.

This example has private Tower proofs struck on the left side of the breech.

LOCK: Flat beveled-edge lockplate measuring 6-3/8" x 1-1/16". Cock missing but other examples have swan-neck type. The feather-spring has a teardrop finial .
Engraved in script lettering ahead of the cock "Ketland & Co." in two lines. There are no other markings.

STOCK: full length walnut, to the muzzle. The comb of the butt measures 7" along the straight section. A rounded edge cheekpiece on the left side measures 6" x 2-5/8".

BRASS FURNITURE: consists of a nosecap, one ramrod pipe, tail-pipe, grip-rail trigger-guard, trigger-plate, sidepiece, butt-trap cover and buttplate. There is also a sling-bar.

The nosecap is plain, 1-5/8" long, secured by a single brass rivet.

The ramrod pipe is collared and faceted 1-15/16" long, with its flared mouth 3-1/2" from the muzzle, held by a single pin.

The tailpipe is similar in form to the other pipe, 3-3/8" long and has a squared-off finial.

The trigger-guard is of "American" form of grip-guard, a curved extension behind the bow acting as a pistol-grip for the hand and passing close to the wrist of the stock before sweeping downwards at the rear; overall length is 9-5/8" and the finials are both squared-off and faceted with horizontal grooves across the ends in "American" style; the guard is held by two pins. The bow is 1" across at its widest point.

The sling-bar mounted on the left side is straight, 7" long, anchored at the rear beneath the rear sidenail and at the front, 6-7/8" from the breech, by a 1/2" wide rounded surface band around the barrel and fore-end.

The sidepiece is of a pattern often seen on American long rifles, flat with a squared-off tail and grooves across the ends.

The cover of the butt-trap is flat and flush with the surface of the wood, has an outline at the front of the hinge like a number of privately-made English military rifles of the period and the Grice Indian rifle; it measures 4-3/4" x 1-3/8" and covers a single rectangular compartment.

The buttplate has a squared-off tang again in the "American" style, faceted and with grooves across the end, and is crudely engraved D N96. The plate measures 4-1/8" long x 1-3/4" across at its widest point. The right edge of the plate is recessed to receive the rear of the butt-trap cover which is released by a spring-catch through the cover.

The heavy steel ramrod has a thick button-head and the tip has a female thread for tools.

PATTERN 1803 BAKER CAVALRY RIFLE (RA XII-1968) (Page 122)
Overall Length: 35"

BARREL: 20-1/4" browned twist iron, tapered round, 1.10" across breech and .860" across muzzle. .65 calibre rifled with 7 angular grooves equal in width to the lands, making one-half turn in the length of the barrel. Barrel-retaining keys (slides) at 5-5/16" and 18" from the break-off breech, measuring to the centre of each key; upper sling swivel screw through the fore-end at 11-13/16" from the break-off.

The break-off tang is 2" long and 1/2" wide at the rear.

The brass blade foresight measures 3/8" x 5/16" and is brazed 15/32" from the muzzle.

The backsight is a block on a baseplate dovetailed and brazed 3" from the break-off.

This example has private Tower proofs struck on the left side of the breech. Lock: Flat lockplate measuring 4-9/16" x 15/16". Flat ring-necked cock, with the edges and those of the lockplate having a narrow bevel. The comb of the cock has a narrow notched pillar form; the oval top-jaw is notched to move along the comb which is 5/32" at its thickest point; the cock-screw is both pierced and slotted. The throw of the cock is 1-9/32". The steel measures 1-9/32" x 25/32", the foot of the steel with an upward curl. The feather-spring has a teardrop finial and is fitted with a roller.

The markings are stamped, not engraved, and consist of the Crowned GR cypher ahead of the cock, and TOWER in small capitals across the tail. There is no double line border engraving. The Crowned Broad Arrow is stamped beneath the pan. Stamped inside with Crowned 3 and number 4.

STOCK: full length walnut, to the muzzle, with a step forming a semi-pistol grip on the underside at the rear of the trigger guard; the butt is plain without handrail, the comb 8-3/4" long with a drop of 1-5/8" at the comb and 2" at the heel. A plain curved edge cheekpiece on the left side of the butt measures 5-3/16" x 2-5/8" but the measurements vary. Distance from centre of trigger to centre of butt-plate is 13-1/2". The flats surrounding the lock and side-piece are 6" long, plain rounded at the front with a simple point at the rear. There is no barrel tang apron. The ramrod channel is 13/32" in diameter and has a slit through the normally closed lower part of the channel 5-7/8" in length by 3/16" in width.

The distance from nosecap tip to entry-point is 10". The single rectangular compartment of the butt-trap measures 2-3/4" x 1-1/4".

BRASS FURNITURE: consists of a nose-cap, two ramrod pipes, trigger-guard, trigger-plate, butt-trap cover and buttplate. There is also an iron sling-bar on the left side.

The nosecap is of the India Pattern without a collar at the rear, 3/4" long and secured by a single brass rivet.

The upper ramrod pipe is of long trumpet form 2-5/16" long with a flared mouth 5/8" in diameter, with an internal diameter of 3/8". Secured by two pins 15-3/16" and 16-1/2" from the break-off. The distance between the rear of the trumpet pipe and the mouth of the tail pipe is 5".

The tailpipe is straight tapered Pratt in form with a collar at each end and without a rear finial, 1-1/2" long, 19/32" diameter at front and 17/32" at rear; secured by one pin 9" from the break-off.

The trigger-guard is of the standard Baker grip-guard form, a curved extension behind the bow acting as a pistol-grip for the hand; overall length is 7-1/2" and the guard is secured by three screws, through the front finial 2-1/8" from the flat tip, the rear finial 7/16" from its rounded tip, and by a woodscrew through the supporting pillar in the centre of the grip extension. A flat ramrod-retaining spring conforming to the forward tapering outline is fitted into the underside of the front finial and held by its dovetail and the upper guard screw. The bow is 7/8" across at its widest point.

The iron sling-bar mounted on the left side is 5-1/2" long, anchored at the rear beneath the rear sidenail and at the front, 5-15/32" from the breech, by a screw through the fore-end.

The cover or lid of the butt-trap is flat and flush with the surface of the wood, has a rounded outline at the front of the hinge, and is secured by a single wood-screw through the hinge-piece. It measures 4-9/16" x 1-7/16".

The buttplate has a two-stage tang secured by a cross-pin; the tang measures 2-27/32" overall. From heel to toe the plate measures 4" and 1-9/16" across at its widest point. The right edge of the plate is recessed to receive the rear of the butt-trap cover.

The heavy steel swivel-ramrod is held by a pair of swivels which are connected to the barrel by a screw passing through a lug on the underside of the barrel at the muzzle. The rod has a wide slightly domed mushroom-head 1-1/8" in diameter. There is a torque hole just behind the head to accept the torque bar when using the ball-drawer. The straight rod is 1/4+" in diameter. The tip of the rod has a female thread without a collar.

PATTERN 1827 BAKER CAVALRY RIFLE (T.A. Edwards & RA XII-1885) (Page 128)
Overall Length: 35"

BARREL: 20-1/4" browned plain iron, tapered round, 1.10" across breech and .860" across muzzle. .65" calibre, rifled with 7 angular grooves equal in width to the lands, making one-quarter turn in the length of the barrel. Barrel-retaining keys (slides) at 5-5/16" and 18" from the break-off breech, measuring to the centre of each key; upper sling swivel screw through the fore-end at 11-13/16" from the break-off.

The break-off tang is 2" long and 1/2" wide at the rear.

The brass blade foresight measures 3/8" x 5/16" and is brazed 15/32" from the muzzle.

The backsight is a block on a baseplate brazed 1-3/32" from the break-off.

LOCK: Flat lockplate measuring 5-3/8" x

1". Flat ring-necked cock, with the edges and those of the lockplate having a narrow bevel. The comb of the cock has a narrow notched pillar form; the oval top-jaw is notched to move along the comb which is 5/32" at its thickest point; the cock-screw is both pierced and slotted. The throw of the cock is 1-9/32". The steel measures 1-9/32" x 25/32", the toe of the steel with an upward curl. The feather-spring has a teardrop finial and is fitted with a roller.

The markings are stamped, not engraved, and consist of the Crowned GR cypher ahead of the cock, and TOWER in small capitals across the tail. There is no double line border engraving. The Crowned Broad Arrow is stamped beneath the pan. Stamped inside with crowned 3 and number 4.

STOCK: full length walnut, to 1" of the muzzle, the butt is plain without a handrail, the comb 8-3/4" long with a drop of 1-5/8" at the comb and 2" at the heel. The grip is formed with a one-piece rounded-bottom pistol-grip in place of the earlier grip-guard. Most of this pattern were made with a two-piece grip, the lower part glued and secured by a screw at the bottom. A plain curved edge cheekpiece on the left side of the butt measures 5" x 2-5/8" but the measurements vary. The distance from the centre of trigger to centre of buttplate is 13-1/2". The flats surrounding the lock and sidepiece are 6" long, plain rounded at the front with a simple point at the rear. There is no barrel tang apron. The ramrod channel is 13/32" in diameter and there is no slit below the tailpipe. The single rectangular compartment of the butt-trap measures 2-11/16" x 1-5/16".

BRASS FURNITURE: consists of a nose-cap, two ramrod pipes, trigger-guard, trigger-plate, butt-trap cover and buttplate. There is an iron sling-bar.

The nosecap is of the India Pattern without a collar at the rear, 3/4" long and secured by a single brass rivet.

The upper ramrod pipe is of long trumpet form 2-5/16" long with a flared mouth 5/8" in diameter, with an internal diameter of 3/8". Secured by two pins 15-3/16" and 16-1/2" from the break-off. The distance between the rear of the trumpet pipe and the mouth of the tailpipe is 5".

The tailpipe is straight tapered Pratt in form with a collar at each end, and without a rear tang, 1-1/2" long, 19/32" diameter at the front and 17/32" at rear; secured by one pin 9" from the break-off.

The trigger-guard is of the Paget form, with the rear tang curved to fit the pistol-grip; overall length is 7-1/2" and the guard is secured by a pin 1-1/4" from the front finial, and a screw through the rear finial 1-5/8" from its rounded tip. A ramrod-retaining spring is fitted into the underside of the front finial. The bow is 7/8" across at its widest point.

The sling-bar mounted on the left side is 5-1/4" long, anchored at the rear beneath the rear sidenail and at the front, 5-9/16" from the breech, by a screw through the fore-end without a baseplate on the right side.

The cover of the butt-trap is flat and flush with the surface of the wood, has a rounded outline at the front of the hinge, and is secured by a single woodscrew through the hinge-piece. It measures 4-9/16" x 1-7/16".

The buttplate has a two-stage tang secured by a cross-pin; the tang measures 2-27/32" overall. From heel to toe the plate measures 4" and 1-9/16" across at its widest point. The right edge of the plate is recessed to receive the rear of the butt-trap cover. The tang is engraved in large shaded letters, X. R. H. [10th Royal Hussars].

The heavy steel swivel-ramrod is held by a pair of Paget-pattern or C-shaped flat swivels which are connected to the barrel by a screw passing through a lug on the underside of the barrel at the muzzle. The rod has a wide slightly domed mushroom-head 13/16" in diameter. There is a hole just behind the head to accept the torque bar when using the ball-drawer. The straight rod is 5/16" in diameter. The tip of the rod has a female thread without a collar.

– POST-1783 INDIAN RIFLES –
Note: In this section the term "presentation" refers to the fact that these rifles were given, presented to, rather than sold; it does not refer to the quality of the rifles.

PATTERN 1816 INDIAN PRESENTATION COMBINATION GUN (RA XII-1460) (Page 183)
Overall Length: 44-3/4"

BARREL: 29" round with full length tapering sighting plane, from .380" at breech to .310" at muzzle, slightly tapered superimposed barrels, the rifled barrel on top. The rifled barrel is .56 calibre, rifled with 10 rounded grooves just wider than the lands, making one turn in the length of the barrel. Rifle barrel .950" across breech, .830" across muzzle. Both barrels fitted with plain breeches and platinum-lined vents.

The silver rounded blade foresight is inlet into the barrel at the muzzle. The backsight is a block on a baseplate with one hinged leaf, dovetailed 6-1/16" from the breech.

The breech of the rifle barrel is inlaid with two gold lines, with one gold line inlaid across the breech of the shotgun barrel. Dovetailed .550" from the breech is a rectangular block measuring 3/4" x .650" containing the Royal Coat of Arms in gold. The top is also inlaid with a gold ribbon in which is engraved "TATHAM LONDON".

The rifle barrel is stamped with London commercial proofmarks, and the initials WF (William Fullerd).

The 14 bore smoothbore barrel is fully round and the barrel walls are thick enough to allow use of a round ball load as well as for shot.

LOCKS: Two flat lockplates with a rounded-outline tail, measuring 4-1/2" x 15/16". Fitted to the rear of the cocks with a sliding safety catch. Double-fence pans, a roller fitted to each feather-spring. Flat ring-neck cocks of the Joseph Egg design with external mainsprings fitted by swivels to the bottom of each cock. Ahead of the cock on each lockplate is engraved "Tatham" in script, partially covered by the mainsprings.

There is a single sidenail located ahead of the cocks entering from the left lock. Stock: walnut, butt only. Comb is 9-1/4" long. A plain curved and moulded edge cheekpiece on the left side measures 6-1/4" x 3". Distance from centre of trigger to centre of buttplate is 14". The wrist has flat chequering.

FURNITURE: of blued iron, consists of three ramrod pipes, thumbpiece, trigger-guard, butt-trap cover and buttplate. The plain cylindrical ramrod pipes are each 1-1/8" long and soldered along the right side at the barrel joint. Each pipe is slightly smaller than the previous: external diameter of front pipe is .580", of the middle pipe .550" and of the lower pipe .480" The mouth of the upper pipe is 5" from the muzzle, and the other two pipes are fixed at 14-1/16" and 22-7/8" from the breech, respectively, measuring to the front of each pipe. The one-piece scroll trigger guard with a flat-fronted bow and pinched-scroll grip has a separate trigger-plate, without a front finial. The bow is engraved with a line border and a shield trophy, and the top of the scroll is decorated with a very simple trophy. A rectangular octagon silver thumbpiece is inlaid across, rather than along, the wrist. The butt-trap cover measures 4-11/16" x 1-3/8", the hinge having a plain rounded front like the Pattern 1805 Baker rifle and similarly secured by a single woodscrew. The cover is opened by pressing a spring-activated button at the base of the buttplate tang. The lid is engraved with a large stag in woodlands with border lines and a flowerhead surrounding the hinge-plate screw. The two-step buttplate tang is 4-1/4" long, the plate measuring 5-1/4" from heel to toe and 2" across at its widest point.

The straight heavy wooden ramrod has a brass cap and a brass capped ball-screw at the tip.

PATTERN 1816 TATHAM INDIAN CHIEF'S RIFLE (RA XII-614) (Page 183)
Overall Length: 46-1/8"

BARREL: 30-9/16" straight tapered, 1.050" across breech, .960" across muzzle, fitted with a patent false-breech stepped on both sides. .56 calibre, rifled with 10 square grooves slightly narrower than the lands, making 1 turn in the length of the barrel. Barrel-retaining keys (slides) with oval silver keyplates at 7-3/8" and 11-1/16" from the break-off, measuring to the centre of each key.

The iron blade foresight is inlet into the barrel at the muzzle. The backsight is a block on a baseplate with one hinged leaf, dovetailed 6" from the break-off.

The top of the case-hardened patent breech, which has a platinum-lined vent, is inlaid with two gold lines across the rear and TATHAM over LONDON in gold.

A rectangular block is dovetailed into the top of the barrel ahead of the patent breech, measuring .730" x .660" and containing the Royal Coat of Arms in gold.

The browned twist-iron barrel is fitted with a rib 16-15/16" long with two plain cylindrical ramrod pipes each 1-3/16" long. The front of the upper pipe is 4-3/8" from the break-off, there is 5-3/16" between the two pipes, and 5-5/16" from the rear of the second pipe to the tail-pipe/fore-end cap.

The underside of the barrel is stamped with London Gunmakers' Company proofmarks, the initial S, and the number 1529.

LOCK: Flat lockplate with a squared tail inlaid flush with the surrounding wood, measuring 4-3/8" x 7/8". Fitted at the rear of the cock with a sliding safety catch. Double-fence gold-lined pan, roller fitted to the feather-spring. Flat bevelled edge so-called "French" cock. The tumbler is not detented. Ahead of the cock the plate is engraved "Tatham" in script. There is a single sidenail countersunk into an engraved circular cup.

STOCK: half length walnut. The comb is 9-1/2" long. A plain curved edge cheekpiece on the left side of the butt measures 6" x 3" but the measurements vary slightly. Distance from centre of trigger to centre of buttplate is 14-3/16". The wrist has flat chequering.

FURNITURE: of blued iron. Engraved nosecap with 2-3/16" tang extending to the rear, serving also as a tailpipe. The two-piece trigger guard has a flat-fronted bow and a scroll-grip in which the scroll is pinched together. The separate combined trigger-plate and finial terminates in a medium-sized engraved pineapple. A shield trophy is engraved on the guard bow. The guard is secured at the rear by a woodscrew just ahead of the pointed rear finial. A rectangular octagon silver thumbpiece is inlaid across, rather than along, the wrist. The butt-trap cover measures 4-5/8" x 1-7/16", the hinge having a plain rounded front like the Pattern 1805 Baker rifle. A spring-activated button release catch for the cover is fitted into the buttplate tang. The cover is engraved with a wide wheatear border design, the central motif being a standing stag; the hinge-plate has a large flowerhead engraved around the central securing screw. The three-step buttplate tang is 4-9/16" long, the plate measuring 5" from heel to toe and 2" across at its widest point.

The tapered wooden ramrod has a horn cap and a brass capped ball-screw at the tip.

PATTERN 1816 TATHAM INDIAN WARRIOR'S PRESENTATION RIFLE (RA XII-1569) (Page 185)
Overall Length: 46-1/2"

BARREL: 31-1/16" slightly swamped, 1.070" across breech, .950" across muzzle, and .930" 4" from muzzle. .58 calibre, rifled with 10 square grooves making 1 turn in 26-1/2". Fitted with a patent false breech, the break-off engraved with a border and trophy of arms. Barrel-retaining keys (slides) without keyplates at 6-11/16", 17-7/16" and 22-3/8" from the break-off, measuring to the centre of each key.

The iron blade foresight is inlet into the barrel at the muzzle. The backsight is a block on a baseplate with one hinged leaf, dovetailed 6-1/4" from the break-off.

The top of the patent breech is inlaid with a platinum line on either side of a rectangular block dovetailed into the top, measuring .730" x .660" containing the Royal Coat of Arms in gold.

The underside of the browned twist-iron barrel is stamped with London commercial proofmarks, and the number 1512.

LOCK: Flat bevelled-edge lockplate with a stepped tail, measuring 4-11/16" x .81". Fitted to the rear of the cock with a sliding safety catch. Raised pan, roller fitted to feather-spring. Flat bevelled edge swan-neck cock. The tumbler is detented. Ahead of the cock is engraved Tatham in script.

There is a single sidenail countersunk into a plain narrow circular cup.

STOCK: full length walnut, to the muzzle. Comb is 8-5/8" long. A plain curved edge cheekpiece on the left side of the butt measures 6" x 3" but the measurements vary slightly between examples. Distance from centre of trigger to centre of buttplate is 14-3/16". The ramrod channel is .450" in diameter. The wrist has flat chequering.

FURNITURE: of blued iron, except for a plain rounded horn nosecap, consists of two collared ramrod pipes 1-1/4" long, and a collared tailpipe with tang 2-1/4" overall. The middle pipe is pinned 19-3/16" from the break-off and the upper pipe 26-13/16" from the break-off, the tailpipe being secured by an internal screw from the barrel-bed. The two-piece scroll trigger guard has a separate combined trigger plate and front finial terminating in a small pineapple and secured at the rear by a woodscrew just ahead of the pointed rear finial. The bow is engraved with a border and a shield trophy, and the top of the scroll is decorated with a sunburst. A rectangular octagon silver thumbpiece is inlaid across, rather than along, the wrist. The butt-trap cover measures 5-3/8" x 1-9/16" including the opening tab at the rear, the hinge having a plain rounded front like the Pattern 1805 Baker rifle. The lid is engraved with an unusual trophy design, the central shield having a tipi-like motif. Stamped on the inner surface with the number 315. The three-step buttplate tang is 3-13/16" long, the plate measuring 5-1/8" from heel to toe and 2" across at its widest point.

The tapered wooden ramrod has a horn cap and a brass capped ball-screw at the tip.

1820s LACY & CO. INDIAN PRESENTATION RIFLE (RA XII-3009) (Page 187)
Overall Length: 46-3/4"

BARREL: 31-5/16" tapered octagon, .970" across breech, .900" across muzzle. .52 calibre, rifled with 7 square grooves half the width of the lands, making one-half turn in the barrel. Plain breech. Barrel-retaining pins without plates at 8-3/16", 18-1/16" and 27-3/4" from the breech.

The iron blade foresight is dovetailed into the barrel 9/16" from the muzzle. The plain block backsight is dovetailed into the barrel 6" from the breech. Birmingham 1813 commercial proofmarks are stamped on the left flat at the breech. The plain-iron barrel is finished blue.

LOCK: Flat bevelled-edge lockplate with stepped squared tail, measuring 5-1/2" x 1-1/8". Plain teaspoon-shaped pan, roller fitted to the feather-spring. Flat bevelled edge swan-neck cock. The tumbler is not detented. Ahead of the cock is stamped LACY & CO. over LONDON.

There are two sidenails with bevelled heads not countersunk into the sidepiece.

— 210 —

STOCK: full length walnut, to the muzzle. The comb is 9-1/2" long. A plain curved edge cheekpiece on the left side of the butt measures 6-3/8" x 2-1/2" but the measurements vary slightly. Distance from centre of trigger to centre of buttplate is 14-3/16". The ramrod channel is .370" in diameter and is stamped I.K. The underside of the butt from the rear finial of the trigger guard to the toe of the buttplate is flat. The right side of the butt is stamped with the Broad Arrow over B.O. and there is also a post-1859 III C.R. [Third Class Reserve] stamp.

FURNITURE: of brass and of American longrifle pattern. Plain nosecap 15/16" long, two collared and faceted ramrod pipes 1-7/8" long and matching tailpipe with flat-ended finial, each held by two pins 1-1/4" apart. The trigger guard with grip rail is 8-5/8" long, held by a pin 2" from the front finial and another 1/2" from the rear finial; these finials are flat ended, with longitudinal facets and transverse grooves. The bow has three longitudinal facets. The sidepiece is flat with a fine bevelled edge and in addition to the two sidenails there is a woodscrew through the flat-ended tail. The buttplate tang is 2-1/4" long, flat-ended with three facets and transverse grooves; the plate measures 4-5/8" from heel to toe and 1-7/8" across at its widest point. The toe is flat to match the underside of the butt.

The steel ramrod is tapered, with a button head.

INDIAN PRESENTATION RIFLE BY ROBERT WHEELER (RA XII-3008) (Page 187)
Overall Length: 47"

BARREL: 31-1/16" slightly tapered, 1" across breech, .870" across muzzle..53 calibre, rifled with 7 narrow square grooves 1/3 the width of the lands, making one-half turn in the length of the barrel. Plain breech. Barrel-retaining pins without plates at 11-1/8", 17-1/4" and 28-9/16" from the breech.

The iron blade foresight is dovetailed into the barrel 3/8" from the muzzle. The plain block backsight is dovetailed 6-1/4" from the breech.

Birmingham 1813 commercial proof-marks and a small crowned IR are stamped on the left flat at the breech. The barrel is finished blue.

LOCK: Flat bevelled-edge lockplate with a stepped tail, measuring 4-7/8" x 1-1/4". Plain teaspoon-shaped pan. Flat bevelled edge swan-neck cock. Ahead of the cock is stamped WHEELER in block letters.

The two sidenails not countersunk in the sidepiece.

STOCK: full length walnut, to the muzzle. The comb is 10-1/2" long. A plain curved edge cheekpiece on the left side of the butt measures 6-1/4" x 2-1/4" but the measurements vary slightly. Distance from centre of trigger to centre of buttplate is 13-7/8". The ramrod channel is 3/8" in diameter. The distance from the nosecap to the front of the tailpipe is 19-1/4".

FURNITURE: of brass and mostly of Baker rifle design. The nose cap is of Baker pattern as is the 3-1/2" trumpet forepipe. The 3" tailpipe is collared and barrel-shaped. The trigger guard is of typical Baker pattern, 8-3/4" long and secured by two pins. The sidepiece is of the same American pattern as on the Lacy & Co. example. The butt-trap cover is of Baker design and measures 4-5/8" x 1-1/2" including the opening tab at the rear. The buttplate tang is 2-1/4" long, the plate measuring 4-7/8" from heel to toe and 1-7/8" across at its widest point.

The steel ramrod is a Baker rod.

APPENDIX 2
British Rifle Gunmakers

The makers of the rifles purchased by the Board of Ordnance in 1746, and by Colonel James Prevost in 1756 remain unidentified at the time of writing. All that can be said with reasonable certainty is that they originated in the German States, and most likely in one of the larger centres specializing in military arms, e.g. Suhl or Zella Mehlis.

The six firms who manufactured rifles for the Board of Ordnance between 1762 and 1777 were located in Birmingham and London, England, and the city of Hanover, in the electorate of Hanover, Germany. Two other gunmakers supplied Indian-trade rifles to the American Department who shipped them to America with other Indian-trade goods, and both these were located in London.

The numbers of rifles supplied by each firm was very small, and the following information on each of the makers will help to place them in the wider context of their general gunmaking activity.

Not included in the list below are Board of Ordnance contractors who made no particular contribution to British rifle design or production, but who simply produced standard pattern (in this case Baker infantry) rifles.

BAKER, Ezekiel. London. (*1758–1836+). Apprenticed to Henry Nock, and worked for him until c.1787. Established himself as a gun-barrel maker in 1789 with premises at 8 Fieldgate St. until moving to 23 Little Alie St. in 1791, from which time he made civilian small arms. How he managed to bring himself to the attention of the Board of Ordnance with regard to the design of rifle barrels is not known; between 1794 and 1798 he had only performed barrel-repair work for the Board, and from March 1798 he also supplied complete Short Land Pattern muskets. In a series of trials in 1800 against other makers such as Egg and Nock his barrels were chosen for the new infantry rifle. He delivered his first rifles to the Board in April 1800. In 1801 the first edition of his book Remarks on Rifle Guns was published; the eleventh edition appeared in 1835, one year before his death. He remained at Alie St. until 1804, by which time he had seen his rifle barrel adopted as the Government pattern for both infantry and cavalry rifles. How much of the remainder of the weapon known by collectors as "the Baker rifle" was actually designed by Baker is unknown. He was also a contractor to the East India Company from 1803 to 1822, and they adopted several useful Baker improvements to the locks of their service arms. In 1804 he moved to 24 Whitechapel Road where he remained until his death. From 1823 he operated as Baker & Son, with both his wife Elizabeth and son Ezekiel John taking the leading role at various periods.

BARKER & WHATELY. Birmingham. Matthias (Matthew) Barker and John Whately (1746–22 July 1794+) formed a partnership for the manufacture of guns, gun-barrels, and the selling of them, in 1775, which was dissolved in 1785. Their premises for the joint operation was at 16 Catherine Street. The bulk of their production was in the "export" market, medium to low-quality fowling pieces, pistols and trade guns. Barker was operating as a gunstocker at least as early as 1755, and became a contractor for barrels to the Board of Ordnance in partnership with Joseph Harris from 9 Jan. 1762 until 20 May 1775. The partnership with John Whately made its first delivery of barrels in October, 1775, with further deliveries until November, 1782. John Whately was a member of a large gunmaking family, a bewildering number of whom were named John. Our subject was a gun-barrel maker, with premises in Smallbrook Street, who became a major barrel contractor to the Board of Ordnance from 28 October 1756. He also supplied a few locks in the early 1760s. The firm continued to supply barrels during the operation of the quite separate partnership with Matthias Barker. From December, 1775, Whately & Son also supplied locks to the Board. After the dissolution of the partnership with Barker he is described as a gunmaker and dealer in metals located in Whittall Street.

The partnership supplied the Board of Ordnance with 200 Pattern 1776 rifles and 25 Ferguson rifles. These were stamped on the left upper sides of the barrels at the breech with the partnership's mark, the letters MB & IW in three lines.

BARNETT, Robert. London. From Kirkby Stephen, Westmoreland. Founder of the Barnett dynasty of gunmakers. Initially apprenticed to William Birkell in 1735, but turned over to Richard Wilson (whose family also came from Kirkby Stephen) to complete his time, in 1737. Made free of the Gunmaker's Company of London in 1742, but did not submit a proofpiece or receive his maker's mark (an asterisk over RB in imitation of Wilson's mark) until 1759. It is assumed from arms bearing his mark internally and Wilson's externally, that he continued to work for Wilson as a journeyman between 1742 and 1759, setting-up for himself by 1765 next door to Wilson, at 157, Minories. He retired from business due to ill health in 1781. Barnett supplied Lancaster-pattern longrifles to the exact pattern also manufactured by his neighbour William Wilson and by Grice & Son, for the American Department, who shipped them to Quebec and Pensacola with other official Indian-gift goods.

EGG, Durs. London. (*1748–1831+). One of the finest London gunmakers in the period 1775–1820. Born in Oberbuchsiten, Switzerland, arrived in London in around 1768–70, initially working for Henry Nock. He had set up independently at Panton Street, Haymarket by 1772, where he made the two pattern Ferguson rifles for the Board of Ordnance in April–May, 1776. Judging from the number of surviving examples, Egg was the principal manufacturer of rifles on Ferguson's design, including a number of officer's rifles and carbines, and a silver-mounted example for the Prince of Wales (later George IV.) in 1784. He did not supply any of the regulation pattern military rifles to the Ordnance. He supplied a small series of Crespi-system breech-loading carbines to the Ordnance for troop trials in 1784–5, but did not become a regular contractor to the Board until 1793, from which time he performed a variety of services including the supply of military-pattern trade arms, edged weapons, rifled barrels, rifles, and virtually all patterns of current regulation arms including Short Land muskets and more than 32,000 India Pattern muskets and carbines. He produced a wide variety of military-style muskets, carbines, rifles and pistols for the many Volunteer and Yeomanry units raised between 1793 and 1815.

GALTON & SON, Samuel. Birmingham. The partnership of Samuel Galton (*1720–1799+) and his son Samuel John Galton junior (*1753–1832+) was formed in 1774, after the death of James Farmer in 1773 terminated the previous partnership of Farmer & Galton. Their chief premises were at 84 Steelhouse Lane, with warehouses in London, Bristol and Liverpool. Their chief markets were for export, and for the slave trade. The mark used on military components was a simple SG, SGS or sometimes SG&S. The Galton family left gunmaking in 1818.

The previous partnership had been contractors to the Board of Ordnance, and when materials were again needed at the outbreak of war in 1775, the new partnership again became contractors from 21 April 1775 for barrels, locks, steel rammers and from April, 1778, bayonets. The only complete arms supplied during our period were 200 Pattern 1776 rifles and 25 Ferguson rifles during 1776.

GRICE & SON, William. Birmingham. William Grice was the son of a Handsworth gun-barrel forger, John Grice. He was apprenticed to the Birmingham gunlock maker John Smith on 7 November 1730 for the traditional seven years. Father and son executed a single contract for carbines and pistols for the Board of Ordnance in 1742-3. No information concerning Grice's activities between 1743 and 1756 has emerged at the time of writing, but a number of weapons signed by him suggest a wide market from middle-quality silver-inlaid pieces to low quality export and slave-trade weapons. Multi-barrelled, breech-loading and rifled weapons, as well as sword-pistols, indicate above-average skills, although thefinish is not of high quality even for the period. By 1759 his premises were at 43 Bull Street, but by 1774 they were at 5 Sand Street. He unsuccessfully contested John Waters' 1781 patent for the spring-bayonet. Grice died on 25 July 1790.

William Grice formed a partnership with Richard Edge gunlock maker of Wednesbury in 1756, to supply locks to the Board of Ordnance. A new partnership, William Grice and Son, became contractors to the Board from 7 April 1760, for the supply of barrels, locks and steel rammers. Grice was credited by the Ordnance with introducing the steel, as opposed to the iron, ramrod, unfortunately with no date indicated. Between May, 1772, and November, 1782, they supplied only gunlocks, steel rammers and some smallwork, apart from an unsuccessful pattern rifle and the 200 Pattern 1776 rifles and 25 Ferguson rifles supplied during 1776.

In 1782 he went into partnership with Joseph Grice his nephew (as Grice & Son again) until 1789. Although no documentary evidence has thus far come to light in support, the dating sequences and firm styles suggest the possibility of a second generation William Grice commencing in business in 1770 and being the manufacturer of the Indian rifles in question as well as contractor to the Board of Ordnance during the American War period. No changes in the markings used throughout shed any light on this possibility. On complete weapons Grice used a barrel marking of a crown over WG, while on barrels supplied an asterisk over WG and for locks only the initials WG struck on the inside of the lockplate. William Grice died 25 July 1790.

HIRST, John. London. (working 1744–1776+) Served his apprenticeship under Jonathan Heron, gunmaker in Darton, Yorkshire, came to London in the early 1740s and worked for William Clarke, a gun-barrel contractor to the Board of Ordnance. Located at the sign of the Two Crossed Guns between Little Tower Hill and East Smithfield by 1744. Developed a large-scale general middle-quality trade in the typical variety of mid-18th-century firearms. Became a contractor to the Board of Ordnance for setting up arms on 22 October 1745, and from 1757 to 1776 held a virtual monopoly in this area of the manufacturing process. The five breech-loading rifles which he supplied to the Ordnance in 1762, were probably from his stock in hand, while the subsequent 20 supplied in 1764 were clearly to an approved pattern. These are the first rifles supplied to the Ordnance for which a maker is clearly documented. Became a contractor to the East India Company in 1772.

HUHNSTOCK, August Heinrich. Hanover. Judging from the three sporting rifles, two pairs of rifled pistol-carbines and a pair of rifled pistols by him in the Royal Collection at Windsor Castle, Huhnstock was a maker well-known to the British Establishment for the manufacture of rifled arms by the time he was selected by Col. William Faucitt to furnish patterns for military rifles to the Board of Ordnance in late 1775. He is believed to have continued working into the mid-1790s. Known pieces are signed on the locks A. Huhnstock or simply, Huhnstock, and on the barrels, A Hannover. Huhnstock supplied at least two pattern rifles which became the basis for the Pattern 1776 rifle, almost certainly including the innovative swivel, or captive, ramrod, in the autumn of 1775, and delivered 200 rifles to the final pattern in the early summer of 1776.

TATHAM, Henry senior. (*1770–1835+) was born at Frith St. Soho, London. He is first described as a sword cutler in 1798, and as a gunmaker from 1799, at the time of his appointment as such to the Prince of Wales, working at 37 Charing Cross. In an insurance policy dated 21 Feb. 1799 covering £1000 worth of property, his address is given as "at the corner of Buckingham Court and Charing Cross." His earliest work for the Board of Ordnance was supplying an order of 100 Malayan kris at 9/- each in May 1801. He formed a partnership with Joseph Egg in 1801, which was dissolved in 1814, just before Tatham was employed to supply a series of sporting rifles for presentation to Canadian Indians in British service. At least two rifles of the over/under type are known with Joseph Egg's signature on them. Tatham & Egg also had premises at 60 Frith St. between 1805–08, which may have been workshops. From 1814 Tatham continued in business on his own until 1824 when his son Henry junior joined the firm. Henry senior died in 1835 and junior carried on the business until 1860.

WILLETTS, Benjamin. Birmingham and Wednesbury. Member of a gunmaking family active since at least 1742 and until at least 1870. Believed to be the son of John, a contractor to the Board of Ordnance 1742-57 for barrels and locks. Benjamin became a contractor to the Board on 14 April 1769 for barrels and locks, holding the position, with a break between 1782 and 1793, until February, 1795. The complete rifles supplied during 1776 totalled 200 Pattern 1776 and 25 Ferguson rifles. His Birmingham premises were in Whittall Street. Barrels were stamped with an asterisk over BW and the interior surface of lockplates simply BW.

WILSON, William. London. (*1732–1808+) Son of Richard Wilson, under whom he served his apprenticeship 1747–54. Made a partner in the firm 1755, and took over at Richard's death in 1766. Traded as Wilson & Co. at his father's address of 154, Minories. He continued to use his father's mark, an asterisk over RW, and continued to sign locks merely WILSON in a variety of styles from plain block-letters to copperplate script. He also continued his father's broad range of mass-produced firearms for the lower part of the civilian trade, and for the upper segment of the export trade, especially the North American Indian trade and that for the Hudson's Bay Company; he also continued to be a contractor to the East India Company. In addition to several civilian Ferguson rifles, he also made a number of Lorenzoni-type magazine breech-loading arms exhibiting a high degree of skill and finish. Held a monopoly for the supply of Indian trade guns to the Board of Trade during the American War, and supplied them with three qualities of longrifles on the early Lancaster pattern. The barrels of these rifles bear Wilson's mark, and proofmarks which are either deliberate attempts at faking London marks, or private Birmingham marks, perhaps both. Richard Wilson and his son William operated probably the largest-scale gunmaking business in London during the period 1750–1790.

Richard Wilson, as an important and active official of the Gunmaker's Company, frequently incurred the displeasure of the Board of Ordnance, and was not as a result one of their important contractors. He set up arms between 1746 and 1749, and again between 1756 and 1761. William inherited the Board's aversion, and his work as setter-up between April, 1777, and 1780 was not significant. His primary service to Government was in supplying arms for the "official" Indian trade.

Note: It is a curious fact that none of the four contractors employed by the Board of Ordnance to supply muzzle- and breech-loading rifles during 1776 had ever been contractors for the supply of complete arms, or setters up, but were in each case suppliers of iron components: barrels, locks, rammers, &c. Apart from barrels and locks which invariably bear the markings of one of the four contractors, there is no evidence, documentary or artifactual, to suggest which subcontractors supplied the brasswork, smallwork, or did the rough stocking and setting up of the rifles.

APPENDIX 3

The Composition of Ferguson's Force at King's Mountain, 7 October 1780

The troops commanded by Major Patrick Ferguson at King's Mountain in October 1780 were entirely Loyalist in origin. His own small unit, which was organized shortly before the Charleston Expedition embarked, consisted of volunteers from Fanning's King's American Regiment, Brown's Prince of Wales's American Volunteers, Robinson's Loyal American Regiment, Axtell's Nassau Blues, (in which Frederick DePeyster was a Captain at one point), Ludlow's 3rd Battalion of DeLancey's Brigade, and the 1st (Barton's), 2nd (Morris's) and 4th (Van Buskirk's) battalions of Skinner's New Jersey Volunteers. This unit was sometimes referred to as the American Volunteers, but generally simply as Ferguson's Corps, which adds to the confusion since the much larger force of locally raised militia is also referred to as Ferguson's Corps. Capt. Abraham De Peyster, noted in his Orderly Book on 14 January 1780, while the troops were still at sea:

One half of the Non Comd Off and Privates of each Detacht who are the most active and best Marksmen, to be fixed upon today by the Officers Comd in order the Inst we land to act as rangers, the front Rank of whom are to have Firelocks; the rear Rifles.

A few days later, on 21 January, he described the composition of the detachments.

The Detacht to be form'd in future with four Divisions.

The K A R and 3rd B Delancys to compose the first or light Division under Capt [-Lieut Abraham] Depeyster. [King's American Regt]

The P Wales & 2 Batt N J V the Second Divn under Capt [-Lieut. Charles] McNeil.[Prince of Wales's American Volunteers]

The 4th Battn N J V the Third under Capt [Samuel] Ryerson. [3/NJV] and the 1st Batt N J V Loyal A Regt and Nassau Blues the fourth or left Division Under Capt Dunlop.[not yet identified]

When formed for action the Comd Officer to be in the center of the front rank of each Division and the Soldiers at all times to rally to him accordingly.

The second in Comd with one half of the officers and all the serjts to be in the rear of the Division the remaining officers on the flanks and Corporals in the Ranks. Close (or charging) order the files to be as near as may be without Touching.

Common (or firing) order the files three feet interval or at arms length.

Open (or skirmishing) order four Yards Interval or twice the length of a Man between the files. [NYHS, De Peyster Papers, vol. 1741–1836, n.p.]

In tabular form the above description breaks down as follows:

First (light) Division Capt Abraham DePeyster (KAR)	Second Division Capt Charles McNeil (PoWAV)	Third Division Capt Stephen Ryerson (3/NJV)	Fourth (left) Division Capt Dunlap
Kings Amer Regt 3rd DeLanceys	PoW Amer Vols. 2nd N.J.V.	4th Bn N.J.V.	1st Bn N.J.V. Nassau Blues Loy Amer Regt

and DePeyster states that half of the NCOs and men from the above unit were to be organized and used as rangers, the rear rank carrying rifles. The sub-unit, christened the American Volunteers but never officially described as such in surviving records, was sent to Savannah under Ferguson's command very shortly after the British forces landed. Allaire records that the unit left Savannah with other troops and began a northward march on Sunday 5 March 1780, via Charleston, which ended for the Volunteers on 7 Oct. at King's Mountain.

Two returns for Ferguson's ad hoc unit indicate its size during the campaign:

	Maj.	*Subalterns*	*Serjts*	*Corpls*	*Drummers*	*Rank & File*
1 Apr 1780	1	7	12	5	2	157
1 Oct 1780	1	4	9	3	1	122

Thus, a week before the battle, the American Volunteers mustered 140 on the ground, but a participating officer, Lieut. Anthony Allaire [Loyal American Regt], states that the American Volunteers went into the battle on 7 Oct. only seventy strong.

Muster rolls of the participating regiments partly indicate men seconded to serve with Ferguson: they reveal 14 privates, 1 serjeant, Lieuts. Duncan Fletcher and Anthony Allaire (the diarist) from the Loyal American Regiment, and 3 privates (including a drummer) from the King's American Regiment. If the tactical arrangements delineated by Capt. Abraham DePeyster on 21 January were still in force, it may be assumed that up to about half of the 70 rank and file may have carried rifles. Since there is no evidence for the withdrawal of the Ferguson rifles from the men to whom they had been originally issued, and who after 12 Sept. 1777 were serving in their various parent companies brigaded in the two Light Infantry Battalions comprised of regular line regiments, there is no reason to believe that rifles other than the Pattern 1776 muzzle-loading rifles were in the hands of these loyalist soldiers.

This core unit of provincial officers and soldiers was supplemented by a large force of South and North Carolina militia. On 31 May 1780 there were "Issued to Major Ferguson per order 300 serviceable French muskets and bayonets and 50 sea service swords" which goes some way towards indicating what the militia forces being raised by Ferguson were armed with at this stage of the campaign. Lord Rawdon mentioned in a letter of 24 October that Ferguson had marched "with about 800 militia collected from the neighbourhood of Ninety-Six", and this is borne out by the surviving muster rolls of a variety of militia units:

Col. John Cotton's Regt., Stevenson's Creek Militia, 96 Brigade: Capt. Henry Rudolph's company = 1 Capt., 1 ensign, 53 privates.

Major Patrick Cunningham's Regt., Little River Militia, 96 Brigade: 36 privates.

Capt. William Payne's company = 1 ensign, 10 privates.

Capt. William Helm's company = 2 captains, 1 ensign, 9 privates.

Capt. Andrew Cunningham's company = 1 capt., 1 adjutant, 45 privates.

Lieut. Col. Zachariah Gibbs' Regt., Spartan Militia, 96 Brigade = 1 major, 1 captain, 17 privates.

Lieut. Samuel Young's company = 1 lieut., 40 privates.

Capt. Joseph Gibbs' company = 1 major, 1 captain, 4 privates.

Lieut. Richard May's company = 7 privates.

Major Daniel Plummer's Regt., Fair Forest Militia = 1 capt., 2 ensigns, 1 adjutant, 19 privates.

The above men are all specifically stated as serving under Major Ferguson for periods covering the Battle of Kings Mountain, and show a total of 20 officers and 237 privates. Daniel Plummer is believed to have commanded all the South Carolina militia which mustered about 320–356 men. Colonel Ambrose Mills is believed to have commanded the slightly more numerous but fatally unreliable North Carolina militia which mustered between 430 and 450 men.

Whether any of the North and South Carolina militia were armed with rifles is unknown, but virtually every account of the battle describes the repeated driving back of the rifle-armed rebel frontiersmen by the musket and bayonet armed troops on the hill; rifles as such are not mentioned amongst the loyalist forces, except as follows.

Captain Abraham DePeyster, Ferguson's second in command at King's Mountain, sent a report of the battle to Lord Cornwallis, from captivity, which sheds some light on the performance of the Loyalist force:

Camp near Gilbert Town, 11 Oct. 1780
I am sorry to acquaint your Lordship that on the 7th instant, Major Ferguson was attack near King Mountain by a body of the enemy. Their numbers enabled them to surround our post and ours was only sufficient to form a single line on the top of the hill. The action lasted an hour and five minutes, when the North Carolina Militia, who were entirely commanded by their own officers on the right, gave way, which not only discouraged the other Regiments, but drove them down the hill before them. Our little detachment of soldiers charged the enemy with success and drove the right wing of them back in confusion, but unfortunately, Major Ferguson made a signal for us to retreat being afraid that the enemy would get possession of the height from the opposite side. The militia being ignorant of the cause of our retreat, it threw the few that stood their post under the officers from Ninety-Six into disorder. Tho the officers cut some of them down, they intermixed themselves with our detachment, and broke us in such a manner that we could no longer act, being then reduced to two sergeants and twenty rifles. The left on seeing us broke, gave way, got all in a crowd on the hill and tho every officer used his endeavours to rally the men, as nothing now offered but to make a breach through the enemy; I am sorry to say was not able to get a man to follow them. The chief part being without ammunition, excepting four men that followed Major Ferguson, while the other officers were doing their best amongst the crowd to collect more to follow them; but I am sorry to say Major Ferguson was killed before he advanced 20 yards. Ensign MacGinnes of Colonel Allen's Corps [Richard McInnes of Captain Hunloke's company, 3/NJV] was also killed soon after the action commenced which rendered the militia he commanded almost useless. In this situation and the small body of soldiers we had being cut up, and finding it impossible to rally the militia, I thought proper to surrender as the only means of saving the lives of some brave men still left. In justice to the officers and men, I must beg leave to acquaint your Lordship that they

behaved with the greatest gallantry and attention, even to a wish; as to the militia, there were many of them both officers and men, who tho the enemy was still within a hundred yards round us, that behaved with a degree of gallantry.

[PRO30/11, 3, 210.]

DePeyster's use of the term rifle in a context where the conventional words would have been muskets or bayonets or even men suggests a specific reference rather than a general one, but still cannot be certainly taken to mean that their remaining force amounted to twenty rifle-armed men. That there were some rifles is suggested by the use of the word in this context, and by the original formation of the unit. DePeyster places the blame for the beginning of tactical disintegration on the North Carolina militia, with a particular reference to the fact that they lacked competent officers, and also indicates that Ferguson's order for a tactical withdrawal up the hill was, at least, mis-timed. He likewise praises the Ninety-Six militia for standing fast.

The other Loyalist participant who left a record of the battle was Lieut. Anthony Allaire of the Loyal American Regiment. The similarities of his report of the 7th October to some parts of DePeyster's letter may mean that Allaire saw that letter before writing up his diary, but he does add further details as to the composition of the forces on the day. He states that Ferguson's force totalled 800 men. Importantly he mentions that "our poor little detachment, which consisted of only seventy men when we marched to the field of action, were all killed and wounded but twenty...", which tallies with DePeyster's statement, but indicates that the American Volunteers had lost half their strength from the last surviving return on 1 October. Allaire states that the American Volunteers lost 18 men killed on the spot, with Capt. Ryerson and 32 privates wounded; he confirms the death of Lieut. McInnes, and says that 2 captains, 4 lieutenants, 3 ensigns and 1 surgeon (Dr. Johnson) were taken prisoners along with 54 serjeants and rank and file, including "the mounted men under the command of Lieut. [James] Taylor".[1/NJV] He says there were 100 militia killed and 90 wounded, some 600 being taken prisoners. In describing the hanging of militia officers after the battle he mentions Lieut. Col. Mills, and Captains Wilson and Chitwood all of whom died, six others being reprieved. Other officers captured included Lieut. Stevenson. [*Diary of Lieut. Anthony Allaire of Ferguson's Corps,* 31.]

APPENDIX 4

Muster Roll of Queen's Rangers Rifle Company first muster, 25 October 1780

Captain	Aeneas Shaw	
Lieutenant	Andrew McCan	
Ensign	(vacant)	William Callender 25 June 81, Charles Matheson 7 Aug. 1781

Serjeant	Thomas Collins	
Serjeant	John Finch	transferred
Serjeant	Henry Rutter	
Serjeant	John King	promoted

Corporal	James Brown
Corporal	Lott Patterson
Corporal	Aaron Olmstead

Drummer   John Ranger

PRIVATES

Thomas O'Niel	Charles Hazelton	Jonathan Richards
Thomas Thoeburn	George Myers	Daniel O'Hara
Nathaniel Bloodworth	Thomas Dean	James MacFerlin
Joseph Lupton	Thomas Smith	James Dunn
Thomas Dunnahoe	John Smith	George Smith
John Bard	Joseph Dayton	Adam MacColgan
William Parr	Thomas Shawford	
William Kelley	Daniel McMahon	
John Dayton	James Gordon	
John Seryver	George Tucker	

Thomas Patterson	enlisted	7 Oct. 1780
James Summers	"	7 Oct. 1780
John Gill	"	9 Oct. 1780
Nathaniel Church		
Josephus Broomhead	"	26 Oct. 1780
John Hamilton	"	26 Oct. 1780
Samuel Boswell	"	26 Nov. 1780

The number of privates listed, 33, tallies exactly with the number of rifles issued to them.

Captain Aeneas Shaw had previously been a Lieutenant in John McKay's Highland Company, and was so carried on muster rolls until 25 Oct. 1780.

Serjeant Duncan McPherson, to whom Simcoe makes several references as being the serjeant of this company, leading them, and being killed with them on 29 June 1781, was always mustered as the senior serjeant of McKay's company, and is never shown in Shaw's rifle company.

Source: Public Archives of Canada, Record Group 81, C series, vol. 1863 (quoted in Murtie J. Clark, II, 536–543.

APPENDIX 5

Muster Roll of New York Volunteer Rifle Company 24 December 1780 – 23 February 1781

No location given

Captain	John Althause
Lieutenant	John Ludwig von Beck
Ensign	John Althause jun.
Serjeant	Donald McNeil
Serjeant	John Stone died 17 Oct. 1781
Serjeant	James McCuin
Corporal	Andrew Kelsey deserted 19 Mar. 81
Corporal	Ludwig Eiseman " 14 July 81
Drummer	John Shelt

PRIVATES

James Britain			Michael Ryan	des. 30 May 81
William Deats			Thomas Quaint	dead 15 Aug. 81
Jacob Busby			Jeremiah McCarty	des. 7 Mar. 81
William Ross (Boss)	des. 27 May 81			
William Hickman			William Walker	
Isaac Deal			Enoch Lewis	des. 19 Mar. 81
Christian Duraing (Duramo)	des. 14 July 81			
John Nichols			David Thomas	des. 19 Mar. 81
George Haynes			John Bryer	"
Benjamin Stivers			Gerhard Hammer	"
John Hurley			Henry Hearse	"
Faithful Luck	enlisted 17 July 81			
James Moore			Abraham Freeland	"
George Hinton			Henry Huthson	pris. 7 Jan. 81
Frederick Rousman			Antony Craser	" "
Allexander Collins			John Bursell	" 8 Jan. 81
Samuel Crowell			Jacob Muth	des. 14 Jan. 81
Robert Gaston			John Metzer	" "
John Sutton	died 9 June 82		William Hine	" 16 Jan. 81
			Charles Rounds	" 27 Jan. 81
			Stephen Ryan	" "
			John Stiels	" "
			George Smith	" 9 Feb. 81
			Francis Pilgo	" "
				and then joined 17 Aug. 81

Thomas King	enlisted 14 June 81, deserted 14 July 81
Nathaniel Duck	" 17 July 81
John Jonson	" 20 June 81
John Burrel	" 17 Aug. 81

20 deserters, 4 enlistees

Source: Public Archives of Canada, RF81, C series, vol. 1874.

APPENDIX 6
British Pattern 1776 and Ferguson Rifle Performance Judged by Test Firing Modern Replicas

Thanks to the engineering and gunsmithing skills of Ernest E. Cowen and Richard Keller we are able to examine in some detail the potential of the British and German rifles used during the American War. I am most grateful to them both for sharing this information with me, and being allowed to present it as part of this study of Britain's flintlock military rifles.

These trials have confirmed what most modern "black-powder" shooters will be aware of, that after a small number of rounds (i.e. about half a dozen) have been fired without cleaning the bore, the accuracy falls off significantly, and further that the design of the Ferguson breech causes the breechloading mechanism to become significantly fouled if not frequently cleaned.

The first of these results applies to any breechloader using gunpowder where there is no lubricant or 'sweeping' built into the loading procedure, while the second is unique to those designs where the moveable parts of the breech are in direct contact with the explosion of the propelling charge.

Whenever test firing is done with replica arms it has always to be borne in mind that, no matter how accurate the replica is in its internal and external details, there are a number of features which simply cannot duplicate the originals. Two are of universal application regardless of the type of arm being tested: (1) modern metals with different characteristics to the original forged iron are used in making the barrels; and (2) the gunpowder being used will differ from the original, if not in grain-size, then in virtually every other characteristic, complicated by our lack of detailed knowledge of the precise burning and pressure qualities of the original.

The Pattern 1776 Rifle

Several years ago the late Kit Ravenshear produced a limited number of reproductions of the P/76 rifle based on examination of all the then-known examples. After most of the work had been completed, a nearly new example of the rifle was discovered and the bore of my rifle was modified to conform to the measurements of this virtually un-fired barrel. The tests which I made with this rifle were fired from a bench with the muzzle rested at 50 and 100 yards. The charge consisted of 3 drams (82-1/2 grains) of an English powder called FO-triangle, officially classed as "Firework Powder" and which, though dirty burning, has been found to shoot closest to the sights on a variety of original flintlock rifles. The powder was loaded from a powder measure. The ball used was .615" diameter and the patching a blue denim material of .017" thickness measured with the micrometer turned as tightly as possible, crushing the material as it would be in the bore, and lubricated with spit. In loading the swivel ramrod was found to work beautifully and to make loading vastly quicker than with a separate ramrod: four smooth arm motions saw the rifle loaded. However, it is easy to see how the swivel screws could be broken or bent if the rod was pulled out too forcefully against the pressure of its retaining spring. The patched ball (square-cut patches with the four corners stitched over the ball) was seated flush with the muzzle and was a sufficiently loose fit in the bore that no separate starter was necessary over the ten-shot firing sequence: a single push seated the ball on the powder.

Loading in the manner described, groups at 50 yards averaged four inches, while those at 100 yards opened up to an average of ten inches. The point of this particular trial was to discover its accuracy potential, hence loading was not done from a paper cartridge.

The Ferguson Rifle

By way of a preamble to the shooting of the Ferguson, some years ago the present writer spent a day with Martin Williams firing his Griffin & Tow screw-plug breechloader of the "pre-Ferguson" style in which the breechplug, also attached to the trigger guard as on the Ferguson, is completely removed from the underside of the rifle to load it, there being no opening in the top of the barrel. In this earlier design the threads are not in contact with the chamber of the rifle, only the circular top of the plug forming a part of the lower wall of the chamber. This rifle was fired more than fifty times without once cleaning the threads of the breechplug and without any significant stiffening of its operation. However, after about the seventh round the accuracy at one-hundred yards deteriorated to the state where striking a man-size target could not be guaranteed. If the bore was cleaned out between shots the accuracy was maintained.

Shooting the Military Ferguson Rifle
by Richard H. Keller and Ernie E. Cowan

The Ferguson rifle, built in 1776 under the directions of Capt. Patrick Ferguson and brought to the United States in 1777, is one of the finest rifles built during the 18th century. It was born out of a need for a rifle which would offset the deadly accuracy of the American long rifle, which, early in the war, the British soldier feared.

The fact that Ferguson, in actual shooting demonstrations before Lord Townshend and King George III himself, was able to dispel all criticisms of the design and convince the British military of its reliability and advantages over any weapon of the day, speaks for itself. He proved the rifle to be even better than it's American counterpart in many ways. Not only was it equal in accuracy out to 200 yards, it had two other advantages not found in the long rifle. It mounted the all important bayonet and could be fired at a steady rate of 3 shots a minute even in the prone position. Thus the shooter did not need to expose any portion of himself to enemy fire while loading, even when caught in the open. Ferguson gives great testament to the advantage of using his rifle in the prone position, writing to his brother in October, 1777, "Such is the great advantage of an Arm that will admit of being loaded and fired on the ground without exposing the men- that I threw my people on the ground under pretty smart firing six times that morning without losing a man, although I had/part of these with me killed or wounded before I was disabled." Those mentioned as casualties were the accompanying light infantry not armed with rifles. The total casualties within his riflemen were only two men wounded, he being one of them, while Wymess's men, armed with muzzle loaders, suffered 17 casualties. Thus through the preservation of his men, Ferguson proved the value of his guns and the wisdom of the British Board of Ordnance in having them built.

In order to build an exact copy of this rifle, an original example had to be located. The only known original specimen of Ferguson's military rifle worldwide resides in the Morristown National Park in Morristown, New Jersey. Since this specimen is in its original unaltered condition, it was the perfect weapon for our project. It is serial number 2 of the 100 built, being one of 25 rifles made by Matthias Barker and John Whately on their contract.

Although many attempt have been made to reproduce this rifle, all have fallen short of the detail that makes the rifle successful, thus resulting in much undue criticism of a superb weapon. It was quickly learned that the key to the success of his rifle lies in its care in building. Each one was carefully hand crafted under Ferguson's keen eye, ultimately receiving his personal mark of acceptance of a crown/PF stamp on the breech. To faithfully recreate this rifle would require the same attention to meticulous detail as the original rifles.

In 1999, we undertook the task of reproducing Ferguson's rifle in the same manner it was done in 1776. Only then could his rifles receive a fair and honest evaluation. Using the Morristown gun as a sample, every minute detail became a reality in a perfectly hand crafted weapon equal in every respect to the original 100 rifles. In four months two rifles were completed, based upon the specifications of the Morristown gun. Devoid of all preconceived expectations, the gun was put through its trials, We soon discovered that if a gun was built exactly as the original 100, the resulting product would perform beyond anyone's expectations and justify the confidence placed in the weapon by both Ferguson and the British military.

The rifle does require special training as no other arm of its time. The average British soldier received inadequate training in firing at marks, and in fact was lucky to fire his musket with live ammunition more than a few times a year. Powder and lead were valuable commodities, and since aimed fire was too little required as part of a soldier's training, it was a new experience for the men into whose hands these first rifles were placed. The rifle required this training, and thus an expenditure of ammunition, resulting in a limited success in teaching his men to shoot accurately, as shown in a demonstration before the King. When his men failed to hit their marks, Ferguson picked up his rifle with a remark that he would not be so embarrassed before the King and his majesty's enemies, and successfully completed the demonstration with his usual coolness and impressive marksmanship. Although Ferguson was capable of firing 6 shots a minute in his demonstrations, he never extolled the advanced rate of firepower exhibited by his new weapon. He concentrated on training his men to take advantage of every bit of cover the terrain afforded them, and, if caught in the open, to fire from the prone position. In addition, he extensively trained his men in the use of the 25-inch sword bayonet specially designed by him. He called it the perfect cut and thrust weapon, being honed to a razor edge. Its size and design shows that it was intended to be used on or off the rifle.

The rifle weighs in at 7-1/2 pounds and has a perfect center of balance. It is very comfortable to carry and to shoot. It is .65 caliber, firing a round ball through a .648 bore. The rifling is 8 groove with a twist of 1 turn in 58 inches.

The key to the success of the rifle is the 70 thousandths bronze tapered plug which opens with one turn of the trigger guard to expose the chamber for loading. We are the first to build this rifle to the exact specifications of the original rifle using the all important 70 thousandths tapered bronze plug. ONLY with a correctly built gun can an honest and fair evaluation be made. The 11 start thread was hand cut on a specially made machine and then carefully fitted into the gun through the lapping process to form a perfect seal when closed, just as it was done in 1776. It takes about a day to lap in each plug, but if done properly, there is very little gas leakage. In fact, the shooter will not even know he is shooting a breech-loader. Even after 800 rounds fired in the test trials, there is no gas leakage to distract the shooter. This amount of shooting is probably far beyond any original rifle of the period would have experienced. The steep taper on the plug allows easy rotation once it breaks free from the seat in the top wall of the barrel, the ONLY place where fouling is any problem.

Bronze was used on the original plugs of Ferguson's Ordnance and East India Company (Nock) rifles for obvious reasons. Firstly, it will not bind with the iron barrel during periods of long storage; secondly, it will not rust into place under the harsh conditions of campaigning in the field where dampness and moisture can cause serious rusting in a very short time; thirdly, the bronze will cool at a quicker rate, thus enabling the plug to be opened more easily when the barrel becomes hot from shooting. The breechplug is the heart of the rifle, thus great care had to be taken for a proper fit. These plugs are not interchangeable between rifles, thus they were serial numbered to each rifle. Should shooting erode the plug to where it leaks gas, it would be a simple matter to fit another plug to the gun, but we have yet to experience any gas leakage, even with over 800 rounds having been fired through a rifle, and we estimate that over 2000 rounds could be fired before any gas leakage problem would occur. If properly maintained, the rifle could have a life span far beyond that of the musket.

The method of loading the Ferguson is very important. It is not simply a matter of pouring in powder to fill the entire chamber and then closing the plug, using the excess powder for priming. Ferguson certainly used this method when shooting 6 shots to impress an audience, but as mentioned above he did not practice nor teach speed of loading rapidly with his men. This type of loading rapidly fouls the upper portion of the threaded barrel wall, requiring a minor cleaning step to continue shooting. Ferguson did a quick cleaning of his rifle in front of Lord Townshend by soaking the lock and breech of a loaded rifle, then clearing it to resume fire in less than half a minute. This was a nice touch to clean the rifle as well as to impress his audience with the advantage his system had over a wet charge in a musket. The temperature and humidity have a lot to do with the rate of fouling. Damp warm days are better for shooting than dry cool weather. Pouring powder directly from a horn into a hot chamber is no recommended for safety of shooting under normal field use. The use of a rolled paper cartridge showed us that he and his men used a better, safer, and long-established method of loading in the field.

The chamber of a Ferguson rifle will hold 90 grains, but the actual shooting charge we used was 65 grains of a mixture of half and half 3FG and 4FG powder, which we believe was about equal to the German powder of the time. In 1776 "superfine double strength powder" supplied by a Kentish powder mill was used. It is important to remember that 18th-century powder used a different charcoal, burning with more moisture and resulting in a softer residue in the barrel, making fouling less of a problem.

Using a 90 grain charge produces excessive recoil and causes the gun to lose accuracy. We know from the equipment carried by his men that there were two methods of loading his rifle. Since they carried a cartridge box, they could use rolled cartridges. In addition they carried a 'ball-bag' on their belt for loose balls and a powder horn with a springcharger for priming and also loading with rifle with loose powder and ball if required. However, as stated above, this practice is dangerous and overcharges the gun, so it was probably only used when the supply of cartridges was exhausted. Use of the cartridge gives a measured charge-normally including priming- and allows the gun to perform at its best. Should the shooter run out of cartridges he can simply drop a lubricated ball into the chamber, pour in powder until the chamber is filled and then close the breech. From experience it was discovered that it was best to avoid pushing powder out the top of the gun when closing the plug. This excess powder becomes ground into the upper threaded portion of the breech, creating the only fouling problem with the system, but even that is not a serious one, being very easy to overcome. When using a 65 grain measured charge, the powder can be kept in the chamber if the plug is closed slowly and the gun kept tilted down.

Using a lubricated ball reduces bore fouling and keeps it soft. Each shot will clean the bore. Lead fouling has never been a problem even with pure lead. Balls should be lubricated with beeswax using a hot ball dipped into the melted wax, which puts a very thin coating on the ball and still allows for easy handling without a mess even if rolled into a cartridge. One interesting way the riflemen lubricated the balls in the field was to carry a piece of beeswax in their ball-bag with the loose balls, which when rolling about would pick up the residue from the wax. The breechplug should also carry a light coating of lubricant for storage; Ferguson mentions the use of a special grease for lubricating the rifles. [!]

If the rifle were to be carried loaded

for any length of time, the ball had to be seated firmly into the front of the chamber to keep it from backing out and allowing the powder to sift around the ball and into the bore. Considering the small stature of the soldier of that time, we believe every man was capable of performing this simple task with his little finger, just as we can easily do today if one is of comparable size with an 18th-century soldier.

Initial loading and immedite firing of the rifle does not require this step, nor does subsequent shooting until the chamber begins to foul. Depending on temperature and humidity, the extra length of the chamber will allow 12–15 shots without having to seat the ball. If the finger tip is too large, a small wooden loading tool can be made to do the trick. It is probable that, if Ferguson had the choosing of his trainees, he will have picked men capable of executing all these various functions.

The rifle can be fired comfortably at 3 to 4 times a minute even when using the little finger or a tool to seat the ball. Unfortunately no contemporary accounts exists of the actual loading method, but from our shooting experience one has to use the same common sense instilled even in the soldiers of their day. One can be certain that techniques were adopted and used just as quickly and simply as we do two centuries later. It was a problem that required a solution, and no doubt a simple solution was found. If the ball is seated to the front of the chamber, it can be carried indefinitely without removing it; at the end of the day the powder may be dumped from the chamber and new powder inserted when needed, even the next day. We have left a gun sit for three days with a ball in the chamber and then recharged it successfully.

A canteen of water will allow the rifle to be fired all day without a thorough cleaning. We have fired the gun thirty times or more before cleaning only the threaded upper portion of the breech. This is done by rotating the plug down about 1/8 inch (not enough to expose the chamber), and then either spitting on the threads or pouring just a little water onto the top of the plug and the threads, working it up and down a few times, then wiping it clean with a finger or a cloth. ANY time the plug starts to tighten-up this method will allow another 8 to 10 shots before repeating the procedure. The gun will never fail the shooter nor will it be put out of action due to fouling. This is where the steep taper on the plug is most important, since the ONLY fouling that will occur is in the upper breech area. Even with a fouled bore, accuracy is such that you can hit a 6–8-inch bull's-eye at 100 yards or a man-sized target at 200 yards, sufficient for the requirements of the day. Using a Ferguson in battle in 1777 would be equal to using the Model 1853 .577 Enfield Rifle Musket. The effect would have been profound, possibly changing the outcome of a battle when used with linear tactics. An advancing line would begin taking hits at 300 yards, and at a rate of 3 to 4 shots a minute, it is doubtful if they could have approached to within volley range.

The Ferguson rifle was 100 years ahead of its time. It would outperform any rifle of its day when considering all factors, viz: they fact that it would never foul if properly used and that it mounted the all important bayonet. Ferguson did not misplace his trust in the rifles: in competent hands and in proper numbers it could have changed the outcome of a battle. Unfortunately it was never tested with linear tactics, and the numbers on hand prevented a thorough evaluation under those circumstances. We can prove, through our use of the rifle, that 100 rifles being fired from a line formation opposing an equal number of the enemy at 200 yards distance, would assure victory. And this can all be done from a kneeling or prone position to minimize casualties from enemy fire. Again, Ferguson specially drilled his men in the use of the prone position that he used so effectively at Brandywine.

Collectors and historians have greatly underrated and underestimated this rifle for over 200 years because an exact copy has never been made and tested properly. We have put on demonstrations with the rifle that made believers of even the most skeptical, just as Ferguson did for Lord Townshend and the King. In every instance the audiences walked away with a new respect for the rifle and most are in awe of the rifle's capabilities. This rifle will never let the shooter down if properly used. It is sad that more people have not had the opportunity to shoot this weapon, as it is a truly remarkable gun. Unfortunately it was born out of the American War and died with the conflict. The British were never fans of the rifle, and the thinking of the day allowed no room for them on the battlefield until the early nineteenth century, when there was again a perceived need for rifles to oppose those in use on the battlefields of Europe and the Caribbean. Even then, knowing what we do today, the Ferguson would have been a much better choice than the Baker rifle.

R.H.K. & E.E.C.

❧ ❧ ❧ ❧

There is no evidence that any form of bullet-seating tool or lubricant was employed by Ferguson's riflemen in loading their rifles, and the author has seen no documentary evidence of a special, or any form of lubricant, in contemporary literature. All we know is that powder flasks formed a part of their special equipment, suggesting the loading of a loose but measured charge; it is also reasonable to assume that the riflemen were issued with the same Superfine Double Strength powder issued with the Pattern 1776 and German jäger muzzle-loading rifles. Without a tool of some sort to force the ball to the same position (fingers are likely to be too large and lack the required leverage) at the front of the chamber, the ball will roll forward less and less with each discharge because of the accumulating fouling, and the point of impact of the shot will change with each shot. Ferguson himself seems to have considered that being able to reload in a prone position without attracting attention in the process was the chief advantage of his system.

As designed and produced for the Ordnance, the Pattern 1776 Ferguson rifle was virtually useless as a military weapon not only because the breech mechanism operated largely in direct contact with the explosion of the propellant charge and would require frequent cleaning of the bore to maintain acceptable accuracy, but also from the fact that the design required far too much wood to be removed from the stock in the breech area, normally weak enough with inlettings for barrel, lock and trigger mechanisms. Had the rifle been produced to a design like, for instance, the so-called "Queen Anne cannon-barrel turn-off" pistols or the Lorenzoni-system breechloaders, with a separate butt and either no fore-end or one fixed separately to the underside of the barrel, with a strong breechpiece holding the lock and breech-plug mechanisms, it might have more closely met the rigorous requirements of "soldier-proof" field use. Even this major re-design would not have dealt with the other fundamental problem of fouling in both breech and bore under military conditions. As it is, both the surviving Ordnance Fergusons and the one known East India Company Ferguson rifle are broken in this weak area, and all seven of those reported in the New York Ordnance Stores in 1783 were "unserviceable," which we may speculate with some confidence was due to breakage of the stock or perhaps loss of breechplugs.

APPENDIX 7

Contract between Lieut. Col. DuPont and A.H. Thornbeck for Rifles for the Prince of Orange's Corps

The 5 June 1800 contract quoted verbatim and in its entirety below is believed to relate to rifles illustrated in Chapter 8. A number of these rifles were transferred from the Woolwich Rotunda collection to the Royal Armouries many years ago. Several of them still retain their "box tools" including powder measures. Each rifle is numbered on the top flat of the barrel near the muzzle with a number in the 800 or 900 range. The only feature which stands out as "modern" is the form of the bayonet bar at the muzzle; they might otherwise date to any time in the last quarter of the 18th century. Whether Andreas Hermann Thornbeck of Cassel was a gunmaker or an entrepreneur has not yet emerged from the records.

AGREEMENT BETWEEN LIEUT. COL. DU PONT OF THE ROYAL ARTILLERY
AT DILLENBURGH AND A.H. THORNBECK OF HESSEN CASSEL
FOR FURNISHING ON THE CONDITIONS MENTIONED
HEREAFTER 850 RIFLES RIFLES FOR CHASSEURS

1st. The undersigned A.H. Thornbeck agrees to furnish at Hamburg the above mentioned 850 Rifles for Chasseurs directed to the Person to be named by Lieut. Col. Dupont.

2nd. Those Arms must be conformable to the approved Patterns seal'd by both Parties to each of those Rifles must be added a Cutlass to be fixed on it occasionally as a Bayonet with a Leather Scabbard to which will be added a knife besides a ball mould, powder measure, worms, Turnscrew and a screw to draw Ball.

3d. The Barrels shall undergo the Proof of the Manufactory by the sworn Proof Master of the Country, and being approved of shall be marked with the usual Mark.

4th. The Rifles shall be examined at Cassel where any little Defect that might be found shall be repaired at the expense of the Contractor.

5th. After due Inspection the Rifles shall be packed up at the Expence of the Contractor in good Chests which previous to their being sent to Hamburg shall be sealed by Lieut. Colonel Dupont or by any Person authorized by him for that purpose.

6th. The Contractor A.H. Thornbeck shall receive for each Rifle furnished conformable to Pattern the sum of 12 Ryks Dollars in Louis Dor's at 5 Ryks Dollars each to be paid by Lieut. Colonel Dupont One Half immediately or at least 3 or 4 weeks after the signature of the present Agreement either in Pistoles or Frederic's D'or at 5 Ryks Dollars or in Drafts on Hamburg or Bremen at one or two Months Date and the other Half in the like manner on the Delivery of the last Arms.

7th. The Patterns shall be included in the number of the 850 Rifles and be paid accordingly but they or one of them shall not be sent but remain at the Manufactory 'till further Orders to serve as Patterns in case any more Arms shall be wanted.

8th. The Contractor engages if nothing Extraordinary prevents it to furnish at Cassel in the space of 8 weeks 400 arms or if possible part of them sooner and the remainder 450 in four or six weeks afterwards and to cause them to be sent to Hamburg. Yet the Freight or Carriage of the same shall be Paid by the Receiver at his own Expence.

9th. For the Execution of the above Articles the undersigned engage their Persons and Properties according to Law without any Exceptions &c. and as thereof 3 Copies made of the same Tenor to serve as, one signed and sealed by both Parties of which Lieut. Colonel Dupont will keep two and A.H. Thornbeck one.
Done at Dillenburgh 5th June and at Cassel 1st June 1800
Signed W. Dupont
And Herm Thornbeck

N.B. It is to be observed that as it is the Intention to complete the Regiment of Riflemen to 1,000 Rank and File the Order has been increased to 1,012 Rifles by the Command of His Royal Highness the Commander in Chief which are at present ready and Delivered. Signed John Sontag, Lieut. Colonel.

A minute of 7 October 1800 states that £1600 had been paid for 1,012 Rifles at Cassel in Germany for the Prince of Orange's Riflemen then at Lymington.

Source: WO/47/2569, 1150-4.

APPENDIX 8

Alphabetical List of Ordnance Contractors with their Production of Baker Rifles & Rifled Carbines, 1800-1838

Abbreviations used:
- blbr = *barrels, locks, bayonets and ramrods; these were supplied to the contractors by the Board of Ordnance.*
- brls = *barrels*
- Cb = *carbine-bore*
- Mb = *musket-bore*
- Lk = *lock*
- R/S & S/U = *rough stocked and set up w/ or w/o = with, or without*
- WI = *West Indies pattern*
- VR = *should have Crowned VR on lockplate and/or barrel*

Contractor, location and dates he supplied				Number	Pattern
ADAMS, John. Birmingham. 1826					
1826	-	50	Infantry Rifles compleat w/o brl & lk	50	1823
ASHTON, Thomas. London. 1805–36					
1805	-	50	all w/o blbr until 1811		
1806	-	50			
1807	-	80			
1810	-	100			
1811	-	100	R/S & S/U		
1813	-	129			
1814	-	<u>11</u>			
		520		520	1805
1824	-	133	Thomas & Charles		
1825	-	136			
1827	-	<u>200</u>			
		469		469	1823
1836	-	60	R/S & S/U Thomas	60	Shah
1838	-	58	Inf R. w/hand bays.		
1839	-	2		60	VR
BAKER, Ezekiel. London. 1800–36.					
1800	-	16	Mb w/boxes, 43 Mb w/o boxes = 59 Mb	59	Mb
		266	Cb w/boxes, 263 Cb w/o boxes = 529 Cb	529	1800
		6	Cb w/boxes for Patterns @ 97/- compleat w/sword-b.		
		2	Pattern barrels @ 24/-		
		305	Barrels rifled, sighted and browned		
		4	Outside Barrel gauges		
		12	Inside Barrel gauges		
		3	Cutting Punches for Spetches @ 7/6		
		2	Pattern locks		
1801	-	48	Life Guards Rifled Carbines	48	L.Gds
		91	Cb w/o b, 31 Cb w/b = 122 Cb	122	1800
		50	Cb West Indies w/o box, Ordnance locks		
		50	Cb " " w/b "	100	WI
		500	flies put into tumblers, 31 Aug.		
		400	boxes fitted to butts, 30 Sept.		

— 223 —

British Military Flintlock Rifles

		272	Barrels rifled, sighted, bayonet bar, & browned.		
1802	-		'boxed 635 Rifles for Manningham's Corps at Weymouth and Blatchington at 4/- all expenses paid.' 20 Feb.		
1803	-	40	PoW LD Rifled Carbines @ 84/- compleat	40	PoW CR
1805	-	75	Infantry Rifles w/o blbr		
1806	-	75	do. 1 Cav. Rifle		
1807	-	80	do.		
1809	-	100	R/S & S/U		
1811	-	100	do.		
		500	Cav. Carb. brls rifled 31 Aug.		
		400	Inf. Rifle do 31 Oct. & 31 Dec.		
1812	-	300	Inf. Rifle brls rifled.		
1813	-	80	Infantry Rifles		
		502	Cavalry Rifles 10th LD @ 40/-	502	PoW CR
		700	Inf. Rifle brls rifled.	80	1805
1814	-	200	Infantry Rifles		
		2	Pattern rifles @ 126/-		
		500	Cavalry Rifles w/swells on the stocks for 10th L.D. 1 May, @ 40/-	500	PoW CR
				200	1805
		502	brls for Cavalry Rifles @ 6/-		
1815	-	1	rifle brl rifled sighted &c.	712	1805
				1002	1813
1821	-	45	Infantry Rifles R/S & S/U	45	1820
1824	-	183	Infantry Rifles, w/hand bayonets		
		1000	Barrels rifled, sighted, fitting hand bayonets & browned @ 18/-, 1 Mar.		
1825	-	184	Infantry Rifles R/S & S/U, 26/-		
1826	-	200	do. @ 26/-. Firm style now Elizabeth & Son		
		567	Pattern 1823	567	1823
		1000	Barrels as last @ 16/-, 10 Mar.		
1827	-	1000	Barrels as last @ 16/-, 14 May.		
		112	Cavalry Rifles new stocked w/own wood & S/U @ 30/- plus 112 sets implements @ 1/6, 17 Sept.		
1828	-	217	Cavalry Rifles as last @ new stocked, 28/- plus implements, 8 Nov. for 10th Hussars	329	PoW CR
1836	-	110	Infantry Rifles,	110	Shah
1838	-	109	Inf. Rifles, @ 27/9		
		50	brls bored, rifled, sighted &c.		
1839	-	1	Infantry Rifle as last	110	VR

BARNETT & SON, John Edward. London. 1836-39

1836	-	160	Inf. R. w/hand bays.	160	Shah
1838	-	153	do.		
1839	-	<u>17</u>	do.	170	VR

BARNETT, Thomas. London. 1800-36

1800	-	75	Cb Infantry Rifles w/o boxes; 10 w/b, rifled		
1801	-	75	Cb w/o boxes; 50 w/b compleat, and rifled	200	1800
		37	Cb West Indies Regt. w/o boxes do.		
		38	Cb do. w/b do.	75	WI
1805	-	26	Infantry Rifles w/o blbr		
1806	-	49	do.		
1807	-	24	do.		
1808	-	56	do.		
1810	-	100	do. R/S & S/U		
1813	-	195	do.		
1814	-	13	do.		
1815	-	<u>32</u>	do.		
		495		495	1805
1820	-	45	R/S & S/U @ 26/-	45	1820
1824	-	183	Infantry Rifles		
1825	-	184	do.		
1827	-	<u>200</u>	do.		
		567	Pattern 1823	567	1823

BLAIR, David. Birmingham. 1800-01.

1800	-	10	Cb Infantry Rifles, w/o boxes, to be rifled 32/-		
		10	Cb do. w/b do. 36/-	20	1800
1802	-	115	West Indies Regt. w/o boxes, compleat		
		125	do. w/b do.	240	WI

BLAIR & SUTHERLAND. Birmingham. 1805-08.

1805	-	117	Infantry Rifles w/o blbr		
1806	-	253	do.		
1807	-	169	do.		
1808	-	<u>409</u>	do.		
		948		948	1805

BLAIR, David. Birmingham. 1809-14.

1809	-	47	Infantry Rifles w/o blbr		
1810	-	60	do.		
1811	-	146	do.		
1812	-	77	do.		
		6	Heavy Cav. Rifled Carbines @ 29/-	6	HCRC
1813	-	45	Infantry Rifles		
1814	-	<u>5</u>	do.		
		380		380	1805

BOND, William Thomas. London. 1836

1836	-	40	Infantry Rifles,	40	Shah
1838	-	38			
1839	-	2		40	VR

BRANDER, Martin. London. 1800-09.

— 225 —

1800	-	63	Cb w/o boxes @ 32/- compleat, to be rifled		
		12	do. w/b		
1801	-	33	Infantry Rifles, w/o boxes, to be rifled		
		92	Cb do. w/b do.	200	1800
		37	Cb West Indies Regt. w/o boxes		
		38	Cb do. w/b	75	WI
1805	-	40	Infantry Rifles compleat w/o blbr		
1806	-	60	do.		
1807	-	80	do.		
1809	-	100	do. R/S & S/U		
		280		280	1805

BRANDER & POTTS. London. 1811-27.

1811		100	do.		
1813	-	140	do.	240	1805
1820	-	45	do.	45	1820
1824	-	183	do.		
1826	-	184	do.		
1827	-	200	do.		
		567	Pattern 1823	567	1823

DAWES, William & Samuel. Birmingham. 1805-14.

1805	-	35	Infantry Rifles compleat w/o blbr.		
1806	-	109	do.		
1807	-	169	do.		
1808	-	347	do.		
1809	-	44	do.		
1810	-	30	do.		
1811	-	152	do.		
1812	-	55	do.		
		6	Rifled Heavy Cavalry Carbine @ 24/-	6	HCRC
1813	-	42	Infantry Rifles. J. & S. Dawes from June.		
		983		983	1805

EGG, Durs. London. 1800-27.

1800	-	100	Cb Infantry Rifles, w/o boxes, to be rifled		
		211	Barrels rifled, sighted, sword fitted, & browned @ 22/-, 30 Nov.		
1801	-	100	Cb, Infantry Rifles, w/ boxes		
		317	Barrels as in 1800		
				200	1800
1802	-	50	Cb, West Indies Regt. w/o boxes		
		50	Cb, do. w/b all to be rifled	100	WI
1805	-	15	Infantry Rifles compleat w/o blbr		
1806	-	40	do. R/S & S/U		
1807	-	60	do.		
1808	-	21	do.		
1811	-	219	do, w/o blbr		
1812	-	65	do, R/S & S/U		
1813	-	200	do.		
1814	-	40	do.		
		660		660	1805
1821	-	45	do. "w/steel rammers & bayonets, R/S&c"	45	1820

1824	-	183	do.		
1825	-	184	do.		
1826	-	1000	Barrels rifled, sighted, bays. fitted & browned.		
1827	-	<u>200</u>	Infantry Rifles		
		567	Pattern 1823	567	1823
		1000	Barrels as 1826, 14 May.		

EGG, Joseph. London. 1820-36.

1820	-	25	Infantry Rifles	25	1820
1824	-	183	do.		
1826	-	150	do.		
1827	-	150	do.		
		483	Pattern 1823	483	1823

FEARNLEY, Robert. London. 1805-11.

1805	-	63	Infantry Rifles compleat w/o blbr.		
1806	-	2	do. R/S & S/U		
1807	-	80	do.		
1809	-	100	do.		
1811	-	<u>100</u>	do.		
		345		345	1805

FEARNLEY, Ann. Widow of last, 1813-24.

1813	-	140	Infantry Rifles	140	1805
1820	-	45	do. Nov. "w/steel rammers & bayonets"	45	1820
1824	-	151	do.	151	1823

GALTON. Samuel Jr. Birmingham. 1801-13.

1801	-	10	Cb Infantry Rifles, w/o boxes		
		10	Cb do. w/ boxes	20	1800
1802	-	60	Cb, West Indies Regt. w/o boxes		
		60	Cb, do. w/b	120	WI
1805	-	36	Infantry Rifles compleat w/o blbr		
1806	-	149	do.		
1807	-	167	do.		
1808	-	361	do.		
1809	-	45	do.		
1810	-	130	do.		
1811	-	163	do.		
1812	-	155	do.		
		6	Heavy Cavalry Rifled Carbines	6	HCRC
1813	-	<u>36</u>	do. w/o blbr @ 40/-		
		1242		1242	1805

GILL, Thomas. Birmingham. 1800-01.

1800 -		30	Cb Infantry Rifles, w/o boxes		
		10	Cb do. w/ boxes	40	1800
		118	Cb twisted Rifle Barrels		

GILL & CO., John. Birmingham. Successor to last. 1805-13.

1805	-	100	Infantry Rifles compleat w/boxes.		
		66	Rifle barrels Cb, plain		

1806	-	137	Infantry Rifles.			
1807	-	39	do.			
1808	-	333	do.			
1809	-	44	do.			
1810	-	40	do.			
1811	-	144	do.			
1812	-	84	do.			
		6	Heavy Cav. Rifled Carbines	6		HCRC
1813	-	<u>7</u>	Infantry Rifles			
		928		928		1805

GRICE, Joseph. Birmingham. 1800–02.

1800	-	20	Musket Proof bore Rifles as Patterns @ 48/- June			
		10	Carbine Proof bore Rifles as Patterns @ 48/- June			
1801	-	10	Infantry Rifles, w/boxes			
		10	do. w/o boxes	20		1800
1802	-	107	Cb, West Indies Regt. w/o boxes			
		104	Cb, do. w/b	211		WI

HAMPTON, Thomas. Birmingham. 1812–26.

1812	-	47	Infantry Rifles			
1813	-	<u>13</u>	do.			
		60		60		1805
1826	-	50	do. w/o bl & lk. @ 42/6	50		1823

HARRISON & THOMPSON. London. 1800–01.

1800	-	100	Cb Infantry Rifles, w/o boxes, 32/-			
1801	-	100	Cb do. w/o boxes, 32/-	200		1800
		38	Cb, West Indies Regt. w/o boxes			
		37	Cb, do. w/b all to be rifled	75		WI

HEPTINSTALL, William. London. 1838–9.

1838	-	38	Inf. Rifles			
1839	-	2	do.	40		VR

HOLLIS, Richard & William. Birmingham. 1812; 1826.

1812	-	43	Infantry Rifles compleat w/o blbr	43		1805
		8	Heavy Cav. Rifled Carbines @ 24/-	8		HCRC
1826	-	50	Infantry Rifles	50		1823

KETLAND & ALLPORT. Birmingham. 1805–13.

1805	-	85	Infantry Rifles compleat w/o blbr			
1806	-	169	do.			
1807	-	179	do.			
1808	-	375	do.			
1809	-	47	do.			
1810	-	98	do.			
1811	-	202	do.			
1812	-	137	do			
		8	Heavy Cav. Rifled Carbines @ 24/-	8		HCRC
1813	-	<u>99</u>	Infantry Rifles w/o blbr			
		1391		1391		1805

KETLAND & CO., William. Birmingham. 1826

1826	-	50	Infantry Rifles w/o bl & lk.	50		1823

KETLAND & WALKER. Birmingham. 1800–08.
1800	-	10	Cb Infantry Rifles w/o boxes compleat @ 32/-		
		10	Cb do. w/b compleat @ 36/-	20	1800
1802	-	106	Cb, West Indies Regt. w/o boxes		
		106	Cb, do. w/b	212	WI
1805	-	169	Infantry Rifles compleat w/o blbr		
1806	-	282	do.		
1807	-	183	do.		
1808	-	<u>387</u>	do.		
		1021		1021	1805

KETLAND, WALKER & CO. [Adams] from 31 Sept. 1808
1808	-	11	Infantry Rifles		
1809	-	48	do.		
1810	-	160	do.		
1811	-	<u>159</u>			
1812	-	120			
		14	Heavy Cav. Rifles Carbines @ 24/-	14	HCRC
1813	-	<u>103</u>	Infantry Rifles		
		482		482	1805

LACY & CO. London. 1838
| 1838 | - | 150 | Infantry Rifles Pattn 1823 | 150 | VR |

LACY & REYNOLDS. London. 1836
| 1836 | - | 150 | Infantry Rifles, Shah of Persia | 150 | Shah |

MARWOOD, William. 1805–09.
1805	-	30	Infantry Rifles compleat, w/o blbr		
1806	-	95	do.		
1807	-	80	do.		
1809	-	<u>100</u>	do. R/S & S/U		
		305		305	1805

MARWOOD, Ann widow of last from Jan. 1811.
1812	-	100	do.		
1813	-	120	do.		
1814	-	<u>20</u>	do.		
		240	do.	240	1805
1820	-	20	do.	20	1820
1824	-	133	do.		
1826	-	<u>136</u>	do.		
		269	Pattern 1823	269	1823

MILLS & SON, William. London. 1836; 1839
| 1836 | - | 40 | Infantry Rifles, Shah of Persia | 40 | Shah |
| 1839 | - | 34 | Infantry Rifles, Pattn 1823 | 34 | VR |

MORRIS, Henry. Birmingham. 1805–09.
1805	-	60	Infantry Rifles compleat w/o blbr		
1806	-	160	do.		
1807	-	167	do.		
1808	-	351	do.		
1809	-	<u>45</u>	do.		
		783		783	1805

MORRIS & GRICE. Birmingham. From 28 Feb. 1810–13.

1810	-	86	Infantry Rifles do.		
1811	-	144	do.		
1812	-	89	do.		
		8	Heavy Cav. Rifled Carbines @ 24/-	8	HCRC
1813	-	50	Infantry Rifles		
		369		369	1805

MOXHAM, Thomas. Birmingham. 1811-26.

1811	-	104	Infantry Rifles compleat w/o blbr		
1812	-	136	do.		
1813	-	21	do.		
		261		261	1805
1826	-	50	do.	50	1823

NOCK, Henry. London. 1800-02.

1800	-	12	Cb Infantry Rifles, w/o boxes		
		108	Cb do. w/b, all to be rifled		
		235	Barrels rifled, sighted and browned @ 22/-		
		100	sets implements		
1801	-	100	Cb Infantry Rifles, w/o boxes		
		180	Cb do. w/b	400	1800
		493	Barrels rifled, sighted, sword-bay. fitted & browned.		
		275	flies put into tumblers of rifle locks @ 6d. 31 Aug.		
1802	-	102	Cb, West Indies Regt. w/o boxes		
		102	Cb, do. w/b	204	WI
		344	boxes fitted to rifle butts, 29 Sept.		

PARKER, William. London. 1811-39.

1811	-	100	Infantry Rifles R/S & S/U @ 40/-		
1812	-	100	do.		
1813	-	115	do.		
1814	-	25	do.		
		340		340	1805
1821	-	45	do. @ 26/-	45	1820
1824	-	183	do.		
1826	-	184	do.		
1827	-	200	w/hand bays.		
		567	Pattern 1823	567	1823
1836	-	60	do.	60	Shah
1838	-	60	do.	60	VR

PEAKE, John. London. 1805-21.

1805	-	14	Infantry Rifles compleat w/o blbr		
1806	-	111	do. R/S & S/U		
1807	-	80	do.		
1811	-	100	do.		
1812	-	100	do.		
1813	-	140	do.		
		545		545	1805
1821	-	45	do.	45	1820

POTTS, Thomas. London. 1836-9.

1836	-	160	do.		160	Shah
1838	-	146	do. do.			
1839	-	23	do.		169	VR

PRITCHETT, Richard Ellis. London. 1824-39.

1824	-	151	Infantry Rifles			
1825	-	150	do.			
1827	-	<u>160</u>	do.			
		461	Pattern 1823		461	1823
1836	-	60	Infantry Rifles		60	Shah
1838	-	38	Inf. Rifles			
1839	-	1	do.		39	VR

PRITCHETT, Samuel. London. 1800-01.

1800	-	100	Cb Infantry Rifles, w/o boxes, to be rifled			
1801	-	50	Cb Infantry Rifles, w/o boxes, to be rifled			
		50	Cb do. w/ boxes do.		200	1800
1802	-	50	Cb, West Indies Regt, w/o boxes			
		50	Cb, do. w/b		100	WI

REYNOLDS, Thomas. London. 1826-7; 1836-8.

1826	-	140	Infantry Rifles			
1827	-	140	do. @ 26/-			
		280	Pattern 1823		280	1823
1836	-	40	Infantry Rifles & SON.		40	Shah
1838	-	40	do.		40	VR

ROLFE, William Isaac. Birmingham. 1811-12.

1811	-	170	Infantry Rifles compleat w/o blbr			
1812	-	117	do.			
1813	-	<u>7</u>	do.			
		294			294	1805

SUTHERLAND, Richard & Ramsay. Birmingham. 1809-26.

1809	-	47	Infantry Rifles compleat w/o blbr			
1810	-	171	do. Cb			
		100	do. Musket-bore			
1811	-	158	do. Cb			
1812	-	122	do.			
1813	-	<u>84</u>	do.			
		582			582	1805
					100	Mb 1810
1826	-	50	do.		50	1823

THOMPSON [THOMSON], James. London. 1806-27.

1806	-	100	Infantry Rifles R/S & S/U			
1807	-	80	do.			

Thompson & Son from Nov. 1808

1810	-	100	do.			
1811	-	100	do.			
1813	-	94	do.			
1814	-	<u>46</u>	do.			
		520			520	1805
1821	-	45	do.		45	1820

1824	-	183	do.			
1825	-	184	do.			
1827	-	<u>200</u>	do.			
		567	Pattern 1823		567	1823
1836	-	40	Infantry Rifles w/hand bays. R/S & S/U for the Shah of Persia, 27/9		40	Shah

WHATELY, Henry & John. Birmingham. 1806–13.

1806	-	16	Infantry Rifles compleat w/o blbr			
1807	-	172	do.			
1808	-	355	do.			
1809	-	45	do.			
1810	-	60	do.			
1811	-	146	do.			
1812	-	92	do.			
		8	Heavy Cav. Rifled Carbines		8	HCRC
1813	-	32	Infantry Rifles			
		918			918	1805

WHATELY, John. Birmingham. 1800

1800	-	10	Cb, Infantry Rifles, w/o boxes, to be rifled			
		10	Cb do. w/ boxes		20	1800

WHEELER, Robert. Birmingham. 1800–26.

1800	-	11	Pattern "Rifled Musquets", Musket proof bore @ 48/-			
		20	Pattern do. Carbine proof bore do.			
		10	Cb Infantry Rifles, twisted iron brl, w/ boxes			
		10	Cb do., plain iron brl, w/o boxes		20	1800
		98	Rifle Barrels, Cb, twisted iron			
1801	-	10	Rifle Barrels, Cb, twisted iron			
1802	-	144	Cb, West Indies Regt. w/o boxes			
		109	Cb, do. w/b		253	WI
1805	-	72	Infantry Rifles compleat w/o blbr			
1806	-	166	do.			
1807	-	174	do.			

Wheeler & Son from August 1807.

1808	-	328	do.			
1809	-	49	do.			

WHEELER, Robert Junior.

1810	-	60	do.			
1811	-	154	do.			
1812	-	120	do.			
		8	Heavy Cav. Rifled Carbines @ 24/-		8	HCRC
1813	-	<u>21</u>	Infantry Rifles			
		1144			1144	1805
1826	-	50	do. w/o brl & lk.			50 - 1823
1835	-	2160	each Implements for Infantry Rifles of Queen of Spain.			

WILKES, James. London. 1800

1800	-	50	Cb, Infantry Rifles w/o blbr, to be rifled.			

| 1801 | - | 25 | | 75 | 1800 |

WILLETTS, Mary. Birmingham. 1800
| 1800 | - | 10 | Cb, Infantry Rifles, w/o boxes @ 32/- | | |
| | | 10 | Cb, do.   w/ boxes @ 36/- | 20 | 1800 |

| 1802 | - | 92 | Cb, West Indies Regt, w/o boxes | | |
| | | 90 | Cb, do.   w/ boxes | 182 | WI |

WILLETTS & HOLDEN. Birmingham. 1805–13.
1805	-	90	Infantry Rifles compleat w/o blbr		
1806	-	126	do.		
1807	-	143	do.		
1808	-	372	do.		
1809	-	45	do.		
1810	-	40	do.		
1811	-	139	do.		
1812	-	92	do.		
1813	-	40	do.		
		1048		1048	1805

WOOLEY & CO. Birmingham. 1806
| 1806 | - | 20 | Infantry Rifles compleat w/o blbr | 20 | 1805 |

WRIGHT, Robert. London. 1800–27.
| 1800 | - | 100 | Cb, w/o boxes, R/S & S/U | | |
| | | 50 | do, w/ boxes | | |

| 1801 | - | 20 | Cb, w/ boxes to be rifled | | |
| | | 50 | do, w/ boxes, | 200 | 1800 |

| | | 37 | Cb, West Indies Regt., w/o boxes | | |
| | | 38 | Cb, do. w/ boxes | 75 | WI |

1805	-	37	Infantry Rifles compleat w/o blbr		
1806	-	38	do. R/S & S/U		
1807	-	80	do.		
1810	-	100	do.		
1811	-	100	do.		
1814	-	140	do.		
		495		495	1805

| 1820 | - | 45 | do. | 45 | 1820 |

1824	-	183	Infantry Rifles		
1826	-	184	do.		
1827	-	200	do.		
		567	Pattern 1823	567	1823

YEOMANS & SON, James. London. 1836–9.
| 1836 | - | 40 | Infantry Rifles w/hand bayonets | 40 | Shah |

| 1838 | - | 39 | Inf. Rifles | | |
| 1839 | - | 1 | do. | 40 | VR |

TOTAL CONTRACTOR PRODUCTION

Pattern 1800 - 2431   Carbine-bore, not counting patterns.
              59   Musket-bore, (all E. Baker) not counting patterns.

West Indies Regiment - 2022: without buttbox or sword-bar   1025
                             with buttbox & sword-bar   997

                             Buttboxes fitted to rifle butts: 744 (1801)

British Military Flintlock Rifles

Life Guards (1801) - 48   (all E. Baker)

Prince of Wales Cavalry Rifle (1803) - 40 (all E. Baker)
(Number made in Tower - 725 in 1805)

Pattern 1805 - 18,819 carbine-bore, counting patterns
                100 musket-bore (1810, all R. & R. Sutherland).

Life Guards Rifled Carbine Pattern 1812 - 102

Prince of Wales Cavalry Rifle Pattern 1814 - 1002 (all E. Baker)

1820–21 - 450

Pattern 1823 - 6248

Prince of Wales Cavalry Rifle Pattern 1814/27) - 329 all Baker re-stocked

Shah of Persia Pattern 1823 (1836) - 1000

Victorian Pattern 1823 - 1012

APPENDIX 9
Baker Rifle Production, 1800-1839

	Complete Rifles		**Barrels**		**Locks**	**Cavalry Rifles**		**Barrels**
1800	1718	Cb	2132	Cb	1193			
	90	Mb	101	Mb				
1801	48	Life Gds (EB)			119	219		
	769							
	2022	W.I. *						
1802	none							
1803	none					40 (EB)		
1804	325	ToL						
1805	190	ToL				259	ToL	906
	359	L				466	ToL	
	804	B						
1806	1281	ToL						
	571	L						
	1527	B						
1807	348	ToL						
	724	L						
	1630	B						
1808	127	L						
	3932	B (Bill bks show 4059-check)						
1809	96	ToL						
	400	L						
	490	B						
1810 Goodman	1139	ToL?						
	400	L 100 Mb	133		1288			
	839	B						
1811	1924	ToL	1886		2690			
	919	L						
	1981	B						
1812	1525	ToL	2260		134			
	365	L						
	1487	B						
1813	497	ToL	466		99	502	L	
	1139	L						
	643	B						
1814	721	ToL	91			1002	L	
	475	L						
1815	727	ToL						
	32	L						
TOTALS	8773	Tower of London						2269
	5611	London trade						
	18059	Birmingham trade including all 1800-01						
	32443							
	20,415	Bill Bks	32,582	Gdmn	37,338	2010	B.B.	

* Half with butt-traps and bayonet bars and half without either.

— 235 —

British Military Flintlock Rifles

POST-1815 Production
(not counting Royal Manufactory Enfield, for which complete figures are not available)

1820-1 -	450	Pattn (?) 1820 (11 Contractors)
1824 -	2032	Pattn 1823 (12 Contractors)
1825 -	2550	Pattn 1823 (20 Contractors)
1827 -	1850	Pattn 1823 (10 Contractors)
1836 -	1000	Pattn 1823 for the Shah of Persia (13 Contractors)
1838 -	930	Pattn 1823 (15 Contractors); 572 new locks, VR
	696	with sword and hand bayonets taken from Store & repaired.
1839 -	83	Pattn 1823 (10 Contractors)

By the Board's Order of 12 Mar. 1838, the first BRUNSWICK Rifles were set up, by Barnett, billed 5 Feb. 1839.

— 236 —

APPENDIX 10

Extract from REGULATIONS FOR THE EXERCISE OF RIFLEMEN AND LIGHT INFANTRY

by Baron Francis de Rottenburg translated into English by Gen. William Fawcett [Faucitt] and published by the War Office, 1798, pp. 6–9. Chapter II.
Of Priming and Loading, and of Firing at the Target.

S1
Of Priming and loading
The words of command for firing and loading are as follows.
1. The Company will Prime and Load.
2. Attention.
At which the fleugelman steps in front.
3. Prepare to Load
For which the fleugelman gives the time in two motions.
1st, Is the same as the first motion in the present.
2d. The soldier half faces to the right, and in the motion brings down the rifle to an horizontal position just above the right hip, the left hand supports it at the swell of the stock, the elbow resting against the side, the right thumb against the hammer, the knuckles upwards, and elbow pressing against the butt, the lock inclining a little to the body to prevent the powder from falling out.
The officer now warns the men in going through the loading motions,
To wait for the words of Command.
At which caution the fleugelman falls in.
At the word One,
The pan is pushed open by the right thumb, the right hand then seizes the cartridge with the three first fingers.
Two,
The cartridge is brought to the mouth, and placed between the two first right double teeth, the end twisted off and brought close to the pan.
Three,
The priming is shaken into the pan, in doing which, to see that the powder is properly lodged, the head must be bent; the pan is shut by the third and little finger, the right hand then slides behind the cock, and holds the small part of the stock between the third and little finger and ball of the hand.
Four,
The soldier half faces to the left; the rifle is brought to the ground with the barrel outwards, by sliding it with care through the left hand, which then seizes it near the muzzle, the thumb stretched along the stock, the butt is placed between the heels, the barrel between the knees, which must be bent for that purpose; the cartridge is put into the barrel, and the ramrod seized with the fore finger and thumb of the right hand.
Rod,
The ramrod is drawn quite out by the right hand, the left quits the rifle, and grasps the ramrod the breadth of a hand from the bottom, which is sunk one inch into the barrel.
Home,
The cartridge will be forced down with both hands, the left then seizes the rifle about six inches from the muzzle, the soldier stands upright again, draws out the ramrod with the right hand, and puts the end into the pipe.
Return,
The ramrod will be returned by the right hand, which then seizes the rifle below the left.
Shoulder,
The right hand brings the rifle to the right shoulder, turning the guard outwards, the left seizes it above the hammer spring till the right has its proper hold round the small of the stock, when the left is drawn quickly to the left thigh.
When the recruits are sufficiently perfect in firing by these distinct and separate words of command, they should be accustomed to go through the motions with the following words of command only.

1. The Company will Prime and Load.
2. Attention.
At which the fleugelman steps in front.
3. Prepare to Load.
To this motion the fleugelman gives the time.
4. Load.
The fleugelman falls in. Every motion in loading as described above, is to be performed; and here officers are required to pay particular attention, that no single motion be omitted, as it is of more consequence that a rifle should be properly, than expeditiously, loaded.

S2.
Riflemen must at first be accustomed to make ready, and present methodically; and in this they should be thoroughly practised, for they will seldom be in a situation to fire by word of command.
The firings may be divided under

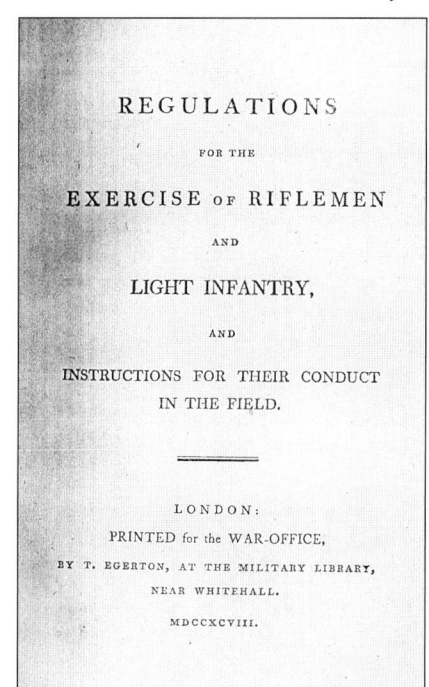

three heads, viz. in advancing, in retreating, and on the spot.

The method of firing in advancing and retreating by signal, will be explained in the following sections.

To fire on the spot with closed ranks, the following words of command will be given.
1. The Company will Fire.

2. Company.
At this word, the right hand file of each platoon takes three quick paces to the front, the rear rank man steps to the right of his file leader.

3. Ready.
At this word, the rifle is brought by the right hand before the centre of the body, the left seizes it, so that the little finger rests upon the hammer spring, and the thumb stretched along the stock, raising it to the height of the mouth, the right thumb on the cock, and four fingers under the guard; when cocked, which must be done gently, the right hand grasps the small of the stock.

4. Present.
The soldier half faces to the right, the butt is placed in the hollow of the right shoulder, the right foot steps back about eighteen inches behind the left, the left knee is bent, the body brought well forward, the left hand without having quit its hold, supports the right close before the lock, the right elbow raised even with the shoulder, the fore finger on the trigger, the head bent, and cheek resting on that of the rifle, the left eye shut, the right taking aim through the sight; as soon as the rifleman has fixed upon his object, he fires without waiting for any command. When he has fired, the right hand quits its hold in facing to the right about, the left swings the rifle round into an horizontal position with the barrel downwards; the rifleman resumes his post in the platoon, in fronting to the left about, brings his rifle into the position to prime and load, half cocks, and proceeds to load, going through the motions as above without further words of command.

As soon as the riflemen are perfect in this, they will be instructed, that at the signal of the horn to commence firing, the two right hand files of each platoon or section, according as the company may be told off, are immediately to take three paces to the front, the rear rank men step to the right of their file leaders, present, and each fires as he gets a proper aim, then resumes his place in the company as above mentioned, and loads again: when the two first files have fired, the two nest advance, and so on through the company.

This mode of firing is necessary to prevent the whole from being unloaded at the same time, when the company therefore has fired once according to the above regulations, every file on being loaded again will advance three paces, and each man will take his aim and fire, and then immediately resume his place in the company, load, &c. When it is required that the firing should cease, the signal to cease firing will be made by the bugle, after which not a shot must be heard. The officers who must invariably remain in the line during this firing, are on no account to stir from the spot, and when the signal to cease firing is made, and every man loaded and shouldered, they will dress their platoons. Too much attention cannot be given to the above rule, for the preservation of the alignment will entirely depend upon the strict observance of it.

S3

Of firing at the target.

The above regulations for firing with cartridges, will only be applicable when a corps of riflemen is required to act in close order, an instance which will very seldom occur, provided this arm is put to its proper use, and officers will observe in all cases, where riflemen act as such, and whenever it is practicable, their men are to load with the powder measure and loose ball; the principal instructions therefore for recruits, will be how to load with the loose ball, and to fire at the target; the loading with cartridge is a secondary object. To this end, the rifle recruit must from the first, in addition to his other exercise, be constantly practised at firing at the target.

In firing at a mark it is to be observed that the target should be at least five feet in diameter; for if it were smaller, the unpractised recruit would be apt to miss so often as to despair of hitting it; and to become expert, a man should find encouragement, and even amusement in this practice. Another disadvantage in its being too small would be, that the rifleman could not become acquainted with his rifle, as in missing the target altogether, he could not ascertain whether he had shot too much to the right, or too much to the left; whereas a target of a proper size, and painted in circles, being easily hit, the rifleman sees at once the fault he has made, and learns to correct it. The rifle recruit must at first be taught to fire at the target without a rest, for if he accustoms himself to make use of a support, he will rarely fire true without one; but as this method will at first be found difficult, and only rendered easy by practice, he should begin by firing at the distance of fifty yards, and increase it by degrees to three hundred. The rifleman must be made acquainted with the nature of the sights and aim of the rifle; he must be taught to use the plaster (i.e. a piece of greased leather or rag) in loading with a loose ball, and how to force it down the barrel, observing that it should lay close upon the powder, without being driven with a degree of force which might bruise the grains; after every shot which strikes the target, the rifleman must observe whether he pointed too high or too low, or too much to the right or left, and correct himself accordingly. The officers will take care that during this practice, every man learns the proper charge for his rifle, and if any rifle should be found faulty, it is to be remarked, that the necessary alterations may be made. Riflemen must also be practised to fire and load as they lay on the ground.
[Regulations.]

Appendices

In addition to the specific information contained in the official regulations, the first Colonel Commandant of the Rifle Corps, Coote Manningham, had the following to say in lectures he delivered to the officers of the Corps in 1800:

It will frequently happen, that to ascertain particular points with regard to the enemy, single riflemen can be used with more effect than a detachment or patrols, which may be liable to discovery; the best men must of course be selected for this service; a man so employed must glide from tree to tree, and from hedge to hedge, and by concealing himself at the smallest noise, he may, by a knowledge of the local, be enabled to ascertain whether or not the enemy are advancing on the side where he is; but such intelligence must be received with caution; it is difficult to meet with individuals sufficiently intelligent and hardy for these sort of enterprizes, and they generally see either too much or too little.

Every individual must be instructed in the method of making up his ammunition, of casting balls, of covering them with rag or leather, and of greasing them; and the commanding officer of a company should take care that he has along with his company bullet moulds sufficient for this purpose. The quantity of powder each rifleman carries will suffice for a long time, and they may frequently, when detached, be able to meet with lead.

[Manningham, Coote. *Military Lectures...* 1803, 59, 71.]

The only reference contemporary with the use of the Baker rifle which gives specific instructions for rifle cartridge using a patch is a work by Col. Macerone published in 1832. Although this is a non-regulation unofficial method devised by Colonel Macerone, it is so rare to find specific references to patching rifle ammunition during the period of Baker use that it is thought worthy of including here. It is also worth noting that the prepared ammunition for the Prussian rifle muskets made by a local Alnwick gunsmith for the Duke of Nprthumberland in 1803 consists of spherical balls wrapped in a punched clover-leaf shaped linen patch which was glued to the surface of the ball. Macerone's plate illustrating the manufacture of rifle cartridges using a square patch is shown earlier in this book. In explanation of his patched ball cartridge Macerone writes:

After various experiments I have found that, with the cartridge I am about to describe, a rifle may be loaded with at least the same precision and efficacy as by the present inconvenient practice, but, at the same time, with very nearly the ease and rapidity of a common musket.
Fig. 1, plate 4, Represents the common paper case, made on a [former] which has its end well hollowed out. Upon the paper being rolled, turned down, and touched with glue, the concavity A is perfected by pressure upon a bullet.
Fig. 2. Is a bit of cotton tissue, of a thickness analagous to the more or less precise agreement of the calibers of the bullet and the barrel. It is a square of two diameters of the bullet, and can be expeditiously made in great numbers, by tearing the calico into strips of the requisite breadth, when a dozen strips, placed one upon the other, may be cut simultaneously into squares with a chisel.
Fig. 3. The bullet enveloped in the square of calico; secured at the corners by a couple of stitches. I find that it is best to glue the bit of cotton on to the end of the paper case first, as in fig. 1, and them, when dry, stitch the bullet into it.
Fig. 4. The cartridge complete.

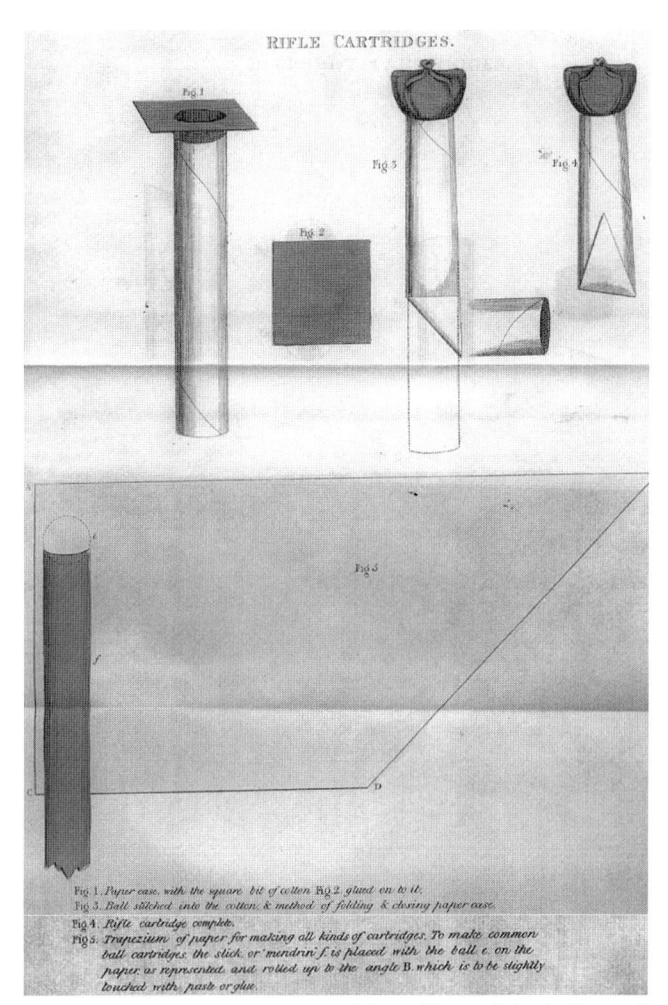

I would recommend the folding-up represented in figs. 3 and 4, instead of any ligature; for even without a touch of glue or paste at the edge B, this fold forms a very secure closing, and is easier than any other to tear off with the teeth, by a gentle turn of the hand, without any jerk or loss of powder.

The rifle cartridge, to be completed, passes to another hand, who, with a brush, or in any other convenient way, gives to the cotton cover of the bullet the necessary greasing of melted tallow.

It is superfluous to point out, that the resistance of the air to the open ears, formed by the folds of the cotton, detaches it from the bullet on the instant of its expulsion from the barrel.

[Macerone, Francis. *Defensive Instructions for the People,...* [1832], 16.]

APPENDIX 11
Cloathing Regulations For Riflemen

Generally speaking, with but few exceptions, rifle-armed units throughout Europe during the period under review wore uniforms based on the colour dark green, and it has come down to the present day as "rifle green." Facings and cuffs were most often red, sometimes black, and other colours more rarely. Accoutrements were generally black, occasionally natural brown. The details of uniforms are a study in themselves and beyond the scope of this study, but the following information relating to the Rifle Corps formed in 1800 under Coote Manningham, which later became the 95th and then the Rifle Brigade, is included to give some idea of a rifleman's outfit. Note that as early as 1802 a general pattern for rifle-armed troops in British service was decreed.

CLOATHING REGULATIONS 1 December 1800 for RIFLEMEN

In a Corps of Rifle Men serving in Europe, North America, or at the Cape of Good Hope each Serjeant shall have annually
For Clothing
A Green Coat, without Lace; a kersey Waistcoat; a Cap, Cockade and Tuft and a Pair of Green Pantaloons; and for Half Mounting
Two Pairs of good Shoes of the Value of Five Shillings & Sixpence each Pair; but he is not to be credited, as in other Corps, with the Sum of Three Shillings for the Difference of Half Mounting, as he receives an equivalent in the Difference between the Value of Pantaloons and of Breeches.
Each Corporal, Drummer and Private Man shall have annually for
Clothing
[same as for sergeant]
Half Mounting
[same shoes] but towards the Price of which the Colonel shall only pay four Shillings and Nine Pence a Pair, the Men paying the Difference in consideration of their being furnished with Pantaloons instead of Breeches.
When the Corps shall be stationed in the East or West Indies they are to conform to the Rules prescribed in the 4th and 7th Sections of His Majesty's Regulations relative to Clothing and Half Mounting dated 9 April 1800. Strict attention is also to be paid to all the other Rules contained in the said Regulations which apply to the case of Rifle Corps, and are not contravened by the particular orders here mentioned.
[WO4/181,188, 3 Dec. 1800.]

25 August 1800

Marksmen to wear the green cockade (4 shots in the target out of 6). Ordinary riflemen to wear the small white cockade (2 shots in target out of 6).

13 July 1802

It is His Majesty's Pleasure that all Companies, Corps, Battalions or Regiments of Rifle Men in His Majesty's Service should be clothed in one and the same kind of uniform Jacket, without any further variation, than the distinction of Facing and Buttons. I herewith transmit to you by the Commander in Chief's order a Pattern Jacket for the general use of Rifle Corps, which His Majesty has approved.... I beg you will be so good as to direct any Patterns of Rifle Jackets, now in your Office, to be returned, as being of no further use.
[WO3/35,119: 13 July 1802, Adjutant General to Thomas Fauquier, army clothier.]

17 April 1809

"*alteration in the Peaks of the Caps of the Rifle Corps has been approved, and that they are in future to be square instead of round, as has hitherto been the case.*"
[WO3/47, 474-5; 17 Apr. 1809, Adjutant General to ?]

APPENDIX 12
Inspection Returns for Rifle-Carrying Regiments, 1817–1852

Source: WO27/143-292

Note:

        BB = *ball bags*
    B&Sc = *bayonets & scabbards*
         C = *carbines*
      Do. = *ditto.*
         E = *Establishment*
   M&B = *muskets & bayonets*
         P = *pistols*
       PF = *powder flasks*
      PH = *powder horns*
      RC = *rifled carbines (cavalry rifles)*
  R&RS = *rifles and rifle sword-bayonets*
       SF = *serjeant's fusils*
       s/r = *steel rammers*
  unsble = *unserviceable*
     WO = *worn out*

Date of Inspection	Stationed at	Comments
8th Light Dragoons		
May 1821.	Cawnpore	507 C (701 E), 715 P. Have Rifles
May 1821.	Cawnpore	Some Rifles have bad locks.
Oct.1821.	Cawnpore	Do.
May 1822.	Cawnpore	Weak springs to some locks of C & R.
Dec.1822.	Ft. William	C all unsble. 80 Rifles good order. Wanting 621 C, 283 P.
May 1823.	Chatham	80 R, wanting 255 Cs/r, complement 335.
11th Light Dragoons		
May, Oct 1820	Cawnpore	80 C. 1238 P. The men are practised in firing Ball with their Rifles and Pistols.
May 1821	Meerut	Target practise with Rifles is but indifferent, only 29 Balls put into Target at 100 & 150 Paces out of 80 fired. 10 Rifles per Troop, all marked & browned.
Oct.1821		T.P. better than last: at 100 yds 756 rds fired, 47 hit near bull's-eye. Practise Powder very bad.
Dec.1822	Meerut	80 C, 1238 P.
May 1823	Do	"An experiment has been made by permission upon several of the Carbines, by altering the Lock according to the late approved Invintion for Fowling Pieces, but it is not found, upon trial, to succeed with arms of this description. Do. Dec. 1823."
13th Light Dragoons		
Oct. 1819	Arcot	"Each Troop has Ten Rifles, perfectly new, not yet served out to the Corps."
Dec. 1834	Bangalore	80 RC still not replaced.
May 1839	Do	Do. unsble, WO.
Sept 1842	Ipswich	322 C s/r & 13 P, perc.
15th (King's) Hussars		
Oct. 1823	Canterbury	247 C unsble. Adj. Gen. says "that Rifles would be issued to replace those that were bad, but none have as yet been received." Whole complement June 1824.
1/12th Foot		
June 1817	Port Louis, Mauritius:	46 R&RS
22d Foot		
June 1827	Stony Hill, Jamaica	24 R&RS (4 SF, 498 M&B). Just out from Fermoy.
Aug. 1828	Up Park Camp, Jamaica	24 R&RS. (as last).
Mar. 1829	Spanish Town, Jamaica	24 R&RS.

— 241 —

Oct. 1829	Do.	Do.	(4 SF, 474 M&B).
May 1830	Falmouth,	do.	Do. 4 515
June 1831	Do.	do.	Do. 4 516
Sept. 1832	Do.	do.	Do. Do.

26th Foot

Jan., May 1821	Gibraltar	5 R&RS rec'd from Gibr. Stores 27 Nov. '20.
Dec. 1821		10 R&RS.
May 1822	Gibraltar	10 R&RS.
June 1823	Cork	10 R&RS. (575 M&B). Do. Oct. 1823.
May 1824	Kinsale. do.	Do. Oct. 1824.
June 1825	Tralee Bks.	do. (576 M&B), 75 actually unsble.
Sept. 1825	Limerick	10 R&RS. (493 M&B s, 83 unsble, 164 A)
Sept. 1826	Dublin	No longer have rifles, possibly by Survey
Dec. 1829	Ft. St. George, Madras	1 R&RS, (5 SF, 921 M&B)

33rd Foot

July 1825	Falmouth, Jamaica.	24 R, 4 B&Sc. (570 M&B)
Mar. 1826, May 1827	Spanish Town, do.	24 R, (485 M&B)
Aug. 1828	Stony Hill, do.	24 R, (4 SF, 482 M&B)
Feb. 1829	Ft. Augusta, do.	24 R, 4 482
June 1830	Spanish Town, do.	24 R, 4 489
May 1831	Up Park Camp, do.	24 R, 4 316 nearly WO

50th Foot

Jan. 1826	Stony Hill, Jamaica.	24 R, B&Sc. (370 M&B)

54th Foot

Dec. 1829	Cannanore	1 R&RS, 5 SF, 774 M&B
May 1830	Do.	1 R&RS, 5 SF, 762 M&B
Jan., May 1831	Do.	5 750.
Dec. 1831	Do.	Do. 5 738
May 1832	Trichinopoly	Do. 33 673
May, Dec. 1835	Do.	

55th Foot

Jan. 1826	Dublin	3 Rifles unserviceable.

1/56th Foot

1817	Falcq, Mauritius	105 R, 103 RS (821 M&B) 4200 rounds of Rifle Ball Cartridge

59th Foot

1817	Ft. William	78 R&RS (605 M&B)

65th Foot

May 1817	Bombay	179 R&RS, (667 M&B). "The Rifles are ordered to be returned into Store as soon as they can be replaced by muskets from the Depots."
Oct. 1819	Ft. George, Bombay	107 R&RS (10 SF, 779 M&B)

75th Foot

Dec. 1822–Dec. 1823	Gibraltar.	4 R&RS. (576 M&B)
June, Oct. 1824	Windsor Bks. Gibr.	do. 128 in use above prescribed period.
Apr. 1825	Fermoy Bks.	4 R&RS. (576 M&B) wanting 164.
Sept. 1825	Dublin	4 R&RS. (740 M&B)
June 1826	Enniskillen	4 R&RS. (740 M&B).
Oct. 1826–Nov. 1827	Castlebar	4 R&RS. (740 M&B)
May 1828	Mullingar	4 R&RS. (740 M&B).
Nov. 1828	Birr	Do.
Oct. 1829	Fermoy	Do. Do.

77th Foot

May 1825	Stony Hill, Jamaica	24 R (570 M&B).
Mar. 1826–Aug. 1827	Falmouth, Jamaica	24 R (492 M&B)
July 1828	Spanish Town, do.	24 R (3 SF, 490 M&B).
Feb. 1829	Up Park Camp, do.	24 R 3 492
June 1830	Ft. Augusta, do.	24 R Do.
May 1831	Stony Hill, do.	24 R Do.
Aug. 1832	Spanish Town, do.	24 R 24 492 (ammo incl Rifle)
Jan. 1833	Do. do.	24 RB&Sc 24 C 492 M&B End.

82d Foot

Oct. 1822	Port Louis, Mauritius	30 R&RS. (3 SF, 459 M&B)
May 1823	Do.	No rifles.

84th Foot
June 1827	Ft. Augusta, Jamaica	24 R, (491 M&B) Last at Buttevant.
Aug. 1828	Do.	24 R, (5 SF, 492 M&B).
Feb. 1829	Stony Hill, Jamaica	24 R, 5 492
June 1830	Up Park Camp, do.	24 R, 28 491
May 1831	Spanish Town, do.	22 R, 2 w, do.
Sept. 1832	Maroon Town, do.	25 R, 1 w, 4SF 491 M&B.

91st Foot
May 1825	Ft. Augusta, Jamaica.	22 R&RS, (559 M&B).
Mar. 1826	Up Park Camp, do.	22 R (2 SF, 506 M&B).
July 1827–Aug. 1828	Span. Town	24 R (2 SF, 450 M&B).
July 1828	Falmouth, do.	24 R (4 SF, 470 M&B of which 296 unsble, 30 rep)
June 1830	Stony Hill, do.	24 R (4 SF 507 M&B).

92d Foot
May 1825	Up Park Camp, Jamaica	24 R&RS, (498 M&B).
Mar. 1826	Ft. Augusta, do.	24 R&B&Sc. (3 SF, 498 M&B)

93rd Foot
Aug. 1841–Mar. 1844	Toronto	36 R&RS PERC. Rifle ammo: belted ball 10,464; plain ball 3381; caps 21,034.

97th Foot
Dec. 1832	Colombo	24 R 5SF 516 M&B
July 1835	Kandy	4 R&RS. 8498
Nov. 1846	C G Hope	7 R&B, issued to Pioneers, flintlock

Cape Infantry
Feb. 1825	Grahams Town, SA.	20 R, 16 RS, (320 M&B). "The expertness of the men in Ball Firing is quite wonderful, their sight is so perfectly correct, that there is scarcely an instance of their missing the object they aim at."

Royal Canadian Rifles
Aug. 1842	Drummondville	1050 RB&Sc. Ball & blank, flint.
Mar. 1843	Do.	Do.
Aug. 1843	Niagara	Do. unsble. New arms shortly expected. None Mar 1844: It is officially announced that new Rifles will be supplied.
Sept. 1844	Do.	840 RRS&Sc. PERC & 210 old Flint for the complement of 1050. The new rifles are 'a beautiful and perfect arm' and are in progress of marking.
Feb. 1845	Do.	1050 RRS&Sc. PERC. incl: ball drawers, brass jags, nipple keys and snap caps.

Depot Battalion
May 1843	Stockton, IOW	126 R&RS, 41 SF, 822 M&B flint
May 1845–May 1846	Parkhurst Bks.	Do. 46 913 not clear
Oct. 1846	Do.	Do. 50 1021 all flint.
May 1847	Parkhurst Barracks.	128 R&RS&Sc. Have both flints and caps.
Oct. 1847	Do.	Do., flints: 3339; CC 59,324.
May 1848	Do.	Do., all copper caps.

Royal West India Rangers
July 1817	St Lucia	212 R&RS (E 262). (986 M&B)
May 1818	Antigua	94 R, (E 212), 81 RS (224 M&B)
Dec. 1818		94 R, (E 112), 8 RS (224 M&B)

Royal York Rangers
July 1817	St. Josephs, Trinidad	188 R&RS, (834 M&B)
Oct. 1818	do.	163 R&RS, (29 SF, 478 M&B)

1st Ceylon Light Infantry
July 1817		Have 111 cut down muskets, (1060 M&B)
Oct. 1820		do. (1256 M&B)
Mar. 1822	Kandy.	120 R complete (1045 M&B)
Sept. 1822	Do.	120 do. (1034 M&B)
Mar. 1823	Do.	120 do. M&B bad, receiving new.
Oct. 1823	Do.	120 do. (1025 M&B). New arms delivered since last insp.except rifles which are nearly new.
Dec.1824	Do.	119 do. Est 1556, 910 M&B new.
June, Dec. 1825.	Do.	199 do. (1556 M&B) of which 910 new, 265 are 3/4 worn.

British Military Flintlock Rifles

July 1826	Colombo	Has Malays and Caffres. 120 R new, (951 M&B new) complement 1532. Sjts have: 5 PF, 5 PH, 5 Bullet bags. R&F have: 115 PF, 115 PH, 115 BB, all have Lock Covers, including infantry. Rifles recently arrived fm Eng are about to be issued to the 9 Malay Co's that have not yet received them.
Dec. 1826		Malays are called Ceylon Rifles.

1st Ceylon Rifle Regiment

July, Dec. 1827	Colombo	120 R new, as last.
June 1828	Trincomalee	400 R complete (1282 M&B) Accoutrement numbers still 5/95. 300 of the muskets were issued them in 1813.
Aug. 1829	Colombo	970 R&RS compl. 903 M&B. still 5/95 accoutrements.
Jan. 1830	Colombo	970 R&RS complete: 870 ea ball drawers, leavers wiping eyes, 1000 lock covers. 773 M&B.
Aug. 1830	Do.	(27/207).
Jan. 1831	Do.	Do. 850 Sc, do. ball drawers, wiping eyes & leavers. Sjts have 5 PH, PF,BB, R&F have 95 of each. 524 M&B.
Dec. 1831	Do.	Do. 678 M&B unserviceable.
Dec. 1832	Do.	Do. as Jan. 1831.
July 1833	Do.	1017 R compl, 917 Sc & tools; ball ctg only. 706 M&B.
Feb., Sept.1834	Do.	1017 R compl, same tools &c. ball ctg. 446 M&B, 260 repairable.
Feb. 1835	Do.	As last, but 706 M&B. Rifles beginning to show signs of use.
Aug. 1835	Do.	1050 RB&Sc, 950 impl., ball ctg only. 660 M&B. Same Rifle comment.
Feb., Sept. 1836	Do.	As last, <u>no PH, PF</u> for either Sjt or R&F.
Feb. 1837	Do.	1050 of everything; 743 M&B.
Sept. 1837	Do.	Do. long time in use; 748
Mar. 1838	Do.	Do. no Ball Bags; Do.
Nov. 1838	Do.	Do. 707
Apr. 1839	Do.	Do. 757
Oct. 1839	Do.	Do. Do.
May 1840	Do.	Do. unsble fm long use, applied for new. 738 M&B
May 1841	Kandy	180 RB&Sc, 870 unsble, 738 M&B unsble. New Rifles are expected from England.
Jan. 1843	Kandy	1470 R, 1050 B&Sc., 420 Rifle Swords & Sc, 210 M&B.
Aug. 1843–Mar. 1845	Do.	Do., 370 M&B
May 1846	Colombo	1470 R, 1050 B&Sc, 370 M&B
Aug. 1846	Do.	Do. Do. 420 Rifle Swords & Sc
Mar. 1847	Do.	1365 R, 105 unsble, 630 w. 370 M&B
May 1848	Do.	1730 R, 532 w. 243 unsble all "New Rifles just received and will be issued immediately."
Nov. 1848	Do.	1805 R PERC RS⪼ 507 w. 570 spare nipples, 190 spring cramps, nipple keys, 1805 brass jags, ball drawers, snap caps and stoppers.
Oct. 1848–May 1849	Victoria, Hong Kong	Serv. cos. 630 RRS&Sc PERC.
May 1849	Colombo.	1425 R PERC., 417 w.
Oct. 1849	Victoria H.K.	Serv. cos. 312 R, 314 RS&Sc, complement 315.
Nov. 1849	Colombo	2050 R&RS&Sc., 417 w.
May 1850	Do.	2105 R&RS&Sc., 367 w.
May 1850	Victoria	Same as Oct. 1849.
Nov. 1850	Colombo	Same as May 1850.
Dec. 1850	Victoria	Serv. cos. 315 R&RS&Sc. full complement same thru' May 1852.
Nov. 1851–May 1852	Colombo	2050 PERC. RRS&Sc.

First Battalion, 60th Foot (Royal American Rifle Regiment)

June 1817	Cape of Good Hope, Cape Castle,	105 R&RS (895 M&B)
Oct. 1818	do.	23 R&RS (759 M&B) w/P Horns
Sept. 1819	Quebec	636 R, 659 RS.
May 1820	Do.	644 R, 628 RS. 39 R unsble; no place to shoot.
Oct.1820	Do.	624 R, 628 RS. 39 R&RS unsble
May 1821	Do.	641 R, 625 RS.
Oct.1821	Montreal	Do. "Very good Rifles."
Sept. 1822	Do.	631 R, 605 RS "in use about 6 years." Ball ctg only.
May 1823	Kingston, U.C.	600 R, 604 RS.
Aug. 1823	Do.	Do.
May 1824.	Do.	598 R, 594 RS.
Oct. 1826	Plymouth	600 R & 596 RS unsble, wanting 776. No insp. since arrival here in Aug. 1824.
May 1827	Depot cos, Coimbra.	540 R&B&SC. Men fire with much accuracy.
Oct. 1827	Serv. cos, Mafra, Port. 540 R&B&Sc.	
May 1828	Fermoy Barracks	775 R, 776 RS, nearly new.
Oct. 1828–May 1830	Limerick	776 R&B&Sc.
Oct. 1830	Cork Barracks	776 R, 755 RS 21 wanting.

May 1831	Gibraltar	540 R, 523 RS, ball ctg only
May 1831	Dublin Depot	236 R, 234 B&Sc.
Nov. 1831	Do.	236 R, 233 B&Sc. 4 swords. Ball ctg 15,277 Blank 12892.
Apr. 1832	Gibraltar	540 R, 523 RS, 17 w.
May 1832	Omagh Depot	272 R, 268 B&Sc. "The target practice is regularly conducted, one co. in rotation being kept off duty for that purpose, the Men are divided into Classes, each firing at different Ranges- the Men in general are very fair shots."
Nov.1832	Gibraltar	540 R, 523 RS, 17 w.
Sept. 1832	Maryborough Depot	272 R, 267 B&Sc, 5 w.
May 1833	Gibraltar	540 R&RS.
Do.	Naas Depot	272 RB&Sc.
Oct. 1833	Gibraltar	540 R&RS. Ball & blank ctg
Do.	Limerick Depot	272 RB&Sc. do.
May 1834	Gibraltar	As Oct. 1833.
Do.	Limerick Depot	272 R, 267 B&Sc. 5 w.
Oct. 1834	Do.	261 R, 256 B&Sc, 5 w; ball
Jan. 1835	Malta	540 R&RS. Ball only
Apr. 1835	Do.	539 R, 1 w; 539 B&Sc,1 w;
May, 1835	Nenagh Depot	235 RB&Sc. Ball & blank
Oct. 1835	Stockport Depot	236 RB&Sc. Do.
Aug. 1836	Corfu	539 RB&Sc, 1 w; all accoutrements unsble. B&Bl. Of 374 fired, 58 missed fire.
May 1836	Newcastle u.T. Depot	236 RB&Sc. Acc. being examined by CO Bd. Ball & blank ctgs.
Nov. 1836	Corfu	539 RB&Sc, 1 w; do.
Apr. 1837	Do.	539 R&B; 539 Scab unsble & wanting. B & Bl.
May 1837	Newcastle u.T Depot	192 RB&Sc.
Oct. 1837	Corfu	As Apr. 1837.
Do.	Sunderland Depot	As May 1837. Ball & blank
Mar. 1838	Corfu	539 R&RS. Ball only
May 1838	Hull Depot	192 RB&Sc. arms are oldB&Bl
Oct. 1838	Zante	539 R, 1w; 539 Scabs unsble
Do.	Pigeon House Fort Depot	192 RB&Sc. Ball only
Mar. 1839	Corfu	510 R&B, 175 Sc, 335 w. Ball only.
May 1839	Beggars Bush Dublin	Dep.272 RB&Sc. Ball & blank.
Sept. 1839	Zante	539 R&B, 539 Sc unsble. Do.
Oct. 1839	Birr Depot	272 RB&Sc.
June 1840	Ft Monckton Depot	Do. "high order" Ball only
Oct. 1840	Windsor	811 RB&Sc, 1 w.
Oct. 1842	Manchester	840 RRS&Sc. & accoutrements 60,312 serv CAPS, 32,100 practice CAPS
June 1843	Dublin	Do., 66,336 CAPS.

Second battalion, 60th Light Infantry

May 1817	St Ann's, Barbadoes,	40 R&RS, (274 M&B)
Oct. 1818	Quebec	47 R, 87 RS, (165 M&B). 1 R condemned by Board of Survey, 35 R rep
May 1819	Quebec	639 R, 636 RS rec'd 1816, those in Store from late 7th Bn. Accoutrem'ts rec'd 1815–16.
Nov. 1819–Nov. 1820	Halifax NS.	100 R&RS, (10 SF, 398 M&B)
May 1821	Do.	150 R&RS, do.
Oct. 1821	Do.	180 R&RS, (10 SF, 453 M&B)
May 1822	Do.	106 R&RS, (10 SF, 269 M&B)
Oct. 1822	Do.	105 R&RS, do.
June 1823	Do.	91 R&RS, (10 SF, 245 M&B)
May 1825	Ft. St. Andrew, Berbice	179 R, 185 RS, (10 SF, 398 M&B) Only 2 co's have Rifles, so wanted to complete to new Establishment. "It is understood that Rifles are on their way from England. Rifle ammunition is wanted, and moulds for casting Rifle Balls- one for each Co.- the same number of graduated Powder Measures. for the different Ranges are also required."
May 1826	Rome Plantation Demerara	179 R, 185 RS (10 SF, 398 M&B) 4 co's still want rifles as reported last year.
May 1827	Berbice, Demerara & Esequibo	179 R, 182 RS (353 M&B). Wanting 17 Rifles; 4 cos still want rifles as reported for 2 years.
May 1828	Berbice, Demerara	175 R&RS, (10 SF, 230 M&B v. old) 4 cos still want rifles.
Oct. 1828	Depot, Portsmouth. 350 R&RS.	
May 1829	Depot, do.	350 R&RS, 24 wanting, also 350 bayonets & scabbards.
July 1829	New Amsterdam, Berbice.	175 R&RS (10 SF, 230 M&B). Wanting 151 swords & belts. M&B v. old, 4 cos wanting rifles, reported since 1825.
1829.	Depot, Portsmouth.	350 R, 348 B&Sc. **[check this!]**
May 1830	Albany Barracks.	693 R, 693 "Hand Bayonets" Cartridges: Ball Blank Service 4,960 13,160 Practice 39,480

Sept. 1830	Do.		693 R&RS.
June 1831	Manchester		693 RB&Sc, 90 w.
Oct. 1831	Do.		783 RB&Sc.
June 1832	Dublin		782 RB&Sc. Ball 84,655; blank 13,250.
Nov. 1832	Templemore		782 RB&Sc.
May 1833	Do.		781 R, 1 w; 782 B&Sc.
Oct. 1833	Dublin		782 RB&Sc. Ball & blank
Apr. 1834	Beggars Bush, Dubl.		780 RB&Sc. Do.
Oct. 1834	Kilkenny		782 RB&Sc. Do.
June 1835	Cork		Do. Ret'd fm WI Mar. 1830. Spring allowance of blank ctg not yet drawn.
Oct. 1835	Do.		510 RB&Sc. Ball only.
Do.	Clare Castle	Depot	192 RB&Sc. Ball & blank.
May 1836	Gibraltar		509 R, 1 w;510 B&Sc. Ball & bl Have been here 6 months.
July 1836	Ft. Regent Jersey	Depot	192 RB&Sc. Old soldiers nearly WO, and recruits.
Oct. 1836	Gibraltar		510 RB&Sc.
Do.	Jersey	Depot	192 RB&Sc.
May 1837	Gibraltar		510 R&B, 175 Sc, 335 sc unsble; B & Bl.
Do.	Jersey	Depot	As Oct. 1836. Ball only.
Oct. 1837	Gibraltar		As May 1837; ball only.
Do.	Jersey	Depot	Do. Ball & blank
Apr. 1838	Corfu		As May 1837.
Oct.1838	Do.		Do. BB&LC. Pouches, Pouch Belts, Bayonet Belts, Slings are std accoutrements.
Do.			Portsmouth Depot 192 RB&Sc. B&Bl. Need browning.
Oct. 1839	Corfu		507 R, 3 w; 508 B&Sc, 2 w; LC&BB. B&Bl.
Do.	Clonmel	Depot	272 R, 65 w for Augm; same for B&Sc & accoutrements. Very expert target practice.
Apr. 1840	Corfu		507 RB&Sc 3 w; good for Garrison duty w/considerable repairs until 1841; same accoutrements.
May 1840	Clonmel	Depot	214 RB&Sc. 2 went to serv co at Corfu. Ball & blank
Sept. 1840	Corfu		627 R, 629 B&Sc note as Apr. B & Bl.
Oct. 1840	Newbridge	Depot	215 RB&Sc, 1 w; LC&BB, ball only. New arms expected next year.
Mar. 1841	Corfu		628 R, 629 B&Sc, for Garr...1841
July 1841	Dublin	Depot	215 R, 1 w; 215 B&Sc, 1 w.
May 1842	New Castle, Jamaica		621 RB&Sc svble with considerable repairs, old & many defective. An issue of Lovells new rifle is looked for towards the end of the year.
Nov. 1842	Do.		Do. New arms expected.
Oct. 1842	Dublin	Depot	216 RB&Sc. flint.
May 1843	Newry.		Do.
June 1843	New Castle, Jam.		624 RRS&Sc PERC., 7613 serv. & 65,662 practice caps.
Nov. 1843	Belturbet	Depot	As last. "Percussion are now issuing to the men in lieu of Flint Rifles."

Third Battalion, 60th Light Infantry
May 1818	Halifax NS	108 R & 128 RS, (457 M&B)
Oct. 1818	do.	125 R&RS (484 M&B)
May 1819	do.	77 R&RS (263 M&B)

Fourth Battalion, 60th Light Infantry
May 1817	Demerara	90 R&RS, (716 M&B) "The men are good marksmen."
Mar. 1818	do.	90 R&RS, (716 M&B)
Oct. 1818	do.	77 R&RS (653 M&B)

Fifth Battalion, 60th Rifle Battalion
May 1817	Gibraltar	623 R (E 887), 264 unslbe. 612 Powder Horns wanting to complete.

Sixth Battalion, 60th Foot
May 1817	Fort Augusta, Jamaica	105 R; 105 RS unsble,(506 M&B)

1st Battalion The Rifle Brigade
May 1817	Bourbon. serv. cos.	583 R, 472 RS, 168 B&Sc.
May 1818	Do.	508 R, 400 RS, 158 B&Sc.
Nov. 1818	Cambrai.	517 R, 381 RS, 169 B&Sc.
May 1819	Do.	680 R, 22 RS, 680 B&Sc.
May 1820	Glasgow.	Do., no RS, 675 B&Sc. in fine order but require browning. "...in general excellent marksmen."
Oct. 1820	Do.	Do., 22 RS, 672 B&Sc. Beautifully browned. Ball ctg only
June 1823	Rathkeale.	600 RB&Sc. No t. practice.
Dec. 1823	Dublin.	Do. "old" general bad construction & materials. "They were originally furnished by contractors. New arms are daily expected."
May 1824	Dublin.	600 R, 599 B&Sc. All new. "Rifles of the very best description."

Oct. 1824	Belfast		600 R, 597 B&Sc. "The locks are not equal in point of excellent workmanship. The Hammers are reported soft as is generally the case with Arms newly issued."	
Oct. 1824	Do.		Do. Just arrived fm Dublin.	
July 1825	Emb for Canada		As last. "I cannot say that the Target practice in Firing Ball, answer'd my expectation, altho' from the few men I saw fire in consequence of the Embarkation, I may not be a competent judge-the present allowance of Ball Ctg is insufficient. The mode of making up this Cartridge, it is conceived, might easily be improved on, by Casting the Bullets perhaps 21 instead of 22 to the lb and when made up in cartridge by having the fustian heading of them <u>well greased</u>. This would make the Bullets fit better the Rifles and the greasing, besides rendering the loading so much more easy, might <u>perhaps</u> tend to their cleansing, as I perceive with the Cartridges now in use, they become <u>very soon</u> foul."	
Oct. 1825	Halifax, N.S.		540 R&RS.	
Do.	Cavan.	Depot cos.	236 RB&Sc. Accoutrements incl. Ball Bags, Lock Covers.	
May, Nov. 1826	Halifax		540 RB&Sc.	
Sept. 1826		Depot cos.	236 R, 231 B&Sc.	
May 1827	Halifax		540 RB&Sc, new and in best state.	
Oct. 1827	Do.		Do.	
July 1828	Do.		538 R	
Dec. 1828	Do.		540 RB&Sc.	
Oct. 1828	Gosport Bks.	Depot	236 RB&Sc.	
June 1829	Halifax		540 RB&Sc.	
May 1829	Portsmouth	Depot	236 RB&Sc.	
July 1831	Dover	Depot	236 R, 225 B&Sc. Ball Bags & Lock Covers mentioned.	
Nov. 1831	Fredericton, N.B.		540 RB&Sc.	
July 1832	Do.		539 R, 1 w; 532 B&Sc, 8 w.	
Do.	Dover	Depot	236 B&Sc. BB&LC	
Sept. 1832	Halifax		539 R, 1 w; 533 B&Sc, 7 w.	
June 1833	Do.		Do. 531 9 w. Ball & blank ctgs.	
Aug. 1833	Chatham	Depot	236 R, 234 B&Sc, 2w. BB&LC.	
Oct. 1833	Halifax		539 R, 1 w; 531 B&Sc, 9w. B&Bl	
July 1834	Do.		540 R, 537 B&Sc., 3w. B&Bl.	
June 1834	Jersey	Depot	236 R, 232 B&Sc, 4w. B&Bl.	
Nov. 1834	Halifax		540 R, 537 B&Sc, 3 w. Do.	
Oct. 1834	Jersey Depot		236 R, 232 B&Sc, 4 w. Ball.	
June 1835	Halifax		540 R, 538 B&Sc., 2 w. B&Bl.	
May 1835	Ft Regent Jersey	Dt	236 R, 232 B&Sc, 4w. B&Bl, Ball Bags & Lock Covers.	
Oct. 1835	Do.	Depot	236 R, 233 B&Sc., 3 w. Ball.	
Nov. 1835	Halifax		540 R, 537 B&Sc, 3w. Ball.	
June 1836	Do.		Do. B&Bl.	
May 1836	Jersey	Depot	232 R, 4w; 229 B&Sc, 7w. Do.	
Aug. 1836	Chatham		696 RB&Sc. Ball only.	
Mar. 1839	Windsor.		700 RB&Sc unsble. No report	
Aug. 1840	Weedon Bks.		840 R&RS&Sc. & accoutrements Ball ctg,	77,550 PERC CAPS.
Sept. 1840	Do. Serv. cos.		624 R&RS&Sc, do.	52,950 Do.
Sept. 1840	Do.	Depot	216 Do.,	12,480 Do.
May 1841	Malta.		624 RRS&Sc. Ball & Blank ctg.	46,162 PC.
Do.	Dublin	Depot	216 Do.	8,655 PC.

2nd Battalion The Rifle Brigade

May 1817	St. Pol. serv. cos.		598 R, 384 RS, 175 B&Sc. One to 7 yrs in use.
May 1818	Do.		584 R&RS. 200 B&Sc. 4–8 yrs in use.
Nov. 1818	nr Valenciennes.		564 R, 384 RS, 180 B&Sc. 3 to 10 years in use.
May 1823	Kinsale.		110 RB&Sc. 490 RB&Sc unsble. "a general change is shortly expected for a Rifle of a better description."
Oct. 1823	Limerick.		As last. Arms were received in 1805 and are in general indifferent.
Apr. 1824	Do.		As last. New arms are about to be furnished.
Oct. 1824	Dublin.		600 R, 598 B&Sc. issued in May, inferior locks.
May 1825	Do.		Do., wanting 176 for Augmentation.
Oct. 1825	Enniskillen.		776 R&RS. Target practice excellent, average 5 hits to 1 miss at 150 & 200 yards.
Apr. 1826	Malta.		540 RB&Sc.
May 1826	Kinsale.	Depot	236 R, 233 B&Sc.
Oct. 1826	Clare Castle.	Depot	Do., particularly bad flints; have no armourer.
Nov. 1826–Nov. 1827	Malta.		540 RB&Sc, new.
May, Nov. 1828	Do. (St Elmo)		Do.
Oct. 1828	Devonport	Depot	236 RB&Sc.
May 1829	Malta (St Elmo)		540 RB&Sc.
Do.	Devonport	Depot	236 RB&Sc. Do. Oct. 1829
Apr., Nov. 1830	Malta (Florian)		540 RB&Sc.

Mar. 1831	Do.		Do. 5400 Ball Ctg, 10,420 Bl.
Mar. 1832	Corfu.		504 RB&Sc.
July 1832	Dover	Depot	236 R, 231 B&Sc.
Nov. 1832	Corfu.		504 RB&Sc, some 9 yrs in serv
May, Dec. 1833	Do.		Do. B&Bl.
May 1834	Corfu.		504 RB&Sc. B&Bl.
Oct. 1834	Ft St Geo., Guern. Dt		272 R, 268 B&Sc, 4 w. Ball. (since 19 Nov '33)
June 1835	Argostoli.		504 RB&Sc. will need renewing
Do.	Guernsey	Depot	272 R, 268 B&Sc., 4w. Ball.
Oct. 1835	Do.	Depot	Do.
Oct. 1835–Apr. 1836	Argostoli.		504 RB&Sc. B&Bl.
May 1836	Guernsey	Depot	192 RB&Sc. Ball only.
Oct. 1836	Argostoli.		504 RB&Sc. B&Bl.
Oct. 1837	Portsmouth.		696 RB&Sc, 14 yrs in use. Ball 4 sjts detached to Persia 27 Apr. 1836.
May 1838	Do.		Do. B&Bl.
Oct. 1838	Woolwich.		Do. Ball only.
June 1840	Windsor.		840 R&RS&Sc., & accoutrements, ball ctg., 46,560 PERC CAPS

APPENDIX 13

Volunteer Rifles and Volunteer Corps Described as "Rifle Men" or "Sharp Shooters"

in the War Office VOLUNTEER LISTS of Jan. 1801, Oct. 1804, Mar. 1807, Sept. 1820 and Sept. 1825.

The Board of Ordnance stated clearly in August 1804 that they did not grant any allowance for rifles to Volunteer Corps. [WO47/2580, 1 Aug. 1804, 2134.] Although it is not the intention in this work to become involved with the many hundreds of privately raised and privately armed Volunteer units raised from 1793, the fact that many of them described themselves, and were armed, equipped and trained, as riflemen, makes it necessary for the sake of completeness to recognize their existence. It is interesting to note that Yorkshire, located considerably further from any likely "front line" of domestic defense, had the largest number of rifle-armed Volunteer Corps, one more than front-line Kent.

In terms of design, volunteer rifles fall into two broad categories: those similar to contemporary sporting rifles, and those made more or less to resemble the Government-issue Baker rifle after 1800. Some differ from the Baker rifle only in lacking a bayonet-bar or a butt-trap. One example seen by the writer conforms entirely to a half-stocked octagon-barrelled sporting rifle, but is fitted with a Baker-style bayonet-bar on the right side at the muzzle. Taken as a group volunteer rifles are not generally equipped to take a bayonet. Many rifles are fitted with improved locks having waterproof pans, rollers on either steel or feather-spring, detents, single-set (or 'hair')-triggers, and refined sights, dovetailed for lateral adjustment, with apertures in the leaves. Most are between .60 and .65 calibre, close to but not always capable of taking the Government size ball; a small number are large enough in the bore to accept the .693" musket ball. Rifling and rifling twists vary from the angular groove and quarter-turn of the Baker to eleven- and multi-groove rounded rifling with up to one and a half turns in the barrel being recorded by the writer. Furniture is overwhelmingly brass and generally similar to the Baker; iron-mounted examples are rare.

Rifles fitted with a combination of such refinements as small sporting-gun style locks, set triggers, aperture tang-sights and adjustable foresights with cuts for a sight-shade should not really be described as volunteer rifles; they belong in a classification of their own: the target rifle.

Despite a diligent search of libraries and institutions, the writer was unable to fill a gap in the published Volunteer Lists between 1807 and 1820. This leaves a good deal of information to be located, especially with regard to the disbanding of most of the volunteer rifle units by 1816.

In the date column of the list given below, the initial date shown is that of the first commission granted to an officer of the unit; the final date is that of the last War Office List in which the unit appears.

The additional notes which appear occasionally are from HO 51/137-139.

Listed alphabetically by counties.
NOTE: the number in parentheses after the unit name is the effective rank and file listed in 1804.

Ayrshire
Ayrshire Volunteer Rifle Battalion (100)	22 Aug. 1803–1807
Kilmarnock Riflemen (60)	22 Aug. 1803

Berkshire
Kintbury (Kentbury) Riflemen (240)	3 Oct. 1803–1807

Cambridgeshire
1st Company of Cambridge & Cambridgeshire Riflemen (2 companies of 60 men each, Jan. 1806)	2 Oct. 1804–1807

Carnarvonshire
Loyal Evionydd (Eifionydd) Riflemen (80)	18 Sept 1803–1808
Loyal Snowden Rangers Riflemen (Snowden Riflemen) (80)	15 Sept 1803–1807

Cheshire
Delamere Forest Riflemen (100)	8 Aug. 1803–1807
Stockport Riflemen (60)	12 Oct. 1803–1807

Cork
Cork Riflemen   23 Dec. 1803–1807
Loyal Cork Legion Riflemen (Cork Supplementary Corps)   25 Feb. 1804–1807

Denbighshire
Ruabon Riflemen   12 July 1803–1807

Devonshire
Devon Riflemen   21 Dec. 1803–1807
Devon Supernumerary Riflemen   n.d. 1803–1807

Dorsetshire
Mapleton Riflemen   4 July 1798

Dumfries-shire
1st Dumfries V. Bn, Closeburn Sharpshooters   12 Sept 1804–1807

Elgin
Forres Riflemen (52)   22 Aug. 1803–1807

Essex
Loyal Ongar Hundred Riflemen (40)   31 Dec. 1803
Terling Riflemen   13 Dec. 1803–1807
Witham Riflemen   6 Aug. 1803–1807
Ongar Rifle Co. disbanded 24 Apr. 1810

Forfarshire
Forfarshire Sharpshooters   25 Nov. 1803–1807
Dunnichen Riflemen   18 Oct. 1803
Montrose Riflemen (60)   18 Oct. 1803–1807
   (disbanded 14 Sept. 1807)

Galway
Tully Riflemen   29 Nov. 1803–1807

Glamorganshire
Forest Riflemen   19 Aug. 1803–1807
Glamorgan Riflemen (336)   12 July 1803–1807

Gloucestershire
Loyal King Stanley Riflemen (63)   5 Sept 1803–1807
Severn Riflemen (104)   12 Aug. 1803–1807
Stroud Riflemen   25 July 1798

Hampshire
Alverstoke Riflemen   20 June 1798–1807
Gosport Volunteers, Rifle Company   July 1807
   (reported disbanded 24 Feb. 1809)

Hertfordshire
Hertford Riflemen (100)   12 Aug. 1803
Kimpton Riflemen   12 Aug. 1803–1807

Isle of Wight
Loyal Newport V.I., rifle company   6 Aug. 1803–1807
Loyal Northwood Riflemen   29 Nov. 1803–1807
West Cowes Riflemen (52)   1804

Kent
Kent Riflemen and Sharp Shooters   23 Apr. 1798
Canterbury Riflemen   30 July 1803–1807
Loyal Deptford Riflemen (56)   17 Aug. 1803–1807
Farningham Riflemen (60)   17 Aug. 1803–1807
Maidstone Riflemen (480)   6 Oct. 1803–1807
Margate Riflemen (40)   29 Aug. 1803
Ramsgate Riflemen (Marksmen) (43)   29 Aug. 1803

Kings Co. Irel.
Mountain Rangers Rifle Corps (32)   1 Sept 1803–1807

Lanarkshire
Glasgow Sharp Shooters (480)   7 Sept 1803–1820
   (10 companies of 80 men, Dec. 1819)

Lancashire
Bury Riflemen (60) (attached to Manchester)	6 Sept 1803–1807
Dukinfield Riflemen	24 Apr. 1804–1807
Liverpool Riflemen (132)	9 Aug. 1803–1807
Loyal Preston Riflemen [Ainsworth] (60)	6 Sept 1803–1807
Manchester & Salford Riflemen (300) (disbanded 24 Dec. 1809)	9 Aug. 1803–1807
Medlock Vale Riflemen (60)	6 Sept 1803–1807
Preston Riflemen (60)	24 Oct. 1803–1807
Wigan Riflemen (87) (received Prussian rifle-muskets 16 Oct. 1804)	22 Aug. 1803–1807

Lincolnshire
Filing & Stainton Dales Sharpshooters	12 Oct. 1803

London
Duke of Cumberland's Sharp Shooters (210)	5 Sept 1803–1807
Gray's Inn Riflemen (300)	15 Aug. 1803–1807
Hackney Riflemen (32) (reported disbanded, 26 Dec. 1808)	9 Aug. 1803–1807
3rd Regt. Loyal London V.I., Riflemen	27 Dec. 1803–1807

Londonderry
Londonderry Legion Rifle Company (40)	5 June 1804–1807

Midlothian
1st Bn 2nd Regt Royal Edinburgh company of Sharpshooters attached (60)	27 Sept 1803–1807
Edinburgh Highland Regt Riflemen	17 Dec. 1803–1807

Norfolk
Blickling & Gunton Riflemen (6 capts.)	19 Aug. 1803–1807
Norwich Riflemen (121)	12 Nov. 1803–1807

Northumberland
Loyal Newcastle-upon-Tyne Riflemen	16 Aug. 1803
Percy Tenantry Riflemen (16 capts.)	30 July 1803–1807

(This unit of 1139 men is known to have been issued with the Model 1787 Prussian rifle-muskets purchased by the Government from 1798, in 1803).

Nottinghamshire
Retford Riflemen (100) (company of 60)	8 Aug. 1803–1819

Oxfordshire
Chalbury Sharp Shooters (80)	3 Sept 1803-disb. 21 Mar. 1804

Peebles-shire
Peebles Riflemen (Sharpshooters, 07)	30 Mar. 1804–1807

Pembrokeshire
Llandicilio Riflemen (98)	10 Aug. 1803–1807
Loyal Haverford West Riflemen	29 Aug. 1798

Renfrewshire
Greenock Sharp Shooters (120)	3 Sept 1803–1807
Paisley Riflemen	1 Apr. 1820–1825

(one company of 120 men authorized 3 Jan. 1820; augmented and formed into 4 companies of 60 men each 8 Apr. 1820)

Rutland
Rutland Legion, dismounted Riflemen	28 Aug. 1805–1807
Rutland Riflemen	22 Aug. 1803
Tainton Riflemen	11 Nov. 1803

Somersetshire
Bath Riflemen (75)	1 Nov. 1803–1807
	28 Aug. 1815–1820

Bridgewater Riflemen
	17 Feb. 1804
Somerset Rifle Company	11 July 1798
Somerset Riflemen (West in '03)	13 Dec. 1803–1807
Taunton Riflemen	11 Nov. 1803–1809

The rifles of the North Somerset Yeomanry Cavalry are to be sold at public auction, 3 June 1826

Staffordshire
Lane End Riflemen — 9 Feb. 1804

Suffolk
Farnham & Bury Riflemen — 30 July 1803

Surrey
Rifle Company, 1st Regt. Vol. Inf. — 14 Jan. 1804–1807
Surrey Yeomanry Cavalry — 24 Sept 1803–1807
   Rifle company dissolved 23 Sept. 1818

Waterford, Ire.
City of Waterford Riflemen — 9 Aug. 1803–1807

Westminster
Duke of Cumberland Sharp Shooters — 5 Sept 1803–1807
Grays Inn Riflemen — 15 Aug. 1803–1807

Isle of Wight
Loyal Northwood Riflemen — 8 Aug. 1803–1807

Wigtownshire
Port Patrick Riflemen (80) — 20 June 1803–1807

East Riding Yorkshire received 40 rifles, Sept. 1803

North Riding Yorkshire
Castle Howard Riflemen — 22 Oct. 1803–1807
Filing & Stainton Sharp Shooters — 12 Oct. 1803
Huddersfield Riflemen — 20 May 1820
Northern District of North Riding of York, Riflemen — 10 May 1798
Stockton Forest Riflemen (56) — 28 Aug. 1803–1807

West Riding Yorkshire Volunteers received Prussian rifle-muskets — 18 Jan. 1805
Bridlington Riflemen — 5 Sept 1803

— ABBREVIATIONS IN THE ENDNOTES —

AB	Abercromby Papers, Huntington Library
Add. Mss.	Additional Manuscripts in the British Library
BL	British Library
CO	Colonial Office Papers, Public Record Office
HL	Henry E. Huntington Library, San Marino, California
HM	Huntington Manuscripts, Huntington Library
HSP	Historical Society of Pennsylvania, Philadelphia.
LC	Library of Congress, Washington, DC.
LO	Loudoun Papers, Huntington Library
NYCD	Documents Relative to the Colonial History of the State of New York. O'Callaghan.
PAC	Public Archives of Canada
PMG	Paymaster General's Papers, Public Record Office
PMH&B	Pennsylvania Magazine of History and Biography
PRO	Public Record Office, Kew
SP	State Papers, Public Record Office, Kew
WLCL	William L. Clements Library, An Arbor, Michigan
WO	War Office Papers, Public Record Office

Endnotes, Listed by Chapter

For an explanation of the abbreviations used in the citations below, please refer to the table on the previous page.

Introduction
1. *A Treatise of Artillery: or, of the Arms and Machines Used in War since the Invention of Gunpowder. Being the First Part of Le Blond's Elements of War: Written in French by that eminent Mathematician, for the Use of Lewis Charles of Lorraine, Count de Brionne, and publish'd for the Instruction of the Young Gentlemen in the Armies of France.* London, 1746, Chap. IX, pp. 62–3. (Reprint by Museum Restoration Service, Ottawa, 1970).

Chapter 1
1. BL, Add. Mss. 5795, 408,421.
2. WO55/352B, 248; SP44/186, 310.
3. WO55/1813, 3 June 1746.
4. SP41/37, 13 Dec. 1746; BL, Add. Mss. 33,046.
5. WO47/43, 35.
6. WO55/353, 25 July and 14 Oct. 1747.
7. WO47/44, 242.
8. WO47/45, 25.
9. Kopperman, P.E. *Braddock at the Monongahela*, 38, 206-7.
10. Printed in: S. Pargellis, *Military Affairs in North America*, 115.
11. HM1717, II, 28.
12. *Ibid.*, 34.
13. LO 4442.
14. Loudoun to Furnis, LO 3623.
15. LO 6688.
16. LO 6897.
17. BL, Add. Mss. 21,643.
18. AB 255.
19. Printed in: N.J. O'Conor *A Servant of the Crown in North America*, 96.
20. Monypenny Orderly Book 1758-9 in: *The Bulletin of the Fort Ticonderoga Museum*, v. XII, No. 5, Dec. 1969, 348.
21. *Ibid.*, 22 June, 353.
22. *Ibid.*, No. 6, Oct. 1970, 435-6.
23. *Ibid.*, 104.
24. HL, AB 407
25. Monypenny, BFTM, v.13, No. 2 (June 1971), 166.
26. HM 687, Orderly Book of Lt. J. Bull 1/NY Regt, 104
27. Willson, B., 367.
28. BL, Add. Mss. 21,652, 24.
29. *Ibid.*, 32.
30. *Ibid.*, 40.
31. *Ibid.*, 21,641, 2.
32. *Ibid.*, 21,640, 66.
33. Forbes' Orderly Book 24 Nov., Washington Papers, Library of Congress.
34. BL, HBP, 21, 644, 80.
35. Information for this paragraph comes from Savory, *His Britannic Majesty's Army in Germany during the Seven Years War*, to which the reader is referred for details of the battles and units, as well as to the excellent bibliography. For numbers see also PRO, PMG 60/1.
36. Waiting for source from author.
37. RAI, ms #1010, General Orders for the Army, Germany, 29 Mar.–20 June 1762: 23 May 1762.
38. *Ibid.*, 9 June 1762. WO51/217, 16 Apr. 1762.
39. Savory, *op. cit.*, 352, 354, 407.
40. *Ibid.*, 371, 400, 511.
41. Printed in: Kauffman, Henry J. *Early American Gunsmiths 1650–1850*, xvii.
42. WO55/2140, 114: 15 Feb. 1762; WO47/59, 134; WO55/363.
43. WO55/2140, 118: 20 Feb. 1762.
44. WO51/217, 16 Apr. 1762.
45. WO47/62, 310, 16 Dec. 1763.
46. Quoted in Lawson, C.C.P., *A History of the Uniforms of the British Army*, v. 2, 195-6, from a PRO reference.
47. WO47/63, 16, 20 Jan. 1764.
48. WO3/3, 102.

Chapter 2
1. Willard, p. 167.
2. Evelyn, W. Glanville. *Memoirs & Letters...*, Oxford, 1879, 67.
3. CO5/92, 568.
4. Historic Manuscripts Commission, Stopford-Sackville Manuscripts, II, 18.
5. *The Iron Duke*, vol. 27, No. 80 (Apr. 1951), p. 65: 3 Sept. 1776.
6. McKenzie, Diary, p. 27.
7. *The Iron Duke*, No. 81 (July 1951), p. 106.
8. *Ibid.*, p. 107.
9. *The Craftsman*, 13 Oct. 1775.
10. WO51/265, 173.
11. WO46/10, 46: Townshend to Germain, 31 Dec. 1775.
12. *Ibid.*, 27: Townshend to Faucitt at Hanover, 4 Jan. 1776.
13. CO5/62, 26: Germain to Townshend, 15 Jan. 1776.
14. CO5/256, 10.
15. WO47/87, 47: 30 Jan. 1776.
16. *Scots Magazine*, 1776, 106: 3 Feb. 1776.
17. WO47/87, 172, 192.
18. WO46/10, 83: Townshend to Howe at Boston, 12 Mar. 1776.
19. WO47/87, 243: 19 Mar. 1776.
20. *Ibid.*, 262: 26 Mar. 1776.
21. *Ibid.*, 339: 17–18 Apr. 1776.
22. *Ibid.*
23. WO51/270, 54: 8 May 1776. Warrant dated 24 Apr. 1776. WO47/87, 357; West, J., 202–3.
24. WO47/87, 423.
25. *Ibid.*, 394, 402.
26. *Ibid.*, 444.
27. *Journal for Army Historical Research*, XVII, 234. From William Clachar's diary of a visit to Birmingham, undated; Clachar was editor of the *Chelmsford Chronicle*.
28. CO324/44, 73.
29. WO47/87, 484-5: 5 June 1776.
30. *Ibid.*, 512.
31. WO55/2147, 10-11,19; 27–8 June, 14 July 1776; WO47/87,541: 29 June 1776; WO47/88, 24: 9/10 July 1776.
32. WO55/2147, 25,43; WO47/88, 112: 28 Aug. 1776; 124: 1 September 1776.
33. *Ibid.*, 15: 9/10 July 1776.
34. WO51/268, 113.
35. WO47/88, 51: 1 Aug. 1776.
36. WO51/270, 337.
37. WO51/269, 316; /270, 175, 73.
38. WO47/87, 158.
39. WO51/271, 135.
40. WO51/272, 16-17: 31 October 1776.
41. WO51/270, 192, paid 7 November 1776.
42. WO52/19, 81: 26 November 1784, No. 1085.
43. WO51/270, 354-5; /272, 114; /273, 47. All on Warrants of Justification dated 7 February 1777.
44. WO47/89, 105: 28 January 1777.
45. WO46/10, 83.
46. *Ibid.*, 117.
47. Harcourt, E.W. (ed), *The Harcourt Papers*, v. XI, 170.
48. WO47/87, 461.
49. WO51/270, 116.
50. Uhlendorf, B.A. (ed) *Revolution in America*, 55.
51. WO47/93, 267: 8 Apr. 1779.
52. "Journal of Serjeant Thomas Sullivan of the 49th Regiment" in: *Pennsylvania Magazine of History and Biography*, v. 34 (1910).
53. Library of Congress, George Washington Papers, v. 6, series 6: Orderly Book 4 Aug.–13 October 1778. I am greatly indebted to James L. Kochan for this entry.
54. *Journal of An Expedition against the Rebels of Georgia in North AmericaÉ* edited by Colin Campbell, Darien GA, 1981, 37, 42, 49, 85.

— 253 —

55. Orderly Book of Frederick DePeyster. New-York Historical Society, DePeyster Papers, vol. 1741-1836.
56. William L. Clements Library, MacKenzie Papers.
57. Ibid.
58. Ibid., and Clinton Papers 155:9.
59. William L. Clements Library, Wray Papers.
60. William L. Clements Library, Clinton's Orders 1778-1782, roll 56, p. 157.
61. PRO30/55, v. 64 (7107).
62. Ibid., v. 60 (6723).

Chapter Three
1. Blackmore, Howard L. *Guns and Rifles of the World*, 60.
2. *Abridgements of the Patent Specifications Relating to Fire-Arms and other Weapons Ammunition & Accoutrements 1588-1858*. London, Holland Press reprint, 1960, 26.
3. WO3/5, 16.
4. *Scots Magazine*, 1776, 217.
5. WO46/10, 136: Courtney to Boddington.
6. WO5/270, 195.
7. WO47/87, 533.
8. WO47/88, 106: 28 Aug. 1776.
9. *Scots Magazine*, 1776, 558.
10. Ferguson, Adam. *Biographical Sketch, or Memoir of Lieutenant-Colonel Patrick Ferguson: originally intended for the British Encyclopaedia*. By Adam Ferguson, L.L.D. ... Edinburgh, 1817, 13.
11. WO4/88, 256.
12. WO47/88, 292: 22 Nov. 1776.
13. *Gentleman's Magazine*, 1776, 574.
14. WO47/89, 136.
15. WO51/270, 354-5.
16. WO47/89, 102: 28 Jan. 1777.
17. Ibid., 111; 31 Jan. 1777.
18. Ibid., 135; 4 Feb. 1777.
19. WO51/275, 16.
20. WO51/284, 18.
21. WO47/89, 126: 4 Feb. 1777.
22. WO4/99, 138.
23. Ibid., 155: 22 Feb. 1777.
24. WO51/273, 109.
25. WO47/89, 261.
26. WO4/99, 217: Barrington to Trapaud 6 Mar.1777.
27. Ibid., 218.
28. WO4/273, 227-8; Barrington to Howe at New York City, 6 Mar. 1777.
29. WO4/99, 220: 10 Mar. 1777.
30. WO55/2009, 253: 3 Mar. 1777.
31. WO4/99, 440: 21 and 25 Mar. 1777.
32. WO55/2009, 262: 23 Mar. 1777.
33. WO55/2147, 177: 26 Mar. 1777.
34. WO47/89, 418: 4 Apr. 1777.
35. Ibid., 672: 6 June 1777.
36. WO55/2010, 55 12 June 1777.
37. WO55/2147, 227: 16 June 1777.
38. Ibid., 230: 22 June 1777.
39. Kipping, Ernst and Smith, Samuel S.(eds) *At General Howe's Side 1776-1778. The Diary of General William Howe's aide de camp, Captain Friedrich von Muenchhausen*. Monmouth Beach, NJ, 1974, 13. Hereafter cited as K&S.
40. British Army Orderly Book 26 Sept. 1776-2 June 1777, New-York Historical Society, No. 40, reel 4, 29 May 1777.
41. Ibid., 30 May.
42. Ibid., 1 June.
43. WO1/10, 114: 1 June 1777.
44. Lydenberg, Harry M. (ed) *Archibald Robertson, Lieut. General Royal Engineers. His Diaries and Sketches in America 1762-1780*. New York, 1930, 136. Hereafter cited as Lydenberg.
45. Lodge, Henry Cabot (ed) *Andre's Journal*, Vol. 1, map between pages 40-1. Hereafter cited as Lodge. Shows Ferguson's corps to left of Bonham Town, With the 71st on the right and Guards on the left, along Brunswick-Bonham Town Road, 21 June 1777.
46. Stephen Kemble's Orderly Book, Collections of the New-York Historical Society, 1884-5, 443, 21 June 1777.
47. Tustin, Joseph P. (ed. & trans.) *Diary of the American War. A Hessian Journal. Captain Johann Ewald, Field Jager Corps*. New Haven and London, 1979, 65, 68. Hereafter cited as Tustin.
48. Kemble, *op. cit.*, 443.
49. Ibid., 25 June 1777, 448, 450.
50. Tustin, *op. cit.*, 69.
51. Kemble, *op. cit.*, 454-5.
52. Ibid., Staten Island 7 July, 466.
53. K&S, *op. cit.*, 18 July, 22.
54. Lodge, *op. cit.*, 59, 71.
55. Tustin, *op. cit.*, 72.
56. K&S, *op. cit.*, 26.
57. Kemble, *op. cit.*, 474.
58. Tustin, *op. cit.*, 74.
59. K&S, *op. cit.*, 25 Aug., 26.
60. Lodge, *op. cit.*, 69, 70.
61. Kemble, *op. cit.*, 477.
62. Tustin, *op. cit.*, 75-6, 77.
63. Kemble, *op.cit.*, 484.
64. K&S, *op. cit.*, 28.
65. Lodge, *op. cit.*, 81.
66. Tustin, *op.cit.*, 79; Kemble, *op. cit.*, 489.
67. Edinburgh University Library, Laing Papers II, 456.2, Ferguson to unknown, 31 Jan. 1778.
68. Lydenberg, *op. cit.*, 146.
69. Tustin, *op. cit*, 81.
70. Baurmeister Letters in: *Pennsylvania Magazine of History & Biography*, vol. LIX, 405-6. Hereafter cited as Baurmeister.
71. Journal of Sergeant Thomas Sullivan, 49th Foot in: *Pennsylvania Magazine of History & Biography*, vol. XXXI (1907), 412.
72. See note 67, *op. cit.*
73. See note 67 Laing II. 456.3.
74. Tustin, *op. cit*, 82.
75. Baurmeister, *op. cit.*, 406-7.
76. Ferguson, A., *op. cit.*, 66.
77. Kemble, *op. cit.*, 495.
78. "A Contemporary British Account of General Sir William Howe's Military Operations in 1777; the original in the Harvard University Library" in: *Proceedings of the American Antiquarian Society*, new series, v. 40 (1930), 78.
79. CO5/94, 881-2, 1 Oct. 1777.
80. Ferguson, A., *op. cit.*, 17-18.
81. Pleasants, Henry Jr., "The Battle of Paoli" in: PMH&B, LXXII (1948), 46.
82. Library of Congress, Orderly Book of Capt. Thomas Armstrong, 64th Light Infantry, 2d L.I. Battalion, 13 Sept.-3 Oct. 1777 in: George Washington Papers. I am greatly indebted to James L. Kochan, for this and the following reference.
83. Ibid., 34.
84. Edinburgh University Library, Laing II.456.4.
85. PRO, PMG14/22.
86. WLCL, Orderly Book of composite Guards Brigade in North America 3 Apr. 1776-1 May 1778.
87. RAI, ms. #1039, General Orders for the Army in America, 13 June 1778-15 Sept. 1778: 24 July 1778.
88. WLCL, Wray Papers.
89. PRO 30/55, v. 64 (7107).

Chapter 4
The major source for this chapter is the papers of William Faucitt, the officer assigned to make the treaties with the German prices, and to oversee and inspect the men supplied under those treaties, specifically his reports to Lord Suffolk, the Secretary of State dealing with German affairs. These are in the Public Record Office, in the State Papers files as indicated. Also consulted were the Rainsford Papers in the British Library.

1. For the American rifle companies' organization and life-spans, see: Wright, Robert K. Jr., *The Continental Army*, Washington, DC, 1986.
2. "The Journal of Lieutenant Johann Carl Phillip von Krafft" in: *Collections of the New-York Historical Society for the Year 1882*, p. 56.
3. For the main references for jäger operations see Bibiography under: Tustin, Baurmeister, Uhlendorf, Kipping & Smith, and also footnote 2.
4. SP81/182.
5. SP81/183: 25 Mar. 1776.
6. Ibid.: 9 Apr. 1776.
7. SP81/184: 3 June 1776.
8. SP81/185, 1776.
9. Ibid.
10. Ibid.: 16 Dec. 1776.

11. SP81/184: 10 Feb. 1777.
12. SP81/188: 27 May 1777.
13. Ibid.: 4 July 1777.
14. Ibid.
15. SP81/189: 10 Dec. 1777.
16. SP81/190; /191: 14 Oct. 1778.
17. SP81/192: 2 May 1779.
18. Ibid.: 3 Apr. 1779.
19. SP81/193: 1 June 1780.
20. Ibid.: 26 May 1780.
21. SP81/194: April 1781.
22. SP81/195.
23. AO3/55, 1.
24. Kapp, Friedrich. *Der Soldatenhandel deutscher Fürsten nach nach Amerika,* Berlin (1864), 235; SP Holland, 592.
25. SP81/105.
26. SP81/184.
27. Ibid.: 12 Mar. 1777.
28. Ibid.: 15 Mar. 1777.
29. SP81/187: 9 Apr. 1777.
30. SP81/189.
31. SP81/190: 23 Jan. 1778.
32. SP81/192: 26 & 29 Mar. 1779.
33. SP81/193: 22 Mar. 1780.
34. SP81/194: Apr. 1781.
35. SP81/195.
36. SP81/194.
37. Ibid.: Apr. 1781.
38. Ibid.
39. McKenzie *Diary,* 2, 587–8.
40. SP81/184: 21 Feb. 1777.
41. CO5/94, 861.
42. SP81/184: 4 Mar. 1777.
43. Ibid.: 28 Mar. 1777.
44. SP81/189.
45. WO4/104, 482.
46. SP81/190: 23 Jan. 1778.
47. SP81/192: 29 Mar. 1779.
48. SP81/193: 22 Mar. 1780.
49. SP81/194: 10 Feb, Apr. 1781.
50. SP81/195.
51. SP81/184.
52. SP81/189: 10 Dec. 1777.
53. Stone, William L. (ed.) *Journal of Captain Pausch Chief of the Hanau Artillery during the Burgoyne Campaign,* Albany, Joel Munsell's Sons, 1886. p. 176.
54. SP81/191: 15 July 1778.
55. Ibid.: 22 Apr. 1778.
56. SP81/192: 20 Apr. 1779.
57. SP81/191.
58. Atwood, Rodney. *The Hessians,* 217.
59. WO55/2009, 116, 137; /2010, 1, 3, 7.
60. WLCL, Wray Papers, 1 Apr. 1780.
61. WO28/7: 19 Oct. 1780, at Quebec.

Chapter Five
1. Kemble Orderly Book.
2. Carter, William. *A Genuine Detail of the Several Engagements, Positions, and Movements of the Royal and American Armies during the Years 1775 and 1776...* London, 1784. Carter was a lieutenant in the 40th Foot.
3. Kemble's Journal: 58, 79, 81.
4. Lydenberg, 88: 7 July 1776.
5. "A Narrative of the Proceedings of a Body of Loyalists in North Carolina" enclosed in Gen. Howe's letter of 25 Apr. 1776 to Germain; quoted in Rankin, H.F. *The Moores Creek Bridge Campaign,* 38. The number includes not only arms of the actual participants (total firearms not more than 650) but also those gathered in during the subsequent disarming. This concentration of rifles in north-central North Carolina is in line with the writer's findings in probate will inventories for the region in 1773-4, which showed the highest concentration of rifles from Massachusetts to Georgia in this very region. This is probably accounted for by its location on the Great Wagon Road which led from Philadelphia through Lancaster County Pa., and on south, and by the activity of Moravian riflemakers in this region of North Carolina. See Jones, Alice H. *American Colonial Wealth,* 3 vols., N.Y. Arno Press, 1977 and Bivens, John Jr., *Longrifles of North Carolina,* 2d ed., York PA, George Shumway, 1988, 7-11, 44-45.
6. Cann, Marvin L. "Prelude to War: the First Battle of Ninety-Six" in: *South Carolina Magazine of History & Biography,* v. 76 (1975) 197-214.
7. Ashmore, Otis & Olmstead, Charles H. "The Battles of Kettle Creek and Briar Creek" in: *Collections of the Georgia Historical Society,* v. 10 (June 1926), 85-126.
8. PRO30/55/36 (4211).
9. WLCL, Clinton Papers, Misc. Corres. 1776-82: 20 Mar. 1776.
10. CO5/557, 3: Indian Accounts, East Florida, 25 June 1775-24 June 1776.
11. PRO30/55, v. 5 (584).
12. WLCL, Clinton Papers, Misc. Correspondence, roll 57: 23 Aug. 1777.
13. PMG14/71, 231.
14. PRO30/55, v. 46 (5238).
15. Simcoe, 230.
16. PAC, RG81, C series, v. 1874.
17. Simcoe, 107-8.
18. LC, Pattison Papers, WO9.
19. PAC, RG81, C series, v. 1863.
20. Simcoe, 230.
21. Ibid., 237.
22. Ibid., 233.
23. WLCL, Wray Papers: Remain of Ordnance and Stores, Savannah 1 April 1780.
24. Quoted from Hamilton's Journal, 23 Aug. 1778 in: Barnhart, John D. *Henry Hamilton and George Rogers Clark in the American Revolution,* 104.

Chapter Six
1. Pennsylvania Colonial Records. IV, 660, 8 June 1745, in *Pennsylvania Magazine of History and Biography,* II, 432.
2. Pennsylvania Council Minutes, IV, 680-5.
3. Historical Society of Pennsylvania, Etting 40, Ohio Co. Vol. 1, 17, 30.
4. Hamilton, Charles (ed) Braddock's Defeat. Norman, 1959, 14 n8.
5. Historical Society of Pennsylvania, Bartram Papers, I, 44, John Bartram to Peter Collinson, 4 Feb. 1756.
6. Pennsylvania Archives 2,643: 24 Apr. 1756.
7. Ibid., 3, 67.
8. as note 6.
9. Pa. Col. Recs., VI, 649, Oct. 1756.
10. McDowell, W.M. Jr. (ed). *Documents Relating to Indian Affairs 1754-1765.* Columbia, 1970, 296.
11. Ibid., 353.
12. Library of Congress, George Washington Papers, reel 30.
13. Pa. Col. Recs., VII, 552.
14. Huntington Library, Loudoun Papers, LO4; PRO, WO34/47, 325.
15. Pa. Col. Recs., III, 293.
16. British Library, Henry Bouquet Papers, I, 341.
17. "Journal of James Kenny 1758-9" in: *Pennsylvania Magazine of History and Biography,* 37 (1913), 422, 420.
18. Pa. Col. Recs., 2d ser. II, 621: 10 Apr. 1759.
19. Historical Society of Pennsylvania, Shamokin Invoice Book #19.
20. Ibid., Shamokin Ledger #16.
21. Ibid., Indian Commissioner's Daybook, Shamokin, 1759-60.
22. Ibid., 1760-1.
23. Ibid., Fort Augusta Ledger A, 8 Apr.-24 Nov. 1762.
24. Ibid., #31, 6 May-10 Aug. 1763.
25. Ibid., Indian Commissioners, James Quaint's Receipts, 16 Aug. 1763.
26. New York Colonial Documents, VII, 61-6.
27. Ibid., 692.
28. Hamilton, et al (eds.) *The Papers of Sir William Johnson,* IV, 496.
29. PRO, CO5/66, 359: 24 Aug. 1765.
30. Pennsylvania State Archives, Harrisburg. Baynton, Wharton & Morgan Papers, Box 24.
31. Ibid., Account Book.
32. Historical Society of Pennsylvania, Cadwalader Papers, George Croghan's Accounts, Box 2.
33. Ibid., Box 3.
34. Schenectady County Historical Society, Letter Book of Daniel Campbel, 71: 4 Aug. 1772.
35. Ibid., 113: 29 Mar. 1773.
36. Ibid., 150: 12 Mar. 1774.
37. Pennsylvania State Archives, BW&M, Box 15.
38. Ibid., Box 23.
39. Ibid., MG19, Box 15.

40. Powell, W.S. (ed.) *The Correspondence of William Tryon and other Selected Papers.* II, 400: 3 Nov. 1769.
41. PRO, CO5/73.
42. Johnson Papers, XII, 968.
43. Bartram, William. *Travels Through North & South Carolina, Georgia, East and West Florida...* London, 1794, 20.
44. PRO, CO5/75: 9 Sept. 1773.
45. Library of Congress, Daniel Claus Papers, I, 162-4: 25 Apr. 1774.
46. as note 32, Box 3.
47. PRO, CO5/77, 22-4, 52, 60.
48. Bailey, Kenneth P. *The Ohio Company Papers 1753-1817*, 338, 410.
49. as note 45, II, 53; and other accounts of the incident.
50. PRO, CO5/94, 223: 3 May.
51. PRO, Privy Council 2.
52. PRO30/55, 21 (2599), 95 (10244).
53. British Library, Haldimand Papers 21,760, 366: 17 Sept. 1780 to Guy Johnson.
54. PRO30/55 (2868).
55. PRO, CO42/40, 331: 19 Oct. 1780.
56. as note 53, 21,783, 62.
57. *Ibid.*, 21,777, 215: 2 July 1780.
58. PRO, WO28/7.
59. as note 53, 21,783, 229.
60. *Ibid.*, 331-2.
61. *Ibid.*, 21,765, 282, Return of 14 June 1782.
62. *Ibid.*, 21,762, 325: 20 Dec. 1782.
63. *Ibid.*, 21,775, 243.
64. *Ibid.*, 21,777, 422.
65. *Ibid.*, 313, 315, 317: 20 Mar. 1781.

Chapter Seven
1. WO47/104, 1 and WO52/20, 50, 1 May 1783.
2. WO47/104, 119, 28 July 1784.
3. WO47/105, 152, 2 Feb. 1785.
4. WO47/107, 464, 5 Apr. 1785.
5. WO47/105, 594-95.
6. WO26/33, 302-08.
7. WO47/107, 272, 1 Mar. 1785.
8. *Ibid.*, 308.
9. WO26/33.
10. WO/26/33, reprinted in JAHR, XXV, 88-89.
11. WO71/11.
12. KCC U269 087/1, Royal Laboratory Courses, pp. 378-387. I am deeply grateful to the late Capt. A.B. Caruana, R.A., for this valuable reference.
13. WO52/58, 264.

Chapter Eight
1. WO1/785, 17, Chatham to Castlereigh, 19 June 1807.
2. HO50/371, 7 June 1794.
3. WO1/780, 217, 10 Feb. 1795.
4. WO1/898.
5. WO6/25.
6. Butler, Lewis. *Annals of the King's Royal Rifle Corps*, London, 1913, 2 vols., vol. I, 253.
7. WO47/2560, 510, 26 May 1796; also 19 May.
8. WO1/782, 155, Crew to Huskisson, 12 May 1798.
9. WO6/142, 734, 20 May 1798.
10. WO52/114; WO52/133; WO52/138; WO52/139.
11. Personal communication from G.M. Wilson, Master of The Armouries, who researched the Alnwick Papers on the rifles and their accessories.
12. Wirtgen, Arnold. *Handfeuerwaffen und preußische Heeresreform 1807 bis 1813*, 126-150, for this rifle musket 134-6.
13. WO52/130.
14. WO6/142, 310, 25 July 1801.
15. WO52/130, 24 Aug. 1799.
16. Personal communication with D.F. Harding, author of *Smallarms of the East India Company 1600-1856*.
17. WO27/93, 15 June 1808; WO27/102, 12 Oct. 1809.
18. Stewart, Charles H. *The Service of British Regiments in North America. A Resumé.*
19. WO6/6.
20. Atkinson, C.T. 'Foreign Regiments in the British Army, 1793-1802' in: *Journal of Army Historical Research*, vol. 21 (Winter, 1942) No. 84, to vol. 22 (Winter, 1944) No. 92, several parts in each volume beginning in volume 21 p. 175. JAHR, 22, 2-3, 322-4.
21. *Ibid.*, 5.
22. *Ibid.*, 320.
23. WO1/898; Atkinson, op. cit., 176.
24. WO4/178; /179.
25. WO3/330, 27 Oct. 1800, 113.
26. WO4/181; Atkinson op.cit., 319.
27. Atkinson, *op. cit.*, 317-18.
28. *Ibid.*, 21, 176.
29. WO1/900; Atkinson, op.cit.,22.
30. Atkinson, *op. cit.*, 22, 240.
31. *Ibid.*
32. *Ibid.*
33. WO1/900, 14 Feb. 1797.
34. Atkinson, *op. cit.*, 22, 240.
35. WO1/900, f.103.
36. *Ibid.*
37. Atkinson, *op. cit.*, 22, 242.
38. Atkinson, *op. cit.*, 22, 248-9.
39. WO1/82; Atkinson, *op. cit.*, 22, 249.
40. WO1/899, 503.
41. Atkinson, op.cit., 22, 250.
42. Milne, S.M. & Terry, A. *The Annals of the Kings Royal Rifle Corps.* Appendix dealing with Uniform, Armament & Equipment. London, 1913, 45.
43. WO4/782, 25 Jan. 1798.
44. Money, Colonel. *Observations on the Use of Chasseurs and Irregulars with an Army in an Inclosed Country, &c. &c.* London, printed by T. Rickaby, 1798, 7.
45. WO1/782, 14 Nov. 1799, 445.
46. Stranks, C.J. (ed.), *The Path of Glory, being the Memoirs of the Extraordinary Career of John Shipp, written by Himself.* London, 1969, 29-31.
47. WO1/894, 686. I am indebted to D.F. Harding for this and the previous references.
48. WO47/2376, 353, to Col. Sontag, 3 June 1800. WO47/2569, 1150-1. See Appendices for the contract for the Prince of Orange's rifles.
49. WO47/2569, 1150-54, 7 Oct. 1800.
50. WO1/664, 199, 7 Oct. 1800.
51. WO1/664, 15 Sept. 1801.
52. WO52/131, 229.
53. WO3/330, 164, 14 Nov. 1800.
54. WO47/2571, 593, 21 June 1801.

Chapter Nine
1. Kent County Council, U269,087/1, p. 384, 14 Feb. 1800.
2. *Ibid.*, p. 384.
3. Baker, E. *Remarks on Rifle Guns;...* London, in all 11 editions from 1802 to 1835, the page varying with the edition.
4. WO52/131; /199; /295.
5. WO52/139, 156.
6. WO47/2568,374, 9 Apr. 1800.
7. WO47/2569, 748, 1 July 1800.
8. WO52/138, 30 June 1800.
9. WO52/139, 31 Aug. 1800; /147, 30 Sept. 1800.
10. WO47/2571, 675, 18 July 1801.
11. WO52/161, 26, 20 Feb. 1802.
12. WO52/159.
13. WO47/2571, 964-5, 29 Sept. 1801.
14. WO47/2584, 2510, 1 July 1805.
15. WO47/2588, 718, 19 Feb. 1806.
16. WO47/2589, 1175, 21 Mar. 1806.
17. WO47/2590, 2003, 12 May 1806.
18. WO47/2618, 4261, 10 Dec. 1810.
19. WO47/2622, 2887, 7 Aug. 1811.
20. WO47/2590, 2634, 23 June 1806.
21. WO52/337, 84, 107.
22. WO47/2621, 2113-4, 7 June 1811.
23. Teasdale-Buckell, G.T. *Experts on Guns and Shooting*, 448.
24. WO3/35, 103, 3 July 1802.
25. WO47/2590, 2634, 23 June 1806.
26. WO3/193, 268, 15 June 1807.
27. WO3/197, 59, 12 June 1809.
28. *Ibid.*, 101, 27 June 1809.
29. WO3/48, 315, 29 June 1809.
30. WO3/199, 22, 14 May 1810.
31. *Ibid.*, 117, 13 June 1810.
32. WO3/203, 115, 28 Feb. 1812.
33. WO3/204, 400, 21 Oct. 1812.
34. WO3/205, 405, 5 Mar. 1813.
35. WO52/231, 30 Sept. 1806
36. WO47/2593, 4516, 21 Nov. 1806
37. WO52/266, 190, 23 Feb. 1807
38. *Ibid.*, 21 Feb. 1807
39. Dupin, Charles. *View of the Military Forces of Great Britain*, London, 1822, quoting The 15th Report of Military Enquiry showing small arms fabricated and received into the magazines of the

Ordnance from the 1st of April 1803 to the 31st December 1809.

Chapter Ten
1. Anonymous [printed for Robert Harford and always referenced as 'Harford'], *English Military Discipline or The Way of Exercising Horse and Foot...* London, 1680, 23. This entire book is actually an admitted verbatim translation of *Le Sieur Louis de Gaya Traite des Armes, des Machinnes de Guerre, des feux d'artifice, des enseignes & des Instrumens militaire ancienne & moderne; avec la maniere dont on S'en Sert presentiment dont les armee tont Fran-coises qu'etranger,* Paris, 1678, where the identical statement is made on page 29. In Harford it reads: "The King commands at present that in every Troop of his Guards be carried eight rifled or screwed Carabins, with Locks like those of Fusils, Mousquetons and Pistols" [i.e. flint locks] My thanks to my wife Sarah for her detective work in sorting this out.
2. WO52/147, 274.
3. James, Charles *Military Dictionary,* n.p., article on "Rifle."
4. Verner, W. *The First British Rifle-Corps,* 101.
5. Baker, E. *Remarks on Rifle Guns...,* 251
6. Royal Artillery Institution Library, G3h/110/1, (14), 40.
7. WO47/2575, 993-4.
8. WO3/152, 68.
9. *Ibid.,* 73.
10. WO3/36, 9 Aug. 1803.
11. WO3/152, 394-5, 21 Sept. 1804.
12. WO47/2582, 489, 8 Feb. 1805.
13. Royal Artillery Institution Library, *op. cit.,* 44.
14. WO47/2589, 1038, 1175, 12 and 21 Mar. 1806.
15. WO3/192, 170, 16 Sept. 1806 to R.H. Crew.
16. WO47/2621, 2112, 7 June 1811.
17. WO3/204, 185.
18. *Ibid.,* 189, 199.
19. WO47/2627, 2618, 24 Aug. 1812.
20. *Ibid.,* 2909, 21 Sept. 1812.
21. WO47/2638, 5235, 26 Dec. 1814.
22. WO3/205, 208, 31 Dec. 1812.
23. WO47/2630, 171, 13 Jan. 1813.
24. WO52/391, 30 Apr. 1813
25. WO47/2633, 6694, 1 Dec. 1813.
26. WO3/207, 290.
27. WO52/414, 250, 31 May 1814.
28. WO52/531, 111, 121, 132.

Chapter Eleven
1. WO47/2641, 2089-90, 22 May 1815.
2. *Ibid.,* 2229, 31 May 1815.
3. *Ibid.,* 2415, 12 June 1815.
4. WO3/212, 340, 28 June 1815.
5. WO47/2642, 2832, 10 July 1815.
6. WO3/213, 19 July 1815.
7. WO47/2642, 3088, 26 July 1815.
8. WO3/213, 48, 27 July 1815.
9. WO3/215, 225, 16 Feb. 1816.
10. Parliamentary Papers, Estimates & Accounts, I, 1816, vol. XII, 148-9.
11. WO52/531, 10.
12. Compiled from several volumes of WO52.
13. Putnam, T. & Weinbren, D. *A Short History of the Royal Small Arms Factory Enfield,* 8-11 ff.
14. WO52/531, 28.
15. WO47/1068, 14 May 1823.
16. WO52/531.
17. See note 12.
18. WO52/531, 53.
19. See note 12.
20. *Ibid.*
21. *Mirror of Parliament,* 1830, 16.
22. Parliamentary Papers, Estimates & Accounts, 1830, vol. XVIII, 309-17.
23. Cope, Sir W.H. *The History of the Rifle Brigade,* 234.

Chapter Twelve
1. WO52/147, 29.
2. WO52/139, 215
3. WO52/147, 294, 30 Nov. 1801
4. Compiled from many volumes of WO52.
5. WO47/2641, 2083.
6. WO52/266, 69, 24 Sept. 1806.
7. WO47/2443, n.p., 4 May 1808
8. WO3/212, 136-7, 19 May 1815.
9. WO47/2642, 2832.
10. WO47/2641, 2229, 31 May 1815.
11. *Ibid.,* 2414-6, 12 June 1815.
12. WO3/212, 309, 23 June 1815.
13. *Ibid.,* 341, 29 June 1815..
14. WO52/435, 182, 31 Mar. 1816.
15. Letter of Adjutant General to General Barnard 19 July 1816, quoted in *The Rifle Brigade Chronicle,* (1933), 236-43
16. WO47/2643, 4653.
17. Howard L. Blackmore "The Baker Rifleman's Sword" in: *Arms Collecting,* vol. 35, No. 1 (Feb. 1997), 9-15.
18. WO47/775, 1125, 1170; WO47/880, 8425, 14 July 1820.
19. WO52/531, 15, 31 July 1820.
20. *Mirror of Parliament* 2 Apr. 1830, 16.

Chapter 13
1. Baker, Ezekiel, *Twenty Two Years Practice and Observations with Rifle Guns,* 1st ed. 1803, 5-6. I am greatly indebted to W.S. Curtis for the correct dating of the first edition of Baker's book. For a full discussion of Baker's publications, see W.S.Curtis "Ezekiel Baker" in "Bibliotorm, the book collectors' column," *Classic Arms & Militaria,* vol. 1, no. 2 (Feb.1994), 36-38.
2. WO52/337, 84
3. WO4/178, 303-4.
4. ADM 160/150, n.p., 11 June 1803.
5. WO27/87, 95th Regiment.
6. *Ibid.* 5/60th.
7. WO27.
8. WO27/97.
9. *Ibid.*
10. Costello, *Adventures of a Soldier,* 1852, 20.
11. Milne, S.M. & Terry, A. *The Annals of the King's Royal Rifle Corps,* Appendix dealing with Uniform, Armament and Equipment, 1913.
12. Adjutant General to General Barnard, 19 July 1816, quoted in: *The Rifle Brigade Chronicle,* (1933), 236-43.
13. WO4/188, 309, 17 Jan. 1803 to agents Cox, Greenwood & Cox.
14. WO2/40, 147.
15. Quoted in Rigaud, G. *Celer et Audax,* 25.
16. WO3/201, 298, 18 July 1811, to R.H. Crew.
17. See note 12.
18. *Ibid.*
19. WO52/435, 427-7 and WO52/531, 2.
20. See note 12.
21. WO52/147, 117, 31 Dec. 1800.
22. *Ibid.* 147.
23. WO4/193, 114, 28 Mar. 1804.
24. Quoted in Rigaud, op. cit., 24.
25. Celer et Audax, 24, 25, as quoted in Verner, Col. Willoughby, *History and Campaigns of the Rifle Brigade,* Pt. 1, 1800-1809, 44.
26. See note 11.
27. *Ibid.*
28. General Orders, Spain and Portugal January 1st-December 31st 1811, published by Authority, T. Egerton, London, vol. III, 1812, 109.
29. WO52/531, 226, 228
30. WO47/2590, 2438, 9 June 1806.
31. Baker, *op. cit.,* 8.
32. *Regulations for the Exercise of Riflemen,* 1798, 12.
33. WO52/146, 242.
34. Manningham, Colonel Coote. Military Lectures delivered to the Officers of the 95th (Rifle) Regiment at Shorn-cliff Barracks, Kent, during the Spring of 1803. London, 1803, 71.
35. WO52/159, 21 May 1801.
36. Portsmouth Gun Wharf records, quoted in *The Rifle Brigade Chronicle* (1900), 243-4. These potentially invaluable records seem to have disappeared since the book was written.
37. See note 4.
38. WO 47/2586, 3578, 27 Sept.
39. WO3/192, 244, 5 Nov. 1806.
40. WO6/142, 468-9.
41. WO3/194, 369, 27 Apr. 1808.
42. WO3/195,156, 20 July 1808.
43. WO6/142, 468-9.
44. Quoted in Butler, L. *Annals of the King's Royal Rifle Corps,* II, 39.
45. Agreement amongst contemporary

sources on the diameters of lead ball is lacking. Capt. George Smith's *An Universal Military Dictionary* (1779) gives .596-inch, Ezekiel Baker's *Remarks on Rifle Guns* (1806) gives .597-inch, Jacob Spearman's *The British Gunner* (1828) gives .60-inch and William Greener's *The Gun* (1835) quoting the 1813 Proof Act, gives .603-inch.

46. WO47/2605, 3280, 1 Dec. 1808.
47. WO6/143, 18, 7 June 1809 to Col. Neville.
48. Verner, II, 11.
49. WO6/144, 18.
50. WO27/122.
    British Indian Military Repository, vol.5, 151: Table No.22, report of a British Government sub-committee, 10 Apr. 1821, on the packing of small arms ammunition. I am indebted to David F. Harding for this reference.
    JAHR, 8, 25 Dec. 1814.
    Ibid., 171, 174
    WO47/2641, 1690, 26 Apr. 1815
    WO3/413.
    Spearman, Jacob M. *The British Gunner*, 1828, 253.
    Ibid., 124–5.

Chapter Fourteen
The standard and most detailed reference for foreign troops in British pay during the French Revolutionary Wars (1793–1802) is: C.T. Atkinson "Foreign Regiments in the British Army, 1793–1802" in: JAHR, vols. 22 and 23 (1943, 1944). My coverage of such units in this chapter is based on these articles, with supplementary information when available. Most unfortunately there is no similarly detailed equivalent for the period 1803–1815. Postwar information is drawn very largely from semi-annual regimental inspection returns (WO 27) and where no citation is given for a piece of information during this period it may be assumed to come from the appropriate return for the date in question.

1. Butler, Lewis. *Annals of the King's Royal Rifle Corps*, I, 254; II, 3.
2. Verner, Col. Willoughby. *History and Campaigns of the Rifle Brigade*, Part I, 13.
3. Butler, *op. cit.*, vol. II, 16.
4. Verner, *op. cit.*, I, 16.
5. WO4/185, 255, 27 Mar. 1802.
6. Verner, *op. cit.*, Part II, 6.
7. *Ibid.*
8. Portsmouth Gun Wharf records, quoted in Milne & Terry, *Annals of the King's Royal Rifle Corps*. Appendix dealing with Uniform, Armament and Equipment, 44.
9. WO27/87.
10. WO27/102.
11. WO27/87, 20 Sept. 1804.
12. *Ibid.*
13. *Ibid.*
14. Butler, *op. cit.*, I, 257.
15. Verner, *op. cit.*, I, 13.
16. Butler, *op. cit.*, I, 273.
17. *Ibid.*, II, 212.
18. Milne & Terry, *op. cit.*, 8, 20.
19. Butler, *op. cit.*, II, 16.
20. *Ibid.*, 28.
21. *Ibid.*, I, 258.
22. Compiled from Inspection Returns, WO27.
23. WO4/185, 255.
24. WO27/143 II, 144 I.
25. WO52/531, 109.
26. WO27/182.
27. WO27/257, 301, 320.
28. Verner, *The First British Rifle Corps*, 117.
29. WO27/147 I.
30. WO27/200.
31. WO27/295.
32. WO/27/320, 325.
33. WO27/329.
34. WO27/147 I.
35. WO27/145.
36. Butler, *op. cit.*, II, 241.
37. WO27/143 II.
38. Butler, *op. cit.*, II, 292.
39. WO27/143 II.
40. Butler, *op. cit.*, 280.
41. WO3/32, 127.
42. Verner, *History and Campaigns...*, I, 19.
43. WO3/21, 216–18.
44. *Ibid.*, 235, 15 Jan. 1800.
45. WO3/32, 397.
46. WO4/182, 54.
47. *Ibid.*, 165.
48. Ross, Charles (ed.) *Correspondence of Charles, First Marquis Cornwallis*, vol. 3, 168, to Maj. Gen. Ross, from Dublin Castle, 21 Jan. 1800.
49. *Ibid.*, 177, 4 Feb. 1800.
50. *Ibid.*, 296, 24 Oct. 1800.
51. James, Charles. *A New and Enlarged Military Dictionary, or, Alphabetical Explanation of Technical Terms...*, n.p., article on "RIFLE."
52. Verner, *op. cit.*, 16.
53. WO52/161, 26.
54. WO4/186, 186.
55. WO4/188, 282.
56. Verner, *op. cit.*, I, 73.
57. *Ibid.*, 74.
58. *Ibid.*, 82 and Calendar in *The Rifle Brigade Chronicle* for 1890.
59. Verner, II, 2.
60. *Ibid.*, I, 22–3. WO27/83, 23 Sept. 1800. The notes are in Manningham's own hand, and the number of effective privates is stated as 532.
61. *Ibid.*, 52.
62. JAHR, 18, 108–9.
63. Verner, *op. cit.*, I, 86.
64. *Ibid.*, 91.
65. *Ibid.*, 120.
66. JAHR, 30, 85.
67. Verner, *op. cit.*, I, 98.
68. *Ibid.*, 140.
69. *Ibid.*, 156.
70. Butler, *op. cit.*, II, 62.
71. Verner, *op. cit.*, I, 173.
72. *Ibid.*, II, 14 and Calendar in *The Rifle Brigade Chronicle* for 1890.
73. Verner, *op. cit.*, II, 14.
74. *Ibid.*, 440.
75. WO3/212, 305, 22 June 1815.
76. WO27/147 II.
77. WO27/143 II, 144 II, 145 II, 147 II.
78. WO27/158 II.
79. WO27/160 II.
80. WO27/161 I.
81. WO27/297.
82. As note 77.
83. WO27/158 II.
84. WO27/161 I.
85. WO27/164 I, 249, 273, 282, 297.
86. WO3/206, 434, 27 July 1813.
87. WO3/207.
88. WO27/152 I, 155 I.
89. WO27/156 I, 157 II.
90. WO3/211, 26 June 1814.
91. WO3/205, 204, 30 Dec. 1812.
92. WO3/207, 290, 2 Nov. 1813.
93. WO27/149 I, 156 I.
94. WO27/157 II.
95. WO27/148 I.
96. WO27/291.
97. WO27/314.
98. WO4/190, 251.
99. WO27/158 I.
100. WO3/199, 1 Oct. 1810.
101. Harding, *op. cit.*, Vol. IV, "The Users and their Smallarms," 28.
102. WO3/203, 10 June 1812.
103. WO3/204, 188, 17 Aug. 1812; 222, 28 Aug. 1812.
104. WO4
105. WO3/193, 217, 16 May 1807.
106. WO3/347, 56.
107. Verner, *op. cit.*, II, 10.
108. WO27/143 II, 150 II.
109. WO27/155 II, 169 II.
110. WO27/192, 202.
111. WO27/258.
112. WO52/531, 249.
113. WO27/297,308.
114. WO47/1899, 7, 271, 4 June 1841.
115. WO27/318.
116. WO27/368, 380.
117. WO27/385.
118. WO47/1907, 11, 273, 27 Aug. 1841.
119. WO27/330.
120. WO27/340.
121. WO27/345.
122. WO6/143, 32.
123. *Ibid.*, 35–6.
124. Verner, *op. cit.*, II, 11.
125. *Ibid.*, 13.
126. Butler, *op. cit.*, II, 215.
127. Yaple, "The Auxiliaries: Foreign and Miscellaneous Regiments in the British Army 1802–17" in: JAHR, 50 (1972), 11.
128. WO3/203, 269; Verner, *op. cit.*, II, 8,

14. See also Harding, D.F. *Smallarms of the East India Company 1600–1856*, vol. IV, Chap. 40, 11.
129. WO3/205, 14 Nov. 1812.
130. Beamish, N.L. *A History of the King's German Legion*, II, 469.
131. WO3/204, 79, 13 July 1812.
132. WO3/199, WO27/91.
133. WO3/206, 12 July 1813.
134. WO3/208, WO27/139.
135. WO27/144 II.
136. Yaple, *op. cit.*, 10–28, 25.
137. WO3/206, 21 June 1813; WO27/139; Yaple, *op. cit.*, 27.
138. WO27/144 II, 145 II.
139. WO27/102.
140. WO27/143 I.
141. O'Donnell, Captain H. *Historical Records of the 14th Regiment*, (Devonport, 1893), 95; WO27/129. Courtesy of D.F. Harding.
142. WO27/171, 181, 191 I, 194, 200, 210, 222.
143. WO27/96.
144. WO27/150 I, 153 I, 168 II, 194.
145. WO27/164 I, 166, 181, 191 I, 201, 210.
146. WO4/199, 215.
147. WO27/167.
148. WO27/195, 201, 211, 215, 219, 248.
149. OIOC: L/MIL/3/1135, 388–9, 15 June 1816; OIOC: P/356/69, 4327, 30 Oct. 1816; 4442, 13 Nov. 1816. Courtesy of D.F. Harding.
150. WO27/129, 143 II. OIOC: P/29/55 BIMP No. 87, 14 June 1822. Courtesy of D.F. Harding.
151. WO27/96.
152. WO27/98.
153. WO27/143 II, 148 II.
154. 69th Foot?
155. WO27/156 II, 160 II, 164, 165 II, 167, 169 I, 182, 186, 197.
156. WO27/164 I, 167, 182, 192, 207, 211, 223, 228.
157. WO3/348, 61.
158. WO27/96.
159. WO27/107.
160. WO27/139.
161. WO27/98.
162. WO27/156 II.
163. See DFH; WO27/172, 186, 192, 202, 212, 224. 164. See DFH.
165. WO27/164 I, 167, 172, 187, 202.
166. WO27/164 I, 167.
167. WO27/224, 258; 362.
168. WO3/205, 229, 6 Jan. 1813.
169. WO3/203, 224, 31 Mar. 1812.
170. WO3/208, 21 Mar. 1814.
171. WO3/213, 28 Aug. 1815.
172. WO3/204, 20 & 31 July 1812.
173. WO3/208, 7 Mar. 1814.
174. WO6/142, 277.
175. WO3/198.
176. WO27/91.
177. WO3/204, 258, 5 Sept. 1812.
178. WO3/201, 17 July 1811.
179. WO3/199, 6 Oct. 1810.
180. WO52/129, 181.
181. WO27/91.
182. WO3/190; WO27/91.
183. WO27/91.
184. WO6/142, 468–9.
185. WO3/194,311, 5 Apr. 1808.
186. WO6/143.
187. WO1/786, 45, 3 Feb. 1810.
188. *Ibid.*, 205, 28 May 1810.
189. WO6/144, 43, 17 Sept. 1810.
190. *Ibid.*, 224–6, 27 Mar. 1813.
191. WO6/145, 12 Sept. 1814.

Chapter Fifteen
1. See my article "The Much Maligned Brunswick" Part 1 in: *Guns Review*, July 1970, 266.
2. Surtees, William. *Twenty-five Years in the Rifle Brigade*, 69.
3. Pennycuick, Lt. Col. John (H.M. 17th Foot) *The Light Infantry Drill*, 13–14. My thanks to David F. Harding for this reference.
4. *United Service Journal*, 1831.
5. *Ibid.*
6. Surtees, *op. cit.*, 42
7. *Kentish Gazette* quoted in Verner, 1912, 76.
8. WO3/198, 310, 7 Mar. 1810.
9. WO52/435, 31 May 1814.
10. Verner, *History and Campaigns of the Rifle Brigade*, II, 368.
11. Surtees, *op. cit.*, 382.
12. WO27/220.
13. I am most grateful to David F. Harding for the Madras figures and a most useful discussion of comparative Baker rifle marksmanship. See his *Smallarms of the East India Company 1600–1856* vol. III, Chapter 25.

Chapter Sixteen
1. CO 42/47, 240–52.
2. CO 42/50, 86.
3. Canadian Government Publication *Indian Treaties and Surrenders from 1680 to 1890*, 2 vols., Ottawa, 1891.
4. CO 42/92, 122.
5. CO 42/99, 325.
6. *Ibid.*
7. CO 42/105, 60.
8. CO 42/108, 22.
9. CO 42/110, 169 and CO 42/109, 325.
10. CO 42/111, 302.
11. CO 42/115, 142.
12. CO 42/124.
13. CO 42/128, 120.
14. CO 42/130, 230, 232.
15. CO 42/135, 15 and CO42/137, 20.
16. WO 47/2632, 3783.
17. Compiled from several volumes of WO 52.
18. Johnston, Charles M. (ed) *The Valley of the Six Nations*, 219–20: Noah Freer, military secretary to Gen. Prevost, to Drummond, Quebec, 1 Mar. 1814.
19. Public Archives of Canada, M.G.11, "Q" series, vol. 135 part 2, 386.
20. *Ibid.*, 355–6.
21. Ontario Archives, Norton Papers, MS94, 23 Mar. 1816.
22. *Ibid.*, 358–9.
23. Public Archives of Canada, M.G.11, "Q" series, vol. 139, 97
24. Ontario Archives, Norton Papers, MS94, 17 June 1816.
25. Ibid., 23 June 1816.
26. Sun Insurance Co. records, Guildhall Library London, vol. 413, policy number 687200.
27. WO 52/224.
28. Public Archives of Canada, M.G.11, "Q" series, vol. 140, 360.
29. *Ibid.*, 362.
30. WO52/531.

Chapter 17
1. WO47/87, 364
2. Bailey, D.W. & Nie, D.A., *English Gunmakers*, p. 48.
3. Nielson, O., *Den norske haers handskytevapen...1750–1814*, 278, 280, 283, 285.
4. For further details on the background to this capture, see *Deutches Waffenjournal*, December 1985, p. 1525. Unfortunately, staff shortages at the Wehrgeschichtliches Museum, which owns the rifle, precluded measurement of the twist of the rifling.
5. Bailey, D.W. "The Gentleman's Rifle – a Definition," in *Guns Review*, Feb. 1971, 53-57.

Bibliography of Printed Works

ABRIDGEMENTS of the Patent Specifications relating to Fire-Arms and other Weapons, Ammunition & Accoutrements 1588–1858. London, 1859. Reprint, London, The Holland Press, 1960).

ALLAIRE, Anthony. *Diary of Lieut. Anthony Allaire, of Ferguson's Corps.* 1881, reprint, New York, Arno Press,1968).

ANONYMOUS. *List of the Volunteer and Yeomanry Corps of the United Kingdom...* London, printed for John Stockdale, 1804.

ANONYMOUS. *English Military Discipline.* London,printed for Robert Harford, 1680.

ATKINSON, C.T. 'Foreign Regiments in the British Army, 1793–1802' in: *Journal of Army Historical Research,* volumes 21 (Winter, 1942) and 22 (Spring/Autumn 1944), several parts in each, beginning with page 175.

ATWOOD, Rodney. *The Hessians.* New York, Cambridge University Press, 1980.

BAILEY, D.W. "The Rifle in the American War 1775–1783" in: *Guns Review,* Jan. 1969, 8–12.

BAILEY, D.W. "The Gentleman's Rifle - A Definition" in: *Guns Review,* Feb. 1971, 53–57.

BAILEY, D.W. "The Baker Rifle", 1–4, in: *Guns Review,* 13, 4–7 (Apr.–Jul. 1973), 142–45; 188–191; 226–228; 285–288.

BAILEY, D.W. & NIE, D.A. *English gunmakers. The Birmingham and Provincial Gun Trade in the 18th and 19th century,* London, Arms and Armour Press, 1978.

BAILEY, De Witt. *Pattern Dates for British Ordnance Small Arms 1718–1783.* Gettysburg, Thomas Publications, 1997.

BAILEY, De Witt. *Board of Ordnance Small Arms Contractors 1689–1840.* Rhyl, W.S. Curtis (Publishers) Ltd., 1999.

BAILEY, Kenneth P. *The Ohio Company Papers, 1753–1817.* Arcata, CA, Edwards Brothers Inc., Ann Arbor, MI, 1947.

BAKER, Ezekiel. *Remarks on Rifle Guns...* London, eleven editions, 1801–1835.

BARNHART, John D. *Henry Hamilton and George Rogers Clark in the American Revolution.* Crawfordsville, R.E. Banta, 1951.

BARTRAM, William. *Travels Through North and South Carolina, Georgia, East and West Florida...* London, 1794.

BEAMISH, N.L. *A History of the King's German Legion, 1807–16.* 2 vols., London, 1837.

BLACK, Jeremy. *The War for America.* Stroud, Alan Sutton Publishing, Ltd., 1990.

BLACKMORE, Howard L. *Guns and Rifles of the World.* London, B.T. Batsford, Ltd., 1965.

BURGOYNE, Bruce E. (ed.) *A Hessian Diary of the American Revolution by Johann Conrad Döhla.* Norman, University of Oklahoma Press, 1990.

BUTLER, Lewis. *The Annals of the King's Royal Rifle Corps.* London, Smith Elder, 2 vols. 1913, 1923. For separately printed Appendix see Milne.

CANADIAN GOVERNMENT PUBLICATION, *Indian Treaties and Surrenders from 1680 to 1890,* 2 vols., Ottawa, 1891.

CARTER, William. *A Genuine Detail of the Several Engagements, Positions, and Movements of the Royal and American Armies during the Years 1775 and 1776...* London, 1784.

CASHIN, Edward J. *The King's Ranger. Thomas Brown and the American Revolution on the Southern Frontier.* Athens GA, University of Georgia Press, 1988.

CLARK, Mertie J. *Loyalists in the Southern Campaign of the Revolutionary War.* Baltimore, Genealogical Publishing Co. Inc., 3 volumes, 1981.

COPE, Sir W.H. *The History of the Rifle Brigade.* London, Chatto & Windus, 1877.

COSTELLO, Edward. *Adventures of a Soldier.* London, H. Colbourn & Co. 1841, 1852.

DUPIN, Charles. *View of the Military Forces of Great Britain.* London, 1822.

FERGUSON, Adam. *Biographical Sketch, or Memoir, of Lieutenant-Colonel Patrick Ferguson: originally intended for the British Encyclopaedia.* Edinburgh, 1817.

HARCOURT, Edward W. (ed.) *The Harcourt Papers.* 14 volumes, Oxford, James Parker & Co., 1880–1905.

HARDING, David F. *Smallarms of the East India Company 1600–1856.* London, Foresight Books, 4 vols. 1997, 1999.

HARFORD, Robert. See: Anonymous.

JAMES, Charles. *A New and Enlarged Military Dictionary.* London, 1802.

JOHNSTON, Charles M. (ed) *The Valley of the Six Nations, A Collection of Documents on the Indian lands of the Grand River.* Toronto, The Champlain Society, Ontario Series No. 7, 1964.

JORDAN, John W. (ed.) "The Journals of James Kenny 1758–59" in: *Pennsylvania Magazine of History and Biography,* 32 (1913).

KAPP, Friedrich. *Der Soldatenhandel deutscher Fürsten nach Amerika.* Berlin,1864. Reprint, Munich, Verlag Lothar Borowsky, n.d.

KEMBLE, Stephen. "Stephen Kemble's Orderly Book and Journal" in: *Collections of the New-York Historical Society for the Years 1882, 1883.* New York, 1883, 1884.

KIPPING, Ernst and SMITH, Samuel S. (trans & eds) *At General Howe's Side 1776–1778. The diary of General William Howe's aide de camp, Captain Friedrich von Muenchhausen.* Monmouth Beach NJ, Philip Freneau Press, 1974.

von KRAFFT. "The Journal of Lieutenant Johann Carl Phillip von Krafft" in: *Collections of the New-York Historical Society for the Year 1882.* New York, New-York Historical Society, 1883.

LODGE, Henry Cabot (ed.) *Andre's Journal.* 2 vols., Boston, Bibliophile Society, 1903.

LUMPKIN, Henry. *From Savannah to Yorktown.* New York, Paragon House Publishers, 1981.

LYDENBERG, Harry M.(ed.) *Archibald Robertson, Lieutenant General Royal Engineers. His Diaries and Sketches in America 1762–1780.* New York, New York Public Library, 1930.

MACERONE, Francis (Col.). *Defensive Instructions for the People; containing the new and improved combination of arms, called Foot Lances; miscellaneous instructions on the subject of small arms and ammunition, street and house fighting, and field fortification.* London, J. Smith [1832].

MC DOWELL, W.M. Jr. (ed.) *Documents Relating to Indian Affairs 1754–1765.* Columbia, University of South Carolina Press, 1970.

MANNINGHAM, Coote. *Military Lectures delivered to the Officers of the 95th (Rifle) Regiment at Shorn-Cliff Barracks, Kent, during the Spring of 1803.* London, 1803.

MILNE, S.M. & TERRY, A. *The Annals of the Kings Royal Rifle Corps.* Appendix dealing with Uniform, Armament and Equipment. London, John Murray, 1913.

NIELSEN, O. *Den norske haers handskytevapen. Gevaerer of Karabiner 1750–1814 of Forandringsmodeller.*, Oslo, Army Museum Yearbook 1960.

O'CALLAGHAN, Edmund B. & Fernow, Berthold (eds.) *Documents Relative to the Colonial History of the State of New York*, 15 vols., Albany, 1856–1887.

PAM, David. *The Royal Small Arms Factory ENFIELD & Its Workers.* Enfield, by the Author, 1998.

PENNSYLVANIA ARCHIVES. 9 series, 138 vols. Harrisburg and Philadelphia, Joseph Severns & Co., 1852–1949.

PLEASANTS, Henry Jr. "The Battle of Paoli" in: *Pennsylvania Magazine of History and Biography*, vol. LXXII (1948).

POWELL, W.S. (ed.) *The Correspondence of William Tryon and other Selected Papers.* 2 vols., Raleigh, North Carolina Division of Archives & History, Dept. of Cultural Resources, 1980.

PUTNAM, Tim & WEINBREN, Dan. *A Short History of the Royal Small Arms Factory Enfield.* Centre for Applied Historical Studies, Middlesex University, for Royal Ordnance plc, 1992.

REGULATIONS for the Exercise of Riflemen & Light Infantry & instructions for their conduct in the field. [translated from the German [[of de Rottenburg]] by Gen. William Fawcett] London, War Office, 1798. Subsequent editions of 1799, 1803, 1808 and 1822.

RIGAUD, Gibbes. "Celer et Audax," *A Sketch of the Services of the Fifth Battalion Sixtieth Regiment (Rifles) during the Twenty Years of their Existence.* Oxford, Hall & Stacy, 1879.

ROBERTSON, Heard & ROWLAND, A. Ray (eds.) *Journal of an Expedition against the Rebels of Georgia in North America Under the Orders of Archibald Campbell Esquire Lieut. Colol. Of His Majesty's 71st Regimt. 1778.* Darien (Ga.) Richmond County Historical Society, 1981.

SAVORY, Lieut. Gen. Sir Reginald. *His Britannic Majesty's Army in Germany during the Seven Years War.* Oxford, Oxford University Press, 1966.

SCULL, G.D. (ed.) *Memoir and Letters of Captain W. Glanville Evelyn of the 4th Regiment ("King's Own") from North America, 1774–1776.* Oxford, printed privately, 1879.

SHUMWAY, George. "English Pattern Trade Rifles" in: *Proceedings of the 1984 Trade Gun Conference*, 2 parts, Rochester, Research Division, Rochester Museum & Science Center, 1985. Part II, 11–49.

SIMCOE, John G. *Simcoe's Military Journal. A History of the Operations of a Partisan Corps, called The Queen's Rangers, commanded by Lieut. Col. J.G. Simcoe, during the War of the American Revolution;* New York, 1844. Reprint, New York, The New York Times & Arno Press, 1968.

SMITH, Capt. George. *An Universal Military Dictionary...* London, 1779. Reprint, Ottawa, Museum Restoration Service, 1969).

SPEARMAN, Jacob M. *The British Gunner.* London, 1828.

STEWART, Charles H. *The Service of British Regiments in North America. A Resume.* Ottawa, Dept. of National Defense Library, 1964.

STONE, William L. (ed.) *Journal of Captain Pausch Chief of the Hanau Artillery during the Burgoyne Campaign.* Albany, Joel Munsell's Sons, 1886.

SULLIVAN, James, Hamilton, Milton W. et al (eds.) *The Papers of Sir William Johnson.* 14 vols, Albany, 1921–1965.

SUMNER, Percy. "Uniforms of the Rifle Brigade, c. 1804" in: *Journal of Army Historical Research*, vol. 20, 38-42.

SURTEES, William. *Twenty-five Years in the Rifle Brigade.* London, 1833.

TUSTIN, Joseph P. (trans & ed.) *Diary of the American War. A Hessian Journal. Captain Johann Ewald.* New Haven, Yale University Press, 1979.

UHLENDORF, Bernhard A. (trans. & ed.) *Revolution in America. Confidential Letters and Journals 1776–1784 of Adjutant General Major Baurmeister of the Hessian Forces.* New Brunswick NJ, Rutgers University Press, 1957.

UHLENDORF, Bernhard A. & VOSPER, Edna (trans.& eds) "Letters of Major Baurmeister during the Philadelphia Campaign, 1777–1778" in: *Pennsylvania Magazine of History and Biography*, LIX, Philadelphia, The Historical Society of Pennsylvania, 1935.

VERNER, Willoughby. *The First British Rifle Corps.* London, 1890.

VERNER, Willoughby. *History and Campaigns of the Rifle Brigade.* Part I, 1800-09. London, John Bale Sons & Danielsson, 1912. Part II, 1809-13, 1919.

VERNER, Willoughby (ed.) *The Rifle Brigade Chronicle* London, 1890–1918, and subsequent editors to 1965.

WEDDEBURNE, Serj.[William], *Observations on the Exercise of Riflemen and on the Movements of Light Troops in General*, Norwich, 1804.

WILLARD, Margaret W. *Letters on the American Revolution 1774–1776.* Boston, Houghton, Mifflin Co., 1925.

WIRTGEN, Arnold. *Handfeuerwaffen und preußische Heeresreform 1807 bis 1813.* Herford and Bonn, E.S. Mittler & Sohn, 1988.

WOOD, Walter. *The Rifle Brigade.* London, 1901.

WRIGHT, J. Leitch, Jr. *Britain and the American Frontier 1783–1815.* Athens, Univ. of Georgia Press, 1975.

WRIGHT, Robert K. Jr. *The Continental Army.* Washington, DC, The Center of Military History, U.S. Army, 1986.

YAPLE, R.L. "The Auxiliaries, Foreign and Miscellaneous Regiments in the British Army 1802–1817" in: *Journal of Army Historical Research*, vol. 50 (1972), 10-28.

Index

Abercromby, General James, 14, 15
Abercromby, Maj. Gen. Sir Ralph, 93, 99
Accoutrements, light infantry, 34, 55-6
Ainslie, Maj. Gen., 87
Albemarle, Earl of, 19
Alsop, Thomas, Ass't Inspector of Small Arms, 114, 117
Althause, Captain John, 72ff, 73
Amboy, 45
Amherst, General Sir Jeffrey, 15, 36, 76
Ammunition
  for Pattern 1776 rifles, 34
  Ferguson rifles, 55-7
  German jäger rifles, 68, 93
  Baker rifles, 147-154
Anna, 72
Annual Register, 36
Armstrong, Captain Thomas, 10, 11
Arnold, Benedict, expedition commanded by, 73
Atkin, Edmond, 76

Backhouse, William, 78
Bailey, James, 119, 134
Bags, ball, 34, 56, 149ff
Barclay, Major Thomas, 74
Barrington, Lord, 41-3
Bartleman, Capt., 118
Bartram, John, 75
Bartram, William, 78
Bathurst, third Earl, 181
Baurmeister, Major, 32, 47
Bayonet makers
  Allport, William, 143-4
  Bate, Thomas, 142
  Chambers, Samuel, 143-4
  Craven & Cooper, 142-3
  Dawes, Samuel & J., 142-4
  Dawes, William & Samuel, 142
  Galton, Samuel, 143
  Gill, Elizabeth, 144
  Gill & Co., John, 142-3
  Hadley, Thomas, 142-3
  Hill, John, 143-4
  Johnstone, Joshua, 108, 141
  Mole, John & Robert, 138, 144
  Osborn, Henry, 108, 141, 144
  Osborn, Gunby & Co., 142-3
  Oughton, J. & C., 143-4
  Reddell, Joseph, 142
  Reddell & Bate, 142
  Rock, John, 143
  Rock, Martha, 143
  Salter, George, 143-4
  Salter, J., 143-4

Wheeler & Son, Robert, 143-4
Woolley, James, 108, 141, 143-4
Woolley, Deakin & Co., 141
Bellis, Jonathan, Master Furbisher, 152
Blomefield, Major, 90, 123
Bonham Town, 45
Boscowan, Admiral Edward, 12
Bouquet, Col. Henry, 14-16, 18
Boxtel, battle of, 97-8
Braddock, General Edward, 11, 75
Bradford, W.&T., 21
Bradstreet, Colonel John, 15, 77
Brandywine, battle of, 47-50ff
Brant, Joseph, 79-80, 180
Bremerlehe, 60-3
Briar Creek, battle of, 33, 69-70
Bridges, Eade & Wilton, 26, 29, 32, 43
Brown, Colonel Thomas, 70
Brunswick, duchy of, 16
Burd, James, 76
Burgoyne, Gen. John, 20, 25, 27, 33, 121

Cahokia, 78
Campbell, Lieut. Col. Archibald, 33, 74
Campbell, Daniel, 78
Canada, Upper and Lower, 178
Carl I, Duke of Brunswick, 63
Carl Wilhelm Ferdinand, Duke of Brunswick, 63
Cathcart, Lord, 11
Cavendish's jägers, 18
Chargers, powder, 149ff, 151
Chatham Barracks, 41-3
Chaumette, Isaac de la, 35
Cherokee Indians, 76
Chickasaw Indians, 78
Christian IV., King of Denmark, 7
Christian Friedrich Carl Alexander, Margrave of Ansbach-Bayreuth, 62, 67
Christiana Bridge (Creek), 46
Christopher, 44
Clinton, General Sir Henry, 33, 70
Courtney, John, 38
Cramon, Captain Christoph von, 63
Creek Indians, Upper, 76, 78
Cresap's Rifle Company, 69
Crespi, Giuseppi, 87
Creutzberg, Colonel von, 61

Croghan, George, 76, 78-9
Cumberland, Duke of, 12, 13

Dartmouth, Secretary of State Lord, 21, 79
Davison, Alexander, 182
Denny, Governor, 76
De Peyster, Captain Abraham, 33, 74
Desagulier, Gen., 36
Deserontyon, John, 79
Detroit, 74, 80, 177
Dongan, Governor Thomas, 75
Donop, Colonel von, 60
Dort, 61
Dragoons, Heavy and Light, 121
Drummond, Lieut. Gen. Sir Gordon, 181
Dublin, 117, 124
Dundas, Capt.W.B., Ass't Inspector of Small Arms, 129, 143

Elliot, General George Augustus, 20, 121
Erskine, General Sir William, 47
Evelyn, Lieutenant, 21
Ewald, Captain Johann, 47, 73

Falconer & Co., John, 80
Faucitt (Fawcett), Colonel William, 22-6, 30, 59, 88, 100
Ferdinand, Prince of Brunswick, 16, 18
Ferguson, Adam, 38, 51-2
Ferguson, George, 49
Ferguson, Patrick, 35-51 *passim,* 74
Ferguson's Rifle Corps, 43-55 *passim,* 214-16
Ferrol expedition, 99
Flasks, powder, 44, 54, 56, 148ff
Fleming, Captain William, 33, 74
Folliott & Co., George, 78
Fort
  Augusta, 77
  de Chartres, 78
  DuQuesne, 14, 15, 70
  Edward, 14, 15
  Lyttelton, 76
  Morris, 76
  Pitt, 76, 78
  Stanwix, 62
  Ticonderoga, 15
Fraser, John, 75
Fraser, Major Simon, 18
Fraser's Chasseurs, 16-18
Frederick II, King, Prussia, 11
French, early use of rifles, 7

Freytag, Heinrich Wilhelm von, 16
Friedrich August, Prince of Anhalt-Zerbst, 63

Gage, General Thomas, 21
Gasser, Capt., 118
Gentleman's Magazine, 36, 39
Germain, Secretary of State for America Lord George, 24, 31
Gibraltar, 169
Girty brothers, 79
Goulburn, Henry, 181
Grey, General Sir Charles, 33
Guernsey, Lord, 189-90
Gunmakers/gunsmiths, *(see also page 133-4 for 1823 barrelmakers and page 133-4, 138 for 1820s and 1830s lockmakers)*
  Adams, John, 223
  Arnold, Francis, 115, 119, 125
  Ashton, Thomas, 114, 138
  Ashton, T.&C., 134-5
  Aston, Joseph, 138
  Baker, Ezekiel, 90, 106, 107-9, 114-5, 119, 122-3, 125, 131-2, 134-5, 150, 171-2, 192-4, 212, 223-4
  Baker, Ezekiel John, 138
  Baker & Son, E., 127, 135
  Barbar, Lewis and James, 35
  Barker & Whately 28-30, 39, 212
  Barnett, John Edward 138-9, 225
  Barnett, Robert, 83, 85-6, 212
  Barnett, Thomas 108, 114, 131, 225
  Barnett & Son, 134-5
  Beckwith, William A., 138
  Blair, David, 108, 114, 125, 225
  Blair, Jane Hannah, 180
  Blair & Sutherland, 119, 225
  Bond, William Thomas, 138, 225
  Brander, Martin, 108, 114, 225-6
  Brander & Potts, 131, 134-5, 226
  Clarkson, James, 35
  Dawes, William & Samuel, 119, 125, 180, 226
  Egg, Durs, 37-8, 71, 87-8, 93, 107-8, 114, 131, 134-5, 203, 212, 226-7
  Egg, Joseph, 131, 134-5, 138, 180, 182-3, 227
  Fearnley, Ann, 131, 134, 227
  Fearnley, Robert, 114, 227

— 262 —

Index

Freeman, James, 35
Fullerd, William, 183, 186
Galton & Son, Samuel, 28, 30, 39, 95, 106, 108, 114, 119, 125, 180, 205 212-3, 227
Geere, Baltzer, 77-8
Gill, Thomas, 107, 227
Gill & Co., John, 115, 119, 125, 180, 227-8
Glasscott, M. & G.M., 132, 138, 144
Grice, Joseph, 107-8, 114, 228
Grice & Son, William, 25-6, 30, 83-6, 213
Griffin, Benjamin, 17, 198
Hampton, Thomas, 135, 180, 228
Harrison & Thompson, 108, 228
Heely, J.&S., 124
Hennem, Jonathan, 88
Henry, Moses, 78
Henry, William, 77
Heptinstall, William, 138, 228
Hirst, John, 19-20, 30-1, 198, 200, 213
Hollis, Richard & William, 125, 135, 180, 228
Huhnstock, August Heinrich, 23-5, 199, 213
Ketland, Walker & Co., 125, 180, 207, 229
Ketland & Allport, 125, 180, 228
Ketland & Co., William, 135, 228-9
Ketland & Walker, 108, 114, 119, 229
Lacy & Reynolds, 138, 229
Lacy & Witton, 187-8, 210, 229
Lagatz, Daniel, 35
Leigh, James, 138
Lowndes, Thomas, 180
Marwood, Ann, 131, 134-5, 229
Marwood, William, 114, 229
Mills & Son, William, 138, 229
Morris, Henry, 119, 195-6, 229
Morris & Grice, 125, 180, 230
Moxham, Thomas, 125, 135, 180, 230
Nock, Henry, 90, 106-9, 114, 119, 191-2, 203-4, 230
Oerter, John Christian, 30, 71
Oughton, Joseph, 124
Parker, William, 131, 134, 138, 230
Parsons, Gad, 124
Peake, John, 114, 131, 230
Penterman, Barend, 36
Pistor, Thomas Wilhelm, 64, 67, 201
Portlock, Thomas, 124
Potsdam Arsenal, 94, 204

Potts, Thomas, 138, 231
Pritchett, Richard E., 134-5, 138, 231
Pritchett, Samuel, 108, 114, 231
Probin, John, 189-90
Reynolds, Thomas, 108, 135, 138, 231
Reynolds, William, 134
Rolfe, William I., 125, 180, 231
Royal Manufactory of Small Arms, Enfield Lock, 131ff, 132, 135, 144
Royal Manufactory of Small Arms, Tower of London, 124, 142
Schwalbach, A., 64-5, 202
Sherwood, Joseph, 109, 119, 135, 174
Smith, William, 184
Squires, J., 138
Sutherland, Ramsay & Richard, 115, 125, 135, 180, 231
Tatham, Henry senior, 180-7, 182-3ff, 209-10, 213
Thomas, William 138
Thompson (Thomson), James, 114, 231
Thomson & Son, James, 131, 134-5, 138, 231-2
Thornbeck, And.Herman, 102, 222
Trueman, Elizabeth, 124
Twigg, John, 30-1
Whately, Henry & John, 108, 119, 125, 180, 232
Whately, John, 232
Wheeler junior, Robert, 107-8, 114, 119, 187-8, 232
Wheeler & Son, Robert, 125, 135, 180, 187-8, 232
Wilkes, James, 102-3, 108, 232
Wilkinson, John, 27
Willetts, Benjamin, 28, 30, 39, 213
Willetts, Mary, 108, 114, 233
Willetts & Holden, 119, 180, 233
Wilson, Richard, 80
Wilson, William, 80-3, 85-6, 178, 202-3, 213
Wisner, Leonard, 80
Woolley & Co., 233
Wright, Robert, 108, 114, 131, 134-5, 233
Yeomans, James, 138 (& Son 139), 233
Gunpowder, 16, 26-7, 29-30, 32, 43, 68, 146

Hamilton, Lieutenant Governor Henry, 74
Hanger, Captain George, 59, 61, 71-2
Hanover, 16
Harcourt, Lieut. Colonel

William, 22, 31-2
Hartwell, Thomas, 26
Harvey, Adjutant General Edward, 20, 35-6
Havana, siege of, 19
Hawkes, Moseley & Co., 134, 144
Heligoland, 170
Horns, powder, 16, 34, 146, 147-8ff
Howe, Sir William, 24-7, 31, 33, 45, 51, 80
Hubbardton, battle of, 63
Hulme (Helme) Mr., 103-4

Indians
  Chippewa, 177
  Delaware and Shawnee, 75, 77-8, 177
  'Five Nations Grand River' Iroquois, 181
  Huron, 177
  Missasaugas, 177-8
  Mohawk, 177
  Ottawas, 177
  Pottawatamies, 177
  Seminole, 78
  Six Nations (Iroquois), 177, 180-1
Irish Board of Ordnance, 117-8
Iron Hill, skirmish at, 46

Jägers,
  Anhalt-Zerbst, 59, 63ff
  Ansbach-Bayreuth, 45-6, 59, 62-3ff, 66
  Brunswick, 16, 59, 63ff
  Bückeburg, 16
  Hanover, 16, 93
  Hesse-Cassel, 16, 59-61ff; (Ewald's) 45-6, 60
  Hesse-Darmstadt, 93
  Hesse-Hanau, 61-2ff; Freicorps, 62, 64-5, 67-8
Johnson, Guy, 78-80
Johnson, Sir William, 76-7, 79
Johnston junior, Lieutenant William, 80
Juno, 46

Kayashuta, 79
Keats, T.M., 148
Kennett Square, 48
Kenny, James, 76
King's Mountain, battle of, 55
Knox, William, 81
Knyphausen, General Wilhelm von, 46, 51, 60

Learmouth [Learmonth] & Beazley [& Co.], 138, 144, 147
Le Mesurier, Paul and Haviland, 94
Lindsay, Captain Effingham 101
Lohrey, Captain von, 60
Long, Captain William, 78

Long Island, battle of, 21, 70
Lord Howe, 44
Lord Townshend, 29-30
L'Orient, expedition against, 11
Loudoun, Lord, 12-14
Louisbourg, 11,15
Lovell, George, Inspector of Small Arms, 144, 172-3
Lovely Mary, 27
Lyttelton, Governor, 76

Macomb, Edgar & Macomb, 80
Mallets, 149-150
Manningham, Col. Coote, 102, 146, 151-2
Mayor, Joseph, 124
McKee, Agent Alexander, 78
McKellar, Patrick, 20
McKenzie, Lieut. Frederick, 62
McPherson, Serjeant, 72-3
Mellish, 27
Meyrick, James, 44
Militia, British, with rifles, 169
Miller, Col. James R.A., Inspector of Small Arms, 114-5, 119, 123-4, 130, 143-4, 180
Money, Col. John, 100
Moores Creek Bridge, battle at, 69, 70
Morgan's Rifle Company, 69
Mortar, The, 79
Mould, bullet, 12-14, 16, 27, 76, 78, 119, 151, 188

Nauheim, battle of, 18
New Orleans, battle of, 153, 170, 175
Nicolls, Maj. Edward, 180
Ninety-Six, first battle of, 69
Norcott, Col., 143, 148-9
Northumberland, second, Duke of, 182
Norton, Capt. John, 180-7

Ohio Company, 76, 80
Osborn, Sir George, 60
Outridge, Mr., 118

Palmer, Lieut. Col., 125
Panton, Forbes & Co., 70
Paoli Tavern, attack at, 33, 52-3ff
Paterson, Adjutant General J., 51
Pensacola, 70, 78-80
Pepper, Agent Daniel, 76
Pinman, John, 79
Point of Forks, attack on, 73
Pontiac's Rebellion, 18, 70
Porter, Deputy Commissary, 61
Portsmouth, 44
Prevost, Gen. Augustine, 70
Prevost, Col. James, 12, 13, 18
Prussia, 170
Prussian Rifle-Muskets of 1798, 94

Quebec, 79-80, 83, 178

Rainsford, Major General, 61-2
Regiments, British Army:
  Life Guards, 121, 124
  7th Light Dragoons, 88, 163ff
  8th Light Dragoons, 163, 241
  9th Light Dragoons, 164
  10th Light Dragoons, 88-9, 122-3, 127, 164
  11th Light Dragoons, 88-9, 164, 241
  13th Light Dragoons, 164, 241
  14th Light Dragoons, 123, 164
  15th Light Dragoons, 87-9, 123, 164, 241
  16th (Queen's, Burgoyne's) Light Dragoons, 22, 31, 33, 88, 90
  17th (Preston's) Light Dragoons, 33
  18th Light Dragoons, 164
  21st Light Dragoons, 164
  23rd Light Dragoons, 164
  Guards Brigade, 33, 45
  4th, 46, 50
  5th, 50
  6th, 42-3
  12th, 241
  14th, 42-3
  22nd, 241
  23rd, 46, 50
  26th, 242
  27th, 15
  33rd, 21, 34, 242
  42nd, 15, 25, 31, 33
  43rd Light Infantry, 174
  44th, 15, 33
  46th, 15
  50th, 242
  52nd Light Infantry, 129, 174
  54th, 242
  55th, 15, 242
  56th, 242
  59th, 242
  60th, 15, 70, 155-158ff
  1/60, 244-5
  2/60, 245-6
  3/60, 97, 246
  4/60, 100, 148, 246
  5/60, 99, 100, 102, 130, 146-8, 150, 246
  6/60, 246
  62nd, (Royal American) 12, 13, 15
  65th, 242
  70th, 42-3
  71st, 25, 31, 33, 45, 47-48, 50, 70, 72
  75th, 242
  77th, 242
  80th (Gage's Light Arm'd Foot), 15
  82nd, 243
  84th, 243
  91st, 243
  92nd, 243
  93rd, 243
  95th Rifles, 118, 146, 153, 158-163ff, 174
    1st Battalion, 130, 134, 246-7
    2nd Battalion, 118, 146, 152, 174-5, 247-8
    3rd Battalion, 118, 146, 174
  97th, 243
  Light Infantry,
    1st & 2nd Battalions, 33, 46, 52
  Grenadier Battalion, 46
    Depot Battalion, 243
    Cape Infantry, 243
    Ceylon Rifle Regiment, 165-6ff, 244
    1st Ceylon Light Infantry, 243
  King's German Legion, 164-5ff
    2nd Line Battalion, 118
    4th Line Battalion, 194-5
    Light Brigade, 152-3
    Royal Canadian Rifle Regiment, 166, 243
    Royal Rifle Dragoons, 33
Regiments, Loyalist
  American Volunteers, 74ff, 215
  Detroit Volunteer Chasseurs, 74ff
  East Florida Rangers, 70ff
  Emmerich's Chasseurs, 33, 34, 72ff
  Loyal American Regiment, 215
  New York Volunteers, 72
  New York Volunteer Rifle Company, 33, 59, 72ff, 73, 218
  North Carolina Highlanders, 70
  Provincial Light Infantry, 72, 74ff
  Queen's Rangers, 33, 45-52 passim
    Rifle Company, 72-74ff, 217
  Westchester Chasseurs (Refugees), 72
Regiments, Foreign in British Pay, 1793-1816
  Bourbon Regiment, 167
  Brunswick Light Infantry, 167
  Brunswick Oels Jägers, 167
  Calabrian Free Corps, 167
  Chasseurs Britannique, 167
  Corsican Rangers, 167
  Count Froberg's Levy, 167
  Greek Light Infantry, 167
  De Roll's Regiment, 167
  Hompesch's Chasseurs a cheval, 98-9
  Hompesch's Chasseurs a pied, 98-9
  Hompesch's Fusiliers, 98
  Hompesch's Hussars, 97-98, 121
  Hompesch's Mounted Riflemen, 99, 122
  Löwenstein's Chasseurs (Jägers), 93, 95, 99
  Löwenstein's Fusiliers, 99
  Löwenstein's Light Infantry, 99
  Power's Chasseurs, 97
  Prince of Orange's Rifle Regiment, 101, 222
  Royal Corsican Rangers, 167
  De Chartre's Royal Emigrant, 97
  De Meuron's Swiss Regiment, 95, 97
  Royal West India Rangers, 167, 243
  Royal York Fusiliers, 97
  Royal York Rangers, 167, 243
  De la Tour's Royal Etrangers, 97
  Waldstein's Waldeckers, 97
  De Watteville's Regiment, 167
  York Hussars, 97
  York Rangers, 96, 99
Regiments, Volunteer, 1793-1820
  Percy Tenantry Rifle Company, 94
Regiments, German (see also Jägers)
  Brunswick Prinz Ludwig dismounted dragoons, 67
Regiments, Portuguese
  Caçadores, 166-7
Regulations for Riflemen, 145-6, 173-4, 237-40
Rests, rifle, for practising, 174
Richmond & Lennox, third Duke of, 87, 90
Riedesel, Colonel von, 18
Rifle companies in British Line Regiments, 168-9
Rifles, captured foreign during 1790s, 94-95
Rio de la Plata, 169
Roder, Captain Friedrich Wilhelm von, 63
Rottenburg, Baron Francis de, 100, 151-2, 237-8
Royal Horse Artillery Pistol-Carbine, 90-92
Rumford, see Thompson

Sackville, Lord George, 15
St. Augustine, 70, 79
St. Clair, General Sir John, 11, 12
St. Leger, Colonel Barry, 62
Schulenburg, Graf von der, 16
Scots Magazine, 38
Shah of Persia (rifles), 137-8, 144, 151
Shamokin, 76-7
Sharp, William, 41
Shaw, Captain Aeneas, 72-3
Shippen, Edward, 75
Sicily, 169
Silver Heels, 78
Simcoe, Colonel John Graves, see Queen's Rangers under Regiments
Spangenberg, Pastor, 75
Spencer's Ordinary, battle at, 73
Stade, 63, 99
Stanwix, General John, 14
Staten Island, 60, 72
Stono Inlet, 73
Stuart, Agent John, 77-9
Suffolk, Secretary of State Lord, 60

Taafe & Callendar, 75
Taitt, Agent David, 79
Targets, 91, 105, 106, 171-3, 175
Teedyuscung, 76
Thompson, Benjamin, 21
Tonyn, Governor Peter, 70
Tovey, Captain Samuel, 22
Townshend, George, Viscount, 22, 31, 79
Traille, Captain Peter, R.A., 30, 70
Trapaud, General, 43
Tryon, Governor William, 78
Turkey Point, 46

Uniforms,
  British, 15, 18, 43, 47
  German, 60, 62-3

Volunteer Rifle Corps, listing by county, 249-52

Waldenfels, Captain Christoph Friedrich Joseph von, 63
Wall pieces, 118-9, 182
War of 1812, 179-80
Ward, Agent Edward, 76
Washington, George, 16, 21, 47-49
Watson, Lieutenant Colonel John, 74
Weiser, Conrad, 75-6
Welch's Tavern, 47
Wensen, battle near, 18
Wemyss, Lieut. Col., 47-9
White Mingo, 79
Wilhelmsthal, battle of, 18
Wilhelm, Hereditary Prince of Hesse-Hanau, 61
William, Duke of Hesse, 7
Wintzingerode, Colonel von, 16
Wolfe, General James, 15
Woolwich Arsenal, experiments at, 19, 22, 36-7, 105
Wreden, Captain von, 60
Wurmb, Captain von, 60

York, John, 26